Socialization, sexism, and stereotyping

women's issues in nursing

Socialization, sexism, and stereotyping

women's issues in nursing

EDITED BY

JANET MUFF, R.N., M.S.N.

The C. V. Mosby Company

ST. LOUIS • TORONTO • LONDON   1982

MOSBY

A TRADITION OF PUBLISHING EXCELLENCE

Editor: Pamela L. Swearingen
Assistant editor: Bess Arends
Manuscript editor: Thomas J. Lochhaas
Book design: Susan Trail
Cover design: Diane Beasley
Production: Margaret B. Bridenbaugh

Cover photo courtesy **American Red Cross,** *Washington, D.C.*

The C.V. Mosby Company
11830 Westline Industrial Drive, St. Louis, Missouri 63141

Library of Congress Cataloging Publication Data

Main entry under title:

Socialization, sexism, and stereotyping.

  Bibliography: p.
  Includes index.
  1. Nursing—Social aspects—United States.
2. Sexism in medicine—United States. 3. Women—
Employment—United States. 4. Feminism—United
States. 5. Nursing—Psychological aspects.
I. Muff, Janet.
RT86.5.S65   305.4'3   81-18690
ISBN 0-8016-3581-0   AACR2

AC/VH/VH 9 8 7 6 5 4 3 2 1   03/D/361

Contributors

Sharon E. Aga received her B.S.N. from the University of Arizona. In addition, she has her C.C.R.N. She is Clinical Planner for Nursing, Hollywood Presbyterian Medical Center, Los Angeles, California.

Nalda Findell Brodegaard received her B.S.N. from Skidmore College and her M.S.N. in Psychiatric/Mental Health Nursing from the School of Nursing, Columbia University, New York City. She is a Mental Health Consultant with the Beth Israel School of Nursing, New York, and an Instructor in the Nursing Program at Hunter College. She is in the process of opening a private practice in New York City.

George Brookfield received his L.V.N. from North Hollywood College of Medical and Dental Careers. He currently works in the Psychiatric Department of Valley Hospital Medical Center, Van Nuys, California.

Sheila K. Byrne received her A.A. from San Bernardino Valley College, her B.S. from California State University, Los Angeles, and her M.N. from the University of California, Los Angeles, in Psychiatric/Mental Health Nursing. She is Director of the Institute for Continuing Education for Nurses, University of Southern California School of Medicine, Postgraduate Division, and a Mental Health Consultant for the Los Angeles County/USC Medical Center Department of Nursing.

Elizabeth Carr received both her B.S.N. and her M.S. from the University of North Carolina. She is a certified Clinical Specialist in Psychiatric and Mental Health Nursing and has a private practice for psychotherapy and consultation in Washington, D.C. In addition, she is Adjunct Assistant Professor, Department of Education, George Washington University.

Stanley J. Cias attended Ursinus College, Collegeville, Pennsylvania. He received his diploma from St. Luke's Hospital School of Nursing, Bethlehem, Pennsylvania. He is a staff nurse in the Critical Care Department, St. Joseph's Medical Center, Burbank, California.

Patricia Geary Dean received her A.A.S. from the State University of New York Upstate Medical Center, her B.S. and M.S. from Boston University, and a C.A.G.S. from Northeastern University. She currently teaches at the MGH Institute of Health Professions and is engaged in doctoral study at Harvard University. She has taught for 12 years in baccalaureate nursing programs.

Andy Douglas received his B.S. from Columbia University, New York. He is a certified critical care nurse and has held various staff, management, and teaching positions in oncology and critical care. He is currently employed at the Hollywood Presbyterian Medical Center, Hollywood, California.

Hester Eisenstein is a graduate of Radcliffe College and Yale University. She taught history at Yale from 1966 to 1970 and was the Coordinator of the Experimental Studies Program at Barnard College, New York, from 1970 to 1980. She is now living in Sydney, Australia, where she is Senior Equal Employment Opportunity Adviser for public employment in the state government of New South Wales. She is the editor of *The Future of Difference* (G.K. Hall & Co., 1980) and is working on a history of the development of feminist thought in the United States from 1970 to the present.

Myrita K. Flanagan received her B.S.N. from the City College of New York, her M.S.N. in Psychiatric/Mental Health Nursing from the School of Nursing, Columbia University, New York, and her Ed.D. from Teachers College, Columbia University, New York. She is currently a partner in Flanagan-Galligan Associates, a consultation firm serving nursing service and nursing education.

Jo Freeman is the author of *The Politics of Women's Liberation* (1975) winner of the 1975 American Political Science Association prize for the best scholarly work on women and politics. Her book,

Women: A Feminist Perspective, provided two chapters for this collection. She has been an organizer and participant in the Women's League movement since its inception.

Maurene A. Harvey is a certified critical care nurse with a private practice, Consultants in Critical Care, Inc., in Los Angeles. She develops, conducts, and evaluates programs in critical care nationwide. She is currently an M.P.H. candidate at California State University, Northridge.

Wilma Scott Heide is a nurse, sociologist, and feminist scholar and activist. A former human rights commissioner, she has also been Chairone of the Board and President of NOW, National Organization for Women, Inc. She is currently Professor of Innovative and Experimental Studies and Professor of Women's Studies at Sangamon State University, Springfield, Illinois.

Nancy Henley received her Ph.D. in Experimental Psychology from Johns Hopkins University. She is Director of Women's Studies and Professor of Psychology at the University of California, Los Angeles. Her book, *Body Politics: Power, Sex & Non-Verbal Communication* (1977) reflects her work in the area of women and body language.

Linda Hughes earned her B.S.N. from Oklahoma Baptist University and her M.S.N. from Texas Woman's University. She is currently an Instructor in Nursing at Oklahoma Baptist University.

Beatrice J. Kalisch received her B.S.N. from the University of Nebraska School of Nursing, her M.S. in Maternal Child

Nursing from the University of Maryland, Baltimore, and her Ed.D. in Human Development from the University of Maryland, College Park. She is currently Titus Professor of Nursing and Chairperson in Parent Child Nursing, University of Michigan, Ann Arbor.

Philip A. Kalisch received his Bachelor of Social Science and his M.S. in History from the University of Nebraska, and his Ph.D. in History from Pennsylvania State University. He did postdoctoral study in the history of medicine at Johns Hopkins University. He is currently Professor of History and Politics of Nursing at the University of Michigan, Ann Arbor.

Norine J. Kerr is a diploma graduate of St. Margaret's School of Nursing, Pittsburgh, Pennsylvania. She received her B.S.N. and M.S.N. in Psychiatric/Mental Health Nursing from the University of Pittsburgh. She has worked as Primal Therapist in Pittsburgh and as Clinical Specialist at the Menninger Foundation. She is currently Adjunct Professor at Oral Roberts University and a Nurse Therapist in private practice at the Christian Family Institute, Tulsa, Oklahoma. She is a doctoral candidate at Tulsa University.

Ella Lasky, Ph.D., is a psychologist in private practice in New York City working with individuals and couples. She is a founding member and Vice President of the Woman's Psychotherapy Referral Service, a nonprofit feminist organization. She is the editor of *Humanness: An Exploration into the Mythologies about Men and Women* (MSS Information Corporation, New York).

Mariann Lovell received her B.S.N. from the University of Michigan and her M.S. from Wright State University, Dayton, Ohio, where she is currently an Instructor.

Alma Lowery-Palmer received her diploma in nursing from Homer G. Phillips Hospital School of Nursing, St. Louis, Missouri. She received her B.S.N. and her M.S. from DePaul University, Chicago, Illinois, and her Ph.D. from the University of California, Riverside. She is Associate Professor of Anthropology and Nursing and holds a joint appointment in Innovative and Experimental Studies and Nursing, Sangamon State University, Springfield, Illinois.

Judith Farash McCurdy received her B.S.N. from the University of Iowa, her M.N. from the University of California, Los Angeles, and her Ph.D. from California School of Professional Psychology. She is Director of Nursing for Kaiser-Permanente Mental Health Center, Los Angeles, California.

Elizabeth G. Morrison is currently a doctoral student at the University of Alabama, Birmingham. She received her B.S.N. from the University of Tennessee, Knoxville, and her M.S. from Rutgers University, New Brunswick, New Jersey. She is an Associate Professor at the University of Alabama School of Nursing and an Instructor at the University of Alabama School of Medicine, Department of Psychiatry. She wishes to express appreciation to Dr. Marguerite Kinney and Dr. Debra Aidun for their support and guidance in the development of this paper.

Janet Muff received her diploma in nursing from St. Vincent's College of Nursing, Los Angeles, California, and her B.S.N. and M.S.N. in Psychiatric/Mental Health Nursing from the School of Nursing, Columbia University, New York. She is currently in private practice as an individual and group psychotherapist in South Pasadena, California, and does consultation and education for health care and business organizations.

Shirlee Passau-Buck is a diploma graduate, currently a doctoral candidate at the Institute for Advanced Study of Human Sexuality, San Francisco and a teaching associate at Wright State University. At present she is a member of the Executive Board of Directors of the Social Health Association and the Dayton Area Heart Association. Her major interests lie in the holistic approach to community health and human sexuality.

Ann M. Rosenow holds a master's degree in Nursing from Emory University and a Ph.D. from the University of Chicago. She is currently Associate Professor in the Graduate Nursing Program at the University of North Carolina at Greensboro.

Marilyn Jaffe Ruiz is currently Associate Professor and Chairperson of the Leinhard School of Nursing BSN Program in New York City. She is also a psychotherapist in private practice and has done curriculum consultation and continuing education workshops. Her M.Ed. and Ed.D. are from Teachers College, Columbia University, and she also holds an M.A. in Adult Psychiatric Mental Health Nursing from New York University.

Susan Riemer Sacks is Director of the Education Program and Lecturer in Education at Barnard College, Columbia University. She holds a Ph.D. in Psychology, Child Development, and Learning from Columbia University and has been engaged in research on feminism and psychological autonomy.

Marie Santander received her diploma from St. Vincent's College of Nursing in Los Angeles and is currently completing her B.H.S. in San Diego. She practiced in various critical care areas before entering the medical sales field.

Natalie Shainess, M.D. has been in the field of psychiatry and psychoanalysis for over 35 years. She is a graduate and faculty member of the William Alanson White Institute and was Lecturer in Psychiatry at Columbia University College of Physicians and Surgeons. Feminine psychology and issues relating to women have been her major area of interest.

Russell Shapiro graduated from the University of Wisconsin with his B.S. in neurophysiology. He received his L.V.N. from the U.S. Navy Hospital Corps School in California. He is currently employed in the Psychiatry Department of the Valley Hospital Medical Center, Van Nuys, California.

Emily E.M. Smythe received her B.S.N. from Cornell University–New York Hospital, and her M.N. in Psychiatric Nursing from the University of California, Los Angeles. She is currently a Clinical Nurse Specialist for the Consultation-Liaison Service, Department of Psychiatry, Kaiser-Sunset Medical Center of Los Angeles; is a Mental Health

Nursing Instructor (part time) at Mount St. Mary's College, Los Angeles; and has a private mental health nursing consultation practice.

Shirley St. Amand received her diploma from St. Anne's School of Nursing, Fall River, Massachusetts, her B.S. from the University of Pennsylvania, Philadelphia, and her M.N. from the University of California, Los Angeles. From 1978 to 1981 she was a nurse practitioner in joint practice with a cardiologist in Los Angeles.

Shermalayne Southard Szasz received her B.S.N. and her M.S.N. from the Medical College of Georgia. Her background includes a variety of positions in oncology, critical care, continuing education, and nursing and hospital administration. She currently practices in the Labor and Delivery Department at St. Joseph Medical Center, Burbank, California.

Lenore J. Weitzman received her Ph.D. in Sociology from Columbia University. She is currently Visiting Scholar at the Center for Research on Women at Stanford University.

For

Jo Ann Ashley

who is with us in spirit . . .

Foreword

I am immensely pleased to have been provided the opportunity to write these words of prelude to this book, for the table of contents reads like a topical outline of some of the courses I have taught over the years in the history of nursing. Indeed, as I read chapter after chapter, I heard the echoes of my own voice in classroom after classroom, relating illustration after illustration of the socialization, sexism, and stereotyping in nursing. Additionally, I have often said that the courses I teach in nursing history are exercises in "consciousness raising" and have bemoaned the fact that I have not had the time to put many of my thoughts about these issues down in black and white. This volume does much of it for me.

An even more important reason for wishing to write this foreward is that this book is dedicated to Jo Ann Ashley, and many of the authors cite Jo Ann's classic book, *Hospitals, Paternalism, and the Role of the Nurse* among their references. Indeed, as the dedication states, Jo Ann *is* with us in spirit, but even more so in word.

In the fall of 1967, I was teaching a course at Teachers College, Columbia University, related to the challenge of professionalization in nursing. In that class of 60 or 70 graduate students there was a tiny Kentuckian who became increasingly interested in the historical roots of the current issues being discussed. She was less than 5 feet tall and weighed less than 100 pounds. With hair graying prematurely at the temples and large luminous eyes, she reminded me of a wise old owl, participating sparsely in the classroom, but writing eloquently and incisively in her assigned papers. As a matter of fact, I did not know until the last day of the course that the author of the excellent papers and the little owl were the same person. I had written a note on the final paper, asking the author to speak to me after class that I might link name with face. She sat down next to me in the cafeteria and said simply, "*I am Jo Ann Ashley.*"

Jo Ann was a student in the master's program in psychiatric nursing, and the professionalization course was taken during her first semester at Teachers College.

Dr. Jo Ann Ashley died of cancer on November 19, 1980, shortly after her forty-first birthday.

During the next 2½ years, while I remained on the faculty at "T.C.," Jo Ann and I spent many hours discussing the importance of historical research in nursing. When she finished her master's degree, she went directly into the doctoral program, taking course work related to her eventual goal, a dissertation in the area of historical research entitled *Hospital Sponsorship of Nursing Schools: The Influence of Apprenticeship and Paternalism on Nursing Education in America, 1893-1948*. I am personally proud to have served as the original sponsor of that work and to have been vicariously associated with Jo Ann as she anguished over the numerous revisions that finally resulted in the book now quoted and cited so frequently.

During these years of 1967 to 1970, the women's movement was gaining strength. I had read Betty Friedan's *The Feminine Mystique* and become interested in the National Organization for Women. My research into the history of nursing had already awakened me to the realities of the socialization and oppression of nurses, but I was still not connecting nursing's problems with *women's* problems. Nor was I too sure that I wanted to connect them, for what I was reading in the press and seeing on television about the women active in "women's liberation" did not fit with my own notions of how women *should* act nor how they *should* dress.

Some time in 1970, I was asked to write an article for the American Journal of Nursing about the involvement of the early nursing leaders with the suffrage movement and the Equal Rights Amendment. I enthusiastically delved into the activities of Lavinia Lloyd Dock and her passionate espousal of these concepts and was chagrined to discover that it took the American Nurses' Association many years before finally supporting Miss Dock, much less the Suffrage Act. I also found that by the time the article was published in February, 1971, the ANA had still not come out in support of the ERA! (They finally did, in the summer of 1971.)

Lavinia Dock consistently stated that the concerns of women had to be the concerns of nurses. Therefore in that year, 1970, I decided to attend an early evening meeting of the National Organization for Women, to see for myself if I could identify with it. Prim and proper prude that I was, I did not want to go alone, for it was a big meeting in anticipation of the Women's March for Equality, to plan the parade up New York's Fifth Avenue. I asked Jo Ann Ashley to go with me. Jo Ann was shocked that I would propose such a thing and warned me of the effect upon my reputation if I were to be associated with women like that. She tried hard to dissuade me but, finally and reluctantly, agreed to accompany me. (To this day I believe she felt she had to protect me in some way!) When we arrived, I wanted to sit somewhere in the middle, where I could see and hear what was going on, but Jo Ann was adamant that *she* would stand in the back. I therefore proceeded alone and took my place between two well-dressed and very feminine-looking women, who looked "safe" to me. As it turned out, one was a stockbroker in a large Wall Street firm, interested in women's rights because, as a woman, she was prohibited from having lunch in the all-male stock exchange restaurant where her company had an established charge account for entertaining customers; *she* had to take *her* customers to a public restaurant and then play the male-female game of "who gets the bill." My other neighbor, a doctorally prepared mathematician, was concerned about oppression in the high school where she was employed; she was permitted to teach only the simplest courses in algebra and geometry, while less academically prepared male instructors taught the advanced calculus and trigonometry.

Just as we had become acquainted, a crew of television newsmen rolled their cameras down the aisle, and I looked back to see Jo Ann frantically signalling to me. Her message was clear: "Let's get out of here!" I shook my head and turned back to see who the cameras were focusing on. Down in the right front of the audience there were perhaps a dozen or so dungaree-clad young women waving a sign that read "Radical Lesbians for ERA." The rest of the 150 or more women were dressed as I, in skirted suits or dresses with hose and proper pumps, pearl necklaces, and earrings— some even wore white gloves! The speakers ignored the cameras, as did the audience, and the meeting proceeded with no disruption, save for some enthusiastic shouting and waving from the radical lesbians. The men wheeling the cameras appeared to be scanning the entire group, although they did seem to focus a bit longer on the right front of the auditorium. They left after about 20 minutes, and the entire meeting broke up about 2 hours later.

Jo Ann, bless her heart, had waited patiently for me in the back, and when we left the meeting, I invited her to join me for a cup of coffee in my apartment while we watched the 11 o'clock news to see what the cameras had caught. I was enthusiastic about the meeting and had paid my dues to join NOW that night. Jo Ann was still not convinced and was worried about my prospective association with such an organization.

When the news came on, we were both initially startled by the slanted version of the content of the meeting being related by the commentator. And a minute or so later we were both instantly radicalized by the images being flashed on the screen. There were no pictures of the 100 or more neatly dressed, articulate women attentive to the business at hand. The dozen or so radical lesbians and their banner were photographed unflatteringly and in such a way that they appeared to comprise the entire audience. Jo Ann and I looked at each other with the same insight—they were dividing us as women, just as the oppressors had always divided and conquered us as nurses! I never taught nursing history again without associating it with the history of the oppression of women. And Jo Ann never wrote nursing history again without interpreting it from a feminist viewpoint. We had experienced consciousness raising.

As nurses, we had to learn to identify our problems with the universal problems of women. But have those women in the women's movement learned to identify the problems of women with the problems of nurses? Muff makes the point in Chapter 10: "Why doesn't a smart girl like you go to medical school?" There is an increasing accumulation of articles and books about unsung "sheroes," to quote Heide, but rarely do they mention anyone connected with nursing. The Lillian Walds and Lavinia Docks, the Adelaide Nuttings and Isabel Robbs remain unknown, and the women's movement appears to remain uninterested.

That is the final reason for the pleasure I feel in writing this foreword. It is my hope that this book will be reviewed in the feminist press and read in feminist circles. Perhaps then more women will see that the plight of nurses is very much the result of socialization, sexism, and stereotyping, and more nurses will see the relationship to the universal problems of women.

If we could get *all* women together, how much power we could wield! And wouldn't Jo Ann be delighted?

Teresa E. Christy

Preface

This book is a reader on women's issues in nursing, broadly conceived. Although there are certainly men in nursing, it has traditionally been and continues to be primarily a woman's profession, characterized by all the difficulties and strengths of women in our society.

The issues that face nursing—"reality shock," "burn-out," "drop-out," job dissatisfaction—are not isolated phenomena and should be looked at within the context of women's issues. Whether we like it or not, whether we hope things will change or not, the fact remains that 96 percent of nurses are women, and they share with all women certain developmental and societal difficulties.

This book will discuss developmental and discrimination issues for women in general and will link them to the problems of nurses. In addition it will explore sexism within nursing, its guises, and its effects. Finally, it will suggest ways of combatting sexism, of improving self-esteem and interpersonal relationships of nurses, and of increasing their job satisfaction and longevity.

Socialization is the process whereby values and expectations are transmitted from generation to generation. The traditional socialization of women to be passive, dependent, and nurturing limits their aspirations and career options. Identity and self-esteem, which are derived in part from the socialization process, play an important role in the achievement-related difficulties of women.

Girls are raised to be wives and mothers. Jobs are seen, not in terms of life-long commitments, but as stopgaps to marriage. Cultural institutions (social, professional, political, educational, and religious) that perpetuate the problem constitute an imposing barrier to professions for women. Nursing, with its stereotypic image of caring, nurturing, and subservience, is almost a caricature of womanhood and as such has long been regarded as a "natural" job for women. Most nurses are women, and those who are attracted to nursing generally fit traditional stereotypes.

The frustrations of being a woman in the male-dominated health care system are great. Physicians and hospital administrators, mostly men, anxiously defend their traditional prerogatives as rulers of the roost. Survival for nurses faced with the physician-nurse game, with the paternalism of physicians and administrators, and with the ethics of self-sacrifice so prevalent in nursing situations, is possible only at great cost to the individual. The problems of "reality shock," "burn-out," and "drop-out" are directly attributable to the stresses produced through conflict, loss of self-esteem, and lack of autonomy.

Nursing shortages make headlines from coast to coast. Recruitment efforts have greatly intensified. The federal government, hospital administrators, and nursing administrators all seek answers. Despite a continuous outpouring of nurses from basic training programs, the number of nurses actually practicing is not sufficient to meet patient care requirements. There are many hypotheses offered as to the reasons why nurses do not remain in nursing:

- Women, we are told, are not career oriented, and nursing is a perfect stop-gap.
- Idealistic new graduates are overwhelmed by the realities of nursing practice.
- The personal sacrifice entailed by long hours, shift rotation, weekend scheduling, and low salaries does not appeal to many women for long periods of time.
- Increased opportunities for women in nontraditional occupations are attracting many bright, assertive women who might have chosen nursing in the past.

I think the issues presented in this book are germane to the problems I have just outlined. The first step toward solution is an awareness by nurses of their own strengths, weaknesses, and psychological dynamics. Second is an awareness of the social, political, and interpersonal issues that impinge on the profession as a whole and each person's job in particular. Once nurses are aware of the reasons for their difficulties, they can relinquish their victim behaviors, stop blaming society and men, and begin to take responsibility for the problems. And finally, once nurses are aware and responsible, they will be able to combat sexism and to improve relations with other health professionals. They will feel better about themselves.

This book was conceived out of a variety of my experiences, as a student, a staff nurse, an educator, and an administrator, over several years. Slowly, as the idea developed, I realized that those who were responsible for my own consciousness raising could be more accurately represented through their *own* words than through mine, and the first contributors appeared. More were added as new dimensions evolved.

The contributors have all been encouraged to express themselves both personally and professionally. You will find that at times we overlap because the individual problems we discuss have common origins, and despite our differing philosophies, we share the belief that solutions to these problems lie in self-awareness and personal activism. You will find, too, that our philosophies *do* differ, sometimes diametrically. We have agreed, then, to disagree and to offer you our varying perspectives from which to choose.

The book is organized in five sections: Female Developmental Issues, Career Choice and Nursing Stereotypes, Social and Political Issues, Psychological Issues, and Out from Under (a look at solutions and alternatives). It is designed for nurses who have gained "partial consciousness"—educators, clinical specialists, and supervisors—those who can share our ideas more fully with their students and colleagues. It is, as I have said, a reader, meaning that some chapters are quite theoretical while others are anecdotal and experiential. There is, I hope, something here for every nurse.

Finally, I feel the need to offer a disclaimer: This book focuses on women nurses, and we use feminine or combined pronouns. We realize that the presence or absence of men in nursing is also a women's issue, but it will only be dealt with briefly here. Our commitment is to draw the parallels between women and nurses. Men, this once, must take second place.

I want to express my sincere appreciation to the American Red Cross whose posters were used for the cover of this book and several unit pages. The images of nursing depicted in these illustrations are emotionally charged, inspiring, and patriotic. Such images were an integral part of the war effort, together with stirring images of home, and Mom, and apple pie. They were appropriate and even necessary for their time. My intention in juxtaposing these traditional illustrations with contemporary issues is *not* to denigrate the former but rather to raise the following questions for each reader:

Do these images accurately reflect nurses today?

Has nursing changed?

Has the *image* of nursing changed correspondingly?

Should the image of nursing change?

And if so, what would *you* keep?

What would *you* alter?

What would *you* discard?

For their help I would like to acknowledge Boyce-y, my husband, who fed me (literally and figuratively), who did the dishes *every* night, who read and edited and found the "perfect words," who accompanied me to bookstores, pornography parlors and antique shows (in search of photographs), and many less interesting places, and who paid my telephone bills; Fette, my mother, and Hatsie, our friend, who reported on soap operas and searched the newspapers diligently for any mention of nurses and who proofread the manuscript; Rita, who proofread the galleys; Nancy, who typed the manuscript, all 600 pages of it, at night and on weekends; Helen, who answered the phone, picked up the slack, and ran interference with Boyce-y so that he wouldn't notice that Nancy was typing during working hours, too; Gary, who "volunteered" his photographic skills; and Madeleine and Montgomery, whose furry puppy kisses, unflagging companionship, and occasional overenthusiasm brought muddy pawprints to the manuscript and a sense of perspective and humor to long days of writing and editing.

For sharing their souls and their ideas over the years, I want to thank Sue and

Hester, former teachers, now contributors, who opened my eyes to women's issues; Marty and Marilyn, also teachers, also contributors, who made nursing colleagueship a reality; Sharon, Shiela, and Shermalayne, old friends, who heard me out and helped me out, who weathered various transformations of this book, and who, together with Emily and Judy, made up my local sounding board. To them and to *all* my other contributors go many thanks for having come up with a fresh perspective and novel ideas that make this book so much more than I as an individual could have made it and for having survived my first editorial efforts (with cheerfulness). Thanks to Brenda, Gail, Gena, Jill, Karen, Kathie, and Vivian, the members of my women's group, many of whom *lived* the nursing issues in this book, and all of whom contributed enormously though not in writing.

Finally, for their unfailing support and mentoring, I want to acknowledge Pamela Swearingen, my editor, who got lost on our "first date" and drove all over town with the wrong directions I had given her, but who didn't drop me on the spot; and Bess Arends and Nancy Mullins, her assistants, who fielded my questions, calmed my ravings, and kept the pertinent articles and books coming my way.

Janet Muff

Contents

UNIT ONE

Female developmental issues

1   Rethinking gender identity: A continuing process, 3
    Susan Riemer Sacks

2   Sex-role socialization, 21
    Lenore J. Weitzman

3   Self-esteem, achievement, and the female experience, 48
    Ella Lasky

4   Let's bury old fictions, 77
    Natalie Shainess

5   The sexual politics of interpersonal behavior, 83
    Nancy Henley and Jo Freeman

UNIT TWO

Career choice and nursing stereotypes

6   On the psychosocial barriers to professions for women: Atalanta's apples, "women's work," and the struggle for social change, 95
    Hester Eisenstein

7   Handmaiden, battle-ax, whore: an exploration into the fantasies, myths, and stereotypes about nurses, 113
    Janet Muff

8   Little girls grow up to be wives and mommies: nursing as a stopgap to marriage, 157
    Linda Hughes

9   An analysis of nursing as a career choice, 169
    Myrita K. Flanagan

10 Why doesn't a smart girl like you go to medical school? The women's movement takes a slap at nursing, 178
    Janet Muff

UNIT THREE

Social and political issues

11 The cultural basis of political behavior in two groups: nurses and political activists, 189
    Alma Lowery-Palmer

12 Caring vs. curing: the politics of health care, 203
    Shirlee Passau-Buck

13 Daddy's little girl: the lethal effects of paternalism in nursing, 210
Mariann C. Lovell

14 An analysis of the sources of physician-nurse conflict, 221
Beatrice J. Kalisch and Philip A. Kalisch

15 Altruism, socialism, and nightingalism: the compassion traps, 234
Janet Muff

16 Toward androgyny, 248
Patricia Geary Dean

17 Feminist activism in nursing and health care, 255
Wilma Scott Heide

18 Some thoughts on being a male in nursing, 273
George Brookfield, Andy Douglas, Russell S. Shapiro, and Stanley J. Cias

UNIT FOUR
Psychological issues

19 Without a wife: the dilemma of social support for women's careers, 281
Ann M. Rosenow

20 The nurse defined as the symbiotic mother, 290
Nalda Findell Brodegaard

21 The narcissistic fit between medicine and nursing, 300
Norine J. Kerr

22 Lack of ego differentiation: its effect on nursing leadership, 307
Marilyn Jaffe Ruiz

23 What is achievement in nursing? 315
Ann M. Rosenow

24 Go ahead, I'm behind you . . . way behind you, 321
Patricia Geary Dean

25 Who's going to take care of the nurse? 337
Emily E.M. Smythe

UNIT FIVE
Out from under

26 Accepting the "red," 351
Sheila K. Byrne

27 Power *is* a nursing issue, 359
Judith Farash McCurdy

28 Power and nonverbal behavior: indicators and alternatives, 366
Elizabeth G. Morrison

29 Joint practice, 378
Janet Muff

30 Brainstorming for job satisfaction, 384
Sharon E. Aga and Janet Muff

31 The tyranny of uniforms, 397
Shermalayne Southard Szasz

32 Breaking out . . . breaking in, 402
Marie Santander

33 Getting a foot in the door: one nurse's experience in obtaining hospital privileges, 406
Shirley St. Amand

34 Private practice as an independent
consultant, 409

Maurene A. Harvey

35 A model for private practice:
requirements for success, 413

Elizabeth Carr

Photo by Michael M. Gill.

UNIT ONE

FEMALE DEVELOPMENTAL ISSUES

Most nurses are women* and have in common with their sex developmental and socialization processes. This section distinguishes gender or sexual identity from sex-role socialization: the fact of being a woman as opposed to what it *means* to be a woman in terms of behaviors, expectations, and roles. Women's traditional roles and lack of self-esteem are discussed in terms of women's difficulties in achievement. This section examines psychiatric shibboleths about women and questions Freudian postulates about women being inferior to men. Finally it explores the sexual politics of interpersonal behavior.

How does a human being discover that it is a boy or girl? Sue Sacks discusses the traditional theories that have been used to explain gender acquisition and development: psychoanalytic, social learning, cognitive, and other theories. She examines biological, psychological, parental, and cultural factors that influence a child's gender identity and raises questions as to whether personality characteristics—masculine or feminine—are innate or learned.

Lenore Weitzman focuses on learned and socialized behaviors and roles. She describes the process of socialization chronologically from infancy through adulthood, examining differences in parental and societal expectations of males and females along the way. She relates female socialization to a lack of intellectual achievement, lower career aspirations, and a fear of success. Finally, she says, women are less oriented toward success not only because they have been socialized to be passive, dependent by-standers but also because they are taught to channel their energies in different ways than are men (toward catching a husband, aiding him in his career) and because there is discrimination in *real* career opportunities for women.

Ella Lasky explores in greater depth the relationship of low self-esteem to women's achievements. The traditional feminine characteristics and sex roles are internalized by women as part of the socialization process. Society's opinion of

---

*The contributors to this book cite figures of 96% to 98% depending on the study used. Such statistics may be significant from a male nursing viewpoint (4% being twice as high as 2%) but have little significance from the female point of view.

1

women as second rate becomes women's *own* opinion of themselves and their sex. Young females learn that assertiveness and achievement-oriented actions are unacceptable. In a society that applauds such behaviors but restricts them to males, girls develop a negative self-image. Dr. Lasky links women's low self-image with expectations that women's roles be restricted to those of wife and mother. Women experience societal sanctions and internalized guilt when they deviate from these traditional behaviors. Clinical examples of the "perfect little girl," the "uncommitted floater," and the "woman workaholic" illustrate the results of such limitations and expectations.

Freud, says Natalie Shainess, neglected the reality of his female patients' experiences (actual incest and rape) and the effects of the society in which they lived. The mores of late-Victorian Vienna in conjunction with his personal background colored Freud's attitude toward women and thus his formulations of female mental health. Freudian theory, however, is the foundation on which contemporary psychiatry has been built and the standard against which the mental health of both sexes has been measured. Yet the principles of Freudian psychology are biased against females. Dr. Shainess gives us a fuller perspective. Women, we begin to see, envy men not their sexual organs but often their more fulfilling, exciting social roles.

"Social interaction is the battlefield where the daily war between the sexes is fought." Nancy Henley and Jo Freeman explore social cues that transmit messages to men and women about themselves. During interactions verbal cues are important, but nonverbal ones are even more important and will supersede verbal cues if they conflict. Women must begin to understand the most subtle forces that influence their lives, including nonverbal messages, if they are to understand issues of power and status in relationships and thus their own positions and options.

SUSAN RIEMER SACKS

Chapter 1

Rethinking gender identity

A continuing process

"Hi! What'd you have?" That was the first question I asked of my colleague when she called to share the news of the birth of her son. That spontaneous question came from the well of my accumulated personal history and from the depth of our culture and shared social experiences. Even in the midst of writing this chapter *and* knowing from results of prenatal tests that the infant would be a boy, my years of socialization superseded my research efforts at thinking and rethinking gender.

People tend to form dichotomies, either female or male. Assignment to a gender identity appears nearly universal in this and other cultures and is almost always initially determined by genital inspection. Thus we live in a world of two gender identities. Is this the only world? Of course, there are times when gender is not the organizing principle, when ethnicity, race, age, religion, or income becomes central and focal. For the purposes of this chapter, however, gender as a primary construction of human reality is the central focus.

How does a human being discover that it is a girl or a boy? How does the child develop a sense of being either female or male? How does the child learn what it means to be a girl or a boy? How does one learn that she or he is related to other same-gender persons? What is feminine or masculine? What does that mean? What is feminity or masculinity? What do they mean? How is a child socialized to behave "in accordance" with being a girl or boy? Feminine or masculine? Finally, why do human beings think and act in terms of the girl-boy, woman-man, feminine-masculine dichotomy?

These questions govern our thinking about the topic of human development of gender identity and identification with others of one's gender. For this discussion to be cogent, the terminology must be used consistently. Social scientists have tended to use *sex* and *gender* interchangeably or to distinguish them as biological as opposed to cultural labels. The use of gender terminology makes us pause to think about the implications of being labeled from birth as girls or boys. The major theoretical formulations regarding gender development are also examined in the following sections, as well as the influences of biological, psychological, and cultural factors.

3

TERMINOLOGY

The word *sex* has been used in the research literature to designate the biological status of a person as female or male. The term is used here only to refer to reproductive and love-making activities.[17]

Gender is the cultural and social classification of a person in terms of feminine or masculine qualities. Like sex, gender has been studied as a dichotomy: either feminine or masculine. Gender involves the following components.

Gender attribution is the process by which one person classifies another as female or male. *Gender assignment* is a special case of gender attribution; it takes place at birth and is the designation of the infant by a doctor, midwife, or parents as baby girl or baby boy. Gender assignment is usually based on the inspection of external genitalia, "the prime insignia."[37] Once the assignment of gender has been pronounced, the attribution of gender to the infant by others, and the implicit attitudes involved in this attribution, remain consonant overall.

Even in the case of children born with ambiguous genitalia, the child once assigned almost always develops an unambiguous gender identity as girl or boy. Thus, whereas genitalia are an important aspect of gender, they are not, in and of themselves, sufficient as a total explanation of gender attribution.

Core gender identity is one's sense of "I am female" or "I am male." One's core identity is *self-attribution* of gender, the feeling that one is a girl or a boy. It is not dependent on how others identify one but is one's own biological self-designation. How is one's core gender identity ascertained? We ask: "Are you a girl *or* a boy?" The nature of the response to such a question is partially determined by the formulation of the either/or question.

Gender role identity is one's sense of "I am feminine" or "I am masculine." One's gender role identity is the self-designation of psychological femaleness or maleness, the degree to which one incorporates the activities and behaviors seen as "appropriate" for her/his gender according to societal standards.

Gender role behavior is the set of expectations about "appropriate" behaviors for persons of one gender or the other. A person is born into the female or male category and is expected subsequently to perform in the female or male role and to behave in accordance with the prescriptions and proscriptions for that gender. People are often defined by their gender role behaviors. A stereotype is a set of beliefs about the characteristics of the occupants of a role.[17]

To understand the relationship between assignment (girl or boy), identity (feeling like a female or male), and role (behaving like a female or a male), we first attribute gender. Kessler and McKenna[17] argue that dichotomous gender attribution is a social construction, a means for ordering perceived reality. We divide the world into two categories, female and male, and that dichotomy controls decisions about one's gender assignment, identity, and role. The compelling significance of the process of genital attribution equaling gender attribution and leading to identity and role is critical for human development in a society that essentially devalues the feminine and values the masculine. A challenge to the two-gender structure, which is traditionally grounded in biology and considered invariant, involves the understanding that gender is a construction of the culture and that gender identity continually evolves throughout one's life span.*

Rethinking the meaning of dichotomy is crucial to conceptualizing gender identity as a process. The concept of life and death, the ultimate dichotomy, is being challenged legally and morally today. When is someone really dead? When the heart stops? When the brain stops? When the monitor ceases? Conceptualizing a living-dying continuum opens the possibility in our thinking of a gender continuum.

Let us keep this in mind as we examine the major theories for the development of gender identity.

TRADITIONAL THEORETICAL EXPLANATIONS FOR GENDER DEVELOPMENT

The three major formulations, the psychoanalytic, social learning, and cognitive theories, share the assumption that there are two discrete genders, female and male, and that they are natural and proper. Furthermore, there are two dichotomous gender roles, feminine and masculine, which are the expressions of the two genders.

Psychoanalytic theory

Expounded first by Freud[13] and continued by his disciples, the psychoanalytic approach espouses a biological deterministic interpretation of gender development. In brief, the child's gender identity is dependent on the evolution of a specifically sexual consciousness of self as female or male. In this theory sexuality is the core meaning of both biological and cultural gender. Person[29] notes that gender orders sexuality and then, at least for men, genital sexuality becomes the mainstay of masculine gender; women's gender identity can be maintained in other ways.

Identification was central to Freud's theory of development. The child between 3 and 5 years of age becomes (1) aware of her or his genitals and (2) makes a self-attribution of gender: "I have a penis, I am a boy" or "I do not have a penis, I am a girl." With this recognition begins (3) the Oedipal fantasy involving one's genitals (or lack of) and parents. The child (4) identifies with the same-gender parent, internalizes the attributes and role behaviors of that parent, and hopes to win the opposite-gender parent. Eventually (5) the boy achieves the "appropriate" gender role to behave like a little man and the girl like a little woman, thus resolving the Oedipal conflict.

Genital identity was originally equated with gender identity. Contemporary

---

*References 1, 17, 23, 29.

researchers in the psychoanalytic tradition have incorporated sociocultural influences. Stoller[38] and others have found that pregenital identification for girls and boys with the mother is central to the development of gender identity. Gender role development evolves from parent-child interactions and the fostering of "appropriate" behaviors, especially independence and assertiveness, and from the replication and reproduction of roles and functions.[10,29] According to this theory gender identity is attained by the resolution of libidinal motivations and the intrapsychic integration of the symbols and attitudes of one's gender assignment. This process guarantees cohesive gender identity.

Social learning theory

As expounded by Mischel and Bandura,[24] gender identity is developed through a learning process based on reinforcement and imitation. The sequence involves (1) the awareness by parents and others in the child's environment of the child's gender assignment. (2) The child then imitates or identifies with the actions, attitudes, and responses of the same-gender parent and later with same-gender peers. (3) Through direct or indirect, verbal or nonverbal, reinforcement, the child learns to discriminate gender-type behaviors and to generalize them to other situations. Once learned, the child performs gender-type behaviors.

Gender identity develops through rewards that follow "appropriate" behavior: "I want rewards, I am rewarded for doing girl (boy) things; therefore, I want to be a girl (boy)."[18] There is some disagreement in the literature about whether parents reward girls and boys differentially; this will be discussed later. According to the social learning approach, gender role development is fostered by imitation and modeling, and the content of the reinforcement, either positive or negative, is more significant than the gender of the model. Gender identity proceeds from external environmental forces as the child learns to behave as others behave and is reinforced for these behaviors.

Cognitive learning theory

First presented by Kohlberg,[18] the cognitive learning theory explains the development of gender identity by incorporating principles from Piaget's work: that children play an active role in organizing the world in accordance with their level of cognitive functioning, and that children's understandings are qualitatively different from adults'. The acquisition of gender identity assumes this sequence: "I am a girl (boy), therefore I want to do girl (boy) things, therefore the opportunity to do girl (boy) things (and to gain approval for doing them) is rewarding."[18]

Kohlberg and others have generated considerable evidence to support the cognitive learning theory.[21] Sometime between the ages of 18 months and 2½ years, children can identify their own picture from a group of pictures of other children. By the age of 3 about 88% of children label themselves correctly as a girl or a boy. A child uses the word *girl* as she might use her name or any other label. According to cognitive theory, 3-year-old children have learned the label for "correct" gender identity but cannot yet classify themselves with others of the same gender; nor do they know what being a girl or boy means.

Between 3 and 5 years of age children are actively organizing their world and their way of classifying things in it. By the age of 4 children tend to assign gender labels to dolls based on their length of hair or clothing rather than by genitalia. One 4-year-old, when asked by his mother whether the new baby he had visited next door was a boy or a girl, replied, "I couldn't tell, it wasn't dressed."

During the period of conceptual growth from 4 to 7 years, children develop an awareness of genital differences along with the concept of self-anatomical constancy. This development is a gradual process of the child's active interaction with its environment. To comprehend that the vagina or penis is a permanent part of the body, children must implicitly understand the principle of conservation, a major cognitive mastery identified by Jean Piaget.[5] Usually by 6 years of age children conceptualize gender as fixed and irreversible anatomy; it is then that gender identity is achieved. This means that children know their identity and understand that they will always be girls or boys. Until then children base their self-gender category on the gender-type attributes in their repertoire—hair length, clothes, toys—and believe that by changing clothes one can change gender.

Briefly stated, cognitive learning theory suggests that between 2 and 3 years of age children learn gender self-labeling. During the next 2 years they learn to generalize the labels to each other. But self-attribution of gender does not indicate constancy of gender identity, according to Kohlberg.[18] Constancy of gender identity can only be attained when the child has achieved the cognitive developmental stage of conservation, when the child is certain of the principle of invariance of physical objects.

Once children know their gender identity, they have the capacity to classify others as being of the same gender. At this point connotations of gender roles become incorporated in the child's thinking. Kohlberg suggests that the masculine role becomes valued for power, aggression, and strength and the feminine role for niceness and attractiveness. The characteristics attributed to the masculine role have been assessed as socially prized qualities; those of the feminine role as not culturally valued qualities.[7]

Young children, even at the age of 5, seek reinforcements dependent on gender-typed values. Boys show consistent same-gender preferences over a range of toys and activities; girls tend to vary, in fact often preferring other-gender toys and activities. Perhaps the inconsistency of girls' choices coincides with their awareness of the valuing of and the inherent interest derived from "boys' toys" and games. Despite this inconsistency, once their gender role is established, both girls and boys tend to identify with the same-gender parent and to behave accordingly.

Table 1   *Three theories of gender development*

Psychoanalytic	Social learning	Cognitive developmental
1. Genital awareness = gender identify (fantasy process)	1. Others' awareness of genitals (reinforcement process)	1. Others' awareness of genitals (labeling process)
2. Identification with same-gender parent	2. Identification with same-gender parent	2. Gender identity
3. Gender role identity	3. Gender role identity	3. Gender role identity
	4. Gender identity	4. Identification with same-gender parent

Cognitive learning theory explains the learning of gender identity and gender role as a part of the rational learning process of childhood. Children are intrinsically motivated and actively seek to acquire "appropriate" gender role behaviors to help organize and understand the world.

• • •

Table 1 summarizes in the terminology of this chapter the steps in gender development according to these three theories. It is important to observe that in each theory the steps in the acquisition of gender and the process of acquisition differ.

Other theories

Others have proposed variations of these theories of gender identity.* The process of gender identity and gender role development is so complex that no one mechanism—identification, imitation, reinforcement, or cognitive learning—fully explains the acquisition of gender. There seems to be fairly general agreement that core gender identity ("I am female," "I am a male") is established in childhood, but the aspects of gender role identity ("I am feminine," "I am masculine") need not be fixed and may continue to evolve throughout adulthood.

Children's knowledge at age 3 that they are a girl or a boy does not demonstrate that they know what it will *mean* to be a woman or a man. In their theoretical formulation Kessler and McKenna[17] suggest that when children understand that transformations do not change an object's physical characteristics, they begin to share adult rules for gender construction. By the age of 6 or 7, when children know that gender is an invariant characteristic of themselves, gender identity is established. Kessler and McKenna argue that the social construction of gender itself, which is like skin color one of the few human characteristics invariant from birth, must be reexamined in the context of dichotomizing reality into two genders.

---

*References 6, 19, 22, 30.

Evidence indicates that at the age of 3 children's preference for gender-type toys and activities is not dichotomized.[21] By 6, children tend to express gender-typed preferences consistently. Toys and activities take on gender-fixed, dichotomized categories. At 4½ my son told me, "You can't be a doctor; mommies are nurses." For him, this was a statement of immutable fact. By the age of 11 or 12 children differentiate between anatomical attributes and role attributes. They understand that the former remain basically fixed and that behaviors and feelings are components of the concept of gender role that are not invariable in the same way.

In studying the attribution of gender, Kessler and McKenna[17] asked three groups of children, preschool, kindergarten, and third grade, to draw a picture of a girl and a boy. The children were shown the three groups of drawings 1 month later. The accuracy of gender attribution was found to increase with age. The 8- and 9-year-olds identified their own drawings and those of their own group with greater accuracy than did 4- or 6-year-olds who examined their own depictions or those of their peers. The most interesting finding was that children in each group were better able to attribute gender correctly for the drawings of their peers. This seemed to indicate that the cues that operated for 4-year-olds were shared by other preschoolers but not necessarily by kindergartners or third-graders. The same held within each of the other two groups.

When asked how they knew a drawing was of a girl or a boy, preschool and kindergarten children gave responses such as "his hands" or "he's big" without characterizing the features. Sometimes they said, "It just is." Once children had attributed gender to a figure, they were asked for a reason for their classification. The researchers concluded children's reasons demonstrated the factual status of gender— as the children constructed the facts. The children were not concerned with giving a "good" reason but simply related their own reasons. Although "the hands" is not a "good" reason for adults because it is not a dichotomous or generalizable feature for gender attribution, it was perfectly "logical" for children. Children treat size and hair length as dichotomous identifiers just as adults use genitalia.

Children's drawings and their identification of their own figures provide evidence of their thinking. Goodnow,[15] after decades of studying children's drawings, maintains that they represent "visual thinking." Her analyses indicate that children's drawings are a form of problem solving. Children think when they draw a figure; though their reasons for gender attribution may not be the same as the cues they use, they are sharing their interpretation of their reality. It is not until the child has incorporated the concept of dichotomous gender invariance based on genitalia that the child and the adult use the *same* rules for gender attribution.

The children's identification of their drawings tends to support the cognitive learning theory of gender development; however, their responses elucidate the learning of cultural valuing of the attributes of gender. Eventually children learn to give "good" reasons for identification by gender. Their interpretation of what is factual is modified to fit the cultural structure of a two-gender world.

Kessler and McKenna[17] suggest that children initially form a belief in two genders as much on the basis of behaviors as on biological differences, even though women and men and even children do not necessarily behave dichotomously. Yet we are no more gender-blind than we are color-blind. We still ask "What'd you have?" and we continue to interpret behavior and make differential attributions regarding motivations based on gender even knowing that the genders behave in similar ways.

Gender attribution leads children to a "discovery" of biological, psychological, and social differences, which are examined in the next sections. Research on human similarities and differences contributes to the understanding of the development of gender role identification and behavior: of how the child learns what it *means* to be a girl or a boy, feminine or masculine.

INFLUENCES ON GENDER DEVELOPMENT
Biological influences

Are there genetically controlled characteristics that predispose a child to learn a particular behavior? Psychoendocrine research has provided data to indicate that some behavioral or tempermental proclivities may be influenced by prenatal hormonal environment, although most dispositions may be modified by social influences.[1] The gender assigned and reinforced by rearing is rarely modified after the age of 3 years, except in the case of transsexuals. (For a full discussion, see Kessler and McKenna[17] and Stoller.[38])

Biological principles determine anatomical differences between females and males. At conception the genetic gender of the fetus is established. The basic structure is female, because of the ovum's X chromosomes. For a male fetus to develop, a Y chromosome from the sperm and androgens must be present; the androgen hormones influence the development of external and internal genitalia as well as the central nervous system.

Money and Ehrhardt[26] studied 25 androgenized girls compared with a matched control group. During pregnancy in the 1950s the mothers of these girls were given progestin (which acted like androgen) to prevent miscarriages. Essentially the hormones influenced the development of masculinized daughters, some infants being born with penises though their internal reproductive organs were female. The penises were removed surgically at birth, and additional hormonal treatment at puberty ensured development of secondary gender characteristics.

Money and Ehrhardt[26] studied these girls to ascertain if prenatal androgens had affected their behaviors. They found that the girls who had been fetally androgenized displayed more tomboy behaviors, though not physical aggression, than the control group. The group more than the controls preferred toy trucks to dolls and a functional style of dress and showed little interest in mothering younger children. The group had chosen careers over marriage, in contrast with the opposite interest of the controls. Money and Ehrhardt concluded that prenatal hormonal treatments influenced the brain and subsequent behaviors of the androgenized group. Both female and male fetuses exposed to synthetic progestins tend to be "ultra-masculine," according to Money. Researchers at Rutgers have found that estrogens taken during pregnancy tend to lead to a stronger group dependency and a disposition for the child to be a joiner.[31]

Research into biological influences continues. There is some indication, especially in the work of John Money and his colleagues, that hormonal differences may predispose certain neural pathways to receive certain types of neural information. Findings from this area of research combined with observations of differences in performance on measures of aggression and visual-spatial tasks has led some scientists to conclude that "male superiority [with respect to mathematical ability] is probably an expression of a combination of both endogenous and exogenous variables."[4]

Conclusive answers to questions of biological contributions to gender development must come from further investigation. The child's awareness and understanding of the constancy of external genitalia, however, are central to the gender identity process; evidence of hormonal influences on gender role development and behavior is still being gathered and its conclusiveness assessed.[39] The very idea that active, tomboy behavior, playing with trucks, and so on is identified and referred to as masculine whereas nurturing is referred to as feminine, suggests that the culture has constructed them as such.

Psychological influences

A world dichotomized in two genders is a world in which scientists can discover differences according to gender. The challenge is to differentiate those beliefs that create the social construction of gender and are based on reliable "evidence" from those that are based on generalized stereotypes and yet have become so deeply embedded as to be self-fulfilling prophecies.

Evidence indicates a greater variability *within* gender than *between* genders.[22] More differences exist among girls and women and among boys and men than between girls as a group and boys as a group. Furthermore, girls and boys are developmentally more similar than they are different.

It is difficult to draw definitive conclusions from the research on gender difference and its relationship to gender development. Researchers note that even repeated findings of gender differences do not necessarily indicate the *origin* of the differences.[21,27] In addition, as noted earlier, the underlying assumptions inherent in scientists' questions (such as "Are you a girl or a boy?") control the parameters of the response. In other instances observers' judgments are influenced by their perception of the gender of the participants in a study. For example, college student observers viewed a videotape of a 9-month-old child. For some observers the child was given a girl's name and for others a boy's name. When the observers believed the infant to be a boy, its strong reaction to a jack-in-the-box was labeled *anger;* when the observers believed the infant a girl, they assessed the reaction as *fear.*[21] It is almost impossible when examining research studies to measure the effects of the gender belief system of the observer. The study cited above should serve to indicate the power of subjective judgments made by observers. These cautions regarding research on gender differences and the power of the two-gender dichotomy must be kept in mind.

Leonore J. Weitzman in the following chapter discusses in depth the socialization to "sex" roles and the process by which children learn the "appropriate" behaviors for their roles.

To summarize briefly, children acquire a growing understanding of gender role expectations as they experience increasingly broader contacts—from the immediate family, relatives, teachers, and peers to adults in other environments, such as shopkeepers, bus drivers, medical people. The pattern of this development is as follows:

1. Children first hold fairly stereotypical notions of gender roles.
2. Children view gender-"inappropriate" behavior as wrong; they hold their peers in tow.
3. After about 9 years of age, children follow "appropriate" behaviors by custom, not moral force; boys exercise few deviations though girls may be tomboys.
4. As children develop cognitively, their ability to expand the categories of gender role behavior expands. Unfortunately, this expansion becomes ultimately limited by cultural beliefs and attitudes.
5. Developing flexible conceptions of gender-"appropriate" behavior may be particularly difficult for children in our society—unless there are continuous efforts by parents and teachers to encourage both girls and boys to achieve a balance between self-assertiveness and a concern for others. Block[6] suggests that the integration in girls and boys through an active socialization process of agency and self-assertion with communion, mutuality, and interdependence would broaden and enrich each child's human potential.

Studies of differentiated behaviors along gender lines indicate the following general tendencies:

1. Preschool children tend to prefer activities and toys that are gender-typed.
2. Preschool children tend to choose same-gender playmates even before 3 years of age.
3. The style of play among preschool children differs: boys tend to exhibit more aggression and rougher play than girls.
4. Girls at the age of about 4 increasingly use rules of procedure, for example, taking turns during playtime.
5. Boys at the age of about 4 become increasingly more gender-typed than girls and avoid those activities and toys labeled "sissy" by peers.

(For a detailed discussion, see Maccoby and Jacklin[22] and Maccoby.[21])

The summary above identifies areas in which research findings have indicated differences between girls and boys. On the other hand, these studies do not indicate the origin or cause for the differences.

Parents' role

Do parents treat children in a way that shapes them toward gender-"appropriate" behaviors? Are some behaviors rewarded and others sanctioned?

Maccoby and Jacklin's review[22] of socialization patterns in parental behavior indicates very few differences. Nevertheless, stereotypes of gender influence adult's perceptions of newborn infants.[33] Thirty pairs of parents were interviewed during the first 24 hours after their child's birth. The infants did not differ in weight, length, or Apgar scores. Yet daughters were rated as pretty, little, and soft whereas sons were rated as robust, strong, and large-featured in comparison. Mothers and fathers physically handle their new infants similarly and are close, gentle, and responsive.[28]

As the infant gets older different styles of interacting do emerge; mothers tend to do more caretaking, diaper changing, and feeding whereas father do more playing, tossing, and wrestling. Block[6] notes that boys are encouraged to achieve, compete, control their feelings; girls are encouraged to be dependent, caring, and verbal about their feelings. These encouraged characteristics can have far-ranging implications for restricting the potential behaviors of both girls and boys. In contrast, adults of both genders who rate high in terms of psychological androgyny accept gender-"appropriate" and "not appropriate" roles without difficulty or self-consciousness, and share, for example, child-caring tasks.[2,3]

Indicative of the dichotomous messages of child-rearing practices, most parents think that it is important for their children's clothes and toys to be gender-identifiable by others. Further, parents discourage their sons from activities considered appropriate for girls. In Marlo Thomas's song "William Wants a Doll," 5-year-old William's desire for a doll "to hug and hold" is the epitome of this taboo. He is called a "sissy" by his friend, a "jerk" by his cousin. His father buys him the traditional basketball and baseball glove. Finally the grandmother explains that William wants a doll so that he may learn the care his own child will need someday. As the song ends, William's grandma buys him a doll.

Parental anxieties regarding indications of homosexual tendencies in their sons, as perceived to be demonstrated by home-making, dressing-up, and playing with dolls, evoke powerful parental restrictions on young boys' play. Nevertheless, in preschool classes for 2- and 3-year-olds, all activities involving dolls, trucks, cooking, and blocks are engaged in by children regardless of gender when teachers foster play and promote the activities as components of the total learning process.[8,12,36] Maccoby and Jacklin[22] conclude that "at least not many behaviors are strong enough to elicit clear differential reactions from caretakers."

Do parents and teachers view the two gender roles differently? It appears that parents and teachers do perceive different "natural" characteristics for the two genders, demonstrated by expressions such as "Just like a little boy." Aggression is seen as natural for boys and dependency as natural for girls. Nevertheless, adults believe it is important for boys and girls to possess similar characteristics. Studying 64 prospective parents from three different delivery environments (home birth, maternity centers, and hospitals), Sacks and Donnenfeld[35] found that over 85% of the parents in each group thought it was important for both sons and daughters

> to have good manners
> to be responsible
> to have good sense and judgment
> to have interests and talents
> to be able to make decisions.

Eiduson[11] studied 200 parents about to have children, a sample group equally divided among unmarried couples, single mothers, living groups, and nuclear two-parent family structures; the families participated for 3 years. Eiduson reported the following:

1. Fathers did not participate in child caretaking as much as they had anticipated before the child's birth. In all groups the fathers contributed the bulk of income.
2. Mothers still performed most of the domestic work and child caretaking, but fathers did help with the former (such as laundry and shopping).
3. Mothers remained in charge of nursing, changing diapers, grooming, and feeding. Fathers, when they were involved, were observed roughhousing and going for a walk with the child; mothers taught, played with, and cuddled the child.
4. Families with expressed gender-role egalitarian philosophies were no different from others with respect to toys, activities, and dress for the children: all were essentially unisex.
5. Children were considered children: any differences in socialization, eating, toileting, or discipline were not treated as a function of the child's gender.
6. In general and regardless of gender, parents were openly affectionate with the children, encouraged their independence, and fostered cooperation.
7. Finally, the data about gender differences among the 200 children revealed similar psychological, social, physical, and nutritional development for boys and girls from infancy to the age of 3 years.

Even in families choosing alternative living structures, parental values and philosophies do not appear to influence child-rearing practices during the early childhood years. From this and other studies, the period from ages 3 to 6 rather than the period of infancy may be crucial for parents who wish to implement egalitarian gender role preferences in their child-rearing practices. It is during the period from 3 to 6, when children's gender identity formulation is consolidating, that flexibility of parents' and preschool teachers' in respect to gender role appropriateness could make a difference. Children encouraged to explore their fullest potential would not be bound by gender-"appropriate" behaviors that are socially constructed on the basis of gender stereotypes.

Overall, Maccoby and Jacklin[22] conclude that there is remarkable uniformity in the socialization of young children. This picture may shift, however, as scientists gather more data on the role of parental influences in child-rearing, especially the influences of fathers and siblings. At this time it appears only that boys have more intense experiences of socialization from both parents and teachers. Boys tend to be restricted from gender-"inappropriate" activities more frequently than girls, and boys receive more frequent reinforcements—punishment, praise, encouragement— from both parents and teachers. Boys evoke more concern regarding their behavior and performance, and whatever the explanation for this may be, the greater amount of socialization pressure that boys experience certainly has consequences for the development of their identity and gender role behaviors.

Gender role stereotyping and the consequent internalization by children hurts both girls and boys. Girls learn to repress their energy and curiosity and to conform to "appropriate" roles as conveyed in the family, school, books, mass media, and peer groups. Boys learn to fill their traditional role or suffer the consequences of deviating from the expected, the norm. Making flexible these traditional role-limiting charac-teristics would allow freedom for children to grow.

This brief review of the psychological factors influencing gender role identity and behaviors suggests the following as areas for further research:

- Empirical research on the influence of same- and other-gender siblings and the gender composition in the family structure could elucidate our under-standing of gender identity development.
- Considerably more work is called for on the influences of fathers as co-parents and on gender role development. Are fathers more lenient with daughters? More demanding with sons? How similar or different are fathers as nurturers compared to mothers?
- Will parents who choose alternative life-styles translate their values to non-gender-specific child-rearing practices? Will these children then differ with respect to gender identity and gender role identity from those traditionally reared?
- More research is needed to ascertain why girls and boys between 6 and 12 years of age engage frequently in same-gender activities. Is their gender identity so fragile during these years that it cannot withstand "testing" by mixing?
- Life span and human development research should address questions of gen-der identity changes. As a person no longer needs to be identified as an egg or

sperm carrier for reproductive purposes, core gender identity may evolve to incorporate other gender attributes. Chromosomes and carrier characteristics may be replaced by other identifying characteristics.

Research issues that seek differences in terms of a two-gender dichotomy make *difference* an irreducible concept. Chodorow[10] states that the focus on gender differences denies "those *processes* that create the meaning and significance of gender." Fundamental research must involve a *re*examination of the construction of gender inherited by and sustained in our culture, with a focus on understanding how gender differences are produced and, consequently, reproduce gender inequalities. We must shift our vantage point and reexamine the fundamental premise of the construction of a two-gender world. In a non-gender organized culture, there is little evidence that biological or psychological gender differences would be identified as salient.

Cultural influences

The position presented here is that neither individual gender identity formation nor gender role development occurs in isolation from the social climate. The environment for gender formation, and in fact the notions regarding gender itself, are integral to the production and reproduction of society's thinking. When concepts of feminity and masculinity cease to be value weighted and the constraints of gender are eliminated, people will be free to be uniquely human, to develop their full capacities.[3]

Then autonomy *and* attachment, agency *and* communion, can be integrated and individually expressed. Girls and boys beyond 3 years of age will *not* be forced to internalize differentially valued "appropriate" behaviors and thus will not carry into adulthood conflicts from being assertive, competent girls and nurturant, help-seeking boys.[34] Clearly children gradually become aware of being girls or boys. Their early play involves switching back and forth in gender identity and role. Sometimes they play "mommies," sometimes "fire chief." When gender role behaviors are not narrowly sanctioned, formation of gender identity is not confounded by limitations on "appropriateness" of roles.

A broad construction of humanness contributes dignity to differences. If a man chooses to become a nurse, he is no less a male; if a woman chooses to become a surgeon, she is no less a female. Possessing the competencies and interests to select a career that deviates from the expected gender role occupation need not conflict with one's gender identity. The point is that gender identity is elastic with respect to the components of one's being that it encompasses. Since nursing and medicine in this country have been traditionally gender restricted, choosing a perceived across-gender occupation tests one's sense of gender identity. One's gender identity as female or male may be expanded or made more complex, but the person makes the choice *within* her or his concept of female or male identity.

Gilman[14] writes, "That the children might be most nobly born, and reared in an environment calculated to allow the richest, freest growth, they had deliberately remodeled and improved the whole state." To remodel and improve the whole state would be to recognize the narrowness of gender pathways. I reacted to my colleague's call after she gave birth with the question, "What'd you have?" And yet the more I think about this question, the more I reflect that what made the question seem inevitable is precisely what creates such difficulty in determining how the human being develops its gender identity.

The question demonstrates the cultural dichotomy: If it is a girl, then. . . . If it is a boy, then. . . . It helps the questioner call upon her/his repertoire of "appropriate" reactions and responses. It governs which behaviors the adult will elicit. Overall, parents and adults *tend* to treat girl and boy infants and children simply as children, but they also tend to permeate their environments with gender-related symbols of dress, toys, reinforced activities, verbal and nonverbal interactions, and handling. In subtle and sometimes not easily measurable ways, adults envision and value a two-gender social order.

If gender is understood as a social construction and the dichotomous view of gender is questioned, adults can question the narrow, constrictive concepts of gender role that are the product of dichotomized thinking. A nongender world would eliminate the need for advice from mothers to daughters, as described by Rich in *Of Women Born:*

> "You can be anything you really want to be"—*if* you are prepared to fight, to create priorities for yourself against the grain of cultural expectations, to persist in the face of misogynist hostility. Interpreting to a little girl, or to an adolescent woman, the kinds of treatment she encounters because she is female, is as necessary as explaining to a non-white child reactions based on the color of her skin.[32]

One's gender identity is ever forming, shaping, and reshaping rather than fixed by the understanding of genital constancy. Rethinking gender means blurring the lines between what is prescribed and proscribed as female or male and feminine or masculine. Opening our minds to such thinking opens the paths for reconstructing human interactions and improving the whole state.

• • •

LABELING

Why do we look and label? With a minimum of "seeing," we size up a person on the basis of limited information and form an almost instant first impression that tends to survive later contacts. There are advantages to labeling; it is efficient, economical, and quick and often serves as a guide to behavior. By rapidly labeling a child a girl, we do not have to redefine attributes or search for more than a salient clue, and we may call upon our responses to girls without regard for the individuality of this particular child.

The assignment of a label poses disadvantages:

□ *Lack of interest.* The thing, idea, or person is found to be uninteresting because one has not fully attended to it. The process of sticking a label on something tends to end one's attention to that something. As well, labels themselves are not interesting; it is the real thing, idea, or person behind the label that is interesting.

□ *Mislabeling can occur.* Since the label was originally based on minimal information, mislabeling happens. What cues were used to assign the label? Is a child who runs around the room a lot thereby labeled "disturbed"? Is advocating tests and grades in itself a "traditional" idea? Is an object with four legs and a back necessarily a "chair"?

□ *Mislabeling can lead to inappropriate behavior.* Creative ideas may be rejected because the mislabel did not encourage close examination.

□ *Mislabeling can become a self-fulfilling prophecy.* The child once labeled comes to believe the label and then tends to behave according to the expectations for the label.

Labels are used in everyday life in almost everything we do. We need labels to organize, understand, and deal with our experiences. We gain efficiency, economy, speed, and knowledge of how to behave by being able to put labels quickly on things, ideas, and people. But we lose richness of experience, full meaning, and interest when we label. We also run the risk of distorting reality and creating self-fulfilling prophecies.

AN EXERCISE

When looking at a child . . .

1. Start with a glance; casually form first impressions.

2. Then slow down, look again, and refine, elaborate, and go beyond your first glance. What did you look at first? What cues did you use to get that first impression? What was most noticeable at first? Why? What did you pick up on at first that holds up on further looking? What did you pick up on that seems distorted or false on further looking?

3. Slow down further—allow yourself to get confused—suspend all labels and categories and ideas and "right" and "wrong" ways to proceed. Forget what you're supposed to find. Just look.

4. Look with full attention. Stop thinking in words or analyzing or cogitating. Just look.

5. Look very closely. Look from all angles. Look at all parts. Look around and upside down. Look sideways and backwards. Just look.

6. Look at everything—talk, actions, smiles, frowns, shoulders tensed, relaxed, quick and slow movements, silences, pacing. Notice the *how* of everything. Take it all in. Really look.

After much looking . . .

1. *Write down* in descriptive form what you saw, as behavioral anecdotes. Use "doing" words richly, such as *smiling, winking, pushing, tripping, hitting, beckoning, running towards* or *away from, teasing, joshing,* and so on. Tell the "how" of every action, every doing, every situation. Children do not just *walk,* for example. They walk slowly, haltingly, awkwardly, unsteadily, reluctantly, purposefully, casually, and so on. Notice expressive nonverbal behavior and record it. Children do not just sit, for example. They slouch, perch, or sit at the chair's edge and are relaxed, tense, eager, happy, squirmy, and so on in sitting.

2. Now think of some *labels* that come out of the experience of looking. These are inferences from the data. Are they the same or different from the labels you used before? How are they different? Why are they different? Did you see things differently after much *slow* observation?

3. What was the *experience* like for you? What were your feelings about the child? What did you learn? How rich or how mechanical was your looking? How interesting and full was your final portrait of the child? How thorough a reproduction was it? What haven't you seen still that you'd like to, to complete the picture?

ACKNOWLEDGMENT

I wish to express special appreciation to Lauren S. Sacks for typing the drafts of this chapter.

REFERENCES

1. Baker, S.W.: Biological influences on human sex and gender, Signs: Journal of Women in Culture and Society 6(1):80, 1980.
2. Bem, S.L.: Sex-role adaptability: one consequence of psychological androgyny, Journal of Personality and Social Psychology 31:634, 1975.
3. Bem, S.L.: Probing the promise of androgyny. In Kaplan, S.G., and Bean, J.F., editors: Beyond sex-role stereotypes: readings toward a psychology of androgyny, Boston, 1976, Little, Brown & Co.
4. Benbow, C.P., and Stanley, J.C.: Sex differences in mathematical ability: fact or artifact? Science 210:1262, 1980.
5. Biehler, R.F.: Child development: an introduction, ed. 2, Boston, 1981, Houghton Mifflin Co.
6. Block, J.H.: Conceptions of sex role: some cross-cultural and longitudinal perspectives, American Psychologist 28(6):512, 1973.
7. Broverman, I., and others: Sex role stereotypes: a current appraisal, Journal of Social Issues 28:59, 1972.
8. Carmichael, C.: Non-sexist childraising, Boston, 1977, Beacon Press.
9. Chodordow, N.: The reproduction of mothering: psychoanalysis and the sociology of gender, Berkeley, 1978, University of California Press.
10. Chodorow, N.: Feminism and difference in psychoanalytic perspective, Socialist Review 9:66, July-August 1979.
11. Eiduson, B.T.: Changing sex roles of parents and children. In Anthony, E.J., and Chiland, C., editors: The child in his family: preventive child psychiatry in an age of transition, New York, 1980, John Wiley & Sons, Inc.
12. Frazier, N., and Sadker, M.: Sexism in school and society, New York, 1973, Harper & Row, Publishers, Inc.

13. Freud, S.: A general introduction to psychoanalysis, New York, 1952, Washington Square Press.

14. Gilman, C.P.: Herland, London, 1979, The Women's Press, Ltd.

15. Goodnow, J.: Children drawing, Cambridge, 1977, Harvard University Press.

16. Hyde, J.S., and Rosenberg, B.G.: Half the human experience: the psychology of women, ed. 2, Lexington, Mass., 1980, D.C. Heath & Co.

17. Kessler, S.J., and McKenna, W.: Gender: an ethnomethodological approach, New York, 1978, John Wiley & Sons, Inc.

18. Kohlberg, L.: A cognitive-developmental analysis of children's sex-role concepts and attitudes. In Maccoby, E., editor: The development of sex differences, Stanford, 1966, Stanford University Press.

19. Lynn, D.B.: Parental and sex role identification: a theoretical formulation, Berkeley, Calif., 1969, McCutchan Publishing Corp.

20. Lynn, D.B.: The father: his role in child development, Monterey, Calif., 1974, Brooks/Cole Publishing Co.

21. Maccoby, E.E.: Social development: psychological growth and the parent-child relationship, New York, 1980, Harcourt Brace Jovanovich, Inc.

22. Maccoby, E.E., and Jacklin, C.N.: The psychology of sex differences, vol. 1, Stanford, 1974, Stanford University Press.

23. Miller, J.B., editor: Psychoanalysis and women, Baltimore, 1973, Penguin Books.

24. Mischel, W.: A social-learning view of sex differences in behavior. In Maccoby, E., editor: The development of sex differences, Stanford, 1966, Stanford University Press.

25. Money, J., and Ehrhardt, A.A.: Prenatal hormonal exposure: possible effects on behavior in man. In Michael, R.P., editor: Endocrinology and human behaviour, London, 1968, Oxford University Press.

26. Money, J., and Ehrhardt, A.: Man and woman/boy and girl, Baltimore, 1972, Johns Hopkins Press.

27. O'Leary, V.E.: Toward understanding women, Belmont, Calif., 1977, Wadsworth Publishing Co.

28. Parke, R.D., and Sawin, D.B.: The father's role in infancy: a reevaluation, The Family Coordinator **25**:365, 1976.

29. Person, E.S.: Sexuality as the mainstay of identity: psychoanalytic perspectives, Signs: Journal of Women in Culture and Society **5**(4):605, 1980.

30. Pleck, J.H.: Masculinity-feminity: current and alternative paradigms, Sex Roles **1**:161, 1975.

31. Restak, R.M.: Birth defects and behavior: a new study suggests a link, New York Times, January 21, 1979.

32. Rich, A.: Of women born, New York, 1976, W.W. Norton & Co., Inc.

33. Rubin, J.Z., Provenzano, F.J., and Luria, A.: The eye of the beholder: parents' views on sex of newborns, American Journal of orthopsychiatry **44**(4):512, 1974.

34. Sacks, S.R., and Eisenstein, H.: Feminism and psychological autonomy: a study in decision making, Personnel and Guidance Journal **57**:419, April 1979.

35. Sacks, S.R., and Donnenfeld, P.: Parental attitudes toward alternative birth environments and child-rearing philosophy. Paper presented at the Birth Psychology Conference, New York, June 1980.

36. Stacey, J., Béreaud, S., and Daniels, J., editors: And Jill came tumbling after: sexism in American education, New York, 1974, Dell Publishing Co., Inc.

37. Stoller, R.J.: Facts and fancies: an examination of Freud's concept of bisexuality. In Strouse, J., editor: Women and analysis, New York, 1974, Grossman Publishers.

38. Stoller, R.J.: Sex and gender, vol. 2, New York, 1975, Jason Aronson, Inc.

39. Wittig, M.A.: Sex differences in intellectual functioning: how much of a difference do genes make? Sex Roles **2**(1):63, 1976.

LENORE J. WEITZMAN

Chapter 2

Sex-role socialization

In our society women are characterized as passive, dependent and emotional in contrast to men, who are considered aggressive, active and instrumental. How can these differences be explained? Are women "naturally" more passive, or are they taught to be more passive? Are men inherently more aggressive, or does our society socialize men into more aggressive roles?

To shed some light on the continued controversy over whether (or to what degree) these observed difference are learned or inherent, this paper will focus on the socialization process. I want to examine how the socialization process shapes the sex roles that women and men come to accept as entirely natural and self-evident.

EARLY CHILDHOOD SOCIALIZATION

Socialization begins at birth. From the minute a newborn baby girl is wrapped in a pink blanket and her brother in a blue one, the two children are treated differently. The difference starts with the subtle tone of voice of the adults cooing over the two cradles, and continues with the father's mock wrestling with his baby boy and gentler play with his "fragile" daughter.[41] Researchers have observed sex differences in behavior of male and female babies at amazingly young ages, most of it directly traceable to parents' differential treatment of infant boys and girls.

Moss's[54] observations of mothers with infants at three weeks and three months show that even the newborn baby is consistently being given reinforcement for appropriate behavior. Moss, in fact, has tentatively suggested that patterns leading to verbal ability in girls and aggression in boys were being selectively encouraged in the infants he observed.

Infant socialization

In observing thirteen-month-old babies, Goldberg and Lewis[20] found that the little girls clung to, looked at, and talked to their mothers more often than the little

Revised from Weitzman, L.J.: In Freeman, J., editor: Women: a feminist perspective, Palo Alto, Calif., 1979, Mayfield Publishing Co.

boys. Each of these behavioral differences, however, was linked to differential treatment by the mother when the babies were younger. The researchers had observed the same mothers with their babies when the babies were six months old. At that stage they observed that mothers of girl babies touched their infant girls more often then did mothers of infant boys. They also talked to and handled their daughters more often.[38] By the time these same children were thirteen months old, the researchers observed that the girl babies had learned to respond to the more frequent stimuli they received from their mothers: they reciprocated their mothers' attention, with the result that by thirteen months they talked to and touched their mothers more often than the boys did.

This research vividly illustrates socialization at its earliest stages. It indicates that sex-role socialization begins before the child is even aware of a sexual identity: before he or she can have an internal motive for conforming to sex-role standards. It also indicates that cultural assumptions about what is "natural" for a boy or for a girl are so deeply ingrained that parents may treat their children differently without even being aware of it. Presumably, if we interviewed mothers of six-month-old babies, they would not tell us that they expected their young sons to be independent and assertive while still in the cradle. Yet, it appears that at some level mothers do have such expectations, and these expectations are successfully communicated to very young babies. Thus, wittingly or unwittingly, parents encourage and reinforce sex-appropriate behavior, and little boys and little girls respond to parental encouragement and rewards. So little boys learn to be independent, active, and aggressive; their sisters learn to be dependent, verbal, and social.

Early cognitive socialization

We have been discussing the first type of socialization an infant experiences: simple behavior reinforcement. A second type of socialization begins with cognitive learning—when the child is able to sort out and make conceptual distinctions about the social world and herself or himself. Around the age of three or four, the child begins to make sex-role distinctions and express sex-role preferences. Rabban[59] found that at the age of three both boys and girls still showed incomplete recognition of sex differences and were unaware of the appropriateness of sex-typed toy objects. Each year, however, children's cognitive abilities increase: by age six they are able to distinguish the male and female role clearly, and to identify themselves appropriately. Sex-role learning in these preschool years may be divided into three analytic processes. The child learns:

1. To *distinguish* between men and women and between boys and girls, and to know what kinds of behavior are characteristic of each
2. To express appropriate sex-role *preferences* for himself or herself
3. To *behave* in accordance with sex-role standards

Distinguishing between male and female roles

Both boys and girls learn to distinguish the male from the female role by observing the men and women around them: their parents, brothers and sisters, neighbors, and friends. In addition to serving as models for the young child, these adults and older boys and girls often provide explicit instructions on proper behavior. Little girls are told what is considered nice and ladylike, and little boys are told what is expected of big strong men.

As already noted, parents are especially influential in defining the male and female role for the young child. They do this both consciously and unconsciously, by example and proscription, by reward and punishment. There is some evidence that fathers are more concerned than mothers with sex-typing in young children. Goodenough's interviews[25] with the parents of two- to four-year-old children indicated that fathers more strictly differentiated sex roles and encouraged stronger sex typing in children than did mothers.

Picture books are another important source of sex-role learning for young children. Through books, children learn about the world outside their immediate environment: they learn what other boys and girls do, say, and feel, and they learn what is expected of children of their age. In a 1972 study of prize-winning pre-school picture books, Weitzman and others[72] found girls portrayed as passive, doll-like creatures, while the boys were active and adventuresome. Most of the little girls engaged in service activities directed toward pleasing and helping their brothers and fathers. In contrast, the boys were engaged in a variety of tasks requiring independence and self-confidence.

Picture books also provided children with role models—images of what they will be like when they grow up. Weitzman and others found the adult women portrayed in these award-winning books were consistently stereotyped and limited. Most were identified only as wives or mothers. The men were shown in a wide variety of occupations and professions, whereas not one of the adult women had an outside job or profession. The authors conclude that in the world of picture books:

> Little girls receive attention and praise for their attractiveness, while boys are admired for their achievements and cleverness. For girls, achievement is marriage and becoming a mother. Most of the women in picture books have status by virtue of their relationships to specific men—they are the wives of the kings, judges, adventurers and explorers, but they themselves are not the rulers, judges, adventurers and explorers.

> Through picture books, girls are taught to have low aspirations because there are so few opportunities portrayed as available to them. The world of picture books never tells little girls that as women they might find fulfillment outside of their homes or through intellectual pursuits . . .

> In a country with over 40 percent of the women in the labor force it is absurd to find that women in picture books remain only mothers and wives . . .

Their future occupational world is presented as consisting primarily of glamour and service. Women are excluded from the world of sports, politics and science. They can achieve only by being attractive, congenial and serving others.[72]

Another influential source of sex-role socialization for young children is television. Gardner's study of the program *Sesame Street* (another supposed ideal) indicated that television contributes equally to severe sex-role stereotypes.

Although the images in children's books and TV programs appear to be more stereotyped and rigid than reality, interviews with young children indicate the extent to which these clearly differentiated sex roles are internalized by the child. Hartley asked a sample of young boys what they thought was expected of boys and girls. Her respondents described boys as follows:

They have to be able to fight in case a bully comes along; they have to be athletic; . . . they must be able to play rough games . . . they need to be smart; they need to be able to take care of themselves; they should know what girls don't know . . . they should have more ability than girls . . . they are expected to get dirty; to mess up the house; to be naughty; to be outside more than girls are; not to be cry babies, not to be softies; and to get into trouble more than girls do.[26]

Girls, according to the boy respondents,

have to stay close to home; they are expected to play quietly and more gently than boys; they are often afraid; they must not be rough; they have to keep clean; they cry when scared or hurt; their activities consist of "fopperies" like playing with dolls, fussing over babies, and sitting and talking about dresses; they need to know how to cook, sew and take care of children, but spelling and arithmetic are not as important for them as for boys.[26]

When Hartley asked her young respondents about adults, she found their images of the two sexes even more disparate. In the children's eyes men are active and intelligent,

strong, ready to make decisions, protect women and children in emergencies. . . . They must be able to fix things, they must get money to support their families, and have a good business head. Men are the boss in the family and have the authority to dispose of money and they get first choice in the use of the most comfortable chair in the house and the daily paper. . . . They laugh and make more jokes than women do. Compared with mothers, fathers are more fun to be with: they are exciting to have around and they have the best ideas.[26]

In contrast, women are seen as a rather tired and unintelligent group.

They are indecisive and they are afraid of many things; they make a fuss over things, they get tired a lot . . . they don't know what to do in an emergency, they cannot do dangerous things, they are scared of getting wet or getting an electric shock, they are not very intelligent. . . . Women do things like cooking and washing and sewing because that's all they can do.[26]

Expressing sex-role preferences

Once the child has learned to distinguish males from females and has determined the types of behavior that are appropriate for each, he or she may begin to express sex-role preferences. Rabban[59] found that both boys and girls at age three decidedly prefer the mother role when asked to choose which parent they would prefer to be like.[59]

But the sex-role preferences of children soon change. By age five most boys, and a significant minority of girls, say they prefer the masculine role. Brown,[11] interviewing five- and six-year-old children, found more cross-sex preferences among girls (indicating a desire to be boys) than among boys. In addition, the boys show a significantly stronger preference for the masculine role than girls reveal for the feminine role. The research of Hartup and Zook[30] corroborates the finding about strength of preference and indicates, further, that with each year more girls prefer to identify with the masculine role than boys with the feminine role.[29]

One explanation for the general preference for the male role is that both boys and girls have learned it is more prestigious in our society. Thus, it is preferable. Hartley's study,[26] cited above, clearly indicates that children perceive the superior status and privileges of the masculine role. They know which sex gets the best chair in the house, and which sex is expected to do the cleaning. Brown,[11] using the values children give to sex-typed toys, also concluded that the children saw the masculine role as having greater prestige and value. Smith[69] has found evidence to suggest that as children grow older, they increasingly learn to give males more prestige. He asked children from eight to fifteen to vote on whether boys or girls have desirable or undesirable traits. With increasing age both boys and girls increasingly ascribed the desirable traits to boys. In addition, boys expressed a progressively better opinion of themselves while self-conceptions of girls progressively weakened.[69]

Thus children learn that it is better to be a male than a female because it is men who exhibit the highly valued traits and are accorded the privilege and prestige in our society. No wonder, then, that girls are reluctant to express "appropriate" sex-role preferences, and instead continue wishing they were boys. Boys, by contrast, find it easy to express "appropriate" sex role preferences.

It is likely that the preferences of some young girls are different today. The women's liberation movement has brought a heightened awareness of the impact of negative sex-role stereotypes, and conscious attempts to change them. In addition, feminists have encouraged parents to raise their children in a sex-neutral manner and to instill a sense of pride in their daughters.

Learning sex-role behavior

The third component of the socialization process consists of learning to act like a girl or a boy. Boys appear to have more difficulty learning appropriate sex-role behavior. Their difficulty stems from three sources: the lack of continuous male role models, the rigidity and harshness of masculine sex-role demands, and the negative nature of male sex-role proscriptions.

Several theorists have suggested that boys know less about the masculine role because of the relative lack of salience of the father as a model. Lynn[44] notes that the father is in the home much less than the mother, and even when he is there, he usually participates in fewer intimate activities with the child than the mother does. Both the amount of time spent with the child, and the intimacy and intensity of parental contact are thought to be important for the child's learning. Since the girl is able to observe her mother throughout the day and has continuous and intimate contact with her, she supposedly finds it easier to use her mother as a model, and to imitate appropriate sex-role behavior.

Lynn[44] has further theorized that because boys have less direct exposure to male models they tend to develop stereotypical images of masculinity. This view has been supported by studies showing that fatherless boys have more exaggerated notions of masculinity than boys who have a father in the home.[43] The tendency of boys to pattern themselves after a male stereotype may help account for the exaggerated forms of masculinity encouraged by male peer groups. In the absence of fuller role models to emulate, boys may view exaggerated "toughness" and aggression as appropriate male behavior.

Hartley has suggested that boys have the additional problem of a more rigorous sex-role definition: "Demands that boys conform to social notions of what is manly come much earlier and are enforced with much more vigor than similar attitudes with respect to girls. These demands are frequently enforced harshly, impressing the small boy with the danger of deviating from them, while he does not quite understand what they are."[26] By contrast, very young girls are allowed a wider range of behavior and are punished less severely for deviation, especially in the middle class. (At young ages it is easier for a girl to be a tomboy than for a boy to be a sissy.) Upon reaching adolescence, however, the behavior of girls is more sharply constricted than is boys'.

In addition to the relative absence of male role models and the rigidity of the male sex role, the socialization of boys is said to be characterized by negative proscriptions.[25] Boys are constantly warned *not* to be sissies, and *not* to engage in other feminine behavior. The literature on learning suggests that it is harder to learn from punishment than from rewards, because the desired behavior is not enunciated in the sanction and therefore remains obscure.[23] Thus some theorists have asserted that the socialization of boys is particularly conducive to anxiety. In Hartley's words,

> the child is asked to do something which is not clearly defined for him, based on reasons he cannot possibly appreciate, and enforced with threats, punishments, and anger by those who are close to him. . . . Anxiety frequently expresses itself in over-straining to be masculine, in virtual panic at being caught doing anything traditionally defined as feminine, and in hostility toward anything even hinting at "femininity," including females themselves.[26]

In contrast to the anxiety-producing sex-role learning of the boy, the socialization literature characterizes the young girl's experiences as easy. She is supposedly provided with more positive opportunities to learn appropriate role behavior through her frequent interaction with her mother as well as the chance to try out her feminine role in her doll play.[28] This idyllic view of the learning process for girls appears naive to any women who has been socialized in a middle-class family. It is clear that the sex-role socialization process is equally anxiety-producing for girls, although for somewhat different reasons. The girl is provided with a female model, and is afforded more opportunity to "play out" the "appropriate" behavior, but the role she is asked to play is clearly not a desirable one. As already noted, children understand the relative worth of the two sexes at quite young ages. The little girl is therefore aware of the fact that she is being pushed, albeit gently, into a set of behaviors that are neither considered desirable nor rewarded by the society at large. For example, she is told that it is feminine to play house: to wash dishes, set the table, dress her doll, vacuum the floor, and cook the dinner. In many middle-class homes these activities are delegated to paid domestics, or performed with obvious distate. Why, then, should the little girl want to imitate those behaviors? I would hypothesize the little girl becomes quite anxious about being encouraged to perform a series of behaviors that are held in low esteem. I would hypothesize further that she experiences considerable internal conflict when she realizes that her mother, a loved model, receives neither recognition nor satisfaction for such activities, and yet encourages them in her.

In addition to perceiving the low evaluation of feminine activities, many young girls find boys' activities instrinsically more enjoyable. For example, boys' toys allow a much broader range of activity as well as more active and adventuresome involvement. "One of my biggest disappointments as a child," wrote a girl in Komarovsky's study, "happened on Christmas. I asked for a set of tools . . . only to find a sewing set."[41]

Since most growing children enjoy being active, running and playing outside, getting dirty if necessary, and being allowed to explore their own interests, it is not surprising that many girls prefer "boys" activities, and resent being restricted to being "a sweet little girl."

In reviewing the socialization literature I was struck by the fact that the harsh restrictions placed on boys are often discussed, but those placed on girls are ignored. In fact, there is no reason to believe that the socialization of boys involves greater restrictiveness, control, and protectiveness.[66] Boys may be punished more often, but girls' activities are likely to be so severely constrained to begin with that they never have a chance to engage in punishable behavior. It is also possible that the kinds of sanctions used to socialize women may be more subtle—but no less severe: boys are spanked, but girls may be made to feel unworthy, deviant, guilty, or queer.[9]

In summary, the socialization of boys and of girls may present different sets of difficulties, but difficulties and anxiety in the socialization process are common to both. Typically, girls have more readily available role models, but they probably have less motivation to imitate those models because they (correctly) view the role as more confining and less rewarding than the masculine role. Boys may have less salient role models, and experience more frequent physical punishment, but they have more motivation to learn the masculine role because they (correctly) view it as more highly valued than the feminine role, allowing more exciting and interesting activities.

Consequently, socialization must be understood as an anxiety-producing process for both boys and girls because it requires them both to conform to rigid sex-role standards that are often in conflict with their individual tempermanents or preferences. To the extent that we continue to define appropriate sex-role behavior for men and women as polar opposites, we will continue to push many individuals into unnatural molds.

The learning process: reactions, rewards, and punishment

Let us now briefly consider how specific characteristics are encouraged in children of each sex. According to Kagan,[37] the typical child seeks the acceptance of parents and peers and wants to avoid their rejection. These motives predispose her or him to shun inappropriate activities, and to choose responses that are congruent with sex-role standards.

Parents say that they want their daughters to be passive, nurturing, and dependent and their sons to be aggressive and independent. Therefore, most parents punish aggression in their daughters, and passivity and dependency in their sons.* For example, the little girl is allowed to cling to her mother's apron, but her brother is told that he can't be a "sissy" and must go off on his own. The dependency and affection-seeking responses seen as normal for both boys and girls in early childhood becomes defined as feminine in older children. The result, as Bardwick[2] has noted, is that girls are not separated from their parents as sources of support and nurturance, and they are therefore not forced to develop internal controls and an independent sense of self. Instead, the self that they value is one that emanates from the appraisals of others. Conseqently girls develop a greater need for the approval of others and a greater fear of rejection than do boys.[2]

Kagan[37] has observed that our definition of feminity *requires* reactions from other people. The young girl cannot assess whether she is attractive, nurturing or passive without continual interaction and feedback from others. She is thus forced to be dependent on people and to court their acceptance in order to obtain those experiences that help to estalish sex-typed behaviors.[37]

In contrast, the boy is encouraged to be self-reliant. Many masculine sex-typed

---

*References 1, 40, 56, 66.

behaviors, especially those involving physical skills, can be developed alone. A boy is taught to stand up for himself and engage in certain behavior because he, as a person, feels that it is appropriate. In fact, men who stand by their individual principles despite opposition and the scorn of others often become cultural heroes.

According to Bronfenbrenner,[10] different methods of child training are used for boys than for girls. Boys are subjected to more physical punishment, whereas psychological punishments, such as the threat of withdrawal of love, are more frequently used for girls. Children trained with physical punishment have been shown to be more self-reliant and independent.[10,65] The other method of child training—the love-oriented psychological method—usually produces children who are more obedient and dependent.[10] As girls are most often trained with psychological methods they are exposed to more affection and less punishment than boys. But they are also made more anxious about the withdrawal of love.

Thus, specific methods of child training and the cultural definition of femininity (which necessitates reliance on the approval of others) both encourage dependency in women. Kagan[37] links the crucial significance of others—and their acceptance or rejection—to the finding that girls are often more conforming and more concerned about socially desirable behavior than boys. Another interpretation of female conformity links it to doll-play training. David Matza[49] has hypothesized that girls are taught to be more conforming and concerned with socially acceptable behavior because they are trained to act as socializing agents with their dolls. By talking to, and "training" their dolls to do the right thing, the girls themselves gain a vast amount of experience in articulating and sanctioning the cultural norms.

VARIATION IN SEX-ROLE STANDARDS AND BEHAVIOR
Individual differences

Thus far we have taken the success of the socialization process for granted and have assumed that most boys and girls eventually adopt the prescribed sex-role behaviors. But most of us can think of exceptions—the self confident achievement-oriented girl, or the dependent boy who cares very much about others' opinions of him. We all know some people who seem to contradict the stereotypes and others, possibly including ourselves, who conform only to a percentage of them. In fact, we may often feel the pull of the extremes of a single trait within ourselves, wanting to be both independent and dependent at the same time, or feeling that we are at times totally oriented toward achievement and at other times holding back for fear of being too successful.

The continuing research debate

Before we continue, it is important to note that there is still considerable disagreement about the extent to which sex-linked behavioral differences actually exist.

Although the earlier research seemed to confirm the existence of differences,[71] many of these findings are now considered open to question.

Maccoby and Jacklin[47] report that the evidence is equivocal with respect to anxiety, level of activity, competitiveness, dominance, compliance and nurturance. In addition, although they find fairly solid support for the long-established behavioral differences in verbal ability, spatial ability, and aggressiveness, they do *not* find substantial support for previously reported findings that: (1) girls are more "social" than boys, (2) girls are more "suggestible" than boys, (3) girls have lower self-esteem, or (4) girls are less motivated toward achievement.

Social class variation in sex roles

Sex-role standards also differ by social class and by racial and ethnic group.[24] And even within these large subgroupings, various aspects of family composition affect both the content and the potency of sex-role socialization.

A parent's social class position is an important determinant of his or her sex-role standards and expectations. Sociologists have generally used a combination of three indicators to measure social class—education, occupation, and income. However, the research on sex-role socialization has been consistent no matter what indicator of class is used. All the studies have found that persons in the higher social classes tend to be less rigid about sex distinctions. In working-class and lower-class families, there is much more concern about different roles for boys and girls and men and women.

As might be expected from these parental expectations, differentiation between boys and girls appears to be sharpest in lower-class families.[24] Rabban[59] found that children from working-class families differentiate sex roles at earlier ages and have more traditional sex-role standards than middle-class children. He showed that working-class boys were aware of the appropriate sex-typed toy choices by age four or five; middle-class boys were not aware of them until age six. The class differences are even greater for girls. Middle-class girls not only showed later awareness of sex-typing than working-class girls, but were less traditional in their sex-role concepts.

Middle-class parents may encourage "traditional feminine behavior" in their daughters, but they also encourage a degree of independence and assertiveness. Not only are middle-class parents willing to "tolerate" daughters who are tomboys, many of them encourage their daughters to do well in sports and to excel in school. Lower-class parents are more likely to view such interests and achievements are "too masculine" and to discourage them.

A similar pattern emerges in the class-related sex-role expectations for boys. Middle-class parents are willing to let their sons be more expressive (to be more nurturant and tender), while working-class parents see these traits as "too feminine" or sissy.[64] Working-class parents want their sons to be instrumental, that is, to be focused on tasks and work.

In summary, then, middle-class parents are interested in seeing both their sons and their daughters develop a greater range of traits *along* both instrumental and expressive lines. In contrast, blue-collar parents encourage traditional sex-role behavior in both boys and girls.

Ethnic variation in sex roles

Further specification of sex-role standards occurs along ethnic and racial lines. Many people have the impression that Italians, Jews, Asian Americans, Chicanos, Irish, Poles, Blacks, and Puerto Ricans have distinctive conceptions or appropriate behavior for men and women.[18] With few exceptions, however, ethnic variation in sex-role standards has been ignored in the socialization literature.[7]

Unfortunately, most of the research on achievement motivation and ethnic differences in socialization focuses exclusively on male samples. As psychologist Matina Horner[35] has noted most social scientists investigating achievement motivation did not consider women's achievement important enough to investigate. Further, those few who originally included women in their samples later dropped the female respondents from their analysis when they found the females' responses did not conform to the male pattern.

Racial variation in sex roles: the case of black women

When one first approaches the research literature on black women one cannot help but be puzzled by two seemingly contradictory findings. Some researchers report that black women have adopted a more masculine sex role than white women and are strong, assertive, and independent. But other studies have shown that their self-images are even more sex-stereotyped than those of white women.

A way of resolving these findings is to recognize that they are not contradictory at all—each may reflect a different aspect of the black woman's multi-dimensional sex role. Thus black women may be more independent, more self-reliant, and more work-oriented than white women, but, at the same time, they may be as sensitive, nurturant, compassionate, and "feminine." The findings are contradictory only if we assume that "masculinity" and "femininity" are undimensional.

Women, and black women in particular, may have some "masculine traits" such as independence and self-sufficiency, *and* some traditional "feminine" characteristics, such as warmth and nurturance. For example, in his study of sex roles in the black community Scanzoni[63] found that he had to consider several different role dimensions—each of which varied independently. Thus he found that blacks were more "traditional" with respect to approved behavior for men and women, but were less traditional with respect to women's individualism. In addition, black women were both more nurturant and more task competent, and had more autonomy and power in the family. Thus these findings, like those reviewed above, indicate that "masculine" and "feminine" attributes cannot be viewed as polar opposites.

Similarly, Bem[3] has shown that individuals can score high on both masculinity and femininity, low on both, or some combination of the two. Further, a lot of sex-role behavior is likely to be *situationally specific*—that is, it is likely to depend on the social context. For example, a woman attorney may be assertive with clients, aggressive in court, tender with her husband and nurturant with her children. In fact, since sex-role attitudes and behaviors are likely to be much more *situationally specific* than the research literature seems to acknowledge, it is surprising that there have not been *more* seemingly contradictory findings—for both blacks and whites.

Family constellation and sex roles

In addition to class and race, another important variable in sex-role behavior is the family constellation—the number, spacing, and sex ratio of the children in the family. Brim[8] pointed out the importance of siblings in sex-role definitions, finding that children with cross-sex siblings exhibited more traits of the opposite sex than did those with same-sex siblings.[39] This effect was particularly strong when opposite-sex siblings were older. Thus, boys with older sisters and girls with older brothers are more likely to exhibit the traits of the opposite sex.

Another significant aspect of family constellation is the number and presence of adults. Many sociologists have assumed that children who grow up without a father or a mother must be inadequately socialized. However, recent research has indicated that father absence does not affect lower-class boys' occupational achievement, although it may have a depressant effect for middle- and upper-class boys.

On the other hand, the single parent mother-headed family may be a spur to occupational achievement in girls. Hunt and Hunt[35] have found that girls in father-absent families are freed from the ideal-typical female socialization. These families establish a new type of female role model, blurring the traditional distinction between male and female roles and the instrumental/expressive division of labor by sex, because mothers are performing both roles and both types of tasks. Thus, father absence, in conjunction with modifications of the mother role, may remove some of the conventional barriers to female occupational aspirations and achievement. When girls are not socialized into sharply differentiated sex roles, they may be freed from the traditional restraints on female achievement.

CONTINUING SOCIALIZATION

Although boys and girls learn sex roles early, the definition of appropriate sex-role behavior changes with age. The female sex role at age five is specific to the attributes of a five-year-old, and different from the female sex role at age twenty-five.[28] Sex-role socialization continues throughout the child's life as she or he learns age-specific sex-role behavior.

Thus far we have focused largely on socialization within the family. As the child matures and begins to participate in social relations outside the family, teachers, peers, and other socializing agents become more significant in defining and sanctioning appropriate sex-role behavior.

The influence of the school

Once the child enters school, her or his experiences there assume great importance. The educational system has generally reinforced sex-role stereotypes. One of the first messages communicated to girls at school is that they are less important than boys. For example, in a 1960 study of all third-grade readers published since 1930, Child and others[12] found 73 percent of the stories were about male characters. Girls' impressions that they are not very important are reinforced by the portrait of the few women who do appear in the texts. Child and others found girls and women shown as timid, inactive, unambitious, and uncreative. Females were not only the moral inferiors of males in these books (they are shown to be lazy twice as often as males), but their intellectual inferiors as well.

More recent examinations of elementary school readers indicate that even the newest textbooks retain the same stereotypes.[16,62,74] Nor are these stereotypes restricted to readers. Weitzman and Rizzo[73] have found that spelling, mathematics, science, and social studies textbooks purvey an equally limited image of women. Rarely are women mentioned in important roles in history, as government leaders, or as great scientists. This study found the stereotyping to be most extreme in the science textbooks, where only 6 percent of the pictures included adult women. Weitzman and Rizzo[73] hypothesize that the presentation of science as a prototypical masculine endeavor may help to explain how young girls are "cooled out" of science and channeled into more traditional "feminine" fields.

Guidance counselors and teachers can either help to reinforce conformity to the traditional female role, or present exciting new role models to impressionable young girls. In the past they have mostly done the former. Most schools have had a sex-stereotyped tracking system in which girls are channeled into the more "feminine" subjects while boys are encouraged to tackle the "hard sciences." This has not only channeled the two sexes into two different vocational directions, but has further served to keep both boys and girls from learning skills useful in later life. Thus girls who have been excluded from shop have not learned how to fix things around the home, and boys excluded from home economics are kept blissfully ignorant of cooking and other domestic skills.

In the past, girls have also been excluded from the most rigorous sports and from school athletic teams. In fact, the disparity in support for boys' and girls' athletic programs is perhaps the single most visible piece of discrimination in American education.

Intellectual and analytic ability

Girls consistently do better than boys in reading, mathematics, and speaking until they reach high school.[46] Then their performance in school and on ability tests begins to drop. Although we have every reason to believe that girls' intellectual achievements do decline during high school, it should be noted that the typical measures of intelligence and scholastic achievement at this age have a strong male bias. Milton[52] found that when adolescent or adult subjects were presented with problems involving primarily mathematical or geometric reasoning, the males consistently obtained higher scores than females. However, if the problem—involving identical logical steps and computations—dealt with feminine content such as cooking and gardening materials, the women scored much better than if the problem dealt with guns, money, or geometric designs. He concluded the typical female believes that the ability to solve problems involving geometry, physics or logic, is a uniquely masculine skill, and her motivation even to attack such problems is low—for unusual excellence in solving them may be equated with loss of femininity.[37]

Since the erroneous finding that women are less analytic then men is often quoted, it deserves some attention here. It has been postulated that analytic thinking is developed by early independence training: how soon a child is encouraged to assume initiative, to take responsibility for herself or himself, and to solve problems alone rather than to rely on others for help or direction.[45] Each of these characteristics, as already reviewed, is encouraged in boys and discouraged in girls. When women are socialized to be dependent and passive, they are supposedly being trained to be more "field-dependent" or "contextual" and less analytic in their thinking.

It is interesting to note that spatial ability appears to be learned, and is especially strong in individuals who have hobbies or jobs of a mechanical or technical nature. Since the sex disparity in skills related to this ability widens greatly at age seventeen, it is tempting to connect the superior performance of males with the training they receive in high school classes in mechanical drawing, analytic geometry, and shop (as well as with their spare-time activities).

If both spatial and verbal ability can be learned, findings of sex differences in these areas should direct us once again to the socialization process. As Professor William Goode has noted,

> Although we encourage the verbal fluency of girls and their ease in writing and speaking, we are more likely to criticize boys for their weakness in logic (we forgive girls that fault; it is an endearing weakness, it is cute). In short, although males have a lower potential we strengthen their (boys') ability in logic. We do not, in contrast, strengthen girls' ability in spatial connections or facilitate girls' growth in the areas in which they appear most talented, i.e., the grasp of language construction, logical progressions, syllogisms, and all the apparatus of clear analytic thinking.[22]

The influence of parents

It is not the school alone that channels girls and boys in different directions and emphasizes certain skills over others. Parents also have different sex-related expectations. Aberle and Naegele[1] have reported that middle-class fathers show concern over their sons' lack of aggressiveness, good school performance, responsibility, and initiative. In contrast, their concerns for their daughters focus on attractiveness and popularity.

The Aberle and Naegele study was done in 1952 and may now seem dated. However, more recent studies of parental influence on their children's educational aspirations indicate that girls are still less likely to receive parental support than boys.

Parental pressures to follow a traditional female role are probably greater on the working-class than on the middle-class girl.[56] The working-class girl who aspires to a professional career is seen as especially threatening because her occupational aspirations (if achieved) would result in her being more successful than her father and brothers, in addition to being "unfeminine."

The influence of peers

The equation of intellectual success with a loss of femininity appears to be common among high school peer groups. According to the Kennistons, high school girls feel they must hide their intelligence if they are to be popular with boys.

> Girls soon learn that "popularity"—that peculiar American ecstasy from which all other goods flow—accrues to her who hides any intelligence she may have, flatters the often precarious maleness of adolescent boys, and devotes herself to activities that can in no way challenge their sex. The popular girls in high schools are seldom the brilliant girls; or if they are, it is only because they are so brilliant they can hide their brilliance from less brilliant boys. . . . Most American public schools (like many private schools) make a girl with passionate intellectual interests feel a strong sense of her own inadequacy as a woman, feel guilty about these "masculine" outlooks, perhaps even wonder about her own normality.[14]

Thus, school, parents, and peers make it clear to girls that the major criterion for feminine success is attractiveness to men. Pierce[58] found high achievement motivation for women related to success in marriage, not, as for males, to academic success. In Pierce's view, girls see that to achieve in life they need to excel in non-academic ways, i.e., in attaining beauty in person and dress, in finding a desirable social status, and in marrying the right man.

The mass media reinforce this perception and provide explicit instruction on attaining these goals. *Seventeen, Glamour,* and *Mademoiselle* provide endless pages of fashion, make-up and dating advice. The girl learns that she must know how to attract, talk to, kiss, keep (or get rid of) a boy, depending on the circumstances, and how to use clothes, cosmetics, and interpersonal skills to accomplish these all-important ends.

Just a decade ago one could summarize the three clear lessons that a well-socialized American girl had learned. One concerned her personality, the second her capability, and the third, her future role. With regard to her personality, she had learned to be nurturing, cooperative, sweet, expressive, not too intelligent, and fairly passive. With regard to her capability, she had learned she would always be less capable and less important than most men. With regard to her future, she had learned she would be a wife and mother, and, if she were successful, she would acquire that status soon. Today, as we shall see, the message has become much more complex for the middle-class college girl.

The "terminal year" of school

The end of high school is a critical juncture at which the lives of girls from lower- and middle-class families diverge. While many middle-class girls will go on to college, the last year in high school is what Sheila Tobias[70] calls "the terminal year." for many lower class girls—their last year in school and their last chance "to find a husband." As Lillian Rubin's interviews with working-class girls reveals, for most of them "getting married was—and probably still is—the singularly most acceptable way out of an oppressive family situation and into a respected social status—the only way to move from girl to woman. Indeed, among working-class girls, being grown up means being married."[61]

As Rubin notes, the terminal year for most middle-class girls doesn't come until the end of college (and for some it doesn't come until the end of graduate school). But whenever it comes, it brings the same pressures to marry and settle down—to find a husband, to buy a home, to have children—and to fulfill one's role as "a woman."

SOCIALIZATION PRESSURES IN COLLEGE

For a long time it seemed odd that young women who staunchly resisted the pressures to put social life and popularity above intellectual and vocational achievement during high school, suddenly changed during college. They switched their majors from Economics to English or Art History and decided that they were not really interested in graduate school after all. What happened? It now seems clear that what distinguished them from their working-class sisters was not a stronger commitment to intellectual pursuits, or to feminism, or to a non-traditional lifestyle, but the fact that they did not face the terminal year pressures until the end of college. For them the end of high school was just one more transition point. As long as they continued in school, they were permitted a moratorium on the pressures of "real life." But when these middle-class girls found themselves in their terminal year of school, and thus in the same structural position as their lower class sisters at the end of high school, their behavior changed.

Peer influences in college

One might speculate that women in college today are not being subjected to [marital] pressures. Although their parents may still encourage them to see marriage as the ultimate goal, it is possible that peer definitions of feminine roles are more liberal. The ideology of the current women's liberation movement certainly supports independent achievements for women.

When I first began writing this review paper (in 1972), I did not know of any study that dealt with this possibility in a systematic fashion. So I decided to collect some data from an experiment in my undergraduate course on the family. After a discussion of the ideology and goals of the women's liberation movement, I asked the students to try out the feminist ideals we had discussed in a heterosexual situation of at least one hour's duration.

The most common response encountered by those who completed the assignment, reported by 27 percent of the female students, was a rejection of the feminist behavior by their male companion. In some cases the women were asked to change their behavior: "So after I told him why I was doing it, he said, 'stop it, please, I don't want you to be a member of women's liberation.'" In other cases, the man treated the women's ideas or actions as nonserious, tossing them off as a joke or "putting her down as crazy."

In several instances, the friends and boyfriends were so angered or upset by the women's behavior that they refused to deal with it. They tried to terminate the interaction by telling the women they would never attract a man if they continued to act in such an unfeminine manner. In contrast to these emotional reactions, some of the men were more intellectual about their rejection, trying to answer the feminist arguments "rationally" by arguing that motherhood was fulfilling, or that a women's career was too disruptive to a marriage. The second most common reaction (17 percent) was that boyfriends or dates were merely surprised and uncomfortable. The third most common response, reported by 12 percent of the students, was subtle resistance by dates and male friends. Although not explicitly challenging the women, the men attempted to regain control of the situation. Most of these men denied trying to regain the dominant position in the relationship, contending that they were "just trying to be helpful." Some of the women (8 percent) reported that their dates or boyfriends did not seem to resent their behavior, but other friends and observers did.

Intellectual achievement: the climate of non-expectations

College should present an opportunity for women to broaden their intellectual horizons and to acquire both the background and motivation for occupational success. But in the past women have received less encouragement than men. Women professors have been underrepresented on the faculties of all colleges and universities in the

United States, even in fields that were sex-stereotyped as female (such as English or Art History), and women received no more than a passing mention in the intellectual content of most courses.

The predominantly male faculty typically assumed that women came to college to find husbands and become well-rounded individuals. Few professors took their intellectual or occupational aspirations seriously. As Paula Bunting, the former President of Radcliffe College observed, in her day the college environment for even the brightest women was one of "non-expectations." Instead of stimulating the bright young women's intellectual and political ambitions, college worked as a depressant. Thus many college women came to believe they were less intelligent (or less brilliant or less creative) than their male peers.

Although the climate of non-expectations did not make all women doubt their own capacity, it inevitably had a depressant effect on their ambitions. Even those who began college with high aspirations found their expectations for themselves lowered by the time they were ready to graduate: Perhaps they should apply for an M.A. program instead of trying for a Ph.D., or perhaps they should take a year off and decide what they "really" wanted to do.

Even those who did well in school, and who therefore had the external validation of high grades, began to question whether they were "truly" as capable or as committed as their male peers. Of course, those women who got high grades had rarely received the kind of professional encouragement that was lavished on their male peers—a fact which could not have easily escaped their attention. Perhaps some of those male professors had really wanted to encourage their bright women students but feared their interest might be misinterpreted (by their colleagues or their wives, if not by their students). Others may have been concerned about dissuading women from what they assumed was the woman's preferred life pattern, for it was widely assumed that women had to choose between a career and marriage.

In light of these expectations it is not surprising that women college students in the past have always been less likely to graduate from college than men, or that women college graduates have less often gone on to obtain advanced degrees.[32]

It is widely believed that the climate of expectations is now quite different. However, the available data do not yet reflect a major increase in the professional aspirations of college women. For example, the percentage of women enrolled in medical school and business school has increased substantially in recent years, and women now constitute a fourth of the students in law school. Nevertheless, they still do not appear to be choosing and pursuing careers in the high-level professions to the same extent as men.

Career orientation

It is also widely believed that college women today are much more career oriented than the women who were in college in the 1950's and 1960's. Here the data are less clear, for while the majority of college women now assume they will be employed in the future, their attitudes toward work and family roles suggest that many of them are still thinking in terms of "jobs" rather than "careers." The distinction between a job orientation and a career orientation is one that sociologist Alice Rossi[60] has pinpointed as a critical difference between college men and women in the past. She notes that even though college-educated women might study and prepare for a future occupation, they viewed these occupations as "jobs," not as lifelong vocational commitments. Their middle-class brothers, in contrast, were clearly future oriented, preparing and planning for lifelong careers. (Of course the women's lack of preparation for a lifelong career did not prevent them from working. It did, however, prevent them from organizing their lives for a "career" instead of a "job.")

It is possible that college women hold back from making lifelong career plans because they expect their careers to be heavily influenced by their future husbands and their family life. If this is so, then the recent upsurge in college women who plan to combine marriage and work does not indicate a fundamental change in women's career orientation. For as long as a woman's work is contingent upon her marriage, or her husband, or her childbearing plans, she is still adhering to women's traditional priorities.

Despite the widespread acceptance of employment for married women, it is useful to explore two ways in which the college woman's traditional socialization may create barriers to her occupational advancement. The first is the psychological fear that if a woman is too achieving or too successful she will not be regarded as feminine and will be rejected by men. The second is the cultural imperative that career women must still "prove" their femininity by being good mothers and wives and by not exceeding their husband's status and achievements.

Fear of success

Matina Horner's now famous experiment[34] on fear of success was conducted in 1965. At that time Horner found that college women responded with more negative stories (than college men) when presented with the verbal cue, "At the end of the first-term finals. Anne finds herself at the top of her medical school class. . . ." The women associated Anne's success with strong fears of social rejection and unpopularity, doubts about her femininity and normality, and themes of despair or guilt over having achieved too much. Horner concluded that most college women, consciously or unconsciously, equated intellectual achievement with loss of femininity and were therefore caught in a double bind. In testing and other achievement situations they worried not only about failure but also about success, for they feared success might lead to unpopularity and loss of femininity.[34,35] "Thus women who were otherwise motivated to achieve experienced anxiety in anticipation of success and this may have adversely affected their performance and levels of aspiration."[51]

Although several researchers have now replicated Horner's experiments (some confirming her findings, others challenging them), I believe that fear of success, if it does presently exist, is a temporary phenomenon that will soon disappear. When young women have more successful role models and more opportunities to observe how much fun (and power and money) success brings, they will rapidly lose their anxiety about success. Furthermore, in contrast to the current stereotype of successful women as unfeminine, I think they will discover that "success is sexy"—it increases rather than decreases one's attractiveness to the opposite sex. Just as women have always been attracted to powerful men (even though they were not necessarily "handsome") in the past, it is likely that more men will find dynamic and powerful women increasingly attractive in the future.

Nevertheless, the continued anxiety that many college women currently associate with success suggests that the ideal of the wife-mother-career woman is not without its own anxiety. Furthermore, this anxiety may be exacerbated by cultural pressures on the career woman to prove that she is also a good wife and mother.

The cultural imperatives

The college woman who aspires to a successful career faces two cultural imperatives to prove that she is also a successful woman: one is to bear children; the other, to make sure her occupational achievements do not exceed those of her husband.

Because the belief that the successful career woman is unfeminine is widespread among both men and women, career-oriented women may feel under particular pressure to prove their femininity.[15] Lois Hoffman[32] suggests that having a baby may provide the proof the career woman feels she needs. (It may also force her to devote a great deal of time and energy to family roles and thereby reassert their priority in her life.) However, if motherhood solves one set of anxieties, its demands, especially in large families, may easily create other pressures and role conflicts for the young career woman.

A second cultural imperative is that wives should not exceed their husband's status and occupational attainment.[42] In fact, Hoffman[32] suggests that for educated women a successful marital relationship often requires that both partners perceive the husband to be the more intelligent or successful in his career.

How can the new woman balance these cultural imperatives with the demands of a career? How can she be and do everything?

One way to resolve the conflict is to have a clear sense of priority. Women's socialization suggests that they should treat work as a "job" and put their responsibilities to husband and family first. Is this what college women are choosing to do?

The limited data on occupational aspirations, career decisions, and dual career marriages suggest that the majority still are.[6,19,33] However, sociologist Laurie Cummings[13] has found that a minority of women are beginning to organize their lives differently. Cummings set out to examine the differences among college women who aspired to combine marriage, motherhood, and work. She found that women who are feminists not only express greater confidence in their ability to combine job, family, and marriage, they also make more concrete plans for achieving their aims. They are more likely to plan to go to graduate school, to aspire to a profession, and most importantly, to plan a continuous rather than an interrupted career. They also seem to have clearer ground rules for an egalitarian marriage.

WOMEN'S ACHIEVEMENT

Although this discussion has emphasized formal academic and occupational achievement throughout, it should be clear that there are other areas in which both men and women are motivated to achieve. For example, some people make lifetime careers of philanthropy or unpaid volunteer work. Some devote their energies to civic affairs. Others aspire to positions of responsibility in religious or recreational organizations. Still others undertake technical or creative pursuits such as photography, rock collecting, or wine-making. And all of these unpaid endeavors may give participants a sense of achievement and success.

Nonetheless, there are limits to the status rewards these activities can bring. For in American society, status is closely related to monetary rewards, which generally come from occupational achievements. And it is clear that men, not women, are socialized to adopt the personality characteristics that are related to success in the more prestigious and financially lucrative occupations.

With the relentless conditioning we have just reviewed, it seems remarkable that some girls do not get the message that they are supposed to be less intelligent and less successful until high school, and that some escape through their college years. Further, in spite of the overwhelming pressures to conform to the traditional feminine role, many women do aspire to intellectual and professional success, and a significant number of them attain it. How can we account for these women? Are they deviants, or have we presented an oversocialized portrait of women in this essay?

In the statistical sense, women who have attained professional success are deviants in that they are distinctly in the minority; but it is important to realize what a significant minority they are. We have already noted the wide range of individual differences in both sexes and the extent to which our summary has excluded the statistical minority of woman achievers. In this section we shall focus on this "deviant" group, composed of female doctors, lawyers, engineers, architects, professors, scientists, corporation executives, writers, etc., and ask what has been difficult about the socialization of these women. The following discussion will, of necessity, be speculative, because there has not yet been a systematic study of the socialization of high-achieving women. It is meant to be suggestive.

Family background

One might speculate on various family situations that would encourage a girl's occupational aspirations: being a successful businessman's only child who has been encouraged to take over her family's business; being the daughter of a female doctor, encouraged to assist in her mother's office; or being the oldest sibling in a large family for whom leadership and authority are natural. Achievement motivation and occupational aspirations may arise from a great variety of sources that are beyond the limited scope of this paper to explore.

Several studies have indicated that the role of the mother is especially important. If the mother works, or has worked, the girl is more likely to see a career as "natural" for a woman. In Hartley's study of girls between the ages of eight and eleven, the girls' future plans were significantly related to their mothers' work roles. When asked what they expected to do when they grew up, significantly more daughters of nonworking mothers gave "housewife" as their primary choice and more daughters of working mothers mentioned nontraditional professional areas (such as medicine, law, creative work) as their vocational choices. Also, daughters of working mothers were more likely to plan to continue after marrying and having children.[27]

Traditional identification theory assumed that the same-sex parent was the more crucial in determining the sex-role identity of the child. This theory, which grew out of Freudian theory, asserted that the child must, in order to identify properly as a member of his or her sex, have a same-sex model to imitate.[55] Thus by imitating the father the boy would learn and internalize masculine behavior. Similarly, it was assumed, the girl would learn how to be feminine by imitating the behavior of her mother. According to this theory, the child internalizes not only the particular behavior observed, but a complex integrated pattern of sex-related behavior.[55] I would suggest instead, that a large amount of sex-role behavior can be learned only through interaction with the opposite sex. This is especially true of the "feminine role," which is often defined in terms of relationships with others. It is thus possible that the father teaches the girl how to be feminine as much as the mother does.

Identification theory may be challenged on another ground as well. Identification theorists have assumed that it is necessary for adult role-models to have clearly differentiated sex roles, so that the child can clearly distinguish what is masculine and what is feminine behavior.[57] However, Slater[68] has indicated that adult role-models who exhibit stereotyped sex-role identification may impede, rather than facilitate, the child's sex-role identification. Children may find it easier to identify with less differentiated and less stereotyped parental role models. It is more likely that they will internalize parental values when nurturance (the typically feminine role) and discipline (the typically masculine role) come from the same source.

Both of these challenges to traditional identification theory indicate that the father may play as important a role as the mother in a daughter's socialization. In fact, Heilbrun[31] has shown that highly successful girls tend to have an especially close relationship with, and identify with, a masculine father.

Although there are no direct data, we might speculate that an especially strong stimulus to achievement motivation in women would be a strong father-daughter relationship in which the father encourages his daughter and makes his love and approval dependent on her performance. Most fathers show unconditional support for their daughers, whether or not they achieve, because most fathers do not consider a woman's achievements crucial to her success in life.

The importance of this father-daughter tie has been noted by family sociologist William J. Goode,[21] who has observed that a large number of successful women were their fathers' "favorite child." This can be a great spur to "masculine" achievement, especially when there are no sons in the family and the father supports and assists his daughter's aspirations. This hypothesis has its parallel in research on male achievement motivation, where McClelland's work[50] has shown that a strong mother-son relationship (in which the mother bases conditional love on her son's success) is most conducive to masculine achievement motivation.

The oversocialized portrait of women

Thus far, we have considered high occupational achievement and achievement motivation in woman as if it were deviant, and therefore required a special explanation. However, an alternative view suggests that, in fact, *most* women are motivated to achieve. This perspective would lead one to conclude that the socialization literature presents an oversocialized portrait of women. It is clear that the literature thus far reviewed in this paper exaggerates in two ways:

1. Women are assumed to internalize the feminine role *completely*.
2. The pressures on women are presented as *unidimensional*.

Let us examine each of these.

The socialization literature has probably overestimated the effectiveness of the socialization process. It is assumed that woman have been successfully socialized and have internalized the feminine role. However, if this were so, women would feel fulfilled within that role, whereas in fact almost every study of women's fulfillment has shown that those who conform most closely to the feminine role are least fulfilled.[48] Both Jessie Bernard[4,5] and Betty Friedan,[17] after reviewing the literature on feminine happiness and fulfillment, conclude that most women are not content with their traditional role.

In addition to exaggerating the effectiveness of the socialization process for women, the literature incorrectly treats the pressures on women as unidimensional. Women are viewed as being consistently rewarded for feminine behavior and consistently punished for or discouraged from unfeminine behavior. Social learning theory, which is the basis for the bulk of the material presented in this paper, holds that sex-appropriate responses are consistently rewarded and reinforced—and sex-inappropriate behavior consistently discouraged or punished—in the young girl until she comes to learn and internalize the feminine role.[53,55]

Without denying the pressures on women to conform to the feminine role, one can see that women are socialized in an ambivalent fashion. At the same time that girls are rewarded for typical feminine behavior, they are also rewarded for some types of "masculine" behavior. This is because what is labeled masculine behavior is generally highly regarded and rewarded in our society. The girl who excels in school, wins the tennis championship, or fixes a broken car receives approval for each of these activities. Although she may be regarded as too aggressive or masculine, she is also admired for her accomplishments. Thus, the feminine role is not consistently reinforced.

If we are correct in asserting that the socialization of women into the traditional female roles is neither totally effective nor totally consistent, then one might legitimately ask why there are not more visible examples of high-achieving women. If, as we have asserted, many women are actually motivated to higher achievement, why has the proportion of women in the professions and in other high-status occupations remained so low?

There are two possible answers to this question. The first is that women's achievement is channeled in a different direction. As noted above, Pierce has shown that women with high achievement motivation are oriented toward finding high-status husbands.[58]

But even though women have been socialized to regard personal occupational success as difficult or undesirable, it seems unlikely that many women with high achievement motivation would be content with vicarious achievement alone. Unless they are allowed to play a significant role in their husbands' or sons' careers, they are likely to channel their energies elsewhere. It is obvious that the energies of many capable women are channeled into volunteer work or into other nonremunerative pursuits. Other high-achievement-oriented women may be found in frustrating jobs that are much below their capability, or in positions that involve power and capabilities that are neither recognized nor rewarded (with either money or position) by their employers.

A second answer to the question of why there are not more visible examples of high-achieving women lies in the structural opportunities available to women in this society. When women are denied real opportunities for advancement and are discriminated against at every stage of the process leading to a professional position, it is not surprising that they have not "made it." Thus, the answer to this question probably lies not so much in the socialization of women as in the structural opportunities available to them in our society.

As long as women are denied real career options, it is a realistic decision not to aim for a career. As long as they lack role models of successful career women, are denied structural supports to aid a career, are told they are neurotic or unfeminine if they are dedicated to an occupation, we cannot expect young women to take the career option seriously. The only way to change their (accurate) perceptions about future options is to create *real options* for them.

REFERENCES

1. Aberle, D., and Naegele, K.: Middle class father's occupational role and attitudes toward children. In Bell, N.W., and Vogel, E.F., editors: The family, rev. ed., New York, 1968, The Free Press.
2. Bardwick, J.M., and others: Feminine personality and conflict, Belmont, Calif., 1970, Brooks/Cole Publishing Co.
3. Bem, S.L.: Beyond androgyny: some presumptuous prescriptons for a liberated sexual identity. In Sherman, J., and Denmark, F., editors: Psychology of women: future directions of research, New York, 1976, Psychological Dimensions, Inc.
4. Bernard, J.: The myth of the happy marriage. In Gornick, V., and Morgan, R., editors: Women in sexist society, New York, 1971, Basic Books, Inc.
5. Bernard, J.: The future of marriage, New York, 1972, World Books.
6. Birnbaum, J.A.: Life patterns, personality style and self esteem in gifted family oriented and career committed women, doctoral dissertation, 1971, University of Michigan.
7. Blau, Z.S.: Exposure to child-rearing experts: a structural interpretation of class-color differences, American Journal of Sociology 69:596, May 1964.
8. Brimm, O.G.: Family structure and sex role learning by children, Sociometry 21:1, 1958.
9. Bronfenbrenner, U.: Some familial antecedents of responsibility and leadership in adolescents. In Petrullo, L., and Bass, B.M., editors: Leadership and interpersonal behavior, New York, 1961, Holt, Rinehart & Winston.
10. Bronfenbrenner, U.: The changing American child: a speculative analysis, Merrill-Palmer Quarterly 7(9):73, 1961.
11. Brown, D.G.: Sex-role preference in young children, Psychological Monographs 70(14):1, 1956.
12. Child, I., and others: Children's textbooks and personality development: an exploration in the social psychology of education. In Haimowitz, M.L., and Haimowitz, N.R., editors: Human development: selected readings, New York, 1960, Thomas Y. Crowell Co., Publishers.
13. Cummings, L.D.: Value stretch in definitions of career among college women: Horatio Alger as a feminist model, Social Problems 25(1):65, 1977.
14. Editorial: An American anachronism: the image of women and work, Daedalus, 1964.
15. Epstein, C.: Woman's place: options and limits in professional careers, Berkeley, 1970, University of California Press.
16. Federbush, M.: Let them aspire, Ann Arbor, 1972.
17. Friedan, B.: The feminine mystique, New York, 1963, W.W. Norton & Co., Inc.
18. Gans, H.: The urban villagers, New York, 1962, The Free Press.
19. Garland, T.N.: The better half? the male in the dual profession family. In Safilios-Rothschild, C., editor: Toward a sociology of women, Lexington, 1972, Xerox College Publishing.
20. Goldberg, S., and Lewis, M.: Play behavior in the year-old infant: early sex differences, Child Development 40:21, 1969.
21. Goode, W.J.: Personal conversation, December 1970.
22. Goode, W.: Personal communication, January 1974.
23. Goode, W.J.: The uses of dispraise. In the celebration of heroes, Berkeley, 1978, University of California Press.
24. Goode, W.J., and others: Social systems and family structures, Indianapolis, 1971, The Bobbs-Merrill Co., Inc.
25. Goodenough, E.W.: Interests in persons as an aspect of sex differences in the early years, Genetic Psychological Monographs 55:312, 1957.
26. Hartley, R.E.: Sex-role pressures and the socialization of the male child, Psychological Reports 5:457, 1959.
27. Hartley, R.E.: Children's concept of male and female roles, Merrill-Palmer Quarterly 6:83, 1960.
28. Hartley, R.E.: A developmental view of female sex-role definition and identification, Merrill-Palmer Quarterly, 10(1):3, 1964.
29. Hartup, W.W.: Some correlates of parental imitation in young children, Child Development 33:85, 1962.
30. Hartup, W.W., and Zook, E.A.: Sex-role preferences in three- and four-year old children, Journal of Consulting Psychology 24:420, December 1960.
31. Heilbrun, A.B., Jr.: Sex role, instrumental-expressive behavior, and psychopathology in females, Journal of Abnormal Psychology 73(2):131, 1958.

32. Hoffman, L.W.: The employment of women, education and fertility. In Mednick, M., and others, editors: Women and achievement, New York, 1975, John Wiley & Sons, Inc.
33. Holmstrom, L.L.: The two-career family, Cambridge, 1972, Schenckman Publishing Co., Inc.,
34. Horner, M.S.: Women's need to fail, Psychology Today, November 1969.
35. Horner, M.S. Toward an understanding of achievement-related conflicts in women, Journal of Social Issues 28(2):157, 1972.
36. Hunt, J.G., and Hunt, L.L.: Race, daughters and father-loss: does absence make the girl grow stronger? Social Problems 25(1)91, 1977.
37. Kagan, J.: Acquisition and significance of sex-typing and sex-role identity. In Hoffman, M.S., and Hoffman, L.W., editors: Review of child development research, New York, 1964, Russell Sage Foundation.
38. Kagan, J., and Lewis, M.: Studies of attention in the human infant, Merrill-Palmer Quarterly 2:95, 1965.
39. Koch, H.: The relation of certain family characteristics and the attitudes of children towards adults, Child Development 26:13, March 1965.
40. Kohn, M.S. Social class and parental values, American Journal of Sociology 64:337, January 1959.
41. Komarovsky, M.: Women in the modern world, Boston, 1953, Little, Brown & Co.
42. Komarovsky, M.: Cultural contradictions and sex roles: the masculine case, American Journal of Sociology 78(4):873, 1973.
43. Lynn, D.B.: A note on sex differences in the development of masculine and feminine identification, Psychological Review 66(2):126, 1959.
44. Lynn, D.B.: Parental and sex role identification: a theoretical formulation, Berkeley, 1969, McCutchan Publishing Corp.
45. Maccoby, E.E.: Woman's intellect. In Farber, S.L., and Wilson, R.H., editors: The potential of women, New York, 1963, McGraw-Hill Book Co.
46. Maccoby, E.E.: Sex differences in intellectual functioning. In Mccoby, E., editor: The development of sex differences, Stanford, 1966, Stanford University Press.
47. Maccoby, E., and Jacklin, C.: The psychology of sex differences, Stanford, 1975, Stanford University Press.
48. Maslow, A.H.: Dominance, personality, and social behavior in women, Journal of Social Psychology 10:259, 1942.
49. Matza, D.: Personal conversation, Winter 1971.
50. McClelland, D.: The achieving society, New York, 1964, The Free Press.
51. Mednick, M., and others, editors: Women and achievement, New York, 1975, John Wiley & Sons, Inc.
52. Milton, G.A.: Five studies of the relation between sex role identification and achievement in problem solving, Technical Report No. 3, Department of Industrial Administration, Department of Psychology, December 1958, Yale University.
53. Mischel, W.: A social-learning view of sex differences. In Maccoby, E.E., editor: The development of sex differences, Stanford, 1966, Stanford University Press.
54. Moss, H.A.: Sex, age, and state as determinants of mother-infant interaction, Merrill-Palmer Quarterly 13(1):19, 1967.
55. Mussen, P.H.: Early sex-roled development. In Goslin, D.A., editor: Handbook of socialization theory and research, Chicago, 1969, Rand McNally.
56. Mussen, P.H., and others: Child development and personality, ed. 2, New York, 1963, Harper & Row, Publishers, Inc.
57. Parsons, T.: Family structure and the socialization of the child. In Parsons, T., and Bales, R.F., editors: Family socialization and interaction process, New York, 1955, The Free Press.
58. Pierce, J.V.: Sex differences in achievement motivation of able high school students, Cooperative research project No. 1097, December 1961, University of Chicago.
59. Rabban, M.L.: Sex role identification in young children in two diverse social groups, Genetic Psychological Monographs 42:81, 1950.
60. Rossi, A.: Equality between the sexes.
61. Rubin, L.: Worlds of pain: life in the working class family, New York, 1976, Basic Books, Inc.
62. Sario, T., and others: Sex role stereotyping in public schools, Harvard Education Review, August 1973.
63. Scanzoni, J.H.: The black family in modern society, Phoenix edition, Chicago, 1977, University of Chicago Press.
64. Scanzoni, L., and Scanzoni, J.: Men, women, and change: a sociology of marriage and family, New York, 1976, McGraw-Hill Book Co.

65. Schachter, S.: The psychology of affiliation, Stanford, 1959, Stanford University Press.
66. Sears, P.R., and others: Patterns of child rearing, Evanston, Ill., 1957, Row Peterson.
67. Sewell, W.H., and Shah, V.P.: Social class, parental encouragement, and educational aspirations, American Journal of Sociology **73** (5):559, 1968.
68. Slater, P.: Parental role differentiation, American Journal of Sociology **47**(3):296, 1961.
69. Smith, S.: Age and sex differences in children's opinion concerning sex differences, Journal of Genetic Psychology **54**:17, 1939. .
70. Tobias, S.: Associate Provost of Wesleyan University: I am indebted to her for suggesting this term to me.
71. Tyler, L.E.: The psychology of human differences, New York, 1965, Appleton-Century-Crofts.
72. Weitzman, L.J., and others: Sex role socialization in picture books for pre-school children, American Journal of Sociology, May 1972.
73. Weitzman, L.J., and Rizzo, D.: Images of males and females in elementary school textbooks, New York, 1974, National Organization for Women's Legal Defense Fund.
74. Women on words and images: Dick and Jane as victims, Princeton, 1972.

ELLA LASKY

Chapter 3

Self-esteem, achievement, and the female experience

Self-esteem and achievement are clearly and unequivocally related. As one would expect, people with high self-esteem achieve more educationally and occupationally than do those with low self-esteem. This chapter reviews the research on self-esteem and achievement.

The traditional female role is devalued in our society. Women learn not to value themselves and therefore have low self-esteem. Poor self-esteem leads to lower aspirations and to lesser achievements, thus reinforcing women's lower self-esteem. It is not surprising, then, that few women have high self-esteem and few women are high achievers in our society. I am, however, optimistic that women can be successful despite the barriers to positive self-esteem and achievements in the work place.

SEX ROLES

The appropriate ways for males and females to act, feel, and think are very clearly spelled out for almost every aspect of life in our society. This section briefly reviews the appropriate sex roles for females in our society, focuses on those sex-typed behaviors that relate to achievement, and reviews several techniques by which sex-role socialization is accomplished. The reader can find additional sex-role material in the chapters by Henley and Freeman, Weitzman, and Muff.

The sex roles

One need only watch television for a few hours to get a clear picture of the appropriate female roles in our society. The first thing one notices is that there are very few women to be seen.* Second, those few women who do appear depict

---

*A study covering 14 years (1953 to 1977) of prime-time television shows found that men were three times as likely as women to be the only star of a television show. When all leading roles were considered, women's visibility was between 25% and 35% (men had 65% to 75% of the leading roles).[39] Given that women are 51% of the population, women are truly underrepresented on prime-time television.

characters who are deferent to men and lack status and power. Third, female characters are less frequently rewarded for their behavior than male characters. Last, the women's behavior often elicits no negative or positive consequence at all; that is, women are ignored![39,41,145] Watching these programs teaches the viewer that women are not important, are not valued by society, and are of no consequence.

Our society holds out two main images for females. For girls, the ideal is a passive, submissive, attractive young creature who receives praise for pleasing her brothers and father. She is a smiling onlooker as her brothers actively participate in adventures requiring independence and self-confidence. She watches them receive praise for their achievements and cleverness. For women, the ideal is the angelic, all-giving mother who is always happy to put her children's and husband's needs before her own. Again, a submissive, masochistic, self-sacrificing image emerges. These images are limited, narrow, and incomplete; they are not fully human.*

These images are reflected in all areas of the media and unfortunately are widely accepted. A woman who sees herself in the traditional role feels she should defer to the needs of others rather than assert her own. A 1980 survey found that 77% of the public concurs that a woman should put her husband's and children's needs first.[5] Further, 90% of married, employed women between the ages of 18 and 35 felt that if it were essential to their husbands' careers they would give up their own careers and relocate.[5] Only 22% indicated, however, that their husbands would be willing to move should the situation be reversed.[5] The husband, it seems, is still more important than the wife in the wife's mind.

Sex roles are learned

Most male and female styles are learned rather than innate. We observe stereotypical images in the world, in the people we observe in person, on television, in books, and so on. We receive direct reinforcement through praise, criticism, or punishment from parents, teachers, siblings, and peers. Girls identify with their mothers and desire both consciously and unconsciously to be "just like Mommy" when they grow up. As their intellects mature, women understand that they are female and seek out additional sources of gender information. Finally, women reinforce themselves by acting consistently within these standards.

The most dramatic data indicating that sex roles are learned and not biologically based comes from Money's work[105] with hermaphrodites. Hermaphroditism is a rare abnormality in which the internal sexual organs and the external ones are different or confused. Since gender is assigned at birth according to the appearance of the external genital organs, in cases of hermaphroditism a child can be mislabeled and raised as a member of the other sex. Based on his work with hermaphrodites and surgery to reassign the sex of the child, Money has concluded that socialization is so strong that

---

*References 81, 96, 131, 145, 148, 157, 163.

one should not reassign the sex of a child after 12 to 18 months.

Much sex-role training is done unconsciously by parents. For example, parents are more protective of girls than of boys although there is no physical reason for this. In one particularly interesting study, the parents of 15 boys and 15 girls were interviewed within 24 hours of their babies' births. Infants of about the same size, weight, and good health were involved in the study. It was found that fathers were significantly more likely to think of the infant girls as smaller, weaker, and less hardy than the equally healthy infant boys.[129] Thus from the moment of birth parents treat their male and female children differently; sex-role training has started.*

This misperception of females as frail and weak leads parents to be protective of their daughters. It has been found that maternal protectiveness of girls during the first 3 years hinders their achievements in adult life. Maternal protectiveness of boys in the first 3 years appears to help their achievements in adulthood.[75]

Parents teach sex roles to children by the assignment of household chores. The tendency is for girls to help with the cooking, cleaning, and grocery shopping, whereas boys help with repairs around the house, carrying out the garbage, and mowing the lawn. Other differences in the way parents treat children involve giving boys more freedom to come and go at earlier ages than girls. Girls need to ask permission to visit friends whereas boys can just go, girls need to be home earlier, and so on. Regardless of whether these rules are fair, they do encourage independence in boys and give boys practice in decision making, whereas they encourage dependence in girls and give girls minimal experience in making decisions. Making decisions on matters that are appropriate to one's age and intelligence is an important skill and critical to the development of achievement.

It is unfortunate that sex-role training begins this early, for it leads to a confounding and intertwining of individual personality development with sex-role characteristics. Specifically, the first 2 years is the period in which two important aspects of personality are formed: trust (or mistrust) in oneself and one's environment and confidence (or shame and doubt) in one's ability to do things.[44,164] Infants learn to trust their environments and themselves by having most of their needs met most of the time. They learn autonomy by being allowed to try things that are within their abilities. Parents of boys typically help them reach for toys they are grasping for, thus encouraging their autonomy; parents of girls are more likely to get the toy for them or to distract them with something else, hence discouraging autonomy and indepen-

---

*Another example of differential treatment of boys and girls was seen in the "Baby X Experiment."[137] One group of adults was told that a 7-month-old baby girl was a boy; a second group was told a girl. They selected sex-appropriate toys for the child to play with. A third group of adults was not told any gender for the baby. All decided on a gender and found some supporting evidence for their judgment. Only 30% guessed correctly. The point is that adults seem to need to know the gender of the baby to know how to treat the child, rather than watching to see what the baby likes and treating it individually. This is unfair to boys and girls alike.

dence. Since this process starts early and is not verbal, it is learned in a very powerful, basic way and is highly resistant to change. Parents continue to exert stronger controls and limits on the freedom of daughters than on their sons through childhood and adolescence. The pattern continues and is reinforced.

Effects of sex roles on achievement

The traits that most clearly relate to achievement are independence, autonomy, interest in tasks for their own sake, and affiliation (the desire for friends and the willingness to be friendly). Individuals who desire to achieve have been found to take personal responsibility for their successes and generally perceive themselves as high in ability.[82]

The two background factors that seem most related to achievement strivings in boys seem to be independence training and achievement training. Mothers of sons with high needs to achieve expected their sons to do things independently at an earlier age than did mothers of boys with low needs for achievement.[167] Other studies have found that parents of boys who were highly achievement-oriented expected their sons to do well and got involved with their work in a way that helped the boys learn how to do things well.[126]

Girls are less likely to develop the traits of independence, autonomy, and interest in tasks for their own sake; again, these traits are related to achievement. Girls are taught to be less independent than boys, to stay closer to their mothers[50] and seek more reassurance than boys; girls are less likely to explore or actively and creatively play with new toys[50]; girls are more likely to approach and complete tasks to learn love and approval whereas boys are more likely to complete tasks because of their interest in them[66]; girls are more likely to seek out friends and other people whereas boys are more likely to explore and work on tasks independently[50,113]; girls are more likely to underestimate their competence, to be less confident and to underestimate their own success probabilities[33]; girls do things independently at later times than boys.[66]

These differences in achievement behaviors are socialized. For example, brothers and sisters in the same family are typically treated differently. Boys are encouraged to be competitive, initiating, achieving, and independent; they are encouraged to think that "hard work is good for you." Their sisters, however, are encouraged to be dependent, conforming, and cooperative.[130]

Very masculine males, as well as very feminine females, have been found to do less well on various achievement related measures.[11,13] Individuals who are androgynous, that is who have many feminine and many masculine traits, have been found to be able to do well at more activities than either traditional males or traditional females, for they can vary their behavior to meet each situation. Androgynous individuals do not avoid cross-sex behavior and therefore are exposed to and learn to handle more tasks and more situations.[12,13] But most important in terms of this discussion is that androgynous adolescents and adults of both sexes score highest in self-esteem. They have been found to be more capable and to feel more fulfilled and happy than traditionally male and traditionally female adolescents and adults.[11]

In summary, the appropriate sex roles for males and females in our society are very clear. They are learned by several methods simultaneously: observation, direct reward and punishment of one's behavior, and identification with the same-sex parent. Parents begin to teach sex-role behavior and treat their male and female children differently from the moment of birth. This differential treatment is more likely to develop independent, autonomous, achievement-oriented boys and dependent, affiliative, love- and approval-oriented girls who underestimate their own skills and abilities. The basics of sex roles are deeply, solidly, and thoroughly established in the first 1½ years of life. These sex roles are learned rather than biologically based. Once learned, sex roles are difficult to unlearn; they are still subscribed to by most of our society, including the most highly educated who claim that women and men are equal in all ways.

SELF-ESTEEM

The self-esteem of females is lower than that of males. Most females in the United States are more anxious, have more fears, are more likely to feel inferior to others, and experience more distress and despair than most males. Self-esteem is a personal judgment of one's own worthiness that is expressed in the attitudes one holds toward oneself. In this section, I will suggest that female self-esteem is lower than male self-esteem because our society sees females as less important than males, gives less social status and respect to the female role than to the male role, and evaluates many female characteristics as having less value than many male characteristics. These evaluations are accepted by most people in our society and internalized so that females think of themselves as less valuable and less worthy than men.

Developmental aspects of self-esteem

Differences in self-esteem according to sex are usually thought to start in adolescence, with girls feeling less positive about themselves than boys. In the senior year of high school (according to a national study of 3183 male and female high school seniors), a greater percentage of girls are more likely to feel less positive about themselves than boys.[115] Here are a few sample statements: "I do not take a positive attitude towards myself," "I cannot do things as well as most other people," "I sometimes think I am no good at all." Girls' self-esteem is not totally negative; there are aspects of themselves that they evaluate positively, just as boys' self-esteem is not totally positive. The overall picture of girls' feelings about themselves, however, is more negative than positive and more negative than boys' self-esteem.

Recent studies indicate that self-esteem differences appear prior to adolescence and have been reported in childhood.[25,114] One recent study found that the self-esteem of boys and girls begins to differ in the third and fourth grades (9 and 10 years old). By the sixth grade (12 years old), boys' self-esteem was significantly higher than girls'.[45] The two major differences between them centered around girls' passivity and emotional lability (capacity for being easily upset).[88,140,141]

It seems to me that female self-esteem in our society must necessarily be poor from the moment of birth. All studies have shown that there is a dramatic preference for boy babies rather than girl babies.[1,61,118] The preference for boys over girls as first or only children is about 5 to 1; that is, 83% of parents prefer a boy as their first or only child.[1] This statistic includes mothers as well as fathers. Further, the interval between the birth of a first child and the conception of the second is longer when the first child is a boy than when it is a girl.[118] And the likelihood of having a third child is greater if the first two children are both girls rather than both boys.[118] We can infer, therefore, that girls are less wanted and less valued in our society.

It is well known that children experience how their parents feel about them. The psychoanalyst Harry Stack Sullivan[149] said this clearly, "The self may be said to be made up of reflected appraisals," meaning that a person's self-concept and self-esteem are formed from the way she/he is treated. If parents are disappointed in their daughter, for example, she will sense this and will feel that she is disappointing. It has been found even among boys that "emotional investment" rather than ordinal position or the relative attention "is largely responsible for differences in self esteem."[32]

Parents are not merely disappointed if they have a girl baby, but the mother is significantly more likely to have a postpartum depression as well.[53] How can girls feel as good about themselves if they are not as valued by society and not as wanted by most parents?

Adult self-esteem

The same pattern of self-esteem differences found among boys and girls continues into adult life. A national study using a sample representative of the total population in age, sex, education, income, occupation, and place of residence found that sex, age, and education were the major determinants of self-esteem; "The relationship is clearest with sex . . . more women than men are coded negative or ambivalent in self perception."[58] They report numerous differences between men and women, including much greater emotional distress among women.

Another study, using several college populations, found that the self-esteem of women was significantly lower than that of men.[128] The men tended to view themselves as aggressive, independent, unemotional, dominant, able to make decisions easily, self-confident, and active. Particularly interesting, in terms of achievement, is that the average male self-concept included ambition and business skills whereas the female self-concept did not. The women tended to view themselves as gentle, tactful, interested in their appearance, aware of the feelings of others, expressive of tender feelings. These self-concepts are very much like the sex-role stereotypes prevailing in our society. The researchers did not expect these results, particularly as

> the data producing the conclusion were gathered from enlightened, highly selected college girls who typically more than hold their own intellectually vis-à-vis boys, at least in terms of college grades. The factors producing the incorporation of the female stereotype along with its negative valuation into the self-concept of the female Ss [subjects], then, must be enormously powerful.[128]

Another study of self-esteem had similar findings. This study used 982 men and women as subjects, ages 17 to 60, of differing religions, educational levels, and marital status. It was found that both men and women incorporated the positive and negative traits of the sex-role stereotypes into their self-concepts. The authors write, "Since more feminine traits are negatively valued than are masculine traits, women tend to have more negative self concepts than do men."[22] Women, in other words, are more likely than men to see themselves as irrational, passive, and incompetent. It is especially important to note, given the focus here on achievement, that women are highly likely to experience themselves as incompetent.[22]

A fourth study of male and female personalities using men and women ranging from 15 to 64 years old, found that women have significantly lower self-esteem than men; women felt significantly weaker, more helpless, more fearful, and more timid than men. There were positive self-evaluations, too, with women feeling warmer and more empathic than men, but the overall picture was as always more negative than positive.[14]

In summary, all four studies of self-esteem found that both males and females have some positive and some negative aspects to their self-concepts, but the self-concepts of females include significantly more negative traits than positive traits. The overall pattern of female self-esteem, then, is significantly more negative than the overall pattern of male self-esteem.

One would expect that people with lower self-esteem would be more likely to be emotionally disturbed and less happy. Studies of mental illness and happiness confirm this. A recent study of mental health found that women, as a group, are less happy than men.[106] Using a sample of 2164 adults over the age of 18, representative of a cross-section of the national population, the study found that about three times as many men as women (36.1% as opposed to 13.5%) report they are highly satisfied with their lives. Similarly, three times as many females report low satisfaction with life (28.1% as opposed to 10.1%). As in all studies, most men (58.4%) and women (53.8%) reported medium life satisfaction.

There are differences too in the aspects of life from which men and women draw their satisfaction: men derive their main satisfaction from their work, whereas women get their main satisfaction from their personal relationships.[46,58,106] Women and men worry about different things as well: men worry about their occupational accomplishments, their career progress or the lack of it, and whether or not they have a meaningful vocation; women worry about more personal things, such as the lack of physical attractiveness, competence in interpersonal relationships, and the need for more approval or the receiving of disapproval.

One would expect to find in the literature about mental illness that people with low self-esteem experience more distress. Gove and Tudor[56] reviewed 17 studies of mental illness carried out between 1954 and 1968 and found that the mental illness rate for women was higher than that for men. Women are admitted to psychiatric hospitals more often and use outpatient clinics and private psychiatric services more often than men. They interpret these findings as resulting "from the characteristics of male and female roles in modern society."[56] One of the reasons cited is that most women occupy one role, homemaker, whereas most men occupy two roles, household head and worker. When one of his roles is unsatisfactory, the male can frequently shift his focus to the other source of gratification. Since most women have only the family role, they cannot shift attention to an alternate area should they become dissatisfied. The major tasks involved in running a house and raising children are often frustrating; the homemaker position has low prestige in our society and is unstructured and invisible. In addition married women who work often do so at less satisfactory jobs than men and then must run the household as a second fulltime job.

Thus the studies of self-esteem, happiness, and mental illness all indicate that females experience more distress and have lower self-esteem than males.

Explanations for female lower self-esteem

There are several ways to understand this data. One interpretation is that women are not less happy, are not more emotionally disturbed, and are not suffering lower self-esteem than men but rather *admit* their unhappy feelings more easily. After all, it is quite acceptable for American women to be more emotional than men. It seems to me, however, that this is not the case since all women in these studies did not express these feelings.

A second way of understanding the differences in male and female self-esteem, happiness, and mental health rates is in terms of society's definition of roles. The male role has been demonstrated to be the same as the healthy adult role by an intriguing study of clinical judgments of mental health.[22] Conversely the female role is seen as unhealthy.[22] Therefore women in our society are in an impossible position. To be appropriately female, one must be unhealthy. What is one to do? The measure of mental health, the measure of self-esteem, and the social role are biased in such a way as to demand low self-esteem of American women.

A third way to look at these differences suggests that using summary data about the average male and the average female clouds the issue. If narrower categories were used, such as married women, single women, or women over a certain age, for example, we would get different pictures with more detail and would learn more about why different categories of people have high or low self-esteem. Since not all women have low self-esteem, studying various subgroups would help us understand the issues more clearly. We would gain insight as to which conditions produce higher and lower self-esteem for men and for women. It might well turn out, given the data that is now available, that the higher rates of mental illness and unhappiness are limited to married women. It may be that something about the social role of being a married woman is what causes unhappiness and emotional disturbances rather than something about being a woman per se.

Finally, we could examine this data in a more technical way. It has been pointed out that these studies omit certain mental illnesses that are more common among men, such as alcoholism, drug addiction, and aggressive antisocial acts. Johnson[74] argues that this omission biases the results against women, an important considera-tion. If we use a more general definition of mental illness and include men who are drug addicts or alcoholics and those who have organic brain disorders or are mentally retarded, the statistics would change dramatically. Men would then have higher rates of institutionalization[54] in hospitals. If we add to this aggressive antisocial (criminal) acts and suicide, men's mental illness rates would soar, since most violent criminals are male and men commit suicide three times as often as women do. There are no research data on self-esteem for these groups. It seems reasonable to assume, how-ever, that it would be low. It is difficult, then, to make a definitive statement about comparative mental illnesses of men and women at this point. We can say, however, that current data indicates emotional distress among both sexes.

The traditional female role and self-esteem

The traditional female is either the demure, helpless damsel in distress (who is passive, submissive, and waiting to be saved by her man) or the angelic all-giving mother (who is only too happy to put the needs of her husband and children before her own). These images of women are widely circulated in our society and have been internalized to some degree by all females. Feeling competent is antagonistic to feeling traditionally female.

The traditional female role is associated with poor self-esteem. College women whose role concepts and role aspirations are oriented toward the home-making role have been found to have medium to low levels of self-esteem.[124] Among women 17 to 45 years old, the most "feminine" women have been found to have the lowest self-esteem, whereas women who have a combination of male and female traits have significantly higher self-esteem[2] and greater psychological health.[143]

Married women, as we have seen, are much more likely to have a mental disorder requiring either outpatient care or psychiatric hospitalization and to be less happy than married men.[54-56] Other frequently found symptoms among married women, especially full-time homemakers, include feelings that they are about to have a nervous breakdown, psychological anxiety, physical complaints, feelings of inadequacy, and self-blame for their own lack of adjustment. This is a rather dismal picture, considering the myth that women find absolute fulfillment in marriage.

These symptoms of unhappiness occur considerably less frequently among unmarried women,[17,54,55] a finding that may therefore indicate that mental difficulties are attributable to marriage rather than to femaleness. It may not be that women who marry have more distress than women who don't marry. After all, 96% of American women marry. Rather, it may be that wives make more of an adjustment in marriage than do husbands.[17] Bernard suggests, "The psychological and emotional costs of all these adjustments show up in the increasing unhappiness of wives with the passage of time and in their increasingly negative and passive outlook on life."[17]

Egalitarian marriages, in which both spouses have equal power in making family decisions, seem to avoid these problems. Research indicates that in marriages in which both partners are highly expressive, both partners also appear to be well adjusted and are highly satisfied.[84] A second type of marriage that escapes these problems is one in which the wife works full time.[20] In considering all this data it becomes clear that the women in these marriages feel they have more options and are not "stuck" in their marriages.

It seems, then, that the traditional housewife role rather than marriage iself injures women. Bernard in summarizing the research literature writes, "the truly spectacular evidence for the destructive effects of the occupation of housewife on the mental and emotional health of married women is provided by the relative incidence of the symptoms of distress in housewives and working women. . . . the working women were overwhelmingly better off than the housewives."[17]

A study comparing middle-aged married professional women having children with an equally gifted group of homemakers who had not worked since the birth of their first child found that the full-time homemakers had lower self-esteem and were less satisfied with their lives in an overall sense. They also felt less competent and less attractive than the working wives, who had positive self-images and high levels of life satisfaction despite the difficulties of coordinating their various responsibilities.[18] It may be that women of high self-esteem dare to combine careers and marriage.

Even more provocative are the findings about the self-esteem of the wives of successful men. The researchers in this study had originally expected that these wives would feel very good about themselves since they had achieved the feminine ideal in our society, marriage to a successful man. Rather, they found that being a traditional housewife (even to a successful husband) is a debilitating experience; the self-esteem of these women was significantly lower than that of married professional women or married professional men. Further, the wives of the most successful men had lower self-esteem than the wives of the moderately successful men. Could it be that these women feel relatively insignificant compared to their husbands and therefore have lower self-esteem? Income was the single aspect of husbands' success that affected their wives self-esteem positively. The researchers interpreted this to mean that housewives use income to enhance their own status through the purchase of clothes and other consumer items.[94]

It has been found that wives who do not work have less power and respect in their marriages, regardless of whether they are in the working class or middle class.[63] It has also been found that (given the same social class and employment status) the more children a woman has and the more closely spaced they are, the less power she has in the marital relationship; that is, her position is progressively undermined.[63,84] In sum, the traditional female role, especially the full-time housewife role, is damaging to women's self-esteem.

Factors producing high self-esteem in women

What creates healthy self-esteem in women? Unfortunately female self-esteem has received little attention until very recently. Therefore, I will summarize the most important studies about male self-esteem and the very few studies on female self-esteem and will generalize these findings in terms of female development.

The most thorough and well-known study on the development of self-esteem involved 1748 boys, and no girls, between the ages of 10 and 12. It was found that boys

> with high self-esteem, reared under conditions of acceptance, clear definition of rules, and respect appear to be personally effective, poised and competent individuals who are capable of independent and creative actions. Their prevailing level of anxiety appears to be low, and their ability to deal with anxiety appears to be better than that of other persons. They are socially skilled and are able to deal with external situations and demands in a direct and incisive manner. Their social relationships are generally good and, being relatively unaffected or distracted by personal difficulties they gravitate to positions of influence and authority. (p. 249)[32]

There is an important circularity to these findings that I want to emphasize. Previous experiences of success help a boy to feel competent. This feeling of competence helps him to feel good about himself. He can now approach new tasks with confidence, which increases the chances of his doing well. Since the boy has had many experiences of doing things well, an occasional failure does not cause undue upset and can be accepted realistically. Thus self-esteem and achievement are intertwined.

High self-esteem boys are brought up in the following four conditions: (1) total or nearly total acceptance by parents; (2) clearly defined and consistently enforced limits; (3) respect, latitude, and freedom within the limits; and (4) parents who had relatively high self-esteem. If we look at these four conditions another way, we can say that boys experience significance (meaning the boys felt acceptance, attention, and affection) and competence (meaning successful performance in meeting the demands that were made for achievement). These two factors, significance and competence, were found by Coopersmith[32] to be the two most important contributors to self-esteem.

The parents of these high self-esteem boys were strict, had clear expectations of the boys, and consistently enforced their rules. At the same time they were loving, affectionate, and tolerant of a wide range of expressions.

The parents were "active, poised and relatively self assured individuals [who appeared] to be on relatively good terms with one another, to have established clear lines of authority and responsibility in dealing with the children."[32] Both parents were involved in activities outside the family, thus having additional sources of gratification and esteem.

The mothers of these high self-esteem boys are particularly interesting for us to think about: First, they were not traditional women in the sense of being only family centered. They allowed themselves major interests and sources of joy in addition to their families. Second, those who worked outside the home wanted to continue and clearly enjoyed working. The boys' self-esteem was not affected by whether or not the mother worked. Third, more mothers (39.46%) of boys with high self-esteem expressed no preference for boys or girls than did mothers of children with medium or low self-esteem; this is especially interesting given the overwhelming preference of parents as a group for male children. It may be that these mothers were more open towards people and experiences than other mothers. Fourth, they accepted their roles and carried them out in an effective and realistic manner.

The parents were highly compatible; that is, they had achieved consensus on financial and religious matters, had worked out a style of life that was comfortable for both, and agreed on their privileges and responsibilities.

The fathers were more concerned and involved with their sons on a day-to-day basis and spent more time with their sons than did fathers of low self-esteem boys. Although there were no differences in social status or occupational status among the fathers of high and low self-esteem boys, the fathers of high self-esteem boys had a steadier employment history.

What can we learn from these boys and their parents that is relevant to girls' self-esteem? It seems to me that these parents would be good parents for high self-esteem girls as well. To be perfect parents, they would need to expect their daughters to achieve and to reward their daughters' achievements and efforts toward independence.

ACHIEVEMENT

To achieve means "to finish, to carry out successfully, to bring to an end, to attain, to reach successfully."[116] Yet in our everyday discussions of a person's achievements we usually mean the power, money, status, or prestige in their professional, business, or political work. Household achievement, being a great cook, giving birth to and raising children, coordinating an efficient household, and other housekeeping tasks no matter how impressive are usually not included in this category.

The following sections discuss achievement in terms of jobs, carers, money, power, and prestige, review the background factors of female and male achievers, and summarize the common threads that emerge.

Women's achievements

According to the definition above women have achieved less than men. In terms of prestige, only 26% of all full-time women workers in 1976 were in the top two occupational categories used by the U.S. Census Bureau: professional and technical (accountants, dietitians, registered nurses, psychologists, physicians, writers) and managers and administrators (buyers, purchasing agents, bank officials). These two categories account for 34% of all full-time working men. As is well known, most women who work full time (41%) are clericals (bank tellers, bookkeepers, stock clerks, secretaries, and teachers' aides).

In terms of salaries, women's incomes fell from 64% of men's in 1955 to 58% of men's salaries in 1975.[24] Even when women hold the same jobs as men, they earn less. For example, in 1976 the salaries of professional and technical women were 68% of those of their male counterparts; the salaries of women in management and administration were 59%. This is even more shocking when one realizes how small the improvement has been. In 1939 women professionals and technicals made 60.8% of men's salaries and women managers and administrators made 54%.[35] This is an improvement of only 7.2% and 5% respectively in 37 years.

It is not clear why women in the same fields as men earn less money. One possibility is that women are recent entrants into these fields and therefore receive the starting salaries, pulling the average salary for women down. Overt discrimination is a second possibility. Another possibility is that women do not receive the recognition they deserve (because of the bias against seeing women as competent) and therefore do not receive appropriate merit raises and promotions.[49] Since our society views salaries with great respect and seriousness, being paid less tells women that they've achieved less and are worth less.

Once a field becomes predominantly female, it pays poorly. Unfortunately there is a good deal of occupational segregation. Nearly half of all employed women in 1970 worked in occupations that were over 80% female; two thirds of all men were in occupations that were over 80% male. A study of women and occupational prestige was found that predominantly female occupations are accorded the prestige they deserve but not the income one would predict on the basis of the job's complexity or training requirements.[43] In fact, the salaries of clerical workers, the most dramatically growing field for women, have dropped from 78.5% of men's salaries in 1939 to 64% in 1976.[35] This relative drop in salaries has accompanied the change in the field from "a man's field" to a "woman's field."

Some hope for the future can be derived from the projected median salaries for recent college graduates. Young women college graduates are expected to have starting salaries of $10,294, or 82% of men's ($12,452) starting salaries in 1981.[78]

In addition, women have accumulated relatively little power in our society. There have been no female presidents or vice presidents of the country, relatively few members of Congress, and very few top executives of large companies. Once again, the view towards the future is positive, for there are more female legislators than ever before and three quarters of the nation's population said that they would vote for a woman President.[5]

Background factors of achievers

SOCIAL CLASS AND EDUCATION   Social class and education have long been considered the two major determinants of eventual occupational status and income.[38,48] A higher social class of origin makes it possible, theoretically, for a person to acquire whatever educational and vocational training is needed for her/his career aspirations. Many studies have shown that additional schooling increases a person's earning capacity and that the average earnings of more highly educated people are higher than the average earnings of people with less education.

Jencks' landmark study[73] of economic opportunity in the United States questions these findings. He found that differences in social class and education explain only half the variation in men's occupational status and that brothers raised in the same home end up with standards of living that are almost as different as two randomly selected individuals. Even more provocative is the finding that the earnings of men in the same occupation vary almost as much as men in all occupations. Therefore the number of years of education and the person's family's social class are insufficient to explain income variations, which Jencks[73] attributes to a combination of luck, desire, and personality. As a psychologist, I think his findings make sense. Certainly we all know people who work harder and longer hours, who get ahead despite their backgrounds. Thus for men at least, we can say that factors such as social class and education account for half of what makes them successful. (Unfortunately, Jencks limited his study to men. Any inferences we make about women would be total speculation.)

There is some evidence that members of different ethnic groups within the same social class aspire to different occupations[15]; however, there are so few studies about ethnic differences that is is too early to generalize from them with any confidence.*

BIRTH ORDER   A high achiever is likely to be a firstborn child or an only child in a family.[40] Firstborn children receive extra pressures to achieve; all of their parents' hopes and anxieties are centered on them. This happens because parents are nervous

---

*Several studies have found that black women, like white women, have lower career aspirations than their male peers; they aspire to traditionally female careers like school teaching, social work, and nursing.[15,118]

about their ability to be good parents, and by the time the second child arrives, the parents can relax somewhat. The child's desire to please and the parents' high expectations of firstborn or only children combine to make high achievers. This phenomenon is true of women as well as men.[65,85]

PARENTAL STYLE   The parents of competent, high-achieving children have been found to treat their children similarly. A study defined three groups of nursery school children: (1) the competent children who were assertive, self-reliant, self-controlled, buoyant, and affiliative (the ability to get close to others); (2) the discontented children who were withdrawn from others, distrustful, and unhappy; and (3) the children with little self-control and little self-reliance, who tended to retreat from novel experiences.[8] The parents of the three groups were quite different from one another. The parents of the competent group tended to have certain characteristics: they were demanding of their children, expecting their children to behave in certain ways; they were controlling, telling them what to do and when; they were highly communicative, telling them what they liked and did not like, as well as talking to them about other things; and they were very loving and warm. The researcher thought that this combination of techniques fostered self-reliance in children by encouraging independence of action and decision making within strictly controlled limits. It was concluded that parental practices that are intellectually stimulating as well as to some extent tension producing develop competent children. This pattern is similar to the pattern of parents of high self-esteem children. Others have also found that children, boys in this study, who strove to attain excellence had parents who encouraged achievement in similar ways.[27]

BACKGROUNDS OF HIGH ACHIEVING WOMEN   A high-achieving woman is likely to be a firstborn child or an only child. Several other background factors are important: her mother tends to be well educated and/or works; she values her daughter's assertiveness, achievement, and femaleness; her father has a significant relationship with his daughter that is separate and independent of his wife's relationship with her; he, too, values her femaleness and independence and encourages both; the parents have a good relationship with one another. In addition, a girl who achieves tends not to be excessively close with her mother; given the American norm of close mother-daughter relationships, a mother who allows her daughter to be emotionally separate is rare.*

A study of 25 top- and 25 middle-management female executives of national companies found not only that were all 50 firstborn or only children but also that the 25 top executives exhibited all of the attributes listed above. In addition, these executives came from homes in which they were not restricted to "sex appropriate" activities. If school teachers tried to limit them to traditional female activities, their

---

*References 6, 64, 65, 66, 85, 110, 123, 142, 154, 166.

parents went to the school to intervene and argue in favor of the girls' less traditional interests.[65]

Other studies, too, find that high-achieving women come from homes in which there was no effort to restrict them to only "female" activities. Thus high-achieving women are products of enriching experiences that lead them to less stereotyped roles and have experienced approval for their interests.[65,85,166]

The present families of achieving women are interesting to look at as well. Women who use their talents and skills fully in adulthood seem to have married a certain kind of man. One study compared 200 married women matched for age, education, number and ages of their children, and the incomes of their husbands.[161] The two most important factors differentiating those married women who worked outside of the home from those who were full-time homemakers were (1) the husband's positive attitude about his wife's working and (2) his actual help with childcare.[161] Just as wives may support their husbands' business and professional efforts by moving to other cities, entertaining the husband's associates, and so on, working wives need support and encouragement as well. This support may come in the form of childcare, empathy, typing her professional papers, whatever. It is the husband's emotional support of his wife's work, or the absence of it, that has a tremendous impact on her, much more than the reverse, because most women grow up with traditional ideas about women and need some support to step out of this stereotypic role.

PERSONALITIES OF ACHIEVING WOMEN High-achieving women have been found to differ from the general population of women in several ways. Data from several studies indicate that a woman who achieves in her job is more independent, more self-reliant, more assertive, more adventurous, more imaginative, more experimental, more flexible, and more intelligent than the typical woman. She is also less conservative and less dependent on others and has interests that are less traditionally female.*

It is interesting to note that although achieving women's personalities may be different from those of traditional women, their early sex-role training does have an effect. For example, female medical students' orientation to their work was found to be significantly different from that of their male peers. The females were motivated by interest, altruism, and self-development whereas male medical students most often mentioned future earnings and prestige as their reasons for going to medical schools; female medical students were found to be significantly more independent and achievement-oriented than the males.[166] It may be that females must be very independent and self-confident to make an unusual career choice such as medicine.

A thread that runs through all studies of achievement is the idea of inde-

---

*References 4, 57, 65, 85.

pendence and the feeling of being in control of one's destiny. In a study of school achievement involving 645,000 pupils in grades three, six, nine, and twelve drawn from 4000 public schools across the country, it was found that a sense of control over one's own destiny had the strongest relationship of any factor to achievement.[31] This feeling of independence and control* is not typically encouraged in females but is often found among women who do achieve.[142] In general we can say that the personalities of women achievers are very much like those of the men in their field, be it psychology, art, writing, politics, or science.[4]

Perception of vocational options

Children begin to make vocational decisions at an early age. By age 3 most children understand the concept of a job; by age 3 most children also know whether they are male or female. Most girls between the ages of 3 and 5 want to be either a nurse or a teacher. Boys at this age indicate a broader range of careers, although they are equally sex typed.[159] Children's stereotyping of jobs by gender is quite accurate by kindergarten age and changes little up to the sixth grade.[134] It is rather amazing that they have learned so well, so young. Within this pattern of stereotyping, children are more ready to exclude women from "men's" jobs than vice versa. It appears, then, that most children limit their career options early, but girls do so more severely than boys.

Girls of all ages seem to know less than boys about the various jobs that are possible. By age 10 boys are significantly better than girls at rating the prestige, income, and importance of various jobs—because boys are already at this age feeling the pressure to learn about jobs.[112]

Most high school students feel they receive little or no help with their vocational decisions. A nationwide study of 32,000 high school students found that most eleventh graders' decisions showed a lack of knowledge about their options.[119] Given this lack of information, it is not surprising that high school students fall back on traditionally female and male jobs or do what their parents did. Over half the nation's eleventh grade girls chose occupations falling in the narrow range of (1) clerical and secretarial, (2) education and social services, (3) nursing and human care whereas nearly half the boys chose occupations in (1) technological areas and (2) the trades. As categories indicate, the aspirations of female high school students tend to be traditionally female and to be lower than their abilities. Even most honor students prefer to be teachers and secretaries, although they are capable of much more.[15]

High school students making career decisions must deal with a substantial amount of misinformation. One study found that 41% of the nation's eighth graders

---

*It was also found that most minority children (except Orientals) have less conviction than whites that they can control their own environments and futures. Those who had this feeling also had high achievement.

believed that *few* women worked outside the home after marriage; in reality, about half (47.6%) of all married women living with their husbands work outside the home, and 41.6% of married women who live with their husbands and have children under 6 years of age were working.[156] It is startling that females are making career decisions with such misinformation and unfortunate that there are not better vocational guidance programs available in the United States for both girls and boys.

Studies of social class consistently indicate that working-class children tend to have more sex-role stereotypes about occupation than do middle-class children.[134] The reasons for this are not clear.

It is unfortunate that these early career stereotypes are rarely corrected later in life; most women choose "female jobs," that is, altruistic and helping jobs, whereas most men chose crafts and manufacturing jobs. Since the seeds of these decisions are made so early in life, they are not based on the person's real abilities but on stereotyped ideas of what males and females can do. The traditionally female fields are nursing, teaching, social work, and secretarial work. Nurses typically make their decisions in grade school or high school whereas social workers typically wait until about the sophmore year in college.[36] Female medical students, on the other hand, are in a nontraditional field and seem to make their career decisions in the last year or two of college.[166] Delaying career decisions, it seems, allows a woman to make career choices that are less stereotyped. Since most studies conclude that females tend unrealistically to select occupations requiring abilities that are low in contrast to their aptitudes and interests,[27,117] it is especially important for females to delay their career decisions until they can make more realistic decisions. The years between ages 16 and 18 have been found to be the most realistic period for occupational choice.[47] At this point in development one knows more about one's abilities and skills and can make a more appropriate job decision.

Women's career choices are significantly influenced by the presence or absence of role models, for example, a mother who works or a female teacher in one's field. Most studies of maternal employment have found that if the mother likes working there are no negative effects on her children, male or female.[32,67] Many positive effects have been found for girls. Among the most important is that girls with working mothers are more likely to aspire to higher skilled and more prestigious jobs than girls whose mothers were full-time homemakers.[6] The daughters of employed women more often choose their own mothers as models, that is, as the person they would most like to be like. In addition, it has been found among both male and female Ph.D.s that those with a dissertation advisor of the same sex, who was therefore a role model, were ultimately more productive.[51]

In summary, we may say that a female child is more likely to achieve in her career if she is the firstborn or only child, if her parents clearly reinforce and encourage her achievement efforts, and if they also appreciate her femininity. It is helpful for career decisions to be delayed until high school or the middle of college so that they can be made on the basis of interests and abilities and *not* on stereotypes of the kinds of work females should and can do. Role models who seem happy and successful are also helpful to female's career development.

SELF-ESTEEM AND ACHIEVEMENT
Relationship of self-esteem and achievement

It has been clearly established that there is a relationship between self-esteem and achievement for men. Men with high self-esteem are more likely to achieve educationally,[120] are more likely to attain a higher occupational status,[3] and are more likely to feel competent[32] than are men with low self-esteem.

There is enough evidence available to suggest a similar relationship between self-esteem and achievement for women.[6,7,10] College women with higher self-esteem are significantly more likely to be motivated to achieve and to have higher aspirations, the desire for power, and the wish to be physicians and scientists, whereas girls with lower self-esteem are more likely to aspire to be teachers, nurses, and secretaries.[7] They are also more likely to be motivated to affiliate (seek out friends) than college women with lower self-esteem.[10] It is widely known that successful male executives, similar to successful female executives,[34] are motivated by power and the need to achieve; their needs for closeness and relatively long, stable marriages have not received as much publicity.

As one might expect, the relationship between self-esteem and achievement also works in reverse. Achieving well in their occupations helps men feel better about themselves.[3] Normally, after a man does well, he feels more self-confident and his performance improves or remains equally good on the next task. A similar pattern exists for females.[7,65] We thus have a "positive cycle," so to speak, in which high self-esteem allows one to work more competently at tasks and to accomplish more; these accomplishments in turn create higher self-esteem.

Common achievement conflicts in women

When a person sets out to do something and completes it successfully, it normally raises her/his self-esteem. When a person of low self-esteem, however, sets out to do something and completes it successfully, it often sets up an unconscious emotional conflict because the feeling of competence and self-derogatory feelings are incompatible. Some compromise must then be made between these two feelings. Several such compromises are described in the following sections, following which the common themes are summarized and some hypotheses about their origins explored.

Achievement conflicts occur in both sexes. Matina Horner[69] in her research into the fear of success has suggested that women have more achievement conflicts than men. She hypothesized that independence and achievement strivings are sex-"inappropriate" activities and therefore make women anxious. This anxiety inhibits their performances, and therefore they actually do achieve less than they would otherwise. Subsequent research has revealed that males exhibit as much fear of success as females.[162] Canaven-Gumpert and others,[27] who suggest that achievement conflicts are as frequent among men as women, hypothesize that people who fear success have a strong three-way ambivalence about success: they simultaneously want to avoid failure, to achieve success, and to avoid success. Thus a very complicated set of unconscious feelings exists. The studies of these researchers found in addition that people with achievement conflicts had low self-esteem.

We will have to await more research to be sure about the distribution of achievement conflicts among men and women. One thing is clear: since work achievement is a relatively new requirement for women, the conflict is painful.

This discussion is limited to problems centering on the conflicts between self-esteem and achievement. Rather than trying to exhaust all the possible achievement conflicts in women, I will describe three personality types involving common achievement conflicts: "The perfect little girl", "the uncommitted floater", and "the woman workaholic." Each type is briefly described and illustrated with clinical examples.

THE PERFECT LITTLE GIRL   The perfect little girl type is usually polite, likable, compliant, submissive to others' wishes, and willing to please. She is good at doing what she is told to do, handing her work in on time, memorizing, getting the right answers, and getting good grades. Although she excells and is often an A student, she typically feels that she is stupid. On some level she knows that she cannot or will not think for herself, and she does not trust her own judgment. This makes her even more needy of getting the "right answer" and an A. She needs to be perfect; if she is not perfect she feels horrible about herself; she is always prey to feeling badly because of her basically low self-esteem.

I will describe one such case, Ann, as I will call her. Ann is the "perfect daughter" and the first child of two very insecure people. Her mother needs her daughter to be "perfect" so that the world will realize she's an OK mother. Her father is argumentative, rigid, and distant. Ann received a great deal of praise from her parents for being "perfect," for example, being neat, dressing prettily, doing things on time, in general for complying with her parents wishes. When she tried to do things on her own, however, both parents would stop her. For example, when she went shopping by herself for the first time, her mother told her the shoes she bought were ugly and told her to return them. Other girls her age might have kept them, but because Ann needed to please and was so dependent, she complied and returned the shoes. Whenever she nervously expressed her own opinions at the dinner table, her father told her she was wrong. Therefore she received no encouragement and a lot of criticism when thinking for herself, which convinced her she was stupid and somehow "bad" and should feel badly about herself. The "good little girl" style was an unconscious way to feel less bad about herself.

At work, Ann, like other perfect little girls, is an excellent assistant or collaborator because she is good at taking direction, doing all of the tasks assigned to her, and doing them perfectly. Once her boss realizes she is capable, however, and asks her to do things requiring independent judgment and some decision making, she becomes very anxious and upset. At this point, her low self-esteem and neurotic dependence on others clashes with her real accomplishments. She cannot mess up totally because that would mean she is a failure and not perfect. But neither can she do very well at this new, more responsible task because that would mean she really was smart and worthy. Thus, Ann is in an emotional bind, anxious and insecure; at such times she is likely to undermine her success.

THE UNCOMMITTED FLOATER   The uncommitted floater type accomplishes a good deal but does not acknowledge it. If something good happens she will say "Who me?" or "It's just luck" or "Yes, but there's so much that's not going right, this doesn't matter," or she might not even notice the good things. An uncommitted floater really does have goals and desires deep down but never admits them; consciously she does not set goals or say what she wants. Making a commitment to something feels frightening and very dangerous.

One such woman, whom I will call Betty, really did want to go to graduate school but would not let herself admit this then or now. She consciously feels that she applied to graduate school "only because all my friends were applying, I did it as a lark: since I got in, I went." It would be too upsetting for her to admit that she really wanted to do this, and it is easy to understand why she needed to act this way. If she consciously experienced herself as successful, she would then have to worry that her husband would feel threatened by her interest that was separate from him. She would also have to worry that her mother would become jealous and critical of her. Floating through graduate school protected her against potential failure and possible criticism. Unfortunately it also prevented her from feeling good when she did well. Thus despite her success in school and numerous positive responses from professors and peers, she never felt good or smart. There was always a reason not to take the compliments seriously. She'd think, "Oh, I fooled them," "They're just being nice, they don't mean it," or something like that.

In fact, floating through school in this uncommitted way did reduce her accomplishments from what they could have been. If she had committeed herself, she would have worked harder, studied more, and probably done even better.

Betty was the second child of a depressed woman who was very critical. There was no way to please her mother. Good things were usually not noticed; bad things were criticized very harshly. Her father did not notice good things either, and although he was not harshly critical, he never told her mother to stop critizing Betty and thus never protected her. She therefore developed a style of not letting herself (or her mother) know what was important to her, thus avoiding the worry about whether she would be criticized.

Her brother was the apple of her mother's eye. Everything he did was terrific as far as mother was concerned. No one seemed to notice how compulsive and insecure he really was. Betty always hoped that if she did things "right" she would receive some of the love and affection she thought her brother was receiving.

Betty's not committing herself to projects was a good compromise in that it allowed her to accomplish without overtly threatening her mother or her husband. It was a less than good compromise in that she accomplished much less than she was capable of and she always felt badly about herself.

THE WOMAN WORKAHOLIC   The woman workaholic is able to work and accomplish with some success. She is usually driven and finds her work less rewarding than it could be. She usually feels unconsciously that if she is a success at work she cannot marry. Therefore she devalues her work success and ends up feeling good about neither aspect of her life.

Carol is an example of the woman workaholic. Carol is an administrator who has trouble delegating tasks. She ends up doing everything herself and working 60 hours a week at a job that should take about 40. She is so exhausted that she has little time for friends and no time for boyfriends, although she says she wants boyfriends, marriage, and children. If Carol delegated better she would accomplish more at work and would probably receive praise and promotions. But this would threaten her low self-esteem since she would then worry that she would not be able to do the new job. If she delegated better she might also have more time for her social life, which she claims she wants.

Carol presents herself as a tower of strength to her friends and occasional dates. She does not let herself become consciously aware of when she needs a favor or when she is lonely and needs company. She had good reason for keeping these needs out of awareness. As a child, whenever she did ask for love, attention, or company, she felt rebuffed. Not that her parents did not want to be affectionate, but it was hard for them to express tenderness, and when asked they became anxious and more distant. From past experience Carol learned that asking for emotional support was emotionally devastating for her parents and pushed them even further away emotionally. Carol thus works many hours to fill up the loneliness and exhausts herself as a way to ensure that she does not let these feelings into awareness. She pretends she is a tower of strength to fool herself and others.

Carol never felt loved by either her mother or her father. She feels that her younger sister was loved and is angry at her parents for depriving her. The times she did receive affection and praise from her parents occurred when she earned good grades at school and when they saw her working hard on something, a school report, or an after-school job. She learned then that working long and hard was the only avenue for praise and love. Hence she became a workaholic.

Although Carol is clearly successful at work, she is less successful than she could be. She also devalues the success she does have by saying things like "This really doesn't matter because I'm not married," and thus she ends up not feeling good about either aspect of her life.

• • •

Some common themes emerge from these three styles. One, the parents of all three were ambivalent about their daughter's achievements. They wanted their daughters to do well in the world, yet they did not praise them for independent acts or achievements. Two, the women could all have been much more successful at work without putting in more hours or more effort. As we worked together in psychotherapy it became clear that if they were less anxious and less upset, their efficiency would increase and they would accomplish even more. Now they all sabotage their success in one way or another—Ann by her dependency and her anxious need to find the "right answer," Betty by never setting a goal so that she did not feel she was working on a project, and Carol by her inefficiency and inability to delegate.

Although these women have achieved a good deal, they never felt good about themselves; that is, they have low self-esteem despite their accomplishments. Ann feels inadequate and stupid, Betty feels she never accomplishes anything, and Carol feels her work success is irrelevant because she is not married. They are not unique. I have seen many Anns, Bettys, and Carols in my psychotherapy practice. Others have, too. Clance and Imes[30] have written about highly successful women who feel that they are not bright or competent, who feel like frauds. Symonds[150] has written about neurotic dependency in highly successful women. And Thompson[153] as early as 1941 pointed out the important role our culture has in helping women to feel "inferior."

One interesting question is why these three females developed different styles and different achievement conflicts. To oversimply the answer a bit, it seems that Ann became the perfect little girl because being "good" and complying with her parents' desires did get her praise, love, and affection. Betty and Carol could not become perfect little girls because their parents did not respond this way. There was no way to please Betty's mother, but there was a way to incur her wrath and harsh criticism. Betty learned how to avoid her mother's criticism by not letting anyone know what was important to her. This is how she developed her uncommitted floating style. Carol received praise only when she got good grades and worked hard, and thus she became a workaholic.

The family constellations that produce Anns, Bettys and Carols might vary, but the families share some basic styles. All of them have some ambivalence about their daughters growing up. Perfect little girls come from families that require a great deal of compliance from girls. Uncommitted floaters come from families in which criticism is strong and often unpredictable. Workaholics come from families in which the only praise is for tasks that are performed well and in which all else is ignored.

SUMMARY

It has been found that high-achieving women are likely to be firstborn or only children, as are high-achieving men. They tend to come from homes in which there was no effort to restrict them to "female" activities; in fact, their interest in both "male" and "female" things was encouraged and supported by their parents. Further, high-achieving women are often married to men who encourage their wives' work, both with moral support and with helpful acts such as full participation in childcare, reading manuscripts, and so on.

Achievement conflicts are common among women because traditional images of women dominate our culture and have permeated our psyches. The research summarized here indicates the sex-role training starts on the first day of our lives. Traditional images are constantly reinforced by most every aspect of our culture. To counteract the overwhelming nature of this training, we must reexamine the way we bring up our children, even our newborn infants. We must check our perceptions of our infant girls as "frail" and "helpless." In the early years, especially the first year and a half when the all-important bases for gender identification and personality are being built, we must encourage our daughters' independence, allow them to take pleasure in doing things for themselves, and not overprotect them, as we are programmed to do. This is no easy task, since we, too, unconsciously subscribe to some of these traditional images.

ACKNOWLEDGMENTS

I would like to express my appreciation to Brenda Tepper, Ph.D., who read several drafts of this chapter and was extremely helpful and supportive. I would also like to thank Marilyn Williams, M.A., for her encouragement throughout this project.

REFERENCES

1. Adelman, S., and Rosenzweig, S.: Parental predetermination of the sex of offspring, Journal of Biosocial Science 10:235, 1978.
2. Antill, J.K., and Cunningham, J.D.: Self-esteem as a function of masculinity in both sexes, Journal of Consulting and Clinical Psychology 47:783, 1979.
3. Bachman, J.G., and O'Malley, P.: Self-esteem in young men: a longitudinal analysis of the impact of educational and occupational attainment, Journal of Personality and Social Psychology 35:365, 1977.
4. Bachtold, L.M.: Personality characteristics of women of achievement, Psychology of Women Quarterly 1:70, 1976.
5. Barron, D.D.: Today's American woman: how the public sees her, prepared for President's Advisory Committee for Women by Public Agenda Foundation, New York, 1980.
6. Baruch, G.K.: Feminine self-esteem, self-rat-

ings of competence and maternal career commitment, Journal of Counseling 20:487, 1973.
7. Baruch, G.K.: Girls who perceive themselves as competent: some antecedents and correlates, Psychology of Women Quarterly 1:38, 1976.
8. Baumrind, D.: Child care practices anteceding three patterns of preschool behavior, Genetic Psychological Monographs 75:43, 1967.
9. Bayley, N.: Consistency of maternal and child behaviors in the Berkeley Growth Study, Vita Humana 7:73, 1964.
10. Bedeian, A., and Touliatos, J.: Work-related motives and self-esteem in American women, Journal of Psychology 99:63, 1978.
11. Bem, S.L.: The measurement of psychological androgyny, Journal of Consulting and Clinical Psychology 42:155, 1974.
12. Bem, S.L.: Sex role adaptability: one conse-

quence of psychological androgyny, Journal of Personality and Social Psychology **33**:48, 1976.

13. Bem, S.L., and Lenny, E.: Sex-typing and the avoidance of cross-sex behavior, Journal of Personality and Social Psychology **33**;48, 1976.

14. Bennett, E.M., and Cohen, L.R.: Men and women: personality patterns and contrasts, Genetic Psychology Monographs **59**:101, 1959.

15. Berman, Y.: Occupational aspirations of 545 female high school seniors, Journal of Vocational Behavior **2**:173, 1972.

16. Bernard, J.: The paradox of the happy marriage. In Gornick, V., and Moran, B., editors: Woman in Sexist Society, New York, 1971, Basic Books, Inc.

17. Bernard, J.: The future of marriage, New York, 1972, World Publishing Co.

18. Birnbaum, J.: Life patterns, personality style and self esteem in gifted family oriented and career committed women, Dissertation Abstracts International **32**:1834, 1971.

19. Birnbaum, D., and others: Children's stereotypes about sex differences in emotionality, Sex Roles **6**:435, 1980.

20. Blood, R.O., and Hamblin, R.L.: The effects of the wife's employment on the family power structure, Social Forces **36**:347, 1958.

21. Broverman, I., and others: Sex role stereotypes and clinical judgments of mental health, Journal of Consulting and Clinical Psychology **34**:1, 1970.

22. Broverman, I., and others: Sex-role stereotypes: a current appraisal, Journal of Social Issues **59**:59, 1972.

23. Brown, D.G.: Sex role development in a changing culture, Psychological Bulletin **55**: 232, 1958.

24. Burstein, P.: Equal employment opportunity legislation and the income of women and nonwhites, American Sociological Review **44**: 367, 1979.

25. Bush, D.E., and others: Adolescenct perception of sex roles in 1968 and 1975, Public Opinion Quarterly **41**:459, 1977-1978.

26. Campbell, F.L.: Demographic factors in family organizations, doctoral dissertation, 1976, University of Michigan. Quoted in Laws, J.L.: A feminist review of the marital adjustment literature, Journal of Marriage and the Family **33**:483, 1971.

27. Canavan-Gumpert, D., and others: The success-rearing personality, Lexington, Mass., 1978, Lexington Books.

28. Cartwright, L.K.: Conscious factors entering into decisions of women to study medicine, Journal of Social Issues **28**:201, 1972.

29. Chodorow, N.: Family structure and feminine personality. In Rosaldo, M.S., and Lamphere, L., editors: Woman, culture and society, Stanford, 1974, Stanford University Press.

30. Clance, P.R., and Imes, S.A.: The impostor phenomenon in high achieving women: dynamics and therapeutic intervention, Psychotherapy: Theory, Research and Practice **15**: 241, 1978.

31. Coleman, J.S., and others: Equality of Educational Opportunity, Washington, D.C.,.1966, U.S. Office of Education.

32. Coopersmith, S.: The antecedents of self-esteem, San Francisco, 1967, Miller Freeman Publications, Inc.

33. Crandall, V., and others: Motivational and ability determinants of young children's intellectual achievement behaviors, Child Development **33**:643, 1962.

34. Cummin, P.C.: TAT correlates of executive performance, Journal of Applied Psychology **51**:78, 1967.

35. Current Population Reports: Consumer income, Washington, D.C., 1978, U.S. Department of Commerce, Bureau of the Census.

36. David, A.J.: Self-concept, occupational role expectations and occupational choice in nursing and social work. In Theodore, A.: The Professional Women, Cambridge, Mass., 1971, Schenkman Publishing Co., Inc.

37. Diagnostic and statistical manual of mental disorders, 3, Washington, D.C., 1980, American Psychiatric Association.

38. Dillard, J.M., and Perrin, D.W.: Puerto Rican, black and Anglo adolescents' career aspirations, expectations and maturity, The Vocation Guidance Quarterly **28**:313, 1980.

39. Dominick, J.: The portrayal of women in prine time, 1953-1977, Sex Roles **5**:405, 1979.

40. Douvan, E., and Adelson, J.: The adolescent experience, New York, 1966. John Wiley & Sons, Inc.

41. Downs, A.C., and Gowan, D.C.: Sex Differences in reinforcement and punishment on prime-time television, Sex Roles **6**:683, 1980.

42. Edge, L.: Eliminating barriers to career development of women, Personnel and Guidance Journal **49:**24, 1970.

43. England, P.: Women and occupational prestige: a case of vacuous sex equality, Signs **5:** 252, 1979.

44. Erikson, E.: Childhood and society, New York, 1963, W.W. Norton & Co., Inc.

45. Fein, D., and others: Sex differences in preadolescent self-esteem, Journal of Psychology **90:**179, 1975.

46. Garai, J.: Sex differences in mental health, Genetic Psychology Monographs **81:**123, 1970.

47. Ginzberg, E., and others: Occupational Choice, New York, 1951, Columbia University Press.

48. Glick, P., and Miller, H.P.: Educational level and potential income, American Sociological Review **21:**307, 1956.

49. Goldberg, P., and others: Evaluation of the performance of women as a function of their sex, achievement and personal history, Journal of Personality and Social Psychology **19:** 114, 1971.

50. Goldberg, S., and Lewis, M.: Play behavior in the year old infant: early sex differences, Child Development **40:**21, 1969.

51. Goldstein, E.: Effect of same-sex and cross-sex role models on subsequent academic productivity of scholars, American Psychologist **34:**407, 1979.

52. Goodenough, E.: Interest in persons as an aspect of sex differences in the early years, Genetic Psychology Monographs **55:**287, 1957.

53. Gordon, R.E., and Gordon, K.K.: Factors in post-partum emotional adjustment, American Journal of Orthopsychiatry **37:**359, 1967.

54. Gove, W.R.: Mental illness and psychiatric treatment among women, Psychology of Women Quarterly **4:**345, 1980.

55. Gove, W.R.: Mental illness and psychiatric treatment among women: a rejoinder to Johnson, Psychology of Women Quarterly **4:**372, 1980.

56. Gove, W., and Tudor, J.: Adult sex roles and mental illness, American Journal of Sociology **77:**812, 1973.

57. Graham, P.A.: Women in adademe, Science **169:**1284, 1970.

58. Gurin, G., and others: Americans view their mental health, New York, 1960, Basic Books, Inc.

59. Harren, V.A., and others: Influence of gender, sex-role attitudes, and cognitive complexity on gender dominated career choices, Journal of Counseling Psychology **26:**227, 1979.

60. Hartley, R.E.: Sex role pressures and the socialization of the male child, Psychological Reports **5:**457, 1959.

61. Hartley, S.F., and Pietraczyk, L.M.: Preselecting the sex of offspring: technologies, attitudes, and implications, Social Biology **26:** 232, 1979.

62. Hecht, A.: Nursing career choice and Holland's theory: are men and blacks different? Journal of Vocational Behavior **16:**208, 1980.

63. Heer, D.M.: Dominance and the working wife, Social Forces **26:**341, 1958.

64. Helson, R.: Personality characteristics and the developmental history of creative college women, Genetic Psychology Monographs **76:** 205, 1967.

65. Hennig, M.: Family dynamics and the successful woman executive. In Knudsin, R.: Women and success, New York, 1974, William Morrow & Co., Inc.

66. Hoffman, L.W.: Early childhood experiences and women's achievement motives, Journal of Social Issues **28:**129, 1972.

67. Hoffman, L.W.: The professional woman as mother. In Knudsin, R.; Women and success, New York, 1974, William Morrow & Co., Inc.

68. Horner, M., and Fleming, J.: Revised scoring manual for an empirically derived scoring system for the motive to avoid success, Cambridge, Mass., 1977, Harvard University Press.

69. Horner, M.: Toward an understanding of achievement-related conflicts in women, Journal of Social Issues **68:**158, 1972.

70. Horney, L.: New ways in psychoanalysis, New York, 1939, W.W. Norton & Co., Inc.

71. Huston-Stein, A., and others: The relation of classroom structure to social behavior, imaginative play and self-regulation of economically disadvantaged children, Child Development **48:**908, 1977.

72. Hutt, C.: Sex differences in human development, Human Development **15:**153, 1972.

73. Jencks, C.: Inequality: a reassessment of the effect of family and schooling in America, New York, 1972, Basic Books, Inc.

74. Johnson, M: Mental illness and psychiatric treatment among women: a response, Psychology of Women Quarterly **4:**363, 1980.

75. Kagan, J., and Moss, H.A.: Birth to maturity: a study of psychological development, New York, 1962, John Wiley & Sons, Inc.

76. Kaplan, A., and Beam, J.: Beyond the stereotypes: readings toward a psychology of androgyny, Boston, 1976, Little, Brown & Co.

77. Katz, P.: The development of female identity, Sex Roles **5:**155, 1979.

78. Klein, J.: Sneak preview: the 1980 census, Working Woman, p. 72, September 1980.

79. Knudsin, R.: Women and success, New York, 1974, William Morrow & Co., Inc.

80. Komarovsky, M.: Functional analysis of sex roles, American Sociological Review **15:**508, 1950.

81. Komisar, L.: The image of women in advertising. In Gornick, V., and Moran, B., editors: Woman in sexist society, New York, 1971, Basic Books, Inc.

82. Lasky, E.: Humanness: an exploration into the mythologies about women and men, New York, 1975, MSS Information Co.

83. Deleted in proofs.

84. Laws, J.L.: A feminist review of the marital adjustment literature, Journal of Marriage and the Family **33:**483, 1971.

85. Lemkau, J.P.: Personality and background characteristics of women in male-dominated occupations, Psychology of Women Quarterly **4:**221, 1979.

86. Lerner, R., and others: Self-concept, self-esteem and body attitudes among Japanese male and female attitudes, Child Development **51:**847, 1980.

87. Lewis, H.B.: Psychic war in men and women, New York, 1976, New York University Press.

88. Loeb, R.C., and Horst, L.: Sex differences in self and teachers, reports of self esteem in preadolescents, Sex Roles **4:**779, 1978.

89. Looft, W.R.: Vocational aspirations of second-grade girls, Psychological Reports **28;**241, 1978.

90. Lyle, J.: Television in daily life: patterns of use. In Rubenstein, E.A., Constock, G.A., and Murray, J.P., editors: Television and social behavior, vol. 4, Washington, D.C., 1972, U.S. Government printing office.

91. Maccoby, E.: The development of sex differences, Stanford, 1966, Stanford University Press.

92. Maccoby, E., and Jacklin, C.: The psychology of sex differences, Palo Alto, 1974, Stanford University Press.

93. MacDonald, N., and Hyde, J.: Fear of success, need achievement and fear of failure, Sex Roles **6:**695, 1980.

94. Macke, A.S., and others: Housewives' self-esteem and their husbands' success: the myth of vicarious involvement, Journal of Marriage and the Family **41:**51, 1979.

95. Mahler, M., and others: The psychological birth of the human infant, New York, 1974, Basic Books, Inc.

96. Martin, W.: Seduced and abandoned in the new world: the image of women in American fiction. In Gornick, V., and Moran, B., editors: Woman in sexist society, New York, 1971, Basic Books, Inc.

97. Maslow, A.: Self-esteem (dominance-feeling) and sexuality in women, The Journal of Social Psychology **16:**259, 1942.

98. May, R.: The courage to create, New York, 1975, Bantam Books.

99. McClelland, D.: Assessing human motivation, New York, 1971, General Learning Press.

100. McClelland, D.C., and others: The achievement motive, New York, 1953, Appleton-Century-Crofts.

101. McKee, J.P., and Sherriffs, A.C.: The differential evaluation of males and females, Journal of Personality **25:**356, 1957.

102. Mednick, N.T.S., Tangri, S.S., and Hoffman, L.W., editors: Women and achievement, New York, 1975, John Wiley & Sons, Inc.

103. Miller, J.B., editor: Psychoanalysis and women, New York, 1973, Penguin Books.

104. Miller, J.B., and Mothner, I.: Psychological consequences of sexual inequality, American Journal of Orthopsychiatry **41:**767, 1971.

105. Money, J.: Sex research: new developments, New York, 1965, Holt, Rhinehart & Winston.

106. Morgan, C.S.: Female and male attitudes toward life: implications for theories of mental health, Sex Roles **6:**367, 1980.

107. Mulvey, M.C.: Psychological and sociological factors in prediction of career patterns in women, Genetic Psychology Monographs **68:**309, 1963.

108. Murray, S.R., and Mednick, M.T.S.: Black women's achievement orientation: motivational and cognitive factors, Psychology of Women Quarterly **1:**247, 1977.

109. Nicholls, J.G.: Causal attributions and other achievement related cognitions, Journal of Personality and Social Psychology **31**:379, 1975.

110. Norfleet, M.A.: Personality characteristics of achieving and underachieving high ability senior women, Personnel and Guidance Journal **46**:976, 1968.

111. Oakey, A.: Sex, gender and society, New York, 1972, Harper & Row, Publishers, Inc.

112. O'Bryant, S., and others: Sex differences in knowledge of occupational dimensions across four age levels, Sex roles **6**:331, 1980.

113. Oetzel, R.: Annotated bibliography. In Maccoby, E., editor: The development of sex differences, Stanford, 1966, Stanford University Press.

114. O'Leary, V.E., and Braun, J.S.: Antecedents and correlates of professional careerism among women, paper presented at the annual convention of the American Psychological Association, New Orleans, September 1974.

115. O'Malley, P.M., and Bachman, J.C.: Self-esteem and education: sex and cohort comparisons among high school seniors, Journal of Social Psychology **37**:1153, 1979.

116. Oxford Universal Dictionary, ed. 3, Oxford, 1955, Clarendon Press.

117. Patterson, L.: Girls careers: expression of identity, Vocational Guidance Quarterly **21**:268, 1973.

118. Pohlman, E.: The psychology of birth planning, Cambridge, Mass., 1969, Schenkman Publishing Co., Inc.

119. Prediger, D.J., and othes: Career development of youth: a nationwide study, Personnel and Guidance Journal **53**:97, 1974.

120. Purkey, W.W.: Self-concept and school achievement, Englewood Cliffs, N.J., 1970, Prentice-Hall, Inc.

121. Reich, S., and Geller, A.: Self-image of nurses, Psychological Reports **39**:401, 1976.

122. Reissman, L.: Levels of aspiration and social class, American Sociological Review **18**:233, 1953.

123. Rezler, A.G.: Characteristics of high school girls choosing traditional or pioneer vocations, Personnel and Guidance Journal **45**:659, 1967.

124. Richardson, M.S.: Self-concepts and role concepts in the career orientation of college women, Journal of Counseling Psychology **22**:122, 1975.

125. Romer, N., and Cherry, D.: Ethnic and social class differences in children's sex-role concepts, Sex Roles **6**:245, 1980.

126. Rosen, B., and D'Andrade, R.C.: The psychological origins of achievement motivation, Sociometry **22**:185, 1959.

127. Rosenberg, M.: Society and the adolescent self-image, Princeton, N.J., 1965, Princeton University Press.

128. Rosenkrantz, P., and others: Sex role stereotypes and self concepts in college students, Journal of Consulting and Clinical Psychology **32**:287, 1968, p. 293.

129. Rubin, J.A., and others: The eye of the beholder, American Journal of Orthopsychiatry **44**:512, 1974.

130. Rubovits, P.: Early experience and the achieving orientation of American middle class girls. In Malhr, M., and Stalling, W., editors: Culture, child and school, Monterey, Calif., 1975, Brooks/Cole Publishing Co.

131. Russ, J.: The image of women in science fiction. In Lasky, E., editor: Humanness: an exploration into the mythologies about women and men, New York, 1975, MSS Information Co.

132. Sappenfield, B.R., and Harris, C.L.: Self reported masculinity and feminity as related to self-esteem, Psychological Reports **37**:669, 1975.

133. Schiff, E., and Koopman, E.J.: Relationship of women's sex role identity to self-esteem and ego development, Journal of Psychology **98**:299, 1978.

134. Schlossberg, N.F., and Goodman, J.: A woman's place: children's sex stereotyping of occupations, Vocational Guidance Quarterly **20**:266, 1972.

135. Schuler, R.: Sex, organizational level and outcome importance: where the differences are, Personnel Psychology **28**:365, 1975.

136. Sears, R., and others: Patterns of child rearing, Evanston, Ill., 1957, Row Peterson.

137. Seavey, C.A., and others: Baby X: the effect of gender labels on adult responses to infants, Sex Roles **1**:103, 1975.

138. Sherman, J.: On the psychology of women: a survey of empirical studies, Springfield, Ill., 1974, Charles C Thomas, Publisher.

139. Sheriffs, A.C., and Jarrett, R.F.: Sex differences in attitudes about sex differences, Journal of Psychology **35**:161, 1953.

140. Silvern, L.E.: Masculinity-feminity in children's self concepts, Sex Roles **4**:929, 1974.

141. Simmons, R.G., and Rosenberg, F.: Sex, sex roles and self image, Journal of Youth and Adolescence 4:229, 1975.
142. Skolnick, A.: Motivational imagery and behavior over twenty years, Journal of Consulting Psychology 30:477, 1966.
143. Spence, J.T., and others: Ratings of self and peers on sex-role attributes and their relation to self esteem and concepts of masculinity and feminity, Journal of Personality and Social Psychology 31:29, 1975.
144. Stein, A.H., and Bailey, M.M.: The socialization of achievement orientation in females, Psychological Bulletin 80:345, 1973.
145. Sternglanz, S.H., and Serbin, L.A.: Sex role stereotyping in children's television programs, Developmental Psychology 10:710, 1974.
146. Stockard, J., and Johnson, M.M.: The social origins of male dominance, Sex Roles 5:199, 1979.
147. Stoller, R.J.: Sex and gender: on the development of masculinity and femininity, New York, 1968, Science House.
148. Strainchamps, E.: Our sexist language. In Gornick, V., and Moran, B., editors: Woman in sexist society, New York, 1971, Basic Books, Inc.
149. Sullivan, H.S.: Conceptions of modern psychiatry, New York, 1953, W.W. Norton & Co., Inc.
150. Symonds, A.: Neurotic dependency in successful women, Journal of the American Academy of Psychoanalysis 4:95, 1976.
151. Terman, L.M., and Oden, M.H.: The gifted child grows up, Stanford, 1947, Stanford University Press.
152. Terman, L.M., and others: Gifted children. In Carmichael, L.: Manual of child psychology, New York, 1954, John Wiley & Sons, Inc.
153. Thompson, C.: On women, New York, 1964, Mentor.
154. Trigg, L., and Perlman, D.: Social influences on women's pursuit of a nontraditional career, Psychology of Women Quarterly 1:138, 1976.
155. U.S. Bureau of the Census: Current population reports 1978, P-60, Washington D.C., 1980, U.S. Government Printing Office.
156. U.S. Dept. of Commerce, Bureau of the Census: Statistical abstracts of the U.S., ed. 100, 1978, Washington, D.C., 1980, U.S. Government Printing Office.
157. U'ren, M.: The image of women in textbooks. In Gornick, V., and Moran, B., editors: Woman in sexist society, New York, 1971, Basic Books, Inc.
158. Veroff, J.: General feelings of well being over a generation, paper presented at the American Psychological Association Convention, Toronto, September 1, 1978.
159. Vondraceki, S.I., and Kirchner, E.P.: Vocational development in early childhood, Journal of Vocational Behavior 5:251, 1974.
160. Weil, E.: Work block: the role of work in mental health, Psychoanalysis and the Psychoanalytic Review 46:2, 1959.
161. Weil, M.: An analysis of the factors influencing married women's actual or planned work participation. In Theodore, A., editor: The professional woman, Cambridge, Mass., 1971, Schenkman Publishing Co., Inc.
162. Weiner, B.: Human motivation, New York, 1980, Holt, Rinehart & Winston.
163. Weitzman, L., and others: Sex-role socialization in picture books for preschool children, American Journal of Sociology 77:1, 1972.
164. White, R.W.: Motivation reconsidered: the concept of competence, Psychological Review 66:297, 1959.
165. White, R.: Female identity and career choice: the nursing case. In Theodore, A., editor: The professional woman, Cambridge, Mass., 1971, Schenkman Publishing Co., Inc.
166. Williams, P.A.: Women in medicine: some themes and variations, Journal of Medical Education 46:584, 1971.
167. Winterbottom, M.R.: The relation of childhood training in independence to achievement motivation, doctoral dissertation, 1953, University of Michigan.

Chapter 4

Let's bury old fictions!

Myths, like old soldiers, seem never to die—indeed, they often refuse even to fade away. When they are a reflection of biases which hurt a large segment of the population, they require active disposal—a special effort at caring for a particular kind of environmental pollution. In spite of the efforts of some to hold on to tarnished images of women, especially in Freudian psychology—as evidenced by a recent article in the *New York Times Magazine* by Anne Roiphe,[10] quoting prominent female "defenders of the faith" who, with "masculine" cunning and manipulative skill, avoided certain questions most cleverly—these images have begun to go, will go, *must* go. They have been damaging to one-half the human race for too long—it is time to put an end to them.

It has always fascinated me that Freud was quite interested in a pleasant, rather mediocre novel of derring-do, a kind of non-detective Sherlock Holmesian opus: Rider Haggard's *She*. In some ways *She* symbolizes the all-powerful bitch-goddess men fantasy and fear; her powers lie in her sexual beauty *plus* in the fact that she has discovered the secret of eternal life and youth, and therefore is invulnerable in ruling over her "lost tribe," often quite cruelly. My hunch is that her interest for Freud lay in the fact that in some ways it countered his perspective on women, while retaining the element most pleasing to men: sexual appeal. *She* was active, assertive, aggressive, sexual but nonmaternal, and sometimes sadistic.

Thinking about all this led me recently to a strange discovery of the obvious: While Freud[6] dilated on his views of women so that they formed a metapsychology of women, one looks in vain for a psychology of men. Where, indeed, is it, other than in his consideration of castration anxiety? In comparing the negatives he set forth as characterizing women, they lead to some strange inferences about men. To state his views of women in brief essence: They are passive, masochistic, more prone to jealousy, have weaker superegos than men and a weaker sense of justice; and one of their major problems is penis-envy, its hallmark being feminine aggression. Freud's penis-envy concept was based quite literally on the girl's observations that it was

From Shainess, N.: Let's bury old fictions, Psychiatric Opinion 9(3), June 1972.

missing and ignored the *symbolic* meaning which contained the *genuine* etiologic roots.[17] His final and most significant point was that a woman gains completion only through obtaining a penis-equivalent—a child, and particularly, a male child.

But although not included in theory and formulated only in case histories, his misinterpretation of feminine erotic fantasies, longings and responses, as in the case of Dora, was profound.[13] I have always doubted his correctness in insisting that the seductions reported by women patients were *fantasies*. Review of patients in my practice leads me to state an agonizing truth: The number of *actual* incestuous seductive activities and sometimes rapes by fathers is much *greater* then would generally be believed. Further, in general these were *not* responses to the little girl's provocation (often she is frozen with fear or meets with denial by her mother if she reports it) but expressive of *problems in the father*—and not only in lower class groups. But again, this view of the "seductive girl-child" is syntonic with male desires. Perhaps that is why this mistaken notion has been perpetuated for so long—accompanied by a similar false belief: that women secretly *enjoy* rape! I would not deny that this, like any generalization, may have its rare exception.

Let us turn around Freud's view of feminine psychology to look at men. It implies by comparison that men are active. If they are not masochistic, are they then sadistic? Are men not given to jealousy—which sex is better known for crimes (murders) of passion? Have their "stronger" superegos and sense of justice led them to be fair to the underprivileged, to eliminate that cruel, aggressive insanity—war? If aggression is a *feminine* problem, are aggressive traits desirable in men? And is there no "womb-envy"? Although Freudian theories of women have been under attack, starting—gently—with Freud's own great disciple Ernest Jones,[8] some last words are yet to be said—perhaps these are the very ones!

That historical and theological heritage served as background to Freud's theory derived from the social slant of patriarchal, late-Victorian Vienna contributes to an understanding of his biased views.[12] But, in addition, there are many indications in his personal life of great ambivalences in his relationship to women—his long engagement to Martha Bernays, his role of father-advisor to her in his letters, his friendships with other women including Martha's cousin, while delaying (always rationalized, of course) his marriage, his friendships with Fliess and others.

But Freud himself reveals, through a few remnants, the roots of discrimination within the family and the basis for penis-envy formation in his own family. In the oft-repeated "family myth" of his pregnant mother's encounter with a gypsy seeress who predicted she would bear a *son* who would be a special person, a hero, one sees the compensatory status of the Jewish woman in a patriarchy.[7] Even more revealing is the story, again recounted by Freud himself, of his abhorrence of music, of his sister's piano-playing, of his complaint to his mother and of her ordering the piano out of the house forthwith. This kind of transaction is likely to be repeated by parents over and over again. If his sister did not develop penis-envy because of this discriminatory treatment (I know nothing further about her), it was a minor miracle. As I have indicated elsewhere,[15] a constructive way to have dealt with such a situation would have been for his mother to ask his sister, where possible, to practice when little Sigi was not around; and she would have told the little "hero" that his sister would only play when absolutely necessary, should he be at home; but if she *had* to—well, it behooved Sigi to stuff cotton in his ears! So much for history—and for modes of treating girls as equals.

But seriously enough, here are two significant roots of Freud's bias and penis-envy concept—they are, of course, *social* roots, not instinctual or biological. They helped him overlook another important concept, especially in his time, because it was "socially syntonic": penis-worship—the fusion identification with the male which was part of the frequently observed brother-worship or son-worship. This may be a substrate to the classical woman psychoanalyst's denial of any problem here, observable as a practical maneuver: "If you can't fight 'em, join 'em." As a final point with regard to penis-worship, the key to its meaning is in the compulsive repetition which continues after marriage, the woman often using worship of her brother or son in castrating fashion against her husband, rather than transferring it to him. This reflects the anger at second-class family position which the worship denies.

But as many have pointed out, the concepts about women Freud inferred from his *accurate observations* have two other roots. One was woman's physical weakness and her reproductive function which gave the man greater *power*—a power he often did not hesitate to use (and what does this say about aggression?). And power, once gained, is rarely, if ever, voluntarily surrendered. Secondly, there is an economic basis to keeping women employed, without real pay, doing the routine chores of the home. Women have tended to accept this situation, finding some compensations within their allotted place.

Erik Erikson[4] has recognized this and has noted that women have difficulty in saying what they feel because of the threat to any satisfactions of their accustomed place; and of the "girl talk" they are used to. This was perceived by Aristophanes[1] in "Lysistrata," where she, summoning women to a serious effort to end the war by withholding their sexual favors, finds their silly "woman talk" ("Darling, you look so ravishing today") a distraction from seriousness of purpose.

Psychiatric and medical literature is full of references to the "proper position" of women, and in some instances psychopathology reflects this. Alexandra Symonds[16] had made an excellent statement on this in a paper whose very title expresses much, "Phobias After Marriage: Woman's Declaration of Dependence." Certainly one of the problems in marriage is that all of the *hidden* premises eventually are tested and become clear. But because old gender stereotypes still dominate in our society, men's expectations and demands are often much greater than are revealed during the dating period, so that as women have a clearer sense of identity and develop a health-ward, self-assertive (not aggressive) trend, they find it difficult to conform to these unvoiced male expectations.

As Jean Baker Miller[9] has pointed out, women have existed as "unnecessary" people, on the periphery of economic and political power; she adds that "it seems that the dominant group must constantly try to suppress, contain, deflect and rob people of their legitimate right to be angry (in such circumstances)." It is my thesis—and that of others, too—that the Freudian "mythic view" or fiction about women has helped to keep them in their place.

In relation to considerations of power, a recent "NET Playhouse" series on Elizabeth R brilliantly portrayed the British "virgin queen" as she probably *really* was: perceptive, skillful, clever, enjoying her powers in the affairs of state and refusing to marry because of the full awareness that once married, her power would be lost. Oh, how the men about her, including the lords she created, plotted and gossiped in the traditionally "feminine" style of the usually reversed situation. Oh, how petty they were, and how weak their superegos. Oh, how jealous of each other, as rivals for her "affections." They even began to use the "editorial we" some women are known for when their husbands gain a certain position and they attempt to enhance themselves through *his* status. And, oh, how they resented her making clear that it was *her* orders which were to be followed, not *theirs*—and, oh, how they played the perfect passive lady, by smiles and acquiescence! It was memorable, and highly enlightening. This is not to say that insistence on or strivings for power are admirable or to be desired. It is simply to note that women can be *effective* in power and that men can take on the allegedly feminine characteristics which come with *structured subservience*. That men and women share all traits and potentials was the point of Virginia Woolf's novel *Orlando*[18]—the hero undergoing a spontaneous sex change to heroine, helping Woolf demonstrate her point.[13] Enough of this. Let me turn to the positive.

What *is* feminine psychology? Is is that area which deals with the psychic components of gender and of the reproductive experience. This includes what I have called the nodal points of feminine development and experience: the development of breasts (ignored by Freud!), the menarche, defloration, sexual experience, pregnancy, mothering and finally the menopause.[11,14] It also includes abortion. The significance of abortion as a woman's right cannot be overestimated, since it permits ultimate *mastery*[12] and control over her reproductive life and to her life directions generally. Passive victims cannot mature to become healthily assertive people—the kind of people described by Freud as genital characters—the end of the libidinal road (if you accept libido theory) but seemingly largely reserved for men only.

Mastery of each step along the way is part of the developing positive acceptance of gender and contributes to the feeling of *joie de vivre*—the dominant mood of a healthy emotional life, and of pleasure and pride in gender. How affronting to a woman to suggest that "puberty is the girl's last stand against femininity."[2,3] I assert that it is her *first* stand as a biologically mature woman and contains the first promise of fulfillment of *one*, but only one, aspect of her life—motherhood.

Are there constitutional differences between men and women? Of course! Are there biological differences? Of course! There are also differences in the psychic representations of their sexual, endocrine and reproductive biology. And there are temperamental differences relating to gender as well. It may surprise many to hear that I believe women are *more placid* than men (this runs counter to the myth of women as hysterical emotional creatures, again the effect of societal forces). Comparison with lower animal forms is revealing: It is the bull or stallion which is skittish, while the mare or cow is the *more placid*. It would be a digression to elaborate—but there is a cyclical reason for this in the *male!*

Is there a particular quality one could consider "masculine" or "feminine?" I would say so, although there are so many variables that this quality rarely shows through. I would call the feminine aspect "receptivity," but it is not a passive quality. It represents the taking in of the penis in sexual intercourse, the "taking in" and envelopment of the fertilized egg, the "surrounding of the child" with supportive, nurturant care. It can represent a quality of "openness" in intellectual work and of "wifeliness" as well.

The equivalent in the man would be the quality of being "penetrating," whether it is to penetrate the woman in sexual intercourse, to be more daring (because of the added physical strength as well) in penetrating into the world and now outer space or in work. But both these feminine and masculine components appear in both sexes. And most important of all: *Intellectual strength* is equally divided. To develop properly requires what any ability or mastery does—proper and sufficient practice.

Freudian feminine psychology has tended to keep women within a special kind of ghetto. It has interfered with the development of all feminine potentials. It has helped to perpetuate gender-role stereotypes. And it has, in some measure, prevented women from "finding themselves" sexually, because the passive view of women has applied to the erotic as well. I say this even as I believe that Freud was right about feminine erotic experience in what has become the current "great orgasm debate." Freud described the clitoris as the pine chip which ignites the hardwood fire. In this aspect, at least, he really understood women!

As a final point, returning to Freud's concept of the "genital character"—how does this apply to women? What is a "genital woman"—or, translated, a "liberated woman"? In its implication of maturity, the term suggests a woman who has been free to develop all of her inherent capacities to the fullest extent possible, and this includes the sexual and the maternal. But it implies much more. In the past, trapped within their allotted gender roles, women lived yearning for male approval, always awaiting male judgment. That is, woman had an externalized superego—the man's, not her own. Liberated woman asserts herself as she *must*, consulting *herself*, insisting on her own autonomy—the foundation of true equality.

Thus, a woman can be liberated from within, without any social goals having been achieved—which is not to minimize their importance. Yet while free from outwardly conforming behavior patterns resulting from the imposed expectations of society, she must be equally free of the defenses imposed by a dominating anxiety, as well as from the rebelliousness, anger or vindictiveness, from the self-contempt and self-hatred or pervasive competetiveness which may be generated early in life within the family, when the girl is less valued than the boy. Free to dream; free to develop; free of compulsion; free of irrationality (to the extent possible); free to love: This is liberated woman.

George Bernard Shaw is reputed to have said that when an Englishman tells an Englishwoman she ought to be satisfied with her lot because Oriental women are more restricted, it is like telling the caged parrot he is free because the canary's cage is smaller.

It is time now for all cages to go, even if they are larger than ever before. And as some are discovering, freedom for women means greater freedom for men.

REFERENCES

1. Aristophanes: Lysistrata, New York, 1964, Mentor.
2. Benedek, T.F.: Psychosexual functions in women, New York, 1952, Ronald Press.
3. Deutsch, H.: Psychology of women, New York, vol. 1, 1944, Grune & Stratton, Inc.
4. Erikson, E.: Inner and outer space: reflections on womanhood. In Lifton, R.J., editor: The woman in America, Boston, 1965, Beacon Press.
5. Freud, S.: The interpretation of dreams. In The basic writings of Sigmund Freud, New York, 1938, Random House, Inc.
6. Freud, S.: Female sexuality. In Collected papers, vol. 5, London, 1950, The Hogarth Press, Ltd.
7. Freud, S.: Psychological consequences of anatomical distinctions between the sexes. In Collected papers, vol. 5, London, 1950, The Hogarth Press, Inc.
8. Jones, E.: Early development of female sexuality. In Papers on psychoanalysis, London, 1938, Bailliere Tindall, Ltd.
9. Miller, J.B.: New political directions for women, White Plains, N.Y., 1971, International Arts and Sciences Press.
10. Roiphe, A.: What women psychoanalysts say about women's liberation, New York Times Magazine, February 13, 1972.
11. Shainess, N.: Feminine identity and mothering. In Masserman, J., editor: Science and Psychoanalysis, vol. 7, New York, 1964, Grune & Stratton, Inc.
12. Shainess, N.: Psychological problems associated with motherhood. In Arieti, S., editor: American handbook of psychiatry, vol. 3, New York, 1966, Basic Books, Inc.
13. Shainess, N.: Images of woman: past and present, overt and obscured, American Journal Psychotherapy 23(1):77, 1969.
14. Shainess, N.: Toward a new feminine psychology, Current Medical Dialog. (In press.)
15. Shainess, N.: Women's liberation—and liberated woman. In Arieti, S., editor: World biennial of psychiatry and psychotherapy, vol. 2. (In press.)
16. Symonds, A.: Phobias after marriage: women's declaration of dependence, American Journal of Psychoanalysis 31(2):144, 1971.
17. Thompson, C.: Penis envy in women, Psychiatry 6(2):123, 1943.
18. Woolf, V.: Orlando, New York, 1960, The New American Library, Inc.

NANCY HENLEY and JO FREEMAN

Chapter 5

The sexual politics of interpersonal behavior

Social interaction is the battlefield where the daily war between the sexes is fought. It is here that women are constantly reminded where their "place" is and that they are put back in their place, should they venture out. Thus, social interaction serves as the most common means of social control employed against women. By being continually reminded of their inferior status in their interactions with others, and continually compelled to acknowledge that status in their own patterns of behavior, women learn to internalize society's definition of them as inferior so thoroughly that they are often unaware of what their status is. Inferiority becomes habitual, and the inferior place assumes the familiarity—and even desirability—of home.

Different sorts of cues in social interaction aid this enforcement of one's social definition, particularly the verbal message, the nonverbal message transmitted within a social relationship, and the nonverbal message transmitted by the environment. Our educational system emphasizes the verbal message and teaches us next to nothing about how we interpret and react to the nonverbal ones. Just how important nonverbal messages are, however, is shown by the finding of Argyle and others[2] that nonverbal cues have over four times the impact of verbal ones when both verbal and nonverbal cues are used. Even more important for women, Argyle found that female subjects were more responsive to nonverbal cues (compared with verbal ones) than male subjects. If women are to understand how the subtle forces of social control work in their lives, they must learn as much as possible about how nonverbal cues affect people, and particularly about how they perpetuate the power and superior status enjoyed by men.

Even if a woman encounters no one else directly in her day, visual status reminders are a ubiquitous part of her environment. As she moves through the day, she absorbs many variations of the same status theme, whether or not she is aware of

From Henley, N., and Freeman, J.: In Freemen, J., editor: Women: a feminist perspective, Palo Alto, Calif., 1979, Mayfield Publishing Co.

it: male bosses dictate while female secretaries bend over their steno pads; male doctors operate while female nurses assist; restaurants are populated with waitresses serving men; magazine and billboard ads remind the women that home maintenance and child care are her foremost responsibilities and that being a sex object for male voyeurs is her greatest asset. If she is married, her mail reminds her that she is a mere "Mrs." appended to her husband's name. When she is introduced to others or fills out a form, the first thing she must do is divulge her marital status acknowledging the social rule that the most important information anyone can know about her is her legal relationship to a man.

These environmental cues set the stage on which the power relationships of the sexes are acted out, and the assigned status of each sex is reinforced. Though studies have been made of the several means by which status inequalities are communicated in interpersonal behavior, they do not usually deal with power relationships between men and women. Goffman has pointed to many characteristics associated with status:

> Between status equals we may expect to find interaction guided by symmetrical familiarity. Between superordinate and subordinate we may expect to find asymmetrical relations, the superordinate having the right to exercise certain familiarities which the subordinate is not allowed to reciprocate. Thus, in the research hospital, doctors tended to call nurses by their first names, while nurses responded with "polite" or "formal" address. Similarly, in American business organizations the boss may thoughtfully ask the elevator man how his children are, but this entrance into another's life may be blocked to the elevator man, who can appreciate the concern but not return it. Perhaps the clearest form of this is found in the psychiatrist-patient relation, where the psychiatrist has a right to touch on aspects of the patient's life that the patient might not even allow himself to touch upon, while of course this privilege is not reciprocated.
>
> Rules of demeanor, like the rules of deference, can be symmetrical or asymmetrical. Between social equals, symmetrical rules of demeanor seem often to be prescribed. Between unequals many variations can be found. For example, at staff meetings on the psychiatric units of the hospital, medical doctors had the privilege of swearing, changing the topic of conversation, and sitting in undignified positions; attendants, on the other hand, had the right to attend staff meetings and to ask questions during them . . . but were implicitly expected to conduct themselves with greater circumspection than was required of doctors. . . . Similarly, doctors had the right to saunter into the nurses' station, lounge on the station's dispensing counter, and engage in joking with the nurses; other ranks participated in this informal interaction with doctors, but only after doctors had initiated it.[12]

A status variable widely studied by Brown and others[5-7] is the use of terms of address. In languages that have both familiar and polite forms of the second person singular ("you"), asymmetrical use of the two forms invariably indicates a status difference, and it always follows the same pattern. The person using the familiar form is always the superior of the person using the polite form. In English, the only major European language not to have dual forms of address, status differences are similarly indicated by the right of first-naming; the status superior can first-name the inferior in situations where the inferior must use the superior's title and last name. An inferior who breaks this rule by inappropriately using a superior's first name is considered insolent.[5]

According to Brown, the pattern evident in the use of forms of address applies to a very wide range of interpersonal behavior and invariably has two other components: (1) whatever form is used by a superior in situations of status inequality can be used reciprocally by intimates, and whatever form is used by an inferior is the socially prescribed usage for nonintimates; (2) initiation or increase of intimacy is the right of the superior. To use the example of naming again to illustrate the first component, friends use first names with each other, while strangers use titles and last names (though "instant" intimacy is considered proper in some cultures, such as our own, among status equals in informal settings). As an example of the second component, status superiors, such as professors, specifically tell status inferiors, such as students, when they can use the first name, and often rebuff them if they assume such a right unilaterally.

Although Brown did not apply these patterns to status differences between the sexes, their relevance is readily seen. The social rules say that all moves to greater intimacy are a male prerogative: It is boys who are supposed to call girls for dates, men who are supposed to propose marriage to women, and males who are supposed to initiate sexual activity with females. Females who make "advances" are considered improper, forward, aggressive, brassy, or otherwise "unladylike." By initiating intimacy they have stepped out of their place and usurped a status prerogative. The value of such a prerogative is that it is a form of power. Between the sexes, as in other human interaction, the one who has the right to initiate greater intimacy has more control over the relationship. Superior status brings with it not only greater prestige and greater privileges, but greater power.

These advantages are exemplified in many of the various means of communicating status. Like the doctors in Goffman's research hospital, men are allowed such privileges as swearing and sitting in undignified positions, but women are denied them. Though the male privilege of swearing is curtailed in mixed company, the body movement permitted to women is curcumscribed even in all-woman groups. It is considered unladylike for a woman to use her body too forcefully, to sprawl, to stand with her legs widely spread, to sit with her feet up, or to cross the ankle of one leg over the knee of the other. Many of these positions are ones of strength or dominance. The more "feminine" a women's clothes are, the more circumscribed the use of her body. Depending on her clothes, she may be expected to sit with her knees together, not to sit cross-legged, or not even to bend over. Though these taboos seem to have lessened in recent years, how much so is unknown, and there are recurring social pressures for a "return to femininity," while etiquette arbiters assert that women must retain feminine posture no matter what their clothing.

Prior to the 1920's women's clothes were designed to be confining and cumbersome. The dress reform movement, which disposed of corsets and long skirts, was considered by many to have more significance for female emancipation than women's suffrage.[25] Today women's clothes are designed to be revealing, but women are expected to restrict their body movements to avoid revealing too much. Furthermore, because women's clothes are contrived to reveal women's physical features, rather than being loose like men's, women must resort to purses instead of pockets to carry their belongings. These "conveniences" have become, in a time of blurred sex distinctions, one of the surest signs of sex, and thus have developed the character of stigma, a sign of woman's shame, as then they are used by comics to ridicule both women and transvestites.

Women in our society are expected to reveal not only more of their bodies than men but also more of themselves. Female socialization encourages greater expression of emotion than does that of the male. Whereas men are expected to be stolid and impassive, and not to disclose their feelings beyond certain limits, women are expected to express their *selves*. Such self-expression can disclose a lot of oneself, and, as Jourard and Lasakow[18] found, females are more self-disclosing to others than males are. This puts them at an immediate disadvantage.

The inverse relationship between disclosure and power has been reported by other studies in addition to Goffman's earlier cited investigation into a research hospital. Slobin and others[28] stated that individuals in a business organization are "more self-disclosing to their immediate superior than to their immediate subordinates." Self-disclosure is a means of enhancing another's power. When one has greater access to information about another person, one has a resource the other person does not have. Thus not only does power give status, but status gives power. And those possessing neither must contribute to the power and status of others continuously.

Another factor adding to women's vulnerability is that they are socialized to *care* more than men—especially about personal relationships. This puts them at a disadvantage, as Ross[26] articulated in what he called the "Law of Personal Exploitation": "In any sentimental relation the one who cares less can exploit the one who cares more." The same idea was put more broadly by Waller and Hill[31] as the "Principle of Least Interest": "That person is able to dictate the conditions of association whose interest in the continuation of the affair is least." In other words, women's caring, like their openness, gives them less power in a relationship.

One way of indicating acceptance of one's place and deference to those of superior status is by following the rules of "personal space." Sommer[29] has observed that dominant animals and human beings have a larger envelope of inviolability surrounding them—i.e., are approached less closely—than those of a lower status. Willis[32] made a study of the initial speaking distance set by an approaching person as a function of the speakers' relationship. His finding that women were approached more closely than men—i.e., their personal space was smaller or more likely to be breached—is consistent with their lower status.

Touching is one of the closer invasions of one's personal space, and in our low-contact culture it implies privileged access to another person. People who accidentally touch other people generally take great pains to apologize; people forced into close proximity, as in a crowded elevator, often go to extreme lengths to avoid touching. Even the figurative meanings of the word convey a notion of access to privileged areas—e.g., to one's emotions (one is "touched" by a sad story), or to one's purse (one is "touched" for ten dollars). In addition, the act of touching can be a subtle physical threat.

Remembering the patterns that Brown found in terms of address, consider the interactions between pairs of persons of different status, and picture who would be more likely to touch the other (put an arm around the shoulder or a hand on the back, tap the chest, hold the arm, or the like): teacher and student; master and servant; policeman and accused; doctor and patient; minister and parishioner; adviser and advisee; foreman and worker; businessman and secretary. As with first-naming, it is considered presumptuous for a person of low status to initiate touch with a person of higher status.

There has been little investigation of touching by social scientists, but the few studies made so far indicate that females are touched more than males are. Goldberg and Lewis[13] and Lewis[22] report that from six months on, girl babies are touched more than boy babies. The data reported by Jourard[17] and Jourard and Rubin[19] show that sons and fathers tend to refrain from touching each other and that "when it comes to physical contact within the family, it is the daughters who are the favored ones."[17] An examination of the number of different regions in which subjects were touched showed that mothers and fathers touch their daughters in more regions than they do their sons; that daughters touch their fathers in more regions than sons do; and that males touch their opposite-sex best friends in more regions than females do. Overall, women's mean total "being-touched" score was higher than men's.

Jourard and Rubin take the view that "touching is equated with sexual interest, either consciously, or at a less-conscious level,"[19] but it would seem that there is a sex difference in the interpretation of touch. Lewis reflects this when he writes, "In general, for men in our culture, proximity (touching) is restricted to the opposite sex and its function is primarily sexual in nature."[22] Waitresses, secretaries, and women students are quite used to being touched by their male superordinates, but they are expected not to "misinterpret" such gestures. However, women who touch men are often interpreted as conveying sexual intent, as they have often found out when their intentions were quite otherwise. Such different interpretations are consistent with the status patterns found earlier. If touching indicates either power or intimacy, and women are deemed by men to be status inferiors, touching by women will be perceived as a gesture of intimacy, since it would be inconceivable for them to be exercising power.

A study by Henley[14] puts forward this hypothesis. Observations of incidents of touch in public urban places were made by a white male research assistant, naive to the uses of his data. Age, sex, and approximate socioeconomic status were recorded, and the results indicated that higher-status persons do touch lower-status persons significantly more. In particular, men touched women more, even when all other variables were held constant. When the settings of the observations were differentially examined, the pattern showed up primarily in the outdoor setting, with indoor interaction being more evenly spread over sex combinations. Henley[15] has also reported observations of greater touching by higher status persons (including males) in the popular culture media; and a questionnaire study in which both females and males indicated greater expectancies of being touched by higher status persons, and of touching lower status and female ones, than vice versa.

The other nonverbal cues by which status is indicated have likewise not been adequately researched—for humans. But O'Connor[24] argues that many of the gestures of dominance and submission that have been noted in the primates are equally present in humans. They are used to maintain and reinforce the status hierarchy by reassuring those of higher status that those of lower status accept their place in the human pecking order.

The most studied nonverbal communication among humans is probably eye contact, and here too one finds a sex difference. It has repeatedly been found that women look more at another in a dyad than men do.[10,11,27] Exline and others[10] suggest that "willingness to engage in mutual visual interaction is more characteristic of those who are oriented towards inclusive and affectionate interpersonal relations," but Rubin[27] concludes that while "gazing may serve as a vehicle of emotional expression for women, [it] in addition may allow women to obtain cues from their male partners concerning the appropriateness of their behavior." This interpretation is supported by Efran and Broughton's data[8] showing that even male subjects "maintain more eye contact with individuals toward whom they have developed higher expectancies for social approval."

Another possible reason why women gaze more at men is that men talk more,[1] and there is a tendency for the listener to look more at the speaker than vice versa.[10]

It is especially illuminating to look at the power relationships established and maintained by the manipulation of eye contact. The mutual glance can be seen as a sign of union, but when intensified into a stare it may become a way of doing battle.[11] Research reported by Ellsworth and others[9] supports the notion that the stare can be interpreted as an aggressive gesture. These authors write, "Staring at humans can elicit the same sort of responses that are common in primates; that is, staring can act like a primate threat display."

Though women engage in mutual visual interaction in its intimate form to a high degree, they may back down when looking becomes a gesture of dominance. O'Connor[24] points out, "The direct stare or glare is a common human gesture of dominance. Women use the gesture as well as men, but often in modified form. While looking directly at a man, a woman usually has her head slightly tilted, implying the beginning of a presenting gesture or enough submission to render the stare ambivalent if not actually submissive."

The idea that the averted glance is a gesture of submission is supported by the

research of Hutt and Ounsted[16] into the characteristic gaze aversion of autistic children. They remark that "these children were never attacked [by peers] despite the
fact that to a naive observer they appeared to be easy targets; this indicated that their
gaze aversion had some signalling function similar to 'facing away' in the kittiwake or
'head-flagging' in the herring gull—behavior patterns which Tinbergen has termed
'appeasement postures'. In other words, gaze aversion inhibited any aggressive or
threat behavior on the part of other conspecifics."

Gestures of dominance and submission can be verbal as well as nonverbal. In
fact, the sheer use of verbalization is a form of dominance because it can quite
literally render someone speechless by preventing one from "getting a word in edge-
wise." As noted earlier, contrary to popular myth, men do talk more than women,
both in single-sex and in mixed-sex groups. Within a group a major means of asserting
dominance is to interrupt. Those who want to dominate others interrupt more; those
speaking will not permit themselves to be interrupted by their inferiors, but they will
give way to those they consider their superiors. Zimmerman and West[33] found in a
sample of 11 natural conversations between women and men that 46 of the 48
interruptions were by males.

Other characteristics of persons in inferior status positions are the tendencies to
hesitate and apologize, often offered as submissive gestures in the face of threats or
potential threats. If staring directly, pointing, and touching can be subtle nonverbal
threats, the corresponding gestures of submission seem to be lowering the eyes from
another's gaze, falling silent (or not speaking at all) when interrupted or pointed at,
and cuddling to the touch. Many of these nonverbal gestures of submission are very
familiar. They are the traits our society assigns as desirable secondary characteristics
of the female role. Girls who have properly learned to be "feminine" have learned to
lower their eyes, remain silent, back down, and cuddle at the appropriate times.
There is even a word for this syndrome that is applied only to females: coy.

In verbal communication one finds a similar pattern of differences between the
sexes. As mentioned earlier, men have the privilege of swearing, and hence access to
a vocabulary not customarily available to women. On the surface this seems like an
innocuous limitation, until one realizes the psychological function of swearing; it is
one of the most harmless and effective ways of expressing anger. The alternatives are
to express one's feelings with physical violence or to suppress them and by so doing
turn one's anger in on oneself. The former is prohibited to both sexes (to different
degrees) but the latter is decisively encouraged in women. The result is that women
are "intropunitive"; they punish themselves for their own anger rather than somehow
dissipating it. Since anger turned inward is commonly viewed as the basis for depression, we should not be surprised that depression is considerably more common
in women than in men, and in fact is the most prevalent form of "mental illness"
among women. Obviously, the causes of female depression are complex.[4]

Swearing is only the most obvious sex difference in language. Key[20] has noted
that sex differences are to be found in phonological, semantic, and grammatical

aspects of language as well as in word use.[21,23,30] In one example, Austin[3] has commented that "in our culture little boys tend to be nasal . . . and little girls, oral," but that in the "final stages" of courtship the voices of both men and women are low and nasal. The pattern cited by Brown,[5] in which the form appropriately used by status superiors is used between status equals in intimate situations, is again visible: in the intimate situation the female adopts the vocal style of the male.

In situations where intimacy is not a possible interpretation, it is not power but abnormality that is the usual interpretation. Female voices are expected to be soft and quiet—even when men are using loud voices. Yet it is only the "lady" whose speech is refined. Women who do not fit this stereotype are often called loud—a word commonly applied derogatorily to other minority groups or out-groups.[3] One of the most popular derogatory terms for women is "shrill," which, after all, simply means loud (out of place) and high-pitched (female).

In language, as in touch and most other aspects of interpersonal behavior, status differences between the sexes mean that the same traits are differently interpreted when displayed by each sex. A man's behavior toward a woman might be interpreted as an expression of either power or intimacy, depending on the situation. When the same behavior is engaged in by a woman and directed toward a man, it is interpreted only as a gesture of intimacy—and intimacy between the sexes is always seen as sexual in nature. Because our society's values say that women should not have power over men, women's nonverbal communication is rarely interpreted as an expression of power. If the situation precludes a sexual interpretation, women's assumption of the male prerogative is dismissed as deviant (castrating, domineering, unfeminine, or the like).

Of course, if women do not wish to be classified as deviant or as perpetually sexy, then they must persist in playing the proper role by following the interpersonal behavior pattern prescribed for them. Followed repeatedly, these patterns function as a means of control. What is merely habitual is often seen as desirable. The more men and women interact in the way they have been trained to from birth without considering the meaning of what they do, the more they become dulled to the significance of their actions. Just as outsiders observing a new society are more aware of the status differences of that society than its members are, so those who play the sexual politics of interpersonal behavior are usually not conscious of what they do. Instead they continue to wonder that feminists make such a mountain out of such a "trivial" molehill.

REFERENCES

1. Argyle, M.: The effects of visibility on interaction in a dyad, Human Relations 21:3, 1968.
2. Argyle, M., and others: The communication of inferior and superior attitudes by verbal and non-verbal signals, British Journal of Social and Clinical Psychology 9:222, 1970.
3. Austin, W.M.: Some social aspects of paralanguage, Canadian Journal of Linguistics 11: 34, 1965.
4. Bart, P.B.: Depression in middle-aged women. In Gornick, V., and Moran, B.K.: Woman in sexist society, New York, 1971, Basic Books, Inc.

5. Brown, R.: Social psychology, Glencoe, Ill., 1965, Free Press.

6. Brown, R., and Ford, M.: Address in American English, Journal of Abnormal and Social Psychology 62:375, 1961.

7. Brown, R., and Gilman A.: The pronouns of power and solidarity. In Sebeak, T.A., editor: Style in language, Cambridge, Mass., 1960, M.I.T. Press.

8. Efran, J.S., and Broughton, A.: Effect of expectancies for social approval on visual behavior, Journal of personality and Social Psychology 4:103, 1966.

9. Ellsworth, P.C., and others: The stare as a stimulus to flight in human subjects: a series of field experiments, Journal of Personality and Social Psychology 21:310, 1972.

10. Exline, R., and others: Visual behavior in a dyad as affected by interview control and sex of respondent, Journal of Personality and Social Psychology 16:265, 1970.

11. Exline, R.: Explorations in the process of person perception: visual interaction in relation to competition, sex, and need for affiliation, Journal of Personality 31:1, 1963.

12. Goffman: The nature of deference and demeanor, American Anthropologist 58:473, 1956.

13. Goldberg, S., and Lewis, M.: Play behavior in the year-old infant: early sex differences, Child Development 40:21, 1969.

14. Henley, N.: The politics of touch. In Brown, P., editor: Radical psychology, New York, 1973, Harper & Row, Publishers, Inc.

15. Henley, N.: Body politics: sex, power and nonverbal communication, Englewood Cliffs, N.J., 1977, Prentice-Hall, Inc.

16. Hutt, C., and Ounsted, C.: The biological significance of gaze aversion with particular reference to the syndrome of infantile autism, Behavioral Science 11:154, 1966.

17. Jourard, S.M.: An exploratory study of body accessibility, British Journal of Social and Clinical Psychology 5:221, 1966.

18. Jourard, S.M., and Lasakow, P.: Some factors in self-disclosure, Journal Abnormal and Social Psychology 56:91, 1958.

19. Jourard, S.M., and Rubin, J.E.: Self-disclosure and touching: a study of two modes of interpersonal encounter and their interrelation, Journal of Humanistic Psychology 8:39, 1968.

20. Key, M.R.: Male/female language, Metuchen, J.J., 1975, Scarecrow Press, Inc.

21. Lakoff, R.: Language and woman's place, New York, 1975, Harper & Row, Publishers, Inc.

22. Lewis, M.: Parents and children: sex-role development, School Review 80:229, 1972.

23. Miller C., and Swift, K.: Words and women, New York, 1976, Doubleday & Co., Inc.

24. O'Connor, L.: Male dominance: the nitty gritty of oppression, It Ain't Me Babe 1:9, 1970.

25. O'Neill, W.L.: Everyone was brave: the rise and fall of feminism, Chicago, 1969, Quadrangle.

26. Ross, E.A.: Principles of sociology, New York, 1921, Century.

27. Rubin, Z.: Measurement of romantic love, Journal of Personality and Social Psychology 16:265, 1970.

28. Slobin, D.I., and others: Forms of address and social relations in a business organization, Journal of Personality and Social Psychology 8:289, 1968.

29. Sommer, R.: Personal space, Englewood Cliffs, N.J., 1969, Prentice-Hall, Inc.

30. Thorne, B., and Henley, N.: Language and sex: difference and dominance Rowley, Mass., 1975, Newbury House Publishers, Inc.

31. Waller, W.W., and Hill, R.: The family: a dynamic interpretation New York, 1951, Dryden Press.

32. Willis, F.N., Jr.: Initial speaking distance as a function of the speaker's relationship, Psychonomic Science 5:221, 1966.

33. Zimmerman, D., and West, C.: Sex roles, interruptions and silences in conversation. In Thorne, B., and Henley, N.: Language and sex, Rowley, Mass., 1975, Newbury House Publishers, Inc.

Photo by Gary Botkin; courtesy Blanche W. Pryor.

UNIT TWO

CAREER CHOICE AND NURSING STEREOTYPES

This section explores issues related to female career choices and the choice of nursing in particular. For all women there are certain psychological and social barriers that limit career aspirations and professional achievement. Many women seek traditionally "feminine" jobs—nursing, secretarial arts, teaching—based on their socialization that such jobs are "acceptable." The stereotypic image of nursing and the fact that nursing has been touted as the perfect stopgap to marriage are examined here in light of their attractiveness to recruits and their effects on others' expectations of nurses. Nursing as a career choice is analyzed.

Handicapped by the notion that marriage and motherhood are the socially acceptable "jobs" for women, and tracked by parents and teachers toward "women's careers," few women have considered lifetime professional commitments. Feminism is beginning to change that, asserts Hester Eisenstein, but the problems are many, including females' own conflict over what is possible for them and discrimination in the world of work. Social, professional, political, educational, and religious institutions perpetuate barriers to career success for women. Dr. Eisenstein suggests that we, as women, begin to examine traditional roles, keeping those that are humane—the good aspects—rather than discarding them all.

Nursing has historically been a female profession. Myths and stereotypes about nursing and nurturance as feminine attributes have restricted the profession to women. The effect has been cyclical—as a predominantly female profession, nursing has attracted few men. Thus the myth continues: nursing is women's work. Janet Muff describes the following process: unconscious fantasies about women become myths; myths of women are given tangible form in stereotypes—the handmaiden, the battle-ax, the whore, the idiot, and so on. Her chapter examines these stereotypes, as they appear in all forms of the media, in an effort to make them so vivid and familiar that readers will recognize them wherever and however they later appear.

Linda Hughes examines society's dictum that woman's place is in the home. She suggests that by encouraging women to enter traditionally female professions, with the added notion that such professions are merely stopgaps to marriage, a situation is created in which women do not think in terms of life-long careers. By making nursing the embodiment of "feminine" qualities, women have been seduced into thinking that nursing improves their chances of finding a husband and prepares them for childbearing. In fact, Ms. Hughes says, it is not *nursing* that is being advocated so much as marriage and motherhood.

Who, then, enters nursing, and how is the choice made? Certainly it is based on the image people have of the profession and also on the propoganda that nursing is a "natural" for women. In her chapter Marty Flanagan describes the dearth of realistic information about nursing available to potential recruits. The choice, she says, is based on faulty knowledge. The number of men in nursing has not increased appreciably regardless of our fantasies or wishes to the contrary. Minorities, too, are underrepresented. Once into the system, students in various nursing programs encounter the associate-diploma-baccalaureate dilemma. Attrition rates are high, supporting the claims that students lack prevocational guidance and that nursing schools have difficulty in selecting appropriate recruits. Often the assertive, questioning students are viewed by faculty as troublemakers rather than potentially autonomous, inquisitive nurses.

Women, then, are going elsewhere as traditionally masculine options become available, a trend that has had many positive results for women but has hampered nursing. In the final chapter of this section, Janet Muff takes issue, not with those who choose nontraditional careers but with those who denigrate women in more traditional ones. She attributes this attitude to women's lack of self-esteem, a result of their socialization that women are second-class citizens. Antiwomanism by women arises out of self-hate. Like minorities who flee and later repudiate their ghettos, women who have succeeded in nontraditional spheres often demean their own kind. They identify with dominant group (male) values and deny those of their own group. This chapter explores antinursing behaviors from feminist and other nontraditional viewpoints and also from those within nursing.

Chapter 6

On the psychosocial barriers to professions for women

Atalanta's apples, "women's work," and the struggle for social change

Atalanta [Gr. myth] A beautiful, swift-footed maiden who offered to marry any man able to defeat her in a race; Hippomenes won by dropping three golden apples, which she stopped to pick up, along the way.
Webster's New World Dictionary

"What do you want to be when you grow up?" Within this traditional question for children lie many unstated assumptions about social life. Not least of these is the belief that an individual can choose what she/he wants to be rather than either inheriting it or having it thrust upon her/him by circumstances. Another equally important assumption is that "to be" is the equivalent of "to work." The answer to the question is supposed to be: "a doctor," "a fireman" (sic), or "President of the United States." Until recently (and perhaps still), a common answer from little girls to this question was "I want to be a wife and mommy."* For little boys, "to be" represented a choice of occupation or vocation; it described the work they wanted to do in the world. For little girls, "to be" meant the existential condition and social role that seemed inevitably attached to having been born female.

In recent years, buoyed by the women's movement, little girls have grown up to be all kinds of things besides wives and mothers. They have become engineers, lawyers, doctors, and corporation managers; they have entered many areas of work previously considered virtually off-limits to women. Much media attention has been devoted to these pioneer women, the "first women pilots, steelworkers, policepersons, and the like. But the reality of the world of options for women in the 1980s is more complex than this glowing media portrait indicates.

---

*Some other answers are a nurse, stewardess, or kindergarten teacher. On the expression of childhood ambitions in women, see Laws.[33]

In this chapter I review some of the remaining barriers to women in the professions and in so doing make some suggestions about how we define the problem of psychosocial barriers to women. Under the influence of feminist ideas, society has begun to move slowly away from the conventional wisdom that little boys do whereas little girls are. We have begun to develop a notion of shared human potential in which all people, regardless of their gender, have access to the worlds of love, parenting, and work. But to realize this vision of the future, I argue, society will need to make more than psychological or conceptual changes. The psychological and the social are profoundly connected to the material and economic base on which they rest and which they reflect. Recent attempts to redefine "women's work" have not produced an instant social transformation. To effect profound and lasting change will require a long and complex campaign, one that may take more than one lifetime to win.

After reviewing the current situation of women, I first, discuss what I call here "Atalanta's apples," that is, issues arising out of the conflict between "femininity" and "achievement." Second, I explore some of the implications of the ideology of femininity for the definition, past and present, of "women's work." And third, I return to an examination of femininity and the female sex role, calling for a deconstruction of the elements that have made it up so as to free women's energies for the long hard struggle ahead.

CHANGES AND CONTINUITIES: THE FEMINIST REVOLUTION VERSUS THE SEX-SEGREGATED LABOR FORCE

In recent years women have been entering the paid labor force in greater numbers and are holding a greater variety of jobs than ever before in the history of Western industrialized societies. At the same time, in a not unrelated phenomenon, for the past 15 years or so there has been a major revival of feminism, in what has been called the second wave of the women's movement.* Both of these social changes have prompted a profound reexamination of the role of women in society and the attitudes and feelings that people of both sexes bring to the category "female." In the light of the thinking, writing, and organizing that have characterized this period, old ideas about "that's just how women are" are no longer tenable.

What exactly has been happening? On the one hand, there has been a highly visible entry of women, at least in small numbers, into jobs that until recently were thought of as exclusively "men's jobs," such as blue-collar work in construction or steel mills and professional positions in management, law, medicine, and

---

*The first wave was the international movement of the nineteenth century that, in the United States, culminated in the winning of the vote for women in 1920.[1,27,36]

politics.* This development has prompted a reevaluation of what has been meant by a man's job and an examination of the origins of such categorization. On the other hand, recent research indicates that the major influx of women into the labor force, particularly in the newest category—married women with young children—has largely been into the so-called female job market, that is, into the areas of work largely dominated by women such as librarianship, elementary school teaching, clerical work, and nursing.[9,14] This persistence of what has been termed a sex-segregated labor force has given rise to speculation about the forces that have overall kept the change in the numbers of women working for pay from becoming a significant change in the distribution of women in the labor force.[10]

Ordinarily the discussion of who gets what jobs has been a matter for economists, who study supply and demand and try to explain the flow of different kinds of people in and out of the labor market, along with the levels of wages, unemployment, and related issues. But the recent changes in the working patterns of women have had ramifications beyond the concerns of economists, since they reflect changes in patterns of individual and family life. The question of what kinds of work women do for pay outside of the home raises in most people's minds the question of what women are or ought to be. As recent debates over the issues of abortion, child care, and the Equal Rights Amendment have demonstrated, not everyone agrees that a wife and mommy can also "be" an engineer.

As Elizabeth Janeway[29] and others have pointed out, our society has had a longstanding mythology about women, encapsulated in the sayings, "It's a man's world" and "Woman's place is in the home." In our conventional thinking about what women and men are or ought to be, we have associated men with the public world of work and political life whereas we have associated women with the private or domestic world of home and family. This is a mythology, a set of beliefs people cling to despite the many empirical facts that can be seen to contradict them. People hold onto a mythology because they want it to be true rather than because it is true. People are most in need of myths, Janeway argues, when their reality is changing too fast for them to grasp it and when they feel they need something to give them stability in a world that is becoming unfamiliar and unreliable.†

Recent statistics indicate that the idealized American family referred to in the

---

*Although the title of this chapter refers to "professions" for women, I have broadened the context here to the question of women's roles in the labor force generally, since I believe that this is a useful frame of reference for this discussion.

†Oakley[42] defines mythology less charitably as a system for the prevention of social change: "As anthropologists have discovered, . . . the primary function of myth is to validate a social order. . . . Myth enshrines conservative social values, raising tradition on a pedestal. . . . Because myth anchors the present in the past it is a sociological charter for a future society which is an exact replica of the present one."

sayings about "woman's place"—with the woman firmly anchored in the home, taking care of the children—comprises only approximately 16% of all households.* The model, then, in which only the father works and is the "breadwinner" while the mother acts her role as *"homemaker" without other obligations,* is an accurate picture of a minority—less than a fifth—of all households. Women are not staying in their "place," in most cases, because they cannot afford to. They are heads of households, or they work to supplement a husband's inadequate income, or they are divorced, usually with children, with inadequate or absent payments for alimony and/or child support. The category of woman who work for a living includes all these kinds of women, as well as women who work in professional or executive jobs, for the same kinds of reasons that men holding these types of job do: out of interest or ambition, for prestige, or in general, for job satisfaction.[1,33]

Encouraged by the feminist movement of the 1960s and 1970s, women have sought increasingly to break down the barriers of access to the most prestigious and rewarding jobs in the United States. Female admissions to law school, medical school, business school, and the graduate schools of arts and sciences have all risen dramatically. The number of women in these fields and in executive and management positions has gone up. Along with these changes has come much public discussion of what women can and cannot do well. Perhaps the most significant discussions, from a cultural point of view, have been those of women in sports and in the military, as measures of women's strength and capacity for physical combat and leadership—areas of male privilege and power par excellence.† But the discussion of these social changes has often gotten bogged down in the "anything you can do, I can do better" variety. This is, the attention has been focused on the "first woman" fireperson or West Point graduate as a challenge to stereotypical notions of what women are capable of physically and emotionally. Some of this has had a salutary effect, in that the achievements of the "pioneers" have raised public consciousness about *antiquated attitudes toward women.* In some cases, ideas about women have had to change, because women are doing things that they have not done before and proving that they can do them well.‡ But underneath the surface of these dramatic changes—still the province, for the time being, of a few exceptional women—lie the deep and long-standing effects of the socialization of women (and men), which are proving less easy to overcome. As women have begun to contest conventional ideas about

---

*"15.9 per cent of all households include a father as the sole wage earner, a mother as full-time home-maker, and at least one child."[51]

†In response to the achievements of women such as Billy Jean King in tennis, for example, and to the opening of the nation's military academies to women for the first time in history.

‡For example, running the marathon. I should note that in this discussion I am limiting myself to modern times. (Even in this context, some of the ballyhoo obscures achievements of earlier women in nontraditional fields.)

what they ought to do and to be, they have encountered barriers of all kinds, not least within their own minds and the minds of others.

ATALANTA AND THE GOLDEN APPLES: THE CONFLICT BETWEEN "FEMININITY" AND "ACHIEVEMENT"

Psychosocial barriers to women include barriers that are internal—that is, psychic barriers that women encounter within themselves—and those that are external—that is, barriers to women's achievement that are outside of themselves, although they may be internal to others (notably powerful men). By barriers I mean things that get in a woman's way, that inhibit her, slow her down, or stop her altogether. The image in my mind is that of the golden apples tossed to Atalanta as she sought to win the foot race against Hippomenes. What keeps a woman from getting what she wants, particularly in the area of work?*

Many writers have argued that the chief internal barrier to achievement for women is the social definition of what a woman is or ought to be. They hold that the chief obstacle to women is the fact of having been "socially constructed" as a female, in Freeman's[23] formulation, in a society that interprets female as inferior. Writers on sex-role socialization have argued that the dominant form this process takes for young women in our society has been (and, generally speaking, continues to be) a preparation for the role of wife and mother, whereas for young men it has taken the form of preparation for the role of active participant in the world of work and public activity. The mythology cited by Janeway of "man's world, woman's place" has been reinforced by sex-role sterotyping that has sought to turn all little girls into potential wives and mothers and all little boys into breadwinners.[6,24,43]

Analysts have traced these sex-role stereotypes to the complex of qualities first outlined by the sociologist Talcott Parsons and his colleagues in their writings on the American family. In the Parsons analysis, the division of labor between men and women in the family runs parallel to and is congruent with the social division of labor, in which men work outside of the home while women remain in the domain of the family. For their work roles men learn to be "instrumental," whereas for their family roles women learn to be "expressive." Instrumental characteristics include the ability to compete, to be aggressive, to cooperate with others on important tasks, to lead, and to wield power. Expressive characteristics

---

*I am using the image of Atalanta here, as the myth strikes me as a rather apt and succinct formulation of the traditional conflict for women between achievement (winning the race) and happiness (sexual success within marriage). In this sense the apples are golden: economically, the pull has been toward marriage. But in using this metaphor I don't mean to imply that all of the barriers to women are so seductive and appealing.

include the ability to nurture, to be affiliative, to be sensitive to the needs of others, and to be passive.*

Feminist psychologists have demonstrated that, taken as a whole, the attributes ascribed to women in this formulation (which all too accurately represent the dominant character structure expected of women) form a cluster that makes up an incomplete, sick, or even an abnormal person.† In particular, some writers have held that the group of behaviors and attitudes associated with "femininity" are in direct conflict with women's achievement. In the late 1960s Matina Horner[28] introduced a set of concepts that became and still remain controversial. In interpreting the behavior of young women with access to college education, she argued, one could find and prove the existence of a phenomenon she named "fear of success." Horner thought that young women would be inclined to sabotage their own efforts at academic excellence, out of a deep-seated conviction that this form of achievement was in direct conflict with their own concept of femininity.‡

Horner's view was that so-called bright women *deliberately, if unconsciously,* sought to fail because their idea of successful femininity, defined in part as attractiveness to men, was in direct conflict with their concept of successful achievement, defined as the academic excellence that would ensure professional success. Other psychologists have raised doubts as to the validity or at least the universality of her original experiment. But although some may be reluctant to embrace this theory of women's fear of success as a proved hypothesis (in the sense of a replicable experiment), Horner's point still has validity from a cultural point of view. It is clear from the examination of sex-role socialization for women that the social expectations of women include a component that in effect steers them away from competing as equals with men. To put this idea more succinctly: as a cultural norm, femininity—being a "real" woman, or (in Marabel Morgan's phrase) a "total" woman—has meant being submissive to men and being dependent on them both psychologically and economically. In that sense, the imperative to be feminine—to follow the "nonconscious ideology" of the female sex role (in the phrase of Sandra and Daryl Bem[6])—has acted as a very effective barrier indeed to those women seeking to reach their full potential, both in school and thereafter.§

---

*See Beechey.[4] O'Leary[43] outlines the "competency" cluster (male) as opposed to the "warmth-expressiveness" cluster (female).

†See O'Leary[43] p. 325: "the female may perceive her very personality qualities as second rate." See also Chesler,[15] Broverman and others,[13] and Millett.[41]

‡Horner's now famous experiment required female and male students to complete a story that began: "After first-term finals, Anne (or John) finds herself (himself) at the top of her medical school class." See Horner,[28] Laws,[34] Stein and Bailey,[49] O'Leary,[43] and Levine and Crumrine.[35]

§References 6, 34, 43, 49.

What needs to be examined, of course, is how much this sense of the conflict between femininity and achievement is merely an internal barrier, a psychological inhibition, and how much it has been an external one, a powerful form of social control of women by men. A women may personally feel no particular conflict between being female and achieving something in the public realm. She may not feel threatened in her sexual identity by working her very hardest, going all out for whatever goal she sets herself. She may find, nevertheless, that those surrounding her, particularly (but not exclusively) men, may indeed feel threatened by her and may try to evoke such a conflict in her by overt or covert means. Thus, for example, she may not believe that a woman cannot be a successful physicist, but she may be forced to give up her aspirations to become one if the pressure from hostile male members of the profession becomes too hard to take.*

To return to the concept of femininity (as distinct from the fact of being female): if we view femininity as an ideology (in the Bems' sense),[6] that is, as a set of values that are socially imposed on women rather than a set of characteristics growing "naturally" out of female biology, then what are the actual components of what a woman is "supposed" to be? What is striking in the analysis of sex-role expectations for women is the curious amalgam of elements that make up the ideally feminine woman. The sex-role prescription for women seems to include a number of components, not all of which are self-evidently useful for their destined purposes. What may not have been closely enough examined in recent discussions of sex-role stereotyping, I would argue, is the combination of attributes that taken as a whole serve to produce and reproduce the ideal character structure of the wife and mother. The linkage first established by Parsons and others among the qualities of passivity, dependence, nurturance, and affiliativeness has not yet really been severed, even by theorists of androgyny, who tend to put "male" and "female" characteristics together without sufficiently analyzing them. To give just one example: mothering, or parenting, requires the capacity to nurture. In her book on the reproduction of mothering, Nancy Chodorow[16] has demonstrated what a complex set of skills this is. She argues that successful parenting requires the capacity to reach back into one's own past psychologically and to relive in some sense the difficult path from symbiosis with the nurturer to independence that one traversed in one's own development.†

The skill of successful nurturing, however, is not coextensive with dependence. Indeed, one could argue that these are radically opposed qualities and that nur-

---

*See the account of Evelyn Fox Keller's experience at the Harvard Physics Department.[31] Keller became a molecular biologist instead.

†Chodorow[16] argues that this capacity is currently reproduced only in women and that the process includes psychological components that lie deeper than those outlined in the theory of sex role socialization. Her argument is too complex to be outlined here.

turing in this fundamental way is a directed and active process. It is the clustering of the qualities of femininity—nurturance, dependence, passivity, and so on—into a kind of package, implying that an individual cannot have one without another that constitutes an ideology of the "true" woman. Taken together, they form a powerful barrier to the independence and autonomous development of women.

In particular I would argue that the crucially damaging element in the sex-role stereotype for women has been subordination. Femaleness has been linked to second-class status with the willingness to be less powerful than and placed under the authority of a man. In its effects on an individual woman's self-concept, this has been a major obstacle to achievement and growth in professional work for women. Most professions require a degree of authority, a sense of powerfulness and legitimacy, in their practitioners; indeed, one could argue that this is one of the defining features of work that is professional. The sense of subordination, of being only an adjunct to someone else rather than being an important and serious person in one's own right, is not necessarily attached to a real-life situation of subordination within a marriage and/or work situation. It is something that many women psychologically carry along with them into successful careers and must spend much time and energy combatting within themselves. Ellen Burstyn, the actress, alluded to this internal conflict when she said, in describing her struggle to develop a successful acting career, that she'd had to overcome "being an assistant person!"[5]

The connection of women to concepts of being "secondary" or "trivial" is not only a part of the cultural baggage of women. It is a generally held assumption that, despite the efforts of feminists to counter it, still informs the acting and thinking of most people. Margaret Atwood,[2] the Canadian poet and novelist, has recently commented on the persistence of this cultural value, which essentially identifies maleness and masculinity with power and authority. "After 10 years of the Women's Movement," she writes,

> We like to think that some of the old stereotypes are fading, but 10 years is not a very long time in the history of the world, and I can tell you from experience that the old familiar images, the old icons, have merely gone underground, and not far at that. We still think of a powerful man as a born leader and a powerful woman as an anomaly, a potentially dangerous anomaly; there is something subversive about such women, even when they take care to be good role models. They cannot have come by their power naturally, it is felt. They must *have got it from somewhere.*[2]

The power exercised by men in positions of authority is theirs as if by right; the power exerted by women is seen as illegitimate and derived—if not from a man, then from the devil! I return in the last part of this chapter to the cluster of attributes that makes up the ideology of femininity.

WOMEN'S WORK IS NEVER DONE—BY MEN:* THE EFFECT OF
THE IDEOLOGY OF FEMININITY IN THE WORKPLACE

Up to this point I have been discussing femininity as an ideology that has limited women psychologically from seeking to achieve their full potential in the public realm and that has tended to encourage women to define themselves primarily in their domestic roles as wives and mothers. But the ideology of femininity has also been at work in the job market. Recent research has begun to uncover, or rather to recover, the history of the concept of "women's work." Although some division of tasks by sex appears to be a widespread and perhaps a universal characteristic of human societies, the specific division of labor that has been characteristic of "advanced" Western industrial society can be traced historically along with the sexual stereotypes that have helped to perpetuate this division until modern times. The concept that "woman's place is in the home" is a relatively recent creation, growing out of the history of the Industrial Revolution, when the home and the workplace were separated for the first time. Further, it appears to be class related, since from the early years of the creation of factories women (and children) made up a portion of the work force, particularly in certain industries such as textiles. The image of the woman presiding over the domestic hearth with her husband returning from the world of aggressive business transactions (or exhausting manual labor) to the haven of his "angel in the house" is relatively new, dating from the early Victorian era, and then, as now, described only a minority of relatively privileged households.†

Nevertheless, the ideal of the woman who devotes herself to home and children and whose role in the economy is limited to the consumption rather than the production of goods and services became a powerful image, one to which people in less fortunate circumstances aspired. This image in turn had a powerful impact on the kinds of jobs that were considered suitable for women who had to work outside of the home. The notion arose that only certain kinds of jobs were "women's work." Women could and did work outside of the home, in considerable numbers. But they were supposed to do work that could be seen as an extension of women's work in the home.‡ For example, jobs that involved working with children, such as teaching, could be seen as an extension of the mothering role. Similarly, a woman doing

---

*Thanks for this title to Margaret Power.[44]

†This paragraph condenses and oversimplifies a great deal of material, some of which remains controversial. For the separation of home and workplace, see Oakley[42]; on the division of labor, see Schlegel[48]; for the European case, see McBride[38]; for the American case, see Kessler-Harris[32]; for an overview of the development of a separate sphere of women's work, see Hartmann.[26]

‡There is evidence that this concept arose in part from a reaction to the horrors of the working conditions to which women and children were exposed in the early years of industrialization in England. As reformers sought to eliminate these abuses, they appealed to the idea that this kind of exploitation was a violation of the purity of women. This in turn gave rise to the creation of "protective" legislation, banning certain abuses such as inhumanly long working hours for women.[26]

"domestic work," that is, housework in someone else's home, could be seen to be doing a job that was an extension of her role as a housewife. In this sense a woman was extending the boundaries of her domestic "place" into other places—the school, the house of another family, the typing pool—where she could continue her "womanly" work for wages.

The interesting fact, however, is that this category of "women's work"—jobs deemed to be suitable for women—appears to have had a certain degree of flexibility.[45] One area now generally seen as "women's work" is clerical: secretarial positions that involve typing, filing, taking shorthand, placing phone calls, and generally carrying out the detailed work that keeps offices in business and government running. In fact, however, as Margery Davies[17] has shown, before the invention of the typewriter in the late nineteenth century these kinds of jobs were held almost entirely by men. By 1900 three quarters of these jobs were held by women. Along with the dramatic change in personnel went a change in ideology: secretarial work, which in previous times had been virtually a male-held monopoly, was, it now appeared, ideally suited for women. In other words, with shifts in the structure of work and with the introduction of new forms of technology come shifts in the job market for women as well as in what can be called the ideology of women's work.

In the cases of doctoring and nursing, this historical process of the extension or limitation of the scope of women's work and therefore of women's place can be seen most vividly. The development of nursing as a profession, which dates from the mid-nineteenth century, is intimately connected with the Victorian ideology of what "befits" a woman. As Eve Gamarnikow[25] has shown, at the time that Florence Nightingale and others were attempting to establish nursing as a legitimate area of work for women, this ideology was made explicit as a way of answering those who argued that women had neither the stamina nor the taste for the difficult and disgusting tasks of treating the war wounds of the Crimean War and the American Civil War. Nursing was therefore defended as a task for which women were eminently suited by their very nature. By the early 1900s this equation was codified in the literature on nursing.

> Nursing is distinctly woman's work. . . . Women are peculiarly fitted for the onerous task of patiently and skillfully caring for the patient in faithful obedience to the physician's orders. Ability to care for the helpless is women's distinctive nature. Nursing is mothering. Grownup folks when very sick are all babies.[25]

So successful was this effort that in the late twentieth century, "everyone knows that 'nurse' is synonymous with 'female.'"[12] The history of doctoring, on the other hand, went in the opposite direction: from the beginning of its establishment as a profession, systematic and generally successful attempts were made to exclude women from its ranks,[12,50] and the common association of "doctor" with "male" is a notorious cultural fact.

From these examples it is clear that the concept of what is appropriately "women's work" outside of the home has changed rather dramatically over time. Of course, the concept of "women's work" within the home—bearing and rearing children and doing the housework (shopping, cooking, cleaning, and other tasks)[1,33,42]— has remained pre-eminently unchanged.* The constant in all of this appears to be that the ideology or rationale of "women's work" remains the same whereas the jobs to which it applies can change around. The argument is circular: "women's work" is an extension of women's domestic role; the qualities that make women suited for motherhood and housework are the qualities needed for jobs defined as "women's work"; and jobs can be redefined as "women's work" in a given era, sometimes quite suddenly. The changes in the categories of nursing and of clerical work illustrate the flexibility of this ideology: "wherever women are needed economically it is quickly decided that they are biologically or even spiritually destined" for that place in the economy.[3]

In the past decade and a half, as women have begun to challenge the limitations on what is considered suitable work for them, the barriers to the expansion of women into "men's" work have become more visible. Some of these, to be sure, have been eliminated, in some cases by means of lawsuits against sex discrimination. For example, the convention of advertising jobs in categories of "for men" and "for women" in newspapers such as the *New York Times* has been changed. But other barriers to women in certain kinds of professions are more difficult to break down. Sometimes prejudices against women are expressed in or concealed by different kinds of behavior, not the least of which is sexual harassment on the job. As documented in some recent studies, these experiences can be interpreted as a form of sex discrimination[22,37]: like rape, they are a cultural means of telling women, "You don't belong here. If you persist in being here, we will remind you, using force if necessary, of your primary identity, which is as a sexual being, not as a worker."†

The attempts to expand the realm of women into all public areas—"A woman's place is in the House and Senate!"—have led to a clarification of the attitudes and prejudices generally held about what women are really supposed to be doing. In addition, studies of women in the labor force have begun to suggest that the ideology about "women's work" has served to keep women available as a reserve army of labor. That is, women can be moved in and out of the labor force, according to the needs of the moment, by convincing them their work is secondary, temporary, a stopgap until marriage or for "pin money" after marriage. The most notorious example of this ideological shift is the case of World War II, when women were used in

---

*Of course some people have begun experimenting with changing this. For an interesting examination of experiments in "co-mothering," see Ehrensaft.[18]

†I am referring to the kind of harassment encountered by women miners or construction workers. But of course women doing traditional "women's work" also encounter this kind of treatment.

large numbers to do the factory jobs left vacant by men in the military and were then hustled back out of the jobs when the soldiers returned, in part by means of the re-creation of what Betty Friedan[24] dubbed "the feminine mystique."[9,45] At the same time this ideology governs wage levels for women. Jobs held predominantly by women pay less well than jobs held predominantly by men. Implicitly or explicitly the concept is that women need less income than men because they will be supported by a man in any case (as we have seen in many cases this is purely imaginary). The ideology of women's work thus helps create and perpetuate a vicious cycle. Women earn less than men because they are primarily seen as housewives; because they earn less than men, they see themselves as primarily housewives, actual or potential, and therefore do not demand the same high wages as men.[1,3,43] (Many other factors are involved in this situation as well, including the attitudes of trade unions toward female members.[39])

I cite this material on "women's work" to show that in discussing the barriers to achievement by women, one has to consider psychological issues and economic issues simultaneously. As Judith Long Laws[33] has pointed out in the social psychology literature there has been an implicit criticism of women for lacking sufficient aspiration to succeed in the male-dominated world of the professions. But in interpreting the results of studies that show young women to be less clear-minded and thoughtful than young men in planning their occupational futures, Laws writes, one has to take into account the real world that one is confronted with. She reproaches social psychologists for holding to the "teleological shiboleth," which assumes that

> young women do not plan for their occupational future but rather, like the devout Navaho weaver, leave the design of their identity unfinished until knitted together by their future life partner. The faulty syllogism here is that since most women do intend to marry (true), and since marriage is the true and only, or at least major, vocation for women (questionable), their occupational intentions will be vague, undifferentiated, and indifferent.[33]

"The germ of truth here," Laws goes on to say (emphasis added),

> is that the bulk of young women do show vocational interests that are undifferentiated and perhaps (although I have seen no empirical verification of this) show less than an all-consuming passion for them. This would seem part of . . . "realism" . . .: *if your options are lackluster, and none of them has irresistible incentives associated with it, why would you be excited about your occupational future?*[33]

In research on women who have achieved professional status, psychologists have sought to identify factors that have helped to determine their success: have they had role models in their family? What elements in their education turned them toward professional achievement rather than "merely" marriage and family? But Laws takes these researchers to task for the unstated assumptions they have made about women and about the world of work more generally. Given the number of obstacles placed in women's path from the sole responsibility for child rearing and housework to psychological sanctions about "staying feminine," she argues, it is a wonder that any women ever get out of the house to a job in the first place, let alone a job with serious professional commitments![33]

Much of the early literature about achievement motivation in women dealt implicitly with a model that blamed women for their inadequacies. But I would argue, with Laws,[33] Kanter,[30] Bernard,[8] and others, that a feminist analysis must take into account the structural factors—political, economic, and social—that stand in the way of women as well as the psychological barriers that women themselves may put in their own path.* As we have seen, there is a contradiction in current circumstances between the economic forces impelling women into the labor market and the social and psychological (and political) forces still pushing them to stay home and fulfill their true vocations as wife and mother. In an extremely complex process that is not yet fully understood, the sex-segregated labor market ensures that high-paying, prestigious jobs go mostly to men, whereas low-paying, nonprestigious jobs go mostly to women. This sex segregation coincides with the division of jobs into professional or career types with regular promotions and high status, and routine, nonprofessional types that are essentially dead-end jobs. There is a variation on this pattern within some of the professions for women, such as teaching and nursing, in which the top positions in a field otherwise reserved for women go to men. And in recent years economists have begun to observe an economic and social process called "job turning":

> In this phenomenon, according to specialists, when positions traditionally occupied by men become sources of employment for large numbers of women, the positions begin to lose the salaries and authority long associated with them.[46]

Job turning is of course nothing but a new term for the well-established historical development outlined above, namely, the changes in categories of jobs into "women's work" uniquely suited for women's domestic skills and lower pay.

Rosabeth Moss Kanter's research[30] has shown the importance of job structure in the determination of behavior. In particular her work indicates that women who are

---

*For an excellent review of the history of sex differences as an area of study, which demonstrates how politicized this research has been, see Bernard.[8] She argues that sex-role research until the last decade was chiefly (if at times unconsciously) concerned with demonstrating the "natural" character of sex differences and thereby with reconciling women to their inferior social position. But she points out that in recent years feminists have been critical of the new "socialization" model, as well as of the older "biological" model, on the ground that this too tends to absolve society and particularly men from their role as active obstacles to women's advancement. They can point to socialization as a way of saying, if women don't achieve, it's their own fault: they are socialized to be noncompetitive. This means that acts of actual discrimination against women—the use of male power to keep women out of the arena of competition for "male" jobs—remains hidden. "So long as the institutional structure of our society favors men, they ask, can women, no matter how well prepared psychologically and intellectually, expect to be dealt with on the basis of their merits rather than on the basis of their sex? . . . Not more and more research on sex differences. . . . is called for by these critics but an attack on the institutional structure which embalms these differences in the form of discrimination against women. The name of the game is power" (pp. 14-15).

placed in positions of power act powerfully, despite their sex-role socialization. On the other hand, women who remain in positions in which they are expected to behave in a "feminine" way—passive, obedient, good at taking orders, poor at showing initiative—do so; but so do the men placed in equivalent positions. Kanter argues that the emphasis on sex-role socialization in childhood as a mode of analysis has obscured the importance of the impacts on women during their working lives of the conditions they experience and their reactions to these conditions. Like men, women respond very much to the expectations placed on them by their work situation.

Among the obstacles to women in the professions, then, we must include both the facts of the sex-segregated labor force—the structure of work as it is currently organized—and the lack of knowledge among women of their own situation. I would suggest that many women do not yet know the history of "women's work" and do not realize that the "nonconscious ideology of sex roles" is a social fact rather than an individual or personal set of attitudes. These psychological, economic, and social barriers have only just begun to be exposed, let alone dismantled.

DECONSTRUCTING THE FEMALE SEX ROLE: WHY CAN'T WE KEEP THE GOOD PARTS?

I return now to the consideration of the female sex role and the socialization process that constructs women as feminine. In recent years feminist theorists have moved away from an analysis showing how women have been handicapped by their socially created differences from men to a concept that some of these created differences may have an intrinsic value. Writers like Jean Baker Miller[40] have suggested that in our rush to show what is "wrong" with women we have neglected to look at the elements in the female sex role that are valuable and that ought to be retained and developed.[19] The cluster of attributes that have gone together to make up "femininity" can be separated into its component parts, and these should be examined one by one. For example, it is arguable that dependency is debilitating for women. It is important for women to develop a sense of autonomy, the strength to make decisions on their own, and to become more self-determining in their daily lives, whether at home or on the job. But in encouraging women to become more autonomous and less dependent, do we want women to acquire the kind of independence that has been taught traditionally to men, with its overlay of competitiveness and aggression toward others? In the traditional emotional division of labor between men and women, women have learned dependence and nurturance, whereas men have learned independence and the inability to nurture.[16] (Of course this is a generalization and is belied by many examples of nurturant men.) Along with the cultivation of a new autonomy for women, can we not develop the more traditional capacity for nurturance and, for a sense of "self-in-relationship" (Chodorow's expression), qualities that have been one of the riches of family life at its best as well as something in which women have been specialists for generations?[20,21(p.102),47]

I would suggest, however, that it is not enough to ask that society begin to revalue the psychological qualities developed by women rather than dismiss them and encourage women to develop only qualities hitherto fostered exclusively in men (such as competitiveness and aggression). The other element in the situation that has to be revalued is "women's work," and specifically, women's jobs. Writers on occupational sex segregation have pointed out that because women are segregated into traditionally female jobs such as nursing and elementary school teaching, they remain underpaid because "the lower status accorded women by society at large [is] carried over to *predominantly female occupations, which are generally regarded as less prestigious or important than other occupations*" (emphasis added).[9] Thus in an article in the *New York Times,* an expert declared that women will continue to be underpaid as long as they "cling" to the traditionally women's jobs instead of following their sisters into the well-paid male professions of law and medicine.*

Some women holding positions in the traditional female-intensive professions have begun to reconceptualize their jobs and to reject the ideology of femininity that has kept these jobs both underpaid and inappropriately related to an irrelevant concept of domesticity. As a 12-year veteran airline stewardess remarked, "I don't think of myself as a sex symbol or a servant. I think of myself as someone who knows how to open the door of a 747 in the dark, upside down, and under water."[36] Similarly, in the profession of nursing women have begun to reexamine the skills actually required for the profession. The competent nurse needs the ability to nurture and care for patients, to be sure, but also needs the ability to administer and to organize. As the automatic equation between "femininity" and certain kinds of work is increasingly challenged, along with these changes should come changes in the lower economic value attached to "women's work." In other words, the automatic connection between "predominantly female" and "less prestigious and important than other occupations" must be contested at all levels: salary, job classifications, and hierarchical relationships in the workplace.

• • •

The preceding discussion implies a critique not only of the division of men and women into instrumental and expressive beings but also of the economic division of labor between "male" and "female" jobs with the concomitant devaluing of the "female" category. But this critique in turn implies a rather broad and comprehensive critique of the economy as a whole. It is well beyond the scope of this chapter to spell this out in detail. I can, however, suggest some of the themes that might be pursued. At the beginning of the chapter, I evoked the common question, "What do

---

*The full passage, quoting from a study by Pearl M. Kamer, chief economist for the Long Island Regional Planning Board, concludes that "if women 'continue to cling to traditional, female-intensive professions,' the gap between their earnings and those of male college graduates will remain wide." The study by Frances Cerra[14] "finds college women still aim for traditional jobs."

you want to be when you grow up?" After examining what makes a little girl want to be "only" a wife and mother, I pointed out that sex-role conditioning or socialization is only one side of the picture. The other side concerns the question, what *can* she be? What is it realistic for a little girl to aspire to? The role of women in the labor force is a window opening into the labor force as a whole and into the structure of work in general. What are the barriers to women? They are the barriers that everyone encounters but are complicated by gender: the barriers of class, of education, of race, and of the pyramidal structure of power and rewards. The women's movement has pointed out the kinds of changes that would take away some of the obstacles to the free choice of women: greater access to child care, access to fellowships and retraining, health care including full reproductive self-determination without economic obstacles (to abortion, for example), and an end to sex discrimination and sexual harassment. But most important of all, of course, is a sufficient number of jobs for all the women and men who choose to work. The number and kind of changes necessary to bring about this situation may well go beyond the degendering of job categories.

There is no doubt, however, that important changes have already begun to take place. One cause of these changes is the new consciousness among women of the options open to them. Bennetts' quotes one student (taking Women's Studies courses in college) to illustrate this process of change:

> It was talking about my life, women's lives, the history, politics and socialization of women. . . . I never knew my heritage of being a woman. There were no role models, just silence on the lives of women. Historians have ignored women's work, women's labor, women's experiences. We've been silenced too long, and Women's Studies is ending the silence.

Ignorance of the fact that "woman's place" and "women's work" were ideologically constructed rather than real and unchangeable facts of nature has up to now stood as one of the barriers to women. Ending that ignorance will remove this barrier. But as this student concludes, it can be an upsetting experience:

> It makes me angry to realize all the things I was never taught that would have been so wonderful to know about—so I could have had my own dreams about growing up and being a famous person, the way little boys have their dreams.[1]

REFERENCES

1. Adams, C.T., and Winston, K.T.: Mothers at work: public policies in the United States, Sweden, and China, New York, 1980, Longman, Inc.
2. Atwood, M.: Witches: the strong neck of a favorite ancestor, Radliffe Quarterly 66(3):4, 1980.
3. Baxandall, R., Gordon, L., and Reverby, S., editors: America's working women; a documentary history, 1600 to the present, New York, 1976, Random House, Inc.
4. Beechey, V.: Women and production: a critical analysis of some sociological theories of women's work. In Kuhn, A., and Wolpe, A.: Feminism and materialism: women and modes of production, London, 1978, Routledge & Kegan Paul, Ltd.
5. Bell, A.: The soft core of Ellen Burstyn, Village Voice, February 3, 1975.
6. Bem, S.L., and Bem, D.J.: Training the woman to know her place: the power of a nonconscious ideology. In Garskof, M.H., editor:

Roles women play: readings toward women's liberation, Belmont, Calif., 1971, Brooks/Cole Publishing Co.

7. Bennetts, L.: Women's viewpoints gain respect in academe, New York Times, December 2, 1980.

8. Bernard, J.: Sex differences: an overview. In Kaplan, A.G., and Bean, J.P., editors: Beyond sex-role stereotyping: readings toward a psychology of androgyny, Boston, 1976, Little, Brown & Co.

9. Blau, F.D.: Women in the labor force: an overview. In Freeman, J., editor: Woman: a feminist perspective, Palo Alto, Calif., 1975, Mayfield Publishing Co.

10. Blaxall, M., and Reagan, B.B.: Women and the workplace: the implications of occupational segregation, Chicago, 1976, University of Chicago Press.

11. Brack, D.C.: Displaced—the midwife by the male physician. In Hubbard, R., and others, editors: Women look at biology looking at women: a collection of feminist critiques, Cambridge, Mass., 1979, Schenkman Publishing Co., Inc.

12. Breu, G.: The one in a suit and tie is a nurse, too, People Weekly, June 30, 1980, p. 46.

13. Broverman, I.K., and others: Sex-role stereotypes and clinical judgments of mental health, Journal of Consulting and Clinical Psychology **34:**1, 1970.

14. Cerra, F.: Study finds college women still aim for traditional jobs, New York Times, May 11, 1980.

15. Chesler, P.: Women and madness, New York, 1972, Doubleday & Co., Inc.

16. Chodorow, N.: The reproduction of mothering: psychoanalysis and the sociology of gender, Berkeley, Calif., 1978, University of California Press.

17. Davies, M.: Woman's place is at the typewriter: the feminization of the clerical labor force. In Eisenstein, Z., editor: Capitalist patriarchy and the case for socialist feminism, New York, 1979, Monthly Review Press.

18. Ehrensaft, D.: When women and men mother, Socialist Review **10**(1):37, 1980.

19. Eisenstein, H.: Introduction. In Eisenstein, H., and Jardine, A., editors: The future of difference, Boston, 1980, Barnard College Women's Center and G.K. Hall & Co.

20. Eisenstein, H., and Sacks, S.R.: Women in search of autonomy: an action design, Social Change **5**(2):4, 1975.

21. Engel, S.: Femininity as tragedy: re-examining the new narcissism, Socialist Review **10**(5):77, 1980.

22. Farley, L.: Sexual shakedown: the sexual harassment of women on the job, New York, 1978, McGraw-Hill Book Co.

23. Freeman, J.: The social construction of the second sex. In Garskof, M.H., editor: Roles women play: readings toward women's liberation, Belmont, Calif., 1971, Brooks/Cole Publishing Co.

24. Friedan, B.: The feminine mystique, New York, 1963, Dell Publishing Co., Inc.

25. Gamarnikow, E.: Sexual division of labour: the case of nursing. In Kuhn, A., and Wolpe, A.: Feminism and materialism: women and modes of production, London, 1978, Routledge & Kegal Paul, Ltd.

26. Hartmann, H.: Capitalism, patriarchy, and job segregation by sex. In Blaxall, M., and Reagan, B.B.: Women and the workplace: the implications of occupational segregation, Chicago, 1976, University of Chicago Press.

27. Hole, J., and Levine, E.: Rebirth of feminism, New York, 1971, Quadrangle Books.

28. Horner, M.: Femininity and successful achievement: a basic inconsistency. In Garskof, M.H., editor: Roles women play: readings toward women's liberation, Belmont, Calif., 1971, Brooks/Cole Publishing Co.

29. Janeway, E.: Man's world, woman's place: a study in social mythology, New York, 1971, Dell Publishing Co., Inc.

30. Kanter, R.M.: Men and women of the corporation, New York, 1977, Basic Books, Inc.

31. Keller, E.F.: The anomaly of a woman in physics. In Ruddick, S., and Daniels, P., editors: Working it out: 23 women writers, artists, scientists, and scholars talk about their lives and work, New York, 1977, Pantheon Books, Inc.

32. Kessler-Harris, A.: Women have always worked: a historical overview, Old Westbury, N.Y., 1981, The Feminist Press.

33. Laws, J.L.: Work aspiration of women: false leads and new starts. In Blaxall, M., and Reagan, B.B.: Women and the workplace: The implications of occupational segregation, Chicago, 1976, University of Chicago Press.

34. Laws, J.L.: The second X: sex role and social role, New York, 1979, Elsevier North-Holland, Inc.

35. Levine, A., and Crumrine, J.: Women and the fear of success: a problem in replication, American Journal of Sociology 80(4):964, 1975.

36. Levine, S., and Lyons, H.: The decade of women: a *Ms.* history of the seventies in words and pictures, New York, 1980, Paragon Books.

37. MacKinon, C.A.: Sexual harassment of working women: a case of sex discrimination, New Haven,Conn., 1979, Yale University Press.

38. McBride, T.M.: The long road home: women's work and industrialization. In Bridenthal, R., and Koonz, C.: Becoming visible: women in European history, Boston, 1977, Houghton Mifflin Co.

39. Milkman, R.: Organizing the sexual division of labor: historical perspectives on 'women's work' and the American labor movement, Socialist Review 10(1):95, 1980.

40. Miller, J.B.: Toward a new psychology of women, Boston, 1976, Beacon Press.

41. Millett, K.: Sexual politics, New York, 1970, Doubleday & Co., Inc.

42. Oakley, A.: Woman's work: the housewife, past and present, New York, 1974, Vintage Books.

43. O'Leary, V.E.: Some attitudinal barriers to occupational aspirations in women. In Kaplan, A.G., and Bean, J.P., editors: Beyond sex-role stereotyping: readings toward a psychology of androgyny, Boston, 1976, Little, Brown & Co.

44. Power, M.: Women's work is never done—by men: a socio-economic model of sex-typing in occupations, Journal of Industrial Relations (Sydney), 1975.

45. Rothman, S.M.: Woman's proper place: a history of changing ideals and practices, 1870 to the present, New York, 1978, Basic Books, Inc.

46. Rule, S.: Women still knocking on the door, New York Times, October 12, 1980, p. 43.

47. Sacks, S.R., and Eisenstein, H.: Feminism and psychological autonomy: a study in decision-making, Personnel and Guidance Journal, p. 419, April 1979.

48. Schlegel, A.: Toward a theory of sexual stratification. In Schlegel, A., editor: Sexual stratification: a cross-cultural view, New York, 1977, Columbia University Press.

49. Stein, A.H., and Bailey, M.M.: The socialization of achievement orientation in females. In Kaplan, A.G., and Bean, J.P., editors: Beyond sex-role stereotyping: readings toward a psychology of androgyny, Boston, 1976, Little, Brown & Co.

50. Walsh, M.R.: Doctors wanted: no woman need apply, New Haven, Conn., 1977, Yale University Press.

51. Who is the real family? *Ms. Magazine*, August 1978.

Chapter 7

Handmaiden, battle-ax, whore

*An exploration into the fantasies, myths,
and stereotypes about nurses*

It is always difficult to describe a myth; it cannot be grasped or encompassed; it haunts the human consciousness without ever appearing before it in fixed form. The myth is so various, so contradictory, that at first its unity is not discerned. . . . Woman is at once Eve and the Virgin Mary. She is an idol, a servant, the source of life, a power of darkness; she is the elemental silence of truth; she is artifice, gossip, and falsehood; she is healing presence and sorceress; she is man's prey, his downfall; she is everything that he is not and that he longs for, his negation and his raison d'etre.*

Myths have pervaded cultures since the beginning of recorded memory and undoubtedly before that. They have evolved verbally and in writing, as history and as folklore, as science and as fantasy, so intricately woven into the threads of our lives—religion, politics, economics, education, psychology—that fact has blurred with fiction and the boundaries between myth and reality are indiscernible. Questions such as "How did they begin?" and "Why do they persist?" are logical and suggest that myths serve a purpose. This is indisputable, but the difficulty with such inquiries is two-fold: First, myths by their nature are illogical, and second, their origins have been obscured with the passage of time. The answers, then, are conjectural and are derived mainly from our knowledge of "human nature."

FANTASIES, THE PRECURSORS OF MYTHS

Myths are thought to develop out of the inability of men and women to tolerate ambiguity and fears of the unknown, their need to explain that which is confusing, to make sense out of and to control events. Human beings are continuously engaged in a quest for understanding, which of course can never be fully achieved. Men and women are different, and thus it is impossible for either to fully comprehend what it

---

*From de Beauvoir, S.: The second sex (trans. and ed. H.M. Parshley), New York, © 1952, Alfred A. Knopf, Inc.

means to be *the other*. This may produce anxiety. In addition, when any two people or groups of people come together, the potential for conflict (also anxiety producing) occurs.[141,180] To fill in the gaps in their knowledge that may be disagreeable, both sexes tend to embroider reality with their own fantasies. Fantasies are endeavors

> toward partial fulfillment or gratification of otherwise difficult or impossible goals or wishes . . . through such avenues as:
> □ Affording unreal, substitutive satisfactions. . . .
> □ Serving as a substitute for inappropriate actions. . . .
> □ Affording partial, secret discharge of otherwise unacceptable inner urges and impulses, especially of a sexual or aggressive nature. . . .
> □ The embellishment of activity which may be otherwise distasteful, so as to make it more acceptable or pleasurable.[127]

This means simply that fantasies assist the individual to cope with anxiety or frustration by allowing her/him to mentally create a relationship where none exists, to act our in her/his imagination sexual or aggressive behaviors that are forbidden in reality or to transform a person or relationship into whatever is desired. Fantasies are not accidents; they are representations of unconscious conflicts and wishes.

Fantasies beget myths. Psychoanalysts, anthropologists, and sociologists all agree that myths reveal our deepest unconscious fantasies[164]; they are society's reflections of the imaginary creations of individuals. They are unreal.

FEMININE MYTHS AND STEREOTYPES

Women in mythology are not simply human but have come to represent both supreme good and basest evil.[193] To understand this seeming dichotomy, we must look at the process of personality development, specifically that of the ego and its defenses.

Psychodynamic origins: the process of splitting

When an adult experiences anxiety, often she/he reacts with the same coping mechanisms (defenses) that were used as a child. The outward expression may be different—the adult has greater control over her/his reactions—but the intrapsychic processes are usually the same, those which have successfully defended against similar anxieties over the years.

One of the earliest defenses used by the developing ego is *splitting*.[122] The young child deals with frustration and anxiety by splitting the image of the frustrating person (usually the mother) into a good, all-giving mother and a bad, pain-producing mother. The good-mother image becomes the recipient of all loving, tender feelings (libidinal drives) and is protected from feelings of anger and hatred (aggressive drives), which are directed at the split-off image of the bad, depriving mother. Small children, who lack well-developed egos, experience rage as an overwhelming emotion capable of destroying the good object (image). Destruction of the good mother, the mother who feeds and cares for the child, is tantamount to self-annihilation. Splitting, then, preserves the good mother *and* the self from destruction; it is life preserving.

As the child matures she/he comes to recognize that the good, loving mother is the same mother who can be frustrating and hurtful. By that time her/his ego has developed sufficiently so that the child can tolerate the fusion of both libidinal and aggressive impulses toward the same object without fearing that either object or self will be destroyed. Splitting occurs in adults when ego functioning is reduced or impaired, for example, during dreams, but is also evidenced in daydreams, fantasies, and myths, the illogical productions of every person's psyche.

The irrational nature of splitting allows an individual to split a group into good people and bad people or to split an individual into an all-good person at one time and an all-bad person at another. The myths of women as supreme good or basest evil are the results of irrational splitting, the use by *men* of an early childhood (prelogical) defense to ward off anxiety, to deal with conflict over their simultaneous primitive longings for and dread of women.[106]

Defensive splitting allows the same man, for example, to believe that some women are good (the "marrying" kind) and others are promiscuous (the "sleeping-with" kind); he may see nurses as angels of mercy and also as sex objects. Contradictory? Illogical? Yes, but comprehensible when viewed from the perspective of splitting.

Woman as basest evil: a study in projection

Unfortunately evil myths predominate. Man's dread, it seems, is more powerful, more irrational, and more difficult to cope with than his longing, which may be satisfied in socially acceptable ways. Man denies his dread and says, in effect,

> "It is not . . . that I dread her; it is that she herself is malignant, capable of any crime, a beast of prey, a vampire, a witch, insatiable in her desires. She is the very personification of what is sinister."[106]

Man has taken his own fears, his own aggressive and sexual impulses and *projected* them onto woman. Projection, like splitting, is an unconscious psychological defense whereby one's own unacceptable impulses and feelings are ascribed to another. They are defended against; they are disowned. Not only are they externalized, but they are seen as coming from the other back toward the self.[127] Projection permits men (in this case) to avoid insight into their own fantasies,[156] to say, in effect: "It is not I who am lustful; it is women who are trying to seduce me!"

Historically, women were both worshipped and feared for their primal powers (derived from their procreative functions). Religions originally were less concerned with mysticism and salvation than with the practical aspects of living, and women as bearers of children were central to the continuity of life. The Great Mother or

Goddess figure appeared universally in literature, history, and legend as a reflection of man's fear and worship of women:[111,118,159]

> Once upon a time there was a wicked witch and her name was Lilith, Eve, Hagar, Jesebel, Delilah, Pandora, Jahi, and Tamar. . . .
>
> . . . and there was a wicked witch and she was also called goddess and her name was Kali, Fatima, Artemis, Hera, Isis, Mary, Ishtar. . . .
>
> . . . and there was a wicked witch and she was also called queen and her name was Bathsheba, Vashti, Cleopatra, Helen, Salome, Elizabeth, Clytemnestra, Medea. . . .
>
> . . . and there was a wicked witch and she was also called witch and her name was Joan, Circe, Morgan Le Fey, Tiamot, Maria Leonza, Medusa. . . .
>
> . . . and they had this in common: that they were feared, hated, desired, and worshiped.*

Masculine envy of women's childbearing power ("womb-envy") led to compensatory mechanisms—masculine emphasis on rational and technological developments.[77] The subconscious conflicts, however, continued, and as Jean Baker Miller[148] says, the myth of woman's evil is a projection of man's difficulties onto women:

> Male culture has built an amazingly large mythology around the idea of feminine evil— Eve, Pandora's Box, and the like. All this mythology seems clearly to be linked to *men's* unsolved problems, the things *they* fear they will find if they open Pandora's Box. Women, meanwhile, have been prepared to stand ready and willing to accept all that evil.†

As formalized religions took hold, the Great Mother–Goddess figure was debased, cults that worshiped her were eradicated, and patriarchy was established. The myth of woman as evil survived, however, as the prototypical myth from which others were developed. Woman was relegated to second place, and religion played an important role in keeping her there.[14,183] Men were created in the image of God: women, as the story goes, came second and were allied with the Devil.

> In the beginning God created the heaven and the earth (Genesis 1:1)
>
> And God said, let us make man in our image, after our likeness; and let them have dominion over the fish of the sea, and over the fowl of the air, and over the cattle, and over all the earth (Genesis 1:26).
>
> And the rib, which the Lord God had taken from man, made he a woman and brought her unto the man (Genesis 2:22).
>
> And the Lord God said unto the woman, What is this that thou has done? And the woman said, The serpent beguiled me, and I did eat (Genesis 3:13).
>
> Unto the woman He said, I will greatly multiply thy sorrow and thy conception; in sorrow thou shalt bring forth children; and thy desire shall be to thy husband, and he shall rule over thee (Genesis 3:16).

---

*From *Woman Hating* by Andrea Dworkin. Copyright © 1974 by Andrea Dworkin. Reprinted by permission of the publisher, E.P. Dutton.

†From Miller, J.B.: Toward a new psychology of women, Boston, 1976, Beacon Press.

Not only Christianity has perpetuated the ideology of women as evil or subservient. The morning prayer of orthodox Judaism asserts,

> Blessed art Thou, oh Lord our God, King of the Universe, that I was not born a gentile.
>
> Blessed art Thou, oh Lord our God, King of the Universe, that I was not born a slave.
>
> Blessed art Thou, oh Lord our God, King of the Universe, that I was not born a woman.

And the Koran, sacred text of Islam, reads, "Men are superior to women on account of the qualities in which God has given them pre-eminence."

It certainly took cunning and political savvy to draft God for the masculine team. His endorsement has sanctioned women's oppression in the name of religious principles; His divine approval has been used by men as a smokescreen to conceal their own defensive psychological machinations. And women, as products of their culture, have believed the lies, have at times accepted the myth of their own evil, and have remained in second place—seen as inferior, treated as servants,[8] tolerated by men as a necessary evil (necessary for sex and for child rearing.)[193] The perpetuation of this myth that women are evil has served men well. It has given them license to indulge their lust and their aggression while avoiding responsibility for their behavior. We have all heard the excuse, "The devil made me do it." In this case it is the *she-devil* who is to blame.

Women as supreme good: a study in idealization

We have also heard the tired question "What were women doing while men created masterpieces?" and we know the answer: that women were barred from culture and relegated to the home; that they had no need to create art or literature (they created children); that the men who thought, wrote, and created did so because women poured their love and energy into those men. It is easy to understand how men might justify their relationships with women (consorting with members of a lower caste) on the basis of *necessity;* it is less easy to understand how they might justify their penchant for placing women on pedestals. How is it that the myths of women as supreme good have evolved?

The answer lies in yet another mechanism of the ego, *idealization,*[72] whereby a person or a group is overvalued and emotionally aggrandized:

> It is the process through which one sets up or creates an ideal. . . .
>
> Idealization can be employed to block awareness of . . . unacceptable aspects of a significant object or relationship. . . .
>
> One's sexual or aggressive urges toward an individual may be more readily denied, disowned, held in check, or regarded as less unworthy or "base," when the person concerned becomes an idealized object and is thereby placed on his special pedestal.[127]

The glorification (idealization) of women has its origins too in man's longings for and primitive dread of women. "The attitude of love and adoration signifies: 'There is no need for me to dread a being so wonderful, so beautiful, nay, so saintly.' "[106] Christianity again institutionalized a masculine myth, through the worship of virginity. This was perhaps more cruel than its debasement of women, for it prevented women from expressing their natural sexuality and humanness.[56]

Idealization explains how man's mental image of a woman (or women) may in fact have little to do with reality; it explains how a man might block out those aspects of a woman's personality that he finds distasteful to preserve his infatuaton with her; it explains how a man might justify his relationship with a woman—by making her more than she is, an ideal. (I particularly enjoy the use of the phrase "sets up" in the quotation above. A Freudian slip? Idealizing a woman, placing her on a pedestal, most certainly sets her up for failure, for no woman can live up to an ideal.)

Unfortunately idealization also creates a barrier to falling or remaining in love.[122] Loving a person means loving our mental image of that person. The closer our mental image comes to the reality, the more honest our love. Feelings that arise out of idealization might better be called adoration or infatuation.

The myths of woman as basest evil and supreme good have their origins less in the reality of women themselves than in man's unconscious fears and desires about women. And myths beget stereotypes.

Feminine stereotypes: myths in tangible form

Both kinds of myths—good and evil—give rise to stereotypes. Stereotypes are vivid illustrations, personifications, of myths, which are more elusive, and may be found in all forms of the media. (I use the word *media* loosely to encompass paintings, books, magazines, newspapers, television, theater, and so on.) Some pervasive feminine stereotypes include the following:

Woman as *Mother Nature* or *salt of the earth* combines aspects of both the woman-as-good and woman-as-evil myths.[193] She is seen as the source of life, nurturing and protecting, but also as violent, unpredictable, and uncontrollable.

Woman as *Bitch* expresses man's antipathy and reduces masculine anxiety over threats to his dominance or virility.[70] When labeled a bitch, her power is diffused and reduced; she becomes a deserving target of male agression. She is "asking for it."

Woman as *Enchantress* is a seducer of innocent men.[70, 183, 193] This stereotype allows men not to be responsible for their own lust and behavior. Again, she is "asking for it."

Woman as *Mystery* is an enigma, impossible to comprehend.[193] This stereotype absolves men even from the need to attempt understanding.

Woman as *Paragon of Virtue* is an angel.[183,193] This stereotype brainwashes women into valuing piety, purity, obedience, submissiveness, and domesticity, virtues that will keep her "in her place." Motherhood becomes a "sacred calling."[154,159]

These stereotypes in their various guises (good/bad, naughty/nice, pedestal/brothel[183]) make up the Madonna/Whore dichotomy—the irrational marriage of two myths—woman as basest evil and woman as supreme good. They may be found in the most sophisticated of works:

> Oh Woman! In our hours of ease,
> Uncertain, coy, and hard to please . . .
> When pain and anguish wring the brow,
> A ministering angel thou.
>
> **Sir Walter Scott:** Marmion

And in the most primitive, a nursery rhyme:

> There was a little girl who had a little curl
> Right in the middle of her forehead,
> And when she was good, she was very, very good
> And when she was bad, she was horrid.
>
> **Henry Wadsworth Longfellow**

Such conflicting and unrealistic images of females, in turn, produce conflicting and unrealistic expectations that can never be met. Women, after all, are neither all bad nor all good; they are women.

Nursing myths and stereotypes

Most nurses, we know, are women and are prey to the same fantasies, myths, and stereotypes as their sex in general. As nursing has evolved so have myths and stereotypes specific to the profession, but they are hardly new creations—just variations on the age-old themes.

Women have always been healers of sorts, more or less accepted by the societies in which they practiced.[62,163] The increasing power of such lay healers threatened the church (men) by encroaching on religious prerogatives and was dealt with summarily. "The church associated women with sex, and all pleasure in sex was condemned, because it could only come from the devil."[62] Evil (sexual) women, it was claimed, wielded evil powers—powers that became crimes—and were denounced as witches. (And we all know what happened to witches!)

Despite many obstacles women continued to nurse the sick. Often these women came from the lower classes; they were servants and prostitutes, drunken and ignorant.[15] The Nightingale Nurse, a product of the Victorian era, was invented out of the need to rid nursing of this degenerate image. Emphasis was placed on femininity; educators inculcated Victorian values and insisted on "ladylike" behavior.[62,86] The ignorant, promiscuous image survived, however, hand in hand with that of the Ministering Angel; the Madonna/Whore dichotomy persists to this day.

As healing became more technical and lucrative, increasing numbers of men were drawn to the field. What had been an art became a science, and caring was separated from curing. Curing, the intellectual function, naturally became the exclusive province of physicians (men), the products of medical schools that taught them science and from which women were barred. Nursing, with its mothering image, continued caring for patients.

The stereotypes of nurses, then, have grown out of both feminine mythology and the realities of nursing's past. The fact that neither has a basis in contemporary reality seems to be irrelevant—the myths and stereotypes persist in which nurses are all good or all evil. The all-good stereotypes include the following:

Nurse as *Ministering Angel* or *Angel of Mercy* promotes the altruistic ethic and teaches nurses (women) to care for others first and themselves last, if at all.[78,130] It is derived from the Woman as Earth Mother stereotype, which depicts women as nurturant protectors. Little imagination is needed to extrapolate that nursing is a "natural" function of women.

Nurse as *Handmaiden* or *Servant to the physician* is the natural outcome of the myth of woman as subservient and the prevalence of paternalism in health care.* This stereotype reinforces the idea that nurses lack intelligence and autonomy and is, unfortunately, perpetuated by nurses' own passivity.

Nurse as *Woman in White* is derived from the stereotype of woman as eptitome of virtue.[78] White, after all, is symbolic of purity and virginity; therefore nurses, who wear white, must possess those characteristics. In addition to promoting nurses as unrealistically virginal, this stereotype encourages the definition of nurses as those who wear a traditional uniform and cap rather than in accordance with the functions they perform.[131] The symbol acquires greater importance than actions.

The stereotypes of the all-bad nurse include:

Nurse as *Sex-symbol* is an extension of the seductive woman stereotype.[6,64] It perpetuates male fantasies that nurses are sexually promiscuous. Wheelock relates their seductiveness to their subservience: "All a general rule, situations in which women are seen as subject to the mandates of male authority provide excellent opportunities for sexual fantasizing."[192]

Nurse as *Old Maid* or *Battle-ax* has its origins in the same kinds of defenses that produce the stereotype of Woman as Bitch.[64] Again, derogatory labeling is the penalty for having threatened masculine prerogatives or personalities.

Nurse as *Token Torturer* is the mechanism by which the nurse, in following doctors orders, becomes the visible agent of painful and destructive treatment to the patient. Nurses "shave women about to give birth . . . give enemas . . . injections . . . withhold pain medication."[40]

Perhaps the most potent stereotype of all is that *Nurses are women;* men need not apply.

•   •   •

It is easy to see the relationship between the mythologies and stereotypes of women and those of nurses. Their purposes are the same: to provide easy solutions to

*References 6, 64, 78, 130, 133.

the complexities of human relationships, to obviate the need for men to understand each woman (nurse) as an individual by providing categories within which to "file" her, and to transform the woman (nurse) into *his* ideal to make her more acceptable and accessible and to lessen his guilt by association. Stereotypes are seductive. Once their use becomes habitual (and it has), the conformity of women becomes imperative. No longer merely defense mechanisms or shortcuts for the lazy, these stereotypes are standards by which all women (nurses) are measured and thus are tools of oppression.

THE MEDIA:
VEHICLES FOR DISSEMINATING NURSING MYTHS
AND STEREOTYPES

Myths and stereotypes pervade all aspects of our culture, transmitted via the media in all its forms. The second part of this chapter examines the elaboration of nursing stereotypes and their dissemination.

Books and toys for children

The socialization of children, particularly female children, has been discussed in Unit One. It is sufficient here to say that children's books serve as powerful tools for conveying stereotypes. Fairy tales, for example, convey primary information about our culture and its myths. They portray the essences of woman as evil (the mothers of Snow White, Cinderella, and Rapunzel) and woman as good (Sleeping Beauty and Snow White); they connect goodness with passivity (good women are awakened from sleep by the handsome prince) and evil with activity.[56]

As Weitzman[184] says, "Children's books reflect cultural values and are an important instrument for persuading children to accept those values." From books children learn about women's roles and the value of those roles; from books children learn that various occupations exist, that many are sex typed, and that each has its own expected behaviors; from books children learn what is *possible* for them.

Girls learn that they can be nurses, schoolteachers, secretaries, waitresses, stewardesses, and models—traditionally female occupations.[13,140,184] But even more importantly, they learn that boys grow up to be men whereas little girls grow up to be mommies. Women in children's books are invariably presented as mothers who perform unpalatable household chores.[63,176] The potent message is delivered that women must relinquish their careers after they marry.

Toys too have traditionally been sex typed. Guns, vehicles, and athletic equipment were for boys whereas dolls and *nurse* kits were for girls. Feminists are currently waging a battle against stores that label toys for boys and girls in an effort to change this tracking of children toward particular interests and career options based on sex.[169]

Books and toys for young children, then, do not convey particular nursing stereotypes, but they do teach children that nursing is a female occupation that must be abandoned in favor of marriage and motherhood.

Cherry Ames and Sue Barton: realistic role models for adolescents?

Stories about nurses designed for school-age children are plentiful, although the image of nursing they convey is obsolete. The Cherry Ames[179,185-191] and Sue Barton[20] series were written in the 1930s and 1940s and depict nursing as it was practiced then; the Kathy Martin[112-117] and Penny Scott[124] series, written in the 1960s, portray nursing in much the same way as the earlier books despite the many intervening changes.

All four of these fictional women attended hospital (diploma) schools of nursing from which they received their "cherished RN" after 3 years of agonizing over school work—memorizing all the bones of the body, learning to give bed baths, and spending grueling hours in hospital service. It was true during the 1930s and 1940s that student nurses were indeed used to staff wards wherever and whenever needed. They worked evenings and nights at the hospital's convenience, often alone in charge of many patients, ill prepared educationally for the responsibilities that were thrust on them. Their duties included such tasks as wrapping and autoclaving instruments, rolling bandages, preparing diets for patients, and scrubbing beds in addition to patient care. These practices and more are vividly described in the series cited.

Nursing is described as *glamorous*. The book jacket of a Cherry Ames story says, "It is every girl's ambition at one time or another to wear the crisp uniform of a nurse. The many opportunities for service, for adventure, for romance, make a nurse's career a glamorous one."[108] Each of the series' stories stresses idealism and places great emphasis on starched uniforms and caps. The nurses are highly involved with their patients. Glamour and excitement, however, come not from nursing but from solving mysteries, finding lost deeds to property, discovering hidden identities, and assisting patients in a myriad of ways outside the scope of nursing practice.

Nursing and medicine are imbued with a sense of *mystery* and *elitism:*

Kathy knew that IV was an intravenous feeding, such abbreviations were an important part of hospital language, a kind of secret code. . . .

When diseases and treatments, equipment, and specialists could all be spoken of in an alphabetical jargon, then Kathy would truly feel she belonged to the mysterious world of medicine.[114]

Such descriptions invest nursing and medicine with an aura of magic that is only now beginning to be questioned. Perhaps to a child or adolescent who delights in sharing secrets with friends, whose sense of belonging and acceptance is enhanced by involvement in a select group of peers, whose life may hold little mystery and drama, this mysterious realm would be appealing. But in a society of sophisticated consumers who demand knowledge of and participation in the care they receive, such an idea is not only naive but legally dangerous.

Nursing is portrayed as *simplistic*. The earlier quotation in which Kathy knows that IV means intravenous feeding is one example. Kathy's responsibilities undoubtedly included functions related to IVs other than merely defining the term, yet these are never described or even alluded to. Oversimplifications such as this, although minor (and perhaps necessary to avoid introducing extraneous material into the story), strip the nursing process of its complexity. In addition, the practice of nursing today requires knowledge and skills far more advanced than Cherry Ames or her cohorts ever dreamed.

Perhaps the strongest message delivered by these books is that nurses are *subservient* and *deferential*. Nurses are supportive labor for physician "bosses"; they follow orders, run errands, and idolize the doctors *for* whom they work:

> Penny stepped back to allow Dr. Scott [her father] to leave the elevator first . . . nurses follow doctors as a mark of respect.[124]

Until recently this was typical of the unwritten code of conduct between nurses and physicians. The doctor has always been viewed with reverence, and nurses were educated to respect the position regardless of the individual involved. Nurses stood when doctors entered rooms, followed them out of doors and elevators, and addressed them as "Doctor" or "Sir" while being addressed by their own surnames and titles.

> The O.R. (operating room) was Penny's particular delight in life. Here was the place where her temperament suited the surroundings. Here was drama, excitement. People came in with something terribly wrong. The surgeon did something bold, decisive. Then usually the patient was on the road to recovery. Surgery was so much more vivid, so much more immediate than medical cases where improvement came gradually, so that the difference hardly showed from day to day.[124]

This statement clearly shows that it is the *doctor* who has acted and who is responsible for patients' improvement or deterioration. The nurse's role is to hand him instruments and to anticipate his needs in doing so. Exciting? Glamorous? Perhaps, but in a vicarious way. The nurse can take no credit for having nursed the patient. Nursing educators have long questioned the validity of utilizing nurses in such a capacity, which is incongruent with the principles of nursing practice. Doctors, as we know, treat illnesses; nurses deal with patients' adaptations and responses to illness, including the physical, social, and psychological. Penny's activities in surgery can hardly be seen in this light.

It is almost as if she enjoys the lack of involvement with patients, for she describes medical cases as slow and frustrating. Although this may be true at times, it is also true that such cases require a much higher level of nursing skill than her rote performance in the operating room. In addition, medical cases can be dramatic and challenging whereas surgical cases are often routine and boring.

Through most of the series books, however, the nurses are highly involved with their patients, often to an excessive degree. They are committed to nursing rather than to romance, and though their beaus are very much in evidence, they are never permitted to interfere with nurses' performance on duty.[160] Unlike the "romance" novels discussed next, these books include a considerable amount of nursing activity; it is their emphasis on unrealistic glamour and mystery combined with a simplistic and subservient image of nurses that is so objectionable.

Finally, the series books depict their heroines as going from job to job (of necessity, I suppose). Of the books reviewed, Kathy Martin had had seven jobs since graduation, each presumably lasting about a year. Cherry Ames spent 4 years following graduation in the army as a hospital nurse,[187] a chief nurse on a Pacific island,[188] a flight nurse,[190] and a nurse in a veterans' hospital[186] (these were the war years). After that she progressed through 17 additional jobs. The message given is that nurses can be *peripatetic*—going from adventurous job to adventurous job—and many nurses do. Unfortunately, most fail to find romance in Alaska or a murder mystery in a convalescent home; that is not the stuff of which real hospital jobs are made, and few nurse recruiters (even those made desperate by today's nursing shortage) would view such job-hopping with approbation.

Young people who read these stories will certainly get a picture of nurses and nursing that is stereotypical and a far cry from reality, yet these are the only books available for this age group. New books are needed that will update the image, depict associate and baccalaureate degree nurses, and explore new nursing roles and functions.

Young, vivacious nurse falls for handsome, arrogant surgeon: nursing in the romance novels

Another type of novel, presumably written for the older adolescent and young woman and found in abundance in drugstores, supermarkets, and libraries, is the paperback romance (sometimes mystery) novel. The main theme of such books is the romance, with a nurse as the heroine. These novels share several characteristics with the series discussed above. First, the nurses are invariably graduates of diploma schools (when their educational background is even mentioned); second, they share the notion of doctor as boss and nurse as subordinate handmaiden; and third, doctors do the curing and nurses the caring.

THE BASIC THEME

Virgin, 18 to 23 years old, beautiful, spirited, intelligent, meets good-looking, intelligent, well-heeled male in his 40's. . . .By the end of 180 pages she has redeemed his cynical view of her sex by her impassioned resistance to his dominant virility and is rewarded by a lifetime guarantee of happiness! And full financial support.[87]

This description fits any romance novel, including those about nurses, the only modification being that nurse stories involve nurses and doctors. The usual theme centers around the experiences of the "Heroine nurse" and "doctor" in a variety of unusual settings, attended by a satellite cast of characters including the "fluff ball," empty-headed, Kewpie doll nurse (often the heroine's roommate); the discarded boyfriend (rejected suitor of the heroine); the "bitch" fiancée of the doctor (frequently an heiress); and a significant patient.

As the story evolves, the doctor becomes increasingly insufferable and offensive, although entirely dedicated to his patients; the heroine nurse becomes increasingly attracted to the doctor but attempts to deny her feelings throughout the major portion of the book. Various subplots intervene—in 6 of the 54 books surveyed, the heroine is escaping previous heartbreak; in 5 she is trapped caring for some member(s) of her family. At the conclusion the doctor suddenly declares his undying love for the heroine nurse, most often precipitated by some confrontation with the soon-to-be-rejected suitor or the significant patient, and the heiress slinks off never to be heard from again. (This appears to be some combination of the Cinderella fairy-tale and the Protestant work ethic—the poor, beautiful, hard-working girl will triumph over the rich, ungrateful, lazy girl and will get her just reward, the handsome prince.)

In a most unscientific study of 54 nurse romance novels, I found that

□ The nurse got her man in 47 out of 54 (87%) of the stories.

□ Of the men, 28 were doctors (52%).

□ In 30 (55%) of the stories, two men vied for the nurse (one was always a doctor).

These capsules tell the story:

It was a dream come true for lovely blonde nurse Gloria Stockwell. Jerry Demarest, handsome young resident doctor, was in love with her and urging her to set the wedding date . . . then came the quarrel that changed everything [and Gloria] watched Jerry walk out of her life. . . . It was then that Dr. Matt Albertson eagerly stepped in to offer solace. . . .[37]

Caught between two men—brothers in name only. Surgeon/surfer Paul Denning, blonde, handsome, cooly professional—who seems more interested in her skills than in herself as a woman. And Ross, the professional surfer—wild, headstrong, his animal magnetism undeniable. . . .[52]

The exciting story of a blonde, blue-eyed nurse who discovers she is also a beautiful woman—a woman who must choose between the love and the demands of her career, between two attractive but very different men. . . .[10]

The cover illustrations of romance novels tell the story at a glance:

□ All except one (98%) depicted a nurse in traditional white uniform and cap.

□ In 39 of the 54 books (72%) the nurse was shown with a man.

□ Of these men, 16 were doctors.

□ 14 of these illustrations showed the couple embracing.

Many of the covers sported captions alluding to love and romance:

> A young nurse is torn between two men and two conflicting emotions—love and compassion. . . .[115]

> A beautiful young nurse plays a handsome doctor against a romantic artist in a dangerous game of broken hearts. . . .[33]

> Who could win her for his own: The man with a mission on earth . . . or the man who would walk on the moon.[50]

THE STEREOTYPES   The heroine nurse, as the central figure in romance novels, is the purveyor of many myths about nursing. As has been said, she is always young, single, high spirited, and attractive.[87] From her we learn that *appearances are most important.* Much is made of her hair—its sleek brown waves, profusion of auburn ringlets, resemblance to shimmering golden silk—and much is made of her figure—tall or short, she is always slender, well proprotioned, and without blemish. She like all women is expected to be attractive,[77] to look fashionable and well groomed[91]; she is encouraged to use artifice, to buy the right product.[183] "The technology of beauty and the message it carries is handed down from mother to daughter," says Andrea Dworkin. "Mother teaches daughter to apply lipstick, to shave under her arms, to bind her breasts, to wear a girdle and high-heeled shoes."[56] A woman learns to disguise her face, her body, her natural odors to become a mannekin, a characterization of stereotpyical attractiveness. Nurses in romance novels are no exception. In addition, what the heroine wears is of prime importance.[88] The nurse's traditional uniform lends itself to romantization from the heroine's earliest dreams:

> She looked forward to the day when, with her R.N. pin shining brightly, her chestnut-brown hair crowned by a perky cap, she would be [her father's, the doctor's] aide.[46]

> [She marked time] until she would have her pin, her starched white uniform, her billowing blue cape, and at last, her cap.[171]

> [She had received] the hard earned diploma, cap, and pin that made her an R.N. . . .[136]

> She belonged in this white uniform, in these white oxfords [?] and white stockings. And she had earned the cap that would be put on her head in a moment.[1]

Isn't it interesting that all the nurses in these stories had "saucy,"[81] "jaunty,"[22] or "perky"[46] caps that perched atop their curls? (Somehow, mine was too big, too unwieldy, and inevitably dragged itself off my head, taking large hanks of hair with it.) Isn't it interesting, too, that their uniforms were always "immaculate" and "crisp"?* (I have been under the impression that starch is out and polyester is in.) In addition to the glamorous aspects of the uniform, the message is also conveyed that without it the nurse is *not* a nurse.

---

*References 41, 44, 45, 98.

"Come on, I'll find you a cap," she offered and led the way to her own quarters. "Can't have one of our nurses going around half-dressed. . . ."[82]

Uniforms are worn in the strangest places—ice skating rinks, dude ranches, and on airplanes—to lend the nurse an air of "authority."

This stereotype of the sweet, virginal *girl in white* is a perpetuation of the Nightingale Nurse image, an attempt to place the nurse on a pedestal high above human (sexual) desires. Nurses, it seems, are still trying to clean up their image. Why is it still necessary to divorce ourselves with such vehemence from the "evil" woman stereotype? Can it be that we protest too much? It could be argued that the authors of these novels are not nurses and that their emphasis on symbols is exaggerated. Perhaps so, but writers can hardly be expected to relinquish stereotypes until nurses themselves do, and there are still many nurses who cling to their caps and uniforms with unquestioning vigor.

Aside from the importance of appearances, we learn that *the main aim of nurses is to get a man,* preferably a doctor:

> She thought about the ideas she'd had about nursing. . . .She'd imagined being busy in a great modern operating room all the time, a heroine to her associates and a favorite of all the doctors . . . and her dream had always included the very special doctor who would notice her most of all. He would be young and handsome and without any faults. He would be regarded with awe and respect by all the other doctors and the staff.[41]

> "Here I decide to become a nurse because I figure it's a good way to meet some nice, rich, bachelor patient, who'll be so grateful for my Florence Nightingale Administrations that he'll fall in love with me, and insist that I marry him and share his lovely millions."[22]

> "Well, why did you become a nurse?" asked Kathie.
> "Men, of course, But men, naturally!" said Marie-Claire.[48]

Those who are not in nursing for the purpose of man-hunting are there for altruistic reasons. Such heroines portray a certain glamour in *duty and self-sacrifice.* They give up secure, well-paying hospital positions to work among the poor;* they nurse patients during off-duty hours and vacations.[139,182] As one heroine puts it,

> "I'm here . . . because I have a year's contract and because I am needed. It's a nurse's main aim in life to be needed."[38]

Cover blurbs, too, tout the glamour of the nurses' sense of duty:

> She found pride and romance in her work among the poor.[79]

> Grim duty forced Rietta to leave the life she loved—and face probable heartbreak.[19]

> Duty called nurse Lindsay back . . . but was it duty that kept her there—or handsome Dr. Corbett?[53]

---

*References 79, 83, 96, 161.

Women have been taught to value others before themselves; they have come to believe that duty that entails self-sacrifice is (somehow) ennobling. The heroine of romance novels is invariably a Ministering Angel; her patients come first. (Doctors also come first.) It is precisely this same ethic of self-abnegation that keeps the nurse subservient to and symbiotic with the physician. The heroines are also Handmaidens. This accessory relationship with the physician is discussed separately in a following section.

Second only to the Ministering Angel and Handmaiden stereotypes is that of the Battle-ax nurse, the supervisor or instructor whose authoritarian manner and icy comments demean and demoralize her subordinates. She is the "frigid woman," the spinster, the older nurse (younger ones being typically cast as ministering angels or prostitutes). She is usually stern and unrelenting; occasionally, however, her demeanor is tempered with an almost condescending kindness, but only if the subordinate nurse has proven herself in some crisis and has risen above her peers.

> A big-boned, middle-aged spinster, she ran her two operating rooms efficiently, demanding perfection of the nurses under her, as she demanded it of herself, in her efforts to give the surgeons the service she believed their due. [137]

> She remembered old Cunningham's withering glance down at her when she had first gone to St. Antholin's. But over the years old Cunningham, variously known as the war-horse, the Battle-ax, and even less complimentary terms . . . had become more human. [48]

A battle-ax supervisor speaks for herself:

> "Right on time! I'm surprised," she said harshly, "I thought you big-city nurses doted on being late at relieving people." [82]

Her only redeeming quality seems to be that she runs a tight ship—patients receive excellent care and the work proceeds smoothly under her efficient organization.

Little is known of the Battle-ax's personal life beyond her spinsterhood. Is she the heroine nurse grown old? Hardened if not embittered by her failure to get a man? Nurses in these novels view her with respect as well as fear. It is as if her purpose is the ensure that all fledgling nurses undergo certain rites of passage of which humiliation, deprivation, and exhaustion seem integral parts. She differs from the Battle-ax nurse of male-authored books in that her aggressions are directed for the most part at nurse underlings (rather than at male doctors, whom she treats with solicitude and pampering). She shares with them, however, a common antecedent, the Woman as Bitch stereotype, and is as such an object of derision and hostility.

Another nursing stereotype, that of the *dumb* or *ignorant* nurse, also appears in romance novels. Often, as has been said, she is the "fluff ball" roommate of the heroine. She seems always to be making mistakes and getting into trouble with the Battle-ax and with physicians. Her main qualities are naivete, an almost laughable awe of physicians, and a penchant for needing to be rescued.

Sherry was not officially a stenographer, but an office nurse. Yet she could serve in either capacity, and was the efficient, obliging, eager to please sort of girl who made him feel that any work she performed for him was sheer pleasure.[137]

A nurse in another book appears stupid and stand-offish. She is contemptuously called "Miss White Cap," the kind of nurse who only makes beds and scurries down halls, "a just-emptied bed pan held with some distaste in one outstretched hand."[144] Yet another nurse makes a suggestion to a young, arrogant doctor. She is rebuked and responds by blushing like "the stupidest young probationer." She stammers apologetically:

"I'm—I'm sorry, doctor . . . I was just—well—so excited by what happened . . . I only wanted to help . . . I guess I didn't think."[98]

And there is Happy, a nurse who is forever putting her foot in her mouth, acting without thinking:

"What did you do that riled the chief, Happy?"
"Overstepped my responsibilities as a nurse and stuck my nose in things that didn't concern me . . . " she confessed, and fought hard against the storm of tears that threatened her. "But I didn't mean to upset Mrs. Rankin . . . honestly I didn't! . . . She threw a fit and went into hysterics and Mr. Rankin ordered me out of the room and reported me to the chief . . . They said I had no right to try to interfere in the personal affairs of patients."[81]

How can nurses like these be taken seriously? How can they be presumed to deliver safe, intelligent patient care? Obviously they can't. It is the stereotype of the Dumb nurse (in conjunction with that of the Handmaiden) that reinforces the public's notion that nurses should remain under the direction (and protection) of the benevolent physician for "their own good" and that of their patients.

The Seductress nurse is less prevalent in the series and romance novels than in general literature and other forms of the media. There are instances, however, when nurses in these stories *are* sexualized or shown in a promiscuous light:

She wore a thin white nylon uniform and the bright lighting of the glass and chrome room limned a shadowy silhouette of her lithe young figure.[137]

or meet Miss Irene Cotton:

The red-haired, green-eyed Casualty charge nurse.

Even in the wards she turned the heads of all the male patients capable of noticing that hip-swinging walk, or the way she had of looking at men, with those provocative green eyes partially closed.[149]

And there is lonely Marvin, the hotel manager who calls his new nurse employee in for a chat. The book describes her sitting in front of him, legs tightly pressed together because of her discomfort with the shortness of her *required* uniform, as this conversation occurs:

"Success is a lonely thing. It's made me a lonely man. That's why I want you to call me Marvin."

"I'd be glad to, if it would help you, Marvin," she murmured.

"You're an intelligent girl, Elizabeth, and very, very attractive," he said. "I'll be surprised if you remain a nurse very long."[49]

Finally, there is the cover illustration that depicts a nurse fully undressed, holding a sheet in front of her. (You can tell she's a nurse because she's still wearing a cap.) A doctor stands gazing over his shoulder at her. (You can tell he's a doctor because of the stethoscope in his hand.) Title: *Doctor's Nurse.*[98] This book, interestingly enough, did not "deliver"; there were no scenes in the story that might have lent themselves to such artistic interpretation.

The fantasy that women are promiscuous seducers of men has been dealt with in the first part of this chapter; the most graphic example of these fantasies (as they relate to nurses) are discussed in the later section dealing with pornography.

Nurses in romance novels, then, are Ministering Angels, Handmaidens, Battle-axes, Fools, and Whores. In addition, nursing is portrayed not only as second class but occasionally as *second choice*. This image of nursing—by default—though not precisely a stereotype, occurs often enough to warrant mention. It is the image of a nurse who wanted to be a doctor but was unable to enter medicine for one reason or another. She may be vocal in her disappointment or long suffering; she may participate in medicine vicariously by reading medical journals, observing surgeries,[75] and assisting the physician with experiments.[173] These words tell the story:

"Staff nurse in a general hospital . . . you, who wanted to study medicine and become a doctor? Ending up doing menial work, nurses are useful and important in their way. But you must admit that being a nurse is a far cry from being a doctor. It's like . . . oh, like someone who meant to be an architect, a builder of beautiful buildings, ending up as a construction worker . . . or like someone who wanted to be an artist ending up as a house painter."[75]

THE LIES: GLAMOUR ON THE JOB   *Glamour* is the operative word—forget realism! Nurses in romance novels do very little if any nursing. Although most are supposedly employed, these stories tend to focus on their private rather than professional lives. In surveying the work of nurses in the romance books, I found three common characteristics.

First, the numbers of nurses in some fields are disproportionate to the actual numbers of nurses in those fields. For example, the heroine in 9 of the 54 books was a private duty nurse (16%); in reality only 3% of nurses are engaged in this kind of work.[142] The operating room too is overrepresented.

Second, nurses in romance novels have glamorous and unusual clients: a senator[172] or a peer of the realm[182]; or they have glamorous and unusual jobs: a resort nurse,[36,49] art colony nurse,[33] beauty contest nurse,[54] ice show nurse,[34] flight nurse,[110,145] prison nurse,[151] Olympics nurse,[124] cruise ship nurse,[51] and nurse to the astronauts.[50] The majority of real nurses work in hositals (nearly 66%),[142] but hospitals as most nurses know lack glamour and the public, it seems, wants to believe that nursing is a glamorous job.

Third, nurses in romance novels travel far from Smalltown, U.S.A., to a Florida bayou,[83] Paris,[74] Acapulco,[173] Alaska,[175] Hawaii,[52] and unknown islands (romance novels are big on islands).[18,58,103]

Aside from these glamorous aspects, nursing is portrayed in other unrealistic ways. For example, a nurse on vacation far from home visits her friend who is hospitalized. While there she learns of an emergency in the maternity ward, borrows a uniform, and rushes to assist.[171] Another nurse, precipitously hired by a physician stranger to work in his office, moves to the state where he practices. An emergency occurs at the local hospital, she hurriedly dresses and pitches in.[143] The need for state licenses is overlooked as is the fact that no hospital would permit a stranger to work under such conditions.

Nurses employed in hospitals do in reality float to various areas but not as inappropriately as do these heroines: an operating room nurse (on her day off) cares for a patient in the emergency room[162]; a medical-surgical nurse takes an injured friend to the hospital and scrubs in on his surgery[41]; another nurse bounces between the operating room and general duty[48]; and yet another manages pediatrics, the medical surgical unit, and obstetrics.[45] Medical-surgical staff nurses are promoted overnight to charge positions in an emergency department,[103] "terminal ward,"[182] and an aerospace training laboratory.[50] These nurses do not belong to a float pool but have regular assignments from which they depart and to which they return at the whim of a physician, the need of a patient, or the dictates of chance. They are not specialists; they do not require orientation to new areas or management training. The message is clear—*nurses can work anywhere.* The question then arises whether this is so because nursing, even in specialty areas, requires such minimal skill that any nurse can do any job or because nurses are capable of taking on any assignment and in fact are supernurses?

Getting a job poses no problems for romance nurses; neither does leaving one. Nurses in these stories are hired without interviews; they depart at a moment's notice.[19,32,172] Where are the nursing supervisors? The head nurses? They are invisible and unnecessary, as the next section shows. It is the physicians who arrange for nurses to be promoted and demoted, to come and go.

ANTIPATHY TO ARDOUR: THE PHYSICIAN-NURSE DYAD   The physician is the hero of nursing romance novels (even on the rare occasion when the nurse falls for the "other man"). The stories convey several messages to readers about the relationship of nurses to doctors.

Most potent of these is the idea that the *physician is the boss.* It is he rather than the nursing administrator who hires nurses:

Linette had stood when Dr. Powell came into the office, her attitude the one taught in training school as befitting the nurse in the presence of the lordly being, the doctor in charge of the case.

"Red hair," Dr. Powell murmured to Dr. Sturdivant, "I think she'll do, don't you?"[79]

And it is he who fires them.[53,79]

Physicians arrange for nurses to be transferred to different floors and to various patients.[22,84] Should home care be required, the hospital nurse is sent, courtesy of the patient's doctor.* (Hospitals in romance novels, we already know, are untroubled by the nursing shortage and exigencies of daily staffing.) Physicians need not restrict their activities to professional considerations, either, but freely meddle in the personal lives of nurses. One characterization frequently found is that of the older, paternalistic doctor who cajoles, advises, patronizes, and occasionally browbeats the heroine nurse.† In one story such a man insists that the nurse allow a local girl, a stranger, to share her apartment. When the nurse refuses, she is treated to a tongue-lashing that concludes, "and you a nurse who is s'posed to be compassionate and understanding."[171] The nurse in her guilt and remorse acquiesces.

In addition to being rugged, brilliant, handsome, and dedicated, the doctor is frequently domineering, aloof, abrupt, insensitive, and even deliberately rude. Yet the climate of many romance novels, and the submissive characterizations of their nurses, is such that *rudeness and abuse of nurses by physicians is tolerated.* It is a norm. Many readers will recall Dr. Gillespie, the termagent from the Dr. Kildare series:

> "Why do you have so much starch in your uniform? So it will rustle? So people will know you're about? Don't try to take a place in the sun around here."
> "No, doctor," she said.
> "Nurses are not human beings. They're merely pairs of hands performing services— usually badly. And don't roll your eyes at Kildare, either. He only pretends about you. He doesn't take you seriously, for him you're only a bit of simple diversion. A man has to have a little diversion, doesn't he?"
> "Yes, doctor," she said.[21]

In another story the nurse asks the physician what certain tests revealed about a patient going for surgery. His response:

> He brushed her off impatiently, almost rudely, "I'm not in the habit of confiding in our nursing staff about things which can't possibly concern them. Shall we leave it at that?"
> "Certainly, doctor."[75]

In yet another story, a nurse is transferred to care for a patient at the doctor's request. She comes in on her evening off to begin the case. Soon afterwards the doctor appears and begins to shout:

---

*References 18, 55, 103, 139.
†References 21, 75, 83, 161.

"You were to phone me a half hour ago, nurse. I received no phone call . . . ,"
Veronica's lips tightened. "No-one told me I was supposed to phone you doctor."
He said, his voice edgy with sarcasm, "Can you read, nurse? It's written on the chart!"
. . . She flushed. "I'm sorry, doctor, I guess I missed seeing it."
Veronica felt anger rising in her. He had no right . . . ! She hadn't been careless! Still . . .
she should have seen that notation.
She succeeded in holding back her anger. "No, doctor."
"Next time," he said, "see if you can perform your functions, as a nurse, the way they
should be performed!"
Veronica's lips tightened, but she managed to say, past their trembling, "Yes, doctor."[22]

What more needs to be said?

Nurses do not question doctors' orders, at least not in romance novels. The word
of the physician is law. In one story a new graduate learns this lesson the hard way,
by being publicly humiliated:

As she moved to obey the order to transfer the small boy her mouth was a thin angry
line. Yet she realized she had no right to be angry. After all, who was she, Jennie
Cosgrove, with her cherished cap and pin still a beautiful novelty, to object to any orders
given her by one of those lordly beings, a doctor? She had been an R.N. for less than a
year . . . so it scarcely behooved her to question any orders given her.[84]

In another story student nurses ask the heroine whether it is ethical to question a
doctor's order if you know it to be professionally unsound?

"How would you know that he was being professionally unsound?"
"Well, assume that he was."
"But you can't make that assumption, you see. You're pitting limited knowledge against
more comprehensive knowledge, and your assumption would be somewhat preposter-
ous."
"Still—"
"You obey orders. Not because he happens to be more intelligent or better trained but
because he happens to be responsible for the life involved. . . ."
"Then what happens to the principle of serving the best interests of your patient?"
"But is it his patient or your patient?" she asked in turn. "And who is better qualified to
determine what is or isn't in the best interests of the patient?"[151]

Or one nurse asks another:

"If a doctor asked you to administer certain medications, even if you didn't approve, what
would you do?"
"Administer them, of course, and pray that the doctor was right and that I was wrong."[83]

Last, a nurse scolds a recalcitrant patient:

"I'm a registered nurse, and I've been rigidly trained to obey a doctor's orders; not the
whims and fancies of a rebellious patient."[83]

Again, what more needs to be said?

The inescapable message of romance novels is that *nurses marry doctors*. A nurse's success is measured not by how her patients fare but by whether she wins the doctor's love. She must be lively, humorous, and well groomed at all times, an unrealistic expectation of any human being. Nursing is not always happy or successful; even barring the tragic aspects, there are frequent administrative and organizational hassles that create friction and frustrations. Fatigue and negative emotions such as anger and depression have no place, however, in these stories.

As the nurse is always sweet and kind, the doctor is ruthless and egotistical. His personality traits do not lend themselves to open communication and caring relationships, yet the nurse is attracted to and falls in love with him. Germaine Greer's description of the process is eloquent:

> The lover in romance is a man of masterful ways, clearly superior to his beloved in at least one respect, usually several, being older or of higher social rank and attainment or more intelligent. . . . He is authoritative but deeply concerned for his lady whom he protects and guides in a way that is patently paternal. He can be stern and withdrawn or even forbidding but the heroines of romance melt him by sheer force of modesty and beauty and the bewitching power of her clothes. He has more than a hint of danger in his past conquests, or a secret suffering or a disdain for women. The banked fires of passion burn just below the surface, muted by his tenderness and omnipotent understanding of the heroine's emotional needs.*

Often the physician hero wields enormous power and is unchallenged by other characters; often the inequities inherent in his romance with the heroine nurse, stemming from the disparity between their positions, is never questioned. In patriarchy "love" (for the male) means having power *over* someone or (for the female) falling *under* the power of another.[159] How can love exist between an inferior and a superior? It can't. The one must constantly be reassured of her worth and lovableness to feel secure; the other must constantly idealize his beloved, see her as someone other than her lowly self, to not feel demeaned. Yet the stories tell us it happens:

> The dream-come-true began the day she had stepped into this very office to be interviewed by a startlingly handsome young doctor. . . . When he had swept her into his arms after their second date and confessed that he had fallen in love with her during the first moment together, Terry had echoed his sentiments. . . .[35]

. . . **AND THEY LIVE HAPPILY EVER AFTER**   Nearly 90% of them do anyway. Occasionally the nurse marries a lawyer, a businessman, or a patient rather than the doctor, but it is always as if lightning has struck, so swiftly does the love develop.

In one story, for example, a flight surgeon and the heroine nurse meet during her first flight. He briefly checks her patients, then spends the remainder of the trip working with another nurse and a critically ill patient. Months later the surgeon and

---

*From The Female Eunuch by Germaine Greer. Copyright © 1971 by McGraw Hill. Used with the permission of McGraw-Hill Book Company.

the heroine meet again on another flight—he rushes her to the galley for coffee and to tell her he loves her.[145]

In another story a war-injured patient on admission to the hospital tells his nurse that he knows he will die. She argues with him that he will live even though she knows his wounds are fatal. Much distressed at her conduct, she then rushes to her supervisor who tells her that she is obviously in love with the man. All is now clear. She realizes that she does indeed love him after only a few moments in his company, and she returns to tell him that she has lied about his prognosis. She wonders how she can "explain to him that she had fallen in love with him the instant their eyes met?" She manages. Miraculously, he feels the same. They marry. He dies. (All in the first few pages.) The story continues—she grieves, recovers, and falls in love with his brother, a dedicated physician who is also a duke.[182] (Sigh. . . .)

And what becomes of the heroine nurse once she has captured the heart of her hero? *She leaves nursing to become a wife and mother:*

> "Will you be leaving the hospital after you're married, Leona?"
> "I suppose so," Leona answered. "Bruce and I haven't discussed it. I'll do whatever he wants me to do, of course."[46]

Of course.

The "glamour" is gone: nurses in popular literature

Writers of popular fiction seem no more creative than romance novelists in developing new images for nurses. The same stereotypes appear.

The Battle-ax nurse, for example, is personified at her worst by Nurse Ratched of Ken Keysey's *One Flew Over the Cuckoo's Nest.*[123] Ellen Goodman, columnist for the Boston Globe, says of her,

> Nurse Ratched represents every well-intentioned destroyer of the spirit, every narrow emissary of civilization who ever ruled over a classroom or brought religion to a South Sea Island. She is every frustrated mother who turned into a benevolent despot, skillful at ruling her children through dispensation of love to those who are "good."*

Her patients warn, "The big nurse tends to get real put out if something keeps her outfit from running like a smooth, accurate, precision-made machine."[123] Nurse Ratched is no accident. She is Woman as Bitch, "controlling and oppressing the free spirit of men"[90]; she is the Battle-ax nurse, riding roughshod over her patients, more concerned with organizational functioning than with human needs; she is the nursing supervisor who has sold out to the establishment, whose worst sin is complicity with the system.

The nurse as Seductress is another favorite. She appears as General Dreedle's nurse in Joseph Heller's novel *Catch-22:*

---

*Reprinted with permission of the Boston Globe Newspaper Company/Washington Post Writers Group.

> As delectable a piece of ass as anyone who saw her had ever laid eyes upon . . . chubby, short, and blond. She had plump, dimpled cheeks, happy blue eyes, and neat curly turned up hair . . . Her bosom was lush and her complexion clear. She was irresistible . . . succulent, sweet, docile, and dumb, and she drove everyone crazy.

> "You should see her naked," General Dreedle chortled with croupy relish, while his nurse stood smiling proudly right at his shoulder. "Back at Wing she's got a uniform in my room made of purple silk that's so tight her nipples stand out like bing cherries."[101]

Heller portrays her as the typical "dumb blond," an object not only of lust but of derision. He so *objectifies* her that she remains nameless, forgettable, a mere servant to the sexual appetites of her employer (and his friends). The reader is absolved from guilt at such insensitivity—she is "smiling," we are told, she enjoys this. Another of Heller's characters, Nurse Sue Ann Duckett, initially emerges as a prude, a "tall, spare, mature, straight-backed woman with a prominent, well rounded ass, small breasts. . . . She was adult and self-reliant, and there was nothing she needed from anyone."[101] Promiscuous? Hardly. Yet while she is making a bed, Yossarian, the "hero," slips his hand between her legs and brings it up to her crotch, a signal for his fellow patients to grab her and bounce her back and forth between them "like a tennis ball." Rather than resenting such treatment, she soon abandons her independence and becomes Yossarian's lover. She begins to tease and flirt with the men, reveling in her ability to arouse them. In her we see the Battle-ax turned Whore. How powerful is the man who has wrought such a transformation! Moral of the story: all women (nurses) are *really* asking for *it*, so it's OK to use force or whatever it takes to unleash their repressed desires.

Even when no seduction occurs, the idea that nurses are easy targets frequently emerges. Perhaps the most maligned group in this respect are nurses in the armed forces whose proximity to men encourages the fantasy that they are promiscuous:

> "There's a cooking editor on my newspaper, hell of a good looking woman. I never could get into her pants when I was her editor. . . ."
> "If you have that sort of problem there's always the navy nurses."[104]

In popular fiction and nonfiction the stereotype of nurse as Handmaiden prevails but loses the glamour it had in romance novels (as rightly it should.) Stripped of its martyrdom, the role is seen for what it really is—derogatory and demeaning. The nurse is a fool whose only interests revolve around housekeeping chores and paperwork. In *Intern* (a supposedly true story) by Doctor X, the author angrily relates,

> "I sure was mad at those nurses, though. They get all wound up in their routine idiot work—morning care, baths, meals, charting little things on the charts—and then they resent an emergency as an intrusion and go right on washing people's mouths out and giving backrubs while some patient is dying off in the next bed."[47]

There's something fishy here. How many of us would give our eye teeth to find a nurse who still gives back rubs? How many of us find it implausible that nurses prefer charting and passing trays to emergency diversions? All of us who have ever questioned the absence of care plans, who have investigated patient complaints of cold meals, who have heard on numerous occasions about the "emergencies" that superseded such routine activities.

Tender Loving Care, [150] the nonfiction account by two army nurses of their peers in the service, promoted as a book of humor, is sexploitation at its worst. Following on the heels of a much-acclaimed book about airline stewardesses, *Coffee, Tea or Me?*, this book chronicles the experiences of several women from their induction into the army through a variety of duty assignments. The cover and all other illustrations depict buxom miniskirted nurses in assorted revealing poses:

- Embraced by the snake on a caduceus
- Jogging in tight sweatshirts
- Perched on a barstool with legs crossed
- Posing naked for a filmmaker
- Sitting coyly on a patient's bed with skirt hiked up and garter showing

The stories fulfill the sexual expectations aroused by these pictures.

There is, for example, the account of a new nurse with a voluptuous figure (the "dumb blonde" type) who goes for an introductory physical examination. Two servicemen direct her to a small room away from her companions and tell her to undress. The reader can guess the rest—from the peephole in the wall to the G.I. who plays doctor and nearly gets caught.

Other stories include that of a nurse-prostitute in Vietnam, a dentist who fondles his nurse-patients' breasts while filling their teeth, a surgeon and a nurse who make love in the operating room between cases, and many more. There is no nursing in this book—just furtive, tawdry, and demeaning sex—and little humor.

Another book on medical humor, *More For Doctor's Only*, [76] exploits the stereotypes of nurses as Idiots and Sex-objects. The cover shows a cartoon of a nurse in uniform, cap, and high heels (?) standing behind an x-ray viewer that, naturally, strips her torso to bra and pants. There is also a cartoon of the male guest visiting a hospitalized friend. Perched in his lap is a bosomy, long-haired nurse. He is speaking on the telephone, presumably to his wife, saying "I'm sitting up with a sick friend, dear." And there is the picture of a doctor listening with his stethoscope to a nurse's ample chest. He says, "Why Nurse Jones! I didn't know you cared!"

The jokes are as bad as the illustrations. There is a nurse working her first day in a doctor's office. She opens the door to a good-looking male patient who has laryngitis and whispers, "Is the doctor in?" She whispers back, "No, come on in." And the (idiot) nurse who wouldn't cross a picket line because "she had heard they were having trouble in the maternity ward."

Stereotypes, as has been said, reflect unconscious fantasies; viewing women (nurses) as negative—stupid, aggressive, promiscuous—is a person's way of dealing with that which she/he both longs for and fears. Humor serves a similar function; it devalues that which is threatening.[127] To disparage a woman is to deny one's fear of her; it is to say, "How ridiculous it would be to dread such a poor creature."[106]

A more realistic image of nursing appears in one recent book, *Nurse*, by Peggy Anderson,[4] the story of one nurse's experiences and philosophies. We as nurses may not all agree with her views, but I think we can agree that the book is "real," the drama is the real drama of patients lives, and the feelings are real feelings. It is a beginning.

Ministering angels need not apply: nurses in television and movies

TELEVISION   Television touches the lives of more people than perhaps any other medium. Throughout childhood and into early teens it is certainly the most dominant.[147]

- More American homes have television than have heat or indoor plumbing.
- The average television set is turned on for 6½ hours per day.
- Most children begin watching television at 2.8 *months* of age.
- Three- to five-year-olds watch television 54 hours per week.
- By the time a child graduates from high school, he or she will have spent less than 12,000 hours in front of a teacher and more than 22,000 hours in front of a television set.*

During their formative years, then, most children are innundated with television stereotypes. These popular images not only reflect popular views (since their aim is to please and persuade the audience) but *reinforce* those views and attitudes.[183] No single television program ever ruins a child; no attitude is ever acquired by viewing a single program. The impact is cumulative; it occurs subtly when themes are repeated and images are portrayed with little variation.[138] We learn about the world before we see it; we observe situations before experiencing them in our own lives; we develop *preconceptions* that determine later perceptions of individuals and events.[135] Television tells us "something about the way the world is: whether it is that men kill each other and women cook, or that women spend their husbands' money on ludicrous hats."[147] Stereotypes emerge—the Western hero, the dumb housewife, the sexy nurse.

Soap operas are gaining increased popularity and their influence in propogating stereotypes can no longer be ignored. The Neilsen ratings show that approximately 5.5 million households tune in on an average day to an average soap opera. Highest ratings go to ABC programs: *General Hospital* (12.3 million viewers) and *All My Children* (11 million viewers).[39] These, along with *One Life to Live*, another ABC show, gross about one million dollars per week.[181] Obviously soap operas are big business. Viewers are younger now, and there is no longer a difference between daytime and nighttime audiences.

---

*From Growing Up Free: Raising Your Child in the 80's, by Letty Cottin Pogrebin. Copyright © 1980, Letty Cottin Pogrebin. Used with the permission of McGraw-Hill Book Company.

The popularity of such programs has been attributed to their ability to (1) fulfill fantasies, (2) provide company and (3) provide a sense of continuity now missing in family life.[39,66] In reviewing soap operas I found six (a large percentage of the total) that involved hospitals and thus nurses. These included the three top shows cited above as well as *The Doctors* (NBC), *As The World Turns* (CBS), and *Guiding Light* (CBS). My observations agree with those of Fernandez[71] and Elms and Moorehead,[64] whose studies found nurses stereotyped as faithful servants ministering to the needs of doctors, as exploited sexpots, and as hard-nosed despots and unrealistic old maids (nurse as Handmaiden, nurse as Sex Symbol, and nurse as Battle-ax). In addition I found the following:

1. Nurses in soap operas do very little nursing. They stand at desks, take phone calls, deliver messages, direct traffic, and act as go-fers. Occasionally they might speak with a patient, but it is generally student nurses or volunteers who provide patient care.
2. Nurses in soap operas do a lot of gossiping about clothes and parties, giggling over doctors and boyfriends, and visiting with friends who come to see them during working hours.
3. Nurses in soap operas wear traditional uniforms and caps, but the length of the uniform skirt varies inversely with length of hair depending on whether the nurse is a sex symbol or a battle-ax.

Nurses on adventure programs and situation comedies convey similar stereotypes. Readers may remember the doctor-oriented shows of the 1960's, *Ben Casey* and *Doctor Kildare*. Nurses in these, the forerunners of current shows, were rarely in evidence, and when they were portrayed it was not as autonomous professionals but as subservient, romantic interests of physicians.[146] *Temperature's Rising*, a program of the 1970s, depicted nurses as sex symbols who obeyed orders and received kisses from foolish-looking interns. In one show a patient was about to jump from a ledge; the chief doctor commented, "sometimes sex works," and the nurse obligingly stuck her head out the window to cajole the patient with her charms.[147]

Current programs in which nurses are consistently seen include *Trapper John, M.D.*, *M*A*S*H*, and *Emergency*, and all three programs depict nurses in stereotypical ways. The following example from an episode (November 14, 1980) of *Emergency* is typical:

□ A student nurse is shown so in awe of the M.D. that she follows him around, mouth agape, bungling even the simplest of tasks. The doctor finally yells, "You're job is to assist, not to get in the way!" Dixie, the charge nurse, defends the student and suggests that the doctor try some of his "off-duty personality" on her.

□ The next scene shows the student assisting him to bandage a patient's hand. "Thank you, Miss Walters. That was very nice," he says condescendingly, and then, in an aside to Dixie as the student departs, "Some of my off-duty personality."

▢ A crash is heard. Dixie and the doctor rush to see what has occurred. The student nurse lies amid scattered instruments on the floor. "It was an accident, doctor," she stammers.

▢ Later a call comes in from the paramedics who describe their patient as having "trichlorethylene exposure." The doctor tells Dixie to get the toxicology manual. She holds it open for him as he reads and then asks, "Trichlorethylene, what is it?" He explains what he has just read.

▢ (Messages: Nurses are enamoured of doctors, they are clumsy, and even the best of them can't read).

Although I did not review the program, this description of "the new *House Calls* Gal" in *The National Enquirer* caught my attention: "Blond bombshell Diane Lander, 28, who plays the sexy nurse Sally Bowman this year on the hit comedy 'House Calls,' displays the knock-out figure that helped her land the role."[152] Pictured was the actress in a revealing crocheted swimsuit.

A glance at the nursing cast of characters on soap operas and situation comedies gives us, for example:

▢ Bobbi Spencer, of *General Hospital*, sex symbol par excellence who "hopes her bedside manner will attract a new man in her life." (She used to be a prostitute before going to nursing school.)[97]

▢ Consuelo, of *Marcus Welby, M.D.*, the good-and-faithful handmaiden (whose activities make it difficult for the viewer even to guess that she's a nurse).[71,86]

▢ Dixie McCall, of *Emergency*, not a battle-ax precisely but a highly efficient (she works anywhere in the hospital), no-nonsense, managing sort of nurse.

▢ "Hot Lips" Houlihan and Lieutenant "Dish" of *M*A*S*H*, the first with battle-ax propensities and the second leaning toward dumb; both are portrayed as sex symbols and both ridiculed.[165,192]

▢ And finally "Starch," the dumpy, organized battle-ax, and "Ripples" (because she creates ripples), the high-heeled, dumb, blonde sex symbol of *Trapper John, M.D.*

The myth of male domination is much in evidence in both kinds of programs: *all* nurses are Handmaidens. All nurses, too, are Women in white who wear traditional uniforms, although, as we have seen, they are not as virginal as that colour might imply. The Sex Symbol and Battle-ax stereotypes predominate. Only one stereotype is absent from most soap operas and situation comedies: the Ministering Angel. Nurses on these programs do little nursing and certainly cannot be seen as dedicated care-givers.

Nurses as the butt of television jokes appear much the same as they do in books and cartoons, as Fools or Whores. Joan Rivers is perhaps best known for her tasteless jibes. On *The Tonight Show* (November 24, 1980) she suggested that the only kind of women men like are stewardesses and nurses, both of whom are tramps. After all, we know that "R.N. means Ready Now"!

Two recent specials on nursing encourage me to believe that reality is beginning to challenge the myths and stereotypes. *Nurse* (CBS, April 9, 1980) was a biographical drama of the life of Margaret Sanger, who pioneered birth control and planned parenthood. *A Matter Of Life and Death* (CBS, January 13, 1981) was the story of nurse Joy Ufema's work with terminally ill patients. The good news about this program was its emphasis on nursing autonomy and the nurse as patient advocate; the bad news was that most nurses were shown as apathetic, inhumane bitches and were berated by Joy on several occasions. Both doctors and nurses were initially portrayed as bad guys opposed to Joy's work, but the doctors came around to be good guys whereas the nurses remained antagonistic. (The story was also covered by *People Magazine*.[23])

Such examples of real nurses are rare, however, but like the few realistic books about nurses they are a beginning.

MOVIES AND THEATER Fantasies of masculine domination and feminine subservience pervade the world of film. Molly Haskell, speaking about the treatment of women in the movies, says,

> The big lie perpetrated on Western society is the idea of women's inferiority. . . .
>
> In the movie business we have had an industry dedicated for the most part to reinforcing the lie. As the propoganda arm of the American Dream Machine, Hollywood promoted a romantic fantasy of marital roles and conjugal euphoria. . . .[99]

Roles for female stars have mirrored traditional female stereotypes. In a study of such roles Baunoch and Chmaj[12] describe four major movie types, parallelling the predominant female stereotypes:

- "Pillar of Virtue" (woman as Paragon of Virtue, woman as Mother Nature) including the "sweet young thing," the "perfect wife," the "gracious lady," and "mother, mammy, mom, ma."
- "Glamour Girl" (woman as Enchantress, woman as Mystery) including the "femme fatale," the sex goddess," the "showgirl," and the "cool beauty."
- "Emotive Woman" (woman as Bitch, woman as Enchantress) including the "long-suffering lady," the "vixen," and the "sexually-frustrated neurotic."
- "Independent Woman" (woman as Mother Nature, woman as Bitch) including the "career woman," the "regular gal," the "durable dame," the "brassy modern," and the "liberated modern."[12]

Nurses per se are not discussed, but then nurses have not been portrayed as major characters in movies. They are glimpsed fleetingly as background figures in occasional hospital scenes and are always traditionally attired. *M*A*S*H* and *One Flew Over the Cuckoo's Nest* are the notable exceptions in which nurses have prominent if not leading roles. As I have said, nurses in the former are depicted as promiscuous objects of ridicule and Nurse Ratched in the latter is a cold-hearted object of fear and scorn.

But if nurses are not major characters in movies, it is because *women* are not (in comparison with men). "I don't know," says Shirley Maclaine, "why the stories are still revolving around men's concerns. I'm so tired of hearing it, and I'm so tired that it's still true."[69]

I am not familiar with nurse characterizations in the theater. A recent visit to the stage play *Evita*[157] offered a glimpse of a starched, haughtly nurse who roughly assisted the star, Eva Peron, to bed. She certainly evoked the Battle-ax image, but the part was too limited for me to develop anything more than a brief gut-tightening reaction to her insensitive manner.

Realism triumphs over fantasy: nurses in the news

Newspapers and news magazines consistently reach a large adult population,[120] and their presentation of nurses and nursing tends more toward realism than fantasy. Consumer interest in and concern about health care issues have provided the impetus for an increased focus on nursing. In Los Angeles between November 1980 and March 1981 (the 5-month period when this chapter was being written), there were, for example, 16 newspaper stories concerning nurses—9 about "the nursing shortage," 5 about new nursing roles, and 2 about nurses who were Vietnam veterans. This is impressive coverage!

The nursing shortage articles presented the following information:

1. Reasons for the shortage, including poor working conditions*; poor salary, hours, and benefits†; lack of child-care facilities[59]; lack of autonomy, recognition, and status compounded by physicians' rudeness‡; fewer nurses entering nursing as other career options become available for women§; and reality shock.[59,60]

2. Results of the shortage, including poor patient care‖ and more nursing errors.[125]

3. Solutions to the problem, including joint practice between physicians and nurses, admitting privileges for nurses with their new roles, and alleviation of all the problems cited.[59]

The situation was presented accurately for the most part, and nurses were shown to be intelligent professionals concerned about the care of their patients. I noticed, however, that in several of the articles physicians or hospital administrators were the spokesmen for nursing and patient problems rather than nurses. This unfortunate example of paternalism reinforces the public's idea that doctors and administrators are somehow in charge of nursing.

---

*References 9, 10, 125, 136, 166.
†References 59, 60, 125, 178.
‡References 9, 10, 59, 60, 136.
§References 59, 60, 61, 125.
‖References 59, 136, 166, 167, 178.

New nursing roles highlighted by several articles included psychiatric nurses in private practice,[11,43] family health practitioners,[43] nurse midwives,[5] a visiting nurse whose baby accompanies her on rounds,[68] and neonatal intensive care unit nurses who transport critically ill infants via ambulance.[119] On the whole such stories were informative and accurate and presented nurses in a positive, autonomous way. One general article about expanded nursing roles, for example, indicated that nurses are becoming more assertive, that more men are entering the field, that hospitals are intensifying recruitment efforts, that nurses' knowledge is expanding with increases in medical technology, that nursing is shifting to degree-oriented programs, and that new nursing roles are being created.[16]

Other articles that ostensibly present the "new breed" of nurses in fact depict not first-class nurses but second-class doctors. They describe nurses laboring in areas where doctors refuse to go at a fraction of the salaries doctors would earn—and loving it![170] One article, for example, on neonatal transport nurses describes their activities in detail, particularly their autonomy in life-saving decisions and their rendering of emergency care.[119] The final paragraph, however, undermines the entire story by saying, "Back at [the hospital] Reese and Clark *resumed* their role as nurses, deferring to doctors' decisions" (emphasis added). What role were they assuming in the ambulance if not nursing? Is it the nursing role only to defer to physicians?

The articles on nurses who had served in Vietnam illustrated the stresses these women faced during their tours of duty and again on reentering civilian life.[65,102] They are forgotten veterans about whom little is known and to whom little attention has been paid.

Not all nurses agreed with the content of these articles. Often the issues were debated at length in subsequent letters to the editor. Alternate points of view were presented. Specific issues notwithstanding the importance of this exposure is that *real* nurses and *real* nursing problems are finally being brought to public awareness devoid of myths and stereotypes through the news media.

Token torturers to the fore: nurses in "get well" cards

Greeting cards for hospitalized patients make nurses the butt of every joke. They are stereotyped as the usual Battle-axes, Sex Symbols, and Fools and in addition as Token Torturers, the instruments of pain.

The nurse as Sex Symbol is depicted, for example, in a card that shows the patient lying in bed and winking. The outside caption reads, "Your doctor says you're doing just fine!" and the inside adds, "However your NURSES say you need some more practice!"[93]

Other cards include several stereotypes. One says the patient will be examined by many people while in the hospital; the line of examiners includes three nurses; a fat, short, middle-aged one with a large syringe (Battle-ax–Token Torturer), a tall (Battle-ax) matron, and a curvaceous blonde (Sexpot) in miniskirted uniform.[94] A second card, "Birdwatcher's Guide,"[92] depicts various hospital personnel as birds. The "wring-neck pheasant," a large nurse-bird with cap, sings out, "Are we comfee?" The caption expresses the trite sentiment that this warbler wakes the patient early in the morning when breakfast won't be served until later. The "Late-night flicker," another nurse-bird, annoyingly wakes the patient at night for the proverbial sleeping pill. Torturers, indeed, disguised as Battle-axes with foolish tendencies. In yet a third card a (Torturer) nurse chases her patient with a syringe.[95]

The Patients have Patience!! Activity Book[132] says it all. It shows a nurse chasing a patient with an enema can: connecting the dots in one activity reveals a posthemorrhoidectomy patient also threatened with an enema from a nurse. Nurses in this book are depicted as fall guys for other departments: one refuses to admit the patient without cash and lengthy questions, a second is accompanied by Dracula to draw blood from a patient, and a third is reprimanded by a physician for transporting the wrong patient to the operating room. The last straw is a naked nurse paper doll with three changes of clothes: for a witch, for a prostitute, and for an angel!

"Try rape, you'll like it": nurses in pornography

Projection of sexual desires as a masculine defense is seen most clearly in pornography in which women are portrayed as insatiably sex hungry or as willing victims of abuse. In either case, men defend against their own lust or sadism by perceiving those desires as arising from women. As Wheelock[192] points out, women who are subject to male authority offer excellent material for sexual fantasies. Nursing certainly fits the bill.

Boerigger,[17] in a pornographic book masquerading as a scholarly treatise (designed for the man who can't even admit he likes dirty books), explores the origins of masculine fantasies about nurses. Most men, he alleges, have never worked through their oedipal desires for their mother or "Nanny." The desire and the taboo against it produce conflict that males experience as a wish to conquer the unobtainable. Who could be more like mother than a nurse? (The word itself conjures up images of breasts and suckling.) Who has traditionally evoked two images, the madonna and the whore? The Madonna/Whore dichotomy is *derived* from the masculine oedipal conflict: the struggle between desires on the one hand and prohibition on the other.

In a similar pornographic book–cum–scientific endeavor, Hauptmann[100] intellectualizes on masculine attraction to nurses. I found this book enlightening despite its thinly disguised eroticism, because it develops in detail the various male fantasies (myths) of nursing promiscuity. The nurse as "surrogate mother and ministrant to the injured and infirm has been unsuccessful in obscuring her femininity in the eyes of male patients, doctors, and employees."[100] She is surrounded by an "aura of sexuality," we are told. Whose sexuality? Here we see the beginnings of projection—we are encouraged to imagine a nurse engaged in hiding *her* sexual urges. To this end nurses wear white, symbolic of virtue. But the traditional uniform, rather than being asexual and antiseptic, is perceived by men as a challenge[17] and may even trigger dangerous impulses in those men whose oedipal conflicts are less controlled.[100] (Not only does the nurse crave sex, but she's asking for violence too!) Once we are convinced of nurses' barely concealed passions, we are cajoled by the notion that it is abnormal for nurses to deny their sexuality. It may even be harmful: they'll develop neuroses, their work will suffer! (Horrors!)

So much for niceties. Hauptmann[100] then rationalizes at length on nursing's promiscuity—he hauls out the big guns—the hard-core projections. The defensiveness is almost palpable. We are told:

1. "Many authorities feel that nurses have not been entirely innocent of contributing to . . . the sexual mystique. . . . More and more medical and social spokes*men* have been admitting that they begin to see justification for the strict rules governing nurses' behavior" (emphasis added).[100] We are being hoisted on our own historical petard. (Read: Once a prostitute, always a prostitute.)

2. Women are driven into nursing because they feel guilty over their sexuality and must join other chaste women as a defense against lustfulness.[100] (Read: Get thee to a nunnery!—Shakespeare.)

3. Nursing allows physical intimacy with patients. The woman who is struggling to repress her sexuality can by becoming a nurse indulge in physical intimacy while remaining safe and ethical. Other women enter nursing precisely *because* of the sexual possibilities.[100] (Read: The only way to get rid of temptation is to yield to it—Oscar Wilde.)

4. Aggressive, matronly types (Battle-axes) can as nurses indulge in "Authoritarian sexual behavior with patients and doctors."[100] (Read: A strong woman is a castrating woman—Freud.)

5. Army nurses often get raped in times of war (even in hospital wards during air raids!). Soldiers, after all, are young and lonely (horny). They view nurses as ideals, as Ministering Angels (mothers), who must be seduced. We are told that men delight in "debasing and corrupting that which [they] idolize most."[100] Also, copulation is a primitive defense against fears of dying.[17] The nurse is not responsible, in this case, but then neither is the soldier—war is the culprit. (Read: Don't take no for an answer; when she says, "No," she means, "Yes!")

6. Did you know, for example, that nurses in Vietnam were given contraceptives and encouraged to relate sexually with patients? And did you know that they enjoyed giving injured soldiers reasons to live again?[100]

7. Many nurses are raped. Army nurses receive this treatment often, but so do nurses in mental hospitals. "Some authorities believe that psychiatric nurses

are sexually maladjusted anyway . . . they despise men."[100] (Read: That makes it O.K.!) Ditto with rape for private-duty nurses. It's almost part of the job description.

8. Student nurses are suggestive of images of daughters, chambermaids, innocents. They flatter doctors who are afraid of more aggressive, full-fledged nurses. And they're not nearly as innocent as one would imagine: "Student nurses who manage to avoid orderlies and other males and females who pursue them are still not necessarily chaste but in many cases may engage in secret erotic activities with their classmates."[100]

Pornography is male myths and fantasies of women and nurses as Whores made *real*, given graphic form. Boerrigger[17] and Hauptmann[100] take the process one step further—they validate the pornographic images with "facts" and illustrations.

Pornography epitomizes the nurse as a sex-crazed woman who can't wait to get into bed with patients: "She'd been short-tempered on the job lately, too. She knew damned well that what she needed was a good f_____."[57] (Eureka! The cure for burnout and dropout has been discovered.) And get into bed with doctors.[26,31,57] She is the victim of rape whose physical arousal during the experience exceeds anything she's experienced before.[26,105] She is a multiorgasmic participant in oral or genital sex, engaged in bisexual, homosexual, sadistic-masochistic, and autoerotic practices with other humans or with devices, alone or in groups.* And this is the same nurse in the span of only a few hours!

Pornographic photography depicts nurses wearing—you guessed it—white uniforms and *caps*. They're also wearing black garter belts and red high heels *and* stethoscopes that are strategically placed on male genitalia.[17,85]

Plots in pornographic fiction are virtually nonexistent; there is no pretense at glamour, at romance, at realistic nursing activity. One heroine (?), however, announced that she didn't want to be a *nurse* at all; she was heading for medical school. It is the ultimate insult to be confronted with the nursing as second choice stereotype—perhaps I am simply overreacting after having been exposed to so much nursing promiscuity (system overload, you know).

Enough of the jokes! The stereotype of woman as Victim (nurse as Victim) of her own sexual appetites of those of others is no laughing matter. She *is* a victim, but of projection. *She* does not desire punishment, taming, or debasement, as much as men would have her believe the lie.[56] Where is the dividing line between mental rape and physical rape? Brownmiller[25] has reported the following out of the mouths of rapists:

□ "All women want to be raped."

□ "No woman can be raped against her will."

□ "She is asking for it."

□ "If you're going to be raped, you might as well relax and enjoy it."

*References 29, 31, 85, 105.

Are these not the very myths we have been discussing in terms of pornography? They are myths, yet men *do* believe them; judges and juries *do* believe them; women and even raped women *do* believe them.

IMPACT OF STEREOTYPES—ON NURSES, ON THE PUBLIC, ON PHYSICIANS

How influential, then, are the media in forming people's impressions about nursing? As mentioned previously, one's concept regarding the image of nursing is probably derived from a variety of sources and experiences—it is a cumulative effect. How do myths and stereotypes affect nursing itself? How do they affect the public? In complex ways.

Dropout, burnout, reality shock, and the nursing shortage: fighting myths and stereotypes is a painful process

All professions are stereotyped by sex in our society. The myths, stereotypes, and traditions—in short, the image—of an occupation profoundly affect the people who select that occupation.[134] To the extent that nursing is conceived of as subservient, nonautonomous, rigid, stifling, and noncreative, it will appeal to people who possess those traits and to whom self-actualization and responsibility are threatening prospects; to the extent that nursing is portrayed as a stopgap to marriage, it will attract women who lack career aspirations and lifelong commitment; to the extent that it is sextyped as a women's profession, it will attract primarily women.

This has been evidenced in studies of nursing students' sex-role identities and reasons for choosing nursing. Traditionally women who selected nursing did so because cultural conditioning made this the perfect womens' profession. Dissonance arose for these women when their educational process promoted the independent role of nursing,[177] and they *dropped out.* Disenchantment with nursing grew out of the women's consciousness-raising movment of the 1960s and 1970s. Nurses who had been educated to be independent were no longer satisfied with second-class status and with poor working conditions and benefits. They experienced *reality shock* on entering the work world and quit in large numbers.[26] For others the process was more gradual; they *burned out,* and attrition rates swelled. The *nursing shortage* began. The situation is exacerbated today as fewer women are attracted to nursing and school enrollments are down. Because nursing continues to evoke traditional images, women who seek creative, exciting, autonomous careers go elsewhere.

Stereotyping has also had had a negative effect on the developing theories within the educational system. Traditionally nursing was considered a practice discipline, and the development of theory was neglected. This grew out of the myth that women were not analytic. As the need for theory became more apparent, nurse educators were themselves caught in the rigid confines of female stereotypes. Theory building, after all, requires leisure—some educators must be freed to work on theory. Women have never been afforded that luxury. Finally, hospitals (under the direction of males), as the employers of most nurses, have rarely supported the need for advanced nursing education and for professional activities such as attending conferences, doing research, and so on.[121]

Living with myths and stereotypes, battling them in ourselves and others, is a wearing process made more difficult by the fact that nurses as women have been socialized to believe in those very images of nursing.[24] The stereotype is so "pervasive and entrenched, even the group it hurts . . . believes in it."[121] Many nurses do not want to change nursing. "An aspect of gender stereotyping is that women themselves, in introjected self-contempt, seem to want to continue it."[174] They fear rocking the boat, and after all there are certain advantages to maintaining paternalism, to being the favorite daughter.

The impact politically, socially, and psychologically of being a nurse in our society is thoroughly explored in the following chapters. It is enough for me to say here that for those nurses who have become *conscious*, who seek change, the struggle is a daily one and takes its toll. To the extent that stereotypes persist of woman and her place in society, and to the extent that nursing is seen as a female profession, it will have difficulty attracting intelligent, independent women and men; it will experience casualties among its ranks. To the extent that nurses increase their autonomy and redefine their practice while stereotypes and myths prevail, they will create dissonance with clients and other health professionals whose expectations are traditionally proscribed.

No wonder it is sometimes easier just to leave.

A nurse is what you want her to be: the image of nurses in public and medical opinion

Public opinion (derived from myths, stereotypes, and personal experiences) influences consumers' expectations and utilization of nursing care.[109] Consumers expect nurses to be women and doctors to be men. Two thirds of Americans, for example, would not mind working for a woman, but they "want police, doctors, lawyers, dentists, and bankers to be men, and salespeople, hairdressers, and nurses to be women."[3] In addition, they see nursing as less prestigious than traditionally male professions and *slightly* more prestigious than teaching and other traditionally female professions.[131]

Nurses seem generally well thought of. In one study 53% of respondents considered nurses as "career women" and nearly 49% said they were "smart."[131] Only 1.4% and 2.4% respectively believed nursing glamorous or nurses promiscuous. The public, it seems, views nurses as professionals (86% do) although still subservient to physicians (70%).[130] Whether the respondent had been recently hospitalized (and thereby exposed to *real* nurses) significantly affected her/his view on nurses as independent or dependent.[128] Another study found that consumers (72%) thought nurses should be educated as professionals (and many believed nurses to be better educated than they actually are.) Half of those queried thought all nurses should have baccalaureate degrees.[2]

Despite media emphasis on "bad woman" stereotypes—the Whore, the Idiot, and Battle-ax—the Nightingale image of nursing persists with the public. The ideal nurse is an Angel of Mercy, is good looking, has a pleasing personality,[130] and is neat and tactful.[109] She is also responsible, knowledgeable, caring, competent, skilled, efficient, and dedicated.[131] The myth that nursing is a natural female profession persists[109] along with the idea that a "good nurse" is someone who can work in all areas without specialized training and education.[6] The public, in short, has idealized nursing. Newton[153] in a particularly insightful article suggests that the public's view of nurses may be a way of giving nursing their *prescription* for what is needed. People are saying, "This is what we want."

It is interesting that doctors' opinions of nurses differ greatly from that of the public. Three fourths of doctors viewed nurses as "their assistants—nothing more."[129] They do not want collegial relationships with nurses. In addition, 78% believe nurses have enough to say in patient care, and another 10% think they have *too* much authority.[129] Most physicians do not think nurses understand disease processes and therapies (as compared with 57% of consumers who do.)[130] Again unlike the public, doctors think that a baccalaureate degree is neither good nor necessary; they believe that nursing educators are changing graduates "from members of a humanitarian profession to a bunch of self-seekers who are educated beyond the point of usefulness."[129] (The bit about "self-seekers is akin to the pot calling the kettle black). Doctors, in other words, have much invested in keeping nurses "in their place"! The doctors' image of nurses is similar to that of the public in that it is also unrealistic. But whereas consumers idealize nursing, doctors debase it. Both mechanisms serve to maintain the illusion that nurses are what one wants them to be.

LET'S PUT NURSE RATCHED, HOT LIPS, AND THE NIGHTINGALE NURSE TO BED (?)—GETTING RID OF STEREOTYPES

This final section examines how nurses can begin to eliminate stifling and offensive stereotypes with both personal and public activism.

Personal activism: a good, hard look in the mirror is indicated

This, then, is why myths and stereotypes persist: they represent unrealistic subconscious desires and, like many dreams, are an exercise in wish-fulfillment. That is not to say that they should be allowed to grow unchecked or that nurses should let the status quo continue, but it is a reminder that the persistence of stereotypes among the public, among other health professionals, and even among nurses occurs *because* they meet profound psychological needs.

Before attempting to change public and professional opinions, before engaging in wholesale destruction of nursing myths and stereotypes, it behooves nurses to examine both individually and collectively their own adherence to traditional images and behaviors. After all, myths and stereotypes about nurses could hardly have prevailed unless they contained some partial truth. Getting in touch with ourselves, our own conflicts, our needs for dependency, our indirect expressions of aggression and sexuality, and our complicity with the myths is a painful but necessary first step. Ask yourself the following questions.

Are there not attractions in being subordinate? There are some who would argue that nurses have been *allowed* (rather than forced) to assume traditionally female characteristics of tenderness, sympathy, and mothering[153]; that nurses themselves prefer less responsibility and accountability. Before you shout, "No!" think about it.

What is it about Nurse Ratched that makes us cringe? Why are we so reluctant to claim her as our own? Might it be that we denounce her so vehemently because there is a little Nurse Ratched in all of us?[90] What is it about her (and perhaps us) that causes such anxiety? The fact that she gave in? Bought into the system? Allied herself with hospital administration? Sold out? Took the easy road? "Why did she do something like that?" we ask, implying "I would never *do* that!" Her defection, her *identification with the aggressor*, is perceived as alien, and yet it was a defense and like many defenses was probably subconscious.[28,67,122] It allowed her to get rid of helplessness, hopelessness, and powerlessness by becoming *like* those who were strong, who had the power, who were threatening. It allowed her to survive in an impossible situation. Can each of us honestly say that to keep the peace we have never agreed with someone with whom we really disagreed, have never said yes when we meant no, have never closed our eyes to avoid having to take a stand? Think about it.

Have you ever used seductiveness or feminine wiles? Have you ever played dumb? Such behaviors encourage traditional stereotypes. The current emphasis on assertiveness and on women's issues makes such admissions embarrassing. It is one thing, however, to hide our foibles from others; it is another to hide them from ourselves. Perhaps it is not your style to sell out; have you burnt out or dropped out instead? What, in other words, are *your* defenses. Think about them.

As many authors will say in this book, the first step to self-respect is the acknowledgement of who we are as individuals and as professionals. Only that knowledge can give us the power to choose how we will act and what we will change. From that position of strength we can begin to think about altering nursing myths and stereotypes, ridding ourselves of them, and giving the public new images more congruent with reality.

Public activism: agitation, education, legislation, and negotiation

I credit Virginia Cleland[30] with suggesting that we as nurses must "agitate, educate, legislate, and negotiate" to end sex discrimination.

This chapter has explored various myths and stereotypes about nursing in a way that will, I hope, bring them to life for the reader. If you have vivid pictures in your minds of the Fluffball, the Sexpot, the Handmaiden, the Battle-ax, and the Torturer you will recognize them in all their subtleties should you encounter them again. And you will. Again recognition is the first step.

When you read books, newspapers, and magazines and watch television and movies, ask yourself:

1. Are women shown in numbers equal to men? Do they say as much? Do as much?
2. Are they portrayed as submissive, weak, and ineffectual or strong and competent?
3. Are their roles stereotypically defined? Are they leaders or adjuncts?
4. Are they exploited?
5. Why are they appealing? Because they are cute or sexy or subservient?
6. Are unmarried women showed as incomplete?
7. What are women's concerns? Clothes? Appearances? Men?
8. Are they portrayed as emotional or irrational?
9. Do they enjoy good relationships with other women?

Undoubtedly I have omitted many pertinent questions, but these are a beginning. Butler and Paisley[27] suggest that women should rate media images on a "consciousness scale," which has five levels from worst to best:

1. "Put her down." This image includes dumb blondes, sex objects, and whimpering victims.
2. "Keep her in her place." In this image women are strong only in traditional roles such as nursing.
3. "Give her two places." These are the "progressive" images in which women are liberated from home only to the extent that they are responsible for *both* home and office (supermoms).
4. "Acknowledge that she is fully equal." Women are shown as at least equal or as superior to men.
5. Beyond the dogmatism of level 4, women and men are shown as individuals, as superior or inferior in different, individual areas (including role-reversals such as househusbands, and so on).

Education means raising the consciousness of others. This involves talking with friends, family, peers, and other professionals and writing to broadcasting companies and news media with compliments and suggestions.[73] Keeping these industries aware of consumer reactions is important (and like everyone else they want to be told when they have done a good job). Nurses can take "advantage of the power of television to improve the public image" by serving as consultants and advisors and by participating on talk shows.[158] As I have already said, the news media in particular seem interested in the problems as well as the achievements of nurses. This interest can be capitalized on by enterprising nurses who want to educate the public.

Agitation, legislation, and negotiation involve using your influence in political ways. Included are economic strategies (hitting them where it hurts) such as boycotts against products that exploit women or portray them offensively, letting offenders *know* they are being boycotted and why, and using legal strategies such as formal and informal complaints against offenders. In other words, activism means denouncing stereotypes and discrimination wherever and whenever they occur and using media opportunities to educate the public about nurses and nursing.

· · ·

Self-awareness and political activism are necessary if we are to begin to change the images of women and nursing. As has been said, myths and stereotypes persist because they meet deep psychological needs or reflect subconscious conflicts of the public, other professionals, and nurses *themselves*. Creating new images will be an arduous process made possible only by the vigilance, personal honesty, and willingness to take risks of nurses whose consciousness has been raised.

REFERENCES

1. Adams, T.: Spotlight on Nurse Thorne, New York, 1962, Ace Books, Inc.
2. Alexander, J.W.: How the public perceives nurses and their education, Nursing Outlook 27(10):654, 1979.
3. America's attitudes on women, Los Angeles Herald Examiner, p. A-5, January 7, 1981.
4. Anderson, P.: Nurse, New York, 1978, St. Martin's Press.
5. Anderson, P.B.: Certified nurse midwives: the human side of childbirth, The Los Angeles Times, p. 1, February 8, 1981.
6. Aroskar, M.A.: The fractured image: the public stereotype of nursing and the nurse. In Spicker, S., and Gadow, S., editors: Nursing images and ideals, New York, 1980, Springer Publishing Co., Inc.
7. Ashley, J.A.: Hospitals, paternalism, and the role of the nurse, New York, 1976, Columbia University Teachers College Press.
8. Ashley, J.A.: Power in structured misgoyny: implications for the politics of care, Advances in Nursing Science 2(3):3, 1980.
9. Barclay, D.A.: Angels of mercy are turning in their wings, The Register, p. E-1, February 11, 1981.
10. Barclay, D.A.: Band-aid solutions aren't luring nurses, The Register, p. F-2, February 12, 1981.
11. Barnes, Y.: Clinical specialists—psychiatric nurses practice on their own, The Los Angeles Times, p. 5-8, November 20, 1980.
12. Baunoch, J., with Chmaj, B.: Film stereo-

types of American women: an outline of star roles from the thirties to the present. In Chmaj, B., editor: Image, myth, and beyond, Pittsburgh, 1972, Know, Inc.
13. Belotti, E.G.: What are little girls made of? New York, 1976, Schocken Books, Inc.
14. Bem, S.L., and Bem, D.J.: Case study of a nonconscious ideology: training the woman to know her place. In Bem, D.J.: Beliefs, attitudes and human affairs, Belmont, Calif., 1970, Brooks/Cole Publishing Co.
15. Bingham, S.: Ministering angels, New Jersey, 1979, Medical Economics Co.
16. Bird, M.: Nurse's role becoming more vital in health care, Los Angeles Herald Examiner, p. B-1, March 31, 1980.
17. Boerigger, J.W.: What you always wanted to know about sex in uniform but were afraid to ask, New York, 1973, Capri Publishers, Ltd.
18. Bowman, J.: Nurse on Pondre Island, New York, 1965, Prestige Books, Inc.
19. Bowman, J.: Door to door nurse, New York, 1967, Prestige Books, Inc.
20. Boylston, H.D.: Sue Barton series, Boston, 1930s through 1940s, Little, Brown & Co.
21. Brand, M.: Dr. Kildare's crisis, New York, 1940, Dell Publishing Co., Inc.
22. Brennan, A.: Nurse's dormitory, New York, 1962, Prestige Books, Inc.
23. Bricker, R.: Joy Ufema's work with the dying has inspired controversy, a TV film, and immeasurable gratitude, People 15:69, January 19, 1981.

24. Broverman, I.K., and others: Sex-role stereotypes: a current appraisal. In Lasky, E., editor: Humanness: an exploration into the mythologies about men and women, New York, 1975, MSS Information Co.

25. Brownmiller, S.: Against our will—men, women, and rape, New York, 1975, Simon & Schuster, Inc.

26. Bruce, W.: S.E.X. nurse, Wilmington, Del., 1978, Encounter Books.

27. Butler, M., and Paisley, W.: Women and the mass media—sourcebook for research and action, New York, 1980, Human Sciences Press, Inc.

28. Cameron, N.: Personality development and Psychopathology, Boston, 1963, Houghton Mifflin Co.

29. Carver, M.: Two horny nurses, San Diego, 1980, Greenleaf Classics, Inc.

30. Cleland, V.S.: To end sex discrimination, Nursing Clinics of North America 9(3):563, 1974.

31. Cockrin, R.: Nighttime nurse for hire, New York, 1980, Carlyle Communications, Inc.

32. Converse, J.: Emergency nurse, New York, 1962, Signet.

33. Converse, J.: Art Colony nurse, New York, 1969, Signet.

34. Converse, J.: Ice show nurse, New York, 1970, Signet.

35. Converse, J.: Terry Allen, nurse in love, New York, 1970, Signet.

36. Converse, J.: Winter resort nurse, New York, 1973, Signet.

37. Converse, J.: Nurse in turmoil, New York, 1974, Signet.

38. Craig, G.: Nurse at Guale Farms, New York, 1964, Prestige Books, Inc.

39. Crow, T.: Watching the soaps becomes a national pastime, Pasadena Star News, Extra, p. 2, November 7, 1980.

40. Daly, M.: Gyn/ecology: the metaethics of radical feminism, Boston, 1978, Beacon Press.

41. Dana, R.: Nurse Freda, New York, 1966, Modern Promotions.

42. De Beauvoir, S.: The Second Sex, New York, 1952, Alfred A. Knopf, Inc.

43. Delatiner, B.: Nurses in practice on their own, The New York Times, March 6, 1977.

44. Dern, P.: Nurse at Burford's Landing, New York, 1967, MacFadden Books.

45. Dern, P.: Nurse's dilemma, New York, 1967, MacFadden-Bartell Co.

46. Dern, P.: Florida nurse, New York, 1968, Lancer Books, Inc.

47. Doctor X, Intern, New York, 1965, Fawcett-Crest Books.

48. Dorien, R.: Noonday nurse, New York, 1957, Lancer Books, Inc.

49. Douglas, D.: Resort nurse, New York, 1969, Signet.

50. Douglas, D.: Apollo nurse, New York, 1970, Signet.

51. Douglas, D.: Sea nurse, New York, 1970, Signet.

52. Douglas, D.: Surfing nurse, New York, 1971, Signet.

53. Douglas, D.: Nurse in disaster, New York, 1972, Signet.

54. Douglas, D.: Beauty contest nurse, New York, 1974, Signet.

55. Douglas, S.: Assistant surgeon, New York, 1962, Signet.

56. Dworkin, A.: Woman hating, New York, 1974, E.P. Dutton.

57. Eastwood, N.: Naughty night nurse, San Diego, 1980, Greenleaf Classics, Inc.

58. Eby, L.: Nurse on nightmare island, New York, 1966, Lancer Books, Inc.

59. Editorial, Nurse! Los Angeles Times, December 8, 1980.

60. Editorial, Wanted: more nurses, Los Angeles Times, December 3, 1978.

61. Editorial, Want more nurses: make jobs more rewarding, Modern Healthcare, p. 5, January 1979.

62. Ehrenreich, B., and English, D.: Witches, midwives, and nurses: a history of women healers, New York, 1973, The Feminist Press.

63. Eliasburg, A.: Are you hurting your daughter without knowing it? Pittsburgh, reprint, Know, Inc.

64. Elms, R.E., and Moorehead, J.M.: Will the "real" nurse please stand up: the stereotype vs. reality, Nursing Forum 16(2):113, 1977.

65. Elvenstar, D.: Mary comes marching home, Los Angeles Herald Examiner, California Living Section, p. 6, December 14, 1980.

66. Embree, A.: Madison Avenue brainwashing—the facts, In Morgan, R., editor: Sisterhood is powerful, New York, 1970, Vintage Books.

67. Engel, G.L.: Psychological development in health and disease, Philadelphia, 1962, W.B. Saunders Co.

68. Estes, J.: Homebound patients find baby's visit is sunshine, Pasadena Star News, p. C-1, February 24, 1981.

69. Farley, E.: Shirley Maclaine—she's not worried, Los Angeles Times, p. 6-1, December 2, 1980.

70. Ferguson, M.: Images of women in literature, Boston, 1973, Houghton Mifflin Co.

71. Fernandez, R.C.: Let's turn off the soap opera image of nursing! RN 43(9):77, 1980.

72. Firestone, S.: The dialectic of sex, New York, 1972, Bantam Books, Inc.

73. Fonseca, J.D.: The public and not so public image of nursing, Nursing Outlook 28(9):539, 1980.

74. Frazer, D.: An American nurse in Paris, New York, 1963, Pocket Books.

75. Frazer, D.: Nurse with a past, New York, 1964, Pocket Books.

76. Frederics, V.: More for doctors; only, New York, 1962, Pocket Books.

77. Frieze, I., and others: Women and sex roles—a social psychological perspective, New York, 1978, W.W. Norton & Co., Inc.

78. Frost, M.: Facts and fantasies—out of date images are responsible for some of the unrest in nursing, Nursing Times 74(43):1779, 1978.

79. Gaddis, P.: Heiress Nurse, New York, 1959, Prestige Books, Inc.

80. Gaddis, P.: Big city nurse, New York, 1963, MacFadden-Bartell Co.

81. Gaddis, P.: A nurse called Happy, New York, 1963, MacFadden Books.

82. Gaddis, P.: Nurse Christine, New York, 1963, MacFadden Books.

83. Gaddis, P.: Bayou nurse, New York, 1964, MacFadden Books.

84. Gaddis, P.: Everglades nurse, New York, 1965, MacFadden Books.

85. Genital Hospital: carry on bedpan babes, Swedish Erotica Magazines and Books.

86. Glass, L., and Brand, K.: The progress of women and nursing: parallel or divergent? In Kjervik, D., and Martinson, I., editors: Women in stress: a nursing perspective, New York, 1979, Appleton-Century-Crofts.

87. Goldstone, P.: Romance novels, chapter 1: Hollywood comes courting, Los Angeles Times, Calendar section, p. 3, February 8, 1981.

88. Goldstone, P.: Silhouette's format for true love, Los Angeles Times, Calendar section, p. 4, February 8, 1981.

89. Goodman, E.: [Title unknown] The Boston Globe Newspaper Company/Washington Post Writers Group.

90. Greenleaf, N.P.: Coming to terms with Nurse Ratched, Supervisor Nurse 7(6):48, 1976.

91. Greer, G.: The female eunuch, New York, 1971, McGraw-Hill Book Co.

92. Hallmark Greeting Card: Birdwatcher's Guide, card no. 90C 343L.

93. Hallmark Greeting Card no. 60KC 140M.

94. Hallmark Greeting Card no. 50C 342Q.

95. Hallmark Greeting Card no. 50C 3964.

96. Hancock, L.A.: West End nurse, Philadelphia, 1943, The Blakiston Co.

97. Hanson, D.: Born to lose? Soap Opera's Greatest Stories 4(3):44, 1981.

98. Harvey, G.: Doctor's nurse, New York, 1961, Pyramid Books.

99. Haskell, M.: From reverence to rape: the treatment of women in the movies, New York, 1974, Penguin Books.

100. Hauptmann, G.: What you always wanted to know about sex and nurses but were afraid to ask, Wilmington, Del., 1973, Eros Publishing Co.

101. Heller, J.: Catch-22, New York, 1963, Dell Publishing Co., Inc.

102. Hendrix, K.: After the war—women Vietnam vets seeking peace of mind, Los Angeles Times, p. 7-1, January 11, 1981.

103. Holloway, T.: The nurse on Dark Island, New York, 1969, Ace Books.

104. Homewood, H.: Final harbor, New York, 1980, McGraw-Hill Book Co.

105. Horde, M.: The black night nurses, USA, no publisher given.

106. Horney, K.: Feminine psychology, New York, 1967, W.W. Norton & Co., Inc.

107. Hot knight nurse, Peachfuzz Pussies 2(1):40.

108. Hott, J.R.: Updating Cherry Ames, American Journal of Nursing 77(10):1581, 1977.

109. Hughes, L.: The public image of the nurse, Advances in Nursing Science 2(3):55, 1980.

110. Humphries, A.: Flight nurse, New York, 1955, Berkley Publishing Corp.

111. Jaffe, D.S.: The masculine envy of woman's procreative function. In Blum, H.P., editor: Female psychology—contemporary psychoanalytic views, New York, 1977, International Universities Press, Inc.

112. James, J.: A cap for Kathy, New York, 1959, Golden Press.

113. James, J.: Assignment in Alaska, New York, 1960, Golden Press.

114. James, J.: Junior nurse, New York, 1960, Golden Press.

115. James, J.: Senior nurse, New York, 1960, Western Publishing Co., Inc.

116. James, J.: Private nurse, New York, 1962, Golden Press.

117. James, J.: Peace Corps nurse, New York, 1965, Western Publishing Co., Inc.

118. Janeway, E.: Between myth and morning, New York, 1974, William Morrow & Co., Inc.

119. Japenga, A.: Intensive care transport for ailing infants, Los Angeles Times, p. 5-1, February 6, 1981.

120. Kalisch, P.A., and Kalisch, B.J.: Perspectives on improving nursing's public image, Nursing and Health Care, p. 10, August 1980.

121. Keller, M.C.: The effect of sexual stereotyping on the development of nursing theory, American Journal of Nursing 79(9):1585, 1970.

122. Kernberg, O.: Object relations theory and clinical psychoanalysis, New York, 1976, Jason Aronson, Inc.

123. Kesey, K.: One flew over the cuckoo's nest, New York, 1962, The New American Library, Inc.

124. Kirby, J.: Olympic duty, New York, 1965, Golden Press.

125. Knaus, W.A.: We can't solve the nursing shortage until we treat nurses with more respect, Los Angeles Herald Examiner, p. 1-18, November 25, 1980.

126. Kramer, M.: Reality shock: why nurses are leaving, St. Louis, 1974, The C.V. Mosby Co.

127. Laughlin, H.P.: The ego and its ideal, New York, 1979, Jason Aronson, Inc.

128. Lee, A.A.: How—and where—the handmaiden image is changing, RN 42(6):36, 1979.

129. Lee, A.A.: How nurses rate with MDs—still the handmaiden, RN 42(7):21, 1979.

130. Lee, A.A.: Nursing's shopworn image: how it hurts you . . . how it helps you, RN 42(9):42, 1979.

131. Lee, A.A.: We want you, we need you . . . RN 42(6):25, 1979.

132. Levy, L.: Patience have patience!! Activity book, Greeting Card.

133. Lewis, F.M.: The nurse as lackey: a sociological perspective, Supervisor Nurse 7(4):24, 1976.

134. Lieb, R.: Power, powerlessness and potential—nurse's role within the health care delivery system, Image 10(3):75, 1978.

135. Lippman, W.: Stereotypes. In Shrodes, C., and others, editors: Reading for rhetoric, New York, 1962, Macmillan, Inc.

136. Loewe, J.: Nurses say work conditions may interfere with care, Pasadena Star News, p. C-10, January 28, 1981.

137. Lowry, N.: Clayton, Richards, M.D., New York, 1962, Paperback Library, Inc.

138. Maccoby, E.E.: The effects of television on children. In Rogers, D., editor: Issues in child psychology, Belmont, Calif., 1969., Brooks/Cole Publishing Co.

139. MacLeod, J.S.: This much to give, Toronto, 1961, Harlequin Books.

140. MacPherson, M.: Rampant sexism found in books for children, St. Paul Dispatch, Family Life Magazine, p. 20, June 15, 1971.

141. Marriner, A.: Conflict theory, Supervisor Nurse 9:12, April 1979.

142. McCarty, P.: Survey shows a million RNs employed, The American Nurse 12(9):1, 1980.

143. McElfresh, A.: Nurse for Mercy's Mission, New York, 1969, Dell Publishing Co., Inc.

144. McElfresh, A.: Doctor for Blue Hollow, New York, 1971, Dell Publishing Co., Inc.

145. McElfresh, A.: Flight nurse, New York, 1971, Dell Publishing Co., Inc.

146. Media present inaccurate image of nursing, The American Nurse 11(8):7, 1979.

147. Miles, B., and others: Channeling children—sex stereotyping on prime time T.V., Princeton, 1975, Women on Words and Images.

148. Miller, J.B.: Toward a new psychology of women, Boston, 1976, Beacon Press.

149. Mitchell, K.: Emergency doctor, New York, 1963, Dell Publishing Co., Inc.

150. Moura, J., and Sutherland, J.: Tender loving care, Edinburgh, 1969, John Bartholomew & Son, Ltd.

151. Neubauer, W.: Prison nurse, New York, 1962, Avon Books.

152. New 'House Calls' gal, National Enquirer, November 25, 1980.

153. Newton, L.: A vindication of the gentle sister: comment on the fractured image. In Spicker, S., and Gadow, S., editors: Nursing images and ideals, New York, 1980, Springer Publishing Co.

154. Oakley, A.: Woman's work: the housewife, past and present, New York, 1974, Vintage Books.

155. Pogrebin, L.C.: Growing up free—raising your child in the 80's, New York, 1980, Mc-Graw-Hill Book Co.

156. Polansky, N.A.: Ego psychology and communication, Chicago, 1971, Aldine Publishing Co.

157. Prince, H., director: Evita [stageplay], Los Angeles, Spring 1981.

158. Rees, B.L.: Television talk shows: an untapped resource for nursing, Nursing Outlook 28(9):562, 1980.

159. Rich, A.: Of woman born, New York, 1976, W.W. Norton and Co., Inc.

160. Richter, L., and Richter, E.: Nurses in fiction, American Journal of Nursing 74(7):1280, 1974.

161. Roberts, S.: Hope Farrell—Crusading nurse, New York, 1968, Prestige Books, Inc.

162. Roberts, W.D.: Nurse a mystery villa, New York, 1967, Ace Books.

163. Rogers, P.: How sexism haunts nursing, RN 42(2):105, 1979.

164. Roheim, G.: Psychoanalysis and anthropology, New York, 1950, International Universities Press, Inc.

165. Rosen, M.: Popcorn Venus, New York, 1973, Avon Books.

166. Salisbury, A.: Hospitals out of patience with sloppy nursing standards, Los Angeles Herald Examiner, p. I-1, Novembre 24, 1980.

167. Salisbury, A.: How to be a nurse without a license: just call a registry, Los Angeles Herald Examiner, p. A-1, November 25, 1980.

168. Salisbury, A.: One hospital's cure: a registry of its own, Los Angeles Herald Examiner, p. I-2, November 24, 1980.

169. Sav-on will end boy/girl toy sections, Los Angeles Herald Examiner, p. A-9, November 18, 1980.

170. Schorr, T.M.: Nursing and the public press, American Journal of Nursing 80(2):235, 1980.

171. Sears, R.M.: Timberline nurse, New York, 1965, Dell Publishing Co., Inc.

172. Sears, R.M.: Jolie Benoit, R.N., New York, 1970, Dell Publishing Co., Inc.

173. Sears, R.M.: Nurse in Acapulco, New York, 1971, Dell Publishing Co., Inc.

174. Shainess, N.: Women's liberation—and liberated woman. In Arieti, S., editor: The world biennial of psychiatry and psychotherapy, vol. 2, New York, 1974, Basic Books, Inc.

175. Smiley, V.K.: Nurse Kate's mercy flight, New York, 1968, Ace Books.

176. Stewig, J., and Higgs, M.: Girls grow up to be mommies: a study of sexism in children's literature, School Library Journal, p. 44, January 1973.

177. Stromborg, M.F.: Relationship of sex role identity to occupational image of female nursing students, Nursing Research 25(5):363, 1976.

178. Sweeney, J.: Nurse shortage hampering hospital, Los Angeles Times, p. 2-6, November 20, 1980.

179. Tatham, J.: Cherry Ames—rest home nurse, New York, 1964, Grosset & Dunlap, Inc.

180. Thurkettle, M.A., and Jones, S.L.: Conflict and systems process: theory and management, Journal of Nursing Administration, p. 39, January 1978.

181. Townley, R.: Are the soaps new and improved? T.V. Guide 28(50):4, 1980.

182. Triebich, S.J.: Burwyck's wander, New York, 1967, Lancer Books, Inc.

183. Wald, C., and Papachristou, J.: Myth America: picturing women 1865-1945, New York, 1975, Pantheon Books, Inc.

184. Weitzman, L.J.: Sex-role socialization in picture books for preschool children. In Lasky, E., editor: Humanness: an exploration into the mythologies about men and women, New York, 1975, MSS Information Co.

185. Wells, H.: Cherry Ames, student nurse, New York, 1943, Grosset & Dunlap, Inc.

186. Wells, H.: Cherry Ames, veterans' nurse, New York, 1943, Grosset & Dunlap, Inc.

187. Wells, H.: Cherry Ames, army nurse, New York, 1944, Grosset & Dunlap, Inc.

188. Wells, H.: Cherry Ames, chief nurse, New York, 1944, Grosset & Dunlap, Inc.

189. Wells, H.: Cherry Ames, senior nurse, New York, 1944, Grosset & Dunlap, Inc.

190. Wells, H.: Cherry Ames, flight nurse, New York, 1945, Grosset & Dunlap, Inc.

191. Wells, H.: Cherry Ames, staff nurse, New York, 1962, Grosset & Dunlap, Inc.

192. Wheelock, A.: The tarnished image, Nursing Outlook 24(8):509, 1976.

193. Williams, J.H.: Psychology of women—behavior in a biosocial context, New York, 1977, W.W. Norton & Co., Inc.

LINDA HUGHES

Chapter 8

Little girls grow up to be wives and mommies

Nursing as a stopgap to marriage

A critical examination of the history of nursing can provide tremendous insight into the process and the consequences of being female in a patriarchal society. As an occupation long viewed as specially suited to women, nursing has mirrored the myths permeating women's existence throughout history. Barriers created by restrictive and oppressive social ideologies about women have served to retard the growth of nursing as a profession and to limit the full development of nursing's potential. The educational, economic, and political struggles that have typified the nursing profession are based to a large extent on the mythical beliefs about women that have been perpetuated by a male-dominated society.

The mass media, reaching millions of people, are a powerful tool that serve not only to communicate current events but to "dispense values and influence social behavior."[24] By communicating attitudes and opinions the mass media have played a significant role in shaping the image of women and in defining their place in society. A graphic example of the manner in which the media have transmitted attitudes and values about women is the interpretation of nurses and their role in newspaper and magazine articles and in popular books.

A recent historical study examined the portrayal of nurses by the print media.[21] This study concluded that an idealistic image of the nurse has been presented and that, although this image often lacked realism, it reinforced specific ideas about women that were commonly accepted by society. Several mythical beliefs appeared as recurrent themes in the media's interpretation of the nurse and her role. Each of these mythical beliefs is based on specific ideas about women that are generally held to be true by society (see Chapter 7). This chapter examines one of these myths—the marriageability of nurses—and discuss its effects on the nursing profession.

157

NURSING: THE NEW (?) ROAD TO MATRIMONY

In *Women and Economics*, published in 1898, Charlotte Perkins Gilman summarized women's socialization with this comment: "Where young boys plan for what they will achieve and attain, young girls plan for whom they will achieve and attain."[16] Marriage and motherhood have been the societal expectations of women. With nursing predominantly a woman's occupation, public interest in the marriageability of the nurse was clearly evident. Indeed, nursing as a vocational pursuit was publicly legitimized on the grounds that it enhanced a woman's chance for marriage and that training as a nurse would provide a woman with excellent preparation for marriage and motherhood.

Improve your chances for marriage: become a nurse

The print media have repeatedly implied that nursing facilitates the attainment of the marriage goal. This was rationalized in two ways. First, by portraying the nurse as a glamorous and romantic figure, the media indicated that nurses were extraordinarily attractive to men. Second, nursing provided women repeated exposure to men who were thought to be the ultimate potential marriage partners, namely physicians.

Many of the articles written about nurses in popular literature depicted the ideal nurse as the romantic embodiment of true womanhood. As a paragon of purity and virtue, the nurse was viewed as particularly attractive to any man in search of a wife. This idea was clearly expressed in an article written by a nonnurse published in *Good Housekeeping* in 1915:

> There is something about the nurse . . . that makes the rest of us women jealous. A man summed it up the other day when he said, "What on earth is it about a nurse that makes a man want to marry her every time?" [Nursing is] that very high development of all qualities known as "womanly." [The nurse] seems to be a sort of embodied womanhood raised to the nth power.[9]

Several "true life" stories about nurses have been printed in popular magazines, each depicting the ideal nurse who, the readers are told at the conclusion of the article, is busily preparing for her upcoming wedding.* These articles subtly implied that the ability of these women to attain a husband was strongly influenced by the fact that they were nurses. In a profile of a student nurse in 1955, for example, *Woman's Home Companion* quoted the student as saying, "I hope to marry eventually. . . . Some of my friends . . . predict that I'll wind up married soon after graduation. . . ."[1] Two years later *Look* published an article about an emergency room nurse and reported that this nurse had met her husband while on duty: "At their first meeting, he caught the twinkle in her eye."[13] Comments like these left little doubt that nursing was the "new road to matrimony" as it had been so aptly described in 1897.[37]

Although the public was encouraged to believe that nursing practice was fraught

---

*References 2, 13, 15, 46.

with romantic encounters, nurses engaged in day-to-day practice were well aware that this romantic view of nursing hardly typified reality. One nurse responded to a "true life" story that had been printed in the *Saturday Evening Post*. In a letter to the editor in 1954, this nurse noted that the article presented an unrealistic image of nursing practice. Commenting on the effect this article could have on potential students, the nurse clearly stated, "If any poor souls . . . seek a career in nursing with the sole intent of nabbing a husband . . . they are making the biggest mistake of their lives. . . . The fool's paradise . . . depict[ed] just doesn't exist. . . ."[7]

Although the "fool's paradise" did not exist in reality, it definitely existed in the popular magazines and books to which women were exposed. Young women interested in nursing as a vocation were highly susceptible to this form of romantic fantasizing. Nonnurses were hardly in an advantageous position to analyze critically the myths about nurses that abounded in the public press.

Becoming a nurse was thought not only to make a woman more attractive to men but also to afford women greater opportunities to find a suitable husband, in short, a physician husband. The print media repeatedly assured women that a nurse had an excellent chance of marrying a physician.[42,43] As an article in *Mademoiselle* pointed out in 1967, "a homely nurse is more likely to marry a young physician or medical student than is a homely secretary or teacher. . . . One nurse . . . estimated that about 75 per cent of her nurse friends are either married to, or about to be married to, physicians or medical students."[19]

The print media clearly implied that finding a physician husband was one of the major rewards of a nursing career. Women were told that "young doctors strove mightily in the sickroom . . . to keep from flirting with [nurses]"[35] and that "most nurses can hardly avoid marrying doctors—not that they are to be avoided."[18] As an article in *Ladies' Home Journal* elaborated, a woman entered nursing "surely not for the money alone. . . . She has a far better chance of finding a husband among the interns or her patients."[49] The same idea was expressed by one woman's mother on learning that her daughter had chosen to enter nursing school. This nurse commented that her mother "wasn't really reconciled until the day came when she could comfort herself with the possibility of my salvaging a doctor-husband out of the fiasco."[38]

On a superficial level the marriage myth appears to be true. The vast majority of women do marry, and nurses are no exception. Indeed, there are many nurses who marry physicians. Herein lies the element of truth that has strengthened and perpetuated the myth. However, the implication underlying the myth is a social lie that stems from the deception created in the minds of women. Nursing is neither glamorous nor a romantic escapade. Nursing is hard work, and certainly the work carries with it a great deal of responsibility. Most professional occupations are advertised on an economic basis, in terms of salary and fringe benefits, and on the basis of the social status afforded to their members. Obviously if nurses marry doctors, then doctors are marrying nurses. The media never implied, however, that young men should enter the medical profession because it would facilitate their chances of obtaining a nurse wife. Nursing has been perhaps the only profession advertised on the basis of the ability of its members to marry. Indeed, the vocation advertised by the marriage myth was actually marriage, not nursing. The fact that most articles were directed to a potential nurse audience clearly points to the role of the mass media in reflecting the social expectation that women marry.

Additionally, the promise of marriage to a physician did little to depict the actual working relationship that has historically existed between physicians and nurses. Physician-nurse relationships are more often fraught with conflict than spiced with love. Ashley[4] clearly documented the sexist and paternalistic attitude of many physicians toward nurses during the first half of this century. In current times, playing the doctor-nurse game in the work setting typifies the neurotic and unhealthy relationship that often exists between nurses and physicians.[41] Many physicians fail to see the value of establishing a collaborative relationship with nurses; rather, they continue to view nurses as their subordinates, inferior to them in status. As one physician commented only 7 years ago, "I am a little bit more careful not to jump a nurse . . . because I hate to overuse my authority. I'm more inclined to get mad at someone of my own status."[14]

Prepare for marriage and motherhood: become a nurse

Nursing as a vocation for women was legitimized because it provided excellent preparation for marriage and motherhood. The print media implied that it did not matter whether a woman actually practiced nursing or how long she practiced, because the training would not be wasted—it would be invaluable to her when she embarked on her "real" roles in life, being a wife and mother. Women were told that for a nominal tuition and "three years of interesting work a girl could buy herself . . . perfect preparation for marriage and motherhood."[28] Only 10 years ago *The New York Times* printed this comment: "[Nursing is] a good vocation for a girl—she can always use it after she gets married."[31]

This rationale was repeated numerous times during the war years in an effort to recruit women to meet the demand for nurses. During World War I, for example, a physician writing to a congressional representative suggested that women be drafted to attend nursing schools. He provided the following justification for his proposal:

> After our girls have taken the course in a training-school for nurses and have served their two years, they will be better fitted to perform their duties as mothers and I unhesitatingly state that infant mortality will be considerably reduced if the mothers have practical knowledge of nursing.[29]

During World War II the same argument was used to promote the recruitment of potential nurses. As an article in *Good Housekeeping* reported in 1942, "Graduate nurses who give up their profession for homemaking will have had a better practical preparation than other young married women. They will have learned invaluable lessons in hygiene and nutrition and in the care of babies."[6]

Although there is little question that a practical knowledge of nursing could be helpful to potential wives and mothers, the purpose of nursing education is to prepare one to be a nurse. Home nursing courses could have prepared women to be wives and mothers in a less expensive and less time-consuming manner. It is again significant to note that the career promoted by these comments was not really nursing. Nursing simply provided women with a vehicle to achieve their ultimate goal: marriage and motherhood.

Inherent in the argument that nurses' training prepared one for marriage and motherhood was the message that nursing was only a stopgap occupation for women. Once a woman had achieved the goal of marriage, there was little reason to continue active nursing practice. The media assured women that at any time they would be able to "trade their caps for a wedding ring."[10] In 1961 *Good Housekeeping*, reporting on the life of a student nurse, commented that she would practice nursing "at least until she gets a start on her personal long-range plan of providing TLC to four children of her own."[27]

In 1918 a war recruitment article printed in *The New York Times* stated that "Even to those who do not care to continue in the nursing profession after the war the training will be of inestimable value."[3] This comment was repeated 32 years later in an anonymous letter to the editor of *The New York Times* from a registered nurse. This nurse stated that "Young women seeking a career would do well to give nursing more than a passing thought. . . . There is nothing to prevent a graduate nurse leaving her profession at any time. . . . If she marries, her nurse's training will be of inestimable value to her in rearing a family."[33]

The print media socialized women long before they entered the profession to view nursing as an occupation that did not require a long-term commitment from its practitioners. This socialization has had a tremendous impact. The work force in nursing has historically followed a sporadic pattern of employment. A study conducted by the National League of Nursing indicates that "most graduates [of nursing schools] work only one to five years before dropping out for marriage or other considerations."[40] Typically, employment of nurses during the childbearing years declines and rises again during the middle years of life to be followed by a decline again as nurses approach retirement age. A recent study conducted by the American Nurses' Association indicated that although younger nurses are remaining employed in nursing longer, the overall pattern of sporadic employment continued to typify the profession. This study also concluded that 30% of the nurses licensed to practice in the United States were unemployed. Within this group of unemployed nurses, 27% were not actively seeking employment in nursing at the time of the study.[32]

The marriage myth implied and supported two basic social assumptions about women: that woman's primary goal is to marry and raise a family and that marriage and the pursuit of a career are incompatible goals for a woman. Superficially women were encouraged to adopt nursing as a vocation, yet actually they were allowed no real freedom to determine their own ultimate futures.

The motivation underlying the print media's emphasis on the marriageability of the nurse was two-fold. The obvious motivation was the attempt to recruit women for nursing work. The second motivation was the need to assure unmarried women that entering the job market as a nurse did not necessarily make a woman unattractive or unfeminine and therefore undesirable as a marriage candidate. Society's ideas about women implied that women, to be successful when entering the job market, were forced to sacrifice their "natural" womanly qualities and take on unfeminine (that is, masculine) characteristics of competitiveness, aggressiveness and independence.[48] Creating the image of the ideal nurse as a parallel to the virtuous woman implied that nursing, as a predominantly female occupation, was one exception to the rule about working women. It is significant, however, that this exception applied only until the nurse married.

"WOMAN'S PLACE IS IN THE HOME": THE IDEOLOGY OF FEMININE DOMESTICITY

The Industrial Revolution contributed to a new interpretation of women and their appropriate place in society.[11,22,34] Women were assigned to a sphere separate and distinct from that of men.[11] The concept of feminine domesticity explained and justified women's special role in society. Public interest in the marriageability of the nurse and the mythical themes that emerged in print relating nursing to marriage were based on the social ideology of feminine domesticity.

Prior to the Industrial Revolution the work roles of men and women were primarily based on home life and were in an economic sense quite similar. The Industrial Revolution separated work from home, and as a result men's work underwent a marked differentiation from women's work. As Oakley elaborates, "the woman became the non-employed, economically dependent housewife, and the man became the sole wage-or-salary-earner."[34] It was within the framework of a changing market economy that the concept of feminine domesticity emerged and gained widespread acceptance.

The concept of feminine domesticity identified the home as woman's "special sphere." In fact, the home assumed a special significance under this concept. Men, because of their aggressive, competitive, and self-reliant natures, were thought far better equipped to deal with the business world; women, virtuous and pure, cultivated a home environment that would preserve religious values, morality, and aesthetics. "Home and family became the emotional receptable for all the sentimental values and feelings middle-class men increasingly felt inhibited from exhibiting"[22] because of their frequent contact with the business world. "Women, through their reign in the home, were to sustain the 'essential elements of moral government' to allow men to negotiate safely amid the cunning, treachery, and competition of the marketplace."[11] As Cott concludes, "Defining [the home] as her province, the canon of domesticity made woman's household occupation her vocation."[11]

Employment outside the home had severe repercussions for women. "Female employment was condemned on moral grounds, on grounds of damages to physical health, on grounds of neglect of home and family, and lastly, simply on the grounds that it contravened the 'natural' division of labour between the sexes."[34] In addition to this, women who worked outside the home risked the loss of social respectability and a decline in their status as "ladies." The concept of feminine domesticity dictated that "women *became* ladies by staying at home, by behaving in what was considered a proper way, by devoting themselves to their husbands and children, and by developing 'feminine' traits."[22]

The concept of feminine domesticity was initially a middle-class ideology.[34] Many working-class women, however, out of economic necessity did work outside the home. Although this ideology emerged as early as the 1840s, it did not filter down to the working class until the latter part of the nineteenth century. Oakley notes that "The idea that work outside the home for married women was a 'misfortune and a disgrace' became acceptable to the working classes only in the last decades of the nineteenth century."[34] Even with the growing numbers of working women in the twentieth century, the ideology of feminine domesticity has prevailed. Being a housewife and mother continues to be a woman's primary vocation, and employment outside of the home is secondary to or at best an addition to her real vocation in life.

The emergence of this concept of feminine domesticity is significant when juxtaposed with the historical development of nursing. The growth of nursing as a profession closely paralleled the growing acceptance of this ideology by society. Nightingale established her training school for nurses at Saint Thomas' in 1860. Three training schools for nurses, modeled after the Nightingale school, opened in the United States in 1873. By 1896 American nurses had created a professional association, the Nurses' Associated Alumnae of the United States and Canada (later renamed the American Nurses' Association). By the turn of the century nurses were advocating improved educational standards and legal recognition of the trained nurse. By 1903 three states had passed nurse registration laws.

At a time when nursing was developing as a suitable vocation for women and was seeking well-bred and respectable recruits, society told women through the concept of feminine domesticity to remain at home and cultivate "ladylike" characteristics. Certainly these messages were conflicting and confusing. On one hand, women were told that their proper place was in the home; on the other hand, they were introduced to a new vocation that was especially suited to them because of their "innate" maternal and nuturing qualities. The marriage myths bridged the gap between these two conflicting expectations for women. These myths made a nursing vocation compatible with the existing ideology of feminine domesticity.

THE REALITY BEHIND THE MYTHS

Social ideologies about women have profoundly influenced nursing, which "suffers from the same oppression, prejudices, and limitations as women in our society."[17] By communicating messages about the marriage potential of nurses and by suggesting that nursing required only a temporary or transient commitment, the print media reflected long-standing prejudices and limitations related to women and their employment.

Assumptions that marriage and motherhood are the only long-term vocations for women have had important consequences for nurses and for women in general. From an economic perspective, women have been faced with cruel and unjust treatment in the job market. As Katz and Rapone summarize this reality, "The legitimacy of women as paid workers is undermined by the assumption that their primary social roles are to serve as wives and mothers. The justification for occupational and wage discrimination has been based on the view that women workers are less committed to their jobs."[25]

In other words, women and nurses are at a stalemate. Women have been socialized to view marriage and motherhood as their primary vocation in life, but when women express a commitment to these vocations, they are economicaly discriminated against. Ironically, the discrimination is based on the very commitment that society expects of women.

Many employers have historically viewed women's work as temporary or a supplement to the husband's income. Therefore there has been little incentive to upgrade the wages assigned to women's work. In an analysis of women in the labor force Blau points out, "There are some who argue that women do not need to earn as much as men. . . . Single women who work are only biding their time before marriage, so the argument goes, and married women are only supplementing their husband's already ample incomes."[5]

Coupled with wage discrimination that exists in nursing and in other women's occupations, the opportunity for job advancement is fairly limited. Certainly this has been particularly true for nurses who have worked sporadically. Job promotion is often based on longevity of employment. Those who have left nursing to raise a family have often sacrificed potential opportunities for promotion. This has kept many nurses in low wage-earning positions.

The basic assumption underlying the view that nursing is only a stopgap occupation is that a career is incompatible with marriage and motherhood. This assumption does have some basis in reality. Nurses with children have faced numerous obstacles in their attempts to work. Inflexible working hours, tours of night duty, and inadequate child-care facilities, for example, have hampered nurses' attempts to maintain their employment after the birth of children. Hospitals, the primary employers of nurses, have historically displayed little interest in providing flexible alternatives to solve the problems working mothers face. In a recent study of the nursing shortage directed by Wandelt,[47] child-care responsibility was cited as an initial and continuing reason for withdrawal from nursing practice.

Ashley Montagu, in a telling statement on the price that women pay as a result of their socialization, noted that "at the time when the male is preparing for that period in his life when his creativeness is likely to be at its highest, the female is turning in a totally different direction. . . . During the years spent in childbearing and child rearing . . . whatever other creative abilities she may have had tend to fall into desuetude, to become dull and atrophied."[30]

Perhaps the most lasting and pervasive effect of the loss of nursing practitioners resulting from marriage and motherhood has been the loss of potential nursing leaders and the stifling of creativity in nursing. Nurses have continually reinvented the wheel where patient care is concerned. Over the years the nursing profession has educated hundreds of thousand of women, many of whom have remained in practice for only short periods of time or, as Kelly aptly noted, functioned as "the 'appliance nurse'—the one who works only long enough to pay for the new household appliance."[26] This type of work history has neither promoted the growth of nurses as professional practitioners nor facilitated the development of new knowledge in nursing.

One obvious consequence of women's tracking toward domesticity or motherhood has been the constant disparity between the number of nurses licensed to practice and the number who actually do practice. The withdrawal of nurses from practice for reasons of marriage and motherhood has added to the shortage of nurses that has existed in varying degrees since World War II. To suggest that the current nursing shortage is the result solely of nonworking married nurses would be simplistic. The reasons are multifaceted and complex. Certainly the shortage has a direct relationship to the low wages and the poor working conditions that have typified nurses' employment. Reports about the nursing shortage printed in the popular media, however, often cited marriage as one of the primary factors in the shortage.

In 1949, for example, a writer for the *Saturday Evening Post* elaborated on the nursing shortage by commenting that most newly graduated nurses are "of marriageable age [and therefore] an unrecorded but considerable proportion of graduates practice but briefly what they learn."[44] Thirteen years later *Changing Times* reported on the shortage and provided the following explanation for the high turnover rate among nurses: "turnover in the profession is fairly high—not because of dissatisfaction but because many women get married and take on family responsibilities."[8] Moreover, *The New York Times* commented in 1974 on the shortage and listed "marriage, pregnancy, dislike of night and weekend duty, and the preference for a favorable job climate" as the major reasons for the high turnover rate among hospital nurses.[20]

The nursing shortage has been translated by the popular media to mean inadequate and substandard patient care. Numerous accounts have been published about neglect of patients resulting from the shortage of nurses. Indeed, several accounts attributed the death of patients to the absence of a nurse in close attendance at the bedside. In 1959, for example *The New York Times* reported that two infants had died of "respiratory ailments" contracted as a result of being fed from propped bottles, a practice undertaken by the nursing staff because of the shortage of personnel.[36] A survey conducted by *The New York Times* in 1966 learned that "digitalis, quinidine, insulin and antibiotics were not given in many municipal hospitals during night shifts because of the shortage of nurses."[45] The phrase "nocturnal death syndrome" was coined in 1970 to describe the nursing shortage because so many deaths occurred at night "when nursing staffs are almost non-existent."[39]

During the past decade health care facilities across the United States have experienced severe shortages of nurses. Newspapers and magazines report that a lack of qualified nurses has led to the closing of hospitals beds and delays in opening newly constructed hospital wards. The public is being told, in effect, that their access to health care is being curtailed by the shortage of nurses.

A hospital administrator in 1952 concluded that most inactive nurses had "prematurely retired."[23] The implication was that if the pool of inactive nurses would only return to active practice, the shortage would be alleviated. The historical expectation of women and nurses, however, has been that they *should* prematurely retire to devote themselves to their husbands and families. Once again, nurses are stalemated in a game in which the rules constantly change. When the public's need for nurses is less acute, nurses are encouraged to express primary commitment to home and family; withdrawal from practice for marriage and motherhood is acceptable and appropriate (after all, nursing is only a stopgap). When the need for nurses is acute, however, nurses should adjust their commitment to reflect their professional obligation to provide care. Nursing requires devotion and allegiance from its members. The failure to respond to the public need can result in harm or even death for patients.

OVERCOMING THE MYTHS

Myths exert a powerful and subtle influence on society. Daly[12] pointed out that myths serve to justify and perpetuate the patriarchal society in which we live and that they "close off depths of reality which would otherwise be open to us." Although the word *myth* implies an imaginary or fictitious basis for a belief, myths are not readily assumed to be false. In fact, mythical beliefs are largely unquestioned by society because they reflect values and beliefs that are consciously and unconciously adhered to by individuals. Questioning the authenticity of myths means examining the authenticity of the values and beliefs on which these myths are based. This sort of critical examination, although painful, is an essential task facing nurses and women in general.

Nurses need to engage in serious consciousness raising in an effort to enhance their own awareness of the extent to which the social ideologies about women have dictated their behaviors and their achievement of professional goals. Nurses have suffered from the same restrictions and limitations that have been imposed on women in general. These restrictions and limitations have narrowed women's options and robbed them of the freedom to make choices that would directly affect their lives. Only by retracing the past can nurses gain the understanding that is necessary to create solutions to the problems that currently face the profession. Understanding the past and its influence on the present can only result in a healthier and more productive society for both men and women.

REFERENCES

1. Acuille, J.: I had to grow up in a hurry, Woman's Home Companion **82:**38, 1955.
2. Ames, L.: Nurses' aide, Life **12:**44, 1942.
3. Army will train nurses for the war, New York Times, p. 7, June 30, 1918.
4. Ashley, J.: Hospitals, paternalism, and the role of the nurse, ed. 2, New York, 1977, Teachers College Press.
5. Blau, F.: Women in the labor force: an overview. In Freeman, J., editor: Women: a feminist perspective, Palo Alto, Calif., 1975, Mayfield Publishing Co.
6. Bromley, D.: Do you want to be a nurse? Good Housekeeping **114:**42, 1942.
7. Byers, B.: Letter to the editor, Saturday Evening Post **226:**4, 1954.
8. Careers in nursing, Changing Times **16:**29, 1962.
9. Comstock, S.: Your daughter's career: if she wants to be a nurse, Good Housekeeping **61:**736, 1915.
10. Conley, V.: RN—those magic initials, Today's Health **38:**66, 1960.
11. Cott, N.: The bonds of womanhood, New Haven, Conn., 1977, Yale University Press.
12. Daly, M.: Gyn ecology: the metaethics of radical feminism, Boston, 1978, Beacon Press.
13. Emergency angel, Look **21:**106, 1957.
14. Fleeson, L.: Doctors diagnose nurses, Ms **2:**71, 1973.
15. Flight angel, Cosmopolitan **134:**112, 1953.
16. Gilman, C.P.: Women and economics. In Rossi, A.: The feminist papers, ed. 2, New York, 1974, Bantam Books, Inc.
17. Heide, W.: Nursing and women's liberation: a parallel, American Journal of Nursing **73:**824, 1973.
18. Higher learning urged for nurses, New York Times, part 2, p. 4, December 8, 1940.
19. Hoffman, R.: The angel of mercy is dead, Mademoiselle **66:**134, December 1967.
20. Hospitals are vying for nurses, New York Times, p. 97, December 1, 1974.
21. Hughes, L.: Nursing and the public: images and opinions of the profession, 1896-1976, master's thesis, Denton, Tex., 1978, Texas Woman's University.
22. Hymowitz, C., and Weissman, M.: A history of women in America, New York, 1978, Bantam Books, Inc.
23. Inactive nurses sought, New York Times, p. 30, September 4, 1952.
24. Kalisch, P., and Kalisch, B.: Perspectives on improving nursing's public image, Nursing and Health Care **1:**12, 1980.
25. Katz, E., and Rapone, A.: American women and domestic culture: an approach to women's history. In Katz, E., and Rapone, A., editors: Women's experience in America, New Brunswick, 1980, Transaction, Inc.
26. Kelly L.: Goodbye, appliance nurse, Nursing Outlook **27:**432, 1979.
27. Markel, H.: SN, Good Housekeeping **153:**34, 1961.
28. Mayor, M: How to get nurses galore, Reader's Digest **56:**116, 1950.
29. Mobilizing women as nurses, Literary Digest **57:**33, 1918.
30. Montagu, A., The natural superiority of women, ed. 3, New York, 1976, Macmillian, Inc.
31. Morris, B.: Some girls feel called to nursing even before grade school, New York Times, p. 16, April 17, 1971.
32. Moses, E., and Roth, A.: Nursepower, American Journal of Nursing **79:**1745, 1979.
33. No unemployment for nurses, New York Times, p. 26, April 12, 1950.

34. Oakley, A.: Woman's work, ed. 2, New York, 1976, Random House, Inc.
35. Perry, G.: Nurses are lucky girls, Saturday Evening Post **226:**24, 1954.
36. Phillips, V.: 2 babies who died in hospital were fed with propped bottles, New York Times, p. 25, September 26, 1959.
37. Priestley, E.: Nurses a la mode, Nineteenth Century **41:**31, 1897.
38. Russell, S.: A lamp is heavy, Philadelphia, 1944, J.B. Lippincott Co.
39. Sibley, J.: Deaths here laid to lack of nurses, New York Times p. 1, November 13, 1970.
40. Signs of an end to shortage of nurses, U.S. News and World Report **72:**94, 1972.
41. Stein, L.: The doctor-nurse game, American Journal of Nursing **68:**101, 1968.
42. Student Nurse, Cosmopolitan **142:**62, 1957.
43. Thruelson, R.: RN, Saturday Evening Post **220:**34, 1948.
44. Titus, H.: The return of the practical nurse, Saturday Evening Post **221:**38, 1949.
45. Tolchin, M.: City may close a major hospital, New York Times p. 1, July 6, 1966.
46. Villet, B.: More than compassion, Life **72:**68, 1972.
47. Wandelt, M., and others: Why nurses leave nursing and what can be done about it, American Journal of Nursing **81:**72, 1981.
48. Weitzman, L.: Sex-role socialization. In Freeman, J.: Women: a feminist perspective, Palo Alto, Calif., 1975, Mayfield Publishing Co.
49. Who has heard the nightingale? Ladies' Home Journal **65:**11, 1948.

MYRITA K. FLANAGAN

Chapter 9

An analysis of nursing as a career choice

Considerations of the *what* of nursing are incomplete without some examination of *who* nurses are and *how* they came to be nurses.

When examining the wealth of literature dealing with nurses and nursing, one notes the emergence of a rather distressing pattern: nursing as a profession yearly admits hordes of inadequately counseled students (predominantly white females) into a variety of educational programs, all ostensibly preparing their graduates to function as professional nurses and all having extraordinarily high dropout rates. Those students who do complete their educational programs are then extruded into workplaces that frequently bear little or no relation to the ideology or the practical preparation provided by the educational institution; then, to the amazement and consternation of all, they burn out, suffer reality shock, or are in some way incapable of practicing nursing as defined by themselves or by the profession.

Because this cycle is repeated endlessly, it is important to attempt to examine it in sequence. There are no hard and fast explanations or any easy solutions for the problems, but an awareness of some of the facts and an attempt to explain parts of the cycle might lead to a better understanding of the whole.

HOW THE CHOICE IS MADE

The latest available statistics show that the enrollment in basic nursing programs throughout the United States is over a quarter of a million students.[5] There seems to be no lack of aspirants to the ranks of nurses, although the level of knowledge about the field possessed by candidates prior to enrollment must be questioned.

The written material available to the individual considering nursing as a career might possibly discourage more students than it entices. The *Occupational Outlook Handbook*, describing the functions of nursing, says a registered nurse "follows the medical regimen prescribed by the physician." It goes on, in an acknowledgement of changes in the field, to state, "Some RN's, after advanced training, become nurse practitioners and perform services, such as physical examinations, that traditionally physicians have handled."[18]

Unfortunately the *Occupational Outlook Handbook*[18] can be considered to paint an exciting, challenging picture in comparison to the description of nursing found in the *Encyclopedia of Careers and Vocational Guidance,* which says the nurse "works under the supervision of a physician and cares for patients."[9] The personal characteristics required of nurses, according to the *Encyclopedia,* are "good health, stamina, an even temperament and a real desire to devote her life to the service of others."[9] The *Occupational Outlook Handbook* suggests the need for "physical stamina because of the time spent walking and standing" and "emotional stability to cope with human suffering."

Describing what nursing is and what nurses do is by no means an easy task; however, the "strong back, weak mind" image conjured up by the vocational literature can only serve to discourage intelligent, independent, creative, caring young people from even considering nursing as a career.

Some evidence indicates that the decision to become a nurse is frequently made before the stereotypical descriptions found in the vocational literature are even an issue. Fox[6] found that the largest percentage of nursing students made their career choices before the age of 17. Only 10% of the study group had chosen nursing as their major field of study after age 17, compared to 41% of college women enrolled in non-nursing majors. Obviously nursing has great appeal to children and early adolescents; however, this appeal is conceivably not coupled with any in-depth knowledge about the specifics of the role.

That many who decide to become nurses lack knowledge is supported by evidence from a nationwide survey of high school seniors, which reported a positive response to nursing in general and extreme ignorance about what it is that nurses actually do. In addition, the study revealed that both students and guidance counselors were uninformed about the academic prerequisites for entry into a nursing program.[20]

WHO CHOOSES NURSING

Given the general ignorance about the reality of nursing and the prevalence of misinformation and stereotyping, who does choose nursing? Most frequently it is the oldest daughter in a family that has two or more siblings and is Christian. The stated reason of most students for their career choice is most often, "to help others."[12]

Males in nursing

Less than 2% of nurses are men, and whereas the latest enrollment figures show a slight increase in numbers of male students, the overall percentage of men in the field does not appear to be changing very rapidly. As one might predict, men in nursing do report experiencing role strain in attempting to reconcile their gender role with their occupational role. Men in nursing most frequently choose psychiatry, anesthesiology, or administration as occupational areas. These areas may serve to diminish the perceived role strain because they require less physical contact with clients, frequently mandate no special clothing that signals "nurses," and often provide a greater degree of autonomy.

It is both interesting and dismaying to note that the men participating in a study conducted by Greenberg and Levine[7] expressed blatantly sexist opinions of their female counterparts, charactrizing them as "husband hunting," suffering "personality instability," and "needing a greater amount of physician approval." Psychodynamically these attitudes might be seen as an attempt at role reconciliation, but the behaviors linked to such attitudes can only intensify the misunderstandings and conflicts within nursing and further drain energy needed to deal with other issues.

With the many role and status contradictions inherent in being a "male nurse," one questions why any men make such a career choice. Greenberg and Levine[7] report that the majority of men in their sample had originally intended to enter medical school but for either financial or academic reasons had gone into nursing. Bush[2] reported that in her survey job security and opportunity, interest in the biological sciences, and the desire to work in a humanistic field were the stated reasons for the choice of nursing for men. Many of the men in nursing have had previous work experiences as medical corpsmen or hospital orderlies, and within the traditional military and hospital hierarchies their status change to registered nurse might be viewed as positive.

Nursing has recently made an effort to actively recruit increased numbers of male students, but attributing this increased recruitment activity solely to the changing perceptions of male and female roles in society at large may at best be premature. At issue is whether nursing, reflective of the larger society, is moving into a less rigidly gender-defined phase or whether nursing continues in a traditionally female mode and perceives the need for increased numbers of men to assume leadership positions and raise the power and prestige of the profession as a whole. Some notion that having men in nursing is a boon might be inferred from the facts that 78.8% of male RNs as opposed to 64% of female RNs hold positions in hospitals and that less that one third of these men hold staff-level positions whereas over one half of female nurses are employed at that level.[5]

Of additional concern is the reported preference of male students for the technical rather than psychosocial aspects of nursing practice.[21] This could be of critical importance as nursing continues its struggle to escape the handmaiden stereotype, and it certainly acquires more importance when the overrepresentation of men in supervisory and administrative positions is considered.

Minorities in nursing

Yet another facet of the question of who chooses nursing is the underrepresentation of minorities. Approximately 5% of the currently registered nurses are identified as belonging to minority groups, with about 3.3% identified as black.[5] The latest available statistics on nursing school enrollments show an increase in the numbers of minority students, but the current percentage of minority students does not approximate the percentage of minorities in the general population. This underrepresentation has been attributed to a number of factors that might be understood as a reflection of larger societal issues. It does not seem to be the case that nursing is rejected as a career choice by minority students because it is regarded as encompassing demeaning, stereotypical "care" responsibilities; rather, it seems that these students are inadequately counseled about the academic requirements and are therefore not prepared to enter schools of nursing.[20] Yet another factor is the reported lack of positive experience with registered nurses and the resultant lack of social-relatedness to the role.[25] This social estrangement seems to persist even among black students enrolled in nursing programs who are reported to feel less related to the school and their peers than are black students enrolled in other departments in the same colleges.[4]

The limited research available suggests that blacks and other minority groups may feel socially uncomfortable in the role of professional nurse, but it is in no way clear whether this discomfort arises from role strain—the status role in conflict with a cultural or societal role—or whether it arises from the profession itself, which is overwhelmingly white and female.

HOW NURSES ARE EDUCATED

The variety of educational programs available in nursing is confusing both to the individual who is making the career choice and to the profession as a whole. In 1965 the American Nurses' Association formally took a stand on the educational preparation required for entry into the profession. It mandated the baccalaureate degree as basic preparation for professional nursing practice and the associate degree as preparation for technical practice. This scheme had first been proposed some 30 years earlier, and now over 15 years later the confusion and the intramural war is still raging—all parties intransigent on the issue of which educational system provides the preparation for the "best" nurse.

The associate-diploma-baccalaureate dilemma

The various educational programs purport to prepare students for different occupational goals within nursing, but it is doubtful whether these functional differences are communicated to entering students. The choice of any program seems to be less an informed career decision than one based on chance. A survey of students in all types of programs indicated that students selecting a baccalaureate program did so out of a desire for both a college education and nursing as a career choice, whereas the majority of students in associate degree programs made their selection on the basis of the convenient location of the school and the shorter length of the program.

Students enrolled in diploma programs reported that their choices were made out of a desire to find a program that would better prepare them to "nurse."[12]

Students' expectations for their future jobs, and in fact their image of nursing, do not appear to differ among different educational preparations.[11,12] The varying educational routes for entry into practice both illustrate and perpetuate the role confusion and ambivalence of the profession as a whole. This confusion exacts a further price from those graduates who have chosen the wrong preparation for their subsequent practice aspirations. Of students enrolled in baccalaureate programs, 14% are graduates of either associate degree or diploma programs,[5] and a survey of diploma program seniors indicated that some 70% were planning to enroll in baccalaureate programs after completing their present program.[3] This seems a tremendous waste of both student time and educational resources and is undoubtedly the source of many nursing dropouts.

Selection and attrition

The attrition rate in educational programs is also of concern; baccalaureate programs have a dropout rate of 41%, associate degree programs 44%, and diploma programs 26%.[12] This suggests that "reality shock" occurs early for many students and lends credence to the thought that there are great deficiencies in prevocational guidance and counseling for students interested in nursing as a career. Withdrawal rates of this magnitude do not indicate a commitment level necessary in choosing a professional career.

Students' selection of programs of nursing must also be questioned. There have been many studies investigating reliable predictors of success in schools of nursing, but to date the evidence is contradictory and inconclusive.

Previous scholastic achievement is a major contributing factor to success, at least partially refuting the "strong back, weak mind" stereotype. Knopfe[12] found a 61.1% program-completion rate for students who were in the top quarter of their high school graduating class, whereas only 8% of the students who were in the bottom half of their high school class completed their nursing programs. Similarly, Seither[22] found that high school grade average was the most accurate predictor of grade point average in the biological sciences and that the grade average in these courses was the most accurate predictor of passing scores on State Board Examinations.

The educational and occupational background of the student's parents may also be a factor contributing to attrition in the educational program. Hutcheson and others[10] found that the higher the father's educational level, the more likely the student was to drop out of nursing program. Conversely, the higher the mother's occupational status, the less likely the student was to drop out. There is no mention of those students who had both a highly educated father and a mother with a high occupational status.

Investigations of specific personality characteristics of nursing school dropouts have also failed to isolate any reliable predictors. Knopke[13] found that nonsuccessful students had greater needs for structure and organization and lower needs for self-assertion and exhibition of leadership than did successful students. In the group studied by Oleson and Whittaker,[19] however, students who dropped out showed more ability in complex thinking, greater impulse expression, and lower authoritarian needs than did their classmates who completed the program.

Since there seem to be no hard and fast predictive criteria, the prevailing admissions practice in many schools of nursing appears to be to take in a broad range of students and live with the high attrition rates, a policy that places an immense burden on faculties and schools in terms of both tangible and intangible resources. This problem will undoubtedly continue until the general public and therefore prospective students have a clearer idea of what nurses do, until nursing can more clearly and definitively delimit its requirements for entry into practice, and until schools of nursing more clearly articulate their philosophies so that students are better able to make informed choices based on their own goals and aspirations.

Admission and completion statistics for schools of nursing provide only an outline of the problems in contemporary nursing. The crucial determinant of nursing's future involves what goes on during the educational experience, affectively as well as didactically.

Faculty influence

There are 1360 schools preparing "professional nurses." These schools employ nearly 25,000 faculty members full and part time.[17] It is most likely that these 25,000 individuals are the most crucial and influential members of the profession, for those who are the gatekeepers control the fate of the profession. It is entirely within the realm of possibility that nursing faculty members hold highly subjective views about precisely who is suitable for nursing and then tailor their admissions accordingly. The characteristics of a suitable nurse set forth by Florence Nightingale still pervade the public image of nurses and nursing, and it is likely that these qualities—moral rectitude, refinement, obedience, diligence, and self-sacrifice—are part of the sensibilities of nursing faculty. Benton[1] points out that the independent, questioning, skeptical student can pose problems for any educator but that it is precisely this student that nursing can and must appeal to. One must ask, however, if the image of nurses and nursing promoted by diploma schools pervades many collegiate schools of nursing where students are still selected for traditional qualities and programs are still geared to produce "Nightingale nurses."

The process of role acquisition occurring within the educational system is ultimately of greater importance than the didactic material taught. Specific pieces of knowledge rapidly become obsolete whereas the more intangible components of professional education attain more permanence; one suspects that a large share of nursing's difficulties are attributable to its seeming inability to educate nurses for the future.

Oleson and Whittaker[19] found that successful students soon become experts at "fronting," that is, determining faculty expectations and then attempting to be ideal students for the faculty. Fronting includes projecting a high level of interest, enthusiasm, and competency at all times. The resulting environment then becomes one of intellectual and affective mediocrity, and the students tend to remain essentially untouched by the educational experience. Gunter's study[8] of self-actalization levels in nursing students supports the observations that growth does not occur during the educational process. She found that the majority of students had not yet reached, by reason of their age, either social maturity or a high level of self-actualization and questioned their ability to establish the therapeutic relationships with patients that were expected of them.

Shortridge[23] investigated the impact of the educational milieu on attitudes and found that students developed an even stronger commitment to the popular image of nurses during the educational process. Students fixed on the nurse as "giver of physical care" and never developed a favorable attitude toward either research or management as activities for professional nurses.

A distressing implication is that part and parcel in nursing's dilemma is the propensity to select inappropriate students and then never truly touch them in the educational process. This engenders an "as if" quality to the entire profession—let us select students "as if" the selection criteria were reliable and valid and "as if" we shared with them an image of nursing as a profession, let us educate them "as if" there was a common level of emotional maturity and readiness, and let them graduate "as if" they were committed to professional values and "as if" nursing practice and nursing ideology were congruent. For nursing to attain the power and prestige it covets, this "as if" behavior must cease. Perhaps part of the problem lies in the role models, or the lack of them, available to the practitioner. There are approximately 1.4 million individuals in the United States who have the educational preparation to practice nursing, yet only about half of these are presently engaged in practice. Kramer[14] cites the critical necessity to provide role models, and Yura and others[26] state, "nurses lack a sense of themselves as leaders and few role models exist."

There is a common belief that educators must serve as role models for the profession. Indeed, many faculty members perceive themselves as role models while believing that staff nurses should function in that capacity. At the same time students believe that faculty members should act as role models yet state they must frequently look elsewhere.[16] This discrepancy seems to further muddy the professional socialization waters with increasing frustration and alienation. Indeed, faculty should serve as role models—for nursing educators, for professional ideals and values, and for ideal and isolated givers of specific care—but nurses need role models in the practice setting.

Vance's study[24] of contemporary nursing leaders provides interesting contrasts between nurses and those who are publicly acknowledged as nursing's leaders. For example, although over 70% of employed nurses work in hospitals or nursing homes, the great majority of influential nurses have no clinical involvement; 81% of all nurses hold less than a baccalaureate degree, but only one designated nursing leader does so.[24] The contrasts are many, illustrating concrete differences between most practicing nurses and those who are the profession's acknowledged leaders.

• • •

And thus we go on, a vast number of individuals claiming membership in nursing. The resolution of conflicts and problems intra- and extra-professionally will most certainly not be either immediate or perfect. Leininger[15] points out that the culture of nursing is evolving and can be characterized as having two divisions, between the traditional "angel of mercy" and the emerging, career-oriented individual who is less angel and more businessperson. Evolution is a time-consuming process, however, and time will not stand still to wait for "the girls." If nursing continues to vacillate, placate, and stall, it will like the dinosaurs find itself extinct. Unless nursing as a profession, is willing to make some hard decisions and provide clear and unambiguous norms, the cycle will continue and nursing will be increasingly unable to attract quality candidates or retain its most able practitioners.

REFERENCES

1. Benton, D.W.: You want to be a what? Nursing Outlook 27:388, 1979.
2. Bush, P.J.: The male nurse: a challenge to traditional role identities, Nursing Forum 15:390, 1971.
3. Career goals of hospital schools of nursing seniors, Chicago, 1975, American Hospital Association.
4. Claerbaut, D.: The black nursing student at the liberal arts college: a study in alientation, Nursing Forum 15:211, 1976.
5. Facts about nursing, Kansas City, 1977, American Nurses Association.
6. Fox, D.J.: Career decisions and professional expectations of nursing students, New York, 1961, Teacher's College Press.
7. Greenberg, E., and Levine, B.: Role strain in men nurses, Nursing Forum 10:416, 1971.
8. Gunter, L.M.: The developing nursing student, Nursing Research 18:60, 1969.
9. Hopke, W.: The encyclopedia of careers and vocational guidance, vol. 2, Chicago, 1975, J.G. Ferguson Publishing Co.
10. Hutcheson, J.D., and others: antecedents of nursing school attrition, Nursing Research 28:57, 1979.
11. Kaiser, J.F.: A comparison of students in two types of nursing programs, doctoral dissertation, 1974, Teacher's College Columbia University.
12. Knopfe, L.: From student to R.N.: a report of the nurse career pattern study, Bethesda, Md., 1972, Department of Health, Education and Welfare.
13. Knopke, H.J.: Predicting student attribution in a baccalaureate curriculum, Nursing Research 28:224, 1979.
14. Kramer, M.: Reality shock: why nurses leave nursing, St. Louis, 1974, The C.V. Mosby Co.
15. Leininger, M.: Nursing and anthropology: two worlds to blend, New York, 1970, John Wiley & Sons, Inc.
16. Melick, M.E., and Bellinger, K.: Role modeling in nursing: a comparison of baccalaureate student and faculty beliefs, Journal of the New York State Nurses' Association, 10:23, 1979.
17. Nurse Faculty Census, New York, 1977, National League for Nursing.
18. Occupational Outlook Handbook, Washington, D.C., 1980, U.S. Department of Labor.
19. Oleson, V., and Whittaker, E.: The silent dialogue, San Francisco, 1968, Jossey-Bass, Inc.
20. Rudov, M.H., and others: High school seniors attitudes and concepts of nursing as a profession, Bethesda, Md., 1976, Department of Health, Education and Welfare.
21. Schoenmaker, A.: Nursing's dilemma: male versus female admission choice, Nursing Forum 15:406, 1976.

22. Seither, F.F.: Prediction of achievement in baccalaureate nursing education, Journal of Nursing Education **19:**28, 1980.

23. Shortridge, L.: Attitudes of freshman and senior baccalaureate nursing students toward professional nursing behaviors, doctoral dissertation, 1977, Teachers College, Columbia University.

24. Vance, C.N.: A group profile of contemporary influentials in American nursing, doctoral dissertation, 1977, Teacher's College, Columbia University.

25. Winder, A.E.: Why young black women don't enter nursing, Nursing Forum **10:**56, 1971.

26. Yura, H., and others: Nursing leadership: theory and process, New York, 1976, Appleton-Century-Crofts.

Chapter 10

Why doesn't a smart girl like you go to medical school?

The women's movement takes a slap at nursing

Wake up! Get conscious! Women are no longer *The Second Sex!*[4] We need no longer believe in *The Feminine Mystique*[6] that idealizes housewifery and traditional subservience. *Sisterhood is Powerful*[21]! Our eyes are opened to the *Sexual Politics*[19] that confined us to *Woman's Estate*[20]: motherhood, wifehood, nursing, teaching, and the secretarial arts. Rejoice! *Man's World* [is fast becoming] *Woman's Place.*[14]

The women's movement deserves a great deal of credit for raising the consciousness of women to their situation, to sexual discrimination, and to opportunities that should be available for all people at home and at work. This book would never have been written were it not for feminists and feminism. We as nurses have gained immeasurably from their influences. We have also lost.

Naturally, as women have become aware of their burgeoning potential, they have abandoned traditional roles and struck out to explore new territories: medicine, law, banking, and the trades. Sisterhood, we have learned, is important because we share a common history (*her*story). And so we have also learned to support each other's struggles, to applaud each other's victories, to feel pride in each other's accomplishments (as much as anyone can take pride in the accomplishments of another), to learn from and respect each other . . . sometimes . . . for in the eagerness of some women to embrace new roles has come a denigration of old ones. No one, these women say, *should* want to be *just* a housewife; no one with brains should want to be just a nurse. Have a career! Be a doctor!

That is not what feminism is about. Feminism mandates that each person be free to choose whatever role she/he desires without discrimination or harassment. Why, then, have women come to see nursing as second rate? Because *some* women have accepted nursing by default when they preferred medicine? Because it is *just* a woman's profession? Because it's a "natural" role that requires nurturing rather than brains? We know why men need to view nursing in demeaning, stereotypical ways, but how is it that newly conscious women are beginning to do the same?

My intention in this chapter is to explore the motivations of nontraditional

178

women who denigrate women in traditional roles, specifically nurses, and to describe how these same motivations exist within nursing and are evidenced in the denigration of some nurses by others. The origins of these behaviors are identical and are derived from early female socialization.

REACTIONS TO FEMALE CONDITIONING: SUGAR AND SPICE AIN'T SO NICE AFTER ALL

The entire first section of this book discusses female development, sex-role socialization, sexual politics, and discrimination; therefore I will touch only briefly on what applies here. We know, for example, that female children are less desirable than male children, that from birth, little girls are treated differently than little boys, that girls learn to be passive and dependent, and that women have problems with self-esteem.

Feminist psychologists and psychoanalysts[12,24] have refuted traditional Freudian postulates that women feel inferior because they lack a penis. "Of course," they've said, "women feel inferior. Who wouldn't given the parental and societal messages girls receive that they are somehow second best?" Little girls don't envy their brother his genitalia; they envy his right to wear jeans, to climb trees, to build model airplanes, to come and go with fewer restrictions, to aspire to anything he wants to be!

Concomitant with a desire for things "male" is the need for girls to identify with other females, especially their mothers. How can little girls *want* to be female when things "female" include washing dishes, ironing clothes, cleaning out refrigerators, sweeping, and dusting—things that are boring and devalued by society? They do learn the appropriate roles, however, if only to survive. They internalize those values that females are second best, subservient, silly . . . whatever! And often they live with ambivalence, low self-esteem, and a disparaging attitude toward their own kind.

The roots of women's own antiwomanism are easy to trace. In addition to society's message that women are second-class citizens, their own ambivalence and passivity hamper achievement.[3,11] They are not as successful as they could be, *and* they know it, *and* they relate it to being female: "I'm not good at math so I couldn't very well be a scientist." The hidden but acknowledged message here is that *girls* are not good at math. Ambivalence and passivity not only hamper achievement but also prevent women from expressing overtly their natural feelings of anger, frustration, and aggression. Women learn to channel such feelings into indirect behaviors and to avoid open conflict because they have been taught that conflict drives others away, and women, more than men, are dependent on the love and approval of others.[11] The difficulty with covert expressions of anger, however, is that they leave the woman feeling "like a bitch," "like a nag," and "petty"; they leave her doubting that she's been heard and angrier still at her own impotence; they leave her vulnerable to depression, the turning in of angry feelings toward herself.[13]

Dependency has other implications: it means that women by needing approval from others are forever vulnerable to hints of disapproval and rejection, it means that women rely on *men* for approval rather than on themselves or other women, and it means that rivalry with other women for male attention flourishes (when the goal is get a man, get a date, get a husband).

The devaluation of females, which women themselves internalize, together with socialized behaviors such as passivity, dependence on males, rivalry among females, and avoidance of success create a culture in which women hate themselves and other women.[21]

UP FROM THE GHETTO: LITTLE MISS MUFFET DOESN'T LIVE HERE ANYMORE

Being discriminated against is one thing. Many women refuse to acknowledge the evidence of sexism in their lives through defenses such as denial and repression. But being discriminated against and *knowing* you're being discriminated against— having your consciousness raised—is another. For these women, awareness of sexism brings with it glimmerings of awareness about themselves; their insecurities, their anxieties, their failed defenses, their self-deprecation. Being discriminated against and knowing it is like being an oppressed minority.

Women are certainly not a numerical minority, but they *are* treated in similar ways and do experience discrimination. Women like minorities have been forced to identify with a group that is devalued by society; they grow up needing to identify with other women, a group that society tells them is inferior. Self-hatred and hatred of one's own group result.[10,17] Studies have shown that the psychological characteristics of oppressed minorities and of women are similar and result in similar behaviors[7,10,21]

- □ Denial of membership in one's own group
- □ Denigration of other members of the group
- □ Glorification of and sympathy for the oppressor
- □ Acceptance of one's own inferiority, self-scorn, and self-blame
- □ Withdrawal and passivity
- □ Slyness and cunning
- □ Strengthening of in-group ties; aggression and revolt

It is easy to recognize the defensiveness of such behaviors. Some are extrapunitive, meaning they turn the hurt and rage of being oppressed outward against others; some are intrapunitive, meaning they turn those same feelings inward against the self. Frieze and others[7] have identified two of these—"identification with the dominant group and aggression against one's own group"—as being most common among women. I would suggest that underlying these behaviors is the defense mechanism of denial, specifically *denial of membership in the female group*. This allows a woman to tell herself, "I'm different. I'm not like *them*. I'm better. I'm special. I'm whatever." She can believe others when they tell her, "You're not like all the other women I know" or "You don't look like a nurse." Little Miss Muffet, in other words, repudiates her tuffet, her background, her origins.

Identification with the dominant group

Sociologists who study oppressed minorities describe their behavior as "identification with the dominant group"; those who study people thrust into foreign, hostile environments call it "going native," by which they mean adopting wholeheartedly the foreign nationality and culture[16]; psychologists speak of a defense mechanism called "identification with the aggressor."[2,5] Regardless of the name, they are all talking about the same defensive (and usually subconscious) process whereby an individual militates against feelings of helplessness, anxiety, or fear by becoming like the feared or threatening person(s). Women assume the desired or envied qualities of men for themselves, denying their weakness or helplessness and feeling strong like the dominant group. Identification involves more than being strong or aggressive or active like men, however; it means taking on the attitudes of men, including their attitudes about women.

Aggression against one's own group

Denial of female ties and identification with men allow women to *turn against other women*. They scorn the "cattiness" or "silliness" of females. Unfortunately, beneath the hostility to other women, lies a repudiation of and hostility to the self.

> Another form of self-hatred may not [appear to] include oneself, but may describe one's feeing for other members of one's group because they possess the qualities that the dominant group devalues. This behavior is common among professional women, particularly those who have achieved high status. . . .These women, who have made it, or are trying to make it in a masculine, often hostile environment, look with scorn at traditional women, as the cause of men's antifemale attitudes.*

Some women, then, view other women as inferior (as do men). They devalue the work of women. They insist that their doctors, lawyers, and dentists be men; they take their problems to men for solution rather than consulting with female peers.

"Horizontal hostility," or violence against one's own peers, as Kennedy[15] calls it, becomes manifest in yet other behaviors: *sibling rivalry* and *competitive dueling*. When the goal is masculine approval, women, of course, become rivals and work against rather than with each other.

Although Frieze and others[7] did not find the other victim behaviors—self-deprecation, self-blame, withdrawal, passivity, slyness, cunning, and obsequiousness—manifest as commonly in women as in minorities, others have. As has been said, passivity necessitates directing one's anger in covert ways, sometimes against oneself. This *leads* to self-deprecation, self-blame, and withdrawal, all symptoms of

---

*Frieze, I., and others: Women and sex roles—a social psychological perspective, New York, 1978, W.W. Norton & Co., Inc.

depression. Slyness, cunning, and obsequiousness, on the other hand, also contain hostility, but it is directed outward in a covert, passive way.

I believe that *all* these behaviors involve women's anger against men for having oppressed them. Denying one's membership in the female group, identifying with men, passive aggression, and depression also include anger against *women*, with whom each woman of necessity has identified in achieving her own female sexual identity. The term for these identifications is *introjects*. They are the mental representations in every person's mind of people who helped form her/his identity. The key to understanding how one turns anger against oneself is the understanding that one is directing that anger at the mental image, the introject, which is part of one's own psyche.

I'M O.K.—YOU'RE NOT O.K.: FEMINIST POTSHOTS AT NURSING

The women's liberation movement has, as I have said, affected nursing in many positive ways. It has also inadvertently, hurt nursing, by opening the door to career opportunities for women. Nursing, with its traditional handmaiden image, no longer has a captive audience and may no longer be able to attract the best, brightest, most creative women. They are going elsewhere. We as nurses cannot blame feminism for that, not if we honestly believe that equality means the freedom of each individual to choose whichever career she/he desires.

We *can* blame those feminists, however, who disparage or attack nursing or who in exploring career opportunities omit nursing altogether; we can point out the antiwomanism and self-hate inherent in such actions. For these women, becoming "conscious" has involved identification with masculine characteristics *and* a denial of females who cling to traditionally feminine ones. Adoption or repudiation of certain traits is the right of any individual, but the expectation that all people become like oneself is wrong. Ellen Strong,[23] in describing her dislike of the cleaned-up ex-junkie, puts it well. She says, "He'd seen the light, and now out-Puritaned the Puritans."

Seeing the light for some women has meant identifying with male oppressors and disparaging traditional groups such as nurses and housewives. This has been evidenced overtly when feminists have openly ridiculed nurses and nursing and covertly when they have avoided or omitted them. It occurs, for example, in the *New York Women's Directory*,[25] which tells the reader, "women's work is no longer limited to . . . nursing" (true); but which in subsequent chapters extolling the virtues of nontraditional careers omits nursing altogether. The message is then that nursing no longer exists as a choice.

Even Letty Pogrebin,[22] a woman well known for her efforts toward nonsexist child rearing, a woman who tries to sound positive about nursing, fails. In her book on working women she discusses the nursing shortage and sympathizes with the difficulties nurses have in male-dominated health care areas. Then she says, "Mothering is the key word used by all the dedicated professional women I interviewed." (Nurturing, perhaps; Mothering, NO!) Worse yet, she cites Dr. Judith Lorber, a sociologist, as saying that nursing is partly to blame for nursing problems (true), *but* (there's always a "but") she goes on to quote, " 'College graduated nurses acquire skills like pharmacology or psychiatry which prepare them to be more than mothers to patients . . . they're ready to be Assistant Doctors.' " There's so much that's wrong here: the emphasis on motherhood, the insinuation that nurses are getting above themselves, the notion that knowledge is the exclusive province of medicine, and even her inaccuracy in citing pharmacology and psychiatry, which nurses have always learned, as being to blame.

Nursing writers have wrongly denounced the women's movement for encouraging women to choose other careers because nursing loses out.[9] Women should be free to choose nursing or medicine (or anything else for that matter). Nursing's job is three-fold: to point out discrimination from any source, male or female; to attract the kinds of women it seeks by altering its image if necessary; and to encourage women in all occupations to retain traditionally feminine characteristics such as caring, nurturing, and humaneness.

I'M O.K.—YOU'RE NOT O.K.: NURSES AGAINST OURSELVES

Nurses too engage in antiwoman and antinurse behaviors; nurses too channel their aggression against others and against themselves; nurses too express anger covertly. Nurses, after all, are mostly women and have not learned to value themselves.[1]

Within nursing and among nurses we find all the behaviors discussed above. There are, for example, continuing battles between nursing education and nursing service, between nursing administration and nursing staff, and among graduates of the three preparatory programs, associate degree, diploma, and baccalaureate degree nurses. Much nursing communication is frought with bickering, fault finding, and name calling.[18]

Aggression against the group is typified by such behaviors. Infighting among nursing educators, for example, involves *sibling rivalry*, as do squabbles between educators and individuals in nursing service, criticisms of graduates of one program by graduates of another, and scapegoating of one nursing unit (or one nurse) by another. Something is usually at stake: tenure, promotions, approval (usually of a male doctor or administrator), or some other gain. The nurses' own self-esteem, however, is the real underlying issue in this game of one-upsmanship (sic). It is as if one nurse can only be up by putting another (or the group as a whole) down.

It is difficult to separate out specific instances of *identification with the aggressor* from instances of aggression against the group because they are closely linked. Aggression against the nursing group usually involves some identification with the values of the aggressor. For example, a nursing director who aligns herself with a hospital administrator against nursing staff has both identified with the aggressor *and* acted against her own kind. The same is true of the nurse who bypasses her colleagues and uses physicians as her source of information and approval. She has openly identified with the aggressor, and covertly she has slapped her nursing peers by not respecting their knowledge and ability to help her.

I am reminded of an alumni dinner I once attended at which an ex-classmate said, "You're in private practice as a psychotherapist? Well . . . I'd never come to you. You're still just a nurse!" "Let's leave off the 'just,' " was my response, and I think that single word is germane to the notion that it is threatened self-esteem that provokes such behaviors as identifying with aggressors and attacking one's colleagues. Finally, it is not only those who have achieved or gotten ahead who denigrate other women. In this case, it was a diploma graduate who took me to task for having gotten above myself. The enmity goes up and down and sideways.

Fragile self-esteem, the product of female socialization, makes nurses vulnerable, makes them them want to identify with doctors and hospital administrators, makes them strike out at other nurses, makes them defend and defend and defend against the realization that they as women and as nurses are devalued. To this end they occasionally deny that they are nurses. For example, Miriam Gilbert,[8] a nurse writing in a feminist book, entitled her article, "Women in Medicine." So that the reader would understand her choice, a footnote explains, "Most 'women in medicine' are nurses, not doctors—so it was thought more realistic to have the following article than any on the same subject by a woman doctor." I applaud their use of an article about nursing, but couldn't they have used *nursing* in the title? It wouldn't have been the "same subject" if a doctor had written it, would it? Why get defensive about wanting to include the article by quoting statistics about the number of nurses? I can almost hear the words: "But some of my best friends are nurses. . . ."

That article, like many others, *tries* to be positive. (But the need to *try* implies the presence of something negative that must be overcome). The author suggests that many women who chose nursing might, if they had had free choice, have chosen medicine. A valid point. She suggests too that there are men in medicine who might prefer nursing. Also valid. She ruins it, however, by phrasing it thus: "I have seen many men who, in my opinion, are third-rate doctors and would, unquestionably, have been first-rate nurses if they, too, had not been victimized by a double standard."[8] Well, *I* question it!

Of course, the most dissociated nurse is the one who evades questions about her job by saying, "I teach" or "I'm a child-birth instructor" or "I'm a therapist." That person is no longer a nurse. And as I have said, there is nothing wrong with not being a nurse. Something is definitely wrong, however, if the same person who avoided calling herself a nurse must defend this avoidance with explanations. Her rationalizations are many, but they tell us, again, that the woman-nurse-whatever is conflicted and anxious about *her* status, about *our* reaction, and probably about many other things.

I would like to say to nurses, then, "Choose! Be a nurse, or don't be one, but make your choice and be happy about it!" The thing is, I cannot say that to women in general for obvious reasons. I would like to say to both "By all means be aware. Share your consciousness. Encourage others to 'see the light.' But if they don't, or won't, or can't, don't do the very thing you're decrying—don't damn them for it." Sisterhood is powerful! And if we learn that, we can participate in the one minority group behavior rarely seen among women: the strengthening of in-group ties.

REFERENCES

1. Bush, M.A., and Kjervik, D.K.: The nurse's self image. In Kjervik, D.K., and Martinson, I.M., editors: Women in stress: a nursing perspective, New York, 1979, Appleton-Century-Crofts.
2. Cameron, N.: Personality development and psychotherapy, Boston, 1963, Houghton-Mifflin Co.
3. Cavenar, J.O., and Werman, D.S.: Origins of the fear of success, American Journal of Psychiatry **138**(1):95, 1981.
4. de Beauvoir, S.: The second sex, New York, 1974, Vintage Books.
5. Engel, G.L.: Psychological development in health and disease, Philadelphia, 1962, W.B. Saunders Co.
6. Friedan, B.: The feminine mystique, New York, 1974, Dell Publishing Co., Inc.
7. Frieze, I., and others: Women and sex roles—a social psychological perspective, New York, 1978, W.W. Norton & Co., Inc.
8. Gilbert, M.: Women in medicine. In Morgan, R., editor: Sisterhood is powerful, New York, 1970, Vintage Books.
9. Glass, L.K., and Brand, K.P.: The progress of women and nursing: parallel or divergent. In Kjervik, D.K., and Martinson, I.M., editors: Women in stress: a nursing perspective, New York, 1979, Appleton-Century-Crofts.
10. Hacker, H.M.: Women as a minority group. In Freeman, J., editor: Women: a feminist perspective, ed. 2, Palo Alto, Calif., 1979, Mayfield Publishing Co.
11. Hoffman, L.W.: Early childhood experiences and women's achievement motives. In Lasky, E., editor: Humanness: an exploration into the mythologies about men and women, New York, 1975, MSS Information Corp.
12. Horney, K.: Feminine psychology, New York, 1967, W.W. Norton & Co., Inc.
13. Jacobson, E.: The regulation of self-esteem. In Anthony, J.E., and Benedek, T.: Depression and human existence, Boston, 1975, Little, Brown & Co.
14. Janeway, E.: Man's world, woman's place, New York, 1971, Dell Publishing Co., Inc.
15. Kennedy, F.: Institutionalized oppression vs. the female. In Morgan, R., editor: Sisterhood is powerful, New York, 1970, Vintage Books.
16. Kramer, M.: Reality shock, St. Louis, 1974, The C.V. Mosby Co.
17. Krech, D., and Crutchfield, R.S.: Elements of psychology, New York, 1965, Alfred A. Knopf, Inc.
18. Menikheim, M.L.: Communications patterns of women and nurses. In Kjervik, D.K., and Martinson, I.M., editors: Women in stress: a nursing perspective, New York, 1979, Appleton-Century-Crofts.
19. Millett, K.: Sexual Politics, New York, 1970, Doubleday & Co., Inc.
20. Mitchell, J.: Woman's estate, New York, 1973, Vintage Books.
21. Morgan, R.: Sisterhood is powerful, New York, 1970, Vintage Books.
22. Pogrebin, L.C.: Getting yours: how to make the system work for the working woman, New York, 1975, Avon Books.
23. Strong, E.: The hooker. In Morgan, R., editor: Sisterhood is powerful, New York, 1970, Vintage Books.
24. Williams, J.H.: Psychology of women: behavior in a biosocial context, New York, 1977, W.W. Norton & Co., Inc.
25. Womanpower Project: The New York woman's directory, New York, 1973, Workman Publishing Co.

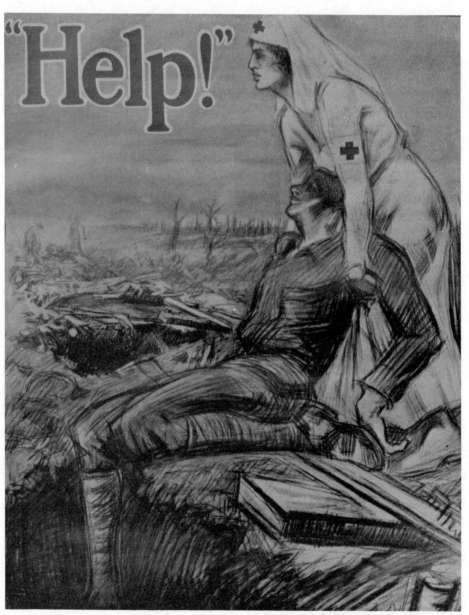

Photo by Gary Botkin; courtesy Blanche W. Pryor.

UNIT THREE

SOCIAL AND POLITICAL ISSUES

Once in nursing, women experience a variety of stresses—social, political, economic, and psychological. This section and the one that follows deal with such issues. The assignment of chapters as social and political or psychological is for the most part arbitrary, because most issues have ramifications in all areas.

Alma Lowery-Palmer contrasts the political orientation of nurses with that of political activists. She suggests that the nursing role often discourages those skills required for political activism. Nurses, she says, are socialized into "feminine" (dependent) behaviors. Her chapter examines the effects of nursing education, American culture, and the work environment of nursing autonomy and opportunity for expanded roles. Awareness of sociocultureal conditioning is a first step toward changing heretofore ineffectual behaviors by nurses.

In the workplace of most nurses, the hospital, Shirlee Passau-Buck likens interpersonal relations to those of the family: the doctor as father, the nurse as mother, and the patients as children. The supporting role of nurses to physicians is based on the patriarchal, familial model that assigns to men the intelligence-requiring jobs and assigns to women those that require only "natural" attributes. Women and nurses, then, receive little credit for their work. Their success, after all, is innate, assured by their very nature. Caring is automatic and requires neither brains nor skill. Curing, the physicians' role, is valued both cognitively and financially. "Physicians are well-paid for curing, but not so nurses for caring."

The relationship of doctors and nurses is not only similar to that of husbands and wives but also reflects another aspect of patriarchy, fathers and daughters. Mariann Lovell explores paternalism—the notion that if nurses will behave like good little girls then physician-daddies will love and care for them—and its effect on nursing autonomy. She gives us an historical overview of its propogation by medicine as a deliberate deception, a means of keeping nurses as subordinate handmaidens.

Specific conflicts between doctors and nurses are analyzed in the chapter by Beatrice and Phillip Kalisch. They explore issues such as the mutual lack of knowledge, differences in treatment emphasis, educational disparities, nurses' lack of commitment (as perceived by physicians), and mutual fears and distrust. Suggestions are

187

made for improving the relationship through better communications, team development, and education.

Female socialization and paternalism are important in keeping women-nurses "in their place." Also of importance, says Janet Muff, are altruism, socialism, and Nightingalism, ethics that repudiate individual rights and hence the self. Women learn that their main purpose is to care for others. If someone "needs," they must give. The self is second to others. This is the basis of altruism. Socialism mandates that the needs of some are a claim or *right* to the goods and services of others. Doctors and nurses and their services become the property of the state and may be distributed according to the needs of others. Nightingalism reflects the peculiar adaptation of altruism within nursing. The needs of patients, again, supersede the rights of nurses to determine when and whom they will serve. Such ethics repudiate the individual right of nurses (and doctors) to their own services and ultimately to their own lives.

These social, political, and philosophical influences, then, have resulted in the victimization of nurses. Victimization, however, required two participants, the victim and the oppressor. In her chapter *Toward Androgyny,* Patricia Geary Dean encourages nurses to foil their oppressors, to become assertive. She outlines a variety of areas within nursing where action is needed: the establishment of practice standards, the resolution of the associate-diploma-baccalaureate dilemma, increased responsibility for care, image building, mutual support and collegiality, and self-exploration, to name a few. Such activities, she suggests, will develop within nurses both "feminine" and "masculine" characteristics. They will become androgynous and able to exceed the traditional limitations of male and female roles.

Wilma Scott Heide in her chapter on feminist activism also looks at ways in which nurses have been and can continue to be active. Her focus takes us into the political arena. She calls for demystification of the "M.D.eity" and for participation by nurses in all health care issues. She affirms "feminine" strengths as necessary and valuable. She also endorses nurses' power in the sense of being capable and taking action. "*All* issues," says Dr. Heide, "are women's issues" and must be dealt with by nurses and women who must stop agonizing and begin organizing.

The last chapter in this section is a composite of the thoughts of several male nurses on their situation as members of a "woman's" profession. Their responses, when first questioned on the subject by Janet Muff, seemed so open and refreshing and hopeful that they were included in this unplanned chapter. Androgyny, it appears, is already a reality for these men. They have learned the value of opposite-sex traits, in this case nurturance and compassion.

ALMA LOWERY-PALMER

Chapter 11

The cultural basis of political behavior in two groups
Nurses and political activists

Nurses are the least political of all people in health care work.[29]
McFarland and Shiflet: *Role and Power in the Nursing Profession*

The nurse's role does not promote the development of the knowledge, attitudes, and skills required to participate actively in the political process. The lack of preparation for political activism among nurses affects them both as regular citizens and as members (or nonmembers) of professional organizations and potential agents of change in the health care arena. The political process, like the nursing process, is primarily interpersonal. How can one account, therefore, for the political apathy of nurses? A partial answer to this question lies in the contrasting societal and professional socialization of women-nurses and men–political activists.

The two groups, nurses and political activists, are subgroups of one larger community, and American society. The cultural ideas and expectations of the two groups have their basis, then, in a common ideological system. The contexts in which these ideas are acted out, however, lead to vastly different outcomes in terms of political behavior.

Each group has its own structural characteristics, its own means of recruiting members, enforcing its formal and informal rules, and governing individual's relations to themselves, to others, and to things.

The purposes of this chapter are to examine the professional socialization of nurses in terms of the cultural conception Americans have on the self, the self-other relationship, work, and the oppositional mode of thought and to show how male and female perceptions of these concepts shape the political thoughts and behaviors of nurses and political activists. More specifically, the chapter describes how the professional socialization of nurses leads to the development of behavior that is considered appropriate in the setting of nursing practice but is inappropriate and ineffective in the political arena. Finally, in the concluding discussion the chapter demonstrates why the rank and file nurse, to paraphrase Beals and others,[4] has come to want to act as she/he must act if the sociocultural system of the workplace is to be maintained.

This study is based on (1) an anthropological interpretation of research concerning professional socialization and political attitudes of nurses, (2) my experience as a participant-observer with the professional staff of United States Senator Daniel K. Inouye[22] (Democrat, Hawaii) during the summer of 1978, and (3) my own experience both as a student nurse and as a practicing nurse.

The professional socialization of political activists is not directly examined but is inferred from the traditional societal socialization of boys for male roles in American culture.

SELF

> Each to each a looking glass
> Reflects the other then doth pass.[8]
> C.H. Cooley: *Human Nature and the Social Order*

One's sense of self develops within a group and is a product of interaction with the social and physical world. In addition to the simple perception of oneself as an object, the self reflects comparisons made with other people. The way in which other people regard us is also central to our self-image. This view of the developing self-image is consistent with Cooley's[8] idea of the "looking glass self"; he asserts that the most important determinant of a person's self-concept is how she/he thinks other people think of her/him. What effects do societal and professional socialization have on the development of the nurse's self-image, and how does that image relate to the nurse's political behavior?

Studies of the socialization of nurses have found that certain "feminine virtues"— responsibility, motherliness, purity, femininity, service, and efficient house-keeping[33]—are highly valued by both society and schools of nursing. These virtues have served as criteria for the recruitment of new students by hospital boards and nursing leaders. It is interesting to note that omitted from the idealized virtues is among others, the success orientation toward political activism. The educational institutions in which the student nurse has internalized these "virtues" have been hospital training schools and, more recently, colleges and universities.

Historically, the model of the American family was transferred to the hospital and its affiliated school of nursing. The roles of nurses and doctors were defined in terms of male and female roles in the home. Ashley[1] describes the hospital as the "household" where nurses were responsible for meeting the needs of all members of the hospital family, from patients to physicians. The family model persists, even in university nursing programs. Cleland[6] found that the actions of nursing directors and deans are often "wifelike" toward the male hospital or university administrator, like housewives asking for grocery money.

The approach to nursing education was that of apprentice education, which not only provided a source of cheap labor for the hospital but served to inculcate the values of the hospital, preserving the institution's reputation, output, progress, welfare, and efficiency. Apprentice nurses were taught to be obedient and docile and to accept poor working conditions and stringent discipline. Repressive educational practices instilled respect for authority and a spirit of unquestioning loyalty to the institution and physicians. Although we have moved nursing programs to the academic environment of colleges and universities, the apprentice model of education essentially persists. deTorneyay describes the nursing education process:

> We have socialized nursing students to the submissive role. We have helped students to be tactful and diplomatic to the point of obscuring their collaborative role. We have so filled nursing students with the fear of making a mistake that they are low risk-takers. Along with fostering this fear of making mistakes, we socialize our students to depend on physicians and to be reluctant to accept responsibility and accountability for their own action. [13]

deTorneyay's description of the present-day socialization process is reminiscent of the early apprentice training programs. An image of self as submissive, dependent, and risk voiding is not likely to motivate participation in political activity either in one's work setting or on the governmental level.

The learning environment in which the student is socialized promotes feelings of dependency directly through teaching methodology and teacher-student interaction and indirectly by the nursing school's inability to influence the interaction between the student and hospital personnel in clinical experiences.

Irrespective of teaching methods, the discrepancy between what is taught in the classroom and what the students experience in the clinical area persists, resulting in large measure from a preoccupation with course content to the almost total exclusion of the actual process of nursing. Course content, loosely defined as "all of the material we have to cover," emphasizes memorization of facts. The nursing process, on the other hand, emphasizes problem solving and the nature of the interaction between two human beings—nurse and patient. Because of the social context of nursing practice and the high prestige accorded science and technology, nursing instructors consciously or unconsciously find it easier and more acceptable to concentrate on teaching "scientific principles" rather than problem-solving methods.

To teach the nursing process, the teacher must have some control over nursing practice, the setting in which it occurs, and the choice of learning experiences provided for the students. Nurses and nursing instructors do not have such power. One way in which the powerlessness of nurses is maintained in the practice setting is the introduction of arbitrariness by those who are powerful. A nurse, for example, may be rewarded today and punished tomorrow for the same act, with no change in the underlying rules.

A registered nurse who is a student in a baccalaureate program recently described a situation in which she observed that a terminally ill patient with cancer wanted to talk with her rather than take the medication that he had requested. Acting in accordance with her observation and the principles of the nursing process, she spent time with the patient, talking and showing concern and support, and did not give the pain medication. Proud of the results, she eagerly reported her experience in the morning report. She was severely reprimanded for failing to carry out the doctor's orders. She never knew the reason for the reprimand, since trying other methods before giving pain medication is the preferred practice in nursing. On further investigation it was discovered that there was a problem between the doctor and the head nurse, whose response to the doctor was to literally execute his orders rather than the usual nursing measure of trying other methods before giving pain medication. The student, of course, had had no way of knowing this.

Nursing instructors are often unwilling to risk revealing their powerlessness to students. Taking their cues from instructors, students do not reveal their own. In some respects teacher-student relationships in nursing are very much like the doctor-nurse game described by Stein.[31] Since the learning environment is characterized by mistrust and self-effacement, students cannot assume responsibility for their own learning. When generalized to political situations, such behavior proves ineffective.

Traditionally, nursing instructors have related to students in a way that suggests mistrust of the student's judgment. Every nursing activity is observed for accuracy and safety to the patient. Cohen[7] has observed that a necessary precaution unfortunately becomes a straitjacket, demanding that all students' behavior be monitored and assuming that every error is equally dangerous.

In my own experience as a student, I wondered why we required so much supervision when medical interns did not. In my first nursing position in a large teaching hospital, I later sought an answer to this question. While assisting interns with various procedures, I would ask if they had done the procedure before. The answer was usually no, accompanied by discussions on the purpose of internship. My unspoken feeling at that time is consistent with that of Cohen,[7] who states that if such elaborate efforts must be made to protect the helpless patient from the nursing student, the student can only conclude she is for some unfathomable reason a congenital hazard to the very people she wants to help. So preoccupied is she with implementing the nursing intervention correctly that there is little time, energy, or will for creativity or initiative. In contrast, as observed by Knowles,[25] a medical graduate is trained to take immediate action with the individual patient and to expect immediate rewards.

In such a learning environment, the student compares herself and her work to a physician and the practice of medicine and comes to view herself as being powerless and having low status. The supremacy of the medical profession serves as a day-to-day reminder of her inferiority.[9] An individual with such a self-image is not likely to participate in political activities. There is considerable evidence linking self-esteem, motivation, expectancies, and opportunities to political activism. The more healthy, efficacious, and confident a person is, the more she/he participates in politics.[32]

Ideally the nursing instructor selects clinical learning experiences to illustrate specific principles under discussion in the classroom, but the implementation of such an approach to teaching is extremely difficult if not impossible. This difficulty results from the persistence of apprentice learning in which a nurse is a nurse is a nurse. Anyone can ask a student to do anything without knowing or even considering her stage in the learning process. If the student can implement the request by whatever means are necessary, she is rewarded. On the other hand, if she refuses, stating that she is unable to fulfill the request or even that it is not within her assignment, she and the whole nursing program of which she is a part are criticized. I should like to emphasize here that nothing has been resisted as strongly in nursing practice as the idea of a planned clinical assignment for student nurses in the clinical setting. Nursing instructors who cooperate with hospital personnel by permitting students to do whatever they are asked are viewed as "good" or "realistic" teachers; the student who not only does what she is asked but also does anything else "her hands find to do" is considered to possess initiative, intelligence, and creativity. Knowing my strong opposition to the apprentice approach to nursing education, one hospital administrator, a registered nurse, said to me, "While I understand and admire what you are doing, I will never be able to pay nurses to do what you are teaching them to do." When I discussed the matter with nursing service personnel, they agreed with the hospital administrator, and the nursing faculty suggested that I continue to stand up for what I thought was right while in fact agreeing with the administrator. One is reminded here of similar double messages nursing instructors give to students.

The examination of the process of nurse socialization reveals no significant experiences that directly or indirectly lead to the development of positive political behavior. The concomitant self-image of nurses is in accord with observations of Kalisch and Kalisch[23] that the nurse does not usually have the time, the energy, the available resources, the self-direction, the confidence, the assertiveness, or the will to move into active roles in our government or, I might add, in our workplaces and everyday lives.

SELF-OTHER RELATIONSHIPS

> Group affiliations add further information about the self through comparisons and contrasts with the members and with other groups.[19]
>
> Hermann and Milburn: *A Psychological examination of Political Leaders*

In American culture primary attention is given to the uniqueness of the individual rather than to the relationships between individuals, to the likes and aspirations of the individual rather than the duties and obligations of one individual to another.[21] Different cultures, however, place greater or lesser emphasis on the individual or the group.

Ideally, nurses place great emphasis on the individual, which is reflected in such expressions as "individualized patient care," "personalized patient care," "meeting the needs of the patient as a person," and so on. In reality, however, because nursing work is defined in terms of complex organizational structures, the nurse is responsible for groups of patients and groups of co-workers and is accountable to groups of doctors and groups of administrators. Although the nurse's work primarily involves an interpersonal or intergroup process, she believes that she can do little to affect the group or the system. Learning the subculture of nursing does not include learning how the system works and does not encourage investigation of the organizational structure. For example, nursing schools in both hospitals and universities by concentrating on task-oriented courses fail to encourage participation in the larger community of scholars. When I called the American Heart Association, for example, to ask if my class might attend their conference, sponsored by the County Medical Association, the program director said, "We have never had student nurses attend these things—but yes. That's a good idea." Students generally view nonnursing classes as "getting electives or extra requirements out of the way," and nursing faculty tend to have little communication with their colleagues in other areas of the university. Social isolation places limitations on one's growth and development in terms of sharing ideas with others. Locked in their own world, nurses isolate themselves from the arena where the power games are played.

There is no real motivation for nurses to pursue the implications of ideas from other classes or academic disciplines for their own lives or work situations. This is not to say that some individual students to not do this, but there is no organized way to do this on a group basis. According to studies in political science, for example, the individual's personal feelings about her/his own competence intereact with her/his assessment of environmental possibilities. One needs knowledge about how one's society works if one is to make any realistic attempt to affect it.[32] To develop any significant plan for change in nursing, Heide[18] has observed, nurses have to understand how male-oriented, male-dominated society has determined the nature of our private and public lives as well as all our institutions.

The political activist, unlike the nurse, emphasizes "groupness." He responds to the constituent not because of an obsession with the individual but because as a constituent the individual represents a group—a group on which the individual has influence. It is the voting mass (constituency) that the politician influences through individuals. Unfortunately, the professional socialization process of nurses has not done as well as it might have in demonstrating the political implications of being group oriented. Ashley[1] has observed that there is recent evidence that nurses in leadership positions are "least effective" in the areas of interpersonal relations and communicating with other nurses. Many fail to cultivate a power base among nurses from which to operate. Instead, without communicating with those they represent and without the concensus of those whom they are supposed to be leading, they make their decisions in relative isolation.

Recently I asked a group of students, "Why do you think nurses are hesitant to join the ANA?" The response: "Membership fees are too high for what you get; they don't do anything for you." Implied in this response is the traditional view of self that leads nurses look to others to make decisions and take actions for them. Such a view of self accounts in large measure for the traditional reluctance of nurses to unite and fight for their personal and professional interest. Only a minority of nurses belong to their professional associations, with the net effect that the American Nurses's Association cannot speak effectively for nursing since the majority of nurses are outside its umbrella. [26]

In terms of Festinger's theory [16] of social comparison, the nurse evaluates herself in relation to powerful others in the environment, for example, physicians. In interpersonal situations she views herself as powerless to influence people or groups. Leininger [27] has observed that many staff nurses and nursing faculty tend to remain passive in discussions and decision making. In the presence of physicians, nurses often remain silent and dependent on physicians for medical decisions and action. Such behavior has limited political value.

More direct and important is the lack of positive role models in the socialization process of the nurse. Feeling powerless themselves, both teachers and practicing nurses communicate powerlessness to the student. In fact, the student is rewarded not for challenging but for conforming. Having no model for change, students come to view change as something to be written about rather than effected. [24] An obedient, dependent individual cannot be expected to be open to new information, to take risks, to tolerate ambiguity, or to engage in compromise, all characteristics of political activists. [19]

The need to maintain the subordinate role in the work setting has been highly valued in nursing under the guise of being for the benefit of the patient. This need, a main concern of nurses, is acted out in many interpersonal patterns—not antagonizing people, not openly displaying power, and above all, using tact and diplomacy. One nurse, after completing a class in assertiveness training, stated, "While I was assisting a physician with a procedure he shouted at me, 'Go and get a male nurse to do this—these female nurses are not worth a damn around here!!'" When asked "How did you handle that?" she stated, "I just stood there speechless. I am not assertive, you know."

The subordinate-superordinate relationship is maintained also through the use of veiled or indirect language. Dachelet, [10] speaking of the doctor-nurse game described by Stein, [31] states that the nurse who was trained little more than a decade ago lives not only with a sense of dependence and subservience to the physician but also with a marked sense of intellectual worthlessness. She was taught the art of communicating recommendations to the physician in such a way as to disguise the fact that she was actually contributing something intelligent to the management of patient care.

The subordinate status in interpersonal relations is regulated and maintained through the belief that the authority accorded to the physician results from his many years of study and superior knowledge and intelligence. Tragically, the same is not true for the nurse regardless of how many years she spends in school.

The group approach, as we have seen, is an exception rather than the rule in nursing. In a study of decision making by coronary care unit nurses in a large hospital in southern California, it was observed that nurses make decisions not, as they reported, based on the patient's need but instead based on the time of day (day, evening, and night shifts), the personality of the attending physician and nursing supervisor, the nature of the nurse's interaction with the physician and nursing supervisor, the interaction between the physician and the nursing supervisor, the number of auxillary nursing staff on duty, and the number of personnel on duty in other departments.[28] The crucial distinction between political activists and nurses in decision making is that the nurse unlike the political activist is unaware of the power implications of her actions. Bowman and Culpepper[5] argue that nurses individually and collectivly have been unable or unwilling to make a conscious decision to assume power.

The weight of the cultural tradition of the nursing community has served as a constraint on the conscious development of a sense of power by nurses. Bowman and Culpepper[5] further assert that nursing, which in the past has occurred in a rigid, regimented, sexually segregated, and often intellectually sterile environment, has not stimulated self-assertion in nursing students. This, combined with their service orientation, has left nurses ill equipped to project themselves as significant health professionals. They have perceived themselves as dependent rather than independent practitioners. The perception of themselves as dependent is implied in the traditional language used to describe their roles. To define the nurse as "handmaiden to the doctor" and her function as "anticipating the needs of the doctor without appearing to do so" or as "carrying out the doctors' orders" hardly prepared the nurse for decision-making roles regarding health care. As a result, generally speaking, when health or health-related issues are brought up in the political community, it is the doctor and the hospital administrator whose advice is requested. If requested, the advice of nurses is not taken as seriously as that of more powerful groups.

The traditional worship of authority, the socialization of the young nurse in the mores of the institution, the reliance on those above to make the right decisions, the fear of questioning and generating open controversy—all combine in developing politically naive nurses.[23] While nurses are embedded in group-based processes that enforce subordinate, dependent roles, they have little understanding of such processes and thus little ability to alter them, which would itself necessitate group behavior and affiliation with other nurses.

WORK

> Work is a serious, adult business, and a man is supposed to 'get ahead' or 'make' a
> contribution to community or mankind through his work.[2]
>
> Arsenberg and Niehoff: *Introducing Social Change*

The manner in which work is defined in different social groups determines in large measure how group members view themselves and their relationship to others. One's sense of influence in the social system is related to the definition and status given to one's work by the community. In American culture work is defined as only those activities that are marketable for money. Goods and services, in contrast to work, are defined as noneconomic. For example, just as the Federal Government omits housework from tallies of the Gross National Product, hospitals omit nursing services from the patient's bill. Nursing and housework are thus relegated to the category of nonwork. In American culture, respect is given to work that is paid for.

Nursing "work"—helping, nurturing, caring, comforting, counseling—is not held in high esteem by the public. Dachelet[10] asserts that the public's view of nursing is somewhat vague and largely undifferentiated. The public's view seems generally to be that anyone, or at least any female, can provide basic nursing service. Reasons usually put forth for this view are that nursing is primarily a female occupation that it is invisible to the public, and that it is not marketable.

In all sociocultureal groups men generally control public power, the creation of symbols, and therefore society itself. Masculinity is associated with the adult status of active domination in the outside world of work. Work becomes important not only for its material reward but also because it symbolizes power and adult responsibility. Extending this type of reasoning to the female role results in cultural restrictions on women and on nurses. Their activities, in contrast to those of men, occur within the private domain of the household, away from power. Housework and caring for others are considered non–revenue producing and therefore nonwork. Although nursing services, largely housework and caring for others, are remunerated, they are hidden in the general category of hospital services. Nursing "work" becomes unimportant and without prestige to the extent that it is not included in the patient's bill. The invisibility of nursing has been perpetuated by powerful groups in the hospital organization. Physicians, the most powerful group in health care, have convinced the public that healing is a discrete, tangible commodity well worth paying for and that the separate and distinct contributions of nursing, a form of supportive labor, are in fact attributable to the doctor's medical skill.[1] Friedson[17] pointed out that the public is not aware of nursing service in terms of the competence, skill, or knowledge of its practitioners.

Hospital administrators, by hiding nursing services within the category of hospital services, are also perpetuating the invisibility of nursing. When a patient pays her/his hospital bill, she/he is aware of paying not for nursing services but only for hospital services that are listed and therefore public. A grave consequence of this mask is its impact on developing positive political attitudes in nurses. The larger society, in combination with nursing education, has socialized the nurse to perceive her work as being of no consequence and to view herself as powerless to make a worthwhile contribution to the community or humanity through her work. This lack of a sense of personal competence has led the nurse to believe that she is powerless to effect changes in the conditions of her work or in her established interaction patterns with others, especially those in authority.

OPPOSITIONAL MODE OF THOUGHT

A special characteristic of Western thinking, fully reflected in American ways, is that of making two-fold judgments based on principle used as a guide to conduct.[2]

Arsenberg and Niehoff: *Introducing Social Change*

In American culture individuals not only think in terms of mutually exclusive categories—male/female, doctor/nurse, thought/emotion, professional/nonprofessional, public/private—but also assign meanings that suggest the first term is qualitatively better than the second term of each set. The term more highly valued provides a justification for positive efforts whereas the one with lower value justifies negative actions.[2] Furthermore, any transgression of these dichotomies signals disorder, danger, and pollution.[14] Doctors, like other dominant groups, tend to suppress conflict. To paraphrase Jean Baker Miller,[3] they see any modification of the "normal" situation as threatening. For example, any behavior by nurses that symbolizes a rejection of the status quo is met with resistance by physicians. If the nurse who was told "female nurses are not worth a damn" had reacted directly to the doctor's verbal assault, the nurse-doctor relationship would have broken down and she would have been punished for insubordination. Holt,[20] in her discussion of the Chicago registered nurse who was fined for refusing to wear her cap, has observed that the nurse's opportunity for free expression is being suppressed on as elementary a level as a hospital rule about wearing that outdated status symbol, the nurse's cap.

The recently expanded role of the nurse can be viewed as another behavioral stance that questions the traditional nurse-doctor relationship. Physicians resist such a stance by their continued effort to define nursing—"under the supervision of the physician"—in such a way as to maintain their power and control. Efforts at defining nursing tasks serve to hide the real battle over the expanded role of the nurse, involving not only philosophy and expertise but power and prerogatives, economics, and politics. Nurses caught in conflict with physicians over new roles should remember this well.[12]

One's perception of the meanings of the dichotomous sets of terms is influenced by one's relationship to them. The doctor-nurse dichotomy, for example, is an artificial separation of health care into distinct parts in either-or terms—in this case, curing and caring. Although no such distinct entities exist in reality, doctors, nurses, and others behave as if they do. The problem with such dichotomized thinking is that members of the contrasted groups are prevented from viewing each other as human beings rather than as titles and status or in a category. In the case of the doctor/nurse dichotomy, each member can use time, energy, and resources to identify, describe, and classify the tasks of both without ever considering the nature of their relationship as persons charged with the responsibility of helping the ill and without considering the impact of that relationship on the care provided. Such preoccupation with tasks serves to maintain the doctor's power and prevent the acquisition of power by the nurse and does little to facilitate effective health care delivery.

Nurses' bid for professionalism also reflects dichotomized thinking. One kind of two-fold judgment made by the American culture is to classify work as professional or nonprofessional. This dichotomy expressed contradictions inherent in the American culture and in the subculture of the hospital. Medicine, a profession, is defined in terms of masculine traits—autonomy, dominance, knowledge, and technical competence—whereas nursing, considered a nonprofession or semiprofession, is defined in terms of feminine traits—submissiveness, dependency, nurturance, and helpfullness.

Nurses, like others in subordinate roles, have internalized the beliefs of the higher-ranking group and the meaning it has assigned to the nurse and nursing work. The low value placed on nursing is also transferred to health care consumers. Studies show that other health workers and patients as a rule have only a general knowledge of what a nurse does or can do.[16] They do not usually understand the nature of the assistance the professional nurse is prepared to offer. Yet an examination of the professional socialization of nurses reveals that it does not confront the public image of nursing. To do so is to transgress the boundary of male/female and public/private dichotomies, thereby turning social order into chaos. Such behavior contradicts culturally appropriate behavior for nurses and women. How can the nurse be an advocate for the patient if the patient is unaware of her role and if that role precludes advocacy?

Another consequence of the oppositional mode of thinking is observed in the attrition pattern of nursing students and its impact on the development of political behavior. One study shows that students who withdraw from nursing programs score higher in terms of achievement, autonomy, succorance, and dominance but lower in deference, abasement, nurturance, and endurance than those who remain.[30] This study suggests that obedience and subservience of nurses continue to be the preferred behavior from the perspective of nursing educators. On the other hand, efforts toward professionalization are exposing role conflicts inherent in nursing culture. Nursing instructors, carriers of the culture, inadvertently perpetuate the development of traditional nursing behavioral expectations. Ironically, in an effort to produce only highest quality nurses, nursing education drives out of the field those students most likely to become true professionals. The system as it is presently constituted is self defeating. Students who are most assertive and more accepting of their own aggression leave the nursing program, whereas students who are more dependent and least likely to develop positive political orientations complete their education. Cohen[7] observes that nursing seems to be involved in a catch-22 situation. The individual most capable of professionalism, the bright, questioning, and assertive female, could change the structure and symbolism of nursing, yet she is the individual most likely to be factored out.

NURSES AND THE POLITICAL PROCESS

The feeling that the behavior of women is inappropriate to the political arena results from this oppositional mode of thought, involving the political consequences of behavior related to dominant culture values concerning self, self-other relationships, and work. The Rural Health Clinics Services Act of 1977 (PL95-210) Title 42 is an example of these consequences. The rules and regulations in this law on the definition of the nurse practitioner were based on 60 comments received from 41 sources, including representatives of national, regional, and state organizations. Of these comments, 30 indicated that the initial definition of the nurse practitioner should be further defined by adding the phrase "who holds a baccalaureate degree in nusing." Other commentors rejected this. Many of them supported the concept of greater uniformity in the programs to prepare nurse practitioners but challenged the assertion tha graduation from a collegiate nursing program was a demonstrated factor related to competence and quality peformance as a nurse practitioner. Further, the published guidelines for nurse practitioner programs in response to the Nurse Training Act of 1975 (PL 94-63) provide for the "award of grants to public and nonprofit schools of nursing . . . for the training of nurse practitioners" and specify that such programs shall be open to registered nurses irrespective of the type of school of nursing in which they received their training.[15]

Disagreement over this issue exists among nurses. Opposition and conflict are natural in all human groups and are necessary for change; properly handled, such conflict may lead to the development of political activism among nurses. Given the nature of the political process, however, it is disadvantageous for groups to present themselves to politicians as fragmented by opposing views. The likelihood of an issue becoming a law depends on the degree to which a group can prove the issue's worth and worth ultimately depends on the number of people committed to it as well as on their power.

Cultural and social values upheld by nursing education are among the essential features underlying the reluctance of nurses to enter the political process. One of the aspects of the political process, as pointed out to me by Dr. De Leon,[11] legislative aide to Senator Inouye, is in a very real sense built on interpersonal relationships. The basic conventions of interpersonal relations in the political community allow disagreement, voicing of opposing views, and committing oneself to a position on issues. The traditional sociocultural milieu in which nurses have been socialized, however, has militated against the development of independent thinking and open dialogue, resulting in a reluctance of many nurses to enter the political process.

Social conditions change and old rules of behavior are modified or replaced with new ones. Nurses, as the largest group of health professionals, are beginning to realize their potential power. This increasing awareness of the need for cooperative efforts will ultimately lead to a sense of group strength, which is necessary for success in the political process. Senator Inouye, in his speech before the American Nurses' Association 51st Convention, June 1978, put the need for group work very succinctly:

> It is the nursing profession that must pursue these ends; it is you with your large numbers and your positive public image who must convince the Congress that nursing practice is unique and that the nurse is a true health care professional. For the health and welfare of the nation and for the future of the nursing profession, you must become more involved in the legislative and policy-setting processes. I urge you to speak out and make your voice heard. We must work together if we are to change the institutional patterns of the past within forthcoming national health insurance; then, together we can reach our goal of assuring accessible, quality health care at a reasonable cost for all our nation's people.[22]

To become aware of the sociocultural conditions in which nursing behavior is rooted is the beginning of change in nurses' political behavior. To fully implement this change, however, is to change the locus of decision-making power.

REFERENCES

1. Ashley, J.A.: Hospitals, paternalism, and the role of the nurse, New York, 1976, Teachers College Press.
2. Arensberg, C., and Niehof, A.H.: Introducing social change, ed. 2, New York, 1971, Aldine Atherton.
3. Baker Miller, J.: Toward a new psychology of women, Boston, 1976, Beacon Press.
4. Beals, A.R., and others: Culture in process, ed. 2, New York, 1973, Holt, Rinehart & Winston.
5. Bowman, R.A., and Culpepper, R.C.: Power: Rx for change, American Journal of Nursing **74**(6):1054, 1974.
6. Cleland, V.: Sex discrimination: nursing's most pervasive problem, American Journal of Nursing **71**:1542, 1971.
7. Cohen, H.A.: The nurse's quest for a professional identity, Menlo Park, Calif., 1981, Addison-Wesley Publishing Co., Inc.
8. Cooley, C.H.: Human nature and the social order, New York, 1902, Scribner. Quoted in Stone, W.F.: The psychology of politics, New York, 1974, The Free Press.
9. Cowden, P.: Dissatisfaction and the changing meaning and purpose of the nurse's work, Nursing Forum **17**(2):205, 1978.
10. Dachelet, C.Z.: Nursing's bid for increased status, Nursing Forum **17**(1):18,1978.
11. DeLeon, P.K.: Personal communications, 1978.
12. Deloughery, G.L., and Kristine, K.M.: Political dynamics: impact on nurses and nursing, St. Louis, 1975, The C.V. Mosby Co.
13. deTourneyay, R.: Two views on the latest health manpower issue: expanding the nurse's role does not make her a physician's assistant, *American Journal of Nursing* **71**:974, 1971. Quoted in Dachelet, C.Z.: Nursing's bid for increased status, Nursing Forum **17**(2):205, 1978.
14. Diman-Schein, M.: The anthropological imagination, New York 1977, McGraw-Hill Book Co.
15. Federal Register, Part VII, **43**(136):30520, July 14, 1978.
16. Festinger, L.A.: A theory of social comparison processes, Human Relations **7**:117, 1954, Quoted in Hermann, M.G., and Milburn, T.W.: A psychological examination of political leaders, New York, 1977, The Free Press.

17. Friedson, E.: The profession of medicine, New York, 1973, Dodd, Mead & Co. Quoted in Dachelet, C.Z.: Nursing's bid for increased status, Nursing Forum **17**:(2):205, 1978.

18. Heide, W.S.: Nursing and women's liberation: a parallel, American Journal of Nursing **73**(5): 824, 1973.

19. Hermann, M.G., and Milburn. T.W.: A psychological examination of political leaders, New York, 1977, The Free Press.

20. Hott, J.R.: Nursing and politics: the struggle inside nursing's body politic, Nursing Forum **15**(4):325, 1976.

21. Hsu, F.L.: Psychological anthropology, Homewood, Ill., 1971, The Dorsey Press, Inc.

22. Inouye, D.K.: Speech presented at the American Nurses' Association 51st Convention, Honolulu, Hawaii, June 1978.

23. Kalisch, B.J., and Kalisch, P.: A discourse on the politics of nursing, Journal of Nursing Administration **6**(3):29, 1966.

24. Kelly, L.Y.: The power of powerlessness, Nursing Outlook **26**(7):468, 1978.

25. Knowles, J.H.: The rationalization of health services. In Knowles, J.H., editor: Views of education and medical care, Cambridge, Mass., 1968, Harvard University Press. Quoted in Dachelet, C.Z.: Nursing's bid for increased status, Nursing Forum **17**(2):205, 1978.

26. Lawrence, J.C.: Confronting nurses' political apathy, Nursing Forum **15**(4):363, 1976.

27. Leininger, M.: Political nursing: essential for health and educational systems of tomorrow, unpublished paper presented at the dedication of the Health Science Building for the school of nursing seminar, University of Indiana, Evansville, April 25, 1975.

28. Lowery-Palmer, A.: Decision making process by nurses in coronary care unit, N.D. On file at Department of Anthropology, University of California–*Riverside.*

29. McFarland, D.E., and Shiflet, N.: The role of power in the nursing profession, Nursing Dimensions **7**(2):1, 1979.

30. Reece, M.M.: Personality characteristics and success in a nursing program, Nursing Research **10**:172, 1961. Quoted in Cohen, H.A.: The nurse's quest for a professional identity Menlo Park, Calif., 1981, Addison-Wesley Publishing Co., Inc.

31. Stein, L.: The doctor-nurse game, Archives of General Psychiatry **16**:699, 1967. Quoted in Dachelet, C.Z.: Nursing's bid for increased status, Nursing Forum **17**(2):205, 1978.

32. Stone, W.F.: The psychology of politics, New York, 1974, The Free Press.

33. Strauss, A.: The structure and ideology of nursing: an interpretation, in the nursing profession. In Davis, F., editor: Five sociological Essays, New York, 1966, John Wiley & Sons, Inc.

Chapter 12

Caring vs. curing

The politics of health care

Discrimination against women pervades our social institutions both at work and in the home. Most people marry, and "naturally" women become mothers. Male dominance begins at home where women have traditionally been unequal to men. From early in life men are encouraged to be active and rational; women are trained to be involved with emotions and reactions of others and are thereby diverted from examining and expressing their own emotions. Men do important tasks and have exciting careers, whereas women do the less-valued work of helping other human beings develop. In Western society men are encouraged to dread or deny feeling weak or helpless. Women are supposed to be accommodators, mediators, adapters, and soothers—but these behaviors are devalued and connote weakness.[20]

Personalities of men and women are socially shaped for a planned order in society. Historically, personalities of men and women have been standardized as contrasting and complimentary, and all institutions in society have been congruent with this standardization. Women's maternal function, including as it has the responsibility for home and family, is at the root of women's oppression. Motherhood has determined the status of womanhood. In a patriarchal society it is a central social and political institution, necessary for maintaining the status quo, male supremacism. Rather than being a choice, motherhood was (and is) viewed as the "natural" role for all women, who are expected to accept it without ambivalence. Men have wanted no part of parenting, an unpaid occupation outside the world of public power that has lower status and involves less control of resources than paid work.

In our society mothers exclusively care for children and are often isolated from other adults. There is a physical separation of men-fathers in the work world from women-mothers in the home. Male dominance has been institutionalized through the socialization of women to affirm laws and sanctions designed to keep themselves powerless. Paradoxically, mothers are attributed within an almost superhuman power over their offspring; they are responsible for children's survival, health, self-hood, and good and evil.[21]

203

This chapter develops the following ideas:

1. The roles of woman, nurse, and mother are viewed by society as similar if not synonymous.
2. The hospital family consists of mothers (nurses), fathers (physicians), and children (patients) and is based on the patriarchal family system of Western society.
3. The subordinate position of nursing is reinforced by the care/cure myth that values caring, the traditionally female-nursing role, less than curing, the male-medical role.
4. This dichotomy is further emphasized by monetary rewards: physicians are well paid for curing, but not so nurses for caring.

THE HOSPITAL FAMILY

Nursing is simply a continuance of the wife-mother role. Women are thought to be instinctive nurses. Since nursing-mothering is a "natural," the nursing profession has been identified chiefly as a women's arena. Nurses as women are viewed as dependent, nurturing, and self sacrificing. The nurse as a selfless mother-substitute provides nurturing care for patients *and physicians*. Roberts and Group have said, "Nursing pioneers emphasized that to work in hospitals the wifely virtues of absolute obedience, the selfless devotion of mother, and the kindly discipline of a household manager were needed."[22] Since nursing is accepted as natural and intuitive, nurses are neither noted for nor credited with intellect.[23] That nursing is (or should be) limited to nurturance is a notion that has been strongly enforced by men in the health care system[22]—physicians and hospital administrators who are only too aware that women of intellect and scientific practice could not be so easily controlled.

The patriarchal marriage is not unlike the marriage of nursing and medicine. According to Lips and Colwill, "the marital roles provide us with an interesting microcosm of our general sex-role structure: men in our society protect, create, initiate, and decide, and women care for and defer to others."[19] As husbands have held dominant power over wives, so physicians have held dominant power over nurses; as wives are expected to serve their husbands, nurses are expected to serve physicians. Ashley asserts, "Myths surrounding the cult of true womanhood permeate patriarchal history. Because of myths accompanying pervasive misogyny, nurses are still the servants of physicians."[4] Nurses have played the "traditional subordinate role of wife to the medical husband, dutiful, overworked, underpaid," and unappreciated.[8] Because nursing has always been viewed as secondary, our society views nurses as carrying out the physician's orders and responding to his demands. The physician is the commander of the nurse and all health care. Nurses neither think nor act on their own.

Society has been deceived into believing that nursing and medicine are one and the same: nursing skills are attributed to medical skills and health care and medical care are interchangeable.[11] The medical profession has supported the societal view of the nurse as the physician's helper. The nurse simply carries out the physician's orders. Therefore the physician is the only one to be relied on for health care on a continuing basis.[17] The physician is viewed as the sole authority and primary provider of health care.

The hospital milieu encourages patriarchy. It is a myth that most hospitals are dedicated to teamwork and collegiality. Relationships are instead based on those of the family and involve similar inequities. In *Hospitals, Paternalism, and the Role of the Nurse*, Ashley writes,

> The role of women (nurses) was very early conceived as that of caring for the "hospital family". . . .Through service and self-sacrifice, they were to work continuously to keep the "family" happy. . . .In addition women (nurses) were expected to look out for the needs of men (physicians) in the hospital family, who for the most part, did not reside in the household, but were free to come and go. . . .Though often absent, through their influence and domination they carried the authority of "master."[2]

In the hospital situation nurses are responsible for meeting the needs of all members of the hospital family. They are to be submissive, passive, and subordinate yet responsible for every aspect of housewifery that goes on in the hospital. The physician's role is very much like that of the pampered father who is in the home only part of the time and then leaves for work; the nurse, like the mother, remains to care for the patients 24 hours a day.

The "rules" in this physician-dominated situation are established for the convenience of the physician. The nurse is expected to be capable of taking care of whatever problems arise within the hospital, regardless of the area in which they occur. This is particularly true at night, when the nurse is expected to function not only as a nurse but also as a doctor, housekeeper, dietician, cook, secretary, pharmacist, and general "u-fix-it."[2]

THE CARE/CURE MYTH

The myth that nurturing and caring traits of women and nurses are innate whereas traits involving scientific skills must be learned stems from the belief that masculine traits are active (curing) and feminine ones are passive (caring.) Recently there has been a growing realization that these traits are learned and belong not to one gender but to both.

Prominent in the dehumanizing health care system is the imbalance of "masculine" and "feminine" principles. These principles are evidenced in the concepts associated with men and women: independent and dependent, analytic and intuitive, dominant and submissive, active and receptive. The "feminine" principles correspond to the historical roots of nursing—caring, nurturance, receptivity. The more they are expressed to the exclusion of "masculine" principles, the more vulnerable, voiceless, and repressed nurses become.

Ehrenreich and English[12] point out that as male-scientific medicine developed, healing was split into two functions, curing and caring. Physicians cure and receive credit for the patient's recovery; nurses care but receive no credit. The authors assert that "healing in its fullest sense consist[s] of both curing and caring, doctoring and nursing."[12]

Caring and curing, although different, are both essential. Unfortunately, our society does not value caring and curing equally. Men value their work and society values men's work. Since most nurses are women, their work is not valued but, as discussed above, is viewed as an intuitive process, a natural feminine attribute. The assumption follows that it requires very little knowledge or skill. Much can be said about the value of caring; however, in a scientific, cost-efficient, product-oriented society, the traditionally masculine values prevail. The dichotomy of caring and curing is not only arbitrary but also erroneous. Caring can foster healing and hence, curing. Nursing encompasses both caring and curing—healing. If an individual has a stroke, the physician diagnoses the stroke. The nurse cares for the paralyzed individual and assists in the restoration of health, thereby curing.

The separation of curing and caring, apparent in the history of medicine, is a myth propogated by physicians (men) to reduce nurses (women) to the status of secondary healers. Bullough and Bullough have said,

> The supporters of this approach felt that the patient care role should be divided into "care" and "cure" components, with nurses giving psychological support and physicians carrying full responsibility for the diagnosis and treatment of the patient. This division was defended partly in an effort to find an individual niche for nurses but also because nurses were felt to be more naturally maternal and expressive than physicians. This philosophy has acted as a major deterrent to the development of the nurse practitioner role, which contains both care and cure components.[7]

Sexism in the health care system is a reflection of sexism in society. "In our society the institution in the most propitious position to perpetuate sexist ideology is the overwhelmingly sexist institution of medicine."[5] Sexist attitudes and paternalistic tactics on the part of physicians have encouraged nurses to internalize the nurse's subservient, inferior status. The plight of most nurses is not really so different from women in general. Only the stage and the actors are different.

MONEY—THE BOTTOM LINE

Nursing with its emphasis on caring and nurturance has not been valued intellectually or monetarily. Nursing has historically been viewed by society as a "calling" (for women, that is). This economically expedient notion stemmed from the centuries-old association of nursing and religious orders that led to the commonly held belief that nursing is a "charitable and merciful gesture to mankind."[16] Self-sacrifice was inherent in this concept, which inevitably led to the viewpoint that nurses would receive "heavenly rather than earthly rewards" for their labors.

Traditionally nurses have been reluctant to seek improvements in their economic status because to do so would have seemed inconsistent with the saintly values to which they subscribed. In her attempt to present nursing as a reputable profession, Florence Nightingale insisted that women in professions must be well compensated; love and charity were not sufficient pay.[18] Her attitude, however, has not always prevailed.

The majority of nursing directors, for instance, do not manage their departmental budgets. They are expected to provide nurses for staff duty but cannot hire more nurses than the budget allows, regardless of the need for adequate patient care. Staying within the male-dictated budget is of primary concern. Cleland[10] observed that nursing directors when dealing with hospital administrators (male) and physicians (also male) often act "like housewives asking for grocery money" to hire nurses and purchase necessary equipment. "In our society the individuals who control the pursestrings control others. They are the ones with recognized power. This tells us once again where women—and nurses—stand: they are powerless."[14]

Nursing has been unilaterally exploited by the medical profession and by hospital administration. "Economically, nursing has been chronically underpaid, inefficiently lobbied for, and not provided with bargaining powers possessed by other professional groups."[24] In *The Female Eunuch* Germaine Greer writes,

> The most depressing phenomenon in the pattern of women's work is the plight of the nurse. . . .That nurses are victimized by the essentialness of their work into accepting shameful remuneration is an indictment of our society, which is daring them to abandon the sick and dying, knowing that they will not do it.[15]

The commercial value of nurses to health care institutions, particularly hospitals, should not be underestimated, nor should their lack of power and freedom within the system be ignored. As the largest group of employed professionals in the health care industry, nurses have been and continue to be victims of profit abuse. In 1977 the average income for nurses ranged from $9,072 in Rhode Island to $14,216 in California—compared with an average of $65,000 for physicians.[13] In a 1976–1977 comparison with the salaries of male-dominated occupations such as auctioneers, machinists, electricians, and plumbers, nurses' salaries ranked considerably lower.[14]

Given this set of circumstances, one can argue that nurses are oppressed group, coping with a "culture of poverty"—"poverty in spirit and in the purse."[3] In addition, the majority of nurses have been content with this oppression, as evidenced by their reluctance to seek power and freedom through collective action.

> Traditional nurses have themselves overwhelmingly viewed it to be "morally right" for them to be self-sacrificing and supportive of other groups in the health field. Their economic exploitation and their subservient role have been universally accepted.[1]

The myth (and reality) of nurses' subordination to physicians, coupled with a social system that values the work of men over that of women, has led to the depreciation of the role of the nurse in the health care field. As a consequence, less monetary value is placed on nursing work and less status and power are ascribed to nurses than physicians.

The symbiotic relationship between medicine and nursing continues to subvert nursing's efforts toward the liberation and legitimization of its distinctive and unique role in health care delivery. Nurses are frequently blind to the fact that their professional identities have been deliberately submerged in this symbiosis by physicians using calculated deception and blatant paternalism. Further exploitation and denigration of nursing's talents, skills, and energies can be anticipated as long as nurses ignore the situation. If nursing is to survive as a viable and essential social service, nurses must persist in their historical attempt to distinguish the practice of nursing from the practice of medicine by entering into the political arena unencumbered by the deceptions of male supremacy. Nurses, as women, can no longer afford to be noted for intuition rather than intellect, for nurturance rather than productivity, for dependence rather than independence. It is essential that nurses realize that the "feminine" personality traits attributed to them as women are confining and debilitating—that they interfere with the development of identity and achievement behavior. In reality, all of the so-called feminine and masculine traits are *human* traits, part of the full human potential.

REFERENCES

1. Ashley, J.: Power, freedom and professional practice in nursing, Supervisor Nurse, p. 2, January 1975.
2. Ashley, J.: Hospitals, paternalism, and the role of the nurse, New York, 1976, Teachers College Press.
3. Ashley, J.: Health care, American style: helter skelter, par excellence, Supervisor Nurse, p. 46, February 1977.
4. Ashley, J.: Power in structured misogyny: implications for the politics of care, Advances in Nursing Sciences 2(3):3, 1980.
5. Benton, D.W.: Obstetrics-gynecology, Nursing Forum 16:269, 1977.
6. Brooten, D., and others: Leadership for change: a guide for the frustrated nurse, Philadelphia, 1978, J.B. Lippincott Co.
7. Bullough, B., and Bullough V., editors: Expanding horizons for nurses, New York, 1977, Springer Publishing Co.
8. Bullough, V.L.: Sin, sickness and sanity, New York, 1977, Garland Publishing, Inc.
9. Chodorow, N.: The reproduction of mothering: psychoanalysis and the sociology of gender, Berkeley, 1978, University of California Press.
10. Cleland, V.: Sex discrimination: nursing's most pervasive problem, American Journal of Nursing, p. 1542, August 1971.
11. Dachelet, C.Z.: Nursings' bid for increased status, Nursing Forum 17:19, 1978.
12. Ehrenreich, B., and English, D.: Witches, midwives, and nurses, New York, 1973, Feminist Press.
13. For 'new nurse': bigger role in health care, U.S. News and World Report, January 14, 1980.
14. Grissum, M., and Spengler, C.: Womanpower and health care, Boston, 1976, Little, Brown & Co.
15. Greer, G.: The female eunuch, New York, 1971, McGraw-Hill Book Co.
16. Hughes, L.: The public image of the nurse, Advances in Nursing Science 2:55, 1980.
17. Kalisch, B.: Of half gods and mortals: Aesculapian authority, Nursing Outlook 23:22, January 1975.
18. Kelly, L.Y.: Our nursing heritage: have we renounced it? Image 8(30:43.

19. Lips, H., and Colwill, N.L.: The psychology of sex differences, Englewood Cliffs, N.J., 1978, Prentice-Hall, Inc.

20. Miller, J.B.: Toward a new psychology of women, Boston, 1976, Beacon Press.

21. Rich, A.: On lies, secrets, and silence, New York, 1979, W.W. Norton & Co., Inc.

22. Roberts, J.T., and Group, T.M.: The women's movement and nursing, Nursing Forum **11:** 303, 1970.

23. Wilson, J.E.: The evolution of nursing education in the United States, Journal of Nursing Education **16:**31, 1977.

24. Wilson, V.: An analysis of femininity in nursing, Am Bhv Sc **15:**213, 1971.

Chapter 13

Daddy's little girl
The lethal effects of paternalism in nursing

Most of nursing's history has gone unrecognized and unrealized by even the nurses living it. The lessons of history have gone unlearned and have been therefore continually repeated. Jo Ann Ashley's two probing historical studies[3,4] have meticulously documented the pervasive effects of paternalism in the hospital system. As her student, I conducted an independent study designed to expand upon her work. Although this study explored an entirely different aspect of nursing history, the themes that emerged strikingly mirrored Ashley's findings and those of many others as well. Permeating all three studies are the multiple manifestations of paternalism in every aspect of nursing, past and present. The purpose of this chapter is to highlight the lethal effects that paternalism has had and continues to have on nurses and nursing care.

PATERNALISM

The concept of paternalism generally involves one person caring for and guiding another in a fatherly way. It is on this concept that society's social system is structured; paternalism flows from patriarchy. The derivation of the word helps one gain an understanding of exactly what patriarchy means. *Pater* means father, possessor, or master. The family is the basic social unit of patriarchy; *family* comes from *famel*, which means servant, slave or possession. *Paterfamilias*, therefore, means owner or possessor of slaves.[12] This patriarchal order of the household is magnified in the profession of nursing and in the lives of nurses. Although it may be painful to acknowledge that the personal and professional identities of nurses have been dictated and diminished by others, such an acknowledgement must be made if nurses are to stop the abuses of paternalism and enter into a politics of care that is not encumbered by the lethal effects of paternalistic practice.

THEORETICAL FRAMEWORK

Ashley[4] proposes that the relationship between nursing and medicine is based on the myth of the holy marriage between nursing and medicine. She explains the physician's assumption that nursing is tied to medicine as a legal, subservient partner much like wives are tied to their husbands. Just as wives are expected to further their husbands' jobs in various ways, physicians' wives and nurses are expected to serve the same function for physicians. Sociologists propogate this myth by analyzing the physician-patient relationship using a paternalistic (father-child) typology.[16] It follows that the nurse is the wife-mother in this relationship. Exploring the objectification and exploitation of female nurses by male physicians, Ashley clearly shows how the physician-nurse relationship mirrors male-female relationships in its paternalistic intent to maintain control:

> The role of women (nurses) was very early conceived as that of caring for the "hospital family." Their purpose was to provide efficient economical production in the form of patient care; they were to be loyal to the institution and devoted to preserving its reputation. Through service and self-sacrifice, they were to work continuously to keep the "family" happy. . . . Like mothers in a household, nurses were responsible for meeting the needs of all members of the hospital family—from patients to physicians. . . . In addition, women (nurses) were expected to look out for the needs of men (the physicians) in the hospital family, who, for the most part, did not reside in the household, but were free to come and go.[3]

Historical inquiry into the paternalistic attitude toward nurses prevalent among physicians and hospital administrators today reveals that the focus on power and control plays an integral part in maintaining social and professional inequality and the persistence of disease. The control mechanisms most frequently used by medicine to keep nurses subservient and "in their place" are to instill fear and to impose ignorance on them. The medical profession then exploits the fears and ignorance of nurses and others to increase the power of medicine and to maintain greater control. A fearful and ignorant group of nurses is easily controlled.

Deception

Sissela Bok[7] adds dimension to the concepts of control, fear, and ignorance. She explores how deception is interwoven with coercion, violence, power, and paternalism. Each of these factors can justify the use of deception to control those who have first been objectified. Both deceit and violence can coerce people into acting against their will. But deceit controls more subtly, for it employs belief as well as action. When deception is used to coerce it gives power to the deceiver. The power and control relationship that results, whether it is between physician and patient, doctor and nurse, father and child, husband and wife, or any two groups or individuals in the medical hierarchy, constitutes oppressive violence.

Bok[7] defines deception as the intentional communication of messages meant to mislead others. It means making others believe what the deceiver does not believe. Deception can be accomplished through gesture and disguise, action or inaction, and even silence. Lying, an intentionally deceptive message that is stated verbally or in writing, is only one small means of deception.

SILENCE AS DECEPTION   Adrienne Rich,[26] poet and feminist theorist, explores how silence as a deceptive force throughout history and literature begets powerlessness in women. Mary Daly[10] suggests deception is so totally pervasive in patriarchal society that it was not even named in the traditional listing of the Seven Deadly Sins. The deception engendered by patriarchy sedates women until their minds and bodies can be controlled and manipulated. Paternalistic lying promotes this female mind sedation by discouraging questions. When power is thought to be divinely granted or ordained by nature, questions remain unasked; the right to coerce and manipulate is then taken for granted. When this right is questioned, the answer given by paternalists is that their authority is justified when it is exercised over persons for their own good.[7]

This type of paternalistic deception is frequently used for those of limited understanding, such as children, mental incompetents, and the uneducated. In the interest of simplicity the truth is bent to convey what the speaker believes is the right picture. It supposedly compensates for the inexperience or the fears of the listener, just as raising one's voice helps the hard of hearing to understand the message.

LIES   Lies designed to protect can ultimately serve to suffocate and exploit those for whom they were ostensibly meant to protect. Bok describes such an example:

> Throughout history, men, women, and children have been compelled to accept degrading work, alien religious practices, institutionalization, and even wars alleged to "free" them all in the name of what someone has declared to be in their own best interest. And deception may well have outranked force as a means of subjection: duping people to conform.[7]

Political lies differ from other forms of deception in terms of the benefits they may confer and the long-range harm they may avoid. These lies may be broadly paternalistic; the altruistic purposes justifying such lies are frought with error and self-deception.[7] Much deceit for private gain masquerades as being in the public interest; deception, even for the most unselfish motive, corrupts and spreads. Daly[10] in her discussion of deception examines the role that myth plays: "Patriarchy perpetuates its deception through myth."[10] She adds that patriarchal myths contain stolen mythic power because they are phallic distortions of ancient gynocentric civilizations.

In our paternalistic society deception is rarely absent from most human practices. There are great differences, however, among the professions in terms of the types of deceit that exist and the extent to which deception is practiced. The historical data presented here indicate that organized medicine has carefully cultivated deception throughout its American history. Bok[7] indicates that honesty and truthfulness have been left out altogether from medical oaths and codes of ethics and are often ignored in the teaching of medicine.

Control

Paternalistic deception is a strong and vital thread in the intricately woven mantle of control. The medical profession has been particularly adept at utilizing a mix of truth and deception to gain and maintain control of nurses and others. Medicine's habit of protecting what it has by paternalistically limiting the full development of nursing potential in the field of health care is a direct result of medicine's fear of losing control of its dominant position. The obtuse logic required to accept this paternalistic control of nurses is viewed by the medical profession as *right* because this practice bolsters that profession's influence.

This unidimensional focus of medicine in regard to nurses is indicative of a patriarchal mentality that decrees the subordinate role of women. Historical theologian Rosemary Ruether describes the position of nurses and other women in patriarchal society:

> Socially, women form a caste within every class, meaning that they share a common oppression as women, but they find it hard to unite across class and racial lines because they are divided by the class and race oppression exercised by the ruling class. . . .As women they serve as the domestic servants of society, freeing the male for the work day by bearing all the auxiliary and supportive chores. When let into the work world they are generally structured into the same kind of domestic services and auxiliary support systems of male executive roles—as nurses, secretaries. . . .Economically, women provide the support system for male mobility and work. Domesticated in the private sector they are not only the auxiliary support system for male work . . . but they also provide the sphere of rest, recreation and erotic life that pacifies male work alienation.[6]

Nurses are demeaned by the medical profession for the sake of exalting the power and self-identity of the domiant medical group. The medical patriarchy has suppressed these women into a subservient category that works for but does not profit from the business of medicine.

Women as subordinate

Miller's analysis[22] of dominant and subordinate groups shows that the dominant group inevitably sets itself up as "normal" in matters of relationships, health, and so on. Indicative of the paternal ideology that views women as inferior, subordinate beings, Freud wrote of the strange asymmetry in nature that had made only one sex fully normal.[13] From Freud's paternal perspective, the "abnormal sex" was female, "naturally." Miller[22] explains that this familiar rationalization for demeaning and demoralizing treatment is based on the paternalistic chant, "We know what's best for them anyhow."

The assumptions that women are a subgroup, that "man's world" is the "real" world, and that patriarchy is equivalent to culture and culture to patriarchy have provided fertile ground for the historical paternalistic exploitation of women. Women who refused to be wooed by the paternalistic assumption of superiority have been soundly silenced. This silencing has taken political, social, economic, and personal (medical) forms. Feminists throughout history have documented the silences imposed by paternalism—Gilman,[18] Nightingale,[23] and Wolstonecraft[29] in the past, as well as a host of more recent writers including Daly,[10] Friedan,[17] Rich,[26] Janeway,[19] Chesler,[8] Corea,[9] and De Beauvoir.[11]

Fragmentation

Daly explains that paternalism silences and splits apart women by embedding fears:

> These contrived and injected fears function in a manner analogous to electrodes implanted in the brain of a victim ("patient") who can be managed by remote control. This is a kind of "silent" control (as silent as the pushing of a button). Women may feel that they are free from certain fears ("liberated") and then bend to the unacknowledged power of these fears with mental knee-jerk responses.[10]

"Daddy's little girl" bends to the unacknowledged fear that she will fall into disfavor with "daddy" and incur his wrath or, even worse, be ignored or dismissed as "ungrateful" and "unfeminine." Daddy's little girl" will mature physically, but the mental knee-jerk response that is triggered by fear and controlled by daddy-figures will keep the grown-up girl emotionally and intellectually immature. This paternal control has effectively kept women and nurses "in their proper place" for over a century.

HISTORICAL OVERVIEW

One of the first nurses to recognize that being "daddy's little girl" was excessively limiting and oppressive was Florence Nightingale. In 1852, as she embarked on her career as the leader of nursing, Nightingale wrote to her father: "I hope now I have come into possession of myself. . . .You must now consider me . . . a son."[23] The paternalism that oppresses nurses is inextricably linked to the paternalistic oppression of women. The historical study of medicine's development as a business and its resulting impact on nursing clearly shows that the framework of paternalism has shaped both the professional and personal lives of practitioners of medicine and nursing.[21] In 1946 physician Robinson[27] reaffirmed the "natural" paternalism that requires medicine to care for and guide nursing in a fatherly way: "The first mother who leaned over the first cradle of leaves in the primitive forest was the first nurse." Robinson suggests that biology made the female the nurse of the species and the male was therefore to look after her: "Before the dawn of agriculture, the male stepped out of his cave . . . the hunter of all living things; the female remained behind, the nurse of the young and the sick.[27]

PATERNALISM IN MEDICINE AND NURSING

In this manner the view of women as "born nurses" was begun. "The history of nursing is an episode in the history of women," Robinson concluded. "The nurse is the mirror in which is reflected the position of women through the ages."[27] Throughout American history the medical profession has cultivated and maintained a male-dominant position over women. Historical data reveal the medical profession's preoccupation with profits, male privileges, and control over others.[21] Much of the supremacy, power, control, and privilege the medical profession seeks to create for itself stems from the notion that the physician is "a man among men." The manifest sexism of the medical profession is not incidental, nor is its sexism merely the reflection of the sexist attitudes of society in general. The medical profession has gone one step further. It is a citadel historically designed to control women and to keep them "in their place."[9,21]

Modern nursing began at a time when Victorian ideas dictated that the role of women was to serve men's needs and convenience.[3] Medicine's use of the family as a model for relationships was certainly motivated by the prevailing patriarchal system, which decreed that all women exist to meet the needs of their men. The relationship between the male medical profession and the female nursing profession was no exception.

In 1897 Sir William Osler,[25] America's only titled physician, delivered a commencement address to graduating nurses at the Johns Hopkins Hospital: "You have made the practice of medicine easier to the physician." Osler neglected to add that nurses have made the practice of medicine more profitable to physicians as well. He continues,

> There is no higher mission in life than nursing God's poor. In so doing, a woman may not reach the ideals of her soul; fall short of the ideals of her head, but she will satiate those longings in her heart from which no woman can escape.[25]

This is a throwback to the patriarchal ideology that women are ruled by their hearts rather than by their heads. In 1917 the *Boston Medical and Surgical Journal* felt qualified to inform graduate nurses of their many "opportunities." The physician-author limited nurses to caring for the poor who were ill, bettering social conditions in very densely populated areas, and feeding invalids.[28] The *Journal of the American Medical Association (J.A.M.A.)* in 1913 also urged nurses into areas that physicians consider undesirable: "The instinct of the eternal feminine for sacrificial service has been her sole saving grace, the guiding light of her star of undoubted destiny."[5] In case physician readers were still unclear as to how they should view nursing, the author bluntly states, "No calling may more fitly adopt the noble motto of the noblest line of the kingly servants of men, 'I serve.' "[5]

Nurses are thought to exist only to serve men—in the form of physicians. The only rewards necessary to keep nurses "serving" are the platitudes from physicians indicating that nurses are "good girls." There is evidence here of medical misogyny and filial spite. Medicine's notion is that nurses, because they are women and tainted by their continued ties to nature, are required to redeem themselves through "sacrificial service." Medicine "guides" nursing toward this sacrificial service by employing deception. With nurses caring for "God's poor," physicians are free to serve God's rich and to make a handsome profit at nursing's expense.

From the beginning, physicians and hospital administrators controlled nursing. A 1913 *J.A.M.A.* article announced not only that physicians were fighting hospital administrators for the paternal "right" to nursing but also that nurses were indeed commodities requiring male ownership:

> With the ever-extending commodities requiring male ownership, certain social groups take on the characteristics of human commodities. They do not produce, but they conserve values. To these groups, the profession of nursing women belongs.
> Human commodities are created . . . by the need for personal service. Some particular agency of social service is frequently employed for the immediate supply of such assistance. The hospital has served as the "creative agent" of the trained nurse and, now the hospital attempts to become the maker and molder of "the thing created"—its "foster mother."[5]

Although the medical profession admits that there are actually four parties interested in this human commodity (the public—for sentimental reasons; the hosital system that it serves; the medical profession "whose essential handmaid it is"; and the group of nursing women itself), the only real contenders are physicians and hosital administrators. Physicians advance the following argument in support of rightful ownership:

> Medicine has exercised but an advisory influence over the birth and training of the nurse. It has been the habitual critic of her development, and rightly so, because the physician is ultimately the only competent judge of the fitness of the nurse, and the chief sufferer . . . for her possible unfitness.[5]

The oppressive paternalism evident in this medical statement is violent and abusive to nurses. Not only are nurses constantly referred to as "it" (which is singularly dehumanizing in itself), but nursing input is not even considered. Nurses are treated as objects to be acted upon rather than as human beings capable of action. Medicine's right to coerce and manipulate nurses is taken for granted because the paternal physician is exercising his authority for the nurse's own good.

In an attempt to lure nursing over exclusively to medicine and to establish control once and for all, medicine offered to "help" with nursing education reform before nursing leaders had a chance to reform nursing education for the benefit of nurses. Prominent physicians in 1913, touted, that educational reform for nurses

> required the combined wisdom of the leaders of the [nursing] profession *and* of their natural allies in the profession of medicine. . . .[Nursing] must determine, with the aid of the profession of medicine, whose handmaid . . . it is, its own educational fitness for the conservation of . . . human health.[5]

Physicians' motivation to "guide" nursing education in the "right direction" was based on their fear of competition by nurses. Prior to the turn of the century nursing was openly recognized as a branch of applied science that promised to be as important to the health of society as the medical profession.[3] Fearing that nursing knowledge would undermine medical stature and authority as well as threaten their jobs, medical professionals tried to dupe nurses into believing that they were an ignorant group who needed the advice and guidance of the "superior" male profession. This paternal exploitation of nurses is riddled with deception. By triggering the mental knee-jerk response with the fear that nurses do not have sufficient knowledge to educate their own people, medicine twisted the information just enough to make them understand.

To prevent further understanding through education, medicine imposed ignorance on nurses by withholding information. Nurse Linda Richards recalls that during her career that spanned the late nineteenth and early twentieth centuries, nurses were forbidden to read the medical histories of patients. Numbers rather than drug names were placed on drug bottles. "Great care was given that we should not know the names of the medicines given," Richards explains.[9]

To be certain that nurses remain ignorant and controllable, medicine employed several methods. *J.A.M.A.* enumerated them in 1906:

> 1. Every attempt at initiative on the part of nurses . . . should be reproved by the physicians. . . . 2. the programs of nursing schools . . . should be limited strictly to the indispensable matters of instruction for those in their position. . . . 3. The professional instruction of nurses should be entrusted exclusively to the physicians who only can judge what is necessary for them to know. 4. The physician, charged with this instruction should . . . in the course of their lectures, insist on the possible dangers of the initiative on the part of nurses . . . inconsiderately stepping out from their proper sphere.[24]

In 1939 Lewis Jarrett, director of the Medical College of Virginia, wrote in a hospital journal, "It must be remembered, however, that the nurse is educated and trained to administer to the patient, but only at the direction of the physician."[20] Nurses were also encouraged to accept an arrangement that made little sense to minds unencumbered by paternalism. J.M. Emmett[14] addressed the 1943 graduating class of nurses at Jefferson Hospital in Roanoke, Virginia. Although he assured the young nurses that there was nothing on the "immediate horizon" to cause them to feel that the close "relationship" between medicine and nursing would be interrupted, he still felt it necessary to caution them not to get out of line. In a paternal way this physician warned the new nurses to be good little girls and obey the physician and the medical profession would not desert them. "The inter-dependence between the nursing profession and the medical profession must necessarily be accepted if both professions are to continue their scientific efforts and promote their dual welfare."[14]

In 1970 the AMA Committee on Nursing set forth to deceive and exploit nurses with their patronizing "Position Statement." Organized medicine once again offered to "help" nurses "increase the significance of nursing as a primary component in the delivery of medical services."[1] This deceptive statement implied that the knowledge of medical tasks would increase the significance of nursing. The statement continued, "Professional nurses, by the nature of their education, are equipped to assume greater medical service responsibilities under the supervision of physicians."[1] By virtue of the fact that "nurses would . . . extend the hands of the physician," medicine limited the full development of nursing potential. This statement also stressed the need for further training of nurses—training that was to be supervised and directed by physicians.[1]

The 1970 AMA statement is a perfect example of paternalism. Medical "fathers" tell nurses what nursing needs without requesting or considering input from the nursing profession itself. Dorothy Cornelius, President of the American Nurses' Association, reacted to the AMA announcement with this reprimand: "It is not the prerogative of one profession to speak for another. We strongly object to this unilateral action by the AMA that they would attempt to meet the physician shortage by compounding the shortage of nurses."[2] The *American Journal of Nursing* news article that reported these events stated that this response had been elicited by the press "before the association could consider the proposal or even find out any details."[2] Nursing leaders across the country reacted with "shock and surprise."[2] They decried the paternalistic motivation and deception that purported to "help" nurses but that actually used nurses to meet burgeoning medical work force problems.

Despite the rebuke of medicine's deceptive paternal tactics by nursing leaders, AMA's 1970 position statement had great impact on the nursing profession, on health care, and on society. This statement provided the seeds out of which the nurse practitioner movement grew. The effects continue to be felt in the 1980s. The nurse practitioner movement is still surrounded by confusion and conflict among nurses as well as physicians.

THE NURSE PRACTITIONER MOVEMENT

Dorothy Fiorino's revealing historical study[15] of one segment of the nurse practitioner movement dramatically exposed its true intent. Fiorino's research into the beginnings and developments of the National Association of Pediatric Nurse Associates and Practitioners (NAPNAP) disclosed a model case for patriarchy masked as progress. She examined the relationship between NAPNAP and its parent organization, the American Academy of Pediatrics (AAP). These two groups worked together to promote child health care. The nursing group maintained a measure of independence but received guidance, support, and advice from the older, wiser medical group. Fiorino concluded that the true intent of the guidance—control—was hidden under layers of the false generosity of paternalism and was authenticated by the very real need to improve child health care. The AAP "guided" its daughter group by imposing controls that medical men deemed essential in attaining this goal.

In the mid-1960s the nation experienced a shortage of physicians as well as maldistribution of medical services. This shortage and maldistribution of physicians was influenced by the increasing population of infants, children, and young adults. The United States Labor Department, after conducting a Manpower Requirements, Resources, Utilization and Training Survey, mandated that physicians immediately take steps to alleviate the identified problem. The AAP responded quickly because the manpower shortage was more acute in pediatrics than in any other field.[30] Pediatricians developed the Pediatric Nurse Associate/Practitioner (PNA) role because it was a cheap, accessible, and quick way to delegate medical tasks.[15]

Fiorino's historical research unraveled the complicated medical deception surrounding the nurse practitioner role. The PNA concept, conceived of solely by physicians, was born and totally developed, approved, and accredited without nursing input. Moreover, this study illustrates how the medical profession purposely avoided nursing input because they knew that knowledgeable nursing leaders would not allow nurses to be used and exploited in this way.[15]

The blatant paternalistic control so pervasive throughout the PNA movement was succinctly summed up in a letter written by a pediatrician reaffirming the importance of pediatricians' involvement in the standards, training, and actions of the PNA. He paternalistically stated that the people in the ANA have only "limited practical experience and cannot be really aware of what is needed."[15] He expressed fear of losing his fatherly control over his nurses and added that the medical profession made a big mistake by allowing nursing education to get away from physician control and come under the control of nurses.[15]

Yet the PNA movement was touted as one of nursing's role expansions. PNAs were informed that they were "a cut above" regular nurses. Most of the nurses had no way to distinguish between benevolent and malevolent motives for physicians' interference in their profession. These nurses did not question deeply enough the chain of events that surrounded the PNA movement. "Daddy's little girl" was used to and eager for the guidance and control that she unquestioningly (but wrongly) assumed is always for her own good.

The paternalism that keeps nurses subservient, underpaid, overworked, and personally and professionally fragmented from each other persists today. The trajectory of nursing's history cannot be challenged without an awareness of the impact of paternalism on nurses and on nursing practice. Nurses can refuse to be wooed by paternal deception and exploitation. We must begin by shedding the fears and ignorance that make us amenable to external control. Our fears must be examined over and over again until they lose their power over us. Ignorance can be effectively decreased through reading, studying, and sharing our knowledge and experiences with other nurses. A united community of nurses actively sharing and working together to improve nursing practice will halt the abuses of paternalism and allow us to regain our personal and professional identities.

REFERENCES

1. AMA Committee on Nursing: Medicine and nursing in the 1970s: a position statement, Journal of the American Medical Association, 1881, 1970.
2. AMA unveils surprise plans to convert RN into medic, American Journal of Nursing **70:**691, 1970.
3. Ashley, J.: Hospitals, paternalism, and the role of the nurse, New York, 1976, Teachers College Press.
4. Ashley, J.: Nursing power: viable, vital, visible, Texas Nursing **11,** 1976.
5. Beard, R.O.: The trained nurse of the future, Journal of the American Medical Association **61:**2149, 1913.
6. Bianchi, E., and Ruether, R.: From machismo to multuality: woman-man liberation, New York, 1976, Paulist Press.
7. Bok, S.: Lying: moral choice in public and private life, New York, 1979, Vintage Books.
8. Chesler, P.: Women and madness, New York, 1972, Doubleday & Company Inc.
9. Corea, G.: The hidden malpractice, New York, 1977, William Morrow & Co., Inc.
10. Daly, M.: Gyn/ecology: The metaethics of radical feminism, Boston, 1978, Beacon Press.
11. De Beauvoir, S.: The second sex, New York, 1961, Bantam Books, Inc.
12. Dworkin, A.: Our blood: prophecies and discourses on sexual politics, New York, 1976, Harper & Row, Publishers, Inc.
13. Ehrenreich, B., and English, D.: For her own good: 150 years of the experts' advice to women, Garden City, New York, 1978, Anchor Press.
14. Emmett, J.M.: Outlook for the nursing profession, Virginia Medical Monthly **71:**29, 1944.
15. Fiorino, D.: An historical study of the National Association of Pediatric Nurse Associates/Practitioners (NAPNAP), 1973-1978, thesis, Dayton, 1980, Wright State University.
16. Freeman, H., and others: Handbook of medical sociology, ed. 3, Englewood Cliffs, N.J. 1979, Prentice-Hall, Inc.
17. Friedan, B.: The feminine mystique, New York, 1963, Dell Publishing Co., Inc.
18. Gilman, C.P.: The yellow wallpaper, New York, 1973, The Feminist Press. (Reprinted from the 1899 edition, Boston: Small, Maynard & Co.)
19. Janeway, E.: Man's world: woman's place: a study in social mythology, New York, 1971, William Morrow & Co., Inc.
20. Jarrett, L.: Professional standards affecting hospital practice, Hospitals **13:**75, 1939.
21. Lovell, M.C.: An historical study of the development of the medical profession as a business: impact on nursing and society, 1896-1979, thesis, Dayton, 1980, Wright State University.
22. Miller, J.B.: Toward a new psychology of women, Boston, 1976, Beacon Press.
23. Nightingale, F.: Cassandra. Old Westbury, N.Y., 1980, The Feminist Press.
24. Nurses' schools and the illegal practice of medicine, Journal of the American Medical Association **47:**1835, 1906.
25. Osler, W.: Aequanimitas: with other addresses to medical students, nurses and practitioners of medicine, ed. 3, Philadelphia, 1932, The Blakiston Co.
26. Rich, A.: On lies, secrets and silence, New York, 1979, W.W. Norton & Co., Inc.
27. Robinson, V.: White caps: The story of nursing, Philadelphia, 1946, J.B. Lippincott Co.
28. Torrence, G.: The trained nurse, Boston Medical and Surgical Journal **176:**573, 1917.
29. Wollstonecraft, M.: A vindication of the rights of women, New York, 1967, W.W. Norton & Co., Inc. (Reprinted from 1972 edition.)
30. Yankauer, A., and others: A survey of allied health workers utilized in pediatric practice in Massachusetts and in the United States, Pediatrics **42:**733, 1968.

BEATRICE J. KALISCH and PHILIP A. KALISCH

Chapter 14

An analysis of the sources of physician-nurse conflict

Nurses moving quietly,
  Voices hushed in awe,
All things silent waiting,
  Obedient to the law
That we have heard so often,
  But I'll repeat once more:
"All things must be in order
  When Doctor's on the floor."[16]

Yes indeed, "Doctor" was about to make his grand entrance, and woe betide the nurse who made light of it. This first stanza of a poem written three quarters of a century ago, when women were regarded as "weaker vessels" who could not survive the rigors of academic discipline and were relegated to nursing, teaching, and secretarial work, is still pertinent for discussions of the contemporary relationship between physicians and nurses. In the meantime, we have somehow discovered that nurses, who are still overwhelmingly women, do not faint from the strain of analytical thinking or necessarily lose the "delicate bloom of womanhood" in the process, and that the questioning of incongruous professional relationships will not yield a drastic decline in the marriage rate and promote "race suicide."

A number of roadblocks to effective communication have always existed between these two professionals, even though a "good" physician-nurse relationship is vital to quality patient care. Other problems have only recently become areas of conflict, and these pockets of disgruntlement seem to be growing rather than diminishing, to the degree that the relationship has been described as a deteriorating one. These roadblocks to effective communication evolve from within nurses and physicians themselves, from the character of the institutions where they work, and from the values of the society at large.

SOURCES OF CONFLICT
Physician dominance and nurse deference

Through the years the predominant behavior pattern between physician and nurse has been dominance by the former and deference by the latter. Tradition alone cannot be blamed for this authoritarian relationship, as the reasons that account for its establishment are manifold.

Consider first the physician. The opportunity to function independently is highly prized by him and is believed to be one of the reasons for the choice of medicine as a career. This expectation of independence apparently stems from an earlier era when the solo practitioner carrying his little black bag was all things to all persons. The idea was born that nurses were freely expendable and that the urgent needs of the physician took precedence over all else, with the nurse doing everything the physician did not do and apparently loving every minute of it.

Today the physician is no longer an island unto himself and is highly dependent not only on other physicians but also on other health care workers, including nurses. Yet it appears that many physicians are not fully aware of the ramifications of this major shift in health care delivery. They usually have little difficulty asking for advice and recommendations from fellow physicians, but the thought of openly consulting a nurse seems incongruous. As a partial explanation for this phenomenon, several writers attribute this reluctance to the fact that doctors feel threatened when they exhibit any signs that they are not completely independent and totally in control of all health care situations.[8,9] This high degree of individualism and desire for independence among many physicians seems to preclude or limit their capacity for being integrated into multidisciplinary teams or for developing interdependent relationships with other health care workers.

There is another characteristic that is typical of physicians, and that trait is omnipotence. In medical school would-be physicians develop deep fears of committing errors which could mean the very life of a patient. This is appropriately realistic, considering the life and death nature of his work. But in an effort to be able to function without being plagued by constant fear and anxiety, the medical student appears to gradually take on feelings of omnipotence in preparation for the world in which he will be confronted with heavy and awesome responsibilities.

This self-concept of omnipotence is also bound up with the highly authoritarian physician-patient relationship. Most physicians dominate patients and exercise a potent and unusual authority over them known as "Aesculapian authority." Patients view the physician as someone who is endowed with almost mystical healing powers.[7] Physicians promulgate such attitudes on the part of patients by keeping them relatively uninformed about their illness and treatment. They are convinced that fear would keep patients from complying with their orders if it were not for the exercise of Aesculapian authority. This general approach to patients spills over into the physician's relationship with coworkers.

Consequently, physicians have long insisted on maintaining the dominant role in the health care scene. The physician regards other health care professionals as mainly serving him in his so-called captain of the ship role rather than the whole team working side by side serving the patient. The physician makes the assumption that health care workers are carrying out delegated functions or tasks which he could perform but will not because it would be an inefficient and overly expensive use of his time. They often seem unaware that other medical workers now possess skill and knowledge which they themselves do not have.

The nurse, on the other hand, has accepted the position of deference to the physician and other authority figures. She has been described as docile, subordinated, and deferent and has traditionally had the reputation of fulfilling a role of blind obedience to orders rather than that of an autonomous professional. Most nurses have become resigned to occupying a position officially subordinate to that of the physician.

In relating to physicians, deference is so marked that nurses seem to literally bow out when physicians are present. It has been observed that if the patient and doctor both speak to the nurse at one time, the nurse will answer the physician, not the patient.[2] There is also a definite tendency for the nurse to speak only when called upon in formal sessions where physicians are present. Duff and Hollingshead[5] concluded that although they expected the nurse and the physician to work conjointly, what they actually found was that the role of the nurse was clearly subordinate to that of the physician.

Why are nurses deferent? A number of factors contribute to the primarily autocratic relationships. One reason is that most physicians are male and most nurses are female. Throughout history the good samaritan connotation of nursing has reflected the status of women in general. Men, and thus physicians, expect to take the lead in our culture and women, and thus nurses, expect to be led. In order to effect change the nurse must confront men, traditionally unacceptable behavior. Since physicians are not only men but constitute a sort of master race of males, the nurse is in for the fight of her life.

Schools of nursing have not been noted for developing independent and fearless thinkers. In fact, faculties have often added to the natural inclination toward physician dominance in many subtle ways. Overly questioning and rebellious students have often been systematically culled out of the nursing school as "troublemakers." Fear of physician criticism is instilled in students, sometimes unknowingly, by faculty who have been unable to analyze the effects of their own earlier education. Not more than a decade or two ago, nursing students were still being taught to give up their seat to the physician. Then, too, the former restrictive atmosphere of schools did not give students much opportunity to develop creativity and independent thinking.

Another reason for nurse deference is due to the level of education of the physicians. They are more highly educated than most nurses. Unlike physicians, who have mandated the highest levels of education for the practice of medicine and for the medical researcher, nurses have only recently begun to see the value of well-educated practitioners, teachers, and researchers. The educational gap, although narrowing more and more, has severely hindered the development of mutual respect.

Nurses are deferent also because as a group they typically come from a lower socioeconomic class than physicians and their incomes tend to keep them lower. Parents of higher social classes have not encouraged their sons and daughters to choose nursing. Before medicine capitalized on the skyrocketing demand for health care by indirectly limiting the supply of doctors under the guise of standards, doctors and nurses were more equal in socioeconomic status. Forty years ago, the average nonsalaried physician earned $4,695 and the average graduate nurse earned $1,220 or the physician earned approximately three times as much as the nurse. Today the average nurse earns about $11,000 while the average physician earns five to six times as much or more. This socioeconomic gap means that there is less likelihood that nurses and physicians in their personal life will interact, since their typical socialization patterns are so divergent.

One result of this pattern of communication of the nurse-physician relationship had been to severely limit the quantity of communication between nurses and physicians. Wessen[15] found that in the hospital unit the physician is three times more likely to speak to another physician than to a nurse, and his interaction with personnel in other occupational groups is minimal. Similarly, the frequency of conversational interaction of a nurse with other nurses on the unit is approximatley twice that of a nurse with other types of coworkers.[15]

Duff and Hollingshead[5] observed the same phenomenon, discovering that it was unusual for nurses and physicians to visit patients together, much less to let the other one know what the plans for care were. The order sheets were the chief means of communication, and those of course were one-way. Such absence of communication between the two groups has been described as characterizing caste-like relations.

The effect of these nurse-physician communication patterns has had dysfunctional consequences on patient care. Alarmingly, Holfing and his associates[6] demonstrated that nurses were willing to comply with an unknown physician's telephone order to give an unknown drug at twice the maximum dosage. Of the 22 instances, 21 nurses proceeded to administer the drug. This experiment clearly indicates that while in theory there should be two professional minds at work to ensure adequate care for the patient, one of these intelligences, the nurse's, for all practical purposes, is not functioning. It seems clear that the nurse's desire to gain gratitude, praise, and approval from the physician supersedes at times her need to be a competent professional in her own right. A large amount of self-deception goes on within the nurse.

Another result of nurse passivity and physician dominance is what has been called the doctor-nurse game. Stein[14] points out that rarely does one hear a nurse say, "Doctor I would recommend that you order a retention enema for Mrs. Brown." Stein adds that a physician, "upon hearing a recommendation of that nature, would gape in amazement at the boldness of the nurse. The nurse, upon hearing the statement, would look over her shoulder to see who said it, hardly believing the words actually came from her own mouth. Nevertheless, if one observes closely, nurses make recommendations of more import every hour and physicians willingly and respectfully consider them."[14] If the nurse is to make a suggestion without appearing insolent and the doctor is to seriously consider that suggestion, Stein says that their interaction must not violate the rules of the doctor-nurse game.

In playing this game the nurse is to be responsible for making significant recommendations while at the same time appearing passive. This must be done in a manner to make her contributions seem to be those of the physician. The physician, in requesting the advice or assistance of a nurse, must do so without it being noticed.

Physicians' devaluation of nursing

Related to the dominance-deference pattern, another source of conflict in the nurse-physician relationship is the growing unhappiness of nurses about the value they perceive physicians place on their independent contributions to patient care. As an observer so aptly put it in verse[11]:

> She must feel like a girl,
> act like a lady,
> think like a man
> and work like a dog.

While the strong back–weak mind concept may have disappeard to a large extent, many physicians still view the nurse's role as primarily one of carrying out their orders and reporting the patient's progress to them. When physicians are asked for suggestions for the improvement of nursing care, they typically answer that they would prefer more precise compliance with their orders. Good nursing care is equated with the fulfillment of physicians' demands.

Patients are much more positive about the importance of nursing care than are physicians. Zaslove[17] found that when psychiatric patients, their residents and the head nurses were asked to list what helped the patients most during hospitalization, 31 percent of the patients identified nursing as most helpful and another 59 percent mentioned it as helpful. By contrast, only 1 percent of the physicians stated that nursing was most helpful, and only 2 percent mentioned it at all.

Shortell[12] at the University of Chicago studied the occupational prestige differeces within the medical professions. He contrasted the views of 117 physicians and 66 patients who were asked to rank order some 41 job categories. Each of the medical specilizations—chest surgery, internal medicine, pediatrics, etc.—represented a job category along with the director of nursing service, the RN, pharmacist, LPN, aide, and others. The only large variation among the two rankings was for nursing, which the patients rated as much more prestigious than did the physicians. The patients ranked nursing 19th, while the physicians rated it 27th. Patients ranked nurses higher than the medical specialties of psychiatry, preventive medicine, dermatology, allergy, and general practice.

Lack knowledge of other profession

A number of other factors cause communication problems between physicians and nurses. One perennial source of difficulty is that physicians do not understand the functions and goals of the nurse and the nurse lacks insight into the scope of the physician's responsibilities. Neither is able to empathize with the other's viewpoint. Physicians and nurses place different values on specific parts of the health care process, and these divergent values lead to differences between professionals in assessing the relative weight of patient problems. Traditionally, medical and nursing students have not studied together, nor have their curriculums provided them with information about the contributions of the other. Consequently they work their entire professional careers side by side without really understanding what the other is about. This fact has prompted the statement that physician-nurse communication is most characteristic of the parallel play of toddlers.

Psychosocial emphasis

A specific area of misunderstanding has been the greater emphasis the nurse has placed on the psychological aspects of patient care. Physicians feel that nurses have moved too far in this direction, that they are guilty of ignoring physical needs; and nurses believe that physicians have forgotten about the patient as a person.

Nurses' retreat from patients

The nurse's retreat from direct patient care to administrative duties has taken its toll on the physician-nurse relationship. The management duties interfere with the nurse's intimacy with the patients. This reduction in time that the nurse spends with the patient has reduced the communication between herself and the physician, which as had a detrimental effect on their relationship. Lack of opportunity to communicate has resulted in a sizeable loss of understanding. Another part of this phenomenon is that the very reason for the nurse-physician relationship, that is, their mutual concern for the patient, has been eroded because the nurse is not giving direct care. In other words, the common ground between the two has all but disappeared.

Wide range of education

The wide range of educational preparation existing among nursing personnel has been confusing to physicians and has led to further communication problems. Moreover, until the recent past the most-prepared nurses were removed from direct patient care, and thus physicians have already had the opportunity to work with them.

Two systems of authority

Stress and tension on the interpersonal level in hospitals can be traced also to clashes that occur due to two existing systems of authority. Students of hospital administration tell us that the organizational chart should be arranged so that the hospital administrator is over both the department of medicine and the department of nursing. On the nursing side, the hierarchical lines should flow from the director of nursing to the nursing supervisors, head nurses, staff nurses, licensed practical nurses, and aides. From the head of the department of medicine, the line of command should be from the attending physician to the chief resident, senior resident, resident, and intern. In reality the nurse receives orders not only through the hospital administration hierarchy but also from physicians.

These lines of authority inevitably come into conflict since they tend to have overlapping jurisdiction over certain areas. Each system is oriented to a different set of values, one emphasizing the maintenance of the operation of the organization, the other emphasizing the provision of service. Many times the nurse receives dual orders which contradict one another, and it is up to her to resolve the conflicts. Furthermore, she is rarely offered much assistance from anyone (including nursing administration) in this anxiety-ridden task. The nurse feels ambivalent as to which way to go. The difficulties stemming from structural arrangements become associated with interpersonal stresses, the level of morale, and with the attitudes of physicians and nurses toward one another.[13]

Lack of professional commitment

The fact that nursing has been a female's profession has created another serious problem. Since society has until recently valued marriage and motherhood for females above any other vocation, nurses, being women, have also valued these goals above their profession. Nurses have not been career oriented, and most often consider their work as secondary. This fact has led to such stereotypes as the "appliance nurse," one who works only long enough to buy a washing machine or dishwasher for the family. It has been said that the prospect of marriage and children has permeated every aspect of nursing, that no part of the profession can be understood "apart from the influence of marriage plans or its frustration."[4] The high turnover rates have led to limited opportunities for the same physicians and nurses to interact as colleagues. Whether nurses choose to admit it or not, this lack of professional commitment has severely diminished respect of nurses by physicians.

Essentially, nursing has been composed of a small proportion of policy makers, nurses dedicated to professionalization and improvement striving to mobilize a group of mostly casual and transient workers. The real leadership in nursing is like the head of a dinosaur, with the massive body of the dinosaur representing by far the largest health profession—some 900,000 persons—but a woefully silent majority.

More education frowned on

Physicians in general have not been enthralled with nurses becoming better educated. Nurses who tell physicians they are going back to school inevitably receive the response: *"Why do you want to do that?"* Nurses have resented this attitude, feeling that physicians are trying to keep them from sharing the medical stage and from gaining more prestige and recognition. Physicians state that they do not value higher education for nurses because they have not seen the improved care which is supposed to result from additional years in school and additionally they believe that more education means decreased patient contact.

Policing one another

Nurses and physicians are in a position to police one another's performance, at least to the degree that their functions overlap, and this policing activity has caused many a ruffled feather on both sides of the patient care arena. It has been alleged that because the nurse is the only person in a position to observe the work of the physician, he has been anxious to keep her in the subservient, and thus unquestioning, role. Nurses, however, have traditionally been subjected to outrages by physicians (often in front of patients) about the quality of their work. Yet they have been highly reluctant to overtly challenge medical decisions.

A growing restlessness among nurses is evident, however. They are beginning to fight the battles necessitated in order to break the shackles that have kept them subservient and powerless all these years. The June, 1975, issue of *Modern Healthcare*, for example, tells the story of a group of nurses at St. Agnes Hospital in Philadelphia. A nurse refusing to administer a medication because she believed it to be harmful became involved in a heated doctor-nurse confrontation which eventually led to the dismissal of the director of nursing. The nurses were alarmed and protested for the director's reinstatement. In the end 30 nurses resigned.[3]

Fear of usurpation of responsibility

The problem of overlapping of functions and responsibilities between medicine and nursing is large. The rise of the nurse practitioner has been especially alarming to physicians who fear that their responsibility will be usurped. The American Academy of Pediatrics, for example, originally subscribed to a AAP-ANA liaison committee statement that pediatric nurse practitioners should be able to function both independently and cooperatively with pediatricians and that the nursing profession would be in charge of training and certification. Thinking about this further, the AAP, apparently fearing too much independent action and competition for patients by nursing, decided to withdraw its support and develop its own certification test. Instead of moving toward collaboration, the battle lines are being drawn.

Nurses lack of control over nursing

Another source of contention is that while physicians resent nurses stepping over the border into medicine, they feel that it is their right to meddle in nursing. This stems, of course, from the concept that they are the overall authority on all aspects of health care. Medicine has been known to block the delivery of nursing care. For example, in one hospital the authors visited in early 1975, no child could be taken to the play room without a physician's order. As a more enlightened physician, Barbara Bates,[1] cogently remarked, nursing only "wants access to the patient and sufficient control over the nurse-patient encounter to deliver its own unique product, full nursing care."

Political conflicts

Organized medicine and organized nursing have been in opposition on a number of important issues, and these policy decisions have sometimes created rifts between physicians and nurses. For years, the American Medical Association did not support federal aid to nursing and was successful in blocking bills that would have gone a long way toward upgrading the educational and practice levels of nursing. The American Nurses' Association dared to endorse Medicare and other national health insurance programs as far back as 1946 in spite of the vehement opposition of the AMA. Some physicians went so far as to require that their office nurses drop membership in ANA when Medicare was endorsed.

TOWARD A NEW RELATIONSHIP

Considering the factors just discussed, it is not surprising that the nurse-physician relationship is conflict-ridden and fraught with problems. Solutions to the dilemmas are not easy, but a variety of approaches must be employed. Some have to do with working on inner attitudes, while others will necessitate attempts on a one-to-one basis with physicians. Still others will involve group action.

Capitalize on women's lib

Women's Lib fortunately is helping to solve some part of nursing's problem by decreasing the subservient role of women in general. The movement has led to a greater role for women in generating the family income, even for those who are married and have children. Knowing that they will be working as opposed to having a choice in the matter, many nurses are more committed to investing the energy essential to gain improvements. The new consciousness of women has led to less acquiescence among the female group in general.

Increased patient care

A "new" relationship between nurses and physicians will not just happen if nurses quietly sit back and wait. Thoughtful action must be taken. To begin with, nurses must continue their movement away from non-nursing managerial duties and toward direct patient care. Primary nursing, clinical specialists, and nurse practitioners are hopeful examples of this trend. Back in the realm of patient care, nurses and physicians will have an essential need to communicate with one another about patient care. Moreover, the better prepared and most competent nurses will be exposed to, rather than hidden from, physicians.

Patients who reap the benefits of quality nursing care instead of the typical non-care received today will become a much-needed nurse advocate. Consumers will be playing an increasingly more important role in determining the type and character of their health care in future years. The day of doctor dominance is on the wane, much like the decline of the "robber baron" businessmen of 75 years ago.

Educating the physician

Since physicians do not fully understand what nursing has to offer, an educational campaign is desperately needed. Every possible method should be used to spread the message—from posters to special seminars. One-to-one contacts with physicians should be capitalized upon as opportunities for nurses to underline their unique and overlapping contributions to the health care process. Another subtle goal of such a campaign would be to reduce the physician's fear that nurses want to become "doctorettes."

Open communication

Typically nurses grumble about physicians only to one another, yet direct confrontation with physicians about problems must occur on both formal and informal levels if an improved relationship is to evolve, whether or not a formalized health care team exists. In order to avoid physician defensiveness, at least a high degree of defensiveness, an angry, sarcastic or hostile attack should be avoided. Since nurses are reputed to have more training in facilitative communication than physicians, they should be clever enough to use their skills, not just with patients and other personnel, but also with physicians. An empathic, nondefensive, but persistent and aggressive approach is likely to be the most successful.

Such an approach is not aimed toward feeding a physician's ego; instead these are the rules for effectively relating with any human being. For example, imagine how differently a physician would respond to these two divergent comments by a nurse: "I noticed you wrote an order for us to turn Mr. Smith every hour. Since this is a nursing care responsibility, I wonder if you have experienced some problem recently where this was not done?" or "Why do you find it necessary to write orders for nursing care? We're sick of you telling us what to do." The former statement, which aims toward an empathic insight into the physician's viewpoint, would open the way for a discussion of the matter; the latter would cut off communication.

Many misunderstandings between physicians and nurses could be solved if both parties would devote the necessary time to discuss them openly. Nursing administrators need to support and help nurses work through these communication strategies.

Team development

Everyone agrees that nurses and physicians, along with other health care workers and the patient, should be working as teams. Everyone agrees but few actually achieve it. There is good reason, too. Smooth and effective team functioning is difficult to develop, and yet it is in this arena that the physician-nurse conflicts will really be solved.

The first order of business is the negotiation of new roles. This process of role realignment is exceedingly painful and time consuming. The interdependent nature of medicine and nursing with the overlap of function means that they must mutually work toward the sorting out of responsibility. Nursing cannot change without affecting medicine and vice versa. On the road to collaboration, competition and controversy are inevitable and somehow nurses must become comfortable with aggression.

This role realignment causes an enormous amount of anxiety, uncertainty, and frustration for each member. Trust in the performance of the others is essential and, to achieve it, open facilitative communication is vital. Conflicts must be dealt with directly; problems cannot be ignored or submerged. When each team member does not take the time and/or does not have the courage to reveal his or her genuine concerns about that is expected of him by the others and what he expects in turn, the results will be a non-team of sorts and the patient is the loser.

Leadership of the team is a major irritant. Physicians automatically assume the leadship of health care teams, and since they are high status in the group their opinions tend to dominate. Malcolm Peterson[10] notes that "if the physician is always the captain of the team, and if everyone else handles only what he chooses to delegate and delivers services only according to his dictates, there will continue to be no team function."

Attack on autocracy

While attempts toward improved communication are essential and will help a great deal, predictably they will not be enough. The hard solution to the physician-nurse relationship is that nurses are going to have to become aggressive. Nurses can blame a large portion of their dilemma on their own willingness to passively accept their deferent position as idealistic "good samaritans" who will always get by no matter how bad the conditions under which they must work and the treatment they are afforded. Physicians are not going to willingly relinquish their authority.

Nurses obviously need more power if they are going to be in a position to act independently and to foster their ideas for improvement of patient care. Fiscal resources are typicaly essential for power, but nursing service administrators have rarely been endowed with an adequate budget to meet their responsibilities. The 4,000 San Francisco nurse strikers of June, 1974, wanted a greater voice in the running of hospitals and the care of patients. The sad reality is that protests by nurses in this and other ways will have to become more common if inroads are to be made. Of course all other methods for achieving the goal at hand should be exhausted first.

There is a great merit in working as groups—the larger the better—because obviously they carry more clout. A strategy meeting to discuss the problem at hand and what to do about it might turn out to be amazingly fruitful. Documentation of the need in rational terms will go a long way toward convincing physicians why changes are needed.

It is absolutely imperative that nurses become assertive at once. The emerging health planning movement along with the impending national health insurance program that is sure to become law in the near future will have the effect of redefining role prescriptions and authority among health care workers. If nurses are not loudly represented in large numbers, when the new rules and regulations are being formulated, they are sure to be locked into tightly defined positions which will drastically limit their upward drive for a larger, more responsible role in health care. Additional action is needed to secure access to third party payments for nurses functioning as independent practitioners. This pool of money long ago mitigated the financial risk to physicians and most hospitals in caring for indigent patients.

REFERENCES

1. Bates, B.: Physician and nurse practitioner: conflict and reward, Annals of Internal Medicine 3(6):703, 1965.
2. Blum, R.: Management of doctor-patient relationship, New York, 1960, McGraw-Hill Book Co.
3. Cleary, D.M.: A nonstrike for patient care, Modern Healthcare 3(6):43, 1975.
4. Corwin, R.G., and Tawes, M.J.: Nursing and other health professions. In Freeman, H.E., and others, editors: Handbook of medical sociology, Englewood Cliffs, N.J., 1963, Prentice-Hall, Inc.
5. Duff, R.S., and Hollingshead, A.B.: Sickness and society, New York, 1968, Harper & Row, Publishers, Inc.
6. Holfling, C.K., and others: An experimental study in nurse-physician relationships, Journal of Nervous and Mental Disorders 143(2):171, 1966.
7. Kalisch, B.J.: Of half-gods and mortals: Aesculapian authority, Nursing Outlook 23(1):22, 1975.
8. Kane, R.L., and Kane, R.A.: Physicians' attitudes of omnipotence in a university hospital, Journal of Medical Education 44(8):684, 1969.
9. Magraw, R.M.: Ferment in medicine: a study of the essence of medical practice and of its new dilemmas, Philadelphia, 1966, W.B. Saunders Co.
10. Peterson, M: Interdependence: how can the team play the game. In Lippard, V.W., and Purcell, E.F., editors: Intermediate level health practitioners, New York, 1973, The Josiah Macy Jr. Foundation.
11. Pratt, H.: The doctor's view of the changing nurse-physician relationship, Journal of Medical Education 40(8):767, 1965.
12. Shortell, S.M.: Occupational prestige differences within the medical and allied health professions, Social Science and Medicine 8(1):1, 1974.
13. Smith, H.L.: Two lines of authority: the hospital's dilemma. In Jaco, E.G., editor: Patients, physicians and illness: sourcebook in

behavioral science and medicine, New York, 1958, The Free Press.

14. Stein, L.I.: The doctor-nurse game, Archives of General Psychiatry 16:699, 1967.

15. Wessen, A.F.: Hospital ideology and communication between ward personnel. In Jaco, E.G., editor: Patients, physicians and illness: sourcebook in behavioral science and medicine, New York, 1958, The Free Press.

16. When doctor's on the floor, Trained Nurse Hospital Review 16:90, 1896.

17. Zaslove, M.O., and others: The importance of the psychiatric nurse: views of physicians, patients, and nurses, American Journal of Psychology 125(73):482, 1968.

JANET MUFF

Chapter 15

Altruism, socialism, and nightingalism

The compassion traps

Is health care a right? Do your services as a nurse *belong* to others? Do the services of doctors *belong* to others? NO!

Nurses, I know, are divided on this issue. Hildegarde Peplau[24] defines a right as a "social invention—an idea that arises from among the people, an expectation or demand formulated as a claim, which attains further power through custom or law." She is wrong. If expectations, demands, or claims constitute rights, then the demand of a mugger for your wallet or the expectation of a nursing supervisor that you work a double shift without your consent would also constitute rights. Anyone would have the "right" to lay claim to the belongings or services of others. Don't be ridiculous, you say: rights are determined by society. But what *is* society if not individuals? There is only one basic right, the right to life, from which all other rights evolve.

HUMAN RIGHTS*

A "right" defines a freedom of action. For instance, a right to a material object is the uncoerced choice of the use to which that object will be put; a right to a specific action, such as free speech, is the freedom to engage in that activity without forceful repression. The moral foundation of the rights of man begins with the fact that he is a living creature: he has the right to his own life. All other rights are corollaries of this primary one; without the right to life, there can be no others, and the concept of rights itself becomes meaningless.

The freedom to live, however, does not automatically ensure life. For man, a specific course of action is required to sustain his life, a course of action that must be guided by reason and reality and has as its goal the creation or acquisition of material

---

*This section is reprinted from Sade, R.: Medical care as a right: a refutation. Reprinted by permission of The New England Journal of Medicine **285**:1288, 1971. Originally published as Is health care a right? A negative response, Image 7(1), 1974.

values, such as food and clothing, and intellectual values, such as self-esteem and integrity. His moral system is the means by which he is able to select the values that will support his life and achieve his happiness.

The right to life implies three corollaries: the right to select the values that one deems necessary to sustain one's own life; the right to exercise one's own judgment of the best course of action to achieve the chosen values; and the right to dispose of those values, once gained, in any way one chooses, without coercion by other men. The denial of any one of these corollaries severely compromises or destroys the right to life itself. A man who is not allowed to choose his own goals is prevented from setting his own course in achieving those goals and is not free to dispose of the values he has earned is no less than a slave to those who usurp those rights. The right to private property, therefore, is essential and indispensable to maintaining free men in a free society.

In a free society, man exercises his right to sustain his own life by producing economic values in the form of goods and services that he is, or should be, free to exchange with other men who are similarly free to trade with him or not. The economic values produced, however, are not given as gifts by nature, but exist only by virtue of the thought and effort of individual men. Goods and services are thus owned as a consequence of the right to sustain life by one's own physical and mental effort.

If the chain of natural rights is interrupted, and the right to a loaf of bread, for example, is proclaimed as primary (avoiding the necessity of earning it), every man owns a loaf of bread, regardless of who produced it. Since ownership is the power of disposal, every man may take his loaf from the baker and dispose of it as he wishes with or without the baker's permission. Another element has thus been introduced into the relation between men: the use of force. It is crucial to observe who has initiated the use of force: it is the man who demands unearned bread as a right, not the man who produced it. At the level of an unstructured society it is clear who is moral and who immoral. The man who acted rationally by producing food to support his own life is moral. The man who expropriated the bread by force is immoral.

To protect this basic right to provide for the support of one's own life, men band together for their mutual protection and form governments. This is the only proper function of government: to provide for the defense of individuals against those who would take lives or property by force. The state is the repository for retaliatory force in a just society wherein the only actions prohibited to individuals are those of physical harm or the threat of physical harm to other men. The closest that man has ever come to achieving this ideal of government was in this country after its War of Independence.

When a government ignores the progression of natural rights arising from the right to life, and agrees with a man, a group of men, or even a majority of its citizens, that every man has a right to a loaf of bread, it must protect that right by the passage of laws ensuring that everyone gets his loaf—in the process depriving the baker of the freedom to dispose of his own product. If the baker disobeys the law, asserting the priority of his right to support himself by his own rational disposition of the fruits of his mental and physical labor, he will be taken to court by force or threat of force where he will have more property forcibly taken from him (by fine) or have his liberty taken away (by incarceration). Now the initiator of violence is the government itself, the degree to which it has eroded its own legitimacy. It is a frequently overlooked fact that behind every law is a policeman's gun or a soldier's bayonet. When that gun and bayonet are used to initiate violence, to take property or to restrict liberty by force, there are no longer any rights, for the lives of the citizens belong to the state. In a just society with a moral government, it is clear that the only "right" to the bread belongs to the baker, and that a claim by any other man to that right is unjustified and can be enforced only by violence or the threat of violence.

ANTILIFE ETHICS: ALTRUISM, SOCIALISM, AND NIGHTINGALISM

Three philosophies—altruism, socialism, and nightingalism—repudiate the rights of individuals in the name of "sympathy for others," in the name of "society," and in the name of "patients." They share a common base in that they sacrifice some individuals for the sake of others, a morally indefensible position.

Altruism

Altruism is the philosophy of valuing others higher than oneself. It is based on "the principle that man is a sacrificial animal, that the only justification for his existence is the service he renders to others, and that any consideration for the men who provide the services is irrelevant." Altruism implies that self-sacrifice is a virtue and that one's own needs should come second to those of others. Nathaniel Branden generously allows me to include his discussion, "Benevolence versus Altruism," which is helpful in clarifying the differences between these concepts:

> A disastrous confusion in the minds of most people concerning the nature of altruism is the belief that altruism represents or derives from the principle of benevolence, good will and kindness toward others. Advocates of altruism take great pains to encourage this belief—to establish a "package-deal," as it were—so as to conceal from their victims the actual meaning of the altruist morality.
> Such a view of altruism is worse than mistaken: like the perversion entailed in the technique of the "Big Lie," it represents the exact *opposite* of the truth; altruism and benevolence are not merely different, they are *mutually inimical and contradictory.*
> The literal philosophical meaning of altruism is: *placing others above self.* As an ethical principle, altruism holds that man must make the welfare of others his primary concern and must place their interests above his own; it holds that man has no right to exist for his own sake, that service to others is the moral justification of his existence, that self-sacrifice is his foremost duty and highest virtue.
> The essence of altruism is the concept of *self-sacrifice*. It is the *Self* that altruism regards

as evil: *selflessness* is its moral ideal. Thus it is an *anti-self* ethics—and this means: anti-man, anti-personal happiness, and anti-individual rights.

A morality that tells man that he is to regard himself as a sacrificial animal, is *not* an expression of benevolence or good will.

By the nature of the altruist ethics, it can engender only fear and hostility among men: it forces men to accept the role of victim or executioner, as objects of sacrifice or profiteers on human sacrifice—and leaves men no standard of justice, no way to know what they can demand and what they must surrender, what is theirs by right, what is theirs by favor, what is theirs by someone's sacrifice—thereby casting men into an amoral jungle. Contrary to the pretensions of altruism's advocates, it is human brotherhood and good will among men that altruism makes *impossible*.

Benevolence, good will and respect for the rights of others proceed from an *opposite* code of morality: from the principle that man the individual is not an object of sacrifice but an entity of *supreme value:* that each man exists for his own sake and is not a means to the ends of others: that *no one has the right to sacrifice anyone*.

Men of self-esteem, uncorrupted by the altruist morality, are the only men who can and do value human life—because they value their own life, because they are secure in the knowledge of their right to it, and because, to them, *"human being"* is a designation of honor. It is one's view of *oneself* that determines one's view of man and of human stature. The respect and good will that men of self-esteem feel toward other human beings is profoundly egoistic; they feel, in effect: "Other men are of value because they are of the same species as myself." In revering living entities, they are revering their *own* life. This is the psychological base of any emotion of sympathy and any feeling of "species solidarity."

But this causal relation cannot be reversed: A man must *first* value himself; only then can he value others. If a man does not value himself, *nothing* can have value for him.*

Altruism is morally wrong. It repudiates the highest value—the right to one's life—by saying that the needs of others constitute a claim or right to one's own services or goods. It says, in fact, that if someone needs, you *must* give. Many of us, as human beings, as nurses, value other individuals and choose to help them. This is benevolence; it involves choice. Altruism, on the other hand, does not involve free choice on the part of the giver. It changes the motivation for helping others from love to mandated obedience, "from handouts to handcuffs."[23] Each of us as individuals has the right to give or not to give, to help or not to help; society as a collective does not have that right.

How is it that individuals have come to believe in such ethics? Often this happens because they are taught that self-interest is wrong, that assertiveness injures others. Rational individuals must act in their own self-interest, must work to achieve their values, and must be responsible for earning their own happiness. Those who cannot are parasites.

If men lack the self-esteem and courage to assert their right to exist, altruism assures them that this is the virtue of self-lessness. If they lack the independence, integrity and

---

*From Branden, N.: Benevolence versus altruism, The Objectivist Newsletter 1(7):27, 1962.

ambition to fight for their value, altruism assures them that this is the virtue of renunciation. If they dread the responsibility of relying on their own mind, and prefer to surrender it to the authority of others, altruism assures them that this is the virtue of faith. . . . It is harder to achieve self-esteem than to practice self-sacrifice. But there is no substitute for self-esteem and no way to achieve it except by working to live up to one's highest potentiality as a rational, integrated, efficacious human being. The secret appeal of altruism for many people is that it offers them the delusion that an alternative is possible.*

Altruism is close to socialism, which is also anti-self. Socialism advocates collective ownership of goods and services. In a socialist society there are no individual rights and there is no private property. One's services, the goods one produces, belong to and are disposed of by the collective. Socialism is also morally wrong.

Underlying the move toward socialized medicine in our society are the ethics of altruism and socialism, the ethic that the needs of some lay claim to the lives of others. Health care, we are told, is a right, a corollary to the basic right to life.[23] And we are beginning to believe it; we are confusing benevolence and compassion with slavery.

"We are witnessing a 'consumer's revolution' in health care," says Evelyn Benson.[4] "There is a growing conviction . . . that the use of health services should not be contingent on one's ability and *willingness* to pay, that health services are not like most other goods and services" (emphasis added). Health services are most certainly like other goods and services; they are the products and toils of human beings, and as such they belong to those human beings to dispose of as they wish. Statements such as these are based on the altruistic-socialistic assumption that the needs of some constitute a claim to the property of others and that this claim is valid. Where will such reasoning end? Food is a basic need (whereas health care is not). Does that mean that you or I can walk into the local supermarket and demand our *right* to milk, bread, or meat? What will happen when we are no longer *willing* to pay for food? Where do we draw the line?

Socialized medicine†

The concept of medical care as the patient's right is immoral because it denies the most fundamental of all rights, that of a man to his own life and the freedom of action to support it. Medical care is neither a right nor a privilege: it is a service that is provided by doctors and others to people who wish to purchase it. It is the provision of this service that a doctor depends upon for his livelihood, and is his means of supporting his own life. If the right to health care belongs to the patient, he starts out owning the services of a doctor without the necessity of either earning them or receiving them as a gift from the only man who has the right to give them: the

---

*From Branden, N.: Intellectual ammunition department, The Objectivist Newsletter 2(10):39, 1963.
†This section is reprinted from Sade, R.: Medical care as a right: a refutation. Reprinted by permission of The New England Journal of Medicine 285:1288, 1971. Originally published as Is health care a right? A negative response, Image 7(1), 1974.

doctor himself. In the narrative above substitute "doctor" for "baker" and "medical service" for "bread." American medicine is now at the point in the story where the state has proclaimed the nonexistent "right" to medical care as a fact of public policy, and has begun to pass the laws to enforce it. The doctor finds himself less and less his own master and more and more controlled by forces outside of his own judgment.

Any act of force is anti-mind. It is a confession of the failure of persuasion, the failure of reason. When politicians say that the health system must be forced into a mold of their own design, they are admitting their inability to persuade doctors and patients to use the plan voluntarily; they are proclaiming the supremacy of the state's logic over the judgments of the individual minds of all concerned with health care. Statists throughout history have never learned that compulsion and reason are contradictory, that a forced mind cannot think effectively, and by extension, that a regimented profession will eventually choke and stagnate from its own lack of freedom.

Any doctor who is forced by law to join a group or a hospital he does not choose, or is prevented by law from prescribing a drug he thinks is best for his patient, or is compelled by law to make any decision he would not otherwise have made, is being forced to act against his own mind, which means forced to act against his own life. He is also being forced to violate his most fundamental professional commitment, that of using his own best judgment at all times for the greatest benefit of his patient. It is remarkable that this principle has never been identified by a public voice in the medical profession, and that the vast majority of doctors in this country are being led down the path to civil servitude, never knowing that their feelings of uneasy foreboding have a profoundly moral origin, and never recognizing that the main issues at stake are not those being formulated in Washington, but are their own honor, integrity and freedom, and their own survival as sovereign human beings.

Nightingalism

> Never send to know for whom the bell tolls;
> it tolls for *thee*.
>
> **John Donne:** *Devotions*

Do not delude yourself into thinking that socialized medicine is the problem of physicians. It is *our* problem, yours and mine as individuals, because it abrogates the most fundamental right—the right to life. We as nurses are not free from the influences of altruism and socialism; they pervade our ways of thinking, the ethics of our profession, and the mores of our workplaces. Only the name is different: in nursing it is called nightingalism. Nightingalism, the philosophy of the handmaiden nurse, is based on the ethics of altruism (selflessness is a virtue) and socialism (the needs of the collective supersede the rights of individuals).

What reason do most women give for entering nursing? They want to "help" people. What an admirable notion. Unfortunately, altruism and good intentions, as every nurse soon learns, are not enough. Nursing requires brains and skill. As Bernard Shapiro[25] puts it, "self-sacrifice on the altar of larger social benefit may appear heroic, but . . . it usually ends in incompetence." I believe that the fact that most nurses are women is fundamental to the ethics of self-sacrifice in nursing.

SOCIALIZED SELFLESSNESS: TEACHING WOMEN "TO KNOW THEIR PLACE" The first unit of this book deals exhaustively with female socialization and its implications for self-esteem and achievement. We are told that girls and boys are raised differently. "A girl," for example, "is taught that she has to be liked if she wants to be a winner. A boy is taught to concentrate on winning if he wants to be a winner."[14] Girls, then, develop high affiliative needs for love and approval from others. These take precedence over needs for independence and achievement. As a matter of fact, girls learn that to *be* independent and to achieve are not necessary (what are males for, if not to depend on?) and are unfeminine.[17] Women learn that to achieve may threaten their womanliness and may anger men and other women. They support their husbands' successes and those of their children—vicarious achievement is safer.[11]

Females learn too that their role is inextricably bound to subservience and selflessness. Society devalues women, assigns them inferior roles, denigrates them, and hampers their development of self-esteem. Mothers pass on their difficulties to daughters. Subservience to males, to children, and to the needs of others without concern for oneself is woman's lot. Perpetual subservience engenders self-hate and other-hate. Women learn that to express hatred toward others, however, is to lose them; therefore anger is denied and turned against the self. Women learn to feel worthless, to blame themselves, and to see themselves (as society sees them) as second rate.

Women, then, are concerned with *giving;* men are concerned with *doing.*[21] Women derive their self-esteem, their sense of worth, from giving to and caring for others rather than from personal achievement. The need of one human being in our society automatically becomes the responsibility of another, usually a woman. And most nurses are women. They have learned to give and to serve—to give because patients need, and to serve physicians.

HISTORICAL SELFLESSNESS: TEACHING NURSES TO BE HANDMAIDENS Nurses derive their self-worth from knowing that they are helping others. The tradition is a long one, originating probably with the creation of the role but gaining stature from Florence Nightingale. The role of the nurse was to be loyal and devoted in caring for the hospital family. "Through service and self-sacrifice, they were to work continuously to keep the 'family' happy."[1] And nurses learn the lesson well, almost to the point of forgetting that Florence Nightingale was more than just the lady with a lamp; she was strong willed, intelligent, forceful, and political.[26]

CONTEMPORARY SELFLESSNESS: THE COMPASSION TRAPS Female socialization and the nursing tradition have combined to give most nurses a legacy of selfless, subservient ethics. Nurses, we know, are not happy: they drop out or burn out; they bemoan their victimization but seem mired in inactivity. They are unable to take pleasure in their work, a mental state called anhedonia, the causes of which have been described by Bloomfield and Kory[5]:

Fear of pleasure	Approval seeking
Stress overload	Self-rejection
Getting stuck	Anger
Guilt	Loss of values
Worry	

These attitudes and behaviors that result in dissatisfaction and the inability to experience pleasure are germane to the situation of nurses.

Do nurses fear pleasure? I think so, at least to some extent. Have you ever heard a nurse say, "Things are going so well, I'm waiting for something bad to happen" or "I'm dreading my evaluation. I mean, *I* think I do good work, but I just get nervous about evaluations." Where do such thoughts come from? Is the world really so malevolent? Probably not, but people, especially women, have been taught that pleasure and putting oneself first (selfishness) are wrong. Morality and religion often equate pleasure with sin and threaten sinners with dire consequences. There is also in such statements by nurses a sense of being judged and found wanting, which is partly a projection of the nurse's own lack of self-esteem onto others but is also partly a reality because women rely heavily on the approval of others for their self-images.

An overload of stress diminishes the nurse's sensitivity to pleasure. How is it that nurses become overloaded? Nurses routinely accept dangerously high patient workloads; they are coerced into working double shifts, coming to work on days off, and rotating to days, evenings, and nights regardless of their own exhaustion. Why? Because patients need care. Certainly patients need care, and certainly women-nurses have been conditioned to render that care in a selfless-subservient manner, but the reasons go even deeper. They lie buried in each nurse's psyche.

To understand these reasons, we must begin to ask ourselves what nurses are *getting* out of their selflessness in serving others. Approval, perhaps? A feeling of self-righteousness?[12] A sense of heroism?[6] Selflessness, after all, is akin to martyrdom.

> Martyrs assume the role of neglected, self-sacrificing individuals who voluntarily neglect their own interests and aspirations to enhance the welfare or careers of others. This not only explains their own lack of eminence but also bestows upon them a saint's mantle of selflessness and devotion. . . . The role of martyrdom may be assumed initially as a reaction-formation against . . . feelings of hostility and resentment or as a form of expiation for the guilt feelings arising from such feelings.[2]

Not very pretty, is it? But delving into our subconscious motivations rarely is. Often we turn up things we would prefer to leave buried. That's why we have done such a good job of repressing them and defending against them. That's why they continue to plague us. Something in the subconscious of every nurse, some need, is met through serving others. Why do nurses have rescue fantasies? Because they see themselves as saving patients' lives and receiving the admiration and approval of supervisors and physicians? See themselves as surpassing other nurses? Perhaps because deep within each adult-woman-nurse are the remnants of infantile omnipotence (babies feel they are very powerful) that are activated as a defense when the nurse feels most power-less and impotent. And nurses often feel that way.

Martyrs, Ausubel and Kirk[2] says, develop that role out of a reaction-formation against hostility or out of guilt over their hostility. In neither case is the anger expressed openly and directly. Women and nurses, we know, experience powerless-ness to which the immediate natural reaction is anger. But women and nurses have been taught that to express anger is to drive away those who are most necessary for their self-esteem. So what happens to the anger and hostility? It is expressed in passive-aggressive ways; it is defended against (reaction-formation); it is turned against the self and is experienced as guilt and worthlessness.

Are these not the very attitudes and behaviors that lead to anhedonia? Anhe-donia, the inability to experience pleasure, is an integral component of depression.[3] Let us briefly explore, then, these ways that we as nurses handle our anger:

1. Passive aggression: this means simply that we use anger or express anger in passive rather than active ways. We don't say exactly what we mean. We beat around the bush. We talk behind people's backs and then are surprised when they *somehow* find out. We stir up "tempests in a teapot" and then wonder how it is that things got so out of hand.
2. Reaction-formation: this is only one of many defenses against anger and like most is subconscious. It is seen in the person who assumes attitudes that are diametrically opposed to forbidden emotions like anger:[7] the person who is very good instead of "bad," the Pollyanna, the person who is so sweet you could kill her, the nurse who would *never* dream of getting angry with a patient. This is not an act. These persons do not experience their anger; the defense is so automatically conditioned that they feel exactly the opposite. It is a passive-aggressive defense.
3. Guilt and self-blame are also passive responses. Rather than directing the anger at the legitimate object, one turns it in against the self.

NURSES' RIGHTS

Having acknowledged the roots of our difficulties, the origins of our oppression, and the philosophies that destroy us, and having begun to examine the defenses that ensure our victimization and powerlessness, we can begin to make changes. We must begin to assert our rights—first as individuals, then as women, and finally as nurses.

No more dutiful daughters and helpless victims

What would it mean to relinquish unrealistic self-blame and other blame? It would mean acknowledging our dependency, our need to be needed, our need for approval, our self-righteous, heroine rescue fantasies, our omnipotence, and our defenses. A tall order.

Giving up self-blame would mean experiencing our legitimate anger toward others, which is a painful process. "Blaming persons who've caused hurt is often more difficult than the old, familiar masochistic circle of self-condemnation, especially if the other person is vital to one's life."[21] (Especially if the other person is a doctor we depend on, a supervisor who evaluates us, or a peer who can make our life miserable). It would mean relinquishing our dependency on the paternalistic and maternalistic figures with whom we have been symbiotic for so long; it would mean confronting our sibling rivalry with peers; it *could* mean standing alone.

Giving up other-blame might sound like a contradiction to what I've just said, but it is simply the other side of the coin. People who blame themselves irrationally often do the same with others. Both behaviors exist in helpless, dependent victims. Giving up other-blame does *not* mean whitewashing those who have exploited nurses or nursing; rather it means relinquishing our victim posture, seeing these others as they really are, and doing something about the problem rather than engaging in endless litanies of complaints. Many nurses decry the coercion of staff nurses by administration to assume responsibilities beyond their professional, physical, and psychological capabilities. Many nurses decry the offensive, arrogant attitude of physicians toward themselves and others. This places the blame solely on the oppressive administration and doctors, and it is not solely theirs. I am the first to denounce such oppressions, but it is true that nurses often fail to see their complicity in such situations. It's the old "rug" story: people can't walk on you unless you make yourself into a rug. Administrators and doctors could not oppress and coerce nurses unless the nurses had judged *themselves* guilty in the first place.

Relinquishing old responses necessitates the building of new ones: taking unpopular stands, speaking up, taking action, and accepting risks. Gloria Donnely[9] suggests the following behaviors to break the "stimulus-guilt-acquiescence" sequence:

- □ Recognizing our patterns of interaction
- □ Removing ourselves from situations until we can handle them effectively; giving ourselves time
- □ Consciously changing our thinking
- □ Refusing to accept responsibility for the responses of others
- □ Repeating assertive behaviors until they feel comfortable

I would add: learning to say an unequivocal "No!"

Propaganda sounds good (it's meant to): know thine enemy

Eliminating nightingalism cannot be done without pulling that proverbial rug out from under our oppressors. Nurses will be denounced as heartless, selfish brutes; there are some who will accuse us of having abandoned "feminine" (read: humane) principles for "masculine" (read: inhumane) ones. All potential guilt buttons will be pushed. Eliminating nightingalism, altruism, and socialism means knowing in our hearts that we are not out to hurt patients but want to take care of ourselves, that we are not abandoning caring, humane principles but are broadening our repertoire of attitudes and behaviors to include those that will allow us to grow as individuals.

There are those who will contradict me. Partridge,[22] for example, defines being masculine as being independent, analytic, dominant, active, scientific, cognitive, and assertive; being feminine, on the other hand, means being dependent, intuitive, submissive, and receptive. She says, "I do not wish to be equal to the [masculine] qualities just cited, because it means abdicating the abiding strengths that women have contributed to society."[22] It does not. Such traits are not mutually exclusive. Even supposedly dichotomous independent/dependent and dominant/submissive traits are usually found together in the same individual, and both traits in each pair should be valued.

I agree with nurses who exhort us to retain our positive, "feminine," humanizing traits,[8,26] but I refuse to acknowledge that many of the so-called masculine traits cited above would somehow diminish the strength of women or make them less humane. They are necessary. From the onset I have tried to make it clear that the benevolence, giving, and helping that each nurse engages in should be the choice of that nurse only, not the mandates of someone else. Each nurse's service should be her own to render or withhold without fear of retribution and without subjection to guilt-oriented tactics. Unfortunately such tactics abound in nursing and medicine; they are the tools of the oppressor, the altruist, the socialist. They cannot, however, be used effectively against the nurse who refuses to accept the guilt, who will *not* be responsible for the actions of others, and who stands firm in her right to refuse services to patients or clients for whatever reason she deems necessary.

By these statements I am not advocating that any nurse abandon patients during a given shift because of a lack of sufficient help. I do advocate that she make the situation known to appropriate authorities, that she take steps to prevent recurrence of the situation by working and planning with those authorities, and should the problem be insoluble, that she remove herself from the situation permanently. Certainly patients have needs. So do nurses. And it is about time that nurses stand up for their own rights. Any supervisor who browbeats a nurse into staying late "because you can't abandon the patients" is wrong. Any nurse who mutely accepts unsafe patient caseloads is wrong. When we as nurses begin to assert our rights, a few patients may suffer, but I suggest that many are already suffering and so are nurses. A stand for nurses' rights will ultimately improve both nursing's morale and patient care.

The current situation fuels the fires of those who would oppress nurses. Patients complain that they receive poor nursing care. Harassed nurses working short cannot possibly deliver safe care, but they try. Then they burn out. Then they drop out. Then we (and patients and doctors) read about the "nursing shortage." Patients complain even more strongly about their lack of care. Doctors complain. Nurses feel more harassed. Where will it end? Nurses ask, "Does a patient have to die?" No. Not if nurses learn to say that one word: *no.* "No, I cannot accept any more patients." "No, I cannot work today, tonight, and tomorrow." What would happen then? Beds might have to be closed. Doctors won't like that. Do they like their patients to go un- attended? Do *they* want someone to die? Probably not. But there are sick people out there who need to be hospitalized. Then tell them. Tell them the beds are not available because the nurses are not available. When they ask why the nurses are not available, *tell them!* Tell them that the salaries of steel workers, postal workers, auto workers, coal miners, and some stenographers have more than kept pace with infla- tion whereas the salaries of nurses have not. We are not in this business out of charity, as altruists and nightingalists would have us believe. We are here to make money, to use our minds and our skills, to provide services to patients on our own terms. We need no longer apologize and feel guilty.

We cannot let things go on as they are. On that issue we all (altruists, socialists, and nightingalists included) agree. But there is no solution in placing doctors and nurses in bondage. It has never worked and never will. To take away an individual's control over her/his services is to take away her/his right to life. It is to take away all motivation, and people will not work if they are not motivated. We can no longer allow ourselves to *be* motivated solely out of concern for the other person, out of guilt, or out of the reprehensible notion that selfishness (concern with oneself) is wrong. For too long we have sacrificed ourselves because we were taught that self-sacrifice is a virtue. Nothing can be gained from the sacrifice of *any* of us any longer.

We must refute those who say that the rights of patients supersede those of nurses or doctors. We are all individuals with the same fundamental human rights, but we are not all equal. We have individual capabilities and many differences. We share the rights to life, liberty, and the pursuit of happiness. *Pursuit* is the key word. We are guaranteed the right to pursue happiness, to pursue health, and to pursue monetary rewards for our services, but we are not guaranteed that our efforts will be successful. No one can guarantee the happiness of another, and no one can guarantee health. We must each earn our own livelihoods, buy our own homes, our cars, our food. We cannot demand that others do that for us anymore than they can demand we do it for them.

Where will we, the workers, be when those who are no longer *willing* to pay for health care become no longer willing to pay for their own food but demand caviar, no longer willing to pay for their own homes but demand mansions, no longer willing to pay for their own recreation but demand radios, televisions, free movies, free vacations, airline tickets, yachts? Absurd? Not as absurd as you might think:

> There's something disconcerting about standing in line at the check-out counter behind someone using food stamps—especially when one is paying for one's own order with the family's mortgage money.
>
> Breathes there a soul so liberal that comparisons do not arise upon watching such purchases? My thought processes work this way: "Hamburger, I'm buying hamburger. She's buying a roast. Potato chips, candy—will food stamps really pay for those?" Then I watch as the cashier rings them through with nary a word.
>
> My basket is full of generic no-names with their depressingly obvious black-and-white labels. Hers, my God, rivals the rainbow—not a cheapie to be found in the bunch.
>
> I find myself thinking that there must be something terribly wrong with the system which causes me to, even for a moment, consider the advantages of being a food-stamp recipient. . . .
>
> While window-shopping at a lobster pound and bemoaning the astronomical prices, I spoke to the owner. "See this?" he said while fanning food stamps. "The only lobster sales I've had today were paid for by these. Sad commentary, hunh?"
>
> Hunh, indeed. I left, half-heartedly clutching a small package of frozen fish.*

Where, as I've already asked, do you draw the line?

And what will happen to those who cannot afford to pay for health services? They will tell us their plight as individuals, and we as individuals of our own free will will adjust our fees, trade our services, or serve them without cost *if* we are truly humane. If we are not, no law that enslaves us to those we serve will make us so.

---

*From Kroll, K: American pie, in some sky, The New York Times, March 15, 1981. © 1981 by The New York Times Company. Reprinted by permission.

REFERENCES

1. Ashley, J.A.: Hospitals, paternalism, and the role of the nurse, New York, 1976, Teacher's College Press.
2. Ausubel, D.P., and Kirk, D.: Ego psychology and mental disorder: a developmental approach to psychopathology, New York, 1977, Grune & Stratton, Inc.
3. Beck, A.T.: Cognitive therapy and the emotional disorders, New York, 1976, International Universities Press.
4. Benson, E.R.: The consumer's right to health care: how does nursing respond? Nursing Forum 16(2): 139, 1977.
5. Bloomfield, H., and Kory, P.: Inner joy: new strategies to put more pleasure and satisfaction in your life, United States, 1980, Wyden Books.
6. Bush, M., and Kjervik, D.: The nurse's self-image. In Kjervick, D., and Martinson, I., editors: Women in stress: a nursing perspective, New York, 1979, Appleton-Century-Crofts.
7. Cameron, N.: Personality development and psychopathology: a dynamic approach, Boston, 1963, Houghton Mifflin Co.
8. Curtin, L.L.: Human values in nursing, Supervisor Nurse 9(3):21, 1978.
9. Donnelly, G.F.: 'Frankly, Ms. Scarlett, I can't work another double' (on getting clear of guilt), RN 42(1):79, 1979.
10. Donovan, L.: What nurses want (and what they're getting), RN 43(4):22, 1980.
11. Frieze, I., and others: Women and sex-roles: a social psychological perspective, New York, 1978, W.W. Norton & Co., Inc.

12. Greer, G.: The female eunuch, New York, 1971, McGraw-Hill Book Co.

13. Hallas, G.G.: Why nurses are giving it up, RN **43**(7):17, 1980.

14. Hemingway, C.: Working women, Los Angeles Herald Examiner p. 17, January 27, 1981.

15. Kalisch, B.J.: The promise of power, Nursing Outlook **26**(1)42, 1978.

16. Kelly, L.Y.: Our nursing heritage: have we renounced it? Image **8**(3):43, 1976.

17. Lieb, R.: Power, powerlessness, and potential: nurse's role within the health care delivery system, Image **10**(3): 75, 1978.

18. Maloney, L., and others: America's middle class: angry, frustrated, and losing ground, U.S. News and World Report, p. 29, March 30, 1981.

19. McClure, M.: The long road to accountability, Nursing Outlook **26**(1):47, 1978.

20. Menaker, E.: The masochistic factor in the psychoanalytic situation. In Lerner, L., editor: Masochism and the emergent ego: selected papers of Esther Menaker, New York, 1979, Human Sciences Press.

21. Miller, J.B.: Toward a new psychology of women, Boston, 1976, Beacon Press.

22. Partridge, K.B.: Nursing values in a changing society, Nursing Outlook **26**(6):356, 1978.

23. Peikoff, L.: Doctors and the police state, The Objectivist Newsletter **1**(6):25, June, 1962.

24. Peplau, H.: Is health care a right? affirmative response, Image **7**(1):4, 1974.

25. Shapiro, B.: The dead end of altruism: a note to nurses, Nursing Forum **16**(4): 384, 1976.

26. Thompson, J.D.: The passionate humanist: from Nightingale to the new nurse, Nursing Outlook **28**(5):290, 1980.

PATRICIA GEARY DEAN

Chapter 16

Toward androgyny

VICTIM PSYCHOLOGY AND THE SOCIALIZATION OF WOMEN
Definition

Androgyny refers to a state in which both sexes feel free to choose from a full range of human behaviors. Neither sex needs to feel restricted to the behaviors ascribed by socialization. Both males and females are free to express both nurturing and problem solving.[2] It would seem that the one percent of the nursing profession who are male may already be androgynous. They are able to express the caring side of their personalities as nurses as well as the traditional behaviors of males. The largely female remainder of the profession, in some cases, may have to actively move toward this state.

Practice standards established

Nurses are a wonderfully wise, competent and caring group of people. As a group, we are far more advanced than any other group of health professionals in setting standards for our own practice. We lead the way in determining outcome criteria for the care we deliver—a significant move toward quality assurance. Our educational programs are advanced in the use of objective-based learning and educational technology. We involve our students in planning and evaluating their programs. We have an advanced accreditation process for those programs. We have direct, legal responsibility for the care of our patients through our licensure.

Responsibility for health care delivery

We carry a significant share of the delivery of health care in this country. We spend approximately fifty hours with the patient for each single hour the physician spends with that patient. Our responsibility for the patient extends twenty-four hours a day. In many institutions no one but a nurse is immediately available to a patient for sixteen of those twenty-four hours. Some of us are single-handedly responsible for the total health care of some rural towns. We make a staggering number of judgments

From Dean, P.G.: Image, 10(1):10, 1978.

minute by minute and day by day which directly influence the lives and well-being of our clients. We are awesome in our sheer numbers. One million nurses could be quite a coalition.

Gap between image and reality

Despite all of this, our contribution to that multibillion dollar industry, health care, remains so unrecognized that the image which the public has of us is that of a woman in white carrying a bedpan. Or we are seen as the handmaiden of the physician. The American Nurses Association has judged that gap between the image and the reality of the nurse to be so critical as to warrant a public relations campaign. We have now finished 1977, the Year of the Nurse.

How can it be possible that a group of one million caring, competent, concerned, and wise people can be so unnoticed? Could it have anything to do with the fact that this vast group is mainly female? Ninety-nine percent of us are women. We could consider ourselves a double minority. We are women in a male-oriented society and nurses in a physician-oriented health care system.

Victim psychology and socialization of women

In examining our situation, we need to look at knowledge gained from two areas: victim psychology and the study of the socialization of women. The following discussion will consider certain occurrences within the profession as symptomatic of the "victimization" of nurses and of their socialization as women.

Nurses, as women, are members of a minority group. As such, they can be considered victims, that is, a group with low status and power.[1] Victims engage in horizontal violence. They are aggressive with one another rather than with the higher status group. The approval of the higher status group may become so important to the "second class" group that the members of victim group may prefer to act like the members of the status group rather than as a member of their own group.[5]

Victim behavior

In this light, it is possible to observe victim behavior within the profession. Take, for example, the long standing split between the two major nursing organizations. It has long been discussed within the profession as a detriment to the actualization of the profession. Most nurses will belong to one organization or the other but not to both. In the meantime, the energy that the profession needs to advance itself is spent on conflicts within the profession. The better situation for the whole of the profession would be the unification of both groups to work on common issues. Both are strong organizations. One plus one could equal four. It would be a positive change if members of both groups would join the other and begin as members to influence the organizations to work together for the whole.

One cannot help but wonder if the tendency for nurses to join no professional organization whatever could be part of the symptomatology of a second-class group which does not wish to acknowledge membership in that group.

Delineation of levels needed

The long-raging, degree-diploma controversy is another example of horizontal violence. We have become, to the outside world, an example of a profession which cannot "get its act together." Thirteen years later we have not yet implemented the ANA resolution of 1965. We open ourselves to the charge that we do not know what we are talking about. We profess two levels of practice, yet all nurses take the same licensure. Graduates of both types of educational programs are now making contributions to the profession. It would be to our benefit to solidify those contributions by delineating levels of practice instead of arguing their superiority. One is not better than the other, but simply a more current one. The degree does provide us with an academic, scientific base, validity and status that the diploma does not. It also provides a foundation for graduate study and specialization. Primary and secondary school educators have long recognized the power of the degree in this knowledge-oriented world. They have also recognized that the beginning teacher needs supervision and assistance. If we could recognize this and provide assistance in becoming a skilled practitioner to the new degree graduate as well as a career-ladder potential for the diploma graduate, we could get on with the business of working together for the good of the whole profession. This unification could enable nurses to join energies and to use them where they would do the most good for the whole: impacting on the health care system and opening up opportunities for every nurse. We can no longer afford to argue among ourselves.

Potential of mutual support

The tendency to look for weaknesses in technical skills in a nurse with a degree parallels the behavior of an oppressed group which looks with hostility on a member who dares to be "better" or to advance. A degree is a step down the road to the professional recognition which we all need. We must help and encourage one another down that road in ever increasing numbers. One million nurses all going down that road together could be a very formidable force in health care.

Problems of self put-downs

We exhibit other behaviors as well. Probably the worst critics of nurses are nurses themselves. This ability to self-criticize has often been healthy to the profession. It has led to a certain honesty and willingness to change. It has, however, also contributed to repeated self put-downs which can slow change and tarnish the public image of the group.

Sad, too, is the fascination of some nurses with the physician role. Nurses who become physicians' assistants and then take on all of the attitudes and values of the physician group right down to the short white coat are practicing a form of self put-down. This denial of one's own identity and origins is common in victim groups. Some nurses even go on to other academic programs and professions and no longer admit that nursing was their original profession.

Programs and workshops presented for nurses by nurses often feature speakers with many backgrounds other than nursing. We often fail to recognize the expertise of other nurses. This is another self put-down.[3] What better way to acknowledge to the world and to ourselves that we have something to say than to have nurses on matters of importance to the profession? We must look to one another for knowledge and recognize our experts.

Problems of stereotypes

As a profession of mainly women, we are influenced by the stereotype of females which occurs in our society. This stereotype labels women as nice, caring, warm, peacekeeping, passive, unknowledgeable and dependent. In fact, the very stereo-type people often have of the nurses is the warm, caring woman.[4]

As nurses, it is important that we look at our profession in this light to determine whether we are falling into the "traps" the stereotypes of socialization set for us.

The nursing profession demands a great deal of knowledge wherever it is prac-ticed. There has long been a dichotomy in the profession between theory and prac-tice, education and service. It is sad that we let this dichotomy continue to exist. It reinforces the stereotype; women are unknowledgeable. Nurses, women, don't know much. They do not have a grasp of the "hard facts," the tough, scientific data. This is far from the true picture.

As long as we continue the split between nursing education and nursing service, it will continue to appear—to ourselves as well as to the public—that it takes a special nurse to be a "thinker" and another kind of nurse to be a "doer." In fact, we all need both. A "doer" who does not think is dangerous. A thinker who never tests her thoughts thinks in a vacuum.

Interchange of abilities

It would seem that if educators could spend some time in practice—as some are—and practicing nurses spend some time teaching, together we could go far. This is a move that the profession as a whole needs to encourage. It will demand some changes in both the academic and the practice settings. All nurses need to be free to show, use and increase their knowledge. This interchange of abilities would allow that.

Colleague behaviors

Because women are socialized to be in competition with other women for the attention of men, we learn not to help one another. We also have learned not to develop one another. This manifests itself in the tendency of nurses not to act as colleagues or mentors. Colleague behaviors include showing competence, giving feedback, recognizing skills and competences of one another, showing respect for one another and consulting with one another. These behaviors are developing within the profession and must be fostered.

We have many skilled and knowledgeable nurses within our ranks. Seldom, however, do we think to consult with one another about a problem. In fact, the consultation, if it occurs, is often with other professionals. We must begin to consult with nurses and develop one another as professional colleagues.

Nurses within organizations rarely think to call in other nurses on consultation. Rarely are funds built into budgets for consultation with nurses on special problems. Instead, nurses tend to rely on the services of other professionals for consultation even though there are nurses with the necessary skills and background. The next time you need a consultant—call a nurse.

The scientific method

The use of the nursing process has a long history in the profession. Yet in many areas in nursing the use of this problem-solving process and the resultant written care plans is still in its infancy. The use of date-related goals as included in the ANA standards of Practice is still unusual. Care plans may be written in a rudimentary fashion and in a grudging manner. How often does one hear such comments as, "If I wanted to become a writer, I wouldn't have become a nurse," or "I want to take care of people, not write about it."

This odious task is no more than a form of the scientific method, a simple problem-solving process. It is a reasoning process, albeit a documented and evaluated one. It is the same procedure each one of us must utilize repeatedly in our daily lives.

Could it be that the problem lies in the socialization of women to be nurturers and doers, not problem solvers? It is the male half of our society which is socialized to problem solve. This function then may not readily "fit" with a group which is predominantly female.

Yet it is this very process which can show the public what it is that a nurse does in a way which no public relations campaign will ever be able to do. By its very existence, a nursing care plan documents the role and work of the nurse.

Accountability and goal setting

The existence of a written plan of care makes us accountable for its contents. Having made a diagnosis and set goals, we are held to meeting those goals. Looking at female socialization, this accountability and setting of goals is not a part of the usual role of women. The antagonism to the socialization of women is built into the process: women are to be present-oriented, they are not to be taken seriously, and they are to be nice. A care plan demands a future orientation. The setting of goals demands a gearing up for events beyond the here and now. Of course, a care plan which is also in reality a contract for services to the client is to be taken very seriously. By writing the plan for all to see, the nurse leaves herself open to criticism. Criticism for the woman can be a withholding of approval and a way of saying she is not nice. This leaves us as a profession of women endorsing and requiring in our standards of practice a function for which we are unprepared by our female socialization. In this sense, the task is strange and uncomfortable.

The care plan, by giving some organization and documentation to our nurturing and care, may well help us do better what we already do so well. It can be a tool for the sharing, consulting and collegial relationships which we need to grow as a profession. It can also help us build the problem-solving skills so necessary both to life and to our profession. But it must be recognized as such.

Problems of self-concept

These are the symptoms. The diagnosis then could be stated as problems of self-concept. The prescription is threefold. First, we need to continue the directions set by the American Nurses Association for nurse power and nurse recognition. We need to "talk ourselves up" both to one another and to the country. We need to consult more with one another and to develop colleague relationships. We would strengthen our own self-concepts and that of the profession if each of us as individuals began to serve as mentors for "younger members of the profession." As mentors, we can extend the nurturing we do so well. By providing for the development of individual nurses, we can also strengthen the profession. Finally, we need to learn to work as a team, all of us. By merging our diverse backgrounds, we can advance the profession. It is that teamwork through which one learns so well and profits by so fully.

Choices about expectations and influences

It would be helpful for us to examine our own situations as both women and nurses. The impact of socialization on women is great. To be able to recognize that influence for what it is, differing expectations, and to go on from there is freeing. It is important to recognize that those expectations can influence nurses. It is even more crucial that we make some choices about the expectations and influences to which we will be susceptible.

Toward androgyny

Nurses have some of the very important skills and traits which have been encouraged in women by socialization: the ability to show emotions, the development of personal power, caring, cooperation, listening skills, and the ability to support others. To be able to add to this some of the positive skills which are usually considered a part of the male role—future orientation and problem solving—would make us much fuller human beings as well as more competent professionals capable of providing better care. Let us move on to androgyny.

REFERENCES

1. Allport, G.: The nature of prejudice, Menlo Park, Calif., 1958, Addison-Wesley Publishing Co., Inc.
2. New Dynamics Associates: Great American female stereotype, New Hampshire, 1977, Laconia.
3. Pierce, C.: Androgyny: a behavioral goal for women and men, New Hampshire, 1977, Laconia.
4. Rogers, J.A.: Struggling out of the feminine pluperfect, American Journal of Nursing **75:** 1655, 1975.
5. Shain, M.: How women put women down, Chatelaine, April 1972.

WILMA SCOTT HEIDE

Chapter 17

Feminist activism in nursing and health care

You, the reader, deserve and need to know something of my perspectives, premises, background, and intentions. I want to share with you some experiences and insights that have radicalized me into becoming a feminist, a political activist committed to indivisible human rights. *Radical* means literally to go to the root or origin of a situation, phenomenon, or problem. It does *not* mean "kooky," bizarre, or irresponsible. Quite the contrary, if one is serious about change in the human and humane interest, it is irresponsible *not* to be radical.

Feminism goes to the sexist root of human oppression consequent to patriarchy (which means male power, rule, and domination in values, in governance, in all institutions). Sexism as the root, the original form of human oppression, sanctioned the *idea* of oppression and made other forms of oppression, such as racism, classism, ageism, religionism, and homophobia, predictable and virtually inevitable. Sexism in health care in general and in nursing in particular is an especially virulent pathology. The sexism that historically and currently defines and oppresses nurses and nursing provided the many insights and experiences for me as a woman and a nurse that compelled me to leave clinical nursing for my psychological survival and political integrity. I worked as a staff nurse, supervisor, administrator, and educator as well as a public health nurse and educator for 11 years.

The oppression of women, nurses (almost synonymous with women), and nursing has been voluminous and overwhelmingly documented elsewhere and in other chapters of this book.[1] I want to focus on the perspectives that guide me in determining both the imperatives for and some of the realities of feminist activism in nursing and health care. In doing so, I want to pay tribute to my foremothers and sisters in nursing, the unsung sheroes* who were, are, and are becoming feminists. I know the courage required and the enormous gratification in translating these profound visions into feminist alternatives to both patriarchal and medical control of health care. My premises are as follows.

Sheroes is a generic word I created for people we admire of both sexes; *heroine* is a derivative word and women are not derivative except from our parents, all Adam's rib mythology being precisely that.

PREMISES

1. It is necessary to demythologize some "old husband's tales" and to demystify the M.D.-eity to understand both the politics of sexism and realize the potential of self-defined nurses and nursing.

2. Medical care is *not* the same as health care and should *not* be used as a synonymous and/or interchangeable word meaning health care. Health care is basically an interrelational or a social phenomenon. It *may* be augmented or aided by medical care, that is, by chemical or medicinal therapies or by instrumental technologies, procedures, or surgery.

"Transcending any medicine, surgery and/or physiotherapy may be the experiential reality of whether encounters by clients/patients with health care practitioners are affectively positive, conducive to healing and/or nurturing of positive self-images of both clients and practitioners."[11]

Medication, instrumental technology, and the relative overvaluing of procedures and techniques that are performed on passive people often dominate the qualitative, expressive components of care that can involve the client or patient in her/his own healing. The involvement itself may be therapeutic and curative.

Further, A. Wildavsky reminds us:

> According to the great equation, (available) medical care equals health, but the great equation is wrong. More medical care alone does not equal health. The best estimates are that the medical system itself affects about 10% of the usual indices for measuring health, i.e., whether you live, how well you live, how long you live. The remaining 90% are determined by factors over which doctors have little or no control, such as individual life style, social conditions, and the physical environment.[17]

3. Health policy decisions and funding are made in the context of a value system that is white, patriarchal, and capitalist; they are made mostly by men, although over 75% of health care providers and a large majority of the consumers are women. Medicine and medical technologies, representing primarily the instrumental and disease-reactive approach to health problems, are often funded and given priority at the expense of expressive, holistic health, proactive nursing care and social programs. Yet the latter are among the factors most crucial in determining the health status of the majority of people. These factors include housing, nutrition, economic opportunities and resources, mental health, and the power to control one's life.

The expressive components reflect the individually and societally nurturant qualities of "feminine" (and generally subordinated) values toward which primarily women have been socialized. The instrumental approach reflects the "masculine" (and usually dominant) values toward which primarily men have been socialized. Naturally (though not yet normally), *both* sexes possess the potential to acknowledge and exhibit *both* repertories of "feminine" and "masculine" behaviors. Feminism is intent on freeing both sexes to be both "feminine" and "masculine." Both repertories have positive dimensions: positive "feminine" principles include compassion, nurturance, sensitivity, the more humane values. Feminism affirms both women and "feminine" values of both sexes for both private and public policies. More on that later.

4. We must understand that being female is a biological *part* of identity; it is *not* the same as or synonymous with "feminine" traits, which are *learned* principles and behaviors. Likewise, being male is a biological *part* of identify and is not the same as or synonymous with "masculine" traits, which are *learned* principles and behaviors. Normally, but *not* naturally, most females are (still) socialized to be "feminine" and not "masculine" and most males are (still) socialized to be "masculine" and not "feminine." The *super*imposed socialization via this sexist process, that is, the very *existence* of the process itself, reveals its *un*naturalness, its artificiality. The medical system derived from patriarchy reflects and institutionalizes this sexism. It further reinforces occupational segregation of the sexes so that most physicians are (still) male and most nurses are female.

Feminism is increasing the numbers of women who are becoming physicians, but the number of men becoming nurses has increased very little, except for the disproportionate number of men appointed as nursing administrators. One of the results of sexism is not only that males are demonstrably more valued than females but also that "masculinity" (learned gender behavior) is more valued than "femininity" (learned gender behavior). Our typical female socialization means we learn the "feminine" behaviors of ministering to (ad-ministering) everyone else much, much more than men learn to minister to others, yet men are considered more qualified even for nursing ad-ministration disproportionate to their percentage (3%) among nursing professionals. I consider experience with nurturance, without subservience, creating nurturant environments, and the valuing of these "feminine" qualities as bona fide occupational qualifications for any leadership, for administration, and for *any* health care providers. Need I remind any reader which sex is more experienced in nurturance or which sex is finally beginning to nurture itself as well? Assertive nurturance of ourselves and others is the concept I would encourage as one more private and public policy implication of feminism.

5. In advocating the affirmation of women, of "feminine" strengths for both sexes, and in critiquing both patriarchy and medical control of health care and of nurses, I insist that one understands that to be pro-women does not mean to be anti-men. It does mean rejection of male control of and power over women and redefinitions and sharing of power itself. Neither do I say that medicine is *good for nothing* or that nurses should practice medicine without a medical license. Along with other nurse and some physician feminist activists, I am insisting that medicine is *not* good for everything and that physicians must stop practicing and controlling nursing without a nursing license. Nursing and medicine must become complementary and coordinated in law and practice and must not continue as subordinate

and superordinate. These are recommendations I made as an invited consultant to the National Joint Practice Commission* in December 1974. Other nurse feminist activists are creating similar changes in various state practice acts.

6. Much of the hierarchy of the still medically controlled health care system derives from the influence of organized religion and the military. Both of these are more archetypically patriarchal than we may like to think in the sex-casts of their leadership and their domination and mutual reinforcement. Both devalue women in institutionalized ways. A tragic paradox in the instance of Christian religions is that Jesus Christ reportedly exhibited the traits of compassion, caring, sensitivity, openness, and nurturance, some of the characteristics thought to be the special prerogatives of women, the so-called feminine factors. I wonder if the real meaning of Jesus' crucifixion is the symbolic crucifixion of woman and the crucifixion of the *expression* of "womanly" or "feminine" behaviors by a man? Jesus also valued women more than usual, particularly for his day. If he had been a woman, he, like most other women then, would have been ignored. If Jesus appeared today, he might well be recrucified for his "feminine" behaviors and his untypical valuing of women. Leading those who would so crucify him would be some so-called Christians. Today, nurses and other feminists of both sexes who affirm women and "feminine" in the sense of humane principles for private and public policies are crucified, albeit in more subtle ways. Agree or disagree, but do think about it.

7. In health care, instrumental, technical, "masculine" behaviors addressed to specific "cures" of specific diseases (reactive) are more valued and funded than expressive, social, "feminine," proactive behaviors addressed to care of the whole person, the health education of the client, and preventative measures that consider the client as an active participant in her/his own healing. Physicians are more instrumental and "masculine" in their approach, and nurses are more expressive and "feminine." Indeed, nursing has been documented as the one profession that is doing the most health consumer education,[18] Instrumental reactive approaches are more financially rewarding; expressive proactive approaches pay less but have more potential for self-care and for developing 90% of the factors that actually determine the health quality of the people. Instrumental cures are often necessary and often considered more dramatic, but in terms of the overall quality of a nation's health, I remind readers of the earlier quotation about the medical system affecting only 10% of the significant indices that influence and measure health quality. The writing of Jean Baker Miller is also instructive here:

> Humanity has been held to a limited and distorted view of itself—from its interpretation of the most intimate of personal emotions to its grandest visions of human possibilities— precisely by virtue of its subordination of women.[13]

---

*National Joint Practice Commission of the American Nurses Association and American Medical Association, consisting of eight members from each.

Think about that as I share Dr. Miller's insights, her notion that by projecting into what is called women's work "some of its most troublesome and problematic necessities, male-led society may also have simultaneously, and unwittingly, delegated to women not humanity's 'lowest needs' but its 'highest necessities'—that is, the intense emotionally connected cooperation and creativity necessary for human life and growth."[13]

Nurses in particular and women in general have been performing this vital work; we must demand its recognition and high value as the beginnings of personal integrity and societal health.

8. My next premise is that empowerment is a vital factor in the health of individuals, of nurses, of nursing. To have power basically means to do or to act, to be able. Self-empowerment means and portends having the consequent power to influence and control one's own life and the life of society including health care. Power has also been defined as the ability to command or control others. The first definition is healthy; the second, in the view of most feminists, is patriarchal, androcentric (male-centered), and unhealthy. There are alternatives.

It has been written that power corrupts and absolute power corrupts absolutely. That's true of the androcentric model regardless of whether it is practiced by men *or* women. I think that the corollary to this is that powerlessness corrupts and absolute powerlessness corrupts absolutely. Women's and nurses' powerlessness is not absolute but too nearly so. Corruption of those nearly powerless takes many forms: the undermining of integrity and self-confidence, the inhibiting of individual and professional growth, identification with agents of control and oppression (mostly males, mostly physicians), and competition with other victims (nurses) for minimal power on others' terms.

Gaining real power for significant change requires that nurses transcend their historically tragic drama of dependence and the artiface of ladylike powerlessness. The inability or unwillingness of most nurses and nursing leaders until recently to identify with feminist imperatives is understandable but not acceptable or effective. Nurses have dedicated their lives to limited reform, to service, to the care of others, to an accommodation to patriarchy and consequent medical control. Some assertive nurturance of nurses and nursing would be a *major* public health measure for nurses and the quality of health care.

In insisting on assertive nurturance of nurses, I am reminded of the always incisive, humane, and visionary writing of Adrienne Rich. She notes the power of the "way things are to denude and impoverish the imagination. Even minds practiced in the criticism of the status quo resist a vision so apparently unnerving as that which forces an end to male privilege and a changed relationship between the sexes."[15] And I would add an end to physicians' privileges and a changed relationship between nurses and physicians.

9. Next, it is my premise that *all* human issues are women's issues, though some

impact on and require the insights of women more than others; in addition, *all* issues need feminist perspectives to delineate the distortions, imbalances, and either/or polarities and pathologies of androcentric thinking and behaving. Likewise, to be fully human and humane all health care issues need the insights and alternative visions of feminist nurses, physicians, and other health care providers. Feminism is a gestalt, an all-encompassing view of human affairs; it makes the connections between the emotional and intellectual, the expressive and instrumental, the "feminine" and "masculine" in both sexes and between private and public affairs and policies.

10. Finally (for this essay) it is my premise that sexist language is both consequence and cause of continual male-centeredness and domination. *He is not* and does *not* include *she*. *Man is not* and does *not* include *woman*. Using male-only language programs people to consider the male only as the standard, the norm, the totality of people rather than a part—less than half—of humanity. It devalues woman by exclusion; it erases images of women and girls and exaggerates the imagery of males and overvalues their importance. If it is too awkward for anyone to use *she/he*, *woman/man*, *her/his*, then use *s/he*, *wom/an*, and *her* for the following reasons: *woman* and *she* include *man* and *he* (unlike the reverse); females comprise the majority of U.S.A. and world populations; the human embryo is basically female for the first 6 weeks of intrauterine life. Use of *man*glish (called English) is a clue that the speaker or writer does not value women, regardless of which sex she/he may be. Language is a powerful way to indicate value and nonvalue.

FROM AGONIZING TO ORGANIZING

Raising consciousness and agonizing about problems, about sexism, and about oppression of women and nurses are healthy beginnings of activism. Agonizing alone is not adequate for significant change though it can clear the air, help the more powerless to find each other, reassure individuals and groups that they are not alone, build mutual support, and generate self-confidence. It can build a nurturant environment necessary for the courage to envision, create, organize for, and implement change. All of this can be enormously energizing. The processes are ongoing and vital; feminist processes are also integral parts of the very lifeblood of the products, the outcomes, the quality and empowerment of people.

A basic tenet of feminism is that the personal is political and the political is personal. The two are not as separable as much political "science" and political theory might have us believe. I here use *politics* in the generic sense of power, its definitions, its definers, its exercise and exercises, its scope and implications from and for personal and occupational life, its uses and misuse, its economic implications, applications, and sources. The word *politics* is usually defined in the more limited sense of public policy making, electoral and appointive positions and processes, and legislative phenomena. The usual concepts are relevant and important but no way adequate to either understand or generate political activism by feminist nurses and their friends.

SAMPLING OF FEMINIST ACTIVISM IN NURSING AND HEALTH CARE

What follows is a small sampling of feminist activism in nursing and health care and activism by nurses. I will focus on that activism which I know best from first-hand experience but will not limit this sampling to that. The full delineation of the latter beyond my personal experience has and will increasingly require volumes of books and articles; fortunately, these are emerging.

1. In the early and late 1940s nurses and hospital attendants at state hospitals for those deemed mentally ill organized to reduce the work week from an average 66 hours to 48 and then 40 hours, to provide more humane care for patients, and to create a nurturant environment for patients and staff. We were considered impertinent, insubordinate, and troublesome. I will not include here the personal harassment and job jeopardy and retaliations experienced by some of us.*

2. In the later 1940s and early 1950s the American Nurses' Association (ANA) embarked on an Economic Security Program for nurses. Barbara Schutt, later the editor of the *American Journal of Nursing,* provided significant leadership for these courageous undertakings almost unheard of by nurses prior to then. I am suggesting not that such organizing didn't happen earlier but only that it was virtually unheard of by nurses who were (and are) expected to serve, to be obedient, to be submissive and subordinate, to be "good" women as interpreted by physicians and hospital administrators. The ANA program was partially successful, but it was never really linked to feminist consciousness (though some of us tried) and did not question the hierarchy and male/female sex segregation of occupations or the patriarchal medical values that oppressed nurses and women and others with little power. Some nurses, however, have learned that the welfare of patients can be served at the bargaining table as well as the bedside.

3. In 1970 I presented a paper on values and decisions at the Population Congress in Chicago. I was there as a scholar and feminist activist, chaired the women's caucus, and worked with blacks, Hispanics, and poor people (mostly women) to turn the Congress around from its essentially affluent white male orientations. Staff from *Imprint,* a publication of the National Student Nurses Association, Inc., were present, knew of my nursing background, and asked me to write an article on what feminism might mean to the nursing profession and nurses. Delighted by their invitation, I wrote "Women's Liberation Means Putting Nurses and Nursing in its Place."[5] This began 10 years of keynoting national, state, and other nursing con-

---

*My biography by ethicist Eleanor Humes Haney, to be published in 1982, includes some of these experiences.

ferences. Finally, nurses were becoming eager to hear, read, and act with their sister nurse feminists, but it was my prominance as a political activist that provided the entree. The feminist consciousness of *some* nursing students makes me relatively optimistic that future nurses will be politically active and effective in insisting that women's studies with feminist perspectives will increasingly become an integral part of nursing education for leadership in health care and society.

Other chapters in this book make clear that profound resocialization of nurses and nursing is imperative for nurses to create their natural place as health care leaders. The connections between this process and what feminism portends (in terms of reconceptualizing health care, affirming women and valuing the work done mostly by women, nurse empowerment and political sophistication, and much more) seem almost too obvious to mention. Yet is is precisely these compelling needs that the normal (*not* natural) socialization of women and nurses has repressed or denied consequent to superimposed or internalized constraints originating from those who are not women or nurses.

4. Prior to 1971 the ANA opposed the Equal Rights Amendment mostly on the grounds that women needed so-called protective legislation instead. Actually, this legislation had never protected nurses from abuses in terms of hours worked, shifts split, weights lifted, and more. In 1971 I asked Barbara Schutt if she thought the ANA might be ready to remove its opposition to ERA and even support it. Believing the timing to be good, she put NOW in touch with ANA legislative people. NOW provided informational material to ANA, which facilitated ANA's finding a graceful way to remove its opposition and to become supporters and even advocates of ERA.

Indeed, by 1978 the ANA supported the economic boycott of states that had not yet ratified the amendment. Further, the ANA was persuaded to relocate an International Council of Nurses Conference they had planned to host in Missouri and an ANA Convention slated for Georgia to ERA-ratified states. The excellent leadership of former ANA President Anne Zimmerman was significant in allowing the ANA to exercise the courage of its convictions in these and other actions.

5. In early 1973, at NOW's Sixth National Conference, nurses and friends of nursing organized Nurses NOW to address sexism in nursing and health care. Registered nurse Kathleen McInerney,[12] an outstanding leader, encouraged Nurses NOW to address many issues, including opposition to proposed institutional licensure of nurses that would have further removed nurses from participation in definition and control of nursing and opposition to racism, classism, and heterosexism in nursing and health care. Nurses NOW recognized anti-unionism in nursing to be the result of nurses' learned classism and concern with "professionalism." One tragic consequence of oppression is that the oppressed identify with those free to be the agents of oppression rather than with their own sex, race, or class. Thus we see the phenomenon of implied or explicit consent to oppression through acts of omission and commission. Although profeminism, prounionism, and pro–racial justice has in-

creased in nursing over the past decade, they have yet to reach the point of critical mass necessary for fulfilling nursing's potential to lead in reconceptualizing, organizing, and transforming the qualitative dimensions of health care and empowerment.

6. Organizing in 1970, feminist nurses and other health activists pressed the National Institutes of Health (NIH) to include nurses in particular and women in general on its numerous public advisory boards. Women were and are over 75% of health care providers; nurses were and are the largest profession or occupation of health workers. Yet women in general and nurses in particular comprised a *maximum* of 10% of these advisors, an underrepresentative token. Letters, visits, presentations, and pressure all seemed to no avail until a coalition of the Associations for Women in Science, the NOW Legal Defense and Education Fund, and 15 individual complaintants (including me) filed suit against Elliott Richardson, Secretary of the Department of Health, Education and Welfare (HEW) to require a substantive change. Only then, as the suit gained standing in court and progressed did NIH begin to respond in still hesitant, reactive ways.

Advisory boards such as HEW (now Health and Human Services) decide what and whose and how health-related research and projects are funded with public money. Their domination by white males or their values has had a profound influence on health care policy and practices. The percentages of women and nurses subsequent to this suit have improved but are still a significant distance from reflecting population demographics, let alone feminist perspectives. Dr. Julia Apter, NOW Legal Defense and Education Fund attorney Sylvia Roberts, and attorney Helen Hart Jones must be credited with much of the effective work on this issue. The American Nurses' Association and National League for Nursing were invited and urged to participate but declined.[14]

7. The National League for Nursing (NLN) has *no* position on the ERA. In 1977 it elected a nonnurse, a hospital administrator, a man, as president of this 95% women's organization in spite of protests by Nurses NOW, this writer, and others. Clearly, the NLN, made up mostly of those identified as "educators," needs education on the imperatives that women experience and develop leadership in (primarily) their own organizations as well as in health care and society. It is *not,* as some in NLN allege, a sign of sex equity to elect men to top leadership posts in such predominantly women's organizations *before* genuine sex equality in health care and society generally has actually been established. It *is* a tragic reflection of male-identified and male-oriented loyalties and a denial of women as sisters and leaders, a most unhealthy and uneducated phenomenon.

8. In 1973, after several years of urging by Barbara Schutt and her successor, *American Journal of Nursing* editor Thelma Schorr, I finally wrote an article on the parallel needs of women and nurses for liberation.[8] Dr. Shirley Smoyak, a registered nurse from Rutgers University, herself a leading feminist and nurse-educator activist, tells me it is the article most quoted by her students at Rutgers. Others have given

me similar feedback. So much for false modesty—a kind of conditioned dishonesty, consequent to women's sexist socialization to affirm the talents of everyone else but ourselves. Obviously I have recovered. It was Dr. Smoyak who took the initiative in arranging for my aforementioned consultancy with the National Joint Practice Commission of which she was a member.

9. In early 1974 I was invited, thanks to Barbara Schutt, to meet with the ANA Board of Directors. Before this meeting I consulted with Nurses NOW to ascertain their recommendations as to what I might share with other nursing leaders. The essence was that the issue for ANA and its membership was *not* whether or not to engage in politics (in the generic sense of power, its redefinitions and sharing.) Intentionally or unintentionally, ANA was already engaged in politics. Opting not to participate in generic politics is *itself* a political decision. The questions for ANA required decisions of *what* politics to pursue. Acts of omission implied consent to, acceptance of, and acquiescence or accommodation to sexist politics of health care so demonstrably damaging to nurses and nursing. The ANA, I suggested, could take the leadership in affirming and demonstrating the healthy potential of feminist politics. At that meeting the only substantive, affirming response came from the only black woman on the Board. Within a few months ANA did establish the Nurses Coalition for Action in Politics (N-CAP) with offices in Washington, D.C. Those in the know report that my meeting with the ANA Board at least contributed to that decision. ANA's activity vis-à-vis legislation was not new; the scope of legislation addressed and the overt recognition that politics is much more than legislation per se are a relatively new dimension for many.

10. In 1975 the late Dr. Jo Ann Ashley, a feminist nursing educator, invited me to write the Introduction to her book, *Hospitals, Paternalism and the Role of the Nurse*.[1] After reading the galleys of this overdue landmark book, I agreed to her welcome request and asked only that what I wrote be published without censorship (though editorial advice to sharpen the writing would be welcome.) The publisher agreed . . . until I submitted my draft. First, I wanted an introductory paragraph and then a short chapter at the end, which I proposed titling "On-words" and "After-words" because my thoughts would be more appropriate after the reader had been informed by Dr. Ashley's scholarly documentation of the oppression of nurses and nursing by physicians and hospital administrators. The publisher would not abide by that bit of innovation. Secondly, contrary to the original agreement, the editor would not accept several of my proposals, only one of which I mention here.

I recommended that organized nursing was more than justified in demanding modest (in relation to the documented damage) financial reparations from white physicians and hospital administrators of *at least* $1 million annually for the rest of this century. The money would be used to develop nursing as a self-defined health endeavor neither dependent on nor beholden to medicine or hospital administrators for its direction and development; it would establish nursing and nurses as collegial peers, complementary rather than subordinate to others. This was and is a serious proposal.

Nursing has the quantitative power and can develop the qualitative clout to implement this or some similar healthy proposal. Physicians and hospital administrators and their associates have the financial resources and the obligations to take at least these restorative and healing steps to compensate nurses and nursing for historical and often continuing repressions as well as to cease such today.

When the publisher declined to honor their initial agreement to publish what I wrote, I did not want my name to go on the milder material (and approach) that *could* be published. It was only in sisterhood for Jo Ann Ashley who pleaded with me (and because she had had to hassle for 3 years to get her book published) that I was persuaded to keep my promise although others hadn't.

It is difficult enough for nurses and women to transcend lifetimes of institutionalized sexism, to overcome deep and pervasive oppression to speak and write the truth, to relive the pain and denial of self-worth in the process. What I've summarized is but one of literally countless examples of the difficulty and often near impossibility of bringing these truths to public consciousness. It is also an imperative part of the processes of healing and education of health care practitioners and consumers.

11. At the 1974 ANA Convention, thanks to Dr. Betty L. Evans, R.N., and her colleagues, sessions were held on "Women's Rights and the Nurse." The fairly large hall was packed, four of us made substantial presentations,* the response was electrifying, and we struck some significant nerves . . . as intended. At the end I asked all to join in singing "I Am Woman" but to substitute the word *nurse* for *woman*. Copies of the lyrics of Helen Reddy's 1973 popular song had been distributed to participants. A few thought this "nonprofessional" and chose not to participate, but *most* did and exuberantly. It was a moving experience; some of us cried openly for the joys of release, of togetherness.

Simultaneous with the 1974 ANA Convention, some San Francisco nurses from a local hospital were openly protesting and publicly demonstrating about the poor quality of patient care and the conditions of their work. To its credit, the ANA Convention came out in public support of these nurses, their actions and objectives. Sisterhood (and new dimensions of brotherhood) were inexorably furthered in nursing.

At about the same time as the 1974 convention and indeed before, gay nurses and their friends were becoming organized for mutual support and to promote the education of nurses about the full potential of sexuality. Heterosexism was and is rampant in nursing and health care. Kathleen McInerney and I met with gay nurses and friends the evening before the session on "Women's Rights and the Nurse" to

---

*References 2, 6, 12, 16.

publicly indicate support and to applaud and participate in the imperatives to educate ourselves and society to the full potentials of human sexuality and to eliminate homophobia.[9] Nursing is still in the early stages of those healthy processes.

MORE FEMINIST CHANGE AND POTENTIAL

How else have (and can) feminist nurses and other health care providers been (and become) activists? Let me count the ways. No, the ways are virtually countless. Let me mention some samples only and trust that readers will augment these and create yet more on every issue of and related to health care:

1. Feminist nurse activists are demystifying the M.D.-eity.
2. Feminist nursing activists and scholars are researching; writing articles and books; teaching; consulting; meeting; networking; producing films, slide shows, and video tapes; doing public affairs programs and programming; introducing and lobbying legislators and *becoming* legislators; speaking up and speaking out publicly at conferences, symposia, conventions, and meetings of hospital and other public boards and commissions; organizing for feminist changes; and sharing via consciousness-raising and support groups.
3. Feminist nurses and other health care activists are introducing and developing women's studies courses and programs from feminist perspectives in nursing schools and other health provider schools including medical schools and public health programs. These are, in my view, imperative to resocialize current health care providers and educators and to integrate these perspectives as core insights and processes.
4. Scholarship and activism (optimally as mutually supportive, *not* mutually exclusive) by feminist nurses and friends address issues such as the following:
   a. Psychosurgery and its experimentation (alleged to be therapy) on the relatively powerless: women, racial minorities, poor, young, and otherwise imprisoned physically or psychologically. For example, one major victim population is women, on whom prefrontal lobotomies are still performed to adjust "uppity" women to "their place." To return women to being "happy housewifes" is judged a "success." First, who marries a house? Second, if such damaging measures as lobotomies must necessarily be *superimposed* on people, who is really "happy" about that?[12,13]
   b. Infant formulas are seductively introduced to poor women in impoverished countries by multinational corporations. Breast feeding is healthier and more affordable, efficient, and available than using a formula. Poor women can't afford a formula and often dilute it, with disastrous if not fatal nutritional consequences for infants. Patriarchy strikes again!

Feminist nurses are part of the coalition to end this practice wherever it exploits poor women and threatens their children.

c. Feminist nurse activists have been and are part of the process of ending the double standard in mental health, creating and implementing bills of rights for clients and patients.

d. Drug therapy, drug misuse and abuse, product mislabeling, drug testing, drug costs, the pacification especially of women by drugs—these and more are all issues in which feminist nurses are activists and scholars.

e. Genetic engineering and manipulation are issues addressed by feminist nurses and other health care activists.[7] Genetic engineering and manipulation do not begin or end with intrauterine life. This issue exists in a socioeconomic, political context that is dominated by white males and their values. Of course, we worry about cloning, synthetic gene construction, and the ability not only to know but to predetermine the sex of the embryo-fetus-child. Males are still preferred to females in the U.S.A. and indeed in most of the world—yet another consequence of sexism. We would be naive and foolish not to resist continuing gynocide (female-killing) whether it occurs through overt abuse and violence or through the use of available technology to limit female conceptions and births.

f. Local, state, and federal public budgets are monitored and need to be influenced by feminist nurses. Health care and human services represent work done (paid, unpaid, or underpaid) primarily by women. It is primarily men who decide such public budgets and whose projects and research receive most of the funding. The results of this obscene imbalance are often disastrous for women, for nurses, for nursing, for the most needy, and for hopes for a humane society. Look at the budget policies and policy makers of the white androcentric Reagan staff. *Administration* is too generous a word for this staff because it literally means to minister to people, and it is women and minorities who have ministered to and nurtured everyone else, though they are seldom ordained as public policy and budget makers.

5. The ANA brought suit against Teachers Insurance Annuity Association and College Retirement Equities Fund (TIAA-CREF) to make their tables sex-neutral rather than sex-biased against women. The issue was that because women generally (not always) lived longer than men (by about 7 years), TIAA-CREF and other carriers required women to pay in more money although they received the same benefits as men (or women pay in the same amount as men *but* receive fewer benefits); women and men, in other

words, paid in the same amount, but women received less. The ANA won a favorable ruling, but the issue is still being questioned and litigated, for example, in New York State. Incidentally, there is *no* such thing as a "unisex" (as in tables) because there remain two sexes, not one: the correct phrase is *sex-neutral*.

In 1972 commissioners of the Equal Employment Opportunity Commission (EEOC) continued to accept the sex-biased policies and practices of TIAA-CREF and other carriers and employers. Some of us from NOW met with EEOC. Part of our agenda was to persuade EEOC to change its own policies to be consistent with Title VII of the 1964 Civil Rights Act, which they are mandated to enforce. I reminded the commissioners that it is also true that white people generally (not always) outlive black people (by about 7 years). It should therefore follow, according to their sex-biased rationale, that white people should receive lower benefits or pay higher premiums than black people. The inconsistency and double standard were apparent to the EEOC. Still, it was not until I promised legal action and a media campaign to bring this to public consciousness that EEOC agreed to change its policies to require sex-neutral tables, payments, and benefits.

The change of EEOC policies and guidelines facilitated efforts by the ANA and others to press the issues and file suit for sex-neutral tables. The EEOC itself also filed suit against the pension company.[3] With the white male club and its mentality reinforcing its own power in the federal government, one can not be sanguine about the prospects in the early 1980s for all women and minority males (including most nurses). Feminist nurses and other health activists must deepen and extend our commitments and numbers and must move from agonizing to organizing for change.

6. Child care and "who cares" are issues that pervade and underlie institutional and most individuals' policies and practices by acts of omission or commission or both. I would suggest that if nurses or anyone else wants to learn something, try to teach it; further, if one really wants to understand something, try to change it. So it is with child care and "who cares." These are gut-level issues. First, the ability to incubate and give birth to an infant does not necessarily mean that one has any ability to nurture and rear that child; likewise, the biological ability to father a child does not mean a man is *dis*qualified to nurture and rear that child. Infant and child care are learned human behaviors; most men need the potentially humanizing experiences of nurturing even more than most women, and males are educable.

There are policy implications in this. For example, places where adults work, study, or otherwise function need quality infant and child care for all employees and students. A lack of or token availability is de facto discrimination against women, who are still the primary if not sole child-care agents.

Among so-called developed nations, the U.S.A. is relatively undeveloped and regressive vis-à-vis child care. Nurses with feminist consciousness should be the national and world leaders in this institutional change.

7. Feminist nurses and other health care activists are among the leaders in the imperatives for reproductive choice, for women's control of their own bodies, for a child's right to be wantèd. Given the realities that women alone experience the work of pregnancy, the labor of delivery, and the major time and energy of infant and child care, compulsory pregnancy to term *against* a woman's wishes for *any* reason is *in* voluntary servitude. This is a violation of the Thirteenth Amendment to the U.S. Constitution. Further, the human sperm and ovum either singly or in combination are *neither* so rare *nor* so precious singly *or* in combination as to supersede the right of the living woman to decide what shall inhabit and receive sustenance from *her* body and for how long. That is part of her genuine right to life. Attempts to give the woman-dependent fertilized ovum, embryo, or fetus any legal rights that diminish or eliminate any women's paramount right to control her body are clearly anti-woman, indeed misogynist, and therefore antifamily and surely not divine.

From the feminist women's self-help health movement has come the initiation and development of menstrual extractions, the forerunners of what is and will surely become do-it-oneself early self-abortions that are self-decided, safe, inexpensive, and hygienic. The questions are not *if* but simply *when* and precisely *how* this knowledge and methodology will spread worldwide. The mission impossible is on its way to becoming the mission accomplished. The opposition will self-destruct of its own anachronisms. Meanwhile the attempt by many conservatives to legislate a so-called human life constitutional amendment must be seen as an intrusion of government into almost every bedroom by the same folks who say they want to get government off our backs.

These people, who would like to so regulate people's private lives, are saying in this proposed amendment that most existing forms of birth control should be banned, as should research on newer and safer birth control as well as morning-after pills, even for rape and incest victims. These are the same individuals who want no control of guns and want more money for military and police hardware, fewer health and safety regulations and their implementation, fewer health and human services unless one is wealthy enough to pay, fewer product and drug safety guarantees, constitutional *in*equality that denies legal personhood (via the Equal Rights Amendment) to all girls and women, capital punishment, elimination of affirmative action except for white males, and much more. May no nurse, no woman, be seduced into believing these philosophies and policies to be anything other than what they are: anti-women, anti-minorities, anti-poor, anti-family, anti-privacy, anti-life, anti–affordable health care and human services, and pro-militarism.

The so-called human life amendment would be the ultimate in government *on* our backs and *in* our bedrooms and (for women) in government's literal invasion of our privacy via our uteri. For government to so act would be a gang rape. Feminist nurses, civil libertarians, health care activists, feminists at large, and those who believe in a child's right to be wanted are organizing to assign this proposed amendment to the oblivion it so richly deserves.

8. What does *not* deserve the near oblivion its opponents have sought for several decades is proposed health care insurance available to people of every income level. Most but not all feminists support the principle of health care as a right, similar to the right to education but even more fundamental. Many feminists insist that such health insurance be supported only on the grounds that publicly financed health care *not* continue the medical model of control, the disease-oriented system. Instead, a holistic approach involving health education, illness prevention, client participation, and coordinated nurse-physician practices (not subordinate-superordinate) needs to be integrated to any publicly funded insurance of quality health care.

9. Feminist nurses and other health care activists generally support and promote the development of nurse practitioners who take and make the time to relate to whole persons, not just "cases" or diseases as physicians often do. The comparison between the technician (physician) and the humanist (nurse) demonstrates notable differences but also remarkable parallels. The results of feminist research into the comparative costs and benefits of quality health care may come as a pleasant surprise: nonprofit health care practitioners (nurses, physicians, and others) are necessary for both quality and affordable health care.

10. Finally is the reminder that the feminist health movement is well on its way to becoming a vital worldwide core of the nearly universal women's movement. The vibrant nongovernmental forum held simultaneously with the official United Nations International Women's decade, Mid-Decade Conference in Copenhagen in July 1980 was alive with health care activists including nurses. The amount of sharing, networking, organizing, and making of commitments was mind expanding and soul healing. The Boston Women's Health Book Collective of Somerville, Massachusetts, is a vital leader in this healthy work nationally and internationally. Nursing and nurses both need to be more informed about and to become participant-leaders in these vanguard transformative phenomena. Nurses who are not

yet feminists must question why they are not. What's so frightening about a movement that values women and the humane part of what is called "feminine" in both sexes and supports these through private and public policies including health care? If not feminism, what? A continuation of sexism with its self-denials and truth-denials?

I predict, rather, that as more nurses know and experience feminism's underlying values, as they perceive the benefit or organizing society according to so-called womanly (really human and humane) principles, nurses will embrace feminism. Then health care and healing can become integral foundations of our common life rather than commodities to be hoarded, sold, and bought if and as one can afford. Crucial in transforming these visions into realities is the recognition that feminism, as a profound values transformation, is a precondition. I wish for you dear sisters and brothers who read this the kinds of experiences that lead to such recognition.

Humanity may literally yearn for what feminism portends. This includes creating a world where the power of love, in the sense of caring about ourselves and others, exceeds the love of power over others. We who have been taught to care must care *enough* to be brave in asserting our feminism. That, not merely our anatomy, may be our real destiny.

ACKNOWLEDGMENT

I would like to express my appreciation to Terry A. Guy, who typed this manuscript.

REFERENCES

1. Ashley, J.A.: Hospitals, paternalism and the role of the nurse, New York, 1976, Teachers College Press.
2. Dumas, R.G.: Women power. In ANA clinical sessions (1974 Convention), New York, 1975, Appleton-Century-Crofts.
3. Fields, C.: TIAA's 'unisex' [sic] pension calculations stalled nationwide by New York ban, The Chronicle of Higher Education 21(22):1, 1981.
4. Goldstein, J.: Psychosurgery: on programming the powerless to love the powerful, unpublished statement, December 27, 1973.
5. Heide, W.S.: Women's liberation means putting nurses and nursing in its place, Imprint 18(3):4, 1971.
6. Heide, W.S.: Feminist objections to psychosurgery, Drug Research Reports, September 1973.
7. Heide, W.S.: A feminist's perspectives on manipulation of woman (woman include man), address to The Genetic Manipulation of Man

[sic] Symposium, University of Wisconsin, Stevens Point, November 8, 1973. Reprint, Pittsburgh, Know, Inc.
8. Heide, W.S.: Nursing and women's liberation—a parallel, American Journal of Nursing, May 1973.
9. Heide, W.S.: Revolution: tomorrow is NOW: presidential address to Conference of National Organization of Women, Inc., Vital Speeches of the Day, May 1973.
10. Heide, W.S.: Feminism for healthy nursing. In ANA Clinical Sessions (1974 Convention), New York, 1975, Appleton-Century-Crofts.
11. Heide, W.S.: Feminism: making a difference in our health. In Nutman, M.T., and Nuddson, C.C., editors: The woman patient, New York, 1978, Plenum Press.
12. McInerney, K.: Sexism is a social disease and nursing is infected. In ANA Clinical Sessions (1974 Convention), New York, 1975, Appleton-Century-Crofts.
13. Miller, J.B.: Toward a *new* psychology of woman, Boston, 1976, Beacon Press.

14. NOW Legal Defense and Education Fund: Records of case of Association for Women in Science et al vs. Elliot Richardson et al; author's own records of the lawsuit and correspondence.
15. Rich, A.: Toward a woman-centered university. In Howe, F., editor: Woman and the power to change, New York, 1975, McGraw-Hill Book Co.
16. Schaefer, M.J.: The dilemma of the nurse administrator. In ANA Clinical Sessions (1974 Convention), New York, 1975, Appleton-Century-Crofts.
17. Wildavsky, A.: Doing better and feeling worse: the political pathology of health policy, Daedulus **106**(1):105, 1977.
18. Women's Equity Action League: Women and health: the care is there but not the power, Washington Report **5**(1):1, 1976.

BIBLIOGRAPHY

Corea, G.: The hidden malpractice: how American (sic U.S.A.) medicine treats women as patients and professionals, New York, 1977, William Morrow & Co., Inc.

Ehrenreich, B., and English D.: For her own good: 150 years of the experts' (sic) advice to women, New York, 1978, Anchor Press.

Heide, W.S.: Feminism for health social work, Smith College School of Social Work Journal, Winter 1976.

Heide, W.S.: Nursing and women's liberation—a parallel, American Journal of Nursing, May 1973.

Howell, M.: A woman's health school, Social Policy **6**(2):50, 1975.

McFarland, D.E., and Shiflet, N., editors: Power in nursing, special issue of Nursing Dimensions **7**(2), 1979.

Ruzek, S.B.: The women's health movement: feminist alternatives to medical control, New York, 1977, Praeger Publishers.

RESOURCES

American Indian and Alaska Native Nurses Association, 231 S. Peters St. Norman, OK 73069.

Chicana Nurses Association, P.O. Box 33376, Los Angeles, CA 90033.

Feminist Women's Health Center, 1112 Crenshaw Boulevard, Los Angeles, CA 90019. Vanguard movers and shakers.

KNOW, Inc., P.O. Box 86031, Pittsburgh, PA 15221. A feminist press with fascinating articles, reprints including "The Reality and the Challenge of the Double Standard in Mental Health," "Advice to the Bridegroom," The Politics of Touch," and beaucoup more.

National Association of Hispanic Nurses, 12044 Seventh Avenue N.W., Seattle, WA 98177.

National Black Nurses Association, Inc., P.O. Box 18358, Boston, MA 02118.

National Gay Task Force, 80 Fifth Avenue, Suite 1601, New York, N.Y. 10011.

National Women's Health Network: "Warning: the National Women's Health Network has determined that our medical system may be hazardous to your health" and other publications/actions, 224 7th Street S.E., Washington, D.C. 20006.

National Women's Studies Association, c/o University of Maryland, College Park, IN 20742. To get women's studies/feminism integrated into curricula.

Nurses Coalition for Action in Politics (NCAP), 1030 15th St. N.W., Suite 408, Washington, D.C. 20005.

Nurses Network, c/o Health/PAC, 17 Murray Street, New York, NY 10007. Address on job issues, collective bargaining, patient care, working conditions, unionism, sexism, and racism.

Nurses NOW, c/o National Organization for Women, Inc. (NOW), 425 13th Street N.W., Washington, D.C. 20004. Part of world's largest feminist organization.

Nursing: The Politics of Caring, the voices of nurses as most folks have never heard them before. Filmmakers Joan Finck and Timothy Sawyer in Collaboration with Karen Wolf, R.N., 23 min, 16 mm, color/sound, ¾" videocassette, rental and sale: ILEX films, P.O. Box 226, Cambridge, MA 02138.

Older Women's League, 3800 Harrison Street, Oakland, CA 94611. Working on health and health insurance issues.

Taking our Bodies Back, Cambridge Documentary Films, P.O. Box 385, Cambridge, MA 02139. A must-see.

GEORGE BROOKFIELD, ANDY DOUGLAS, RUSSELL S. SHAPIRO, and
STANLEY J. CIAS

Chapter 18

Some thoughts on being a male in nursing

Being a male in an occupation that has traditionally been dominated by females
is quite a unique experience. Although it has been previously assumed that only a
woman could function as a nurse, it is now being realized that a man can also be
caring and sensitive enough to understand people's needs and fulfill the nursing role.

It is interesting to see how society conditions people to hold certain beliefs and
to practice certain traditions. For example, the middle-aged female patient is, in my
experience, quite bashful when being attended by a male nurse and in most cases
would rather be assigned to a female. Young female patients, on the other hand,
seem to have few qualms about being cared for by a male nurse, perhaps because of
the changes in societal expectations about male and female employment roles. I have
also discovered that older male patients often feel more comfortable with a male
nurse; however, younger adult males prefer a female (some because of the "sexual"
contact, and some because they think of themselves as macho and believe that male
nurses must be homosexual or effeminate).

Although working as a man in nursing has many drawbacks, I believe that it has
certain advantages. As society begins to accept the inevitable male/female role adjustments, there will be a concommitant realization of the limitless opportunities for
both men and women in the nursing profession.

George Brookfield

"Do you anticipate any problems having a female supervisor?" I have heard this question so many times that I have begun to think that it must be carved in stone somewhere. I try hard not to strangle such interviewers while responding, "I have found, in 11 years of nursing, that when female nurses are organized, they seem far more organized than males; but when they are disorganized, they are also much more disorganized." I always have some doubts about how this statement will be received, but I risk saying it, knowing that this has been my experience.

I know that men are good for nursing and can help the profession to prosper, not because we are so terrific or because of our stereotypical "business sense." Those are societal rationalizations. I believe that a mixture of traditional male *and* female characteristics would lend a better balance and help to elevate the profession.

I have always considered the rest of the world to be people, not men or women, not greater or lesser, but simply human beings. I realize too that it is neither simple for an entire society to view things that way nor practical to expect it. More important than the male/female issue is the issue of people beginning to know what they want from life. Through working with terminally ill patients and their families, I often found that people could tell me what made them *un*happy but saying what made them happy was more difficult. People, I found, frequently do not know what they want or what makes them happy. Sometimes what people want and what makes them happy are two different things; sometimes they enslave themselves working toward that which makes them miserable. Society, with its traditional stereotypes, with its restrictions on "appropriate" male and female roles, with its sanctions, has forced both men and women to choose that which they do not want, that which does not make them happy. Society's changing and people's changing will make the difference in people knowing and choosing that which they truly want. The nursing profession needs to change, and I believe that it will take both men and women to do it.

Insight is a broad term for beginning to understand—things about your personality, your profession, your way of life. It means *really* seeing and understanding. Often we do not *really* see; we lack insight. (The prisoners Plato describes, for example, were chained to the walls of a cave and believed that things were just as they perceived them to be, even though they saw only the shadows.) We must begin to look beyond the shadows, to gain insight into ourselves, our desires, and our world. The changes in women and in nursing necessitate that we perceive both differently and that we develop new understanding. The same is true of ourselves.

Andy Douglas

As a child growing up in a family of lawyers, physicians, social workers, and dentists, I was continually prompted by my parents to pursue a similar endeavor. Fate took matters into its own hands. The year was 1969, the place was Viet Nam, and I, as a U.S. Navy Special Forces Corpsman, became involved in health care.

In addition to being a corpsman I have been a fire department paramedic, a nursing assistant, an operating room technician, a medical photographer, and a licensed vocational nurse. The gratifications of these varied experiences have shaped my perceptions of men in nursing. The stereotype of a "man in trousers, tunic, and white buck shoes" conjures up for many the label "medical student" or "orderly." Nursing has historically been a starting point for men pursuing their M.D. (after all, they had to eat and pay bills), but nursing has not often been an end in itself for men.

So what kind of man would choose to remain in nursing? A medical school misfit? A business world dropout? A mechanical incompetent? Or worse? The hostile stigma of being thought of sexually deviant is frequently attached to a man in nursing. Though there may be homosexuals in any profession, nursing, because it is associated with "feminine" qualities, lends itself to such biases more readily.

Only recently has there been increasing enrollment of men in schools of nursing. Our philosophy has begun to change. Nursing may no longer be synonymous with women. Men are being seen as an important part of the profession. As equality of the sexes and acceptance of the true capabilities and needs of individuals evolve, nursing will become an increasingly viable career choice for men.

So much for philosophy and fantasy. I have experienced the total horror of combat nursing, the stresses of "curbside" nursing as a paramedic, and the perfunctory responsibilities of an operating room technician. All of these are congruent with "masculine" roles. Medical-surgical wards, however, seem to encourage questions about the appropriateness of my being a male nurse. Females react with wonder, males with abhorrence. I learned that I was better tolerated in emergency rooms, critical care, and psychiatry. I have even been encouraged and welcomed in these areas. Yet I still hear, "Surely you're going to pursue your M.D.!" or "Why Nursing?"

That's a good question: why nursing? Because nursing has purpose and meaning for my life and offers me diversity. There is potential for both vertical and lateral mobility; some areas provide handsome remuneration. My motivation for being a nurse is predicated on these factors. Men (and women) need mobility in their jobs. Nursing provides this.

Men are now actively pursuing careers as nurses. I am fairly independent, and I feel comfortable as a nurse. Men have made an impact on the profession and will continue to do so as acceptance of their talents increases.

Russell S. Shapiro

Being a man in nursing has accustomed me to the politics that occur when a male enters a female-dominated profession. In my nursing school (a diploma school on the East Coast), being one of three men in my class afforded me certain privileges not granted to my female peers. I am naturally outspoken, a factor that contributed to my assumption of a leadership role. For a while I was a rebel, challenging the system, questioning policies and protocols. Along with the leadership role came greater freedoms in dictating student policies as well as greater freedoms in the scope of my clinical practice. I was chosen as the school representative to various student nurse functions in the state.

During my student experience the staff on clinical units allowed me greater autonomy in the care of patients. They tended to identify me as a member of their own group as well as a student. Occasionally my physical abilities were utilized in lifting heavy patients, but I never felt that I was abused or misused in this sense. Overall I was treated in a very professional manner. Unfortunately, many of my peers received much less consideration. How much of this differential treatment was the result of my own personality and how much of my maleness is hard to determine. I found the reverse discrimination to be enhancing, much as women do who pioneer the way in male-dominated professions. My minority status, then, was pleasurable.

The question of my masculinity also arose in this early experience. What type of man would willingly choose to be a nurse? Didn't I really want to be a doctor? Couldn't I *make it* as a doctor? Was there *really* something *wrong* with me (meaning was I a homosexual)? I dealt with these issues then and continue to do so.

I chose nursing for its excellent career opportunities. I could involve myself in the medical field at a professional level and yet avoid 24-hour responsibility and being married to my job. I also liked the diversity nursing offered. Specialization, I knew, would give me additional options and experiences should I find myself bored or in need of further challenge. A good understanding of nursing opportunities, combined with an understanding of my own desires and need to give, made nursing the logical career choice for me. Naturally I have encountered both narrow-minded staff and patients in my experience. In any field in which sex segregation exists such biases are to be expected, but self-understanding has helped me to endure the few negative experiences I have had. My biggest objection is being referred to as a "male nurse." I am a nurse. Period. My sexual appendage plays no part in my job. Labeling of this kind distorts the overall functions of individuals. My responsibilities are the same as those of my female counterparts, so simply referring to me as a nurse should suffice.

"Male nurses" are purportedly able to advance up bureaucratic career ladders faster than female nurses. Qualifications, I am sure, play a part in such decisions, yet it still appears that men have greater opportunity within the field of nursing. It has been suggested that discrimination occurs. This may be partly true, but I think that most men in nursing have chosen this career as an alternative to past working environments. Their past experiences may be partly responsible for their quicker advancement in nursing. In addition, society still teaches men that they have innate leadership abilities that can be used in work situations. Some men have such abilities; others do not. Some men attain positions based on ability; others attain positions because they are *supposed* to have ability. I think the same may be true of women.

The debate over the roles of men in nursing will continue for some time. There will always be men who think their physical capabilities are being abused, and there will always be women who believe that they did not get certain jobs because preference was given to men. We can say that sexism should not exist, but it does, and we must face it. I hope that as more men choose nursing, and as nursing becomes more autonomous, we will be able to attain a balance in which both men and women can meet their own needs and can achieve their goals of delivering optimal patient care.

Stanley J. Cias

"Your Angel of Mercy," original oil painting by Howard Chandler Christy
(1873-1952), from the private collection of Nancy and Robert Risen
(Risen's Fine Art), Glendale California.

UNIT FOUR

PSYCHOLOGICAL ISSUES

The chapters in this section focus on nursing and women's issues whose impact is psychological (and often social and political as well). Their common denominator is the fact that nurses are predominantly female. These chapters form a collection and are all indirectly related through this central issue.

Ann Rosenow begins with a discussion of the common lack of social and personal support for women with careers. Women, she says, have particular support needs because career orientation is not appropriate to traditional female sex roles and deviance brings with it guilt and social sanctions, the stresses of which are great. For women too there are many practical problems inherent in having a career and running a household. Assistance in the form of practical support at home, emotional support, and direct career aid are important if women are to succeed.

The mothering aspects of nursing are examined by Nalda Brodegaard through the framework of Margaret Mahler's developmental stages. Nurses, like mothers, often have symbiotic attachments to those for whom they care *and* to those with whom they work. Nurses seek gratification of their own needs through such relationships and see themselves as omnipotently able to meet all the needs of others. Hospital or professional groups perpetuate this symbiosis through subconscious and conscious processes. The vulnerability of nurses to symbiotic attachments results from their socialization as female care-givers and from the paternalistic health care system.

Norine Kerr examines the doctor-nurse relationship from a psychological perspective and describes the "narcissistic fit" between the professions. The key elements include the narcissist (physician) and other (nurse) colluding in an overvaluing/devaluing split. The narcissist receives the admiration of the other; the other exchanges self-doubt and a lack of identity for identification with the seemingly well-defined narcissist. They become fused and cannot tolerate the emergence of aspects of reality that conflict with the images of each other they have developed. The relationship is precarious and easily disrupted.

Also from a psychological perspective, Marilyn Jaffe Ruiz analyzes the lack of nursing leadership as a problem in ego development and differentiation. Nurses, she says, have failed to become independent and assertive because of sociocultural influences that affect their separation-individuation. Dr. Ruiz suggests that nurses learn to respect each other, that they use professional relationships to rework earlier difficulties in separating and individuating, and that they develop mentoring systems and examine educational processes. Consciousness raising and nursing's involvement in social, political, and practice issues are imperative.

In Unit One Ella Lasky related female lack of self-esteem to achievement difficulties. Ann Rosenow now examines achievement *within* female professions in general and specifically nursing.

Nurses are often their own worst enemies. The profession is rife with conflicts; these are explored in a chapter by Patricia Geary Dean, who focuses on the problems of nurses against themselves on a professional level. The lack of support for nursing colleagues, the encouragment of passivity and conformity, and the conflict between nursing education and nursing administration are important issues she addresses and for which she proposes solutions.

On a more personal level, Emily Smythe looks at the internal conflict and stresses of individual nurses. She describes burnout, despair, and rage as responses to stress and examines the cognitive, emotional, and motivational processes that make nurses vulnerable and impotent.

ANN M. ROSENOW

Chapter 19

Without a wife

The dilemma of social support for women's careers

Establishing and maintaining a professional career as it is currently envisioned requires a great deal of time, energy, and commitment. Support from others is almost essential for those engaged in this endeavor. An acknowledgment of this need is reflected in our occupational and family structures.

In American culture it is assumed that men are the ones who have professional careers. The support they need to achieve professional success is largely provided by their supportive wives. Other social structures and norms provide additional support or exempt men from certain responsibilities so that they may concentrate on their careers. These assumptions have been decisive in shaping professional work requirements, policies, and ethics.[27] These structures and standards complement the role of the professional man, but they conflict with the social role of the professional woman, for she has no wife.

THE SUPPORTIVE WIFE

A number of writers have claimed that having a career in our society is not an individual phenomenon.[14,18] Rather, the careerist is able to devote time to her/his work because of the support of others. Traditionally wives provide a major portion of this support for their husbands.

The vital supportive functions performed by the wives of professional men to sustain their career successes have been outlined by Fowlkes.[14] Among them are (1) *the adjunct role* in which the wife contributes directly to her husband's work, (2) *the supportive role* in which she nurtures her husband's career commitments, and (3) *the double-duty role* in which she provides her husband with the time and independence needed for professional work by assuming major responsibility for childrearing, family life, and household management. The double-duty role is identified by Fowlkes as being particularly crucial. The lack of this support may be most critical for the professional woman: She not only does not have a wife but may be expected to be one.

281

THE PROFESSIONAL WOMAN'S NEED FOR SUPPORT

Women who decide to pursue professional careers have the same needs for support as men. This support may be more difficult, however, for women to obtain. In addition their feminine role responsibilities may result in special needs for support.

Women have been culturally assigned responsibility for home management and child and family care. They are socialized to believe this is their major responsibility. In addition they are expected to provide support for their husbands' careers. These responsibilities are not compatible with the demands of a professional career. To pursue professional careers women must avoid home and family responsibilities or have help with them. Either alternative represents a violation of sex-role norms that prescribe that women should consider marriage and motherhood their primary role. This violation of sex-role norms creates stress, which must be counteracted by emotional support from others.

The failure to behave sex-role-"appropriately" is likely to be met with the disapproval and perhaps outright hostility from others. Condry and Dyer[7] suggest that the controversial fear of success attributed to women, developed by Horner as an addition to McClelland's achievement theory, may simply reflect expectations about the negative consequences of deviancy from sex-role norms. Negative sanctions constitute a threat to a woman's professional success unless support from others buffers their impact. Others' praise for accomplishments and encouragement for career activities are important in counteracting this negative impact.

Women who marry and have children have practical problems that must be solved before they can devote the necessary time to their professional careers.[1] They must have help with child care and household management or face severe role overload, which reduces their effectiveness in both career and family roles. Situations that require extra hours at work, trips out of town, and late meetings are all potential problems for the working mother. If she fails to attend to these aspects of professional work, her professional achievement is threatened.

The single woman's needs for support for her career are somewhat different but are still significant. Although she may not have traditional family responsibilities to hamper her professional achievement, she too is without a wife. In this respect she can be compared to the single man: she too is without built-in emotional support and a social partner.[8]

Women also need assistance from superiors and colleagues to "learn the ropes" and get ahead within the profession. The professional system was not structured with the professional woman in mind. Therefore, some of the important supports men can count on may not be available to women. The mentor system is an example. Fawcett[12] reports there is a whole range of informal social relationships through which professionals communicate and provide assistance to one another. In male-dominated professions, women are sometimes closed out of these support systems.[11] Women often work fewer hours in the professions because of other feminine role responsibilities, thus decreasing their visibility and their inclusion in formal responsibilities and informal networks.

In female-dominated professions such as nursing, however, another problem arises. Mentor support may simply not be available. Fawcett[12] contends that the scientific community in nursing is just beginning to emerge and that such a patronage system is just beginning to develop. Women may also need role models for combining family and career roles and may need advice and support in resolving dilemmas stemming from conflicts between the two roles.

SOCIAL SUPPORT FOR A PROFESSIONAL CAREER

A review of the literature indicates that support from others is considered an important factor in career development and success. A theoretical formulation of the concept of social support is useful in understanding the role that support plays in a professional career.

Social support can be defined as information leading an individual to believe that (1) she/he is cared for and loved, (2) she/he is esteemed and valued, and (3) she/he belongs to a network of communication and mutual obligation.[6,20] Recently the role of social support as a moderator of life stress has become an important concept in areas as disparate as the etiology of physical illness and coping with unemployment.*

In a review of social support literature Cobb[6] identifies evidence that social support can protect people in crises from a wide variety of pathological states. Social support may play a role in mental health as well.[13,15,22] It is reasonable to infer that social support also plays a role in buffering the stress the professional woman incurs through her violation of sex-role norms and her role overload. In addition social support can provide women with other types of assistance needed to sustain their professional careers.

Social career support is the sustenance of one's career by family, friends, colleagues, organizations, and others. The social career support potentially needed by professional women is of three major types:

1. *Practical support:* assistance with or advice involving her household management, family life, child care, or care for ill parents or family members so that the woman can have the time and independence needed for her professional work.

2. *Emotional support:* interpersonal support, advice, sympathy, and encouragement for her professional role.

3. *Direct aid:* direct contributions to the management or content of the woman's professional work or to the status or reputational aspects of her career establishment.

*References 6, 9, 10, 13, 15, 20, 21, 22.

Practical support

Practical support is probably most vital for women who have heavy home and family responsibilities that interfere with their career activities. Marriage and children are two factors with heavy impacts on women's career involvement.

One aspect of practical support involves help with household and personal chores. Finding dinner ready when one comes home from a particularly long and stressful day at work is pleasant and helpful. Running errands such as taking the car to have its oil changed or getting the refrigerator repaired can be difficult when one has a busy work schedule. Spending a weekend doing laundry, cleaning, and grocery shopping is not ideal. Most working women manage these chores without giving them much thought—but at what cost to their professional achievement? Professional men traditionally have supportive wives to take care of many of these responsibilities for them. The single professional woman has no spouse support. The married professional woman may even, in fact, be expected to take care of these things for her husband.

Another aspect of practical support involves assistance with social and recreational activities, including planning and making preparations for activities and being a reliable social partner. Giving parties and dinners and meeting other social obligations such as buying gifts and sending cards can be very time consuming. Of course, many social and recreational activities can be omitted so that time can be devoted to career activities instead. The busy professional man, however, can usually manage both if his wife handles all the details.

The married professional woman may have additional needs for practical support. How extensive these needs are depends on how many demands stem from her husband's orientation to marriage and the nature of his career. The husband who sees his wife's career as secondary to her family responsibilities will most likely make demands with little consideration for career requirements. If the husband is involved in a career that requires active participation by his wife, such as the ministry, politics, or executive managment, further difficulties arise. The professional woman who finds herself in one of these situations needs extra practical support to sustain her professional career.

A married professional woman with children requires some assistance with child care. Unexpected events such as a child's sickness or a late meeting may be the most difficult to manage. Schools and churches generally assume mothers do not work and are therefore available during the day and on short notice when schedules are changed. A reliable means of child care is a vital form of practical support for the professional woman with children, for it is likely that she rather than her husband bears the major responsibility for taking care of their children.

Emotional support

Emotional support is especially important for the professional woman because she is following a deviant life-style. Because she has a career, others may view her as less feminine or as a less competent wife and mother. These negative evaluations can be very distressing.

Social approval for a woman's career is uncertain. Her achievement may even be met with disapproval. Emotional support is important for counteracting the potential inhibition of her career aspirations by social reactions. Achieving success in a feminine sex-typed occupation such as nursing may engender less social disapproval than success in a masculine sex-typed occupation in which the violation of sex-role norms is more apparent. The desire to comply with sex-role norms and avoid social disapproval may, however, have been associated with some women's choice of nursing, an acceptable feminine occupation, as a career. Thus nurses are not immune.

Positive attitudes toward the woman's career by those close to her are important. If significant people in her life do not agree with her career aspirations and instead expect her to be directing her energies elsewhere, a role conflict will result. Role conflicts are stressful and inhibit career success.

Another important aspect of emotional support is the encouragement of others for a woman's career achievement. Those close to the professional woman may not openly oppose her career, but if they have indifferent attitudes toward her success, this too can inhibit her achievement. Their encouragement at strategic points can make a critical difference in her career development.

Closely aligned with the need for encouragement is the need for opportunities to discuss career concerns and aspirations with someone else. This is especially important for career planning. Emotional support can lead to a valuing of the professional woman's career aspirations to the point that they become part of total family planning.

Once adequate practical support is available so that the woman can devote the necessary time to career activities, emotional support to proceed with these activities becomes important. Given sufficient practical and emotional support, direct assistance with career development can then be useful.

Direct aid

Direct aid involves a variety of activities that help a woman get ahead in her career, including services connected with her professional work such as advice on clinical and educational programs, proofreading manuscripts, and aid with speeches, research, written work, and legwork. A colleague with whom she can engage in joint work can be very helpful. Such a relationship provides not only direct assistance with professional work but emotional support as well.

A mentor or peer relationship through which the woman can obtain advice, encouragement, role modeling, and contacts and opportunities for career advancement is also very helpful. Someone within the profession who holds a high opinion of her professional potential and has a position of influence can promote her professional work. This kind of direct assistance can be a key ingredient in career success. Finding adequate career support, however, may not be easy.

SOURCES OF SOCIAL CAREER SUPPORT

Although wives are a vital source of support for their husbands' careers, husbands do not generally fill the same role for their wives. They may provide emotional support, but most husbands give only a limited amount of practical support to their professional wives. The approval and encouragement of husbands for their wives' employment have been identified by numerous writers as an important source of support for married women.* Most studies of husbands' participation in traditional domestic responsibilities of women in the home have, however, found husbands lacking.[23,30]

In addition the norm that a wife support her husband's career seems firmly embedded. Poloma and Garland[24] report that even professional women felt their careers were secondary to their husbands' careers. This attitude results in family decisions and activities revolving to a disproportionate degree around the husband's career. In such an environment social support for the wife's career may be more difficult to secure.

Studies of dual-career families provide some insight into support mechanisms within families in which both husband and wife have demanding careers.[17,18,25] Outside help is frequently employed to assist with domestic chores and child care. In addition an altered and more equitable pattern of status and decision making is generally present in these families.

The dual-career family model has been questioned, however, as a vechicle of support for women's careers. Hunt and Hunt[18] claim that with two careers to support, the family may not be able to provide both careerists with the supportive services necessary to allow them to be competitive in the career market. Traditionally, successful professional men have the benefit of extensive supportive services, provided by wives, that although not formally required are important if not essential for optimal career performance. This correlation suggests that a career is a two-person phenomenon. Support from wives allows men to devote a tremendous amount of effort to career success, an important factor in the productivity of a profession.[3] Female-dominated professions such as nursing can be expected to have a very low incidence of the two-person career. The importance of that factor in the professionalization of nursing deserves further investigation.

Not many professional women have husbands who are willing to play the traditional "wife role" for them, given current cultural norms. This constitutes a serious gap in social support for the professional woman. Even is she chooses to remain single, she must still cope without a spouse's support. If she marries, she faces the dilemma of depriving her husband of support for his career so that she can pursue hers or sacrificing her own career to meet her feminine role responsibilities. As long as the current occupational structure exists a substitute support system will be needed.

---

*References 2-5, 16, 19, 25, 29.

My own study of outstanding nurses provides some insights into substitute sources of social support that may be tapped by women with professional careers.[26] I found that practical support may be obtained through creative combinations of employed help, family assistance from parents and children as well as from husbands, and assistance from neighbors. Emotional support may be supplied not only by husbands and other family members but also by professional colleagues, coworkers, and friends. Professional and social organizations may also be a source of emotional support and encouragement for career achievement. A wide range of new magazines and television programs now addreses the special needs and problems of the career women. Emotional support was found in this study to be more readily available than other types of social support, and the majority of respondents considered it to be the most important support in their career success as well.

Direct aid was generally the type of support most difficult for those successful nurses who were studied to obtain.[26] A few reported having mentors or important role models. Professional colleagues within and outside the profession were the major sources of direct aid. Many nurses, however, reported that they received almost no direct aid. Findings from this study suggest that a professional support network is badly needed by nurses and other women with professional careers. The concept of networking, through which women can make contacts and receive career assistance, has received much attention recently.[31] It may provide a partial answer to the paucity of direct aid in nursing.

FACTORS AFFECTING SOCIAL CAREER SUPPORT

The life choices and attitudes of the individual woman affect her need for social support for her professional career. Her need for practical support depends on the degree to which her other responsibilities interfere with her career activities. Home and family responsibilities constitute a major barrier to women's career participation. It is possible to reduce interference, however, through choosing not to marry and/or not to have children.

A woman's attitudes are also important in determining how much practical support she may require to sustain her professional career. If she is able to let housework and social activity slide when career demands are heavy, her need for practical support will be lower. Her attitudes toward her feminine role responsibilities have a major impact on the degree of role overload she will experience in combining family and career roles, as well as on the amount of practical assistance she will need to prevent sacrifice of her career.

The inner motivations of some women are strong and the need for encouragement from others for career achievement low. Some women accept the fact that their goals are different from what others think they should be and do not allow this to deter them. Individual attitudes and characteristics affect the importance of emotional support for individual women. The importance of direct aid is similarly affected by the individual's assertiveness in making her own contacts and working to establish her own career.

Not only does the need for social support vary, but the degree to which it is sought, accepted, and utilized also varies. Schreiber and Glidewell[28] contend that accepting help from others often requires that one also accept extra trouble, inconvenience, the restraint of one's own desires, or even more vexing costs. They concluded from a study of social norms that constrain interpersonal helping that accepting help involves resolving the conflict between the wish for support and the resistance to being controlled. Perceiving the cost of social support may prevent some women from seeking, accepting, or using it effectively.

THE DILEMMA

Social support can make a difference in career achievement. Nurses, 98% of whom are female, do not have wives to provide this support. Until the current occupational and family structures change, substitute sources of support will be needed by nurses who strive for professional success. The future productivity and advancement of the nursing profession will be strongly affected by how well this need for support is met. The support of husbands does not appear to be the total answer. The discovery of alternative mechanisms of support is a concern not just for individual nurses but for the profession and society overall as well.

REFERENCES

1. Bailyn, L.: Family constraints on women's work. In Kundsin, R., editor: Women and success, New York, 1974, William Morrow & Co., Inc.
2. Barnett, R.C., and Baruch, G.K.: The competent woman: perspectives on development, New York, 1978, Irvington Publishers, Inc.
3. Bernard, J.: Women and the public interest, Chicago, 1971, Aldine Publishing Co.
4. Burke, R.J.: and others: Husband-wife compatibility and the management of stress, The Journal of Social Psychology 94:243, 1974.
5. Cleland, V., and others: Social and psychologic influences on employment of married nurses, Nursing Research 25:90, 1976.
6. Cobb, S.: Social support as a moderator of life stress, Psychosomatic Medicine 38:300, 1976.
7. Condry J., and Dyer, S.: Fear of success: attribution of cause to the victim, the Journal of Social Issues 32:68, 1976.
8. Davis, A.G., and Strong, P.M.: Working without a net: the bachelor as a social problem, Sociological Review 25:109, 1977.
9. Dean, A., and Lin, N.: The stress-buffering role of social support, The Journal of Nervous and Mental Disease 165:403, 1977.
10. Dohrenwend, B.S., and Dohrenwend, B.P.: Stressful life events: their nature and effects, New York, 1974, John Wiley & Sons, Inc.
11. Epstein, C.F.: Women's place, options and limits in professional careers, Berkeley, 1970, University of California Press.
12. Fawcett, J.: On development of a scientific community in nursing, unpublished paper, Pittsburgh, 1980, University of Pennsylvania.
13. Figueira-McDonough, J.: Mental health among unemployed Detroiters, Social Service Review 383, 1978.
14. Fowlkes, M.R.: The wives of professional men: a study of the interdependency of family and careers, unpublished doctoral dissertation, Amherst, 1977, University of Massachusetts.
15. Gore, S.: The influence of social support and related variables in ameliorating the consequences of job loss, unpublished doctoral dissertation, Pittsburgh, 1973, University of Pennsylvania.
16. Higginson, M.V., and Quick, T.L.: The ambitious woman's guide to a successful career, New York, 1975, AMACOM.
17. Holmstrom, L.L.: The two-career family,

Cambridge, Mass., 1972, Schenkman Publishing Co., Inc.

18. Hunt, J.G., and Hunt, L.L.: Dilemmas and contradictions of status: the case of the dual-career family, Social Problems 24(2):407, 1977.

19. Martin, T.W., and others: The impact of dual-career marriages on female professional careers: an empirical test of a Parsonian hypothesis, Journal of Marriage and Family 37:734, 1975.

20. Murawski, B.J., and others: Social support in health and illness: the concept and its measurement, Cancer Nursing 365, 1978.

21. Nuckolls, K.B., and others: Psychologic assets, life crisis and the prognosis of pregnancy, American Journal of Epidemiology 95:431, 1972.

22. Pinneau, S.R., Jr.: Effects of social support on psychological and physiological status, unpublished doctoral dissertation, Ann Arbor, 1975, University of Michigan.

23. Pleck, J.H.: The work-family role system, Social Problems 24:417, 1977.

24. Poloma, M.T., and Garland, T.N.: The myth of the egalitarian family: familial roles and the professionally employed wife. In Theodore, A., editor: The Professional woman, Cambridge, Mass., 1971, Schenkman Publishing Co., Inc.

25. Rapoport, R., and Rapoport, R.N.: Dual-career families re-examined: new integrations of work and family, New York, 1976, Colophon Books.

26. Rosenow, A.M.: The dilemma of achievement in nursing. A woman's profession, unpublished doctoral dissertation, Chicago, 1981, The University of Chicago.

27. Safilios-Rothschild, C.: Dual linkages between the occupational and family systems, Signs: Journal of Women in Culture and Society 1:51, 1976.

28. Schreiber, S.T., and Glidewell, J.C.: Social norms and helping in a community of limited liability, American Journal of Community Psychiatry 6:441, 1978.

29. Van Meter, M.J.: Role strain among married college women, unpublished doctoral dissertation, 1976, Michigan State University.

30. Walker, K.E.: Time spent by husbands in household work, Family Economics Review 4: 8, 1970.

31. Welch, M.S.: Networking: the great new way for women to get ahead, New York, 1980, Harcourt Brace Jovanovich, Inc.

Chapter 20

The nurse defined as the symbiotic mother

Nurse, nurture, nourish. Think for a moment about the implications to a profession of sharing its name with the fundamental task of mothering. A "nursing mother" sustains her infant's life in a way that no one else can. Subsequent to being nursed and nourished at his mother's breast, the child develops an attachment to her that is so unique in its intensity, closeness, and concomitant expectations that it can never be duplicated in his lifetime. Margaret Mahler has called this attachment symbiotic.[3] While a child enjoys a symbiotic attachment to his mother he does not clearly differentiate between his body and hers or between his impulses and their source of gratification: If the child wishes to be fed or comforted, he has every reason to believe that this wish will cause his mother to feed or comfort him. An adequate mother, by virtue of her alertness and prompt attention to her child's needs, unwittingly allows this delusion of symbiosis to develop. Ultimately, as the child's intellectual and physical development proceeds, he will discover his separateness and will be eager to develop his individuality. If the symbiotic attachment was satisfactory, it will leave behind it feelings of security and well-being. This residue provides the foundation from which a healthy adult ego can develop. All adults maintain some longings for the symbiotic phase, which they attempt to gratify in other relationships. If an individual experienced satisfaction of dependency needs as an infant, these longings will not interfere with his ability to fulfill adult responsibilities. Rather, these longings will be helpful in providing impetus toward the establishment of mature, lasting interpersonal relationships. If the symbiotic attachment was not satisfactory, the frustration of the child's needs will cause conflicts that will adversely influence the development of his adult personality and seriously impair his ability to meet adult responsibilities and form satisfactory interpersonal relationships.

Many parallels can and have been drawn between the profession of nursing and the maternal act of nursing. It has been suggested that in ancient communities the nurse was a competent and compassionate mother whose energies and inclinations allowed her to expand her role to meet the needs of sick or needy community members outside of her own family.[7] Like mothering, nursing has been essential to the preservation of life since ancient times. Nursing was the first health care profes-

290

sion, nurturing and sustaining life when little was known about the workings of the human body. As medicine became a science and knowledge of pathophysiology expanded, new professions developed to take over functions that nursing had previously though rudimentarily encompassed: physical therapists developed specialized skills to limit musculoskeletal dysfunctions, occupational therapists specialized in neuromuscular functioning, psychiatrists and psychologists were concerned with emotional and psychic health, and physicians specialized their care for each of the body's systems.

Though the nurse had been the first to assume care for human beings, she was the last to specialize her care. Factions within the nursing profession currently argue the relative merits of the nurse remaining a generalist versus the nurse limiting her practice to specialty areas. Regardless of the faction to which a nurse belongs, it is more or less agreed that nursing care is planned with a concern for the "whole person" and the environment within which she/he must function. Few health care professionals would dispute the validity of this holistic concern. But few professions have encountered the difficulties nursing has encountered in developing its skills in speciality areas. I propose that this problem is a result of nursing's close association with motherhood. In my experience as a psychiatric nurse I have found that the residual need for symbiotic attachment that exists to varying degrees in all individuals can and often does find its object in the nurse. It has been my experience that patients, other health care disciplines, and the nurse herself sometimes collude to allow the nurse to be defined as the symbiotic mother. By this I mean that the nurse becomes expected to meet the needs for total care and comfort characteristically met during that early phase of the mother-child attachment. Characteristic of that attachment is a vague and primitive perception of one's need combined with an absolute belief that mother can omnipotently respond to the need, however, poorly articulated, and soothe all physical and psychic tensions. When, as must realistically happen, the nurse is not able to meet these felt needs, she becomes the target of the frustrations of both staff and patient. For the nurse herself attempts to work within the symbiotic mother role lead to a fragmentation of her efforts, inability to define or meet the patient's legitimate nursing needs, and no time or energy left over to develop specialized skills and knowledge.

I suggest that the reason the nurse is so often cast in the role of the symbiotic mother can be found in the delicate interaction between the intrapsychic and interpersonal needs of the individual, the demands made on the individual by her/his various group associations, and the covert dynamics of groups. I have already discussed the intrapsychic need for a close maternal attachment that persists throughout adult life. In the following pages I will show how patterns of family interaction teach the individual to use interpersonal relationships and group associations to meet this need and the consequent effect this has on the roles that individuals in groups must play.

Group associations are an unavoidable part of every individual's life, beginning as soon as he relinquishes his symbiotic delusions and becomes aware of the family members with whom he must share mother. The family is the first and most important group association an individual experiences. The patterns of interaction learned there will provide a model for behavior in future group memberships. The personality that the individual develops is greatly influenced by the role that he learns to play in the family. One's role describes the way one acts in his position vis-à-vis others: his behavior is determined by both internal and external expectations and pressures. [15]

Family members, because of their close association over a long period of time, become hyperalert to each other's needs, both the conscious, easily articulated needs and the subconscious needs that are felt but not necesarily clearly articulated or understood. Subconscious needs usually coexist with conflicts regarding whether and how they should be met. They exist in the subconscious because a full awareness of them would create unmanageable anxiety. Because these needs are kept out of one's conscious awareness, it is impossible to deal with them in the same direct way that one usually deals with conscious needs. Subconscious needs are usually dealt with by subconscious means. One way that families meet their subconscious needs is through irrational role assignment, [9] or projective identification. [20] These two terms are not synonomous, but they are quite similar and for the purposes of this chapter will be used interchangeably. They refer to a situation in which an individual becomes expected to enact a certain role not because of *his* needs, desires, or internal tensions but because of needs of others that can be met through his enactment of this role. The most common of the irrationally assigned roles is that of the parent. The term *parentification* is used to describe a situation in which an individual subjectively distorts his relationship with his child or spouse as if that person were his parent. [4] This process allows the individual to re-create his parents by encouraging their representation in a current real family member. Thus the individual denies the frightening feelings of abandonment experienced on separation from the actual parent. [9] The assigned role or identification usually represents someone with whom the original relationship was highly conflicted. The conflict is then recreated in the relationship between parent and "parentified" child, serving the dual purpose of keeping the object alive and renewing the opportunity to work through the old conflict. It must be stressed that this is a subconscious process, occuring outside of the conscious awareness of its participants.

Irrational role assignments and projective identifications are an inextricable part of all family systems. They are important vehicles through which behavior is molded and family values are incorporated into the personality. [4] By assuming a parentified role, a child learns to identify with the responsible roles that he will fill in adult life. By projecting a parentified role onto a child, the parent can find occasional necessary relief from the stress and responsibility of parenting. [9] According to Boszormenyi-Nagy and Spark, parentification "describes a ubiquitous and important aspect of most human relationships [and] should not be assigned to the realm of 'pathology' or relational dysfunction. It is a component of the regressive core of even balanced, sufficiently reciprocal relationships."[4] Parentified role assignments do become pathological, however, when they do not allow satisfaction of the child's dependency needs or strivings toward autonomous personality development. When this occurs, the child will move into adult life with an overdetermined need to use interpersonal relationships to meet her/his own frustrated dependency needs. The child will not have a sufficient sense of her/his own identify and may seek self-definition through irrational role assignments made by the groups to which she/he belongs.

For the purposes of this chapter, these are important concepts to keep in mind because as Zinner and Shapiro[20] point out, they provide an important conceptual bridge between individual and interpersonal psychology, helping us to understand specific interactions between persons in terms of specific conflicts within individuals. These concepts help us to understand the individual's motivation to seek parentified objects in group associations. They also provide a basis for our understanding of how these motivations ultimately affect the nurse.

The individual moves from the family to other group associations with the subconscious assumption that new interpersonal relationships will include the opportunity to assume and project identifications or roles and consequently allow him to work through and/or defend against inner conflicts. In other words, the individual expects to repeat the patterns learned in the family. Whether these identifications interfere with his ability to fulfill adult responsibilities depends on whether the projective identifications in the family of origin were pathological and deprived him of supplies needed for healthy personality development.

Various theories have been proposed to explain the subconscious processes that occur within an individual entering a group and the effect of these processes on the functioning of the group as a whole. Clearly, when individuals come together as a group, they bring with them a diversity of thinking and behavior patterns that is broader than that which exists in any one individual.[11] From its inception, the group must struggle to integrate these diverse elements into a behavioral pattern that will allow it to proceed with the task for which it was formed. That process of integration has been likened by some group theorists to the process of integration that occurs in the developing personality of the young child.[13] Like the young child, the group must deal with its dependency needs. Individuals, even those functioning on a mature level, seek out group attachments as a way of meeting their latent dependency needs. For the individual, the group entity may become a symbolic representation of a nurturing mother. "In a broader sense, the hypothesis can be advanced that the universal human need to belong, to establish a state of psychological unity with others, represents a covert wish for restoring an earlier state of unconflicted well-being inherent in the exclusive union with mother."[17] Although the leader may be viewed as a father figure, the group as a whole is viewed as a mother.[18] The members of the group struggle to maintain an all-good image of the "mother-group," an image that they hope will allow them to reexperience the gratifications of their earlier symbiotic attachment. They struggle against the leader who attempts to introduce reality into this perception. When the leader refuses to enact the good-mother role, the members may assign that role to another member.[16]

Bion[2] developed a theory of group behavior that is not concerned with the individual. He saw all group phenomena as a function of what he called mass group processes. He believed that within every group there exist three subconscious emotional states, or "basic assumptions." These states remain dormant while the group is working. When the group becomes diverted from its task, one of these basic assumptions emerges and appears as the operating principle of the group. The three basic assumptions are dependency (the need to be dependent on the leader), fight/flight (the need to fight within the group or alternatively to leave it), and pairing (the need to see sexualized union between two members of the group in the hope that new leadership will emerge as a product of the union). Only one basic assumption appears at a time. Which one appears is determined by the internal and external forces impinging on the group. Bion has been criticized for not giving enough consideration to the individual and for attempting to classify mass group phenomena too narrowly.[19] But a great deal of theoretical support has been given to his theory of subconscious processes that cross individual boundaries to involve the entire group. Freud[10] called this the collective mind of the group. Yalom[19] refers to mass group processes such as scapegoating, emotional contagion, role suction, subgroup formation, and regressive dependency, to name just a few. For the purposes of this chapter Bion's theory is helpful in illuminating the difference between the conscious, task-oriented behavior of groups and the subconsciously motivated behavior employed in the service of avoiding work. When the group is working, its energy is diverted from its subconscious processes, irrational role assignments are less problematic, and basic assumption groups are not apparent.

It is now possible to apply these theories to examine the process within a specific group, an interdisciplinary team of psychiatric clinicians brought together to work with emotionally disturbed patients and families. Kernberg[14] believes that the nature of the task carried out in psychiatric institutions where severely regressed patients are treated has a powerful influence on the group processes of both staff and patients. Further, he states that the stress of caring for the borderline or psychotic patient can induce a replication of the patient's pathology within staff group processes. Under these circumstances a regression to basic assumption group processes may occur.

In my experience as a psychiatric nurse in a day treatment center for emotionally disturbed teenagers, extraordinary demands were made on the nursing staff to meet the dependency needs of the patients. I believe this was the result of a process similar to the one described by Kernberg.[14]

The patients in this center had diagnoses in either the borderline or psychotic range. Most of them had experienced severe early maternal deprivation, and 90% were currently living in a group home setting. For these reasons, dependency needs were of primary concern to them. The painful realities of the children's dependency needs and of the social and intrapsychic factors that constantly denied satisfaction of these needs were naturally difficult for the staff to face. This difficulty was compounded by administrative structures that made it impossible to maintain a consistent working philosophy. As the staff found themselves more and more frustrated in their attempts to meet the children's needs, the group's mature working behavior frequently seemed to be superseded by basic assumption group processes. Because issues of dependency were so blatant in the patient group, dependency was the basic assumption most often operating in the staff group. One form that this basic assumption group process took was an intensified demand that the children's dependency needs be met. To this end, the staff felt a need for *their* leaders to provide structure within the agency and to intervene with outside agencies. For a variety of reasons, the leadership could not meet these needs to the staff's satisfaction. Consequently two things seemed to happen: the staff compensated for the leaders' failure to meet their dependency needs by increasing their attempts to idealize the good nurturant mothering aspects of the group, and the leaders attempted to divert attention from their own inability to meet the staff's needs by demanding that the nursing staff be constantly available to meet the dependency needs of the patients.

The requests made of nursing included the following:

- "Mrs. Brodegaard, X is barefoot, would you see to it that he gets some slippers." (There was no concern regarding why X was barefoot or the implications of encouraging a teenager in an outpatient setting to think that slippers will be supplied whenever shoes are missing.)
- "Mrs. Brodegaard, Y has stomach ache. Z is upset today. Would you make them some tea and let them lie down for a while." (These were possibly legitimate requests but did not necessarily need to be carried out by nursing staff.)

The nursing staff consisted of two nurses with master's degrees, one whose area of expertise and interest was individual and family therapy, the other's being health education.

Nursing staff attempted to assign priorities to the children's needs and to determine which could most effectively be met by the nursing staff themselves, which could be delegated to other staff, and which could not realistically be met by anyone on the team. Leadership saw such attempts as an effort on the part of the nursing staff to shirk totally their nursing responsibilities. To be sure, our efforts were largely motivated by self-interest: we wanted to free our time for the work that was of interest to us and for which we knew we were professionally prepared. But we also believed that it was in the patients' best interest not to be encouraged to believe that a nurse was available at all times to intervene in stomachaches or bare feet. This was not a realistic expectation and would not prepare the children for life in the world to which they belonged.

It seemed that the request for nursing to fill this nurturant role did not develop out of a carefully considered unit policy. The issue seemed to develop spontaneously and served the purpose of diverting some of the tension between staff and leadership. Benfer[1] makes the point that "at times when there is stress, there is sometimes a tendency to focus on someone else who may be more vulnerable. And in many instances, the vulnerable discipline is nursing, because most of its practitioners are female." I believe that nursing was vulnerable to the focus of this particular stress not simply because its practitioners were female (in fact the majority of the staff were female) but because they were female members of a profession that is so closely aligned with mothering. The role of the early symbiotic mother is to be constantly available to meet basic dependency needs. The role of the nurse is to help patients learn how to satisfy their own needs. This means encouraging patients to function at their highest level of independence, even if this does not initially reduce their level of stress or increase their comfort. This distinction between the role of the mother and the role of the nurse is frequently forgotton by interdisciplinary staff as well as by patients. It is far easier to reduce the stress in a volatile ward situation by meeting patient's stated demands than by exploring the intrapersonal and interpersonal dynamics that are involved in those demands. Deloughery and Gebbie[6] claim that society expects the nurse to function as a tension reducer or maintainer of equilibrium rather than to seek to achieve specific goals. My experience certainly lends credence to that theory.

Though the leadership initiated the irrational role assignment described above, the staff group also seemed to endorse it. The need to see the group as a good and nurturant mother (a process that I have theorized was going on in this group) frequently includes the designation of a vulnerable and/or willing member of the group to act out the mother role.[16] As individual and family therapists, our staff was frequently in the position of having to deny patients' stated demands in the interest of encouraging personality growth. Though the staff knew this was sound clinical practice, that knowledge did not reduce the tension such denials created within and between patients and therapists. When the tension became intense, as it frequently did, the members of the staff were sometimes seduced by subconscious processes to make the irrational role assignment of mother to the nurse. This allowed them to take comfort in the belief that although *they* could not meet their patients' demands, there was someone on the staff who could do so.

Cumming and Cumming[5] in *Ego and Milieu* explain that the psychiatrist sets rigid limits on her/his role with the patient that guard against falling into a diffuse personal relationship in which the patient expects the doctor to abandon her/his healing role and take on the role of comforter and personal friend. Such a role removes the objectivity that allows the healer to encourage self-care. The nurse has no such safeguards in her job, and consequently, without vigilant role definition, she is easily seen by the patient as the nurturant mother. For the nurse who is also a psychotherapist, this mistaken identity can be disastrous. Energy that should be used by patients to solve the problem of meeting their own needs will instead be channeled into anger and disappointment with the nurse-therapist.

I believe that the situation that I describe above could have been better managed if both the staff and leadership had been able to conceptualize their difficulties according to Kernberg's philosophy. If the tension on the ward could have been seen as a result not of any one person's failures, inabilities, or unwillingness to work but rather as an understandable response to the overwhelmingly painful reality of the lives of our patients, and if we could have understood that our patients' incessant and urgent expressions of need sparked anxiety in all of us about our own residual dependency conflicts, then perhaps the group could have come to terms with its shortcomings without feeling either guilt or blame. Under such circumstances, irrational role assignments would have been far less problematic.

In this chapter I have drawn on existing theory to show how factors in the dynamics of individuals, groups, and organizations contribute to the general perception of the nurse as the symbiotic mother. These factors lay a foundation that interacts with nursing's own vulnerability to cause role confusion. I believe that two major components of a nurse's vulnerability are stereotypical attitudes toward women and their place in the work force and the paternalistic nature of the health care system. Compounding the effects of both of these factors are personality traits within nurses themselves that may cause them to embrace the mother role.

The traditional hospital arrangement closely parallels the traditional nuclear family.[12] The nurse, like a mother, is available throughout the day to attend to the patient's needs. The doctor, like the traditional father, visits the ward only occasionally, leaving to do work that is presumed to be more important than the nurse's. He maintains an authoritarian posture, leaving orders behind him and being consulted regarding all but the most insignificant decisions. The nurse's role, therefore, becomes very confusing. Because of her constant proximity she has a tremendous amount of responsibility for her patients. Her training and her intimate knowledge of the patient may afford her very accurate perceptions with which to make decisions about her patient's care. Her decision-making ability, however, is not legitimized by authority.[8] Physicians retain the ultimate authority for the patient's care. This leaves the nurse with a feeling of insignificance and helplessness that is inconsistent with her actual abilities and responsibilities.

The situation on the hospital ward is analogous to that of the working mother. Though she is contributing to the domestic economy of the family, she usually does not share the social and economic privileges of the working man. She carries on a dual role, maintaining responsibility for home and family as well as for her job.[12] We are all aware of the still pervasive social conviction that a woman's first and foremost responsibility is to be a good mother. One reason that nursing has remained a woman's profession is that it is seen by so many as an extension of that responsibility. This has made it easier for young women to pursue nursing then any other profession. Within nursing they are protected from "the negative social and/or parental pressures that other professional woman students must endure, because [their] work is accepted and viewed as an extension of what women should do—care for others."[12] Ultimately this protection works against the nurse's best interests. The intelligent and well-trained nurse, particularly if she chooses to pursue a specialty in which she should become a primary therapist, will find herself constantly frustrated. She will be frustrated by her lack of sanctioned authority and, more importantly, by the mother role that is irrationally assigned to her and its concomitant demands. In my experience as a nurse-therapist, sessions were frequently interrupted by requests for bandages, pills, and so on. My time was fragmented by activities that could have been carried out by others but that because of their nurturant qualities were designated "nursing responsibilities."

It is not my suggestion that nurses should cease to be caring, giving, and nurturant; rather, they should cease to be diffusely and indiscriminately so. Caring does not have to exclude carefully planned, goal-directed activities. Neither should it cause the nurse to disqualify herself from training and practice in specialty areas. If specialty practice conflicts with other demands made of the nurse, then these demands have to be reevaluated and tasks delegated. The nurse cannot expect herself to be available to meet all needs. She is not the symbiotic mother. To try to be will result in false expectations within herself and her patient that can only lead to disappointment and frustration.

REFERENCES

1. Benfer, B.A.: Defining the role and function of the nurse as a member of the team, Perspectives in Psychiatric Care 18(4):166, 1980.
2. Bion, W.R.: Experiences in groups, New York, 1959, Basic Books, Inc.
3. Blanck, G., and Blanck, R.: Ego psychology: theory and practice, New York, 1974, Columbia University Press.
4. Boszoremy-Nagy, I., and Spark, G.M.: Invisible loyalties, Hagerstown, Md., Harper & Row, Publishers, Inc.
5. Cumming, J., and Cumming, E.: Ego and milieu, Chicago, 1962, Aldine Publishing Co.
6. Deloughery, G.L., and Gebbie, K.M.: Political dynamics: impact on nurses and nursing, St. Louis, 1975, The C.V. Mosby Co.
7. Dolan, J.A.: Nursing in society, ed. 14, Philadelphia, 1978, W.B. Saunders Co.
8. Edelson, M.: Sociotherapy and psychotherapy, Chicago, 1970, University of Chicago Press.
9. Framo, J.L.: Symptoms from a family transactional viewpoint. In Sager, C.J., and Kaplan, H.S., editors: Progress in group and family therapy, New York, 1972, Brunner/Mazel, Inc.
10. Freud, S.: Group psychology and the analysis of the ego. In The complete psychological works of Sigmund Freud, vol. 18, London, 1955, The Hogarth Press, Ltd.
11. Gibbard, G.S., Hartman, J.J., and Mann, R.D., editors: Analysis of groups, San Francisco, 1978, Jossey-Bass, Inc., Publishers.
12. Grissum, M., and Spengler, C.: Womanpower and health care, Boston, 1976, Little, Brown & Co.

13. Kaplan, S.R., and Roman, M.: Phases of development in an adult therapy group, International Journal of Group Psychotherapy **13**:10, 1963.

14. Kernberg, O.F.: Leadership and organizational functioning: organizational regression, International Journal of Group Psychotherapy **28**(1):3, 1978.

15. Levinson, D.J.: Role, personality and social structure in the organizational setting, Journal of Abnormal and Social Psychology **58**:170, 1959.

16. Ruiz, P.: On the perception of the "Mother-Group" in T-groups, International Journal of Group Psychotherapy **22**:488, 1972.

17. Scheidlinger, S.: Identification: the sense of belonging and identity in small groups, International Journal of Group Psychotherapy **14**: 291, 1964.

18. Schindler, W.: The role of the mother in group psychotherapy, International Journal of Group Psychotherapy **16**:198, 1966.

19. Yalom, I.D.: The theory and practice of group psychotherapy, New York, 1975, Basic Books, Inc.

20. Zinner, J., and Shapiro, R.: Projective identification as a mode of perception and behaviour in families of adolescents, International Journal of Psychoanalysis **53**:523, 1972.

NORINE J. KERR

Chapter 21

The narcissistic fit between medicine and nursing

Narcissism—a term no longer limited to the narrow confines of the psychiatric treatment situation—is fast becoming a popular contemporary term. It is used to describe the very culture in which we live, a world where appearance is all-important, where success is measured by possessions and power, and where image has become more important than action. It is no longer rare to find individuals with such an intense interest in themselves that they are actually incapable of loving others.

Traditionally, narcissism has been viewed as an intrapsychic phenomenon with little emphasis placed on the complementary nature of the narcissist's and the "other's" styles of interacting. Although the narcissist's behavior has been well defined, the other's has not. Otto Kernberg writes,

> The pathological narcissist cannot sustain his or her self-regard without having it fed constantly by the attention of others . . . people count only as admirers. The applauding crowd is welcome, but not people in and of themselves. . . . [she/he] will anticipate receiving tribute from others and may, for a time, be very charming to them. But once the tribute is given, [she/he] quickly becomes restless and bored. In general, [the narcissist's] relationships with other people are exploitative or parasitic, although this may be masked behind a surface which is often engaging and attractive.[1]

The behavior of the other often indicates a willingness to assume the exploited position. Although intensely miserable, the other may take no steps to extricate her/himself from a relationship that is clearly destructive. Why is this so? When viewed in the context of a system, the other in the relationship is not an innocent victim but instead ensures the narcissist's pattern of behavior in the same sense that the spouse of an alcoholic facilitates or enables the drinking behavior of her/his mate.

The narcissist, who seems to have so much self, draws into her/his sphere those who suffer confusion about their identities. The other thrives on the narcissist's grandiose self-view precisely because her/his own self-identity is confused, unformulated, or negatively perceived. Thus complementary roles are created that lock the two into a kind of "narcissistic fit" that ensures a characteristic style of relating. Without this narcissistic fit, without the other assuming a complementary role in the

300

relationship, a predominantly narcissistic style is less likely to exist.

The identifying features of a narcissistic relationship or system involve three main ingredients: an overvaluing of one part of the system, a simultaneous devaluing of another, and an intolerance for any difference or separateness among the parts. A central dynamic in sustaining the narcissistic system is the collusion between the narcissist and the other in preserving the overvaluing/devaluing split and the taboo against differentiation.

I believe that the concept of the narcissistic fit explains something about how nursing and medicine relate to each other. This is not meant to imply that all physicians are narcissists or that all nurses are others; rather, it suggests that a narcissistic dynamic operates between the two professions in the sense that traditionally medicine has been overvalued and nursing undervalued. Since the basic dynamic of the narcissistic interaction involves this overvaluing/devaluing split, perhaps there is something to be gained from a better understanding of this. In addition, since nursing has struggled so laboriously to evolve an image of itself as a profession of competent, individuated practitioners, it becomes appropriate to ask why the struggle has been so prolonged and difficult. Could it be that nursing has perpetuated its own difficulties precisely because nurses have acted in such a way as to ensure the narcissistic system?

This question cannot be answered, nor can the issue of overvaluation and devaluation be understood, without first making clear the factors that give rise to narcissistic growth. In essence, narcissism reflects a disturbance of self-esteem that is compensated for through the building up of an inflated sense of self-importance. Normal self-esteem is jeopardized when the actual self has been rejected so severely that without the particular narcissistic defenses that evolve, the integrity of the individual would be compromised beyond repair. This rejection does not usually result from one event but signifies the damage accrued from chronic nonacceptance of a growing child's feelings, physical being, perceptions, and thoughts. This rejection is life threatening precisely because it is one's feelings, body, perceptions, and thoughts that define both the reality of the self and of others. Without that core reality, annihilation of self is threatened.

To protect against this threat, a replacement for the actual self is needed, and a new image of self begins to emerge. Attention is turned toward fashioning a self that is more acceptable to those who have done the rejecting. This new self is given form through a process of self-inflation, and its main function is to neutralize the rejection of the actual self and to compensate for the injury sustained. The more devastating the initial rejection, the more inflated the pseudoself becomes. By endowing the self with unlimited powers, the narcissist creates a fantasy world in which she/he is the hero, because only the status of hero can console her/him for not being valued or loved. The reasoning of "I am too superior to be understood" lifts the self above others and compensates for a profound sense of insignificance.

Through the creation of an idealized self, the narcissistic individual attempts to receive admiration in lieu of love. Only the actual self can be loved; at best the pseudoself can be admired. Once admiration has become a substitute for genuine love, then flattery, attention, special treatment, confirmation, and applause become the factors that sustain the narcissist's very existence. As Karen Horney says, "From then on he feels unwanted if he is not admired. What falls short of blind admiration is to him no longer love; he will even suspect it of being hostility."[2] Without this confirmation and applause, the narcissist finds her/himself in an extremely precarious situation. Any failure to elicit the needed admiration brings to the surface all her/his underlying insecurity, and thus she/he must sustain this idealized self at all costs; that is, she/he must find confirmation of this self in the external world.

To accomplish this the narcissist entices others to enter into a "fused" relationship in which they function as a mirror to the idealized self. In the name of love the narcissistic individual projects her/his own idealized image onto another and then "loves" and admires the other. In reality, the narcissist is actually loving *her/his* own idealized *self*. The other is merely valued to the extent that she/he serves as a reflection or extension of the narcissist's own idealized self. Once the other assumes that function, it becomes imperative to the narcissist that the illusion of fusion not be broken. Any assertion of difference or separateness will destroy the narcissistic fit and will invalidate the mirroring relationship. A mirror, after all, is supposed to reflect only what it sees, not give forth its own image. Thus fusion is the means by which the narcissist's idealized self-image is maintained in the external world.

I will illustrate this dynamic with an example from my own practice. One of my patients entered the initial phase of treatment with a blissful sense of assurance that she had finally found the "perfect" therapist. Information from the referral source initially allowed me to respond to her needs and concerns in a highly empathic manner, but this was not responsible for the idealization that occurred. In her own mind this patient held an idealized image of herself as an all-good, all-knowing, nurturing "earth mother." Because she had projected this self-image onto me, she became almost ecstatic in my presence as she basked in the reflected glory that this image provided her.

The inevitable injury and disappointment resulted not because I failed to maintain that "earth mother" image but because I failed to maintain the fusion. One day I mentioned that I have little if any artistic talent. Since the patient was highly artistic, this revelation immediately breached the fusion between us. That I was separate from her, that is, that I possessed different talents, shattered her capacity to project her own idealized self onto me. This separation was experienced as a profound shock and abandonment and resulted in intense acting-out behavior both during and outside of our sessions. The patient began contacting hospital staff to tell them that day-treatment staff were dreadfully incompetent. During our meetings she became demanding and hostile; she alternated between refusing to speak and lashing out in a bitter attack. I was initially mystified but soon identified what had occurred just prior to the dramatic change. When I suggested that her anger seemed related to my statement that I was unlike her in the sense of having no artistic talent, she confirmed my suspicions: "When you said that, I hated you. It was as if I lost something I can never again regain."

I learned from this experience that there were certain advantages in my remaining in the role of narcissistic extension. First of all, the patient's idealization of me *felt* good and seemed to infuse my work with power and energy. I experienced myself as more than effective in my helping role. In addition, as long as the fusion was maintained, the therapy went smoothly and I had no angry or acting-out behavior to deal with. And finally, the patient's charges of incompetency were unsettling; I felt I had lost something when she stopped telling everyone what a wonderful therapist I was. The breach of fusion, then, threatened my own self-esteem.

The issue of self-esteem is crucial to understanding why the other stays hooked in the narcissistic fit. When an individual has experienced chronic self-doubt and the lack of a clear identity, exchanging a separate self for identification with a seemingly well-defined and valued self is attractive. Thus through fusion the other gains an identification with the narcissist's idealized self, an identification with the overvalued part of the system.

Has nursing ever been tempted by this kind of "bargain"? Without question nursing *has* experienced self-doubt and an identity confusion so basic that it has been unclear whether nurses should think of themselves as saints or sinners. This predicament relates to the history of nursing, whose roots go back to the Christian Era when the sick were first visited in an organized way by deaconesses. Since the Church was the central charitable organization, these deaconesses were the first "nurses." They distributed food and medicine, performed bedside nursing functions, and ministered to patients' spiritual needs. When the order of deaconesses died out, a group of wealthy Roman matrons assumed their functions. These early Christian nurses emerged from a high social status and were motivated by strong spiritual values.

In the sixteenth century the Reformation began and ended as a revolt that had cleaved Christianity. Church properties were confiscated, and immense wealth was taken from the monastic orders. Suppression of Catholic religious orders, whose members staffed and administered hospitals, left these institutions in chaos. Hospitals became places of horror, and nurses, needed for patient care, were drawn from the illiterate classes. Many of them were prostitutes. Saint or sinner, good or bad, angel of mercy or Nurse Ratched (in *One Flew Over the Cuckoo's Nest*), the conflicting images of nurses emerged. With such confusion is it any wonder that nursing may have sought refuge in merging with medicine and becoming a narcissistic extension of physicians?

Whether intentional or not, nurses have been just that, a narcissistic extension as reflected in the label "physician's handmaiden." This relationship has denied the nurse a separate identity, for the role requires fusion and relinquishing of the individual self. Fusion is maintained in the doctor-nurse relationship as long as nurses do not engage in independent, autonomous thinking and behavior. Fusion, when it occurs, ensures that nurses cannot function without a doctor's order. Physicians are accorded not esteem or respect but blind admiration and awestruck attention. Nurses in turn are treated with paternalistic benevolence and feel a boost in their own sense of importance because of the "acceptance" received from the powerful physician.

The same advantages I experienced in being a narcissistic extension of my patient may be relevant to nursing also. Paternalism is not unpleasant, for it contains elements of kindness, protection, and affection. If merging with a powerful profession infuses nurses with a borrowed power and sense of effectiveness, is this not good? Besides, as long as nursing is seen as an adjunct of medicine, there seems to be a relative calm between the two professions. Conflict arises only when nurses attempt to define themselves as separate and autonomous, for separation means losing identification with the overvalued part of the system. Nurses who do this risk being devalued, which makes the choice difficult.

Nursing is devalued when nurses are defined by the task they perform, tasks that physicians are too busy to do. In such a context health care tasks are assigned a hierarchical value: those who carry out high-level tasks are considered important, and those who carry out low-level tasks are devalued. Among nursing tasks, giving a bed bath becomes "aide's work" and starting an IV takes on importance. Reasoning that correlates self-value with this hierarchical order fails to see that the nurse's value lies in meeting patients' needs in a way qualitatively different from the approach of medicine (not better or worse, just differently).

In healthy relationships, differences reflect the unique capabilities and characteristics of each individual. In narcissistic interactions, such differences threaten the very equilibrium of the "fit" and must be avoided at all costs. If two professions interact narcissistically, one can be seen not as providing a function that is different but merely as performing a more diluted form of the same function. This is evident when nursing growth is perceived as assuming physicians' functions rather than expanded nursing ones. The nurse then becomes a junior doctor who in some diluted form is treating the patient's illness rather than assisting the patient in her/his response to the illness, as is the appropriate role of nursing.

Any system in which there is a denial of difference in function is a narcissistic system. An intense devaluation of nursing occurs when nurses attempt individuation. For some nurses, being devalued is worse than being a narcissistic extension. The apparent advantage of the devalued role over the merged role is the illusion it gives of greater independence. Devaluation, however, actually indicates that the narcissist is still perceiving the other as part of the self, albeit the despised part rather than the idealized part. Nurses who attempt to assert their independence by devaluing medicine similarly have not at all freed themselves from the narcissistic fit. By putting medicine down and elevating nursing to idealized status, they have changed nothing but the side of the coin with which they are identified.

One further characteristic of narcissistic interaction needs to be mentioned. Because of her/his inflated notion of her/himself, the narcissist develops excessive expectations about what the world owes her/him. Confirmation of this grandiose self-concept demands that the world treat her/him as if she/he were entitled to special consideration. The narcissist develops a set of attitudes toward others that reflect her/his expectation of being treated specially and unconsciously reasons, "Because I am extra-special, I am entitled to. . . ." This sense of entitlement gives way to intense anger when expectations are frustrated. Quick flare-ups of emotion are followed by a sudden dispersal of feelings. The narcissist cannot relinquish the expectation that she/he is entitled to special consideration without being thrown into a painful awareness of the illusory nature of her/his idealized self.

This characteristic tendency toward flare-ups of anger causes the other to attempt to circumvent such occurrences by anticipating and responding to the demand for special treatment. The more attuned the other becomes in this respect, the more validation the narcissist receives that such expectations are reasonable and realistic. Thus the narcissist's sense of entitlement becomes more deeply entrenched and her/his fury more pronounced when these expectations are frustrated. How many times have nurses become the targets of an outburst that reflects the underlying attitude, "Because I am important, I am entitled to . . ."? Although it may be difficult to avoid being in that unfortunate position, the nurse does have a choice of responding in the reinforcing role of the other or of breaking the narcissistic fit vis-à-vis a self-valuing and other-valuing response.

In the first case, the response would reinforce the narcissistic assumption of entitlement. A nurse, for example, would offer profuse apologies to the irate physician for not being available when he needed her despite the fact that she had been busy elsewhere. The nurse who responds in a self-valuing and other-valuing manner, however, does not buy into this basic assumption of entitlement. She respects both herself and the physician and recognizes the irrationality of such claims. She might say, "I am aware that you need me to tell you about your patient. I have been unable to do that because I have been attending to a patient emergency that I believe to be my first priority at this time. However, the situation is under control, and I do have a few minutes now." If she had instead responded in any angry, devaluing way, she would merely have moved back into a narcissistic style of interacting.

The task of nursing today is to gain strength from within by learning to cultivate an affirmative sense of our own value. We can choose either narcissistic or healthy paths to achieve this. The two options are not merely qualitatively different but are diametrically opposed. Since psychic energies in the narcissist go toward denying the real self and creating an unreal one, narcissistic growth is based on illusion. The unreal self is idealized and the actual self despised. In healthy growth, on the other hand, the essence of the individual has been affirmed, and thus the creation of a pseudoself is not necessary to compensate for damaged self-esteem. This kind of growth is based on an acceptance of the truth about oneself, which then frees energies to be directed into the realization of one's own unique potential.

Nursing is at an exciting stage in its evolution because it is daring to suffer the pains of individuation and separation so that realization of its own potential can be achieved. But has its growth thus far been free of narcissistic contamination? Has the actual "self" of nursing been nurtured or annihilated? Is a pseudoself emerging to compensate for a damaged self-image? Do we tend either to overvalue or to devalue ourselves? What value system do we use to measure our worth? Have we chosen to merge with the powerful profession of medicine to conquer our self-doubt? Have we entered into narcissistic interaction with physicians because we have chosen a narcissistic path for our own growth?

The degree to which the interaction between nursing and medicine is characterized by a narcissistic fit is for each reader to decide. There is no question, however, that to be free of narcissistic styles of interacting, nursing must, paradoxically, learn to value itself and others genuinely and without compromise. For as we know, the narcissist does not love her/himself in reality. Just as Narcissus loved the image he saw reflected in the water, the narcissist loves the created, idealized self. It is the image that is loved rather than the actual self. Freed from the shackles of a narcissistic fit, perhaps nursing can finally embrace the kind of self-esteem that allows for genuine self-actualization.

REFERENCES

1. Kernberg, O.: Narcissism: why some people can't love, Psychology Today, p. 59, June 1978.

2. Horney, K.: The neurotic personality of our time, New York, 1937, W.W. Norton & Co., Inc.

MARILYN JAFFE RUIZ

Chapter 22

Lack of ego differentiation

Its effect on nursing leadership

Nursing suffers yet benefits as well from being a predominantly female profession. Of all registered nurses 98% are women.[16] As a female group, nursing reflects the attitudes, attributes, limitations, and concerns of women in our society; as a profession fighting for recognition, autonomy, and respect, nursing's problems are inextricably woven with the problems of women who are also fighting for recognition, autonomy, and respect.

Historical trends in the evolution of nursing and the evolution of women in society go hand in hand in contributing to the paucity of recognized female leaders. Leaders reflect the values, strengths, and weaknesses of their groups and of the larger society. Leadership behavior in women is not valued and leads to discriminatory attitudes toward women who display such behavior. Traditionally women have not been viewed as authoritative sources of leadership in American society.

Sociological and historical characteristics interact with the particular "psychology of women" to produce the oft lamented situation of a lack of leadership in nursing. I am proposing that this lack of leadership reflects a psychological tendency of women to resist differentiation of self and to remain in the homogeneous bosom of the collective, or shall I say, to remain part of the undifferentiated ego mass of the group.

BACKGROUND

The problems of leadership in nursing have been well documented.* Nursing has been characterized as relatively passive, powerless, and resistant to change. Various reasons have been given to describe and explain the problems related to leadership in nursing. These include the femaleness of the profession, is relative newness in the academic world, its lack of professional direction, nurses' lack of

---

*References 1, 3, 4, 5, 7, 8.

mentors, an inherent process in the education and training of nurses that extinguishes leadership traits, discrimination by others in the profession toward those who are deviant and demonstrate leadership ability, and many nurses' low self-esteem and desire to serve and care rather than lead.

All of these reasons, as well as many others, reflect the myriad factors that characterize the profession and account for its difficulty in developing leaders. None of the stated reasons, however, speaks to the underlying psychological dynamics of what occurs when a group of women come together to serve others and then themselves. Nursing as a small society is a group with all of the needs typical of any group, including the needs to maintain itself, to satisfy its members' needs, and to allow for growth of the individual while advancing the group's or profession's goals.

Nursing, comprised of women, typifies the difficulties women have individually and collectively in being autonomous, independent, self-directed risk takers. The fear of "loss of other" hampers the differentiation and self-definition necessary for being a leader.

THEORETICAL FRAMEWORK

Mahler's theory[10,11] of separation-individuation and McDevitt's work[13] on object constancy can be used as a framework for discussing the psychological and developmental dilemma of nursing and its problems in producing leaders for the profession. The use of the separation-individuation and object constancy processes as a paradigm here by no means implies that nurses or women are infantile, immature, or babyish. These concepts do, however, provide an opportunity to examine with a developmental model a particular female professional group's leadership needs in a different light.

Separation-individuation

Separation-individuation was described by Mahler[10] as a process that "normally takes place within the child's developmental readiness for and pleasure in independent functioning together with the physical and emotional availability of the mother, who also, under optimal conditions, encourages the child's growing autonomy."[13]

"Separation" begins as the child breaks out of the symbiotic orbit. This is an intrapsychic process whereby she/he learns to differentiate self from others. "Individuation," a complimentary (and lifelong) process, allows the self or the ego to develop autonomous functions. Differentiation and definition of the self and the body optimally occurs in a climate where the child continues to rely on the mother. The sense of increased autonomy and independence continues and is enhanced by neuromuscular maturation and control.[10,11] Each developmental task throughout a person's life involves further separation and individuation.

The phases of the separation-individuation process in early childhood are further divided into the practicing subphase (beginning and proper), rapprochement, and the rapprochement crisis. The practicing subphase allows the infant, now a toddler, the opportunity to test out the world at some physical distance from mother while checking in with her, or "refueling," as frequently as necessary by physical, verbal, or visual contact.[11]

According to Mahler,[11] by the age of 25 to 36 months the toddler has upright locomotion, a fairly good sense of self and other, and an awareness of the separateness of the love object. In addition to this awareness is the fear and anxiety associated with abandonment and the accompanying rage of experiencing her/his aloneness in the universe. This is rapprochement, then, a time when the toddler strives for constant connectedness with the mother in contrast to the intermittent contact of the practicing subphase.

The crisis of rapprochement involves the awareness of one's own separateness and the pleasure thereof and a simultaneous yearning to be symbiosed with the mother to avoid the anxiety of losing her and her love.[11] Developmentally, the implications of this process go on through life. For girls, whose self-esteem and feelings of achievement are associated with affiliative skills, the rapprochement crisis is further aggravated each time a new step is taken. Girls remain dependent on the mother for love while identifying with her and competing with her for desired love objects (men). This dynamic contributes to adult women's fear of being devoured, annihilated, or abandoned by other females while still wanting their love and support. This simultaneous fear and desire has made it difficult for women to be separate and objective enough to be mentors for other women. Women are reluctant to address their competence in front of each other and suffer from lack of support in the area of assisting one another with individuation and competence mastery.

Object constancy

Object permanance and object constancy as described by McDevitt[13] involve two concepts: first, the child is aware that people exist even when out of sight, and second, the child is able to maintain and utilize her/his memory of others even when they are not present or when conflict occurs. In other words, the child feels psychologically connected to another despite geographical or emotional distance. Only by struggling through periods of conflict and reconciliation with the mother can the young girl grow to learn that the differences between mother and child can be tolerated, enjoyed, and encouraged.

SEPARATION-INDIVIDUATION AND OBJECT CONSTANCY RELATED TO NURSING LEADERSHIP

When involved with aggressive strivings it would seem that nurses and women in general lose their "hold on mother." The stability of a positive memory can be shattered when the nurse strives for autonomy. Fear and anxiety are a part of speaking out, going forth, taking risks, and being competent. The nurse might seek to reduce such tensions by clinging rapprochement behaviors, thus limiting her effectiveness as an emerging leader.

Self-development and maturation are necessary for leadership. One must be sufficiently separate to stand comfortably on her/his on while feeling attached to significant others. During periods of conflict and adversity, when one is experiencing the differences between oneself and the other, danger looms for those individuals whose basic ego structure does not allow them to be emotionally attached while experiencing the aloneness of their separateness. Patterns may develop in which a girl, for example, is frightened of being herself and can only be a compliant, dutiful, obedient, passive, albeit frustrated and angry daughter.

For women and nurses whose modus operandi has been self-sacrifice, pleasing others, and merging with the identity of others, assertiveness can be very difficult. Nurses who have been socialized into a passive, self-abrogating, subservient role follow orders, receive limited financial reimbursement for professional services, and rarely are involved in decision or policy making. Nor do they have the skills necessary to advance their own causes or move the profession forward.

MENTORING

People do not accomplish the individuation process in a vacuum. Initially it is crucial that the mother be able to determine consistently and flexibly her child's needs for dependence and independence, closeness and distance, to provide the type of environment in which the child can master autonomy comfortably and without the anxiety and fear of permanent object loss as a sequel of individuation.

For adults, mentors serve a similar purpose as mothers—to guide the young professional through initiation and socialization into the profession, to assist the neophyte to find her/his place without fear of abandonment. Crucial to the mentoring process is the ability to let go of the youngster or neophyte when it is appropriate rather than holding on for one's own sake.

Friday[6] and Levinson[9] discuss inadequate female-to-female mentoring, which may in part result from women's difficulties respecting and being role models for one another. They experience ambivalence over wanting to be separate from "mother" and competing with her while still being dependent on her for nurturance. Women devalue other women. These behaviors have led to men, bosses, husbands, and fathers becoming mentors for women.

Mothers tend to have more difficulty letting go of girls than boys. Nancy Friday[6] states that mothers raise daughters in the "principle of two"—the two of us against the world—and have difficulty letting others in. The principle of two implies symbiotic blissfulness and safety. Since it satisfies the need of the adult to not be abandoned as well as the child's need, this process often imposes sanctions that restrict the freedom of the child or younger person.

Within nursing education and service, innovation, change, and independence are militated against. Often the group bands together in anger against outside male authority figures, either doctors or administrators, instead of focusing its energy on the group itself. The close bond that is felt is really a pseudocloseness since real closeness can come about only through separation-individuation, attachment, conflict, and negotiation in a spirit of trust, mutuality, and support.

Conflict between females or in a female-dominated group is often destructive and characterized by "trashing" and character assassination.[12] Impotent rage gets played out in power struggles, abandonment, depression, and somatization.

LEADERSHIP

Leadership skills involve speaking out on issues that may not be comfortable, facing conflict, planning for the future, and facilitating change. When women behave in these ways, they think that to incur another's displeasure is to be abandoned by the other. Women in nursing need practice valuing themselves and each other and viewing each nurse as powerful and aggressive without being destructive. The fear associated with autonomy and independence is frequently and wrongly based on the assumption that one needs to give up affiliation and the satisfaction of warm relatedness if one is to be self-directed.[14]

In contrast to boys, girls learn to rely on others through symbiosis, anticipation of the other's needs, strong attachments, and affiliative behaviors that limit self-development. Boys, on the other hand, learn to differentiate a self predicated on self-reliance, aggressiveness, competence, mastery, and independence. Complicating this difference is the fact that girls grow up learning to be valued for their femaleness, which then is *devalued* by our society except for the ways in which it can serve others.

Those same girls grow up wanting to be nurses. Nursing is a profession characterized by low status, an ambiguous definition, and collective low self-esteem. In the usual definition a nurse is "a person, especially a woman, who has the general care of the sick or infirmed, a woman who has the general care of a child, or children; a day nurse."[15] In our culture serving others is for losers—it is considered to be on a low level—yet it is the basic principle around which nurses' and women's lives are organized. Women's work is not of the "real world" and is defined as inferior; thus the role of caretaker and nurturer does not have much attractiveness or potency.[14]

In the literature, leadership has been defined in many different ways. Leadership is associated with autonomy, independence, risk taking, accountability, organizational effectiveness goal-oriented behavior, decision making, and the ability to communicate ideas effectively to influence others to move toward setting or attaining goals. Regardless of the definition, all of these concepts involve behaviors that have been traditionally defined as male in contrast to those behaviors such as caring, empathy, nurturing, mothering, and sensitivity that have been traditionally defined as female.

Moreover, the descriptive words for females all serve to support an affiliative-oriented endeavor in contrast to achievement- and independence-seeking behaviors typical of males. This difference is important when examining why women are afraid to take risks and court alienation from others along with the loss of love and self that is perceived to follow. This lack of a clear-cut self contributes to low-level professional initiative and autonomy and to overly protective and possibly smothering wives, mothers, and bosses.

Girls learn to achieve through becoming involved with others. Successes in dating, marriage, and child rearing are still the criteria society uses to measure a woman's worth. To seek work or a career outside of marriage was and is still frowned upon, especially if the traditional roles are neglected. The woman interested in job or career options often faces conflicts involving her own basic strivings and identity and the appraisals of others.

Bardwick[2] has stated that women can achieve greater success if they professionalize their interpersonal skills. How many women entered nursing because it seemed the best of both worlds? On the one hand, it offered a chance to be productive and earn a living while allowing, on the other hand, a woman to do what she did best—take care of others. As nursing has changed and become more of a profession, increased commitment on the part of individuals in terms of life-long career-mindedness and identification is required. There has been a simultaneous change in women and in women's views of themselves. With increased self-worth, better and different opportunities for education, improved technology for the home, and changing responsibilities for men, more women who are committed to careers and have leadership potential are selecting career options other than nursing.

CONCLUSION AND RECOMMENDATIONS

Leadership in nursing requires an effective, mutually satisfying, and reciprocal relationship among all its members. Negative views of the profession can be changed only when people within the professional group develop a more positive regard for themselves and each other. The group must work to overcome sexual stereotyping, discrimination, low self-esteem, low self-confidence, and isolation from men.

In a female professional group such as nursing, the opportunities for replaying the difficulties of separating from mother (or child), individuating and developing the self, identifying with mother, and yearning to satisfy love and dependency needs are endless. With the opportunity for such "replay," however, also comes the opportunity for corrective learning experiences in which the new mother–authority figure can mentor and encourage the younger nurse to experience differences and conflicts with guidance, support, and trust.

Respect for one's own intelligence and worth and for the intelligence and worth of other nurses can come about through educational programs providing curricula that include opportunities for self-definition, direction, innovation, and change rather than rigidly prescribed programs. Educational criteria in university-based programs should be of a high caliber. Applicants to schools of nursing should possess an excellent intellectual ability and a desire for competence and career commitment; they should be achievement oriented and have high energy levels and an active orientation to life. These traits differ from the present-day attributes of a "desire to help people" and "doing well in the sciences."

Faculty should be forerunners in defining their own roles within the profession and academia and should be willing to share their knowledge, concerns, conflicts, and fears among themselves and with others. Developmental readiness on the part of faculty in their generative years should make the mentoring process a natural component of the educational experience.

Built into the curricula of schools of nursing and continuing education programs should be courses in communication, both spoken and written, since leaders should be able to present ideas articulately, especially when "on the hot seat." Panel discussions, debates, and role playing are teaching strategies that could be used (rather than lecture and discussion methods) in a controlled environment. This would afford nurses practice in dealing with differences and conflicts, asserting themselves, and taking a stand without fearing personal loss, rejection, and abandonment for expression of differences and risk taking.

Consciousness-raising sessions for parents, nurses, faculty, and nursing students, in which didactic and experiential situations could be shared, would serve to bring to cognitive awareness the parallels between early childhood development and career development for nurses. Process groups with skilled, objective leadership for all members of the nursing community would be helpful to identify underlying fears and anxieties associated with separation and individuation. Sexual stereotypes related to leadership could also be addressed, explored, and perhaps resolved.

Every effort should be made to involve nurses in the mainstream of political, social, and economic processes in whatever arena they are found. It is time to bring about the end of female "pseudoinnocence" and bring forth the collective power of nurses to have influence on every level while continuing to grow, develop, and lead themselves and their profession.

Nursing as a female profession has been plagued by a lack of leadership. Mahler's theory[10,11] of separation-individuation and McDevitt's work[13] on object constancy are useful in showing the parallels between early childhood development and nurses' psychological dynamics, helping bring about a greater awareness needed to address and solve this leadership problem.

This chapter has explored the lack of leadership in nursing as a reflection of lack of ego differentiation in a female professional group. My aim has been to make you, as nurses, conscious of the problems and aware of some solutions.

REFERENCES

1. Bailey, J., and Claus, K.: Preparing nurse leaders for the world of tomorrow, Nursing Leadership 1(1):19, 1978.
2. Bardwick, J.: Psychology of women, New York, 1971, Harper & Row, Publishers, Inc.
3. Diamond, H.: Patterns of leadership, Image 11(2):42, 1979.
4. Diers, D.: Lessons on leadership, Image 11(3): 67, 1979.
5. Fagin, C.: Refocus on leadership, Nursing Leadership 2(4):6, 1979.
6. Friday, N.: My mother, my self, New York, 1977, Delacorte Press.
7. Kjervik, D.: Women, nursing and leadership, Image 11(2):34, 1979.
8. Leadership: problems and possibilities in nursing, American Journal of Nursing 72(8):1445, 1972.
9. Levinson, D.: The seasons of a man's life, New York, 1978, Alfred A. Knopf, Inc.
10. Mahler, M.: On human symbiosis and the vicissitudes of individuation, New York, 1968, International Universities Press.
11. Mahler, M.: On the first three subphases of the separation individuation process, International Journal of Psychoanalysis 53:333, 1972.
12. Marriner, A.: Assertive behavior for nursing leaders, Nursing Leadership 2(4):14, 1979.
13. McDevitt, J.: Separation-individuation and object constancy, Journal of the American Psychoanalytic Association 23:713, 1975.
14. Miller, J.: Toward a psychology of women, Boston, 1976, Beacon Press.
15. Random House Dictionary of the English language, New York, 1968, Random House, Inc.
16. Vance, C.: Women leaders: modern day heroines or societal deviants, Image 2(2):37, 1979.

ANN M. ROSENOW

Chapter 23

What is achievement in nursing?

Although the answer to the question posed by the title of this chapter may seem obvious, it is not as straightforward as it may seem. The notion of professional achievement is fairly well internalized in American society, but so too are ideas of what constitutes the female sex role. Therein lies the problem for most nurses, who are both women and professionals. This dual identity creates a dilemma because characteristics and behaviors associated with the female sex role are contradictory to those required for professional achievement. It is this contradiction that creates confusion over the meaning of achievement in nursing.

THE CONTRADICTION BETWEEN THE FEMALE SEX ROLE AND PROFESSIONAL ACHIEVEMENT

It has been well documented that a basic conflict currently exists in American society between female sex-role prescriptions and professional achievement.* The incompatibility of the ideal feminine role and the professional role inhibits professional striving by women and is a source of stress for them. The primary source of this stress is ambivalence. Ambivalence and ambiguity arise from contradictions posed by images of the female role, occupational and professional roles, and American society's values of equality and achievement.

The socialization of females in American society inhibits professional achievement in women. Block[7] in a study of adult females found an inverse relationship between occupational achievement and femininity. He concluded that the socialization of women, regardless of their level of femininity, was associated with a renunciation of achievement and autonomy.

A major problem cited by a number of authors writing on feminine socialization and achievement is that central preferred female personality traits are the opposite of those required for professional achievement. In American society, preferred feminine attributes include personal warmth, empathy, sensitivity, emotionalism, grace,

---

*References, 4, 5, 7, 8, 10, 12, 16, 22, 25, 26.

charm, compliance, dependence, and deference.[12] Although not all these traits are antithetical to career success, some, such as emotionalism, compliance, dependence, and deference, are. The traits commonly assumed to be required for professional success include the stereotypically masculine traits of independence, autonomy, assertiveness, competetiveness, and ambition.[12]

Another problem is the incompatibility of women's family responsibilities with the male-oriented professional system. The professional role calls for a strong commitment of time and energy and the subordination of other roles to work. Women, however, are expected to make family responsibilities their primary focus, a role that also necessitates a strong commitment of time and energy. One solution to these problems can be found in those women's professions that are structured differently from male-dominated professions.

SOCIETAL NORMS FOR WOMEN'S PROFESSIONS

Past and current societal norms have created a situation that generally makes the professional role in female-dominated professions such as nursing more compatible with the female sex role. Etzioni and others[13] in describing this situation refer to the female-dominated professions of elementary school teaching, nursing, and social work as "semi-professions." These authors contend that the claim of these occupations to full professional status is neither fully established nor fully desired. Greater compatibility between the professional role and the feminine role is achieved in these semi-professions through assuming that the woman is more committed to her feminine role responsibilities than to her career and by altering the structure of the professional role accordingly. This assumption is supported by the normative expectation that this is as it should be.[12]

Women in American society are assigned major responsibility for household tasks, child care, and emotional and practical support of the husband's career. The professional role, however, as it has evolved in modern society has come to call for full-time, continuous work from the end of one's education to retirement, the desire to actualize one's potential to the fullest, and the subordination of other roles to work.[21] The aspiring professional woman must resolve this conflict between the feminine role and the professional role.

Societal norms provide one resolution to this conflict by changing the professional role in women's professions so that the incumbent can continue to fulfill her feminine role responsibilities. Interrupting her career for marriage, childbearing, and child rearing and dropping out when family needs arise are tolerated and even expected. It is assumed that should her husband require a move because of his career, the family will leave the area and she will quit her job.

The woman is expected not to display the masculine characteristics of ambition, assertiveness, competetiveness, and independence or to engage in the normative behaviors that are required for professional achievement. Career commitment is not an expectation for the professional role in women's professions. Rather, the role is viewed as temporary or secondary to other roles such as those of wife and mother. Women's professions are often billed as "good preparation for marriage and a family" or as "something to fall back on if necessary." This view of women's professions helps prevent disruption in the current male-dominated occupational and familial systems.[9]

Exemption from a strong career commitment and from many of the normative behaviors required of professionals, such as a continuous, full-time work history, changes the structure of the professional role in women's professions. When a primary career commitment and associated behaviors are not required, autonomy and the usual professional rewards such as money and prestige are not granted.

The work role in female-dominated occupations is closely identified with the feminine role and is structured in a manner similar to the woman's role in the family. As the wife-mother is traditionally expected to play a supportive, dependent role in the family, deferring to the decision making of her higher-status husband, the nurse role is structured as supportive of, dependent on, and subordinate to higher-status doctors and hospital administrators.[2]

In this structure the nurse's work role lacks the independence that would facilitate professional achievement. An important feature of many spheres of practice within the profession is the relative lack of autonomy. Davis and others[11] contend that nowhere is this more evident than in the situation of nurses in clinical practice. Most contemporary health agencies have a rather rigidly organized bureaucracy that emphasizes obedience rather than autonomous behavior by nurses.[17]

The reward system in nursing reflects this orientation. The supportive nature of the role results in a system in which rewards come for performing supportive functions rather than for independent professional achievements. Kramer reports that the reward system in nursing is a significant source of tension for the new graduate.[18] She contends that although the nurse expects to be rewarded for the professional nursing behavior she learned in school, she is expected to carry out doctors' orders and follow hospital routines because it is these behaviors that result in the rewards and punishments. Generally little or no provision is made for salary and privilege adjustments in accordance with individual professional achievements by nurses.

Further, the financial and prestige rewards in nursing are relatively low. Nursing is considered a feminine sex-typed occupation because a very large majority of nurses are women and thus it is expected that nurses will be women.[20] Epstein[12] holds that sex typing reflects sex ranking. Men's work, whatever it is, tends to be more highly regarded. Women's work holds less prestige and receives less financial compensation. Achievement, when it does occur in a feminine sex-typed occupation, counts for less. The relatively low rewards, notwithstanding the personal satisfaction the nurse may have, serve to ensure that women will maintain family responsibilites as their primary commitment. This structure leads to confusion over the meaning of achievement in nursing.

THE DILEMMA OF ACHIEVEMENT IN NURSING

Feminine achievement has been a problem because most people consider achievement a male rather than female behavior.[14] Epstein[12] contends that woman are not supposed to acquire valued things independently but rather are to be "vicarious achievers." Women are expected to achieve through supporting their husbands and children in their endeavors and sharing the joy of their successes. The key characteristic of ideal feminine achievement is a selfless giving to others while subordinating one's own self-interests.

The masculine model of achievement, in contrast, stresses money, power, and influence.[12] Ginzberg[15] contends that the key measure of an individual's occupational achievement in a competetive society is the amount of money earned. Associated characteristics are the supervision of a large number of subordinates and a job title that signifies a high level of responsibility.[1] Epstein[12] claims that both men and women value such accomplishments as signs of career success. This model of achievement differs from that of feminine vicarious achievement in a fundamental way. Service to others is not precluded and in fact is often the result of masculine achievement. The driving force behind this type of achievement, however, is the actualization of one's own potential and the pursuit of the personal rewards and recognition that this may bring. It is this masculine model of achievement that has traditionally been the ideal of accomplishment in the professions.

Thus a dilemma concerning achievement exists in women's professions such as nursing. This dilemma can be viewed as a conflict between the feminine role and the professional role. Levinson's concept[19] of role is useful in analyzing this conflict and the consequences it has for the definition of achievement in nursing. Levinson defines a role not as a unitary concept but as a process involving three components related to a person in a given social position:

1. Structurally given demands: norms, expectations, and pressure from others for role behavior.
2. Personal role conception: the individual's personal definition of what someone in her/his social position should think and do.
3. Role behavior: the way a person acts in accord with or in violation of norms and expectations.

The woman in nursing holds a social position that contains conflicting structural role demands—those stemming from the female sex role and those stemming from the professional role. Thus she is confronted with a role dilemma. Her socialization for the role of adult female dictates one set of characteristics and behaviors, whereas her socialization for the role of professional nurse dictates another.

When such dilemmas exist, according to Levinson,[19] there is no optimal mode of adaptation. Each mode has different advantages and costs. The nurse's personal role conception of how she should think and act in her role as a nurse is crucial in shaping her behavior. Societal norms and reward systems also have a strong influence on her resolution of this dilemma.

POTENTIAL MODELS OF ACHIEVEMENT FOR NURSES

Nurses could follow the feminine vicarious model of achievement. Vicarious achievement for a nurse might consist of assisting doctors in their work and then sharing vicariously in their achievements. This stereotype of the nurse as the doctor's helper is in fact widely held. A variation involves being obedient to rules, regulations, and task performance requirements and then sharing in the good reputation of the employing agency. Helping others to accomplish what they wish to accomplish, whether they are physicians, patients, hospitals, nursing students, or others, in the absence of any self-interest, is also a form of vicarious achievement. This model of achievement, however, is not compatible with the ideal of professionalism for nurses.

An alternative would be to adopt the masculine model of achievement, which entails money and prestige. Numerous studies, however, have shown that women's earnings and prestige are not as closely tied to their accomplishments as are men's.* This disparity has been attributed to, among other factors, discrimination against women and the cultural valuation of men's work as more important than women's work.

The devaluation of women's work has affected career patterns in nursing and other female-dominated professions. The Simpsons[23] report that as one goes up the ladder in female-dominated professions, administrative tasks tend to replace core tasks, a tendency in marked contrast to the pattern for physicians, who when they reach eminence continue to treat patients.

This pattern in which the primary tasks of nursing lose prestige reflects the adoption by nurses of the achievement orientation of another occupational group, administrators, as cited by the Simpsons. Another example of this phenomenon can be found among nursing educators, who often adopt the masculine achievement model of university professors. The achievements of nurses as administrators or educators do not enhance the prestige of primary nursing tasks, nor do they provide an achievement model for nurses in practice who are caught in the conflict between their feminine role and their professional role.

The vicarious model of achievement, which is compatible with the feminine sex typing of the occupation, is incompatible with the emerging professionalism of nursing. The masculine model of achievement is not the answer for nurses at the present time because of the current division of labor within the family and the devaluation of

---

*References 3, 6, 12, 24.

women's work. Thus there is some confusion over just what constitutes achievement in nursing. What is needed is an alternative model of achievement that neither requires the denial of self-interest nor devalues women's work. A resolution to the achievement dilemma must be found if the professionalization of nursing is to continue to advance.

REFERENCES

1. Aronson, S.G.: Marriage with a successful woman. In Knudsin, R.B., editor: Women and success, New York, 1974, William Morrow & Co., Inc.
2. Ashley, J.: Hospitals, paternalism and the role of the nurse, New York, 1976, Teachers College Press.
3. Astin, H.S., and Bayer, A.E.: Sex discrimination in academe. In Mednick, M., and others, editors: Women and achievement, Washington, D.C., 1975, Hemisphere Publishing Corp.
4. Backtold, L.M.: Women, eminence and career-value relationships, The Journal of Social Psychology. **95**:187, 1975.
5. Barnett, R.C., and Baruch, G.K.: The competent woman: perspectives on development, New York, 1978, Irvington Publishers, Inc.
6. Bell, C.S.: Alternatives for social change: the future status of women. In Epstein, L.K., editor: Women in the professions. Lexington, Mass., 1975, Lexington Books.
7. Block, J., and others: Sex-role and socialization patterns: some personality concomitants and environmental antecedents, Journal of Consulting and Clinical Psychology **41**(3):321, 1978.
8. Condry, J., and Dyer, S.: Fear of success: attribution of cause to the victim, The Journal of Social Issues **32**(3):68, 1976.
9. Coser, R.L., and Rokoff, G.: Women in the occupational world: social disruption and conflict, Social Problems **18**:535, April 1971.
10. Darley, S.A.: Big time careers for the little woman: a dual-role dilemma, Journal of Social Issues **32**(3):85, 1976.
11. Davis. M., and others, editors: Nurses in practice: a perspective on work environments, St. Louis, 1973, The C.V. Mosby Co.
12. Epstein, C.F.: Woman's place: options and limits in professional careers, Berkeley, 1970, University of California Press.
13. Etzioni, A., editor: The semi-professions and their organization, New York, 1969, The Free Press.
14. Feather, N.T., and Simon, J.G.: Stereotypes about male and female success and failure at sex-linked occupations, Journal of Personality **44**:16, 1976.
15. Ginzberg, E.: Life styles of educated women, New York, 1966, Columbia University Press.
16. Gold, A.R.: Reexamining barriers to women's career development, American Journal of Orthopsychiatry **48**(4):690, 1978.
17. Jacox, A.: Professional socialization of nurses. In Chaska, N.L., editor: The nursing profession: views through the mist, New York, 1978, McGraw-Hill Book Co.
18. Kramer, M.: Reality shock: why nurses leave nursing, St. Louis, 1974, The C.V. Mosby Co.
19. Levinson, D.: Role, personality and social structure in the organizational setting, Journal of Abnormal and Social Psychology **58**:170, 1959.
20. Merton, R.K.: Personal communication in Epstein, C.F.: Woman's place: options and limits in professional careers, Berkeley, 1970, University of California Press.
21. Pleck, J.H.: The work-family role system, Social Problems **24**(4):417, 1977.
22. Rosen, B., and others, editors: Achievement in American society, Cambridge, Mass., 1969, Schenkman Publishing Co., Inc.
23. Simpson, R.L., and Simpson, I.H.: Women and bureaucracy. In Etzioni, A., editor: The semi-professions and their organization, New York, 1969, The Free Press.
24. Stevenson, M.H.: Wage differences between men and women: economic theories. In Stromberg, A.H., and Harkness, S.: Women working: theories and facts in perspective, Palo Alto, Calif., 1978, Mayfield Publishing Co.
25. Ward, C.: Is there a motive to avoid success in women? Human relations **31**(12):1055, 1978.
26. White, M.S.: Psychological and social barriers to women in science, Science **170**:413, October 23, 1970.

Chapter 24

Go ahead, I'm behind you . . . way behind you

Look at us. As a profession we retain the public's confidence (for good reason) while other professions have lost it. Yet we are subject to continuing internal and external problems that we cannot seem to resolve. We do not have our own confidence. We lack solidarity as a group. This is particularly puzzling when one realizes how common our base of experience is. Our educational backgrounds contain many similarities. Some similarities are necessities, such as taking the same licensing exams; we learn many of the same things; we have had the same dreams, the desire for caring; we probably remember the same concerns such as giving the first bed bath, noticing our instructor's white shoes on the other side of the curtain, giving the first shot, and so on.

Despite a movement toward responsibility and accountability we remain a profession whose day-to-day practice is largely dependent. Think, for example, about care plans. They are an independent function. They should document our practice and guide the care of each client. How many are begun? Completed? Become part of the records? How many reflect a real assessment of the client? How many are truly well thought out and individualized? How many are hurriedly completed on the day of discharge? How many well-considered plans are *consulted?* In contrast, how many physicians' orders are left off the records and the Kardex? How many are not carried out? What does that say about ourselves and the way we consult with one another? What does that say about the relative value we place on dependent and independent education?

Look at the systems within which most of us practice—hospitals. Hospital systems traditionally epitomize male patriarchal, authoritarian bureaucracies. The workers are largely female, and the authorities are almost without exception male. The organizational style is typically the pyramid. Anyone who has been in the army would recognize the hospital bureaucracy instantly and know its rules: the top is the top, the father, the ruler. Authority flows from the top down. Those of us who are educators are not much better off. We teach in systems that have been transferred almost intact from the priest- and Church-centered medieval universities. Analyze the modern educational institution and you again find the army's structure. Both the army and Church have in their history an ignorance and denial of women and of their relevance.[5] Look at the nursing system as it exists in the larger system. Is it the same pyramid? Often it is. Often it has the same problems and disillusionments as the system it copies. What significant changes have been made in authoritarian bureaucracies? Studies show that such systems tend to perpetuate themselves, to maintain the status quo. Here we are, a profession seeking to change itself, to review itself, to evolve new roles, and we are embedded for the most part in rigid, authoritarian structures that resist changes.

As nurses we know the often crushing responsibility we take on each time we begin a shift. We all remember the times we ran or prayed our way through a shift short of help and heavy on treatments, medications, and patients in tears. All of us know the exhaustion of that sort of day. Even on good days with good staffing it is impossible to know at the beginning of a shift what may happen during that 8 hours. Each shift is a challenge that calls on our knowledge, wisdom, and skills in its own unique way. Count how many times you've finished your day with energy to spare. Count how many times you've made decision after critical decision with little or no time in between. The stresses are many, yet nurses receive lower pay than painters, tree trimmers, and tire servicemen, as the Denver nurses have pointed out to us. We are reminded daily that what we do is not valued by the society of which we are a part—our status is low.

Repeatedly we deal with a lack of professionalism within our ranks. How many of us are committed to career and work? How many of us still expect to leave nursing when we have a family? How many of us aim at excellence in practice? How many of us belong to our nursing organizations? How many of us participate in those organizations? How many of us subscribe to journals? How many of us are truly committed to a lifetime of learning? How many of us are truly colleagues and consult with one another?

Of course, professionalism means action. Those of us who are professionally oriented have different problems. We may not be accepted by our peers. We may be called idealistic, crazy, or other distancing epithets. We work hard to become skilled clinicians—reading, studying, taking courses—and for this we are poorly rewarded both in money and status. The only access to status and financial gain in many institutions is to move up the administrative ladder. Of course, on that ascent we need different skills, and our hard-won clinical skills are still not rewarded. We face starting over, so to speak, in order to move up. It is strange paradox: move up with fewer skills. It is bound to make for further insecurity.

As nurses we know the importance of caring and nurturance. Our first lessons most likely were in giving skilled bed baths and listening well. We know the importance of developing good relationships, of belonging to a group, of being needed. When we are able, given the conflicting demands on our time, we use this knowledge for our clients' benefit. How do we use it for our own? How much solidarity do we have? How much support do we offer a ground-down, discouraged colleague? What networks do we create—or even allow—for ourselves? How well do we stick together to accomplish common goals despite our diversity? What *are* our goals? How much time do we spend together? How much do we positively reinforce a colleague for a job well done? How often do we set goals for our own achievement and then meet them, a form of self-nurturance?

Studies show that one third of us have dropped out and are not working as nurses. The disparity between the ideal and the real is cited as the cause. The job simply does not fulfill nurses' dreams and hopes—for achievement, for helping others, for intellectual stimulation. Nurses find the patient contact they value diminishing.

What happens to our leaders? Do the natural leaders, the nurses with a vision, survive the educational process? What happens if they ask "Why?" too often? If a nurse takes a stand, is she likely to be supported? How many of our leaders are willing to break with tradition? If our leaders *do* represent us, are they likely to feel the force of the group behind them or must they stand in front, alone in their risk taking, with the cold feeling of wind at their backs because their colleagues are timidly backing away or supporting them only from a distance? Why don't we have more leaders? Why do so few carry the responsibility for so many?

Much is said in our educational systems about critical thinking and creativity, yet we know that American school systems in general reward conformity, passivity, and correct answers.[7] Are *our* educational systems so different? What happens to the nursing student who questions and challenges? The student who is different? Or independent, active, or highly curious? Count the creative nurses you know, or the nurses who use critical thinking. If they survive the educational system, what happens to them in the work place? How long do they last?

We're behind all right—way behind—in many ways. We allow nurses to take risks for the group and then don't back them. We hold to the safety of tradition and "the way it's always done" and therefore ensure our failure to change. We need leaders and trailblazers. We have nowhere near our quota. The general public sees us as handmaidens; enlightened people see us as dominated and even as causers of pain.[3,4] We seem unable to articulate our needs and to demand they be met. We even question whether we have rights.

Why? What are the reasons for the problem? So often we hear the blame ascribed to be one nursing group or another: educators aren't preparing students correctly, nursing leaders aren't planning well, nursing organizations aren't responsive—perhaps this is all true. But why? What are the causes? Perhaps it is time to look at who and what we are.

We are women.

So what? That is an obvious fact. Is it? Have we really defined ourselves as women? Although this reality is acknowledged in statistical terms—most nurses are women—does it really enter into our conscious thoughts and planning? Have we defined ourselves as women with the dreams, hardships, and experiences of women? Without this definition and the understanding that derives from it we are engaged in a kind of cultural and professional borderline psychosis.

OPPRESSIVE SOCIALIZATION OR WOMEN'S HERITAGE: TWO VIEWS OF THE SAME PROCESS

As women we have been formed by the socialization of our culture. We cannot escape it. From the time someone put a pink sleeper on us or a pink ribbon is our hair we have learned the lessons that go with being female. Women are passive recipients, we *are* rather than *do*. We are second class—the male of the species is superior in strength, intellect, rational thinking, economics, and so on. A woman's place is in the home. A woman gives selflessly, even to her own detriment. A woman meets needs. She does not voice them. A woman is valued through her interpersonal relationships. Because we are second class we learn the lessons of any minority: to admire and emulate the power group and to mistrust ourselves, to tear down one another rather than the dominant group. We exist within patriarchal systems, and thus those early cultural lessons are constantly repeated and reinforced in our lives and our practice.

We are women. We are doing woman's work. We care, nurture, and help people grow. It is time to stop denying it. It is time to confront it. It is time to glory in it. It is time to have a feminist perspective in nursing. It is time to stop defining ourselves in male terms. We must begin to question our traditional aspirations. We are making the mistake many women make. We accept the assumptions of the culture that denies us. Adrienne Rich[7] powerfully points out that women live their lives according to the dichotomy imposed by the patriarchal society: caring exists in the home. Outside the home the rules are to control and exploit others and hide our own feelings. Women still feel they must follow those rules. Adrienne Rich writes,

> I have also known nonfeminist women who have looked long and hard at masculine society and its competitive, paranoia rules and who say, "there's something wrong here. Better to stay at home where at least some semblance of emotional life remains, then go out there and become another emotionless flunky." For them the choice is based on the old assumptions. Either you stay at home where you can hope to express tenderness, give and receive warmth, behave spontaneously and generously, or you enter the male world and play the game like a man: the game being control, impassivity, ends above means, exploitation.*

Many of our problems can be traced back to playing the game like a man. When

---

*From Rich, A.: On lies, secrets and silence, New York, 1979, W.W. Norton & Co., Inc.

we do that we cause ourselves problems and double the repression. We are repressed by the bureaucratic and patriarchal system, and we further repress one another. Rather than caring in the workplace we seek to control and exploit others and hide our feelings—just like the army, just like many men.

What would happen to a world without nurturance? Just what is happening to it now—stress and unhappiness. As Jean Baker Miller[6] observes, our culture has so denied men the capacity for nurturance and the expression of feelings that a new profession has been created to provide these: the psychologist. Women provide a necessity. In fact, one could say that it is the fear of *loss of nurturance* that leads to women being controlled. It is the fear of the loss of nurses' (cheap) necessary services and competition with physicians' (expensive) services that necessitates our being controlled in the health care system. Sadly, we no more recognize our value than the larger society does.

It is time to recognize our heritage, our roots. It is time to know who we are and to design structures and systems that provide for what we want and need. It is time to change the assumptions. Of course, we need to know about power and its uses, the organizational framework, and so on. We need to know these to deal with the structures in which we practice; we do not need to turn those lessons on ourselves, to use power in the traditional masculine sense against one another. That is far from freeing. It drives us further apart. The further apart we are, the smaller our relative numbers and the less our chances of being able to have a successful impact on the health care system and to make the changes necessary for quality patient care and satisfying professional lives. The further apart we are, the more controlled and powerless we are as a group. We become locked in a destructive cycle.

SELF-APPRAISAL AND SELF-ACCEPTANCE: BASIS FOR CHANGE

We all know the value of a full assessment of a client. It is time to make that full assessment of ourselves. We must name and weigh everything we see and use that data to plan, to go forward. We must confront aloud both the happiest truths and the most painful truths and let them out of the shadowy corridors of our minds and whispered conversations. We need the power of ourselves. We need to allow the full growth of each of us individually and of all of us together. We must be able to applaud and support that growth rather than view it with suspicion. We can not afford passivity and division. *We need take no guilt or blame.* We do need to identify what is, take responsibility for what we want, and plan to create it. We must recognize that as nurses we want what other women and other minorities want: a knowledge of ourselves and our history, recognition for what we are and what we do, authority and responsibility, status, movement. We face the same problems as other women and minorities: we live in a culture that has different definitions, expectations, and realities; we are easily convinced of our own lack of value and easily allied with the power group; we have learned to mistrust one another and ourselves; we are divided; we do not have a sense of our history; we are suspicious of any of our number who dare to be different; we become anxious, deny realities when they are pointed out to us and hold even more closely to stereotyped and self-defeating but familiar, safe, and sanctioned behaviors.

It is time to stop bemoaning our fate and move ahead. We must realize that it is just this pattern that retards our progress. The patriarchal systems in which we are embedded can turn around and accuse us of being divided, of dragging one another down, and of not knowing what we want. This accusation, of course, overlooks the origins of these behaviors in the reality of being a repressed minority group within those patriarchal systems. It keeps the oppressors free of guilt and us still guilty, powerless, and oppressed. It is time to see ourselves as strong, our skills as important. It is time to act on that vision.

What then must we do? First we must recognize how we are behind and where we are ahead. We are a second-class profession made up of mainly second-class citizens (females). We do not stick together, we do not allow trailblazers. We do not back our leaders. We do not back our peers.

We do nurse. We do care. We are essential in the health care system. Without us people would hurt, become infected, remain ill. We provide an important service.

The time is here to change. The time is here to overcome. The time is here to declare our validity.

UNITY VS. DIVERSITY: NEW DIRECTIONS

In grade school we all learned the ancient axioms: "Divide and conquer" and "United we stand, divided we fall." These are not mere slogans, not mere history lessons. They are daily facts of life and power. Look at how our divisiveness keeps us powerless. These are the running rules of bureaucratic organizations.

> We had better face the fact that our hope . . . depends upon seeking and giving allegiance to a community of women co-workers. Beyond the exchange and criticism of work, we have to ask ourselves how we can make conditions for work more possible, not just for ourselves, but for each other. This is not a question of generosity. It is not generosity that makes women in community support and nourish each other. It is . . . a context in which our strivings will be amplified, quickened, lucidified, through those of our peers.*

The bureaucratic system keeps us divided. Therefore, we must learn the lessons of power, which will let us survive and grow within the system. We must be able to assess and manipulate that system. We must have the will to do it. We must back the leaders who are willing to take those risks for us. We must educate those who do not. But we can not replicate those systems within our own culture. Those systems

---

*From Rich, A.: On lies, secrets and silence, New York, 1979, W.W. Norton & Co., Inc.

divide, stress, and burn us out. We have ample proof of this in ourselves, our profession, and our clients. Many of the illnesses we see are stress related. We must create for ourselves the type of systems we need rather than the hierarchical models we now have. We need clusters of nurses each directly responsible for a reasonable number of patients. Each cluster could be made up of nurses with various areas of expertise in patient care so that nurses could consult with one another on aspects of care. Perhaps each cluster could have a skilled, senior clinician who would have not only a client caseload but also a responsibility for helping less experienced practitioners advance in clinical skills. The old team nursing concept was somewhat similar, but it deteriorated into task units.

We must begin to help other nurses grow. Rather than letting new practitioners and students "sink or swim" we must begin to share the strokes that keep us afloat. Each of us has something we can share with another nurse—some knowledge, advice, experience. Each of us in turn can learn something from another nurse.

As we evaluate one another as peers or evaluate our students, we must recognize and point out strengths. That process takes a more skillful and concentrated evaluation. In the long run, however, it builds a stronger practitioner who knows that tools and skills she has and helps correct weaknesses. Constantly pointing out weaknesses builds only defenses and divisions. Our socialization already assumes and reinforces weakness. It is time to turn the tide. We must build on strengths.

Further, we must use the skills of nurturance, learned for use with our clients, with ourselves. We must give one another time, patience, listening, understanding, and respect for individuality and caring. We know the value of these things. We know from experience with our clients how these can calm anxiety, facilitate positive movement, and even allay physical symptoms. We can no longer deny their potency and growth-producing effects to ourselves. It is time to use what we know to salvage and advance our own profession.

We must break that terrible cycle in which a nurse remembers and repeats the behavior of nurses who "broke" her or "rode" her to force her to conform, increase output, or be less idealistic. We must be able to look back on our experiences with one another with warmth and pride rather than anger and rejection. We all have a great deal to share, and sharing it will bring us much further along. It is essential that we acknowledge and build on our strengths. Not only will we increase both individually and as a body our ability and skill, but we will also have built that respect and solidarity that allows us to unify and use the force of our numbers. If we can unify ourselves and create healthy systems for ourselves, we can use our unity to influence the creation of positive systems for others and for our clients.

On a unit where I taught as a faculty member I saw one of the healthiest systems I have every experienced. The head nurse was a diploma graduate and had been a head nurse for 25 years. Her staff had a range of ages and preparations, and she viewed their skills and strengths with pride. They were expected to orient new staff.

Evaluation was done not in the punitive terms of whether a new member would "make it" or not but in terms of how far along she had come and what was necessary to move her further. I will always remember her comment to me as she introduced me to a new staff nurse: "She's *good* for a young one." I will also remember the glow on the face of that nurse. I observed nurses there consulting with each other on care problems; I saw nurses move from one area to another and help one another voluntarily when the workload was particularly heavy; I noticed patients coming back to visit; I noticed nurses remembering patients they cared for years ago; I noticed nurses scheduling time for conferences, inservice, and workshops and enthusiastically sharing what they learned; I saw nurses reading professional journals during slow times. I salute them all. They are wise. They live the lessons we must all learn.

CHANGING WORK RELATIONSHIPS

We must experiment with new types of employment patterns. Or perhaps we need to go back to old patterns. It was not so long ago that most registered nurses did private duty. Most nurses now are employees and have all the attendant problems of that status. We have responsibilities to an institution as well as to our clients and our profession. Too often there are conflicts. Perhaps we need to become independent contractors. Our responsibility then would be to ourselves as professionals and to our patients. We could provide our own benefit programs (retirement, health insurance, and so on) through our professional organizations. We would not be as dependent and controllable as we are now. We could also strengthen our organizations.

If we remain as employees, perhaps we must organize into bargaining units. Perhaps it is only through this mechanism of strength and a single voice that our message will be heard and we will be able to influence the conditions of patient care. In that event, however, we must be careful to avoid being used by unions looking for new horizons and new power. We need our own power. We need nurses bargaining for nurses. We do not need to join another army—a union can be just that.

Hospitals themselves are undergoing a change. Gone are the days when the director might be a nurse or a physician—someone who understood the realities and complexities of care delivery. Now the administrator is usually trained as a business person and has a primary focus on facts and figures. Financial realities are upon us. We cannot deny them. But we must recognize the administrator's increasing distance from service. Hospitals are an army in which the general has not come up through the ranks. He does not know our problems. We must educate nursing administrators to *our* needs and to the necessity of remaining allied with nursing. We can not afford to have them identify with the bureaucratic structure. To the extent that they do, they will be blinded to the experiences and concerns of nurses are caring. A recent survey showed that only 56% of nursing administrators have full administrative responsibility for their budgets.[1] How can they be effective in making changes and responding to nursing needs without having control over the pursestrings? No one ever became independent on an allowance! We must support our nursing administrators and help them gain control of nursing. They must see the strength of nursing as their own strength and not as a threat.

We must insist that the programs educating our administrators teach them the formation of growth-producing systems. Even corporate executives have recognized the problems built into the authoritarian, autocratic, militaristic style of organization. We must be sure to avoid that same militaristic, ulcer-producing trap. If our administrators do not learn the formation and maintenance of healthier systems, how can we expect them to support such systems?

We must begin to work for conditions that allow and encourage skilled nurses to stay in nursing. We must recognize the skilled clinician with advances in salary and status, retaining her in clinical practice rather than forcing her into an administrative position. We might consider ways for patients to have "their nurse" again should they reenter the hospital or agency. We should recognize our good clinicians with awards from hospitals, agencies, and state nurses' associations. It is encouraging, for example, to note the recognition being given to nursing leaders by *Image*. In addition, we need to recognize our past. It is time to reemphasize nursing history, which has been considered dull and boring for too long. It is our life. To understand our present realities we need to know whence we've come. The wisdom and knowledge of the past is important in the present; it adds to the pride and resolve that move us to the future. It gives strength.

We need to form networks with one another to share information, problems, solutions, hopes. We need to help one another manage the patriarchal systems in which we find ourselves and the stresses and frustrations they engender. We need to form ties not only to one another but with other colleagues and resource persons outside nursing. We can not afford to be isolated.

We need more consciousness raising. We need to recognize our own value and contributions. Then we need to repeat them to ourselves and to the world. We need good press.

We must look at the crushing reality we share with all married working women: *two* full-time jobs. And we need quality care for our children. We should be helping to establish alternative forms of child care. We must begin to talk to ourselves, our young practitioners, and our students about the stresses and strains. We need to live our solutions and demonstrate the reality and possibility of them. We must work with other women to explore alternatives in working hours, lifestyles, and relationships.

Although we must continue to professionalize nursing in terms of its commitment, aspirations, and theoretical base, we must avoid the dichotomy between personal life and work that the patriarchal system imposes. Although we need to retain objectivity in assessing our patients, we cannot afford to cut ourselves off from our own experiences and what they tell us about our needs and goals. We must remain genuine and congruent with ourselves as well as with our clients. If we cannot, we reinforce our separation and isolation from one another and between aspects of ourselves. We have the right to our needs and their fulfillment.

We must base our practice on something more than the traditional reasoning of "it has always been done that way." We need to ask the *whys* and *wherefors* that have never been asked. We need our own researchers. We need to work with them in building theory and studying interventions. At the very least each of us needs to become an intelligent consumer of research in our practice. Some of us may even become researchers. We must insist that our practice be based on answers to questions of *why* rather than on long-held assumptions. Such behaviors will reinforce our value and validity both for ourselves and for our colleagues in the other health professions.

RETHINKING THE EDUCATIONAL PROCESS

We need to look at how and where we recruit nursing students. It is time we stopped leaving recruitment to guidance counselors. We need to let young women and men know that nursing is a grand profession with many and varied opportunities. We neeed to let them know it is intellectually and physically tough (and we need to make it worth the work!).

If the emphasis on intellectual skills and the demands of our programs and practices discourage disadvantaged students (as well it may), then we need to be sure that there are remedial programs to prepare such students to meet the expectations of nursing education. We need to be flexible in the length of time it takes to complete our programs so that students will not be defeated by heavy loads. We cannot afford to be as rigid or repressive as the larger society.

We need to communicate to our students that a nursing program is tough and they will have to work hard. They must learn the value of that work. Often we are too concerned with providing time for their social lives and so on, and thus we reinforce the very cultural standards that enslave us. Can you imagine the faculty of an engineering program worrying about their students' free time? We must emphasize intellectual growth and physcial health. Again Adrienne Rich puts it well:

> We can refuse to accept passive, obedient learning and insist on critical thinking. We can become harder on our women students, giving them the same kinds of "cultural prodding" men receive, but on different terms and in different styles. Most young women need to have their intellectual lives, their work legitimized against the claims of family, relationships, the old message that a woman is always available for service to others. We need to keep our standards very high, not to accept a woman's preconceived sense of her limitations; we need to be hard to please, while supportive of risk-taking, because self-respect comes only when exacting standards have been met. At a time when adult literacy is generally low, we need to demand more, not less, of women, both for the sake of their future as thinking beings, and because historically women have always had to be better

than men to do half as well. A romantic sloppiness, an inspired lack of rigor, a self-indulgent incoherence, are symptoms of female self-depreciation. We should help our students to look very critically at such symptoms, and to understand where they are rooted.

It is not easy to think like a woman in a man's world, in the world of the professions; yet the capacity to do that is a strength which we can try to help our students develop. To think like a woman in a man's world means thinking critically, refusing to accept the givens, making connections between facts and ideas men have left unconnected. It means remembering that every mind resides in a body; remaining accountable to the female bodies in which we live; constantly retesting given hypotheses against lived experience.*

We are no longer training the "ladies" of our original schools but educating tough-minded professionals.

EMPHASIZING PHYSICAL AND MENTAL HEALTH FOR CLIENTS AND OURSELVES

We must become much more active in the cause of women's health. We are latecomers to a full understanding and study of women's physical and mental health. We cannot afford to assume that the health of over half of the population is adequately studied in courses and texts that cover childbearing, medicine, and surgery. Remember, women's health is *assumed* to be covered by these areas; it is not. We have much to contribute and much to learn. We must help women become more comfortable with their bodies. We cannot afford to perpetuate mental health problems originating in the male culture. We must become advocates for our female clients and be in the forefront of changes in women's health care.

We must look at those who enter nursing, knowing that the socialization of women does not encourage achievement and competition. Nursing is a "safe" career choice for many. It allows a woman to succeed without much ambivalence over her role and femininity. It is considered good training for marriage and family, and men approve of it as a choice for wives and daughters. Women with the highest achievement needs generally choose nontraditional career roles rather than nursing.[2] A colleague of mine recently described a program she developed to educate women in a prestigious women's college about nursing. These women were achievers and were oriented to medical school. It took a special program to convince them of the opportunities in nursing.

We need achievers. We need the bright, assertive women who are being drawn to engineering and business. We are struggling to establish our professionalism. Our neophytes must possess the qualities necessary for success in a profession. We are seeking to define our work and implement our plans for both ourselves and our

*From Rich, A.: On lies, secrets and silence, New York, 1979, W.W. Norton & Co., Inc.

clients. We coordinate care. All this takes self-esteem, mastery of skills, and assertiveness. We know that although skills are relatively easily learned, their correct use
demands a great deal of knowledge and understanding. We know that to further the
knowledge base of the profession we need intelligent consumers of research and a
body of skilled researchers. We know that the day-to-day practice of nursing demands a secure sense of self. If a nurse must in the classic feminine mode, derive her
self-esteem from the reflected comments of others, her self-esteem will fluctuate
month to month, week to week, day to day, even minute to minute, as a result of the
pressures and conflicts of the job.

A nurse who depends on interpersonal success to define her self-esteem will be
dependent on clients, peers, superiors, and significant others for affirmation. This
cannot help but cloud decision making and retard growth. We need to develop
self-esteem by accepting our achievements and beginning to value ourselves.

ASSUMING A PROFESSIONAL ROLE

A profession cannot succeed without professionals. If nursing is to be a profession, we must be somewhat radical in our view of the feminine role. We must
continue to study and grow in the profession over a lifetime, to see ourselves in a role
outside the home even when we are married, to delegate child-care and home-care
responsibilities, and to experiment with alternative divisions of labor in the home.
The trend has been otherwise. For example, Davis and Olsen found that students in
university nursing programs actually decreased in professionalization during their
education. Their attitudes became more conservative and job centered.[2]

What happens to students? Or perhaps one should ask what doesn't happen.
How does a young woman who has been socialized to believe in the supremacy of the
home learn the validity of other roles? We must remember that nurses are probably
more conservative and "femininity"-oriented than other groups of women. Thus they
need remedial work in professionalism: early experiences in setting their own goals
and being responsible for meeting them, faculty role models who show and discuss
the combination of home and career roles, and democratic models of shared decision
making. In addition they need experiences in collegiality such as peer sharing of
ideas, approaches, and knowledge and peer consulting; assertiveness skills and rewards for assertive behavior; leadership experiences and opportunities to follow up
on their own interests; discussions of changing sex roles and the consequent stresses
(how to handle them) and rewards; even opportunities to experiment with combinations of home and career; and perhaps discussions of career commitment and what it
means in terms of responsibility, social life, and so on. They need to learn to set their
own goals, plan to meet those goals, and evaluate their own progress.

Look at your local nursing program. Are these elements there? Are faculty free
to experiment with ways to combine home and career? How many nursing in-

structors would frown upon the thought of a baby in the office? How openly are these many professional issues discussed in the first course? In succeeding courses? In admissions criteria or high school recruiting?

How often is a student's first evaluation by an instructor subjective? How often are students taught the value and skill of *self*-evaluation? How often is the self-evaluation respected? What kinds of evaluations are done in the workplace? What input does a nurse have? How often are evaluations negative? The pattern begun in school is often repeated in the job.

Among all the communication techniques a student learns, is assertiveness given a place? How much teaching involves values clarification? How overt are faculty about the need for professionalism? What behaviors are considered "professional" on the part of the student? Does the faculty exhibit them? Are independent, achievement-oriented, and professional behaviors recognized and rewarded, or are they squelched? Does the maternal child health course, for example, support the traditional home and family subtly or not so subtly? Does the psychiatric nursing course present the traditional picture of female mental health? Are alternative models presented?

We must reward the professional behavior of our students and continue to reward that of our new practitioners. If they make us uncomfortable, we must remember that this is a sign of our success. If students and new colleagues question and challenge us, we must refrain from putting them in their place, for if we do, we will all be in the same place: nowhere. Repression is old order. We must muster our wisdom and our reasons and answer them, gently and respectfully. They must continue to question and assert and get answers. We all must. That is the new order.

We must allow our students the security of having time to learn, of failing, and of surviving. She who takes risks is bound not to succeed every time. We must all learn that failure means not disaster but new learning. We must assess carefully the ways in which our students and our new graduates learn. I believe our systems underscore insecurity rather than reinforcing a feeling of competence. Both the educational system and the work system are responsible. In the educational system the student is often not allowed to remain in any one area long enough to build a base of skill and familiarity. Often the concern for safety and excellence leave her too closely supervised to feel secure. Faculty members focus on maximizing the number of different experiences rather than the transferability of skills and experiences once mastered. Not only must we discuss concepts, but we must also make them live and show how they occur in *all* speciality areas rather than retreating into the safety of our own specialities. This means work and challenge for us, but it is worth it. Too often students are shown only their mistakes. We must point out their accomplishments.

We must support our new graduates for what they know and avoid castigating them for seeming "dumb" or "unskilled." It happens again and again. We are the only profession that expects our new practitioners to be as skilled as our seasoned ones. And look how we recognize our tried and true practitioners—minimally, if at all. No wonder they are bitter about the new idealists and are tempted to put them "in their place."

The workplace causes similar insecurities for seasoned nurses. A nurse reports to her floor, for example, full of plans for what she wants to get done today, and then she is "floated" to a strange unit. There she is behind all day because she started late, she doesn't know the patients, and she has to ask where everything is—hardly a way to foster security. Often too it is the least secure nurse who is floated, the youngest and newest, because she has the least seniority. So we perpetuate the anxieties of student days during work days.

DEVELOPING UNITY: NEW ASSUMPTIONS AND NEW SYSTEMS

We must look at new ways to combine forces, to concentrate on what unites us rather than what divides us. One of the most exciting activities I have participated in recently was the New England Regional Project for Maternal and Child Health entitled "To Improve Nursing Services and Nursing Education in Maternal Child Health Care," sponsored by the University of Connecticut School of Nursing with funding from Maternal and Child Health Services of the Bureau of Community Health Services. This project provided a series of conferences and consultations for nursing educators and nursing service representatives. Educators and practitioners teamed up to work on care issues and concerns. First we identified areas for improving quality of care on the units where we worked and taught. Then we proceeded to make changes together. The working together was an invaluable lesson: we recognized our common concerns with patient care and knew and relied on one another's skills; we became friends; we grew, learned, and accomplished our goals; and we grew in our respect for our profession and for one another. Ultimately the experiences of our individual students were enhanced immeasurably. Our experiences as nurses and our concern and involvement with the profession were influenced positively.

I believe that as educators we are too possessive of our students. Sometimes it is as if they provide us our only self-affirmation. We do not have all the answers. We cannot be the only role models. Students need practitioner models. I am not advocating wholesale abandonment of students to apprenticeships as in the past, but I am advocating that our students have some experiences with practitioners who serve as preceptors. As educators we are responsible for the distance the new graduate must bridge between the student role and the graduate role. Often students are not permitted to experience the nurse's role without faculty serving as buffers. In this way we reinforce the mistrust between education and service and among nurses in general. I have had excellent success with about 15 students taking clinical independent studies over several years. Based on each student's own objectives, we found a preceptor in a clinic or hospital setting with whom the student would work and become increasingly independent. I would monitor her progress with conferences and so on but was not present during her periods of clinical practice. These students became secure in their practice and in their ability to gauge their progress and needs. Staff were excellent preceptors and enjoyed the role. They felt that they too had learned. Students thought they were able to make more easily the transition to beginning staff roles.

This is one way to recognize excellence in practice—to ask the excellent clinician to share her skill with the developing practitioner. In addition, clinicians can give conferences on their own and other units about their areas of expertise. Thus we can build up facilitative cycles to replace the current destructive ones.

We must build into our systems a recognition for those nurses who have achieved and who have skills. They can become preceptors for new nurse employees. They can be cited in evaluations, given pay raises, and allowed time to attend workshops. They can teach others their special skills. They can be written up in institution newsletters and by the state nursing organizations. We also need to go public with more articles in newspapers, magazines, and so on. We must recognize and be proud of one another.

We must give our potential leaders reason to stay in nursing. Recently in a graduate class I was startled to discover that I was not, as I thought, the only nurse in the group. Two other people identified themselves privately to me as nurses after I had introduced myself to the group as a nurse. Both these women are doctoral students, and both are changing careers. They identify themelves as members of their new fields, not as nurses. We have lost two talented women, both of whom have had traumatic experiences at the hands of nursing peers because they were somehow "different." We have lost the spice of their differences. Two other professions have gained seasoned and experienced members. We must learn to value deviants for all they have to offer both personally and professionally.

We must join professional organizations. We need the force of numbers. We need the effort of individuals. We need that feeling of confidence and exhilaration that comes from being a part of a larger group working together.

Exciting, encouraging things are beginning to happen. Some hospitals and facilities have made major strides (and have not faced the nursing shortages that less positive institutions have). A major study has just been completed on the reasons nurses leave nursing,[8] and some necessary changes have been proposed.[1] The nursing shortage is getting national attention. The things we have long said among ourselves are now being published in newspapers and on television.

It is time for us all to go ahead—together. We must be individually and collectively right behind those nurses who are identifying the problems. All of us must commit ourselves to the effort. Each of us must convince a dubious colleague. We must unite on our common concerns or perish in our diversity.

REFERENCES

1. Aiken, L.H.: Nursing priorities for the 1980's: hospitals and nursing homes, American Journal of Nursing **81**(2):72, 1981.
2. Bardwick, J.M.: Psychology of women, New York, 1971, Harper & Row, Publishers, Inc.
3. Corea, G.: The hidden malpractice, New York, 1977, Jove Publications, Inc.
4. Daly, M.: Gyn/ecology, Boston, 1978, Beacon Press.
5. Harragan, B.L.: Games mother never taught you, New York, 1977, Rawson, Wade, Publishers, Inc.
6. Miller, J.B.: Toward a new psychology of women, Boston, 1976, Beacon Press.
7. Rich, A.: On lies, secrets and silence, New York, 1979, W.W. Norton & Co., Inc.
8. Wandelt, M.A., and others: Why nurses leave nursing and what can be done about it, American Journal of Nursing **81**(1):324, 1981.

EMILY E.M. SMYTHE

Chapter 25

Who's going to take care of the nurse?

The nurse works in a highly stressful environment that bombards her with an unending array of stimuli. Many of these stimuli are out of her control, yet they directly influence her ability to provide nursing services and contribute to her sense of, or lack of, job satisfaction. Nurses have determined that the greatest stressors are those that involve interpersonal interactions.[8] Yet most of nursing occurs in an interpersonal setting characterized by energetic sex-role stereotyping, the lack of nursing power, and the highly charged emotional context of working with people who are ill.[10,11] The stresses are many.

There is a growing awareness that nursing is in serious trouble. The evidence is abundant: fewer people are choosing nursing as a career; there is a nationwide nursing shortage, many trained nurses are dropping out of the profession, and nurses are moving from one job to another looking for satisfaction. Reality shock and burnout are the villains, we are told.

Since 98% of nurses are female, there is little question that societal expectations of women in general strongly influence the nursing profession. Several authors have suggested that "anatomy equals female destiny." Because we have female sex organs we are expected to behave in certain ways and have only certain avenues of achievement open to us, yet in reality all women and men have the same basic human strivings and needs.*

The nurse, as a female, has been well conditioned to have low self-esteem, to avoid asserting herself, to fear power, and to ignore her own concerns in favor of the needs of others. She has been taught to avoid independence and leadership and instead to obtain much of her personal validation from affiliative relationships that reinforce her stereotyped sex-role behaviors.[1,3,14] Various social sanctions ensure that she will behave in "acceptable" ways consistent with the values of the male-dominated system.[9]

What any woman feels herself to be is in part a function of what others expect of her; the same is true for men. Thus behaving in an acceptable manner endorses a woman's sense of worth and esteem[16] whereas deviating from social expectations places her personal value in question and causes anxiety and internal conflicts. The

337

pressures to conform may be so deeply ingrained that the woman may not even be aware of their subtle yet pervasive influence. She is aware only of the results: conflict and stress.

Not only has the nurse as a female been subjected to these societal forces, but the nursing profession itself has reinforced the "feminine" attributes of passive compliance with the male-dominated health care system. The "good nurse" portrayed in nursing education and in the mass media is the all-sacrificing nurse who is agreeable with everyone, lacks assertiveness, and is as loyal and faithful as a companion dog. Her sole objective and the source of her satisfaction is pleasing others regardless of the cost to herself.*

Recently this image and its subsequent expectations have begun to change. Another image is emerging—that of the "militant nurse," who is willing to strike for better patient care and more equitable pay, who feels comfortable asserting her beliefs and is willing to assume leadership responsibilities.[7] Although this new trend is slowly developing in the nursing profession, the individual nurse who works in the community is still subjected to and evaluated on the basis of the old traditional standards of conduct. If she is militant she may find herself making changes with little support from other nurses. All nurses experience stress, but hers is intensified for having dared to buck the system.

The socialization of women, specifically nurses, sets the stage for stress. Naturally one's susceptibility and responses to stress are the result of socialization and education. These processes are discussed elsewhere in this book; this chapter focuses on the individual, first by discussing three patterns of responding to stress—burnout, despair, and rage—and then by examining the intrapersonal and interpersonal dynamics that make the *individual* nurse either vulnerable or resistant to stress.

RESPONSES TO STRESS

Many nurses respond to stress by burning out, becoming depressed, or becoming rageful. These are not constructive responses, nor do they significantly reduce stress for the individual or the system in which she works.

Burnout

Burnout is a particular type of stress response that has increasingly been identified as a problem among nurses. Burnout is a stage of exhaustion caused by chronic stress that typically results from human service work.[12] The signs and symptoms of the burnout syndrome can be divided into four major categories: (1) stress-related symptoms, (2) emotional detachment, (3) dissatisfaction with work and a resultant decrease in job performance, and (4) diminishing self-esteem.†

---

*References 9, 21, 22, 26.
†References 12, 17, 24, 25.

Stress-related symptoms are usually the easiest to recognize and may be the first indicators of incipient burnout. These symptoms are related to the autonomic nervous system's "fight or flight" response and include increased muscular tension, increased anxiety, changed eating and sleeping patterns, headaches, and gastrointestinal problems, to name a few. Some individuals use alcohol or tranquilizers in an attempt to decrease these symptoms, thus creating an additional problem.

Initially the use of drugs or alcohol may give the nurse the impression that she is controlling her stress and performing well. This may in fact be the case as a result of the anxiolytic effect of these substances. Eventually, however, the nurse develops a tolerance to the particular substance and needs continually to increase the amount used to "survive the pressures of the job" as well as to avoid an uncomfortable abstinence syndrome. Furthermore, as she begins to use larger and larger amounts of pharmacological comforts, her general psychomotor capabilities deteriorate, placing the health and safety of her patients in jeopardy.

Emotional detachment occurs when the nurse reacts to overwhelming job demands by distancing herself and becoming less involved. This is a protective response, an attempt to deal with a situation in which she sees no successful way to cope. Her detachment can take many forms. She may objectify patients by referring to them as a disease, a room number, or some other derogatory label. She may retreat into paperwork, sickness, or absenteeism or may avoid co-workers, apathetically divorce herself from the job, and switch jobs to avoid hassles.

Dissatisfaction with work, if it continues long enough, results in decreased job performance. As the nurse feels more stressed and unable to cope with job demands, she begins to withdraw from her work and may be no longer able to function at a satisfactory level. She finds that it takes longer to do her job, is more forgetful or tends to procrastinate, begins to dislike the job, develops a negative attitude toward anything job related, and probably becomes disillusioned with nursing. She frequently makes errors and finds that her thinking is not as sharp as usual and that she cannot concentrate well. At this point supervisors may become critical of her poor job performance, adding further to the stress.

One third or more of a person's waking hours are spent at work. If a nurse is dissatisfied with her work and functioning poorly, eventually her *self-esteem suffers*. She begins to question her competence, becomes highly self-critical, and feels that she has nothing to offer anyone. She may feel worthless or stupid and become depressed. Low self-esteem is usually the most difficult symptom with which to cope and certainly is the most difficult to change. Once a person's self-esteem is damaged, the stress responses tend to carry over into other areas of her life.

Despair and rage

Aside from developing burnout, nurses who see themselves as victims in a high-stress environment respond with hopeless despair or seething rage against what they perceive as an unjust system.[3,4]

A sense of hopelessness develops from the nurse's perception that she is unable to influence the environment and is powerless to alter events, even those directly related to herself.[20] Most people who feel hopeless become resigned to the status quo, lifelessly going along with whatever happens—as if they are anesthetized. They begin to ignore their own inner strivings and needs because they believe that no matter how hard they fight, they can achieve nothing productive. In addition they believe they are truly doomed to their present existence *forever*. As one nurse I saw in therapy put it, "I'm just going through the motions. I feel like most of me isn't even here . . . maybe there isn't even any me anymore. I don't even hurt or get disappointed, I just don't feel anything now." What actually happens is not necessarily as important as the nurse's perception of it; reality is not as crucial as her *perception* of whether or not she can influence the course of events.

Other nurses become infuriated when they perceive problems and inequities in the health care system. These angry nurses frequently are labeled trouble-makers and considered difficult to work with because they act out their frustrations in a nonproductive manner. Unfortunately they themselves sometimes accept the notion that something is wrong with them because they are not able to adjust and accept the system as it is. In our society the failure to adjust is often seen as a sign of an emotional or mental problem in the individual rather than as a reflection of possible dysfunction within the system.

When a nurse does not fit into the stereotypical behavior pattern, she may receive recommendations to seek professional psychiatric help to deal with *her* problems in adjustment. As Maslow[16] has so aptly said, however, "personality problems sometimes are a loud protest against the crushing of one's psychological 'bones.'" The nurse's failure to adjust to the status quo may in fact be a healthy striving for personal expression and growth that has been misdirected into acting-out behavior that is self defeating.

· · ·

Becoming burned out, resigning oneself to hopeless despair, and lashing out in blind anger are responses that rarely accomplish anything; indeed, these behaviors leave the individual viewing herself as a helpless victim who has no personal control.[25] It is as if she has accepted the societal message that she is a low-status, dependent female who is incapable of adult problem solving or assertiveness. It becomes inevitable that her professional life is then destined to continue in a downward spiral.

Although socialization and stereotypical sexual expectations are influential, there is no direct causal relationship between these forces and the development of one's self-concept. Despite deprived, dysfunctional backgrounds some people are able to succeed and live relatively happy lives; others actually do their best when they are functioning in high-stress environments, seeming to flourish with adversity.[2,16,18]

An awareness of societal influences allows the nurse to make conscious choices, to gain control over her life, and to take active steps to correct dysfunctional influences. Furthermore, she can choose not to collude with the status quo. She needs to accept the past and begin to examine how she can avoid similar problems in the future. It is pointless for a woman (or nurse) to waste energy complaining about how things are when she has little control over others or society at large. Playing the "ain't it awful" game does little to give her a sense of control or power over factors that affect her work.

Many of the problems within nursing can be viewed from a systems orientation. Certainly many of the changes that will have the most impact on the profession will result from a broad-scale approach to professional problems. Other chapters here explore these systems issues and their developmental relationships to problems in nursing practice. This chapter focuses on the individual nurse, her ways of coping with the chaotic environment, her difficulties in achieving job satisfaction, and the threats to her professional survival.

Although the socialization of women and the education of nurses has had a pervasive negative influence on nursing practice, each individual nurse has a choice of how she will work; in fact, she has the ultimate responsibility for her own accomplishments and self-esteem. Furthermore, an individual cannot deal with systems issues unless she first strengthens her sense of self-worth and gives herself permission to assert her basic rights and beliefs.

VULNERABILITY TO STRESS

The remainder of this chapter examines some of the variables that contribute to the successful functioning of some nurses as well as some of the traps to which other nurses succumb. What is it that makes one nurse vulnerable to stress and another seem totally resistant?

Perception

"Man is not troubled by events but by the view he takes of them," Epictetus wrote.

Selye[23] has described stress as the "non-specific response of the body to any demand made upon it." One of the critical variables that determine which demands are stressful is the individual's perception or cognitive appraisal of the stressor. Stress is a unique, subjective experience—what is distressing to one individual may actually be energizing, a positive stimulus, for another person.[2] There are potential stressors all around, particularly in the demanding job of nursing, yet some nurses seem "stress resistant." Many of these individuals have specific sets of attitudes toward and perceptions about life that give them a sense of psychological hardiness.[18] These attitudes include an openness to change whereby change is viewed as a challenge rather than a threat, a sense of commitment to and involvement in what one is doing rather than a sense of alienation, and finally a sense of control over one's life stemming from the belief that her behavior has a positive impact on her environment. With these attitudes an individual can experience enormous stresses and suffer no ill effects; in fact, this individual usually flourishes and has a sense of well-being.[18]

The individual, then, has the choice of perceiving situations as distressing (with a resultant depletion in energy) or as challenging (with a resultant increase in energy and productivity).

Perceptions are based on a cognitive process that is learned from past experiences and thus are amenable to educational intervention. The nurse's knowledge and intelligence are resources for handling potentially stressful situations and can give her a sense of control over them.[2] It is interesting to note that in the Chinese language the symbol for *crisis* is a combination of the symbols for the words *danger* and *opportunity*. All stress-producing situations are potentially hazardous, and yet they also provide an opportunity for growth, mastery, and increased self-esteem.

Clearly, the sexual socialization that has conditioned women and nurses to perceive their accomplishments on the basis of pleasing others, to squelch personal motivations to meet the needs of others, and to evaluate themselves on the basis of male-dominated constructs of stereotypical behavior plays an essential role in influencing one's perceptions and ultimately one's behavior. A nurse's sense of interpersonal competence and her perception of herself are intimately related to the socialization process[9,14]—many nurses derive their self-worth from the approval of others. Therefore interpersonal interactions are potentially hazardous; they may become sources of further personal devaluation.

One means of dealing with stress, then, is for each nurse to become aware of and to question her perceptions of herself, of others, of her interactions, and of events. If she knows that her socialization and education may contribute to faulty perceptions, she is better able to appraise situations realistically and to respond appropriately.

Self-talk

Self-talk is intimately related to perception. The way we see ourselves comes out in the way we talk to ourselves. Unfortunately, this process develops into a vicious circle: the way we talk to ourselves about ourselves reinforces and solidifies our perceptions.

Frequently a nurse may think of herself as a helpless victim at the mercy of people and events. Much of her language reflects this irrational reasoning; for example, she may say, "Dr. Jones *makes me* feel so dumb" or "that patient is really *depressing me*" or "because I am a woman whenever I speak up they *make me* feel foolish." Just an issue of semantics? Perhaps. But these statements reflect a nurse's unfounded belief that events and people have more control over her life than she does herself. All of us engage in self-talk. If the self-talk reflects an accurate appraisal of the world around us, we tend to function well; if, however, our self-talk is irrational or based on misperceptions, we experience undue stress and uncomfortable emotions such as feelings of guilt, worthlessness, anxiety, and depression.

Albert Ellis[13] developed "rational emotive therapy" as a means of replacing irrational self-talk with more realistic statements about ourselves and our world. His basic theory is that the emotions we experience have very little to do with our life events but instead reflect our interpretations of these events as evidenced in the things we tell ourselves about them. Irrational self-talk, based on irrational or inaccurate perceptions and beliefs, produces an emotional response. Engaging in this behavior results in a physiological arousal experienced as muscle tension or anxiety.[19]

The two most common types of irrational self-talk are statements that "absolutize" or "awfulize."[13]

Absolutizing statements connote the idea that everything has to be a specific way and allow no deviations from the perfect standard. If a nurse fails to achieve some standard, regardless of whether it is reasonable, she believes herself to be a total failure. Many of the absolutizing standards in nursing are derived from unreasonable expectations learned through our professional education, the socialization process, and the mass media. Regardless of their source, the nurse who evaluates herself in terms of these absolute, perfectionistic standards can only find herself wanting.

The second type of irrational self-talk, awfulizing, expands temporary problems or discomforts into catastrophic events. Simply forgetting to give a medication on schedule becomes "probably killing the patient"; speaking up to a doctor whose judgment seems mistaken becomes "probably being fired." Naturally, once the nurse starts awfulizing situations, she becomes paralyzed and cannot take initiative or assert herself. After all, no one in her right mind would willingly risk murder over a mistake or ridicule over an expression of opinion.

Both awfulizing and absolutizing open the door to destructive self-criticism, self-beating. Once this has occurred, the nurse doesn't need anyone else to criticize her or keep her in her place—she does a good job of it herself.

Another problem resulting from negative self-talk is that it never allows the nurse to develop a reasonable self-appraisal of her professional functioning. She becomes susceptible to the criticisms of others, justified or not, and loses her ability for self-observation. This tendency is particularly destructive when the nurse is attempting to be an agent of change or to develop herself in ways that do not follow traditional stereotypical behaviors. Whenever an individual makes waves, she needs strong self-esteem as a basis from which to work. If she is continually tearing down her self-confidence, then the criticisms, and even the questions of others render her defenseless.

Certainly it is unfortunate that nurses have been socialized to distrust their own intellectual abilities, have been viewed as at their best when they are passively acquiescing to the dictates of males, and have been taught to give generously in needless sacrifices. The task of each nurse is to understand and accept her own introjection of these values and ideals before she can develop realistic expectations against which to measure herself. Simply learning assertive skills or taking leadership workshops will not produce the desired change; she must first change her self-talk such that she tells herself she has a *right* to be assertive. She must give herself permisssion to grow and to speak up. If nurses cannot alter their perceptions and self-talk, they will not need outsiders to keep nursing "in its place"—they will do it themselves.

Expectations

Unrealistic expectations of others and ourselves create a climate in which stress in inevitable. There is nothing wrong with the fundamental values and standards presented in nursing education as long as they are viewed as goals toward which we should strive. Their menace arises when nurses measure themselves against such standards on a daily basis and find themselves lacking, especially since many of these ideals may not be feasible in the realities of individual work environments.[15] Nurses cling to unrealistic ideals; an individual who does not trust her own perception cannot abandon the security of dogma no matter how unrealistic it is. The clash of these ideals with job expectations leads to a sense of frustration and failure because both cannot be accomplished. Rather than questioning the standards, rather than questioning the system, the nurse most often questions her own competence.

One of my students described it this way: "The good nurse is all things to all people at all times! The good nurse is expected to know everything, to make no mistakes, and certainly to be self-sacrificing without any personal negative reactions or feelings toward her patients." There is no way to succeed with these kinds of expectations; failure is inevitable.

The problem, however, lies not as much in failing to reach the goals as in the significance nurses attach to the failure and the degree of their disillusionment. The level of disappointment when we fail to meet our expectations is related to the level of our expectations: the higher a nurse's expectations, the greater her potential disappointment and sense of failure.

Many people, nurses included, need to be in control. They become frustrated when they are not, and stress increases. Frequently a nurse allows things and people beyond her control to cause her great stress. Many of these things are givens, people and problems beyond her sphere of influence. They may simply be facts of life, or they may be nursing situations that for the moment (or forever?) cannot be altered—lack of staff, the number of admissions to one's unit, or the attitudes of another person. A nurse who constantly pits herself against the givens experiences powerlessness. She allows events beyond her control to influence her happiness and mental well-being. Perhaps the healthiest realization a nurse can have is that the only person she can control is herself.

Nurses who are satisfied with their jobs tend to have personalized, realistic goals and the ability to separate their sense of self-worth from the outcome of events beyond their control. This means, for example, that a patient's death is not experienced as a personal failure. The nurse develops an objectivity that allows her to reasonably assess her own responsibility for events and the responsibility of others.

Assertiveness

Assertiveness is the process by which each person develops her/his identity; a child, for example, asserts its independence from the mother and becomes a separate individual. The processes of assertion and individuation continue throughout life. Being able to assert oneself is a necessary ingredient to becoming self-actualized and to developing and maintaining self-esteem.[5] Basic human instincts or needs cannot be suppressed; only their expression can be withheld or altered. Assertiveness is essential for meeting one's needs. A nurse who denies her own needs denies and becomes alienated from herself. She disowns herself. Often women (and men) find their needs at odds with societal stereotypes and sex-role expectations. Conflicts occur. Assertiveness becomes threatening. Individuation falters. It is paradoxical: assertiveness encourages identity-formation, and identity-formation encourages greater assertiveness. This process gives us power over ourselves and our destinies.

Orientation to power

The issue of power is discussed in other chapters and thus is mentioned only briefly here as it contributes to stress. Most nurses have yet to discover their ability to handle power; they are reluctant to take control. Often low-status people are forced to demand their rights loudly and to wrest power from others.[3,7] Nurses find this abhorrent because as women they have been all too aware of the masculine abuses of power. Power implies control. Traditionally this has meant male domination and masculine control of women. But power can also mean the ability to control oneself—a feminist definition. For this kind of power the nurse needs to take the initiative rather than waiting to be asked to share the power with physicians and hospital administrators. Nurses are a silent majority who have traditionally had little voice, no vote, and minimal control over issues that affect their situations. Good intentions do not produce changes, for doctors and administrators are not easily motivated to relinquish their domination. Accepting power as individuals and as a group is the sole way to change the status quo of nursing.

Women who are successful in using power behave differently from others; they expect to be treated as equals. They risk speaking up, knowing their positions may not be shared. They do not wait silently, hoping to be asked to participate. They support their opinions with facts.

To remain silent is to collude with those whose power is oppressive; it is to support the status quo. By remaining passive a nurse misses the opportunity to increase her self-esteem and accomplish her goals. This passivity perpetuates the vicious cycle that produces a sense of helplessness and hopelessness about the nurse's own practice and the nursing profession as a whole.

Contagion

Contagion is the spreading of a disease, idea, or feeling from a contaminated person to a receptive new host.[12] Disgruntlement and negative attitudes spread easily and obscure reality. As the disease advances, objectivity is lost. Often a nurse who works in a unit where pessimism prevails finds herself accepting the consensus that there is no hope for change, that assertiveness won't work.

Contagion occurs when griping and other nonproductive coping strategies are used. A new person in such a situation often joins the crowd rather than risk being ostracized.

Fighting contagion, like anything else, requires recognizing its existence and its effects. The next step is to observe its operation in the environment. Talking out a problem is different from continual griping. The former leads to problem-solving behaviors; the latter leads nowhere. Simply pointing out the contagion process is sometimes enough to break its hold; sometimes, as a last resort, a nurse might decide to avoid a colleague whose attitude is always negative. (Who needs the energy drain?)

• • •

Our attitudes, beliefs, and values, the products of socialization and education, are clearly related to what we perceive as stress. Stress is inherent in nursing. We have little ability to control many potential stressors in the environment, but we *do* have control over our perceptions of these stressors and our responses to them. The choice is ours to see them as challenges to be mastered or as threats to our self-esteem.

REFERENCES

1. Adams, M.: The compassion trap. In Gornick, V., and Moran, B.K., editors: Women in sexist society: studies in power and powerlessness, New York, 1971, Basic Books, Inc.
2. Antonovsky, A.: Health, stress and coping, San Francisco, 1979, Jossey-Bass, Inc., Publishers.
3. Brooten, D.A., and others: Leadership for change: a guide for the frustrated nurse, New York, 1978, J.B. Lippincott Co.
4. Bush, M.A., and Kjervik, D.K.: The nurse's self-image. In Kjervik, D.K., and Martinson, I.M.: Woman in stress: a nursing perspective, New York, 1979, Appleton-Century-Crofts.
5. Butler, P.E.: Self-assertion for women: a guide to becoming androgynous, New York, 1976, Harper & Row, Publishers, Inc.
6. Chevy, L.: On the real benefits of eustress: an interview with Hans Selye, Psychology Today, p. 60, March 1978.
7. Clark, C.C.: Assertive skills for nurses, Wakefield, Mass., 1978, Contemporary Publishing Co.
8. Claus, K.E., and Bailey, J.T., editors: Living with stress and promoting well-being: a handbook for nurses, St. Louis, 1980, The C.V. Mosby Co.
9. Cohan, M.B.: Personal identity and sexual identity. In Miller, J.B., editor: Psychoanalysis and women, New York, 1973, Penguin Books.
10. Corea, G.: The hidden malpractice: how American medicine treats women as patients and professionals, New York, 1977, William Morrow & Co., Inc.

11. Dean, P.G.: Toward androgeny: victim psychology and the socialization of women, Image **10**(1):10, 1978.
12. Edelwich, J., and Brodsky, A.: Burn-out: stages of disillusionment in the helping profession, New York, 1980, Human Sciences Press, Inc.
13. Ellis, A.: A new guide to rational living: North Hollywood, Calif., 1975, Wilshire Books.
14. Henley, N., and Freeman, J.: The sexual politics of interpersonal behavior. In Freeman, J., editor: Woman: a feminist perspective, Palo Alto, Calif., 1978, Mayfield Publishing Co.
15. Kramer, M.: Reality shock: why nurses leave nursing, St. Louis, 1974, The C.V. Mosby Co.
16. Maslow, A.: Toward a psychology of being, New York, 1968, D. Van Nostrand Co.
17. Pines, A., and Aronson, E.: Burnout: from tedium to personal growth, New York, 1981, The Free Press.
18. Pines, M.: Psychological hardiness: the role of challenge in health, Psychology Today p. 34, December 1980.
19. Rimm, D.C., and Litvak, S.B.: Self-verbalization and emotional arousal, Journal of Abnormal Psychology **74**:181, 1969.
20. Roberts, S.L.: Behavioral concepts and nursing throughout the life span, New Jersey, 1978, Prentice-Hall, Inc.
21. Seidenberg, R.: Is anatomy destiny. In Miller, J.B., editor: Psychoanalysis and woman, New York, 1973, Penguin Books.
22. Seidenberg, R.: The trauma of eventlessness. In Miller, J.B., editor: Psychoanalysis and woman, New York, 1973, Penguin Books.
23. Selye, H.: Stress without distress, New York, 1975, Signet.
24. Shubin, S.: Burnout: the professional hazard you face in nursing, Nursing 78 **8**(7):22, 1978.
25. Storlie, F.J.: Burnout: the elaboration of a concept, American Journal of Nursing p. 2108-2110, December 1979.
26. Weitzman, L.: Sex-role socialization. In Freeman, J.: Women: a feminist perspective, Palo Alto, Calif., 1978, Mayfield Publishing Co.

Photo by Gary Botkin; courtesy American Red Cross, Washington, D.C.

UNIT FIVE

OUT FROM UNDER

Nurses are affected both by their female socialization and by the social, political, and psychological issues inherent in nursing and the health care system. These difficulties and some solutions have been set forth in the first four units. This final unit offers suggestions for change and presents alternative roles. It is meant not to be exhaustive but as a beginning.

In the first chapter Shiela Byrne describes nurses' defenses against self-awareness: denial, projection, playing stupid, unrealistic expectations, inappropriate expressions of anger, and disassociation from peers. She suggests that the only way for nurses to alter their situation is to be aware of themselves and to *accept* themselves for what they are. Only then can they have the power to be something else, to change themselves and their situations.

Power, says Judy Farash McCurdy, *is* a nursing issue. She describes power as the ability to get things done and refutes the notion that power is limited to finite quantities. Power is gained through doing extraordinary tasks, being visible, having relevance to organizational goals, and forming alliances. Power brings greater power, and powerlessness generates powerlessness Relating to others and behaving as a powerful, competent person and sharing power with others increase each nurse's personal power.

Elizabeth Morrison examines power as it appears in nonverbal contexts. She differentiates patriarchal power (power over others) from feminist power (power over oneself). By examining kinesics (how we move our bodies) and proxemics (how we place them in relation to others), nurses can begin to understand the nonverbal messages they send about their own power or lack of it. It may not be possible for each nurse to be openly assertive; she can, however, learn to use her body in ways that enhance rather than undermine her image as a competent professional.

Doctors and nurses *can* develop collegial relationships. Janet Muff explores the development of joint practice committees and practice settings. Specific guidelines are given for establishing and maintaining a working relationship between nurses and physicians, including such diverse elements as consciousness-raising groups, the selection of committee members, and the need for primary nursing.

349

In their chapter, "Brainstorming for Job Satisfaction," Sharon Aga and Janet Muff outline a multitude of approaches to the problems of job dissatisfaction and attrition among nurses. Child-care facilities, clinical levels of practice, flexible shifts, monetary inducements, and benefit packages are all discussed.

Shermalayne Szasz asks some thought-provoking questions in her chapter about nursng uniforms. She describes their historical beginnings and the part they have come to play in nursing myths and stereotypes. Nurses have been taught that their "professionalism" is dependent on a white uniform, yet other professionals do not wear uniforms. Could this be yet another way to keep nurses in their place? What message do uniforms convey? What image? Is this the image each of us as nurses wants to communicate?

The final chapters in this section deal with various issues and models of independent practice including positions involving sales, partnerships with physicians, consultation, education, and professional services. These are the stories of individual nurses who share their experiences partly as a source of information but also as a source of encouragement, hope, and creativity. They are saying, "This is how we did it. You may choose to do it differently. The point is that there are tremendous opportunities for nurses in nontraditional roles!"

SHEILA BYRNE

Chapter 26

Accepting the "red"

Women are socialized into dependent and submissive roles from infancy on. Even before they are old enough to have any awareness of a sexual identity, the sex-role socialization has begun. Little boys learn to be active and aggressive whereas little girls learn to be passive and dependent. This behavior develops with both the conscious and unconscious encouragement of parents.[26]

Goldberg and Lewis[11] found that 13-month-old girls cling to, look at, and talk to their mothers more often than little boys; they linked these behaviors to the different ways the infants' mothers treat them.

From children's books little girls learn they receive attention for being pretty and for becoming like mother. They learn their social status and prestige comes by way of a relationship with a special man. Their reading does not mention that intellectual pursuits or life outside of marriage brings fulfillment. They learn that for them, future success comes from being glamorous and congenial and from giving service.[27]

Little girls learn to think of themselves as passive and supportive participants in the scheme of life. They are the "dutiful wife" when they play house or the helpless damsel in distress rescued by the aggressive and powerful prince. Never are they a strong figure around whom others rally. Consequently, little girls rarely see themselves out in front with someone backing them up. Rather they perceive themselves as hitching their wagon to someone else's star and gaining status through that association.

In adolescence boys are expected and encouraged to seek activities outside the home whereas girls are more carefully watched and protected by special rules that apply only to them. While boys are encouraged to separate from their parents in preparation for autonomous and responsible adult behavior, girls are encouraged to maintain a dependent relationship with their parents and families and to transfer that relationship to their husbands and children.[8,16]

In early adulthood when both men and women are encouraged to get a good education, society expects men to select a career and work hard in achieving that goal. Women, however, receive the implicit or explicit message that an education for them is merely a form of intellectual preparation for meeting a good husband and for later use for added family income.[8,13] Little if any time is spent supporting and encouraging women in the selection of a career they will continue to practice through their lifetime. Consequently, few women actively plan their careers beyond the confines of home and family. Their career aspirations are low and most often involve temporary jobs and little or no thought for career planning. Women tend to believe employment is optional and expect that someone else will earn the income.[8,13]

Horner,[12] who tested men and women from 1964 to 1971, demonstrated that both sexes behaved in ways consistent with the dominant cultural stereotypes; that is, intellectual achievement, competition, independence, competence, and leadership were congruent with the mental health of men but were basically inconsistent and in conflict with that of women.[12]

An aspect of the core female personality in our culture, then, is dependency. Women learn to be compliant, lovable, and self-effacing. They learn that survival and acceptance means limiting their life space and repressing their own healthy desires for growth and self-expression.[12,22,24]

How then does this dependency of women fit their choice of nursing as a career? In its earlist beginnings in religous orders, nursing established a model for all-giving, self-sacrificing, and self-effacing behaviors. Those who nursed repressed all thoughts of self; their focus was totally on giving service to the patient and unquestioningly complying with the physician's orders. The heritage of nurses who "gave their all," who mirrored the Florence Nightingale image of the "Lady with the Lamp," further demonstrates this all-sacrificing, selfless ethic.

Through the early years of nursing's educational history, the rites of passage into nursing were fraught with rigid and fixed rules.[5] The aspiring nurse was required to live in the hospital dormitory, had her limited hours of free time controlled by her superiors, and when not in classes had to work long hours at the hospital's convenience to gain the "required experience." The nurse's personal life was further controlled by the dictate that marriage was forbidden and would lead to immediate expulsion. Still today, many older nurses compare their training experiences with those of more recent graduates, whom they find lacking for not having *worked* or *suffered* enough to be worthy of the title "nurse."

The image of the all-serving, dependent nurse has been further perpetuated by the expectation that nursing functions are determined by the orders of physicians who have total control over patient care. The role of the nurse is seen merely as that of a handmaiden. Although nurses no longer relinquish their chairs or stand when a physician enters the room, many more subtle forms of subservient, dependent behavior continue to be expected.[25] When we examine the image of nursing in conjunction with the socialization of women to be passive and dependent, it does not take a great deal of imagination to understand why women choose nursing as their work.

Nursing provides many of the features attractive to the dependent woman. It most certainly is a socially sanctioned occupation. The nurse can be completely directed by others, can receive her gratification from serving others, and can rely on the physician as the dominant member of the team when a decision is required. In this fashion the nurse is able to maintain a low, dependent profile that demands little more of her than that she follow orders.

Many nurses see their work as a temporary occupation until a husband comes along. They also view it as something they can always fall back on if their families' financial needs increase. Consequently nursing is infrequently chosen as a *career*. It is not selected as a profession in which one can excel and gain the prestige and recognition of peers over a lifetime.

In recent years the women's liberation movement has created unrest and questioning among women who have been given permission to be who they are and to explore their feelings and wishes. With this movement has come similar unrest and questioning in the ranks of nursing. Many nurses are searching for a new identity as women and professionals; many are attempting to work with their dependent characteristics and move toward becoming more independent.

As nurses seek autonomy in their profession and take on more responsibility, they begin to experience some of the anxieties and doubts of increased accountability. In the past their dependent behaviors protected them from these anxieties: they could always call the doctor. Men grow up with these same anxieties about facing the world and working successfully at their careers, but they have been socialized from an early age to anticipate them and work through them. Women are just beginning to address these issues.[8,13]

As I see it, nurses are experiencing a form of adolescence. Their desire for individuation and autonomy is fraught with ambivalence and anxiety over separation, and it precipitates a regression to familiar forms of behavior. Although many nurses are now experiencing the drive to become responsible and independent professionals, they are also experiencing the pull of old injunctions and expectations from their early socialization. These dicta admonish them to remain in socially established and acceptable roles. A struggle ensues.

When working with nurse support groups, my goal has been for participants to begin to *recognize* and *own* their feelings, to derive support from their peers, and to move toward more responsible and autonomous functioning. In these groups I have noted a number of behaviors derived from feelings of dependency: the denial of these feelings, the use of projection, "playing stupid," unrealistic self-expectations, inappropriate expressions of anger, and the rejection of one's peer group. These behaviors limit nurses' personal and professional growth. In no way do I suggest that this list is all inclusive, but it does include those behaviors I have found most prevalent. In the following sections I discuss their origins and manifestations and propose some alternatives.

DENIAL OF FEELINGS OF DEPENDENCE

Based on the premise that nursing is a profession appropriate for the dependent individual, it seems safe to assume that all nurses fall at some point on a continuum of dependency. This need for dependency is stronger for some than for others, but it is common for many nurses to deny such feelings, just as the adolescent does. Although they may function in a manner that appears autonomous, in many situations their independence is a facade. When the pressures increase beyond their capacity to cope, the mask crumbles. The inability to accept their dependency prevents them from seeking assistance (or even recognizing their need for it) and inhibits the development of adaptive strategies. That which they have used for protection—denial—becomes their downfall.

PROJECTION

Projection is most commonly used as a defense mechanism by nurses who want to maintain their dependent stance. They find the thought of independent action too threatening to consider but yet are unable to admit this fact to themselves (denial again). They fear failure in taking risks with new behaviors and fear the rejection of those whom they depend on and whose approval they seek.[17,19] They protect this fragile area of their ego by blaming others for their circumstances; they become victims. They bemoan their situation with a pathetic helplessness or a righteous anger over what others have done or are doing *to* them. When others come to them with offers of assistance and suggestions, they respond, "Yes, but . . ." and give various reasons why the offers and suggestions will not work. In this fashion nurses abdicate all responsibility for their dependent position or for doing anything to change their situation. They are therefore able to maintain their dependent stance without owning the feelings of dependency.[3,28]

Common examples of the use of this form of projection involve blaming "them." "They do this" and "they do that." Often "they" are never identified. "Physicians," "the administration," and "the system" are also frequent culprits blamed for keeping nurses in such "one-down" and helpless positions. Society is also frequently blamed as the persecutor. If it weren't for what their parents told them or for society's treatment of women, things would be different. "Ain't it awful" and "If it weren't for you" are frequent games used by victims.[4] They identify these situations as causes of their plight, yet they clutch at them with threatened egos. Projection becomes an armor against accepting their own feelings of dependency and taking responsibility for their own actions.

PLAYING STUPID

Dependency is closely associated with low self-esteem, which leads to a fear of failure, a fear of success, and a fear of rejection, all of which inhibit risk-taking behaviors. [13,17,19] If, for example, nurses feel that they are intellectually inferior to others, as many do, they create a no-win situation for themselves. When confronted with problems that challenge them intellectually, they automatically assume that they will be unable to solve them. Before making active attempts at a solution they give up and call the supervisor or the doctor.

The pay-offs for this behavior are that potential failure or rejection by those seen as important is avoided and the anxiety created by these fears is kept at a tolerable level. Any movement, toward independent action, however, is thwarted, and the dependent mode of behavior is maintained. This regressive action reinforces nurses' beliefs that they are indeed intellectually inferior to others, and the same ritual is repeated when they encounter the next problem.

Another aspect of playing stupid is the nurse's reluctance to question physicians' clinical decisions or to offer information from their own knowledge base that could benefit the client. Nurses purposely keep their knowledge to themselves to avoid aggression or rejection from physicians on whom they depend. The increased visibility resulting from their expression of knowledge could lead to the health care team having greater expectations of them. To many nurses the prospect of becoming more accountable and responsible is still too threatening. They prefer to maintain a dependent position by keeping a low profile and playing stupid.

UNREALISTIC SELF-EXPECTATIONS

Nurses frequently fail to meet their own expectations. This behavior has its roots in the dependent personality with low self-esteem. In an effort to compensate for and defend against their feelings of inadequacy, nurses often create expectations beyond their reach. [19] With this inability to set reasonable goals comes an inability to judge their own performance realistically and to set limits on their own expectations or the expectations others have of them. [2,7]

When they do not achieve their goals, they feel they have failed and that they are lacking. It does not occur to them that the task may have been unattainable. Nurses who set unrealistic expectations for themselves or accept those of others most often feel incompetent, guilty, and a failure. Even when they are able to prioritize and complete *some* tasks, they feel little sense of accomplishment and belittle themselves for not having completed them *all.* [7] Here again, nurses reinforce their own feelings of dependency and low self-esteem.

INAPPROPRIATE EXPRESSIONS OF ANGER

In attempting to develop independent behaviors, nurses often confront situations of discrimination against them as women and as nurses. Because they have been socialized to repress feelings of direct hostility, they often react from a position of dependence, much as a child rages, or they react in a passive-aggressive manner and are left confused by the responses they evoke in others.[14,15,24] The expression of direct aggression is difficult for most individuals to cope with but is especially difficult for women who are just learning to deal with it. Men have been learning to handle anger since they were children.

Aggression that continues to be repressed can lead to feelings of helplessness, victimization, and depression.[24] It is difficult for nurses who are struggling with their dependency to express hostility directly toward those whom they perceive as more powerful than themselves or on whom they depend. Again, they fear retaliation, rejection, and being left on their own. This is an extremely threatening prospect.[24]

DISSOCIATION FROM PEERS

As nurses begin to develop new modes of independent behavior, many frequently dissociate themselves from their peer group.[9] This ego defense mechanism is often found in members of groups that are discriminated against.[1] Nurses who are attempting to exercise more autonomy and independence and to whom others repeatedly respond in a manner indicative of the stereotype of *all nurses* begin to experience feelings of hatred toward their own kind. They begin to view all other nurses as *responsible* for creating their struggle and impeding their progress.[6]

In their efforts toward individuation these nurses often dissociate themselves from other nurses and begin to respond to them as a stereotypical collective rather than as individuals. They ridicule and demean them for their lack of and fear of independence. These attitudes arise, however, because of their attempt to deny their own dependence. They are in reality disowning themselves and engaging in a form of self-hate.[21,33]

CONCLUSION

Central to each of these behavior is some form of denial: of dependency, of ability, of hostility, of *self*. Central too are mechanisms that reinforce nurses' abdication of responsibility for their thoughts, feelings, or self and that maintain their dependent one-down position.

How, then, can we as nurses work with these feelings and dependent responses so that we can grow in new directions? As long as we continue to disown ourselves by blaming others for our victimization, we will continue to be victims. To what end do we lament and painstakingly document the early socialization of women and the subservient model established by nursing pioneers? Is not this behavior in itself yet another way in which we point the finger of blame and further abdicate responsibility? Nurses, we are of age and Florence Nightingale is dead! Isn't it time for each of us to point to herself and ask, "Now, what am *I* going to do about it?"

We can continue to deny ourselves, but the reality does not change—we *are!* I am reminded of the parlor game in which players are instructed not to think of the color red. As long as they consciously try to avoid the image, the red glares on. At the moment when they accept the red, however, and dwell on the color, they can let it go and move forward. Denial requires energy that could more profitably be spent elsewhere; acceptance is the key to letting go and moving on.

I am not suggesting that the past is unimportant or that changing our dependent feelings and behaviors is an easy task. Simply knowing the reason for these and achieving an insight into them does not assure change. Altering well-established, socially reinforced behaviors is difficult and provokes a good deal of anxiety. Familiar patterns of behavior, after all, were established for a reason, but becoming aware of that reason can be a step in changing the patterns. This endeavor requires motivation, a conscious choice, and action; it requires taking responsibility for how we think, feel, and act. If we are to take responsibility for ourselves, we must first accept our dependency needs. This does not mean surrendering to a lifetime of being one-down and passive. On the contrary, it means accepting who we are. It is the very act of self-ownership that moves us from a position of impotence to a position of strength. [18,20]

If we admit our dependency and accept it as a part of ourselves, then we can begin to examine how it is adaptive and how it is maladaptive. We can develop an awareness of those key situations in which we are vulnerable to regression, in which we sabotage our own efforts toward success and growth.

The routes to self-awareness and self-acceptance are many: consciousness-raising groups, yoga, assertiveness training, psychotherapy, and meditation are but a few that have been found useful. The route itself is unimportant. As Mahatma Gandhi said, "We all take different roads up the mountain, but when we get to the top, the same sun shines on all of us." What is important is that each of us becomes aware of those feelings that color our behavior.

Becoming aware of ourselves allows us, then, to make conscious choices about our lives. Once we begin to do this, we are no longer "victims." [4,18,20] Even though certain situations evoke great anxiety, we will be able to decide on plans of action. Should we decide at times not to act, that decision too is conscious and is based on our recognition of ourselves rather than on what we think others *make* us do or do *to* us. When we are able to make such conscious decisions, we will no longer need to blame others for our circumstances. We will recognize that we are where we are because we choose to be there. [10]

We will engage in self-dialogue in determining realistic expectations, and our actions in each situation will be spontaneous and come from the integration of our feelings and thoughts of the moment. Feelings of anger will be more easily expressed, and it will no longer be necessary to reject our own kind. Developing self-awareness will lead us to a clearer sense of identity, and we will recognize that this identity cannot be altered by the actions or responses of others.

Nurses, we are indeed in our adolescence. Fraught with the anxieties and stresses of becoming more independent, more visible, and ultimately more responsible and accountable, we often retreat to former modes of dependent behavior. This is not a problem if we are *aware* that this is what we are doing and if we have made a *conscious choice* to act thus. It is when we act without this consciousness that we have lost our*selves* and old patterns will prevail. It is through the development of self-awareness and conscious choice that we will finally begin to move out from under.

REFERENCES

1. Allport, G.: The nature of prejudice, Garden City, N.Y., 1958, Doubleday & Co., Inc.
2. Bandwich, J.: Psychology of women, New York, 1971, Harper & Row, Publishers, Inc.
3. Berger, M.M., and Rosenbaum, M.: Notes on self-rejecting complainers. In Rosenbaum, M., and Berger, M.M.: Group psychotherapy and group function, New York, 1975, Basic Books, Inc.
4. Berne, E.: Games people play, New York, 1964, Grove Press, Inc.
5. Cohen, H.: Authoritarianism and dependency. In Flynn, B., and Miller, M.: Current perspectives in nursing, St. Louis, 1980, The C.V. Mosby Co.
6. Daddio, S.: Oh! the obstacle to women in management. In Jongeward, D., and Scott, D.: Affirmative action for women: a practical guide for women and management, Reading, Mass., 1975, Addison-Wesley Publishing Co., Inc.
7. Edelwich, J.: Burn-out: stages of disillusionment in the helping professions, New York, 1980, Human Sciences Press, Inc.
8. Epstein, C.: Woman's place, Berkeley, 1971, University of California Press.
9. Fromm, L.: The problem in nursing: nurses! Supervisor Nurse 8(10):15, 1977.
10. Glasser, W.: Reality therapy, New York, 1975, Colophon Books.
11. Goldberg, S., and Lewis, M.: Play behavior in the year-old infant: early sex differences, Child Development 40(1):21, 1969.
12. Horner, M.: Toward an understanding of achievement-related conflicts in women, Journal of Social Issues 28(2):226, 1972.
13. Horner, M., and Walsh, M.: Psychological barriers to success in women. In Kundsin, R.: Women and success, New York, 1974, William Morrow & Co., Inc.
14. King, P.: A strategy for change. In Jongeward, D., and Scott, D.: Affirmative action for wom-en: a practical guide for women and management, Reading, Mass., 1975, Addison-Wesley Publishing Co., Inc.
15. Koltz, C.J.: Private practice in nursing, Greentown, Md., 1979, Aspen Systems Corp.
16. Low, I.: Family attitudes and relationships: a summary. In Kundsin, R.: Women and success, New York, 1974, William Morrow & Co., Inc.
17. Mauksch, I.: Paradox of risk-takers, AORN Journal 25(7):1312, 1977.
18. May, R.: Man's search for himself, New York, 1967, W.W. Norton & Co., Inc.
19. Mishel, M.: Patient problems in self-esteem and nursing intervention, Los Angeles, 1974, B and P, The Trident Shop.
20. Resnick, R.: Chicken soup is poison, Voices 6(2):75, 1970.
21. Seidenberg, R.: For the future-equity? In Miller, J.: Psychoanalysis and women, New York, 1977, Penguin Books.
22. Seidenberg, R.: Is anatomy destiny? In Miller, J.: Psychoanalysis and women, New York, 1977, Penguin Books.
23. Stone, H., and Winkelman, S.: Voice dialogue: a tool for transformation, The Journey (Sherman Oaks, Calif., Delos, Inc.) 13:1, 1978.
24. Symonds, A.: Neurotic dependency in successful women, American Academy of Psychoanalysis 4(1):95, 1976.
25. Varga: The nurse-doctor relationship, Nursing Times 70:44, January 10, 1974.
26. Weitzman, L.: sex-role socialization. In Freemen, J.: Women: a feminist perspective, Palo Alto, Calif., 1975, Mayfield Publishing Co.
27. Weitzman, L., and others: Sex-role socialization in picture books for preschool children, American Journal of Sociology 77:1125, 1972.
28. Yalom, I.D.: Theory and practice of group psychotherapy, New York, 1975, Basic Books, Inc.

JUDITH FARASH McCURDY

Chapter 27

Power *is* a nursing issue

Power is alternately worshipped, feared, longed for, and mistrusted as well as eternally misunderstood. We learn about power and its acquisition, management, and dispersal through our first experiences with a system of power: The family. Through interations with parents, who for purposes here represent management, we gain a sense of our relationship with power. Children's roles are similar to those of subordinate employees. The parent's power relationship to the child may be benevolent, dependent, democratic, dictatorial, tyrannical, or perhaps even submissive (as in parental role reversal). Furthermore, this relationship may be contradictory and confusing if it is alternately benevolent and dictatorial.

Each relationship or combination of relationships involves emotional attachments and teaches children who makes decisions and how they are made. The methods and maneuvers of power acquisition are demonstrated in parental interactions and are emulated by children; our feelings toward those in power are formulated at this time. Thus we develop concepts not only about subordinates but about power holders. Both positions may be experienced as both positive and negative.

From these first experiences with power we gain a sense of our ability or lack of ability to influence the world around us. We learn that power can be used as a tool or as a weapon in relationships with others. These lessons are translated into other interpersonal activities such as communication, leadership, management, and collaboration—all vital activities for effective adult living. A positive or negative familial power experience affects one's ability to deal with power systems in adulthood. Thus an understanding of one's personal relationship with power is the cornerstone for effective management and use of power in personal and work environments.

POWER AND THE HOSPITAL "FAMILY"

Having both an understanding of the family power system and an ability to analyze and view it objectively is especially relevant to developing similar skills in a hospital power system. Hospital employees assume various roles within the immediate and extended hospital "family." In fact, most organizations are run like

359

families and share similar characteristics. It is important to be aware of one's own response to power figures and of how past relationships have influenced one's present behavior and style of leadership.

The hospital is for many a symbolic representation of the family; traditionally, the mother, father, and sibling roles are reenacted by various types of employees. Just as power is covertly and overtly expressed between mother and father in the home, so too is power expressed between the stereotypical male and female roles of the hospital administrator or medical director and the nursing director. The contrasting modes of power acquisition and usage can be often observed. The male figure often uses direct methods such as issuing orders or commands, assigning tasks, and being intolerant of questions or assaults on his position. These "masculine" behaviors are described as confidence, assertion, and a sense of direction. The female in contrast more often uses indirect or covert ploys such as suggesting and questioning rather than declaring to avoid projecting ideas as her own. Intense, direct verbalizations are viewed as aggressive, hysterical attacks. Males who perceive a threat to their power generally restore it through an attack on the *personhood* of the woman rather than the idea or product she presents.

By using the family as a basic model for the development of our personal relationships with power we gain a greater understanding of our use of power as nurses. Power is defined here as the ability to get things done, to mobilize resources, to get and use whatever is needed to meet one's goals.[2] Power may entail the use of internal or external resources; power is not a finite quality.

The family is the educational center for teaching females submission as opposed to dominance. Few little girls gain a sense of power or competence through their achievements or accomplishments. Power is more likely associated with passive qualities such as being "good," "pretty," "smart," or "nice"; competition and achievement are usually considered aggressive and unfeminine. Women develop a sense that their survival comes from being associated *with* a power figure rather than from acquiring power in their own right. The power figure's approval is viewed as a necessity for survival, and thus submissive behavior is reinforced.

For most women power is associated with personhood because they were socialized to think it is primarily acquired from personal attributes rather than accomplishments. Thus when a woman's ideas, actions, and products are not accepted, she views this as a personal rejection and defeat. Her self-confidence and self-esteem are undermined, and she often resorts to previous modes of enhancing power, much as she did as a little girl. She is ill prepared to compete at the organizational level.

Because power is often considered dependent on one's personal or physical attributes rather than skill or competence, women are competitive with each other. Power is viewed as a sum-zero commodity: If one woman has it, another seems to lose it. This attitude results in a sense of vulnerability and anxiety because loss of power seems inevitable. Power is not viewed as a universally available resource that all may tap and share. Since women seldom feel they inherently possess power, they rely on others for its acquisition. Women sense that power manages them rather than that they may use and benefit from it.

Female nurses enter the power system of the hospital with sex-role socialization handicaps. They relate to power differently from men, a fact that explains many maneuvers within the hospital nursing subsystem. Because of their mental set regarding power, female nurses often sabotage nursing as a group to feel adequate as individuals; some degree of power, in the sense of mastery and control over one's fate, is necessary for feelings of self-esteem and well-being.[1] When the nurse's exercise of power is thwarted or blocked, when she is rendered powerless in the larger arena, she tends to exert power over her subordinates. Thus a pecking order is established within the nursing group as a power hierarchy in which nurses have some control.

The larger hospital system rarely rewards those who exercise individual power. Caught up in the ambiguity of conflicting relationships often existing between the hospital administrative and medical systems, the compliant, submissive nurse is usually the one who reaps the rewards of praise and approval; the assertive, overt, direct, communicative nurse does not. This is again reminiscent of familial patterns—no wonder many nurses feel trapped in a hopeless downward spiral of powerlessness and vulnerability. Understandably such a nurse may turn on herself or her peer group with displaced feelings of anger. Often the individuals who achieve power in the nursing hierarchy are those who are most restrictive, coercive, and covetous of their positions. Surely nursing has demonstrated its inability to solidify as a cohesive working group. Both the powerless and the powerful react against their own colleagues. Because they have risen through a nursing system wherein power may have been acquired through covert and often subversive styles, nurses feel precarious and insecure holding power positions. They "identify with the aggressor" by adopting the style of male leaders as one means of securing their positions. Unfortunately, few nurses in these power roles are models of positive behaviors or facilitate the development of new styles in their subordinates.

Being in touch with one's own power and competence can be frightening. One anticipates attcks froms a variety of fronts that will result in a loss of power. Unfortunately, women and nurses who hold powerful positions often undermine themselves by regressing rather than progressing. Such women perceive threats from peers and fear a loss of femininity and self-esteem when male figures use tactics involving personal defamation to challenge their power. These women experience other losses as the result of the isolation and depersonalization of having a powerful position.

Many theories have been advanced to explain why women experience themselves as subordinate, powerless, inferior, inadequate, or menial. These theories can be used as a foundation for developing new behaviors.

ACQUISITION OF POWER

There are a number of ways in which women can use or operate through organizations to increase their power.[2] They can learn to acquire and use power effectively. Habitual behaviors resulting from early lessons, passivity, and focusing on wrong targets can be replaced with new behaviors. These new behaviors result only from an intellectual effort and the assumption that one is responsible for how one operates and affects others. Women need to expand their repertoire of behaviors and to incorporate or adapt "masculine" and business concepts of power for their own use. They need to develop new skills in team play and innovative intellectual pursuits. Both activities and alliances may be resources for enhancing one's power base.

Power may be gained through the performance of one's job-related activities. For these activities to increase one's power, however, they must meet three criteria: (1) they must be extraordinary, (2) they must be visible, (3) they must be relevant to the solution of pressing organizational problems.[2]

Not everyone in an organization can accumulate power through competent performance, because most people simply do the ordinary and the expected—even if they do it very well. The extent to which a job is routinized is the extent to which it fails to produce power, because success is considered an *inherent* quality of the job and the organization. Neither individuals nor organizations get credit for simply doing the expected.[2] Because many nursing responsibilities are derived from physicians' orders or hospital policies and procedures, the opportunities for originality or innovation in job duties are minimal. Often daily shift activities seem like an assembly line. The quality of performance in carrying out these routine responsibilities must not, however, be discounted. Excellence that reflects knowledge and demonstrates skill enhances a nurse's credibility and self-esteem and determines how she is viewed by peers and subordinates. Self-respect and the respect of others are critical to the development of trust, and trust is the cornerstone of a power base.

Doing the extraordinary

There are opportunities for extraordinary activities for the nurse who is the first in a new position, who makes organizational changes, or who takes major risks and succeeds. As new positions or changes become increasingly familiar and routine, they involve less recognition. Change as a means of achieving power occurs within organizations when individuals are hired or promoted.[2] Reorganization is a common way to manipulate an institution's structure and thereby increase the power flow. Reorganization ensures the new leader that her/his team is well placed, removes or renders the opposition less effective, and provides the new leader with rewards to dole out in the form of new opportunities and job changes.[2]

Being successful with extraordinary risk is also power enhancing, as is classically seen in the awe inspired by charismatic leaders. High risk takers are organizationally valued for job-related actions because they can be relied on to perform in the most difficult circumstances and they do more than is expected. Socially they develop charisma in the eyes of the less daring.[2]

Power, then, seldom results from routine daily activities but more commonly from developing new methods, approaches, or solutions to existing problems. The amounts of time, intellectual effort, and resources necessary to achieve noteworthy outcomes usually involve activities beyond those of an 8-hour shift. Because few nurses desire to expend the extra effort, the majority have minimal power. To increase one's power, one must proportionately increase one's effort. One must remember that power is acquired not through passivity but through one's personality and through extraordinary activities.

Being visible

If activities are to enhance one's power, they must be visible and must attract notice. Jobs that straddle the boundaries between organizational units or between the organization and its environment tend to be more noticeable than those within a unit. These straddling jobs often become power positions because of their visibility.[2] Nurses also have many opportunities to gain visibility by serving on interdepartmental committees or in community programs, positions that can make them known beyond the familiar boundaries of nursing not only as individuals but through their group identity. Nurses may acquire referent power as part of a larger body.

Having relevance for the organization

Even extraordinary and visible activities do not necessarily contribute to one's power if they are not relevant, that is, if they cannot be identified with a solution to a pressing organizational problem. Activities engaged in for their own sake do not lead to gains in power, even if they are brilliantly performed. The wider system's goals and ideology must always be considered.[2] The nurse, for example, must perceive organizational goals, values, needs, and problems and must direct her efforts toward activities congruent with these. She must extend her energy and action beond her personal and group interests and benefits. Unfortunately, nurses often fail to develop the insight that working on behalf of the organization does not necessarily mean assuming an adversary relationship with their professional group.

Forming alliances

Power may also be acquired through alliances with others. In a large, complex system it is often necessary to achieve power through social connections, especially those outside the immediate work group. Such connections must be long lasting and stable and must include "sponsors," peers, and subordinates.[2]

Sponsors are important because they provide advice and because they are often in a position to fight for their protégées, stand up for them in meetings, and promote them for promising opportunities.[2] Physicians are available to nurses and are often used as sponsors. In their quest for independence and autonomy nurses frequently mistake having a mentor for being subservient. This relationship should instead be viewed as an apprenticeship during which the nurse becomes secure enough that she can maintain such dependent or interdependent relationships without feeling threatened. "Going it alone" is not in itself a virtue. Credibility flows from the sponsor to the nurse and can foster opportunities for the nurse to participate in activities that might otherwise be unattainable.

Sponsors provide an important signal to others, a form of reflected power. Sponsorship demonstrates to others that one has the backing of an influential person, that the sponsor's resources are behind one. Much of the power of relatively new nurses comes not from their own resources but from "credit" extended to them because there appears to be a more powerful set of resources in the distance.[2] Through the sanction of a sponsor the nurse may gain entrance to committees or be entitled to initiate activities previously not open to her on the basis of her own merits. These oportunities may enhance her esteem, respect, and trust, all of which afford power. In some situations being sponsored may allow lower-level organization members to bypass the hierarchy's initiation rites and credibility tests; they may be allowed to get inside information, to short-circuit cumbersome procedures, to cut red tape, or to get special performance opportunities.

Once the nurse has developed her credibility through her performance and excellence, her reliance on sponsors as a source of power often diminishes. The importance of one's quality output cannot be overemphasized. A lack of achievement or competency reflects not only on the individual but also on the sponsor. Second chances are rarely forthcoming in such cases because the damage to the nurse's and the sponsor's self-esteem is difficult to repair.

Often neglected in the striving of nurses for power are peer alliances that work through the exchange of favors. On lower levels information is traded; on higher levels bargaining and trade involve good performers and job openings.[2] Facilitating the good performance of others and affording them opportunities for recognition provide a climate of good will, which in turn increases power. Such behavior, however, requires that one view power as an entitlement all may share and enjoy. If all members of a team experience a sense of power, the effectiveness of the group as a whole is enhanced.

One's formation of alliances should not always be oriented upward. Different rates of hierarchical movement may mean that one's subordinates or peers today may become one's bosses tomorrow. It can be to a person's advantage, then, to make alliances downward in the hierarchy with people who seem to be on the way up. [2] Developing the power and performance potential of subordinates results in one being surrounded with effective, productive colleagues. Subordinates who feel they have power are more apt to collaborate and cooperate with team members and to form working alliances with their leaders. The distribution of power facilitates *alliances* rather than adversary relationships.

Such working alliances develop effective work groups that will achieve recognition. Their contribution to overall organizational goals will increase, as will the likelihood of the higher echelon bestowing power on them. The nurse who is able to relinquish power to subordinates will find it a circular process: power is reciprocated. It is interesting to note that one attracts power not through coercion and holding on but by letting go and allowing power to flow.

· · ·

Power is likely to bring more power in an ascending cycle, and powerlessness is likely to generate powerlessness in a descending cycle. The powerful have credibility supporting their actions and thus have the capacity to get things done. Their alliances help them circumvent the more restricting aspects of bureacracy. They can be less coercive and rules-bond in their exercise of leadership, and thus their subordinates and peers are more likely to be cooperative.[2]

Relating to others and behaving as a competent professional is the cornerstone of acquiring power, resulting from a combination of empathy and a positive personality integrated with intellectual and cognitive skills. Most nurses do possess these attributes. Holding a position of power entails having the corresponding responsibility. Each nurse who wishes to develop her power must therefore be willing to take risks, bear the anxiety of changing old scripts, and relinquish the safety net of the traditional dependent-woman position. Experiencing one's own power and self-esteem is the reward of practicing as a competent, autonomous, professional nurse.

REFERENCES

1. May, R.: Psychology and the human dilemma, New Jersey, 1967, D. Van Nostrand Co.
2. Swingle, P.G.: The management of power, New York, 1976, Halsted Press.

ELIZABETH G. MORRISON

Chapter 28

Power and nonverbal behavior
Indicators and alternatives

Power is an issue for women by virtue of the fact that women have very little of it. Since the overwhelming majority of nurses are women, power is also a nursing issue. This chapter speaks to women and therefore to nurses. What are the advantages and disadvantages for women of examining power and its nonverbal indicators? In its most elemental form, power is "the ability to influence and enforce decisions."[23] For a variety of reasons women need to be more aware of what power is, how it operates, and how it can be used.

For centuries women have been taught to consider themselves powerless relative to men and societal forces. Our lives are controlled by others, and that control is so deeply entrenched that most of the time we are unaware of it. Within the last 2 decades, however, more and more women have become and are becoming aware of something amiss in the patriarchal dominance of all areas of life. To understand power is to understand how that dominance is perpetuated. Once one achieves this understanding, options and choices become apparent, and one can make decisions about how one does or does not participate in the maintenance of the status quo. Nurses live and work in systems controlled by men. At a time when nursing is striving for more professional recognition, it is essential to understand the dynamics of power.

As women have begun to study more intensely the basis of feminine behavior, the stereotype of women's passivity and submissiveness is consistently an object of analysis. It is impossible to be passive and submissive in a vacuum, for this behavior is evidenced in relationships: "in general our nonverbal signals help to clarify the relationship between two communicators. Matters of status or dominance, sexual receptivity, kinship, and aggression are made evident by nonverbal signals."[26] A growing body of literature on assertiveness for women focuses on identifying and changing verbal response patterns. A more subtle and perhaps more important area of behavior is nonverbal behavior, the study of which includes but is not limited to kinesics (how we move our bodies) and proxemics (where we place our bodies in relation to others). Communication theorists have maintained that when we are faced with an incongruence between another's verbal message and nonverbal message, we pay attention to the nonverbal and disregard the verbal.[28] Therefore it is appropriate for women to increase their awareness of how they use body movements so that they can consider their options and make choices about their behavior.

Women cannot generate alternatives and make choices about their behaviors without doing so consciously. When one does not recognize what one is doing, when one's behavior is automatic, then one does not even consider the possibility of alternatives.

Some people maintain that male and female behaviors are gender linked and instinctual and that choices cannot be made with instinctual behavior. Birdwhistell,[7] one of the recognized authorities in kinesics and kinetic research, has distinguished sexual characteristics in the forms of *"Primary* sexual characteristics which relate to the physiology of the production of fertile ova or spermatazoa, the *secondary* sexual characteristics which are anatomical in nature, and the *tertiary* sexual characteristics which are patterned social-behavioral in form. These latter are learned and are situationally produced." Nonverbal behaviors are tertiary sexual characteristics, according to Birdwhistell,[7] and therefore are social rather than instinctual in nature. Therefore choices can be made about behavior, once the behavior is identified and acknowledged.

The only disadvantage of the study of power and its nonverbal indicators by women is expressed in the old adage: power corrupts and absolute power corrupts absolutely. If we use power the same way it has traditionally been wielded by males, we are liable to continue on a course of destruction of our planet, destroying ourselves in the process. It is imperative to find transforming approaches to power.

The objectives of this chapter are to discuss different types of power, nonverbal indicators of dominance and submission, and alternative ways for women to use behavior. The alternatives discussed here are not exhaustive but are a beginning effort to generate a list of possibilities to be revised, refined, and expanded.

TYPES OF POWER

Two categories of power are discussed here: patriarchal types of power and feminist types of power. The first involve power over others, whereas the latter involve the power to control and regulate oneself.

Patriarchal power

Five bases of power have been delineated by French and Raven[15]: legitimate power, reward power, coercive power, expert power, and referent power.

Legitimate power is synonymous with authority and is grounded in one's "perception of legitimate right with a reciprocal obligation [of others] to accept" that right.[15] This is the power we give our elected political representatives when we agree to abide by the laws they pass. It is also the power we give to hospital administrators and supervisors when we agree to abide by institutional policies and procedures. Women have little experience with wielding this kind of power, as Bunker and Seashore explain:

> The exercise of legitimate power requires behaviors that may not be well practiced by some women. It requires clear decision making, assertiveness, and accountability. It is sometimes a lonely task. Becoming more assertive, expressing her own views first rather than soliciting others', being pro-active rather than re-active, indicating clearly the degree to which she is willing to share power, being decisive, all these behaviors are less a part of the socialization of women than of men.[9]

Reward power is the capacity to distribute rewards. Mothers are familiar with this type of power since they are charged with raising children and rewarding them for various behaviors. Millett[22] aptly points out that women's influence exists primarily in the family and not in the larger society. Mothers may not receive many rewards for child raising since the traditional view is that if the child is not socially successful, this is the mother's fault, but if the child does succeed, this occurs despite the mother's influence. An analogous situation occurs in nursing. Although nurses are aware that nursing care makes a difference in patients' recovery time, chances are the doctor gets the credit for making the patient well. If the patient does not get well or gets well too slowly, the blame is put on poor nursing care.

Coercive power is the ability to punish and is associated with the use of covert or overt force. It is the bottom line of power, used when all else fails. Henley[19] describes a continuum of the applications of force, from subtle to blatant: (1) internalized control, (2) environmental structuring, (3) nonverbal communication, (4) verbal communication, (5) mild physical sanctions, (6) long-term restraint, and (7) use of weapons, killing, war. Rape or the threat of rape is also a form of social control applied specifically to women. Coercive power is a form of power that women have experienced—on the receiving end. We are taught we are physically and intellectually the "weaker" sex, and we all learn we must avoid "provoking" men (who are "naturally" aggressive) to violent acts against us.[25]

Expert power is influence based on one's knowledge and expertise. With few exceptions expert power in our society is reserved for men. It is interesting to note that almost all literature defining women's psychological, emotional, physical, and intellectual functioning has been written by men[10,29] and that male behavior is considered the standard or norm to which female behavior is compared; in this comparison women emerge as less than human.[8] There is, fortunately, an emerging body of literature written by women, for women, and about women from women's perspective,[4,11] a formidable task in view of the fact that women's expertise is not usually recognized or supported by men or other women. This fact is demonstrated in nursing by nurses who call on physicians (men), who are perceived as more knowledgeable, for consultation; it is rare that nurses (women) consult other nurses. We talk about how competent other nurses are, but we do not recognize each others' competence with appropriate behavior.

Referent power is influence based on one's identification with another, more powerful person. Women are familiar with this type of power. We are socialized to believe that we attain power and status by attracting, associating with, or marrying powerful men.[6] We are known not by our own accomplishments but by the accomplishments of the men who are our fathers, husbands, and co-workers. As an exercise, one can note how women are described in news articles or introduced socially and professionally: commonly included is information about a woman's husband, such as his profession or standing in the community. Parallel information about a man's wife is not customarily included when men are described or introduced. The implication of these messages is that women are powerless or nonexistent unless they are associated with a male.

Patriarchal forms of power, then, exclude women from power; women are the other, the powerless, in relation to men. Although women are aware of these types of power, they are socialized to be more conversant with referent and coercive power and are not taught the skills necessary for the exercise of legitimate and expert power.

Feminist power

Feminist forms of power mainly concern one's ability to control oneself. Steinem[27] defines feminist power as the "power to control one's own life but not to dominate others." Bardwick[5] describes personal power as "a feeling of power that resides within a person and comes from maturity, ego-integration, security in one's relationships with others, lack of need to gain from others, and confidence in one's impulses"—an admirable goal but not easily attainable when women exist in a state of socialized inferiority and oppression.

Ashley[2] believed nurses have personal power but misuse it by directing it covertly and against each other. Geyer and others[16] claim that nurses discount the power they do possess by "discrediting their ability to be in charge of their lives, discrediting their ability to think or allowing others to do so, and considering their own needs less important than the needs of others."

Feminist power is first concerned with taking charge of one's own life, an experience not familiar to many women, in contrast to patriarchal power, which involves taking charge of the lives of others (including all women). Women's taking charge of their own lives can predictably have enormous social as well as personal consequences. If we do develop a sense of our own power, we will no longer be willing to give men power over us. The consequences of decreased submissiveness and willingness to be controlled may lead, however, to increased coercion by men to put us back in "our place."

The next section identifies nonverbal indicators of submission and dominance related to coercive power. This area of behavior is discussed here because it involves the most difficult type of power for women to deal with and because as women become more assertive, they must learn to confront coercion directly or face an increasing use of force in their daily lives.

NONVERBAL INDICATORS OF DOMINANCE AND SUBMISSION

The definitive study of power and nonverbal communication was accomplished by Henley,[20] whose book reviews, describes, and collates an enormous amount of research in the area of communication. The following discussion focuses on kinesics (the study of body movements, including facial expressions) and proxemics (the study of spatial relationships, including touching).

Even though we are relatively unaware of our nonverbal behavior, when it is called to our attention women are better judges of the meaning of behavior than men. In a study conducted by Cunningham,[12] females judged emotional reactions consistently more accurately than males. Cunningham also reported that females scored higher than men on a neuroticism scale and that neuroticism scores are correlated with judging ability. He speculates that "the higher performance of females on the judging task could also stem from a developmental history emphasizing a social orientation."[12] It is a valid supposition that women are more sensitive than men to nonverbal behavior as a result of their conditioning to attend to relationship issues. Unfortunately, women also learn not to trust their own perceptions of what is occurring in a developing relationship and thus may find themselves in an uncomfortable or difficult situation.[25] Nonverbal communication, like verbal communication, occurs within a relationship and must be observed and judged accordingly.

Kinesics

Discussing how we move our bodies and what body language means has become a popular social game in the last decade. Various books purport to tell us how to "read" the behavior of others and by implication how to gain the upper hand in a relationship. That is not the intent of this analysis; the point is to identify contextual behaviors that indicate postures of dominance or submission.

Givens[17] has studied the nonverbal clues involved with flirtation, courtship, and seduction. He observed unacquainted heterosexual couples in their first meeting and reported behaviors he considered dominant or submissive in their interaction. Dominant behaviors included backward head tilts, indicating "arrogance, superiority, and disdain,"[17] and lateral gaze cut-off. Submissive behaviors included lateral head tilts, forward head tilts, pouting lips, self-clasping (folding one's arms around the body or touching oneself), downward gaze aversion, and smiling. Many more submissive gestures were noted than dominant gestures. Also noted were socially negative cues and behaviors to end the interaction, such as "blank-faced stare, lateral gaze-cutoff, and tongue show."[17] Most though not all of the submissive gestures were exhibited by women; most of the dominant gestures, by men.

An interesting aspect of this study was the difference between a downward gaze aversion and a lateral gaze aversion. Women learn to avert their eyes when approached by men, but the direction of the aversion may be an indicator of how women perceive themselves. Averting their eyes downward may be construed as a submissive gesture or a come-on; averting their eyes laterally may be construed as dominance or as a cut-off to future communication.

Givens[17] includes a case study of a woman whose nonverbal submissive behavior was strikingly inconsistent with her verbal behavior. She entered therapy because she was being approached by men in situations she deemed inappropriate. The goal of her therapy was to establish congruence between her verbal and nonverbal behaviors: "the woman need not become more assertive—she need only arrest the submissiveness."[17] The reader is left wondering, however, whether this is intended as a recommendation for that woman alone or for all women. If women exhibit more dominant kinds of behaviors, will these threaten men?

Henley's exhaustive review[20] of the research lists other nonverbal cues of dominance and submission. Dominant behaviors include pointing, staring, leaning back in a chair, placing the hands at the back of the neck or on the head while speaking, sitting with a leg over the arm of a chair, straddling a chair, putting the feet on desk or chair, standing with arms akimbo, standing over someone to talk, and steepling the fingertips. Submissive behaviors include slumping the body, tightening the body, folding the arms, holding the hands behind the back, looking up to the other, bowing the head, and crossing the legs.

From a comparison of these dominant and submissive gestures it can be generalized that dominant behaviors involve expansiveness, openness, and relaxation of the body whereas submissive behaviors involve tightening, closing, and tensing the body. Obviously body movements are related to the use of personal space.

Proxemics

How we use and are accorded space are measures of status and dominance. Consider how much space is left around prominent public figures. Consider corporate executives with large corner offices and hospital administrative staff with carpets and large offices. As individuals move upward on the power ladder, they are accorded more space. On the other hand, as individuals consider themselves more dominant, they tend to take up more space and to infringe on the space of others.

All of us have around us in interactions a comfort zone, a certain amount of space between ourselves and others that is not noticeable unless it is violated. All of us have had the experience of another standing or sitting too close to us when conversing and have been vaguely aware of the accompanying discomfort although we were perhaps unable to identify its source. The source of the discomfort may have been the violation of our personal space.

Hall[18] defines four areas of distance: intimate distance, personal distance, social distance, and public distance. Intimate distance is the amount of space between us and our lovers, family members, and close friends; it involves mutual physical contact. Public distance, at the other extreme, involves how far we stand from strangers and how far we sit from speakers at a meeting. Public distance is mediated by the density of the situation; for example, it is impossible to maintain the usual distance in a crowded subway or bus. Personal and social distances fall somewhere between the extremes of intimate and public distances.

We not only have our own zone of comfort, but we also negotiate with the other's zone of comfort when we engage in interaction. There are cultural and geographic variations in comfort zones. The use of space is a contextual aspect of interaction, just as body movements are. Engebretson[14] provides an example of what can happen when the context is ignored. He describes a woman whom he diagnosed as deviant the minute she sat down as far away as possible from him in his office. That he neglected to consider the context, his own behavior in the situation, is unfortunate. That he had the power to diagnose and treat the woman is frightening.

Henley[20] explicates five ways that one's use of space reflects dominance or submission: (1) dominant individuals control more space, (2) dominant individuals are freer to move into the space of others, (3) dominant individuals are accorded more space, (4) subordinate individuals yield their space to dominant individuals, and (5) dominant individuals occupy positions that control resources. The fact that dominant individuals are freer to move into the space of others is of particular concern in male-female relationships, for this behavior may involve touching and its implications.

According to Allen, "touch is involved with status. Anyone can touch a child, and a physician or dentist can touch a patient, but the patient would never consider reaching for the physician or dentist."[1] Since higher status is accorded to men in our society, they are freer to touch women than women are to touch men. Another invasion described by Davis[13] is prolonged visual contact within a close range. This behavior is slightly different from staring and refers to two people walking toward each other. Apparently there is a certain distance at which eye contact is normally averted by both parties, yet every woman has had the experience of being "looked over" on the street and has felt exposed or violated.

The submissive behaviors that complement the invasion of space are yielding space, giving up space, shrinking one's physical space, leaning away, and "accepting touch, failing to . . . reciprocate touch."[21] Women are taught to sit in such a manner as to minimize the amount of physical space they take up. Subordinates are expected to yield their space by giving up their seat to someone with authority or moving out of the way when an authority figure approaches.

The use of space is a nonverbal indicator of power and dominance. Superordinates expect and are accorded the control of space, including the personal space of others, whereas subordinates are expected to yield or submit to the invasion.

Many other nonverbal indicators of dominance and submission are beyond the scope of this paper. Factors such as the use of time, tone of voice, inflections, manners, style of dress, and the structure of the environment all play a role in the communication of nonverbal messages. Kinesics and proxemics are discussed here as a starting point for achieving an awareness of behavior, for understanding our bodies and how we use them is essential if we are to communicate verbal and nonverbal messages congruently. The following lists summarize dominant and submissive behaviors and demonstrate how they are complementary.

NONVERBAL BEHAVIORS

Dominant	Submissive
Backward head tilt	Lateral head tilt (head cocking), downward head tilt (bowing), forward head tilt
Staring, lateral gaze aversion	Downward gaze aversion
Blank face	Smiling
Standing over	Looking up to
Expanding space	Contracting space
Invading space	Yielding space
Leaning forward	Leaning backward, moving away
Touching	Allowing touch, not reciprocating touch

ALTERNATIVES

When considering alternative behaviors one must "recognize that *the powerlessness of feminine actions exists only relative to the power of masculine ones.*"[21] This caution implies we should not use information about how power operates to become more dominant or more like men but should examine our own behavior and make choices about what we do. Certainly, one of the alternatives is for women to become more like men and to assume and perpetuate dominant positions vis-à-vis other women. That, however, is to replicate the oppression of each other and, hopefully, will not be seriously entertained as an alternative for women. It is difficult, however, not to entertain that idea, since we have all been acculturated to believe that the way things currently are is the "natural" way for them to be and since there is no precedent for what relationships would be like between people if power over others were not an issue.

Based on the premise that the power to control oneself is our goal, I present the following suggestions for consideration.

1. Use the information from your observations and research to monitor your own behavior. Keep a journal, take notes, negotiate with a friend to observe each other's behavior, or form a discussion group for the purpose of collecting baseline data about how you use your body and your space in different circumstances. Are your non-verbal messages congruent with your verbal messages? Are you conveying what you intend to convey?

2. Make decisions about your behaviors noted during this data collection. Not all submissive behavior is bad, nor does it always carry submissive messages. Do we want to stop smiling completely? Probably not, but we might want to assess the times when we use smiling for purposes of appeasement and when we smile to convey warmth, comfort, and affection.

Do we want to yield space? Sometimes yes, or we might get run over. Sometimes the decision should be made to stand our ground, not give up our seats, not automatically shrink our personal space. Many nurses are socialized to defer automatically to physicians: we stand when they enter the room, give up our chairs, and give up our space. On some hospital units it is not unusual to find a room set aside for the specific use of physicians. Nurses use such a room only with the clear understanding they will vacate the premises immediately if a doctor appears. We might consider negotiating for such space, for after all it is the nurses who run the unit.

Are we willing to accept uninvited touching? Chances are we are not, but how can we make that clear without making a scene or seeming ridiculous? Part of the problem is that touching conveys so many messages, ranging from aggression to sexuality, that it is frequently difficult to sort out what is intended. Trust your own perceptions. Women are in a situation of double jeopardy in the sense that being submissive is also interpreted as an invitation to touch. We are taught to please people (particularly men), and if they want to touch us that is supposed to be a compliment to our attractiveness and desirability.[25] If your decision is that you do not want to be touched, say so clearly and calmly. And repeat it as necessary.

3. Be prepared for the consequences of behaving differently. Chances are you will be accused by men and some other women of being less feminine. Since submissiveness is a stereotypically feminine trait, it is true you will be less feminine if you are less submissive. But that does not make you any less a woman. You also might experience an upsurge in dominant behaviors from others when you behave less submissively. If you are prepared and recognize what is going on, you will be able to maintain your own behavior. Be aware, however, that when anxiety is high you might inadvertently revert to your former stance. That is to be expected, for none of us is used to some of these behaviors; they take practice. This is a time when a

support group is of valuable assistance for talking things over and maintaining courage.

One should also be prepared for the threat or use of physical force. Women need to learn to use their bodies to defend themselves against physical attack. Most of us have been taught to rely on men to protect us—from other men. It is time we learned to protect ourselves. Take a self-defense course, practice with friends, and learn the extent and limits of what you can do with your body. Boys are socialized to use their bodies offensively and defensively through organized team sports. They develop an appreciation of what they can do and what they can count on teammates (or opponents) to do; thereby they gain competence and confidence in their bodies. Provide your daughters the same opportunity.

4. Attend to other women.[21] If we gave each other the kind of attention we give to men, we could do much to support each other in the quest for personal power. We have been taught that men are prizes and that we must compete with each other to get the prize. Do not continue to compete but cooperate instead—not for a male prize, but with and for each other. In the process you may discover you are worth more than you thought. You will discover that other women are knowledgeable, interesting, and worth knowing.

Ashley[3] commented that "women nurses are *women* first" and that we must strengthen and support each other. Think about the nonverbal ways you communicate acceptance and appreciation. In the past year, what percentage of your own health care dollars have you invested in nursing? Do you see a nurse colleague for your own health care maintenance, or do you see a physician? Would you consider contracting with a nurse instead? When you need consultation for a patient care problem, do you turn to a nurse colleague or to a physician? Do you attend continuing education offerings sponsored by nurses? Do you submit articles to nursing journals? Do you belong to and participate in nursing organizations? Encouraging each other as women and as nurses has the added effect of reinforcing both personal and professional competence and effectiveness.

5. Participate in research and tell others what you are doing. Though the literature on power and nonverbal behavior is voluminous, very little is known about women's relationships with other women (with the exception of what men have said about them). Lesbians are women who have decided to relate exclusively to other women and by so doing are developing and publishing a body of knowledge about women's relationships. Read it. If we are going to claim power for ourselves, we need to help, support, and learn from one another.

SUMMARY

This chapter discusses the relationship between power and nonverbal behavior and proposes alternative ways for women and nurses to consider their behavior.

Power is considered in both the patriarchal sense of power over others and in the feminist sense of power to control oneself. Women need to be aware of the types and uses of power if they are to understand it and to make decisions about how to use it and how to respond to it. Women and nurses have been socialized not to use power but to submit to it.

Nonverbal indicators of dominance and submission are important to women's understanding of their behaviors because (1) women are relatively unaware of their nonverbal behavior, (2) dominance and submission are directly related to the use of coercive power, and (3) if verbal and nonverbal communications are incongruent, people rely more on the nonverbal. Assuming that one's awareness of behavior can lead to a wider variety of personal choices, women have alternatives to traditional behaviors. There are many ways women can take control of their bodies and their space.

I recognize that this chapter covers only a small part of the investigation that needs to be carried out by women, for women, and with women. As nurses, as women professionals, we are in a unique position to contribute to a growing body of knowledge about ourselves. In the process we will grow and affirm ourselves and each other in new and as yet uncharted ways.

REFERENCES

1. Allen, T.: Body language in the dental office, Tic 35(10):1, 1976.
2. Ashley, J.: This I believe about power in nursing, Nursing Outlook 21(10):637, 1973.
3. Ashley, J.: Power in structured misogyny: implications for the politics of care, Advances in Nursing Science 2(3):3, 1980.
4. Baker-Miller, J.: Toward a new psychology of women, Boston, 1976, Beacon Press.
5. Bardwick, J.: Some notes about power relationships between women. In Sargent, A., editor: Beyond sex roles, St. Paul, 1977, West Publishing Co.
6. Bardwick, J., and Douvan, E.: Ambivalence: the socialization of women. In Gornick, V., and Moran, B., editors: Woman in sexist society: studies in power and powerlessness, New York, 1971, Basic Books, Inc.
7. Birdwhistell, R.: Kinesics and context: essays on body motion communication, Philadelphia, 1970, University of Pennsylvania Press.
8. Broverman, I: Sex-role stereotypes and clinical judgements of mental health, Journal of Consulting and Clinical Psychology 34(1):1, 1970.
9. Bunker, B., and Seashore, E.: Power, collusion, intimacy-sexuality, support: breaking the sex-role stereotypes in social and organizational settings. In Sargent, A., editor: Beyond sex roles, St. Paul, 1977, West Publishing Co.
10. Chesler, P.: Women and madness, New York, 1972, Avon Books.
11. Cox, S., editor: Female psychology: the emerging self, Chicago, 1976, Science Research Associates, Inc.
12. Cunningham, M.: Personality and the structure of the nonverbal communication of emotion, Journal of Psychiatry 45(4):564, 1977.
13. David, A.: Body talk, Supervisor Nurse 9(6): 36, 1978.
14. Engebretson, D.: Human territorial behavior: the role of interaction of distance in therapeutic interventions, American Journal of Orthopsychiatry 43(1):108, 1973.
15. French, J., and Raven, B.: The bases of social power. In Cartwright, D., editor: Studies in social power, Ann Arbor, 1959, Research Center for Group Dynamics, Institute for Social Research.
16. Geyer, J., and others: Person power: the power you have to be in charge of your life (how to reclaim it and make it work for you), Pediatric Nursing 4(2):17, 1978.
17. Givens, D.: The nonverbal basis of attraction: flirtation, courtship and seduction, Psychiatry 41(4):346, 1978.
18. Hall, E.: The hidden dimension, Garden City, N.Y., 1966, Doubleday & Co., Inc.

19. Henley, N.: Nonverbal communication and the social control of women, Science for the People 8(4):16, 1976.

20. Henley, N.: Body politics: power, sex and nonverbal communication, Englewood Cliffs, N.J., 1977, Prentice-Hall, Inc.

21. Henley, N.: Changing the body power structure, Women: a journal of liberation 6(1):34, 1978.

22. Millett, K.: Sexual politics, New York, 1969, Ballantine Books, Inc.

23. Ryan, W.: Blaming the victim, New York, 1971, Pantheon Books.

24. Shafer, C., and Frye, N.: Rape and respect. In Vetterling-Braggin, M., and others, editors: Feminism and philosophy, Totowa, N.J., 1978, Littlefield, Adams & Co.

25. Stanford, L., and Fetter, A.: In defense of ourselves: a rape prevention handbook for women, Garden City, N.Y., 1978, Doubleday & Co., Inc.

26. Starkweather, C.: Disorders of nonverbal communication, Journal of Speech and Hearing Disorders 42(4):535, 1977.

27. Steinem, G.: The way we were—and will be, Ms., p. 60, December 1979.

28. Watzlawick, P., and others: Pragmatics of human communication, New York, 1967, W.W. Norton & Co., Inc.

29. Weisstein, N.: Psychology constructs of the female. In Gornick, V., and Morgan, B., editors: Woman in sexist society: studies in power and powerlessness, New York, 1971, Basic Books, Inc.

Chapter 29

Joint practice

Welcome to the hospital family! The nurse is wife to the doctor husband; she is dutiful daughter to the paternalistic physician; she is symbiotic mother, meeting everyone's needs, and the doctor expects that of her.

Welcome to the study of interpersonal relations! The nurse is powerless victim to the oppressive physician; she is coy participant in the doctor-nurse game; she identifies with the aggressor in a defensive attempt to overcome her helplessness.

Welcome to the world of sexual stereotypes! The nurse is angel of mercy, handmaiden, battle-ax, sexpot, and idiot. The doctor is knight in shining armor, big daddy, sugar daddy, saver of lives, and vile oppressor.

Welcome to chaos! The nurse has an associate degree, a diploma, a baccalaureate degree, a masters' degree, or a doctorate. She is technical; she is professional.

Welcome to nursing school/medical school! The nursing model/medical model. Caring/curing. Whole person/body part. Art/science. Empathy/antipathy. Woman's profession/man's profession.

• • •

How can two such disparate professions (much less individuals) come to an understanding of their independence, dependence, and interdependence? How can they overcome their biases against one another? Through self-awareness, naturally. And through an understanding of social, political, economic, and interpersonal phenomena. Through education. Through working together in a climate of mutual respect. Through joint practice.

"Joint practice is nurses and physicians collaborating as colleagues to provide patient care."[6] It involves shared goals, authority, and responsibility.

HISTORICAL DEVELOPMENT OF JOINT PRACTICE

The National Commission for the Study of Nursing and Nursing Education recommended in 1972 that the American Nurses' Association and the American

Medical Association begin to collaborate. The National Joint Practice Commission was developed:

1. To examine "the roles and functions of *both* professions"
2. To define "new roles and relationships"
3. To recommend "changes in professional education to support new roles"
4. To remove "sources of professional differences"
5. To assist "in the development and support of State joint practice committees"[5]

The Commission was composed of equal numbers of practicing nurses and physicians. Supported by a grant from the W.K. Kellogg Foundation, this group established model settings for the development of joint practice units in four hospitals of different types (a medical center, a large community hospital with few resident physicians, a large community hospital with a large house staff, and a small hospital) in different geographic locales. Their purpose was to develop, observe, and evaluate joint practice programs and to publish guidelines for others who might wish to pursue similar projects. Subsequently the National Joint Practice Commission published statements on various topics relevant to physician-nurse collaboration.

JOINT PRACTICE: FOUR NECESSARY ELEMENTS

For nurses and physicians to collaborate as colleagues in a hospital situation, four criteria are necessary: the establishment of a joint practice committee, the examination and perhaps revision of state nurse practice acts to allow greater nursing autonomy, parity of nursing and medicine in the hospital hierarchy, and the establishment of primary care nursing.

Joint practice committees

Joint practice committees include equal numbers of physicians and nurses and provide a formal network for collaboration. Their purposes are to define and redefine the roles and functions of both professions and to make recommendations to hospital administrations and governing boards about issues of patient care. Optimally they integrate nursing and medical observations, diagnosis, and plans for patient care; they enhance communication through consultations and conferences; they establish standards of care; and they provide joint continuing education.[9]

Nurse practice acts

With a realignment or readjustment of physician and nurse roles comes the need to examine state nurse (and medical) practice acts. The legality of such changes must be ensured for the protection of both the professionals and the public. The National Joint Practice Commission recommends that practice acts be broad and flexible enough to incorporate changes in roles and functions as they occur.[7]

Nursing parity in hospital hierarchies

Perhaps the most controversial issue raised by the National Joint Practice Commission has been its recommendation that nursing be given the same status as the medical staff in the organization.[1] The Commission suggests that professional nursing staffs be responsible for the quality of nursing care and for the conduct of their members. In addition it recommends that nursing departments, like medical departments, be directly accountable to hospital governing boards rather than to hospital administrators.[8]

Primary care nursing

Primary care, in which professional nurses are responsible and accountable for nursing patients, provides optimal patient care and an environment in which physicians and nurses can best work jointly. Dr. Schaffrath, Director of the National Joint Practice Commission, says, "There should be a patient-nurse relationship in which a professional nurse renders the nursing service to the patient and does not delegate nursing tasks to people who are not professional nurses."[1]

JOINT PRACTICE: THE PRACTICALITIES

To establish joint practice systems within a given hospital requires the commitments of medicine, nursing, and hospital administration. Change, as we all know, takes time. Because in this case roles, functions, and relationships are expected to change, it also requires education, communication, patience, and perseverence. The process includes a series of steps, as follows.

Administrative joint practice council

Perhaps the first step in developing joint practice is the formation of a group of equal numbers of nurses and physicians at the administrative level. The *nurses* should be administrators and clinical experts who can best articulate the position of nursing. The *physicians* should represent various specialties and interest groups in the medical staff. Both nurses and physicians should be respected and viewed as powerful by their peers; these factors become important in determining how recommendations and changes are received.

These individuals should share the philosophy that an improved collaboration will result in better patient care. Their goals include the following:

1. Encouragement of nurses to develop clinical skills and decision-making abilities.
2. Development of guidelines for medical and nursing roles and functions.
3. Establishment of primary care nursing, beginning with one unit and expanding to others.
4. Integration of the nursing and medical records to reflect this collaboration.

5. Continuing education of physicians and nurses, jointly and each by the other.

6. Maintenance of open lines of communication between the two disciplines.

Issues such as who will be the council chairperson (a nurse and a physician could be co-chairpersons, or the chair could alternate between medicine and nursing for set periods) and how conflicts are to be resolved (an ad hoc committee could be established to investigate and make recommendations when conflicts arise) should be agreed on early. Goals, objectives, and protocols should also be considered.

Development of pilot unit

The choice of a unit in which to pilot a joint practice system should involve nursing and medicine (the council discussed above) as well as hospital administration. Types of patients, the availability of nursing staff, the physical plant, and many other factors should enter into the decision. Once a unit has been chosen, the next step is to begin to educate physicians and nurses about the expected changes in their roles and functions. Formal classes, consciousness-raising groups, and visits to other facilities that have successful joint practice systems are a few ways to prepare these individuals.

A joint practice committee should be established at the unit level, again composed of equal numbers of nurses and physicians who are directly involved in providing patient care on that unit. The function of this committee is to develop policies and procedures for that specific unit, to deal with conflicts that may arise, to establish guidelines for nurse and physician roles, to institute primary nursing, and to work with the administrative council.

Physician and nurse education is essential for the success of primary care nursing. Physicians should begin to see nurses not as their assistants but as autonomous practitioners whose services are interdependent with their own. Nurses should become responsible for "taking health histories, performing assessments, conducting health education, counseling and referring patients to community agencies."[3] For specifics about the development of primary care, I urge interested nurses to review the many articles and books on the subject.

In addition to seeing nursing as a profession separate from medicine, physicians in a primary care situation will begin to realize they can no longer assume every nurse knows (or ought to know) about every patient. Conflicts between the disciplines should be resolved on a clinical basis, in terms of what is best for the patient. This process precludes personality clashes, one-upsmanship (sic), and reliance on traditional expectations.[2] Together with legal counsel the unit committee can develop guidelines for expanded nursing functions. These, of course, must reflect those activities that even the least prepared nurse can perform so that physicians can develop consistent expectations of what nurses will be relied on to do.

Once the nursing and medical staffs are familiar with primary care and have begun to feel comfortable in their new relationships, consideration should be given to integrating medical and nursing records. A problem-oriented method is ideal; the literature contains many examples. Interdisciplinary progress records should be utilized to reflect the collaboration of all members of the patient care team. One hospital, for example, instituted a clinical flow sheet to reflect routine treatments, procedures, medications, and other activities that did not need to be recorded in the progress notes.[2] The progress record covered 24-hour periods and required that the primary nurse, like the primary physician, make a chart entry only once in that time and that other entries be made only if significant changes occurred in the patient's status.

Joint continuing education in the form of case presentations by both disciplines, consultations, lectures, and discussions is vital not only for increasing the knowledge of practitioners but also for creating a climate of mutual respect. The success of the pilot venture will soon result in eager requests for expansion to other units. Again the process should be undertaken in a logical series of steps to ensure that the foundations of knowledge and effective relationships have been built before primary nursing and integrated patient records are attempted.

JOINT PRACTICE: OTHER IMPLICATIONS, OTHER AREAS

The principle of joint practice, that physicians and nurses should work together as colleagues for the betterment of patient care, can be applied to a variety of settings. Private practices, for example, composed of nurse practitioners in partnership with physicians are beginning to develop.

> The nurse practitioner and physician who elect the joint practice model usually espouse the philosophy that a combined effort will result in better patient care. They are interested in providing a broad range of services to include preventive, diagnostic, therapeutic and rehabilitative services; they use their combined education, experience and skills to meet these comprehensive needs.[3]

Joint practice services might include office care and home and hospital visits as well as visits to businesses, industries, and schools. The responsibilities of each partner are mutually determined.

The issue of fees is often important. It has been suggested that both partners in a joint practice charge the same fees for office visits, hospital visits, and so on. It has been found that the nurse practitioner frequently spends more time with patients than her physician counterpart, and on this basis equal fees can be justified. In addition some patients view a lower fee as an indicator of a lower standard of care—the nurse, in other words, might be thought to provide less service than the physician.[3] Such interpretations should be discouraged. The need for hospital admitting privileges by nurse practitioners is also an isue in private practice but may be more easily resolved as hospitals develop joint practice committees that mandate pariety and collaboration between the disciplines.

REFERENCES

1. Appelbaum, A.L.: Commission leads way to joint practice for nurses and physicians, Hospitals **52**:78, July 16, 1978.
2. At this hospital, 'the captain of the ship' is dead: an interview with Sarah A. Blackwood, RN, MSN, RN p. 77, March 1979.
3. Brown, K.C.: Nature and scope of services: joint practice, The Journal of Nursing Administration, p. 13, December 1977.
4. Brunner, N.A., and Singer, L.E.: A joint practice council in action, The Journal of Nursing Administration, p. 16, February 1979.
5. The National Joint Practice Commission: Brief description of a demonstration project to establish collaborative or joint practice in hospitals, 1977-1980.
6. The National Joint Practice Commission: Statement on joint practice in primary care: definition and guidelines.
7. The National Joint Practice Commission: Statement on medical and nurse practice acts.
8. The National Joint Practice Commission: Statement on nursing staffs in hospitals.
9. The National Joint Practice Commission: Statement on the definition of joint or collaborative practice in hospitals.

RESOURCE

The National Joint Practice Commission
35 East Wacker Drive, Suite 1990
Chicago, Illinois 60601

SHARON E. AGA and JANET MUFF

Chapter 30

Brainstorming for job satisfaction

Nurses are making headlines!

NURSES QUIT HOSPITAL FOR CASINO[15]
NURSE SHORTAGE HAMPERING HOSPITALS[17]
NURSE RECRUITMENT ON THE CRITICAL LIST[3]
BAND-AID SOLUTIONS AREN'T LURING NURSES[2]
ANGELS OF MERCY ARE TURNING IN THEIR WINGS[1]

The problems of nurses are finally being reported by the media, but this coverage often reflects the views of hospital administrators and physicians rather than nurses themselves. In addition, now that the problems have been identified, other professionals, labor unions, and government agencies are only too willing to step in and solve the problems of nursing.

Here, first, are some of the facts:

☐ There are 1.4 million registered nurses in this country.[1]
☐ Of these, only 66%[1] or 67%[8] are working.
☐ Only 44% work full time.[1]
☐ 10.8% of *working* nurses are "very satisfied" with their jobs; 54% are "fairly satisfied." The rest are "somewhat" or "not at all" satisfied.[7] (What about nurses who are not working—were *they* satisfied?)
☐ Turnover rates are high, varying from 25%[7,10] to 45%[3]
☐ The vacancy rate for budgeted RN positions in 20%.[3,20] The American Hospital Association estimates there are currently 100,000 RN vacancies in this country.[1,20]
☐ The movement of nurses from job to job reflects career advancement in only 1/5 of these cases.[6] The rest are lateral moves.
☐ The average annual salary of a full-time RN is $12,938[13]—less than that of computer operators, grocery clerks, meat cutters, tree trimmers, parking meter repairmen, auto parts clerks, animal control wardens, and so on.[7] In 1977 a group of nurses brought suit against the city of Denver for discrimina-

384

tory pay and employment practices because graduate nurses were making less than many male-dominated occupations that involved fewer responsibilities and required less educational preparation. In April 1978 the Chief Judge of the U.S. District Court, Fred Winner, brought forth his decision: "We're confronted with history which has discriminated unfairly and improperly with women. . . . [The nurses] have established by and large that male-dominated occupations pay more for comparable work than is paid in female-dominated occupations." Sounds hopeful, right? Wrong! Judge Winner ruled against the nurses because "a decision in their favor could end by disrupting the entire economic system of the United States of America." He supported his decision on the technicality that the nurses' charges were made on grounds of occupational rather than sex discrimination. The nurses are appealing.[7]

Obviously the supply of nurses is not keeping up with the demand. Has this occurred because there are not enough nurses or because nurses do not remain in nursing? If nurses do not remain in nursing, is this the result of personal reasons or job dissatisfaction? This chapter first discusses those ideas about the nursing shortage (red herrings) that have been propogated by those who prefer not to confront the reality of job dissatisfaction, then examines nurses' own reasons for job dissatisfaction and the nursing shortage. Solutions to these problems are discussed, and finally, we address further issues for nurses to consider.

WHY IS THERE A NURSING SHORTAGE? RED HERRINGS

The following explanations have been offered for the nursing "shortage." They are patently false or evade the *real* issues of why nurses leave nursing, have a high turnover rate, work only part time, or otherewise contribute to the lack of a sufficient number of nurses to meet patient care needs.

"We cannot staff our hospitals because of a severe nursing shortage"

This statement is the grandfather of all red herrings. There is no *real* nursing shortage! The fact is simply that many nurses are not working (for a variety of reasons discussed later). By defining the problem as a nursing "shortage," hospital administrators, nursing supervisors, or whoever avoid looking at the real reasons why there are not enough nurses: that women are socialized to place their families first and careers second (these are called "personal" reasons for leaving nursing) and that nurses are unhappy in nursing (reasons of job dissatisfaction). Not only are nursing problems evaded, but nurses also are viewed as scapegoats. The nursing "shortage" becomes a pat excuse for every failure to render necessary care and for every vacancy that can't be filled. It is the ultimate answer that absolves the people responsible from dealing with problems here and now.

"Nurses don't care about money—just give 'em a pat on the back once in a while"

Of course nurses want to feel appreciated, and money isn't the only reason why nurses are dissatisfied, but unfortunately pats on the back don't put food on the table or pay the mortgage. Low wages have not traditionally been a major reason for nursing dropout, but times and nurses have changed.[11] A recent study of 3500 nurses found that 45% of unemployed nurses cited salary issues as an important reason for leaving nursing and 60% of unemployed nurses cited low salaries as a major reason for remaining out of nursing.[19] Thanks in part to the women's movement, women and thus nurses are beginning to value themselves and their work and are beginning to expect adequate compensation for their services.

"Hospitals are experiencing a nursing shortage because unscrupulous nursing registries are luring nurses away"

In psychiatry this kind of statement is called *projection:* "It's not *me* that's got problems; it's that bad guy out there who's doing it to me." There is no need for registries to lure nurses away; they are already *running* away in droves! For the first time, through registries, nurses can be in control of their work, and they love it.

Before examining the real reasons for the nursing shortage, however, we would like to add that nurses themselves have contributed to the development of these red herrings by failing out of apathy or a fear of reprisals to indicate their *real* reasons for leaving their jobs.

WHY IS THERE A NURSING SHORTAGE? NURSES ARE MAD AS HELL AND THEY'RE NOT GOING TO TAKE IT ANYMORE!

Many nurses continue to see nursing as a stopgap job rather than as lifetime career. Earlier chapters discuss this problem, which arises from the socialization of women to be primarily housewives and mothers. Those chapters suggest ways of understanding nurses' own reactions to socialization and stereotyping and ways of changing learned patterns of behavior. This chapter examines reasons other than those "personal" reasons why the supply of nurses has not kept pace with the demand. There are two major areas of concern here: production and retention.

Are we producing enough nurses?

The answer to this question is both no and yes. No, because not as many people are choosing nursing today as in the past. Admissions have dropped. The women's movement again is partly responsible, first because women are no longer willing to subjugate themselves to others and to repudiate their own needs as nursing often requires, and second, because nontraditional fields are opening up for women. Yes, because schools are having problems choosing the "right kind" of people and preparing them to work effectively in the real world.

Are we retaining our nurses?

Nurses do not for the most part remain in nursing full time for their lifetimes. The socialization of women to put marriage and family before careers is covered elsewhere; this chapter focuses on those issues that make nurses unhappy or dissatisfied and that contribute to high attrition rates. The folowing factors are culled from several studies of nurse job dissatisfaction.

Nursing schools attract and reinforce passive individuals who find themselves out of their depth in work situations that require decision making, autonomy, conflict management, and so on. (And what nursing situation does not?) These new graduates then experience reality shock.[9]

Work situations themselves contribute to nurses' unhappiness in the following ways:

- Poor conditions such as understaffing, overloading, inflexible work hours, floating, shift rotating, and frequent overtime cause unhappiness. Such conditions reduce contact between the nurse and patient and result in increased errors and poor patient care, outcomes nurses find intolerable.
- Salaries and differentials (for shifts, weekends, and holidays) are low. For example, at an average salary increase of $100 per year, a nurse with 20 years' experience makes only $2000 more per year than she did as a new graduate.[21]
- Hospital and nursing administrators are often inattentive to nurses' needs for education and intellectual stimulation.
- Physicians and others are often insensitive or disrespectful. Passivity and compliance are valued rather than initiative and creativity. "God," says Vale, "is a hard act to follow."[18] Not only are nurses disregarded or devalued individually, but this problem is institutionalized through the devaluation of the nursing department in the hospital hierarchy. Hospital administrators and physicians, for example, report directly to the board of directors; the nursing department reports to the hospital administrator (or worse yet, to one of his associates). Nurses usually are not voting members of hospital committees. In addition, there are few formally instituted lines of communication between nurses and their medical peers. The nursing director is not, for example, coresponsible with the medical chief of staff for patient care, and the assistant director of nursing for medical services is not on a par with the chief of medicine. Collegial relationships naturally develop, but there is rarely a formal structure to encourage this to occur.
- Benefit packages are not attractive. Health insurance is usually offered, but maternity or psychiatric coverage may not be covered adequately or at all. Other types of insurance frequently are not offered.
- Nurses themselves contribute to nurses' dissatisfaction. Nursing administration frequently purges the staff of "troublemakers" (nurses who ask too many questions or rebel against the status quo). Nurses do not respect other nurses as individuals or as professionals; they call a psychiatrist, for example, rather

than a nurse from the psychiatric unit when they have difficulty dealing with patients. Too often nurses refuse to acknowledge their own part in being unhappy; they instead blame nursing leaders, educators, doctors, and hospital administrators.

We are not, then, retaining our nurses: they dropout, they burnout (they are physically present but professionally incapacitated), and they grow apathetic, angry, and dissatisfied with their role.

WHAT CAN BE DONE ABOUT THE NURSING SHORTAGE AND NURSES' DISSATISFACTION?

Approaches to the problems of the shortage and dissatisfaction are many. Hospitals entice nurses with monetary bounties, trips to Hawaii, automobiles, and the like. Nurse recruiters travel to Canada and Europe, advertising the unparalleled attractions of this country. In California legislators are considering lowering nursing board scores to permit more nurses to practice. None of these approaches are *the* answer. First of all, there is no single answer. Second, answers that have not been well thought out, are hit or miss, or deal with scattered problems often cannot solve the basic problems. These answers are based on the red herrings; they attempt to solve the nursing "shortage" by pulling more bodies into the system rather than by solving problems within the system itself. Such solutions may work to alleviate a crisis temporarily, but their effects are often short lived.

Long-term solutions to the problems of the nursing shortage and nurses' job dissatisfaction must be reached methodically using problem-solving methods. Although further research is needed into the issues of why nurses leave nursing, there are sufficient data now to begin to address the issues. This is the job of the nursing profession, not others. On a smaller scale each hospital must begin to examine the reasons for job dissatisfaction and dropping out among its own nurses in its own locale and must then begin to deal with those issues.

The following sections include some suggestions. They offer a point of departure, a nudge to start the creative juices flowing; they are not intended to be comprehensive or to solve every problem.

Attracting and educating appropriate kinds of people

Who are attracted to nursing? What attracts them? Who do we *want* to be attracted to nursing? What will attract these kinds of people? Does what we *say* we want (autonomous, accountable nurses) differ from the kinds of nurses produced by nursing education? If so, where does the problem lie? In the people we recruit to nursing or in the educational process? There are so many questions we need to ask, and just as many answers we need to find. The first four units of this book begin to answer some of the questions; they state the problems. The following are some solutions.

1. Make nursing attractive to intelligent, questioning, assertive women and men of all classes and races by changing the job situation and the role of nurses in it and by changing the image and stereotypes of nurses (see Chapter 7).

2. Unify the profession on issues of entry into practice. We have been attempting to solve this problem for more than 20 years. In psychodynamic terms, when someone indulges in the same behavior over a long period of time without moving ahead, there is a reason. What is getting in the way of nursing's moving ahead? Why do we continue to struggle with this issue? Either the problem is insoluble and thus we should accept that fact and drop the issue, or we can attack the problem and put it behind us. Our need for a perfect solution that does not anger or upset other nurses says something about us: we need the collective, we fear taking risks—in short, we do not want (however subconsciously) to move ahead.

3. Increase the number of nursing graduates in accordance with established criteria for entry into practice. This may involve opening more nursing schools. It may mean changing the standards for admission to nursing programs and giving credit in baccalaureate schools for certain facets of associate degree and diploma training and for life experiences. This is a call not to *lower* admission standards but to reexamine the educational system and institute widespread changes.

4. Recruit assertive, independent, career-minded individuals into nursing programs and reward these behaviors.

5. Within the educational process make the following changes:
   □ Begin self-exploration into students' anxieties over assertiveness and give assertiveness training.
   □ Provide healthy doses of reality for students. Take steps to end the split between nursing educators and nursing practitioners. Give students greater autonomy in clinical experiences and use clinical experts as resource people (see Chapter 24).
   □ Develop faculty as role models of independence and assertion.

6. Accept that a nurse is not a nurse is not a nurse. A nurse may view her patients or clients as whole individuals, but it is impossible to expect her to deal with all facets of the individual. Specialization may be necessary. The credentialing of specialists, then, is an issue that must be addressed.

Changing the nursing role and the nursing work environment

There are many questions about the nursing role and work environment and just as many answers. Again, the problems are defined in earlier chapters. Here are some solutions:

1. Encourage nursing's autonomy. This means nursing is responsible for its own practice and has the authority to manage that practice.
   □ Equalize nursing and medicine formally in the hospital hierarchy. If medicine reports directly to the hospital board of directors, then nursing should as well. Nurses should be voting members on all hospital com-

mittees that affect personnel in general, nursing practice, or patient care.
Establish a joint practic system (see Chapter 29).

□ Give the nursing department responsibility and authority for the nursing
budget. Initiate a fee-for-service system whereby patients are charged
separately for nursing care. The inclusion of nursing services in a general
room rate means that nursing cannot demonstrate the revenue it produces
for the hospital, and the ability to generate revenue is directly linked to
power in budget negotiations. A nursing department that can demonstrate
its worth in dollars and cents has something tangible with which to bargain.
The ultimate in fee-for-service systems is a situation in which nurses contract independently or as a group to provide services to a hospital. This is
also the ultimate in autonomy and responsibility, because such nurses
would be self-employed. (This is similar to the concept of nursing registries
in that registry nurses are not employees of the hospital itself, have greater
control over their schedules and areas of practice, and charge a fee for their
service; it differs, however, in that registry nurses are still employees of the
agency rather than independent contractors.)

□ Flatten the nursing hierarchy through greater decentralization and the
delegation of responsibility and authority to individual nursing units. Give
head nurses who have appropriate education and training autonomy over
nurses and nursing care in their areas.

□ Institute primary nursing.

□ Encourage the kind of climate in which *all* nurses have input into practice
and policy issues.

□ Change the traditional procedures whereby head nurses have the thank-
less job of scheduling nursing staff. One way might be to have the staff on
individual units be responsible for their own schedules. Another way
might be centralize the responsibility for overall scheduling in one individual such as a staffing coordinator or the nursing department. This
change does not contradict the move toward decentralization. It provides
an equity for and a unified perspective of the department as a whole,
which individual units cannot achieve, yet it also provides for individual
responsibility in that nurses submit only vacation and leave of absence
requests to the coordinator. All other requests for time off can be resolved
among the nurses themselves, the changes then being submitted.

□ Institute a "care team" composed of administrative, supervisory, educational, and consultant nurses who respond to emergency or critical situations on any nursing unit.* These are the situations that alter the smooth,

---

*The care team concept was proposed by Judy Snook, Director of Nursing at San Dimas Community
Hospital, San Dimas, California.[14]

safe, timely, and continuous delivery of patient care. They may originate from one incident or several. Their result is often, however, that the unit is thrown into a highly frustrating, stressful frenzy in which the staff cannot cope and get behind, tempers rise, and the possibility of errors is great. Imagine the effect of four or five RNs appearing to bail out the distressed unit and its overloaded nurses. Such situations are usually handled and resolved within 45 to 90 minutes, and the care team then returns to their normal duties. This system increases the contact between nursing administration and nursing staff, enhancing the credibility of both and facilitating more dialogue between them.

□ Utilize nurse planners to develop and implement goals and projects within the nursing department.

□ Establish quality assurance programs with the evaluation of individual nurses' performance as one component.

□ Recognize standard nursing practice and do not require physicians' orders for nursing therapies.

□ Develop a per diem float pool rather than relying on outside agencies. Possibly divide the pool into specializd divisions so that critical care nurses, for example, would not be expected to work in the maternity department. Encourage per diem nurses' participation in departmental policy making and problem solving by planning regular meetings to elicit their contributions.

2. Provide attractive salaries, benefits, and perquisites, as follows:

□ Fight the myth that nurses are not interested in monetary rewards. *Competitive salaries* are important—competitive not only with other hospitals but also with other professions whose levels of responsibility for services and personnel supervision are similar. Establish sufficiently high *differentials* for evening and night shifts so that rotation of daytime nurses is unnecessary; do the same with weekends and holidays. Some hospitals use the *bounty* system to attract nurses, including money ($100 to $1000), gifts, automobiles, and vacations. Provide *relocation assistance* and *housing* for nurses from other states and countries. Give a *referral bonus* to staff nurses who recruit their colleagues. Develop a competitive *benefit package,* considering such items as meal discounts, a uniform allowance, pharmacy and optical discounts, medical care, comprehensive insurance coverage (including maternity, psychiatric, and dental benefits as well as life and disability insurance), and a retirement plan with profit-sharing or stock options. Allow nurses to exchange unused sick days for a cash bonus at years' end or for additional vacation days.

□ Be flexible with scheduling. Control over when they will work is an important issue for many nurses. Integrate *4-, 8-, and 12-hour shifts.* Some hospitals have successfully used the *4-40* system, in which nurses work 4 10-hour days. This system can be implemented for individuals or for the whole department (overlap time is used for conferences, patient teaching, staff education, and so on). Other hospitals prefer the *7-70* system, in which one group of nurses works 7 8-hour days (for 70 hours' pay) and then has 7 days off while the alternate group works. Contrary to the speculation of critics, the incidence of errors does not increase and extreme fatigue is not a problem in this system.[4] Patients in fact receive better care because their nurses are consistent over a period of 7 days. Another choice is a system of *12-hour shifts*, in which there are only two shifts (day and night) and nurses work three 12-hour shifts (for 42 hours' pay). (The seventh day is often taken care of by those nurses who want to work overtime.) Baylor University Medical Center pioneered the use of two *12-hour shifts on weekends* with full-time pay.[2] The regular staff works Monday through Friday on 8-hour shifts; the weekend staff works days or nights for 12 hours on 2 days. Both staffs are satisfied: one has weekends off, and the other has more money for less work. Yet another variation is to *work 4 nights and get paid for* 5. The possibilities are endless, and the system chosen should be tailored to the paticular situation.

□ Provide child-care facilities. Consider offering such services free to the night shift and at a discounted rate for the evening shift.

3. Develop clinical ladders to reward with both money and recognition those nurses who remain in the clinical area. It is important to include all nurses in this clinical ladder concept. To leave out, for example, emergency department nurses because there is no shortage in that area or to develop only critical care ladders because these nurses seem more assertive and ask for more than medical surgical nurses only accentuates the division and isolation that exist in nursing. It is also important that criteria developed for clinical ladders are expressed in concrete, behavioral terms and that nursing credentialing committees are established to review and approve all applications for clinical level differentiations, thereby establishing a system of peer review.

4. Make education a high priority. The possibilities are numerous:

□ Provide continuing education programs and money for nurses to attend programs at other facilities.

□ Offer tuition reimbursement for nurses wishing to obtain baccalaureate or master's degrees. Partial fees can be paid, or the entire tuition can be paid and pay-back reductions made for each year of the nurse's service.

□ Develop new graduate internship programs, review classes for Nursing Board Examinations, and refresher courses for nurses returning to work after an absence.

□ Establish a network among facilities for exchanging nurses for educational experiences.

- Work with educational institutions in developing baccalaureate and master's programs given at times more accessible than during day-shift working hours, given on a part-time basis, and given at the hospital rather than the college campus.
- Utilize clinical specialists for on-unit education in addition to the classes offered by the education department.
- Give supervisory and management people specific training. Theoretical information is just as important as life experiences.
- Provide consciousness-raising or stress-management groups utilizing people other than direct supervisors so that interaction is facilitated. The goal, more than mere catharsis, can include personal and professional education, conflict resolving, and problem solving.

5. Delegate nonnursing functions to nonnursing personnel.
- Develop coordinators to supervise unit clerks and to be responsible for environmental aspects and supplies.
- Develop a separate system to transport patients, deliver specimens, retrieve x-ray films, garner supplies, and so on.
- Consider using dietary hostesses to pass patient trays, the housekeeping department to deliver linen to individual patient rooms, exchange carts for central supply items, a unit-dose pharmacy system, and so on.

Changing interpersonal relationships

The practical, concrete issues of nursing's professionalism discussed above play a big part in nurses' job satisfaction or lack ot it. Equally important are the interactions between nurses and others, including other nurses, other professionals, doctors, and administrators. For nurses to be happy, changes must be made.

1. Examine our individual problems and address the problems of nurses who are peers, subordinates, and leaders. Develop our nursing organizations to be representative of nurses' needs. An organization, after all, is composed of individuals. If it is not representative, whose fault is that? If its fees seem too high, should we not examine our priorities to see whether this is an excuse for apathy—or can we not change the fees? Can we develop new organizations if the current ones will not change to meet our needs?

2. As individuals, nursing departments, and a profession, establish better working relations with physicians and hospital administrators.
- Encourage medical schools to educate their students about nursing roles and responsibilities. We can participate in this educational process (who better than nurses can teach about nursing?).
- Develop joint practice systems within our institutions.
- Educate physicians with whom we work on a day-to-day basis about nursing.
- Stop thinking of politics as a four-letter word, as something unhealthy, something to be overcome, the enemy. We can debunk the myth that one

either has or doesn't have a political outlook. People are not *born* with savvy! Politically astute people know their organization, its formal and informal lines of communication, its goals and values. Politically astute people do their homework. They gather the facts to support proposals *before* submitting them. They know that no one gives you anything because you're a nice person; you get what you need when you can prove in concrete, statistical, dollars-and-cents terms why you need it and how giving it to you will benefit the organization.

3. Become politically aware and active.
   □ Know what health care legislation is before Congress and your state legislature. Write state and federal Legislators to voice your concerns and support or opposition.
   □ Speak or testify at public hearings on health care issues or support nursing leaders who are doing so.

CONCLUSION

We have presented a few ideas for your consideration. It is beyond the scope of this chapter to describe how any one of these solutions may be instituted. Nursing and other literature has much on the subject. Other nurses have answers. Start reading, start talking—do *your* homework.

There are a few related issues we would like to mention before closing.

1. We must decide what we as individuals and as a profession want from nursing. We must respect the fact that others are different and that what satisfies them may be different from what satisfies us. Unfortunately, there are no perfect solutions. On an organizational basis, however, it is perhaps better for nurses to agree philosophically about their practice. It is difficult to establish primary nursing in situations where nurses actually do not want to give patient care. Whatever our choice is, we must be honest about it so that care can continue and nurses can be happy about their work.

2. We must learn to value the written aspects of our work, for even though, as Moses and Roth comment, "the complaint is frequently heard that registered nurses are immersed in paperwork, it is apparent from the sample surveys that nurses *are* involved predominantly in direct patient care."[13] Care plans and charting are important, and so are research and record keeping (if we record statistics that are useful in budget preparation and proposals for increased staffing or necessary equipment).

3. We must stop being the "gimme kids." We do not *deserve* anything because we are nice. Hospitals do not *owe* us benefits, salaries, whatever. As professionals we can expect certain compensation and respect for our work. But we *must* produce.

4. We cannot allow standards within nursing to be lowered by other nurses or those outside of nursing. A recent advertisement in the classified advertising section of the Los Angeles Times read as follows[12]:

MORE MONEY for the work you're doing

LVN earn RN

RN earn BSN

NO Class Room Time Required

California and NLN approved programs

What does this mean? It means, in plain English, that LVN work is the same as RN work is the same as BSN work. It means, "you're doing the work, why not get the title and get paid for it?" It implies you needn't go to school to advance yourself. The pendulum, it seems, has swung too far toward giving credit for experience and devaluing classroom educational material. How does this sound?

Nurse Aide→LVN→RN→BSN→MD

No Class Time Required

Do you think physicians will go for that?

Physicians as well as administrators and legislators are behind the effort to blur the lines and facilitate the advancement of ancillary personnel into nursing's ranks.

There is now a movement in California to lower Nursing Board passing scores to below 350. Barring that, California may utilize its own examination rather than the national one. What will this do to the mobility of nurses holding California licenses? If the measure passes, new graduates who fail the Board examination may be able to continue working for up to 2 years using interim permits. What are the reasons behind this movement? The national examination, we are told, discriminates against those who do not speak English as a first language. Will lowering the standards improve patient care? Will hiring people who cannot speak to patients improve patient care? We must define our values.

Let's stop being professional pessimists and start being mature nurses—positive, self-confident, self-contained, and self-governed.[5] Nurses must address the issues of the nursing shortage and nurses' job dissatisfaction. Others, we can see, are only too ready to do it if we do not.

REFERENCES

1. Barclay, D.A.: Angels of mercy are turning in their wings, The Register, p. E-1, February 11, 1981.
2. Barclay, D.A.: Band-aid solutions aren't luring nurses, The Register, p. F-2, February 12, 1981.
3. Beyette, B.: Nurse recruitment on the critical list, Los Angeles Times, p. V-1, September 30, 1980.
4. Bigham, J.: They're learning to love the seven-day work week, The Register, p. E-4, February 11, 1981.
5. Curtain, L.: Enough of reality shock, burn-out, and identity crisis, Supervisor Nurse 2(10):7, 1980.
6. Donovan, L.: Can you really make more as a grocery clerk, RN 43(3):50, 1980.
7. Donovan, L.: What nurses want (and what they're getting), RN 43(4):22, April 1980.
8. Hallas, G.G.: Why nurses are giving it up, RN, p. 17, July 1980.
9. Kramer, M.: Reality shock, St. Louis, 1974, The C.V. Mosby Co.
10. Low pay cited in nurse shortage, American Medical News, p. 6, January 16, 1981.
11. McCloskey, J.C.: What rewards will keep nurses on the job, American Journal of Nursing 75(4):600, 1975.
12. Medical Advancement Center (advertisement), Los Angeles Times, Job Opportunities, p. 69, April 26, 1981.

13. Moses, E., and Roth, A.: Nursepower: what do statistics reveal about the nation's nurses? American Journal of Nurses, **79**(10):1745, October 1979.
14. Nielsen, B.G.: "The nursing shortage" [memo to chief executive officers], Hospital Council of Southern California, July 7, 1980.
15. Nurses quit hospital for casino, American Medical News p. 18, January 16, 1981.
16. Osinski, E.G., and Morrison, W.H.: The all-RN staff, Supervisor Nurse **9**(9):66, 1978.
17. Sweeney, J.: Nurse shortage hampering hospital, Los Angeles Times, p. II-6, November 20, 1980.
18. Vale, V.L.: Letter to the editor, Los Angeles Times, p. II-6, February 9, 1981.
19. Wandelt, M., and others: Conditions associated with registered nurse employment in Texas Center for Research, Austin, 1980, School of Nursing, University of Texas.
20. Weiss, R.E., and others: Nursing shortage: a solution, Hospital Forum **23**(5):19, 1980.
21. Work conditions cause nurses to leave, The American Nurse **12**(12):5, 1980.

BIBLIOGRAPHY

Claureul, G., and Caviness, S.: Keep that nurse, Hospital Forum **22**(5):11, 1980.

Christman, L.: Professional nursing practice/impediments to practice=satisfaction quotient, Journal of the New York State Nurses Association **10**(4):25, 1979.

Deloughery, G.L., and Gebbie, K.M.: Political dynamics: impact on nurses and nursing, St. Louis, 1975, The C.V. Mosby Co.

Garfield, C.: Coping with burn-out, Hospital Forum **23**(1):15, 1980.

Grimm, L.J., and Crawford, J.J.: Viewpoint: assertiveness training for nurses, Nursing Administration Quarterly **2**(3):59, 1978.

Heinen, B.: Job satisfaction for the float staff, Supervisor Nurse **10**(1):48, 1979.

Nielsen, B.: Agencies fill a need but are not the answer, Hospitals **55**(6):66, March 16, 1981.

Nurse registries—part of the problem or part of the solution (editorial). Hospitals **55**(6):65, March 16, 1981.

Silber, M.B.: The motivation pyramid in nurse retention, Supervisor Nurse **12**(4):45, 1981.

Spencer, C.E.: Nurses need liberation—but from whom? RN **42**(7):63, July 1979.

Ulsafer-Van Lanen, J.: Lateral promotion keeps skilled nurses in direct patient care, Hospitals **55**(5):87, 1981.

Watson, L.A.: Keeping qualified nurses, Supervisor Nurse **10**(10):29, 1979.

SHERMALAYNE SOUTHARD SZASZ

Chapter 31

The tyranny of uniforms

. . . the patient opens his eyes and finds a nurse by his bedside. Without a word being spoken he receives a number of messages. Here is someone who is professionally trained, who knows how to handle his particular troubles, knows the correct treatment and how to give it, who is competent, kind, efficient, gentle. He is safe in her hands. She may speak to him and give reassurance or instructions but the words are secondary and merely add to a message which has already been given, conveyed by the uniform itself.[10]

THE ORIGIN OF UNIFORMS

Historically nursing began as a penance practiced by convent men and women. But "professional nursing"—nursing for pay—was predominantly practiced by those who could earn their living no other way, by women who were destitute, widowed, or elderly. When Charles Dickens in 1844 introduced Sairey Gamp and Betsey Prig as caricatures of professional nurses of his time, a hue and cry went out to reform nursing. Ten years later a study conducted in England recorded the reactions of physicians and superintendents to the professional nurses of their time:

If I can but obtain a sober set, it is more than I can hope for.

I inquired about the character of the nurses and Dr. X says they always engage them without any character, as no respectable person would undertake so disagreeable an office. He says the duties they have to perform are most unpleasant and that it is any wonder that many of them drink, as they require something to keep up their spirits.[8]

Because of this negative perception of professional nurses, uniforms were developed for nurses to convey an image of respectability, cleanliness, and servitude. The uniform and cap originated in the dress of convent nuns. The cap originally included an attached veil, which was symbolic of humility, service, and obedience— a custom that has been retained by most Catholic orders and by many marriage ceremonies. The meaning of nurses' caps is usually considered a remnant of this custom, the cap being a symbol of humility and service to humanity.[5]

Uniforms were developed not only for nurses, however, but also for others in the health care field. Men interested in the healing arts became physicians, women

397

interested in the healing arts became nurses, and what both wore in the hospital setting distinctly symbolized their roles as well as their ranks. A man in a long white lab coat was assumed to be a physician. A woman in a white dress and white cap was obviously a nurse.

Times have changed and the composition of the classic health care team is different. Institutions now boast social workers, psychologists, dieticians, medical technologists, and a host of assistants in addition to physicians and nurses. Any of these health workers may wear either the traditional white coat that once distinguished physicians from other providers or the white uniform that was once uniquely nurses'. Nurses still wear white uniforms, but the physician's white coat has become optional. Reversals of the traditional occupational roles further accentuate the confusion as one finds more male nurses and more female physicians.[6]

WHAT THE UNIFORM MEANS: ASSOCIATIONS AND STEREOTYPES

When asked to describe the term "professional nurse," those within nursing and those outside it both tend not to describe nurses' attributes, educational level, or values but instead to define the professional nurse by her appearance: white cap, white uniform, white stockings, white shoes, white female. The "professional nurse" remains a stereotypical media image defined not in accordance with who the nurse is or what she does but with how she looks. Is this not the characteristic way women have been defined all along? As Siegel states, "The identity of the nurse has become so closely intertwined with the symbolic nursing attire, that her identity hinges on the wearing of the traditional garments."[9]

People often greet nurses with the remark, "It's so nice to meet a nurse who looks like a nurse." But the uniform can evoke both positive and negative associations and symbolizes meanings based largely on one's previous experience or on images fostered by the profession or the press. These meanings and associations may have no relation to any individual nurse. Typically the uniform is associated with the roles of waitress, servant, or mother and the traits of being receptive or authoritarian.

Boerrigger[2] discusses the sexual associations of the white uniform worn by nurses and brings out some of the meanings assigned to the white uniform reinforced by current fiction, television, and movies.

> Historically, white has been the hue which designates chastity and purity. . . . man is piqued sexually by the quirk of wanting to possess and conquer that which is unobtainable or virginally untouched and hence pure.
>
> Although it has often been generalized that the hospital nurse dressed in white stockings, cap, and uniform may have an antiseptic and asexual effect upon the male, it is now being realized that a number of males find erotic arousal in exactly . . . that type of attire.[2]

MYTHS ABOUT UNIFORMS

The white uniform has been promoted as a *means of instant identification* of nurses by the patient. This assumption, however, is false. Since identical dress has long been adopted by workers in allied health fields and vocations unrelated to health care, the uniform is no longer a reliable cue. The typical hospital patient has considerable difficulty differentiating nurses from other hospital personnal. This identification difficulty is still greater if the person has relied almost exclusively on the uniform and is not sensitive to other situational cues.[9]

The white uniform has also been promoted as a *means of immediate access* by nurses to the patient; it is as a license to enter the territory of the patient and address highly personal issues. Research tends to contradict this assertion, however, when *real* access to the patient is considered. It has been found that the uniform tends to establish a distance, difference, and ranking between nurses and patients, professionals and lay people, officials and constituents. Wearing a uniform thus often creates a distance between the nurse and patient rather than promoting closeness.

On the one hand, the patient's identification can be at least partially assisted by a uniformed appearance; on the other hand, closeness may more easily develop between interacting persons if they have similar appearance or dress. Psychiatric nurses, community health nurses, and even some Catholic sisterhoods (from which much of the nursing tradition is derived) are adopting lay dress based on these findings.[9]

MYTHS TO HIDE BEHIND

The uniform *serves as an affiliative tool* and gives many nurses a sense of belonging. Because of this outward conformity, nurses identify with the group, not realizing that the group itself is mostly ill defined. Many think the uniform makes them part of a group. The irony here is that there is no one group in nursing just as there is no one goal. There are little cohesion and unity in nursing. We are kidding ourselves when we think the uniform serves as a signal of a unified nursing identity.

To some people the uniform *identifies the nurse's functions* as well as her role. If one "looks like a nurse," one doesn't have to define what a nurse is. There is a tendency to hide behind the uniform: "I look like a nurse, therefore I am a nurse." We assume that while we are wearing a uniform, people automatically know us by looking at us. Everyone, however, has a different perception of what the uniform signals. Thus we leave ourselves open to others' interpretations. ("This is how a nurse is supposed to look" or "This is how a nurse is supposed to act" or "This is how a nurse is supposed to feel.")

The traditional white nursing attire *allows some nurses to remain role-bound and anonymous.* The nurse does not have to define herself; she feels the uniform does this for her. Since this process involves little ego differentiation, the nurse as an individual fades into the background, leaving the empty shell of a stereotype. The only advantage, if one chooses to accept it, is that a nurse as a blob of white does not have to take an individual stand on who she is. The uniform allows us, then, not only *not to be conversant* with who we are but also, since we are anonymous, even *not to be responsible* for what we are. With all the ambiguities and associations of the uniform, nurses must recognize that we cannot be content to allow a uniform to tell us and others what a nurse is and what a nurse does.

UNIFORMS AND "THE PROFESSIONAL"

Members of a true profession such as medicine, law, divinity, engineering, and teaching need no distinctive badge. As sociologist Eliot Friedson[4] indicates, "the license and mandate to control its work, granted by society" is foremost to the idea of a profession. In American culture the more a person attains professional stature, the less distinct and conforming her/his outward appearance need be.

Few professionals wear uniforms. Members of military and quasimilitary organizations such as the police do wear them. Within civilian professions, however, nurses are among the unique few who cling to the tradition of wearing uniforms. The milieu of the hospital encompasses many groups of professionals, but the only group of professionals who maintain a prescribed uniform continues to be nurses.

Physicians wear no identifying symbols other than occasionally a white jacket or lab coat. Patients trust physicians not because of a uniform but because they have presumably attained a certain level of specialized knowledge and education. In addition, they are figures of authority and command respect from the public not by virtue of what they wear but by their demeanor. It is evident that those with the highest authority, except in the military, seldom wear any type of distinguishing dress at all.[1]

The nursing uniform is not used in a positive way, as a business suit is, for example. The nursing uniform does not promote an image of an autonomous person. As Hughes and Proulx point out, "Nurses today are abysmally naked in their display of authority apparel."[6] It is interesting to note that the more a nurse specializes, the less traditional her appearance becomes. In the areas of intensive care, labor and delivery, the operating room, pediatrics, and psychiatry, in all of which nurses have increased autonomy, they seem to conform less to the traditional white uniforms.

A study by Klein and others[7] in 1972 attempted to evaluate the self-esteem of nursing staff by studying nursing's self-image and patients' perception of nursing staff when the traditional white uniform was replaced by street clothes. Klein surmised from the data that

> the fact that nursing staff members feel better about themselves when wearing street clothes apparently permitted them to rely more heavily upon their interpersonal skills for

dealing with patients. . . . Their forced change back into uniforms . . . appeared to disturb an emerging, more satisfying sense of self. . . . Thus while mode of apparel in itself appears to be a relatively unimportant variable, it clearly has considerable symbolic value . . . it seems to be closely related to matters of professional role, morale, and prestige.[7]

Two studies conducted at the University Hospital and Clinics in Gainesville, Florida, reported positive reactions to pediatric nurses wearing pastel attire. It was concluded that this attire was helpful in the nurse-patient-parent relationship, particularly in reducing the anxiety of children. In addition pediatric nurses had a more personal view of their role.[3]

But most nurses still desire to wear uniforms despite the evidence that the traditional white uniform is in fact *unprofessional* and prohibits many nurses from developing a unique and professional role in the eyes of physicians, administrators, the public, and nurses themselves.

Why does this occur? Naturally there are people within the health care system who have much invested in keeping nurses in white uniforms. These people encourage nurses to wear uniforms and caps and tell them this makes them "more professional." But are caps and uniforms actually more professional, or do they still function psychologically in terms of the original intent—a reminder of obedience, servitude, and humility?

Many questions, then, emerge that must be answered by each individual nurse:

What does your uniform mean to you?

What does your uniform seem to mean to other people?

Is the uniform appropriate to your job?

Does your uniform still fit into your life-style?

Does the nursing uniform necessarily have to be white?

I do not mean to suggest that uniforms should be abandoned entirely. It is time, however, for nurses to begin to think about *all* aspects of their situation, including their dress, so that they can make intelligent decisions about their future.

REFERENCES

1. Bevona, C.G.: The nonfunctional nursing cap.
2. Boerigger, J.W.: What you always wanted to know about sex in uniform but were afraid to ask, London, Capri Publishers, Ltd.
3. Cheng, N., and others: A second look at nurses in colour, Hospitals **39**:59, June 16, 1965.
4. Friedson, E.: Profession of medicine, New York, 1971, Dodd, Mead & Co.
5. Goodnow, G.: Nursing history, Philadelphia, 1949, W.B. Saunders Co.
6. Hughes, E., and Proulx, J.: You are what you wear, Hospitals **53**:113, August 16, 1979.
7. Klien, R., and others: Psychiatric staff: uniforms or street clothes? Archives of General Psychiatry **26**:51, January 1972.
8. Robinson, V.: White caps: the story of nursing Philadelphia, 1946, J.B. Lippencott Co.
9. Seigel, H.: The nurses uniform—symbolic or sacrosanct? Nursing Forum **7**(3):315, 1968.
10. Watson, G.: The uniform that brings confidence, Nursing Mirror **147**:34, July 20, 1978.

Chapter 32

Breaking out . . . breaking in

Ships are safe when they are docked in harbor . . . but that is not what ships are for. I was once safe in my job as well, but I sought something more when I began my sales career 3 years ago. Until that time I had worked in or managed several specialty departments, including a cardiac catheterization laboratory in a small hospital.

My entry into sales was serendipitous. A sales representative with whom I was acquainted asked me, "When are you going to get out of the hospital?" She suggested I contact the national sales manager of a hospital equipment supply company. I called him and we met for lunch. We discussed travel rather than business. A few weeks later he offered me the first territory that opened. Later he told me he had hired me because of my ease in conversing with him (a sales prerequisite). I became the second woman in a sales force of 35 men and the first nurse . . . an experiment.

As I was to discover later, all of the essential elements of a good salesperson-company match seldom come together as easily as they had in my situation. These elements include the right time, the right company, the right employee-supervisor chemistry, and an atmosphere for creative work. With beginner's luck I embarked on my new career in the world of medical sales.

My territory consisted of all the hospitals within three states. It was my responsibility to manage, sell, and in-service five product lines of cardiovascular equipment—equipment with which I was familiar, a fact that eased my transition from cardiovascular nursing to cardiovascular sales. What made me think I could sell? I wasn't sure, but I thought of all the patients to whom as a nurse I had "sold" faith in the medical-nursing team and faith in their ability to get well.

I was petrified but convinced myself that the worst that could happen would be failure—and that wasn't fatal. I mustered my managerial know-how, and that together with the credibility I achieved through my nursing experience and familiarity with the equipment got me started. Nurses often ask the same questions:

"Are the products good?"

"Are they readily available?"

"Can I trust the salesperson to give me accurate information?"

"How will the company and salesperson respond in an emergency?"

I made the answers to these questions my platform and ran on it. It worked.

I cannot stress enough the importance of providing good service. I remembered too well some of my nursing days, which I would love to forget, when the patients were unstable, the equipment wouldn't work, the doctors were screaming, half the staff was "sick," and I needed *something* to be right. I recalled picking up the phone on a few of these occasions to request a pacemaker, catheter, or whatever and being relieved to hear the salesperson say, "Relax. I'm on my way." I have never forgotten the importance of being available. Consequently I made up for my lack of electronics knowledge with service and teaching.

I have noted then and notice still a syndrome that occurs between salespeople (usually those who are female) and nurses. I call it the "three piece suit, I've made it, you haven't game." Sometimes a salesperson gives this impression, and sometimes a nurse anticipates it from past experiences. Either way it means trouble and can only be avoided by aligning oneself with the nurses.

I think it helpful at this point to describe what I sold: physiological pressure transducers, arterial line kits, electromagnetic blood flow devices, cardiac output computers, thermal dilution catheters, and portable monitoring systems. I mention this to make it clear that women can and do sell electronic equipment, although there are not many who do. I had much to learn about these instruments and their application when I entered sales, a realization that made me aware of the need to teach the nurses with whom I worked. I am not, repeat *not*, an electronic genius, but I learned.

On the other hand, the knowledge I had gained in nursing of hemodynamic parameters was an advantage in troubleshooting. When I received a call concerning supposedly malfunctioning equipment, I could help the nurse reevaluate the patient's physiologic status, medications, other equipment, and so on. Often the real problem was discovered in these areas.

My familiarity with hospital procedures was also helpful. Again, my years of interdepartmental interaction served me well as a salesperson.

All was not perfect, however—the feeling of personal rejection, common in sales, was difficult to handle at times. Working for months on a proposed strategy only to have the competition get the sale was galling. I had to change my values. My criterion for success was no longer how hard I worked or how many patients I assisted to recover but *how much revenue I generated*. This is the issue that concerns a corporation when considering a nurse for employment. Can she make the crossover? (More on this later.)

In nursing, time is very important: medications, meals, doctors' rounds, and therapies are monitored by effective nurse managers, and team and shift planning involves time considerations. As a salesperson I found myself in an environment where my time was my own. I was heady with my new-found freedom! And I was frightened. There was no one to check the fruits of my daily work, no one to review my time card—my sales figures at the end of the month were of sole importance.

My being female did not become an issue with clients in this first position. There are some medical sales specialities, however, that lend themselves to male-female games.

I could write a saga entitled "Single Woman on the Road" to describe the tremendous adjustments I needed to make in my life as I began traveling extensively. Most salespeople quickly discover whether or not they enjoy traveling; there seems to be no middle road. It is lonely. When the work is done, there is only a hotel room to return to. I have survived by familiarizing myself with the cities in my territory, making them homes away from home. I have found that a woman alone is often perceived as a "sitting duck" and that her survival depends on her ability to handle that kind of situation.

After 2 years another opportunity presented itself, and again I managed to escape the usual interviewing process. The new company was familiar with my work and sought me out. I used the transition period, however, to investigate and interview with other companies. I learned that the interviewing process can be tedious, frightening, and much work. It is an art that must be learned. I suggest that before beginning one should talk with salespeople and executive placement agencies and read books and articles on the subject. During these interviews I was asked, "Why are you so successful?" and first began to analyze my success. The previous pages reflect my answers.

With this second firm came the opportunity to learn a new medical specialty and to develop another side of my personality. I no longer had the security of 10 years' cardiovascular nursing experience to hide behind. Suddenly I, the woman, the salesperson, was selling to Dr. John Doe, the man, the physician. I had no parallel experiences as a nurse on which to rely. I was no longer working with nurses. Unpalatable as this may be to some, I learned that being a woman was a definite advantage in my new situation. I learned too that being female might open a door but will never keep it open unless that fact is accompanied by a good product, knowledge, and service. Why are women in sales often so successful? Because we have to be.

Other chapters discuss nursing stereotypes and the public image of nursing. In the corporate world the unfounded attitude prevails that nurses and sales don't mix. I emphasize *sales* positions here, because most firms have recognized the contributions a qualified nurse can make in the areas of education, field training, troubleshooting, advising about products, and liaisons with medicine. It is in sales that nurses still fight the all-giving, gentle nurturer image. The bottom line in sales is money, and for nurses money has traditionally been a dirty word, something that might tarnish one's image. Businesses succeed by making money, and nurses who sell must reject the self-sacrifice (company-sacrifice) ethic. I hope that the entry of more nurses into sales will help further change these corporate attitudes, for it can be done: the two companies for which I was an experiment have both hired more nurses.

If you are thinking about sales as an alternative to nursing, consider the following questions:

Can you adjust to a new value system?

Can you be self-motivated? Self-managed?

Can you handle rejection without taking it personally?

Do you have a drive to make money?

Do you have the traits necessary to deal with different people every day?

Are you willing to take risks?

Can you turn off the job at night?

Are you secure in your own womanhood?

If you have answered the above questions positively, sit in your favorite quiet place at home and think about what you like most in nursing—then get someone to pay you for selling or teaching about related products. (If you don't like pediatrics, for example, don't choose pediatric products to begin your business career.) Choose a field in which your background and knowledge can be an asset. Talk to your present sales representatives. *Ask yourself whether or not you can adjust to traveling* and be honest in assessing the travel requirements of potential companies. This is one way of avoiding unnecessary pressure—examine all the aspects of the fit between you and the position.

A fine resume is essential. There are companies that specialize in helping one turn out a sophisticated product; use them if you're unsure about this aspect of selling yourself. Graphic designers do unique and memorable work (and you do want to be remembered). These investments can pay off when you finally begin the interviewing process.

An employment agency with a medical sales division might be a good place to start. Or you might wish to investigate positions through salespeople familiar to you. Often they can refer you to someone they trust even if they can't help with specific job information. Some companies rely on placement services exclusively, but others avoid them—do your homework.

In closing, I quote the advice of W.E.B. DuBois on his ninetieth birthday to his great grandson:

"It is of prime importance that you learn what you want to do, how you are fit to do it and whether or not the world needs the service. . . . The return from your work must be the satisfaction that work brings you and the world's need of that work . . . income is not greenbacks, it is satisfaction, it is creation, it is beauty. . . ."

To that I would add: if business is right for you, and you are right for business, you can have the greenbacks too! Good luck.

Chapter 33

Getting a foot in the door

One nurse's experience in obtaining hospital privileges

Change is inevitable, but planning for change is a process that can be learned. Nurses in independent practice need to learn the process of planning for change if they are to implement their practice effectively.

A case in point is the obtaining of hospital privileges by independent nurse practitioners. The planning for this change must include considering the possible resistance to change, the lack of awareness manifested by others, and procedural delays. Only arduously did I learn this myself.

I am an independent nurse practitioner, a consultant to a cardiologist. The change in my instance involved obtaining hospital privileges at one of the local private hospitals into which we admit our office patients. Hospital privileges are a critical element in our concept of the continuity of care and would enable me to continue to care for our office patients during their hospitalization. Obviously, hospitalization for an acute illness does not mean that patients cease to have other chronic health care problems requiring nurse practitioner consultation.

Fortunately in my case, the required change was already in progress. Hospital administrators were aware that nurses were beginning to apply for hospital privileges as one aspect of nursing's expanded role. I learned that the Medical Review Committee had just received an application for attending privileges from a nurse practitioner and that a Joint Practice Committee had been formed to evaluate the applicant and make appropriate recommendations. That someone else was breaking ground in such an important area was encouraging.

When I applied for hospital privileges, I assumed the application would be processed in 3 to 6 months. Never did I suspect it would require 2½ years for the hospital to establish a procedure for evaluating and implementing this proposed change.

Many changes had to occur before the hospital reached the point of seriously considering nurses' applications for hospital privileges. All the institution's barriers to

406

this change had to be identified and surmounted. Becoming aware of the hospital's internal structure and functioning was of utmost importance. The medical bylaws had no provision for nonphysician staff privileges. Moreover, these bylaws could be changed only by a majority vote of the entire medical staff at its annual meeting.

Another obstacle was the lack of knowledge on the part of hospital health personnel about the independent nurse practitioner's role within the institution. Physicians feared the competition, nurses worried about the lack of control, and the hospital community overall did not understand the role of an independent nurse practitioner in an acute care setting.

Planned change also requires identifying key people in positions to make policy decisions. I made it a point to introduce myself to nursing administrators and to convey to them my nursing philosophy and commitment. By working closely with the nursing staff in instituting nursing rounds and by giving pathophysiology lectures, I helped the nurses see that I functioned from a nursing perspective and that I was not trying to be a "minidoctor."

Sometimes apparently powerless people turn out to be facilitators of change. One such example was the medical staff executive secretary. Through her attendance at all medical staff meetings she knew the policies and politics of the institution. She was regarded favorably by many of the medical staff and therefore had significant political clout. I spent time with her at lunch making sure she understood the concept of nurse practitioners. I then forwarded to her copies of educational articles about nurse practitioners.

A top priority was to win the confidence of the medical staff. At first, the physicians on the Joint Practice Committee saw no place for nurse practitioners in an acute care setting. Their lack of knowledge about nurse practitioners made the task of setting up policies and procedures for attending privileges virtually impossible. Educating the physicians about the expanded role of nursing in a hospital setting was another area of frustration. Because they were all independent medical practitioners, it was impossible to meet with them as a group for any type of instruction. They had to be educated about my role first on a one-to-one basis and then indirectly through the acceptance of patients and the hospital network system.

Another key person was the Associate Nursing Administrator. I met with her several times to discuss ways of establishing a procedure to allow hospital privileges for nurse practitioners. In these discussions I drew on my experience at the state and regional levels of the State Nursing Association in dealing with new legislation and Association policies regarding nurse practitioners.

Finally, it was essential to apprise key people in the hospital continually about the progress of my application. As in any major institution, the hospital's administrators had other priorities besides dealing with a small group of individuals seeking hospital privileges. Their responsibilities within the institution were so overwhelming that months would pass before the Joint Practice Committee met again. I wanted them to realize that I was sympathetic to their concerns but that I had not lost interest in obtaining hospital privileges.

Two and a half years after I first applied, the institution changed its medical bylaws to allow allied health professionals to apply for hospital privileges. Both the Joint Practice Committee and the Medical Executive Committee adopted policies and procedures. The Joint Practice Committee was finally ready to process its first applicant.

The process of obtaining hospital privileges required identifying and working through many particular factors: overcoming resistance, educating hospital personnel, briefing key people, waiting persistently. The final result was that nurse practitioners could apply for hospital privileges in a system of well-defined hospital guidelines for application and review.

The following are the key elements to consider when attempting to bring about planned change in an institution:

Knowledge of planned change theory

Review of the literaure

Assessment of the power structure within the institution

Knowledge of the medical bylaws

Understanding the functioning of the Joint Practice Committee

Specific plans for instituting change within the institution

Educating all health personnel about nursing's roles

Working closely with nursing services to bring about the change

Keeping the issue visible

BIBLIOGRAPHY

Bergeson, P., and Melvin, N.: Granting hospital privileges to nurse practitioners, Hospitals **49** (16):99, 1975.

Friedman, E.: Staff privileges for nonphysicians, Hospital Medical Staff 7(3):22, 1978.

Huber, G., and Romoff, J.: Repayment regulations limit use of physicians, Hospital Medical Staff 9(8):2, 1980.

Melvin, N.: Power: nursing's challenge to change. Developing guidelines for clinical privileges for nurse practitioners. American Nurses Association Publications (G-135):62, 1979.

MAURENE A. HARVEY

Chapter 34

Private practice as an independent consultant

As nursing increases in depth and breadth, nurses are searching for alternative ways to utilize their skills and are establishing new roles within the health care delivery system. Consulting is an alternative that appeals to many, but few know where to begin or how to predict whether they will reach success.

With no training or experience as independent contractors, many consultants have learned by trial and error. Suprisingly, common sense and intuition have sufficed. For those now considering this role, certain observations and generalizations regarding the factors involved in becoming a successful and satisfied independent consultant can be made from these early efforts.

POSSESSING A MARKETABLE SKILL

The key to successful consulting is providing a needed skill or service *better* and *more economically* than the institution itself can. The ability to provide better services is acquired through experience, preferably in a variety of settings. It would be highly unlikely for a new graduate to establish a successful consulting practice.

The ability to provide services economically results from specializing and capitalizing on intermittent needs for specialists. General skills can probably be provided by someone already on staff. And if the demand for a specialist is continuous, then the institution often finds it more efficient to employ someone full time to meet the need. For example, institutions have no need for a consultant to conduct orientation classes. This is a general skill, is tailored to the institution, and is needed on an ongoing basis. An annual stress management seminar, however, could best be provided by an outside specialist. Even though the hourly expense for a consultant is high, the total cost is still less than that of having a staff member spend 3 or 4 days planning and developing a 1-day workshop that might not reflect firsthand knowledge.

GAINING ENTRY

Once a marketable skill is developed, the next step is making prospective clients aware that the expertise is available. Those agencies most likely to be in need can be identified on the basis of past experience. The most difficult barrier is gaining a meaningful entry.

Rarely are blind mail or telephone contacts helpful in developing clientele unless such contacts happen to occur when specific needs have already been identified. The usual sequence is that someone on staff identifies a need and asks colleagues and others on staff for a referral. If someone asked for a referral has knowledge of the consultant's skills from some previous professional involvement, the initial contact comes more easily.

Since word of mouth is so important, getting started is easiest in a location where recognition already exists through the contacts and exposure of prior employment, for independent practice can include participation in professional organizations and speaking before various groups. Once consulting is begun, each client becomes a referral source.

CONSTRUCTING A PROPOSAL

The initial meeting with a potential client should involve exchanging information about the client's needs and the consultant's services and discussing avenues for meeting these needs. The consultant should be open and flexible, working with the client first to define the need and then to explore ways to meet it. It is not advisable to attempt to sell a client a predetermined package.

After this meeting the consultant can construct a specific proposal outlining the goals and objectives of the program, the way in which it will be implemented, the time frame involved, and the responsibilities of each party.

Consulting fees are at first difficult to set. Since it generally takes an inexperienced person three or four times longer than a consultant to provide the same service, begin by charging about three times the hourly wage of the staff person who would otherwise provide the service. The client may actually save money in such contractual agreements because there are no payroll taxes or employee benefits to add to the cost.

Fees can be set by the hour or by the contract. It is important to be consistent in charges for all clients. Fee schedules should be set and adhered to whenever applicable.

FULFILLING THE PROMISE

Probably the most important aspect of successful consulting is the quality of the work. Clientele is developed by not simply meeting obligations but by exceeding the expectations of clients. Quality leads to quantity.

To make the client more aware of the benefits of the consultation, and to heighten the consultant's awareness of ways to improve, an evaluation meeting should be held after the consulting is completed. Periodically repeated contracts with clients make up the bulk of most consulting businesses.

THE ADVANTAGES

The advantages of full-time independent consulting are numerous. A major benefit is the ability to control the service. Once the proposal is designed and the agreement signed, the delivery can proceed without interference. The contract is the only real pragmatic concern. Although it is necessary to be aware of the agency's power structure and internal politics, these factors are extraneous and rarely burden the consultant.

The financial rewards of consulting are good, even when the cost of providing self-insurance and other necessities is taken into account. High in-house expenses make contracted services cost-efficient for the client and profitable for the consultant.

Professional rewards include the recognition of acquired skills, personal growth through concentration on a specialization, and the more efficient use of time. As a salaried employee, a nurse is often called on to meet a host of demands that require expertise or talents that cannot be found in any one person, resulting in less efficient interaction, poor performance, and decreased job satisfaction. For an independent consultant, uninterrupted work on projects that best utilize unique skills and training is possible. Since an agency does not hire a consultant to meet a need of only a handful of people, larger numbers of nurses are reached, thus expanding professional contribution.

THE DISADVANTAGES

There are negative aspects of consulting that turn many nurses away from full-time independent contracting. If the intention is to consult on a part-time basis, however, most of these drawbacks are insignificant.

First, the problem of the risk involved must be overcome. Work is not guaranteed and is subject to periods of too much and too little demand. Therefore income will not be steady, and a lack of confidence in the overall income from consulting may cause some anxiety. Another problem is the fear of failure. It is difficult to leave the security of a respected position and put a reputation on the line.

A nurse who becomes a consultant may miss that which was once frustrating— relationships with patients, peers, and colleagues. As an outsider, however, associated with each institution on a short-time basis, a consultant can achieve true independence and isolation from the frustrations of nursing.

QUALITIES THAT FOSTER SUCCESS

Having examined the process of consulting, it is important to look at the qualities of the consultant. Although the following list is not all inclusive, these traits are helpful in developing a successful career in private practice:

Self-motivation to high levels of quality and quantity

Ability to organize

Flexibility and creativity

Self-confidence

Assertiveness and the judgment to know when to use it

Ability to perform objective self-evaluation

Also helpful are those skills related to the business aspects of consulting. Keeping accurate and detailed business, tax, and insurance records takes time. This skill can be acquired through self-education, but it may be advisable to retain an accountant or tax attorney. This expense is justified by the fact that the time spent keeping records can be more profitably spent consulting. This principle applies to all other support services as well.

WHERE TO BEGIN

If consulting seems appealing and a marketable skill and the requisite personality traits are possessed, a local reputation should be developed. Gradually contracts can be made with outside agencies on a part-time basis. If success and enjoyment result, a gradual transition to full-time consulting can be undertaken. Salaried employment can be decreased as consulting commitments increase.

Consulting is an option open only to a few nurses, but to them it offers autonomy and professional growth. It is a way of growing or changing without dropping out. Through consulting an increased contribution to nursing can be made.

Having an outstanding professional reputation is necessary to enter consulting. It must be maintained and expanded to produce success.

ELIZABETH CARR

Chapter 35

A model for private practice

Requirements for success

During the last decade the nursing profession has made a tremendous movement toward independence and autonomy. Several interrelated factors have influenced the direction of the profession, including the emphasis on graduate education,
a proliferation of expanded nursing roles, legislative changes in many states' Nurse
Practice Acts to sanction autonomy and accountability, the women's liberation movement, and consumers' demands for health promotion and self-care. These developments have provided the impetus for the movement of many nurses throughout the
United States into independent practice.

As women's role in society is dramatically changing, so too is the role of the
nurse as she moves from semiprofessional status to full professional status. The
history of nursing shows it has evolved in concert with medicine; the nurse's traditional relationship with the physician has been as handmaiden—subservient, submissive, and dependent.

This chapter presents a model of independent nursing practice that calls for a
change from the traditional, dependent role to an expanded, autonomous one. The
development and implementation of innovative professional opportunities for nurses
is discussed, as are issues of nursing autonomy, female conditioning, practice development, and requirements for success. The nursing profession is entering an exciting
period as it moves toward full professional status. The future holds opportunities and
demands we have just begun to realize. We are starting a journey into unexplored
territory that will challenge us personally and stretch our professional capabilities.
This passage promises financial reward, personal fulfillment, and professional en-
hancement; it requires courage, determination, and much hard work. The future of
nursing is in our hands.

AUTONOMY IN NURSING

For 15 years the literature has discussed independent practice as a nursing
concern. The private practice setting, in which the nurse assumes complete re-

sponsibility for her practice, is one road to autonomy in nursing. The independent nurse rather than being an extension of the physician practices a unique discipline.

Kinlein[9] provides a thoughtful analysis of the independent nursing role in comparison with the traditional role. In the traditional model the consumer has no direct access to the nurse's services, and the nurse is dependent on the physician for direction. In contrast, the independent nurse practitioner is directly available and accessible to potential and actual consumers, maintains direct communication with clients regarding her services, and is responsible for all professional activities including assessment, decision making, care giving, and evaluation. Expert knowledge and specialized skill in *applying* that knowledge are key ingredients in the independent nursing role.

Full professional status demands control of the profession over its practice, education, and research. The private practice setting provides an opportunity for the clinical nurse specialist and the advanced nurse practitioner to function autonomously. As such, private practice represents a major move toward self-direction and professional parity.

DEVELOPING A PRIVATE PRACTICE

Agree[1] interviewed nurses in private practice and found that most had developed their businesses for similar reasons: a frustration with institutional practice, the determination to achieve greater personal and professional fulfillment, and economic motivations. These themes recur throughout the literature as nurse practitioners, psychiatric and mental health clinical specialists, and nurse midwives have described their motivations for developing private practices. [11,12,16] All of these issues influenced my decision to open a practice in Washington, D.C., which I will discuss to illustrate the process.

Before coming to Washington I lived in Los Angeles, where I had developed a successful and rewarding nursing career. My practice in Los Angeles involved three settings: I was director of consultation and education for five community mental health centers, had a private psychotherapy practice, and was on the faculty of the medical school at the University of Southern California. What I learned from these positions was useful in establishing my current independent practice.

I created the position of director of consultation and education in conjunction with the local mental health administration. The position involved developing and coordinating a program of consultation and education services for a large geographic area (a population of 1.5 million over 222 square miles). The program was designed to deliver comprehensive services based on mental health priorities and community needs. I was the first nonphysician and the first woman on the management team. It was an exciting and challenging experience that required diligent efforts to develop a combination of management, leadership, and marketing skills. The work involved meeting with administrators and staff of community agencies to provide consultation services and to develop preventative care projects, several of which have received national recognition.[2,4]

During the same period I developed a private psychotherapy practice. Success in such an endeavor requires a high level of professional competence and adequate referral sources. Presentations at professional meetings and ongoing contacts with colleagues were effective in developing referrals. For example, my involvement in a third-party reimbursement project with other psychiatric nurse specialists had a secondary benefit in the establishment of a mutual referral system.

My third position as a faculty member of an interdisciplinary, postgraduate training program further enhanced my practice. The prestige of being associated with a university afforded me recognition as an expert consultant and led to being introduced to other professionals who continue to assist me in my career.

The Los Angeles experience influenced the development of my Washington practice in several ways. Josefowitz[7] in *Paths to Power* discusses the need for women to recognize and translate their specialized skills into generalized competencies to advance their careers. She emphasizes that women must increase their awareness of their career aspirations. For example, developing the mental health agency consultation program increased my business and marketing skills, which I then utilized to develop my consultation practice in Washington. The satisfaction of earlier roles helped me recognize my ongoing career goals and that I prefer a variety of independent nursing roles and enjoy being my own boss. My Los Angeles background gave me both confidence and experience as I embarked on new endeavors in Washington.

Assessing the community

As the center of the federal government, Washington is a beautiful and dynamic place to live and work in. As I began to inquire about its opportunities for psychiatric nurse specialists, I was quickly informed that the city had more mental health professionals per capita than any city in the United States. Another revelation was that the Washington metropolitan area had a closed and competitive market for public and private mental health services. I was not discouraged, however, and began my own assessment of the community.

I had only one contact when I moved to Washington. My approach to exploring professional opportunities was to telephone colleagues and other professionals and ask for an opportunity to meet with them. Individuals whom I met suggested others to contact. I soon became familiar with Washington and its potential business opportunities. I found that most people were willing to meet with me and share their knowledge of the system.

While I was investigating employment opportunities, a contact in the field informed me of an interdisciplinary mental health private practice group which for a nominal initiation fee and monthly charge provided an office and beginning referrals. Within 7 months I had my own office in a downtown location and had developed my own referral sources. A year has now passed since I saw my first patient in Washington. My psychotherapy practice has grown to approximately 12 hours per week and provides a substantial percentage of my monthly income. My fees are negotiated in accordance with the patient's financial situation and insurance program. Third-party reimbursements for nurses remain a problem because many policies do not include nurses. Consequently I reduce my fee so that the patient in such cases is not penalized. This means a considerable loss in income: approximately $100 per week based on my current practice.

Approximately 90% of my referrals come from nurses.

Developing a consulting business

It quickly became apparent during my exploratory efforts that Washington holds substantial business opportunities for organization consultants. To take advantage of these, however, I needed to be flexible regarding potential clients and services and willing to provide consultation to areas of business rather than only to human service organizations.

My initial efforts included contacting training and personnel officials in several federal agencies. Although I was unfamiliar with the federal system and unclear about how to market my services to potential clients, the individuals I met with were both encouraging and helpful. They gave me good advice such as the suggestion to join The American Society for Training and Development, to which belong most organization consultants in the Washington area. Involvement in this group provided me with more contacts who educated me about the marketing of professional services and gave me opportunities to speak at meetings.

My Los Angeles work in consulting and training had mainly involved providing gratis services to schools, nursing homes, halfway houses, probation departments, and other community organizations. Although my consulting skills were strong, organization consulting was a new area for me and had a new language. For example, my basic approach to consulting had involved Gerald Caplan's[3] concepts of mental health consultation. I was not aware of the theory and practice of organization development. I later came to realize, however, that this type of consulting is essentially the same as Caplan's model for consultee-centered administrative consulting. The following vignette underscores the importance of having transferable knowledge and skills when one expands one's role.

Getting the first contract

Through my initial efforts, I discovered an organization that trains federal employees in skills such as management, leadership, communication, and assertiveness. In an interview with the program director I presented myself as a competent consultant and was told I would be called if "something came up." A few months later she asked me to provide a 3-day training program on assertive communication skills. This was my first break.

I also discovered the Women's Consultant Network, a subgroup of the American Society for Training and Development, and was immediately invited to join an effort to revitalize the group. My first project was to design and present a program on stress, networking, and support systems, following which I was approached by the faculty of a local university who were looking for someone to teach consulting in their education department. I accepted the position.

Through the Women's Network I met experienced female consultants who shared their knowledge with me. Their advice was particularly useful in developing a resumé that translated my mental health background into terms potential business clients would understand.

I also contacted nursing colleagues. I met with psychiatric nurse specialists in private practice, nurses in public and private psychiatric institutional settings, and nurse educators. Through formal and informal associations with nursing colleagues I have received significant patient and consultation referrals. For example, I have provided a consultation skills workshop and a seminar on psychodynamic assessment for two nursing continuing education programs. A colleague referred a client to me for a one-time stress management workshop, a referral that now has the potential of developing into a major consultation project that will be personally, professionally, and financially rewarding. I have been able on occasion to hire nurse associates to assist me in providing workshops and consultation services. I give referrals to colleagues as well and have found this to be a mutually enriching process.

My initial efforts also involved exploring the local community mental health system for possible consultation contracts. My assessment, however, was that there were no resources available to pay for my services even when an organization expressed a desire for my expertise. Following this assessment, I channeled my efforts into more economically viable sources.

Participating in professional organizations, continuously seeking new contacts, and speaking at professional meetings are the ongoing activities I utilize to develop my business, which now includes universities, public and private agencies, and associations. My consulting skill and experience, combined with a strong clinical base, are viewed by clients as unique professional assets. They frequently comment on the depth of my background and express respect for nurses as a professional group. They are supportive of my expanded nursing role in many practical ways, including referring new clients and projects to me. I have developed a professional package that is diverse and includes the behavioral sciences, consulting skills, organization and management theory, adult education concepts, issues of health and wellness, stress management, psychopathology, and psychotherapy.

Academic involvement

My efforts at assessment included contacting local schools of nursing. This produced results. I currently teach a graduate course in mental health consultation at a local university, a position I find particularly gratifying because of my commitment to high professional standards in nursing education. Both the students and the school are pleased to associate with an active practitioner, and I am equally delighted with the academic association. I also teach an undergraduate course on consultation at another university. I alternate semesters for the two positions.

I welcome professional contacts with colleagues after my relative isolation in private practice. The academic involvement has helped develop my consulting practice as faculty members have referred clients to me. Another advantage of an academic affiliation is that it is prestigious and endows the practitioner with a standard of professionalism. Organization clients often express respect for academic positions. Teaching, however, involves a great deal of preparation and work, and its remuneration is small when compared to the time one invests.

ISSUES IN CONSIDERING PRIVATE PRACTICE

If nurses are to adequately determine the scope and nature of their practice, they must be aware of the options and consequences of available practice models. Nurses in private practice have written extensively of their experiences in developing their businesses.[8,9,12] The assessment of community needs for nursing services, the development of referral sources, legalities and nurse practice acts, accounting and billing issues, banking and financial resources, initial business costs, marketing and business promotion, and relationships with nurse and physician colleagues have all been described from various private practice perspectives.[14] A review of the literature on private practice models and the experiences of practitioners can help the uninitiated outline the issues, problems and reasons for success or failure.[9,14,17]

The need for economic security in the face of the fiscal uncertainty of business ownership is real and should not be underestimated. Although the economic rewards of independent practice may exceed institutional salaries, it often takes a new business several years to develop. In the interim, the income from private practice may be considerably beneath institutional salaries, and thus the private practitioner must be fiscally and emotionally prepared for this possibility if she is to keep the business operating. (For example, my income for the first year of practice in Washington was less than half of my last year's earnings in Los Angeles.) The tax benefits, however, are considerable.

A nurse who wants to be independent must be prepared to take risks and invest considerable time and money in her professional and business development. Thus it is necessary to have available capital for business essentials. She must have the cash available to take advantage of business developments and expansion opportunities as they arise. The adage "you have to invest money to make money" is certainly true for nurse consultants and may be essential to one's ultimate business success.

Private practice creates specific stresses including those of professional isolation, the sole responsibility for patient care, possible negative reactions from colleagues and others, and an uncertain income. Perhaps the most difficult of these is one's sole responsibility for patient care. The nurse in private practice has a continuous (24 hours a day, 7 days a week) responsibility that may involve life-threatening situations. The luxury of giving one's responsibility for patients to another professional at the end of a shift does not exist in private practice. This accountability requires an advanced education and supervised postgraduate clinical experience. I believe that a graduate degree in nursing is a minimal requirement for independent practice.

Any nurse considering such a move must evaluate her capabilities and readiness for the demands of solo practice. Experience in independent nursing roles and leadership positions can provide the beginning skills. Certification as a clinical specialist in the specialty area is an important professional accomplishment and will likely become a qualification for third-party reimbursements of nursing services.

NURSING AND WOMEN'S ISSUES RELATED TO PRIVATE PRACTICE

Nursing leaders and health officials call for nursing to take the initiative in defining its services and increasing its autonomy.[9,10] The high turnover rate for hospital-employed nurses is related to job dissatisfaction stemming from a lack of independent nursing functions and inadequate opportunities for career advancement. The struggle for autonomy in nursing mirrors the battle of women for independence and equality. Other chapters here address socialization processes that teach females to suppress their excellence and track them toward marriage and motherhood rather than careers. Such influences have profound implications in terms of the preparedness of nurses (mainly women) to assume independent practice.

There are differences between males and females in terms of their career development.[6] Men typically conceptualize careers as a series of accomplishments leading to recognition and reward. Women, on the other hand, conceptualize careers in terms of their personal growth, satisfaction, self-fulfillment, and giving to others. Women usually do not include financial reward or professional recognition in their attitudes toward careers. In addition, men and women assess risks in strikingly different ways. Men see risk as two-sided: winning or losing, opportunity or danger. Women see risk as one-sided: danger, injury, loss, and ruin. Risk is something to be avoided at all costs. Women, then, are often more comfortable in dependent roles and are less motivated to achieve. This, too, has implications for independent practice.

THE PROBLEM OF DISCRIMINATION

It is interesting to note the phenomenon of some feminists' reverse discrimination toward the nursing profession. Feminists seem determined to devalue nursing as a submissive and subservient occupation. For example, a recent article in *Savvy*, a magazine for "Executive women," encourages professional women to write for publication. The author notes that increasing numbers of scientists, bankers, businesswomen, and *even nurses* are writing books and articles to advance their careers.[5] Such demeaning references to nurses in a women's magazine are particularly interesting because feminists are supposedly supportive of all women.

Nursing and other predominantly female professions are devalued by the women's movement as "support roles" for men.[7] Although a positive value is given to women who move into traditionally male professions, there has been little recognition by the women's movement of the professional advances and expanded role of nursing.

Other nurses believe that many nurses are their own worst enemies. This claim has some validity and is relevant to the subject of private practice because many advanced nurse practitioners have experienced difficulties with their nursing colleagues (including the sabotaging of hospital privileges). State boards of nursing too have not supported as they might have the reimbursement efforts of private practitioners.

Such discrimination from colleagues can best be understood by recognizing that many nurses continue to identify with and accept the traditional role of women. The movement of peers toward autonomy is anxiety-producing for these nurses because it threatens the status quo. Even nurses who struggle for professional autonomy experience conflicts between the demands of professionalism and the prevailing sex-role stereotypes of obedience and dependence. Independent practice requires that nurses be self-sufficient, assertive, and decisive—qualities that are in opposition to cultural norms.

Women's need for approval is a result of the socialization process, in which self-evaluation depends on meeting others' expectations. Most nurses are aware of the "proper" role for women and may be overly sensitive to actual or implied criticism as they move toward independence. Their desire for approval, especially that of physicians, may be quite unrealistic, especially as many physicians are threatened by the changes within nursing.

Although I am aware that many nurses question independent nursing roles, my personal experiences have shown that colleagues can be supportive and helpful in developing a private practice. I have already indicated that the majority of referrals to my psychotherapy practice come from nurses. Another example of nursing's support involved a nurse who supported me in a conflict over my fee for a consultation service. Her support was based on the view that my sole source of income is service fees, and that I must be adequately compensated for my time. I could mention numerous examples of nurse colleagues who have assisted me in my career and business development.

PRIVATE PRACTICE: REQUIREMENTS FOR SUCCESS

Private practice requires that nurses have the following qualities: clinical and consulting expertise, business and marketing skills, political savvy, self-confidence, flexibility, energy, and a professional network.

Clinical and consulting expertise

Clinical and consulting expertise together with ongoing professional development are essential and should be viewed as minimum requirements for private practice. Perhaps the best way to build a business is by providing outstanding professional services. Excellence speaks for itself. Giving presentations at professional meetings is an opportunity to demonstrate to colleagues and potential clients one's expertise as a clinician and a consultant.

Business and marketing skills

Business acumen and marketing knowledge are essential for private practice. A nurse who enters private practice must identify those of her skills that can be transferred to her new setting. The abilities to present oneself and to clearly articulate the range of one's services to potential consumers are necessary components of marketing. Building referral sources, expanding one's scope of practice, and investing in one's practice are business decisions that must be carefully and rationally made. Private practice is, after all, a small business operation.

Networking and political savvy

Discrimination against nurses and the lack of support from feminists, colleagues, insurance companies, and others must be dealt with directly. Nurses must recognize discrimination and develop strategies to combat it. We cannot afford to feel sorry for ourselves but must devote our energies to remedying problems and meeting our own needs. Much can be accomplished with a rational, problem-solving, goal-oriented approach.

Networking activities in which colleagues organize to exchange information, develop strategies for political action, and educate consumers about professional nursing services are essential to private practitioners. Formal and informal networking is an excellent way to build one's business and involves a mutual helping process. Networks also reduce one's isolation.

Political savvy becomes increasingly important in the effort toward obtaining third-party reimbursements. Nurses in private practice should be prepared to invest time, energy, and money in political activities that will benefit them professionally. Following a 2½-year effort, psychiatric and mental health specialists in California have recently introduced a bill for third-party payments into the State Assembly. Their strategies included developing a statewide network of nurses to work on the project, meetings between nurse specialists and all California legislators to educate them about the role of specialists and the reimbursement problem, a letter-writing campaign by consumers and nurses, and soliciting the support of allied mental health disciplines. Nurses in this instance organized to meet their own needs and to change discriminatory economic practices.

Self-confidence and a flexible, energetic approach

Developing and marketing one's services in a complex society involve skill and flexibility. Schlotfeldt[13] defines nursing as a field of professional activities that assist people to attain, maintain, and regain health. This broad definition certainly covers a wide range of practice opportunities. Nurses in private practice must begin to think beyond simply providing traditional health services and must create innovative services in new areas to fully utilize their many talents.

Operating a small business is risky, and thus the need for self-confidence is great. Flexibility and the determination to face disappointments go a long way toward ensuring one's survival. Nurses must be prepared to change their direction as is necessary. For example, although most of my consulting work has been with the federal government, I now expect such work to become dramatically less available in the wake of recent budget cuts. I must therefore assess present conditions and anticipate future directions to develop strategies for building my practice. The ability to live with uncertainty and change is a must. It can be an exciting and energizing process to find within oneself the substance and direction to meet ongoing challenges. Personal drive, ambition, and optimism as well as the ability to be a self-starter are all personal requirements for private practice.

CONTINUING THE JOURNEY

The latter sections of this chapter reflect a business approach to the development of a private practice. Some nurses may be uncomfortable with this seemingly cold-hearted approach to providing nursing services. I prefer to call it realistic. Certainly I take pride in my professional work and gain satisfaction when patients and clients develop and improve their health through my efforts. I find, however, that I must be realistic if I am to succeed. Female conditioning has created barriers to thinking in business terms; nurses traditionally think of serving others for altruistic reasons rather than for financial rewards.

As the role of women in society continues to change, so too will the role of nursing. Along the road to professional autonomy many more nurses will build private practices, especially as nurses' frustrations increase within physician-dominated health care settings. The consumer's demand for participation in health care will create substantial business opportunities for creative nurses. The business world demands hustling and selling oneself or one's services. Nursing has services of distinct value that can be sold to potential consumers. Our journey to independence must be through the promotion and delivery of highly valued professional nursing services.

REFERENCES

1. Agree, B.: Beginning an independent nursing practice, American Journal of Nursing **74:**636, April 1974.
2. Berkovitz, I., and others: Attending to the emotional needs of junior high school students and staff during school desegregation: contributions of mental health consultants. In Powell, G., Editor: The psychological development of minority group children, New York, Brunner/Mazel, Inc. (in press).
3. Caplan, G.: The theory and practice of mental health consultation, New York, 1974, Basic Books, Inc.
4. Carr, E.: A model of child abuse prevention, paper presented at American Orthopsychiatric Association, New York, 1981.
5. Gott, T.J.: Published anything good lately? Savvy **1**(11):22, 1980.
6. Hennig, M., and Jardim, A.: The managerial woman, New York, 1977, Anchor Press.
7. Josefowitz, N.: Paths to power, Reading, Mass., 1980, Addison-Wesley Publishing Co., Inc.
8. Keller, N.S.: The evolution of a successful partnership, Journal of Nursing Administration, p. 6, October 1977.
9. Kinlein, L.M.: Independent nurse practice with clients, Philadelphia, 1977, J.B. Lippincott Co.
10. Kohnke, M.F.: The case for consultation in nursing, New York, 1978, Wiley Medical Publicatons.
11. Lane, H.C.: Promoting an independent nursing practice, American Journal of Nursing, p. 1319, August 1975.
12. McShane, N.G., and Smith, E.M.: Starting a private practice in mental health nursing, American Journal of Nursing p. 2068, December 1978.
13. Schlotfeldt, R.: This I believe—nursing in health care. In Browning, M.: Expanded role of the nurse, New York, 1975, American Journal of Nursing Co.
14. Simms, E.: Preparation for independent practice, Nursing Outlook **25:**114, 1977.
15. Simms. L., and Lindberg, J.: The nurse person, New York, 1978, Harper & Row, Publishers, Inc.
16. Webster-Stratton, C.: The nurse practitioner in private practice, Pediatric Nursing, p. 24-30, January-February, 1978.
17. Wong, D.: Private practice at a price, Nursing Outlook **25:**258-259, 1977.
18. Zahourek, R.: Two management systems in a nursing private practice group, Journal of Nursing Administration **9:**48-51, 1979.

Index

A

Abuse of nurses by physicians, 132
Academic involvement and private practice, 417-418
Accountability, 252-253
Achievement, 59-70
  conflict(s)
    common in women, 66-70
    with femininity, 99-102
  effects of sex roles on, 51-52
  intellectual, in college, 37-38
  of nurses, potential models for, 319-320
  nursing
    definition of, 315-320
    dilemma of, 318-319
  professional, in contradiction with female sex role, 315-316
  self-esteem and, 66-70
  of women, 41-44
    family background in, 41-43
Achievers; *see* Achieving women
Achieving women
  background factors, 61-64
  birth order, 61-62
  education of, 61
  high, backgrounds of, 62-63
  parental style and, 62
  personalities of, 63-64
  social class and, 61
Activism
  feminist; *see* Feminist, activism
  personal, 149-150
  public, 150-152
Activists, political, and nurses, 189-202
Acts, nurse practice, 379

Adjunct role of supportive wife, 281
Adolescents, role models for, 122-124
Aggression against one's own group, 181-182
Agitation to end sex discrimination, 150-152
Aid, direct, in support of professional career, 285
Alliances, forming, 363-365
Altruism, 236-238
Ames, Cherry, 122-124
Analytic ability and socialization, 34
Androgyny, 248-254
  definition, 248
Anger, inappropriate expressions of, 355-356
Antilife ethics, 236-242
Assertiveness, 345
Associate-diploma-baccalaureate dilemma, 172-173
Assumptions, new, and developing unity, 334-335
Atalanta's apples, 95-112
Authority and physician-nurse conflict, 227
Autocracy and physician-nurse conflict, 231-232
Autonomy in nursing, 413-414

B

Baccalaureate-associate-diploma dilemma, 172-173
Barton, Sue, 122-124
Battle-ax, 113-156
Behavior
  colleague, 251-252
  gender role, definition, 4
  interpersonal, sexual politics of, 83-91
  nonverbal, and power, 366-377
  political, cultural basis of, 189-202
  sex role
    learning of, 25-28
    variation in, 29-32

Behavior—cont'd
  victim, 249-250
Birth order and achieving women, 61-62
Black women and sex roles, 31-32
Books for children, 121-122
Brainstorming for job satisfaction, 384-396
Breaking out, breaking in, 402-405
Burnout, 338
Burying old fictions, 77-82
Business skills for private practice, 421

C

Care
  cure/ myth, 205-206
  health; *see* Health care
  of nurse, by whom, 337-347
  of patient, and physician-nurse conflict, 230
  primary care nursing, 380
Career
  choice, nursing as, 93-185
    analysis of, 169-177
    making the choice, 169-170
    who chooses nursing, 170-172
  orientation in college, 38-39
  professional, social support for, 283-285
    direct aid, 285
  social support for
    dilemma of, 281-289
    factors affecting, 287-288
    sources of, 286-287
Caring vs. curing, 203-209
Change, self-appraisal and self-acceptance as
      basis for, 325-326
Changing work relationships, 328-330
Childhood socialization, early, 21-29
Children, books and toys for, 121-122
Class; *see* Social, class
Cognitive
  learning theory of gender development, 6-8
  socialization, early, 22
Colleague behaviors, 251-252
College
  career orientation in, 38-39
  peer influences in, 37
  socialization pressures in, 36-41
Communication and physician-nurse conflict,
      230-231
Community, assessing, and private practice, 415-
      416

Compassion traps, 234-247
Conditioning, female, reactions to, 179-180
Conflict(s)
  between femininity and achievement, 99-102
  common achievement, in women, 66-70
  physician-nurse; *see* Physician-nurse conflict
  political, and physician-nurse conflict, 229
Consultant, independent
  advantages of, 411
  beginning, 412
  constructing proposal, 410
  disadvantages of, 411-412
  fulfilling the promise, 410-411
  gaining entry, 410
  possessing a marketable skill, 409
  private practice as, 409-412
  success, qualities that foster, 412
Consulting
  business, developing, and private practice, 416
  expertise for private practice, 421
Contagion, 346
Contemporary selflessness, 240-242
Contract, first, in private practice, 416-417
Control in paternalism, 213
Council, administrative joint practice, 380-
      381
Cultural
  basis of political behavior, 189-202
  imperatives, 40-41
  influences on gender development, 16-17
Cure/care myth, 205-206
Curing vs. caring, 203-209

D

Daddy's little girl, 210-220
Daughters, dutiful, nurses as, 243
Deception
  in paternalism, 211-213
  silence as, 212-213
Deferential, nurses as, 123
Delivery of health care, 248-249
Dependence, denial of feelings of, 354
Despair, 339-341
Development; *see* Gender, development
Developmental
  aspects of self-esteem, 52-53
  issues, female, 1-91
Dilemma, associate-diploma-baccalaureate, 172-
      173

Diploma-baccalaureate-associate dilemma, 172-173

Directions, new, and unity vs. diversity, 326-328

Discrimination and private practice, 419-420

Dissatisfaction
of nurses, solutions for, 388-394
with work, 339

Dissociation from peers, 356

Diversity vs. unity, new directions, 326-328

Doctor; see Physician

Domesticity, feminine, ideology of, 162-163

Dominance, nonverbal indicators of, 370-373

Double-duty role of supportive wife, 281

Dutiful daughters, nurses as, 243

Dyad, physician-nurse, 131-134

E

Education
of achieving women, 61
to end sex discrimination, 150-152
of nurses, 172-176
attrition, 173-174
faculty influence, 174-176
selection, 173-174
nursing, 228
wide range of, 226-227
of physician about nursing, 230

Educational process, rethinking of, 330-331

Ego differentiation, lack of, 307-314
background, 307-308
theoretical framework, 308-309

Elitism in nursing and medicine, 122

Emotional
detachment, 339
support, 284-285

Ethics, antilife, 236-242

Ethnic variation in sex role, 31

Evil, woman as basest, projection in, 115-117

Expectations, 344-345
choices about, 253
unrealistic self-expectations, 355

Extraordinary, doing the extraordinary and power, 362-363

F

Faculty influence in education of nurses, 174-176

Family background in women's achievement, 41-43
constellation and sex role, 32

Family background in women's achievement
—cont'd
hospital, 204-205
power and, 359-361

Fantasy(ies)
exploration into, 113-156
as precursors of myths, 113-114
realism triumphing over, 142-143

Fear of success, 39-40

Feelings of dependence, denial of, 354

Female role; see also Women
distinguished from male role, 23-24
traditional, and self-esteem, 56-58

Feminine
domesticity, ideology of, 162-163
myths, 114-121
stereotypes, 114-121
as myths in tangible form, 118-119

Femininity
conflict with achievement, 99-102
ideology of, effect in work place, 103-108

Feminist
activism
from agonizing to organizing, 260-261
in health care, 255-272
in nursing, 255-272
in nursing, sampling of, 261-266
premises, 256-260
change, 266-271
potential, 266-271
potshots at nursing, 182-183
power, 369-370
revolution vs. sex-segregated labor force, 96-99

Fictions, burying old, 77-82

Floater, uncommitted, 68-69

Fragmentation due to paternalism, 214

G

Gender
assignment, definition, 4
attribution, definition, 4
definition, 4
development
biological influences on, 10-11
cognitive learning theory of, 6-8
cultural influences on, 16-17
influences on, 10-17
psychoanalytic theory of, 5-6, 8
psychological influences on, 11-13

Gender—cont'd
  development—cont'd
    role of parents in, 13-16
    social learning theory of, 6, 8
    theoretical explanations for, traditional, 5-10
  identity
    core, 4
    rethinking, as continuing process, 3-20
  role, 4
  self-attribution of, 4
  used interchangeably with sex, 3
"Get well" cards, nurses in, 143-144
Getting a foot in the door, 406-408
Girls; *see* Little girl(s)
Glamour
  as gone, 135-138
  on job, 130-131
Glamorous, nursing as, 122
Goal setting, 252-253
Group
  aggression against one's own group, 181-182
  dominant, identification with, 181

H

Handmaiden(s), 113-156
  teaching nurses to be, 240
Health
  mental, emphasizing for clients and nurses, 331-332
  physical, emphasizing for clients and nurses, 331-332
Health care
  delivery, 248-249
  feminist activism in, 255-272
  feminist activism in, sampling of, 261-266
  politics of, 203-209
Helpless victims, nurses as, 243
Heritage, women's, two views of, 324-325
Historical selflessness, 240
Home, "woman's place in," 162-163
Hospital
  family, 204-205
    power and, 359-361
  hierarchies, nursing parity in, 380
  privileges, nurse's experience in obtaining, 406-408
Human rights, 234-236

I

Idealization of women, 117-118
Identification with dominant group, 181
Identity, gender; *see* Gender, identity
Ideology
  of feminine domesticity, 162-163
  of femininity, effect in work place, 103-108
Image
  of nurses in public and medical opinion, 148-149
  and reality, gap between, 249
Individuation-separation, 308-309
  related to nursing leadership, 309-310
Infant socialization, 21-22
Intellectual
  ability and socialization, 34
  achievement in college, 37-38
Interpersonal
  behavior, sexual politics of, 83-91
  relationships, changing, 393-394
Issue(s)
  female developmental, 1-91
  nursing
    power as, 359-365
    related to private practice, 419
  political, 187-277
  psychological, 279-347
  social, 187-277
  women's, related to private practice, 419

J

Job
  glamour on, 130-131
  satisfaction, brainstorming for, 384-396
Joint practice, 378-383
  committees, 379
  council, administrative, 380-381
  elements of, four necessary, 379-380
  historical development, 378-379
  implications, 382
  pilot unit, development of, 381-382
  practicalities, 380-382

K

Kinesics, 370-371

L

Labeling, 17-18
Labor force, sex-segregated, vs. feminist revolution, 96-99

Leadership, 311-312
  nursing
    effect of lack of ego differentiation on, 307-314
      object constancy related to, 309-310
      separation-individuation related to, 309-310
Learned, sex roles as, 49-51
Learning
  process in socialization, 28-29
  sex role behavior, 25-28
  theory
    cognitive, of gender development, 6-8
    social, of gender development, 6, 8
Legislation to end sex discrimination, 150-152
Literature, popular, nurses in, 135-138
Little girl(s)
  daddy's, 210-220
  growing up to be wives and mothers, 157-168

M

Male(s)
  in nursing, 170-171
    thoughts on, 273-277
  role, distinguished from female role, 23-24
Marketing skills for private practice, 421
Marriage
  chances for, improved by being nurse, 158-160
  nursing as preparation for, 160-162
  nursing as road to, 158-162
  nursing as stopgap to, 157-168
Media disseminating myths in stereotypes, 121-147
Medical
  opinion, image of nurses in, 148-149
  school vs. nursing, 178-185
Medicine
  mystery and elitism in, 122
  narcissistic fit with nursing, 300-306
  paternalism in, 215-218
  socialized, 238-239
Men, women's work never done by, 103-108
Mental health, emphasizing for clients and nurses, 331-332
Mentoring, 310-311
Minorities in nursing, 171-172
Mislabeling, 18
Model(s)
  potential, for achievement of nurses, 319-320
  for private practice, 413-423
  role, for adolescents, 122-124

Money
  as bottom line, 206-208
  nurses' attitudes toward, 386
Mother(s)
  little girls growing up to be, 157-168
  symbiotic, nurse as, 290-299
Motherhood, nursing as preparation for, 160-162
Movies, nurses in, 141-142
Mystery in nursing and medicine, 122
Myths
  care/cure, 205-206
  exploration into, 113-156
  fantasies as precursors of, 113-114
  feminine, 114-121
  fighting, as painful process, 147-148
  nursing, 119-121
    media disseminating, 121-147
  overcoming, 166-167
  reality behind, 164-166
  in tangible form, feminine stereotypes as, 118-119
  about uniforms, 399

N

Narcissistic fit between medicine and nursing, 300-306
Negotiation to end sex discrimination, 150-152
Networking and private practice, 421-422
News, nurses in, 142-143
Nightingale nurse, getting rid of, 149-152
Nightingalism, 239-242
Nonexpectations, climate of, 37-38
Nonverbal
  behavior and power, 366-377
  indicators of dominance and submission, 370-373
Norms, societal, for women's professions, 316-318
Novels, romance
  nursing in, 124-134
  stereotypes in, 126-130
Nurse(s)
  abuse by physicians, 132
  achievement of, potential models for, 319-320
  against themselves, 183-185
  care of, by whom, 337-347
  chances for marriage improved by being, 158-160
  deference and physician dominance, 222-225
  as deferential, 123
  dissatisfaction of, solutions for, 388-394

Nurse(s)—cont'd
  as dumb, 128
  as dutiful daughters, 243
  education of; see Education, of nurses
  experience of, in obtaining hospital privileges,
      406-408
  in "get well" cards, 143-144
  as helpless victims, 243
  as ignorant, 128
  image in public and medical opinion, 148-149
  impact of stereotypes on, 147-149
  lack of control over nursing, 229
  in literature, popular, 135-138
  love relationship with surgeon, 124-134
  marrying physicians, 133-134
  mental health, emphasizing, 331-332
  money, attitudes toward, 386
  in movies, 141-142
  in news, 142-143
  Nightingale, getting rid of, 149-152
  not questioning physician's orders, 133
  as peripatetic, 124
  physical health, emphasizing, 331-332
  -physician conflict; see Physician-nurse conflict
  -physician dyad, 131-134
  political activities and, 189-202
  political process and, 200-201
  in pornography, 144-147
  practice acts, 379
  practitioner movement, 218-220
  psychosocial emphasis by, 226
  retaining nurses, 387-388
  retreating from patients, 226
  rights of, 242-246
  rudeness to, by physicians, 132
  stereotypes about; see Stereotypes
  as subservient, 123
  as symbiotic mother, 290-299
  teaching nurses to be handmaidens, 240
  in television, 138-141
  in theater, 141-142
Nursing
  achievement
    definition of, 315-320
    dilemma of, 318-319
  autonomy in, 413-414
  as career choice; see Career, choice, nursing as
  education; see Education, nursing
  elitism in, 122

Nursing—cont'd
  feminist activism in, 255-272
    sampling of, 261-266
  feminist potshots at, 182-183
  as glamorous, 122, 130-131
  issue(s)
    power as, 359-365
    related to private practice, 419
  leadership; see Leadership, nursing
  males in, 170-171
    thoughts on, 273-277
  minorities in, 171-172
  mystery of, 122
  myths, 119-121
    media disseminating, 121-147
  narcissistic fit with medicine, 300-306
  in novels, romance, 124-134
  nurses' lack of control over, 229
  parity in hospital hierarchies, 380
  paternalism in; see Paternalism
  physicians' devaluation of, 225-226
  as preparation for marriage and motherhood,
      160-162
  primary care, 380
  as road to marriage, 158-162
  role, changing, 389-393
  shortage, 147-148
    reasons for, 385-388
    solutions for, 388-394
  stereotypes, 93-185
  as stopgap to marriage, 157-168
  vs. medical school, 178-185
  women's movement taking a slap at, 178-185
  work environment, changing, 389-393

O

Object constancy, 309
  related to nursing leadership, 309-310
Oppositional mode of thought, 198-200
Oppressive socialization, two views of, 324-325
Organization, having relevance for the organiza-
    tion, 363
Oversocialized portrait of women, 43-44

P

Parents
  influence of, in socialization, 35
  role in gender development, 13-16
  style of, and achieving women, 62

Parity, nursing, in hospital hierarchies, 380
Paternalism, 210-220
  control in, 213
  deception in, 211-213
  fragmentation due to, 214
  historical overview, 214-215
  in medicine, 215-218
  in nursing, lethal effects of, 210-220
  theoretical framework, 211-214
Patient care and physician-nurse conflict, 230
Patriarchal power, 367-369
Peer(s)
  dissociation from, 356
  influence(s)
    in college, 37
    on socialization, 35-36
Perception, 341-342
Peripatetic, nurses as, 124
Personal activism, 149-150
Personalities of achieving women, 63-64
Physical health, emphasizing for clients and nurses,
    331-332
Physician(s)
  abuse of nurses, 132
  as boss, 131-132
  devaluation of nursing by, 225-226
  dominance and nurse deference, 222-225
  education about nursing, 230
  impact of stereotypes on, 147-149
  -nurse conflict; see Physician-nurse conflict
  -nurse dyad, 131-134
  nurse in love relationship with, 124-134
  nurses marrying, 133-134
  orders of, nurses not questioning, 133
  rudeness to nurses, 132
Physician-nurse conflict, 221-233
  sources of
    analysis of, 221-229
    authority, two systems of, 227
    lack of knowledge of the other's profession,
      226
    more education for nurses frowned on by
      physicians, 228
    nurses' lack of control over nursing, 229
    nurses' lack of professional commitment, 227-
      228
    nurses' retreating from patients, 226
    nurses' wide range of education, 226-227
    physicians' devaluation of nursing, 225-226

Physician-nurse conflict—cont'd
  physician dominance and nurse deference,
    222-225
    policing one another, 228
    political conflicts, 229
    psychosocial emphasis by nurses, 226
    responsibility, fear of usurpation of, 228-229
  toward a new relationship, 229-232
    autocracy, attack on, 231-232
    communication in, open, 230-231
    education of physician about nursing, 230
    patient care increase, 230
    team development, 231
Pilot unit, development, and joint practice, 381-
    382
Political
  activists, and nurses, 189-202
  behavior, cultural basis of, 189-202
  conflicts and physician-nurse conflict, 229
  issues, 187-277
  process, and nurses, 200-201
  savvy and private practice, 421-422
Politics
  of health care, 203-209
  sexual, of interpersonal behavior, 83-91
Pornography, nurses in, 144-147
Power
  acquisition of, 362-365
  alternatives, 373-375
  feminist, 369-370
  hospital "family" and, 359-361
  nonverbal behavior and, 366-377
  as nursing issue, 359-365
  orientation to, 345-346
  patriarchal, 367-369
  types of, 367-370
Practice
  joint; see Joint practice
  nurse practice acts, 379
  private; see Private practice
  standards, 248
Practitioner, nurse practitioner movement, 218-
    220
Primary care nursing, 380
Private practice
  academic involvement and, 417-418
  assessing the community, 415-416
  business skills for, 421
  clinical expertise for, 421

Private practice—cont'd
  as consultant, independent, 409-412
  consulting business, developing, 416
  consulting expertise for, 421
  continuing the journey, 422-423
  developing, 414-418
  discrimination and, 419-420
  energetic approach for, 422
  first contract in, 416-417
  flexible approach for, 422
  issues in considering, 418-419
  marketing skills for, 421
  model for, 413-423
  networking and, 421-422
  nursing issues related to, 419
  political savvy and, 421-422
  self-confidence and, 422
  success in, requirements for, 413-433
  women's issues related to, 419
Professional
  achievement, in contradiction with female sex role, 315-316
  career, social support for, 283-285
    direct aid, 285
  role, assuming, 332-334
  uniforms and "the professional," 400-401
  woman's need for support, 282-283
Professions for women
  psychosocial barriers to, 95-112
  societal norms for, 316-318
Projection, 354
  in woman as basest evil, 115-117
Propaganda, 244-246
Proxemics, 371-373
Psychoanalytical theory of gender development, 5-6, 8
Psychological
  influences on gender development, 11-13
  issues, 279-347
Psychology, victim, and socialization of women, 248-254
Psychosocial
  barriers to professions for women, 95-112
  emphasis by nurse, 226
Public
  activism, 150-152
  impact of stereotypes on, 147-149
  opinion, image of nurses in, 148-149
Punishment and socialization, 28-29

R

Racial variation in sex role, 31-32
Rage, 339-341
Rape, 144-147
Reactions and socialization, 28-29
Realism triumphing over fantasy, 142-143
Reality
  behind myths, 164-166
  gap between image and reality, 249
  shock, 147-148
Red herrings, 385-388
Relationships
  interpersonal, changing, 393-394
  work, changing, 328-330
Relevance, having relevance for the organization, 363
Research debate, continuing, concerning sex role, 29-30
Responsibility and physician-nurse conflict, 228-229
Retaining nurses, 387-388
Rethinking the educational process, 330-331
Revolution, feminist, vs. sex-segregated labor force, 96-99
Rewards and socialization, 28-29
Rights
  human, 234-236
  of nurses, 242-246
Role(s)
  adjunct, of supportive wife, 281
  double-duty, of supportive wife, 281
  female
    distinguished from male role, 23-24
    traditional, and self-esteem, 56-58
  gender; see Gender, role
  male, distinguished from female role, 23-24
  models for adolescents, 122-124
  nursing, changing, 389-393
  of parents in gender development, 13-16
  professional, assuming, 332-334
  sex; see Sex, role(s)
  supportive, of supportive wife, 281
Romance novels; see Novels, romance
Rudeness of physicians to nurses, 132

S

School
  influence in socialization, 33
  "terminal year," and socialization, 36

Scientific method, 252
Self, 190-193
Self-acceptance as basis for change, 325-326
Self-appraisal as basis for change, 325-326
Self-concept, problems of, 253
Self-confidence and private practice, 422
Self-esteem, 52-59
  achievement and, 66-70
  adult, 53-55
  developmental aspects of, 52-53
  high in women, factors producing, 58-59
  lower, female, explanations of, 55-56
  traditional female role and, 56-58
Self-expectations, unrealistic, 355
Self-other relationships, 193-196
Self putdowns, problems of, 250-251
Self-talk, 342-344
Selflessness, 240-242
Separation-individuation, 308-309
  related to nursing leadership, 309-310
Sex
  discrimination, 150-152
  role(s), 48-52
    behavior, learning of, 25-28
    behavior, variation in, 29-32
    in contradiction with professional achievement, 315-316
    deconstructing, 108-110
    effects on achievement, 51-52
    ethnic variation in, 31
    family constellation and, 32
    as learned, 49-51
    preferences, expression of, 25
    racial variation in, 31-32
    research debate concerning, continuing, 29-30
    social class variation in, 30-31
    socialization, 21-47
    standards, variation in, 29-32
    -segregated labor force vs. feminist revolution, 96-99
  used interchangeably with gender, 3
Sexual politics of interpersonal behavior, 83-91
Shock, reality, 147-148
Shortage of nurses; see Nursing, shortage
Silence as deception, 212-213
Skills, business and marketing, for private practice, 421
Social
  change, struggle for, 95-112

Social—cont'd
  class
    of achieving women, 61
    variation in sex role, 30-31
  issues, 187-277
  learning theory of gender development, 6, 8
  psychosocial; see Psychosocial
  support; see Support, social
Socialism, 234-247
Socialization
  analytic ability and, 34
  childhood, early, 21-29
  cognitive, early, 22
  continuing, 32-36
  infant, 21-22
  intellectual ability and, 34
  learning process, 28-29
  oppressive, two views of, 324-325
  oversocialized portrait of women, 43-44
  parents in, influence of, 35
  peer influence on, 35-36
  pressures in college, 36-41
  punishment and, 28-29
  reactions and, 28-29
  rewards and, 28-29
  school in, influence of, 33
    "terminal year," 36
  sex role, 21-47
  victim psychology and, 248-254
Socialized
  medicine, 238-239
  selflessness, 240
Societal norms for women's professions, 316-318
Splitting, process of, 114-115
Standards, practice, 248
Stereotypes, 93-185
  feminine, 114-121
    as myths in tangible form, 118-119
  fighting, as painful process, 147-148
  getting rid of, 149-152
  impact on nurses, public and physicians, 147-149
  in novels, romance, 126-130
  nursing, 93-185
    media disseminating, 121-147
  problems of, 251
  uniforms and, 398
Stress
  -related symptoms, 339
  responses to, 338-341

Stress—cont'd
  vulnerability to, 341-346
Stupid, playing stupid, 354-355
Submission, nonverbal indicators of, 370-373
Subservient, nurses as, 123
Success
  fear of, 39-40
  in private practice, requirements, 413-423
  qualities that foster, for independent consultant,
    412
Support
  emotional, 284-285
  practical, 284
  professional woman's need for, 282-283
  social, for careers, dilemma of, 281-289
Supportive role of supportive wife, 281
Supportive wife, 281
Surgeon, nurse in love relationship with, 124-134
Symbiotic mother, nurse as, 290-299
Systems, new, and developing unity, 334-335

T

Talk, self-talk, 342-344
Teaching
  nurses to be handmaidens, 240
  women "to know their place," 240
Team development and physician-nurse conflict,
    231
Television, nurses in, 138-141
Theater, nurses in, 141-142
Theory
  learning; *see* Learning, theory
  psychoanalytic, of gender development, 5-6, 8
Thought, oppositional mode of, 198-200
Toys for children, 121-122

U

Uncommitted floater, 68-69
Uniforms
  associations and, 398
  meaning of, 398
  myths about, 399
  origin of, 397-398
  "the professional" and, 400-401
  stereotypes and, 398
  tyranny of, 397-401
Unity
  developing, new assumptions and systems in,
    334-335

Unity—cont'd
  vs. diversity, new directions, 326-328

V

Victim(s)
  behavior, 249-250
  helpless, nurses as, 243
  psychology, and socialization of women, 248-254
Visible, being visible and power, 363
Vocational options, perception of, 64-66

W

Whore, 113-156
Wife(wives)
  little girls growing up to be, 157-168
  supportive, 281
Woman as basest evil, projection in, 115-117
"Woman's place is in the home," 162-163
Women; *see also* Female role
  achievement of, 41-44
    family background in, 41-43
  achieving; *see* Achieving women
  black, and sex roles, 31-32
  idealization of, 117-118
  oversocialized portrait of, 43-44
  professional, need for support, 282-283
  professions for
    psychosocial barriers to, 95-112
    societal norms for, 316-318
  as subordinate, 213-214
  as supreme good, 117-118
  teaching women "to know their place," 240
  workaholic, 69-70
Women's heritage, two views of, 324-325
Women's issues related to private practice, 419
Women's lib and physician-nurse conflict, 229
Women's movement taking a slap at nursing, 178-
    185
"Women's work," 95-112
  never done by men, 103-108
Work, 197-198, 352
  dissatisfaction with, 339
  environment, nursing, changing, 389-393
  place, effect of femininity ideology in, 103-108
  relationships, changing, 328-330
  "women's," 95-112
    never done by men, 103-108
Workaholic, woman, 69-70